BYRON

BYRON

Selections from Poetry

Letters & Journals

1949

Edited by Peter Quennell

for THE NONESUCH PRESS

LONDON

Sir John Murray has generously accorded permission to The Nonesuch Press to reprint selections from 'Lord Byron's Correspondence' in this book.

PRINTED AND MADE IN GREAT BRITAIN
BY ROBERT MACLEHOSE AND CO. LTD.,
THE UNIVERSITY PRESS, GLASGOW

CONTENTS

CONTENTS

CONTENTS

BIOGRAPHICAL INDEX

1788. January 22nd. Born.
1801. April. Is sent to Harrow.
1805. July. Leaves Harrow.
1805. October. Goes up to Cambridge.
1808. July. Leaves Cambridge.
1809. March. *English Bards, and Scotch Reviewers* published.
1809. July. Sets out for the Near East.
1811. July. Returns to England.
1811. August. Mrs. Byron dies.
1812. March. *Childe Harold*, Cantos I and II published.
1814. April. Medora Leigh born.
1815. January. Marriage to Anne Isabella Milbanke.
1815. December. Ada Byron born.
1816. January. Lady Byron leaves Piccadilly Terrace.
1816. April. Separation. Byron leaves England.
1819. December. Leaves Venice.
1822. April. Death of Allegra Byron.
1823. July. Sets out for Greece.
1823. August–December. Living in Cephalonia.
1824. January. Reaches Missolonghi.
1824. April 19th. Death.

FOREWORD

WHILE preparing this selection of Byron's prose and verse, my intention has been to include as many of the letters as space would allow, and all four journals, but to omit every poem that does not seem to me to possess genuine poetic quality. I have tried, in fact, to produce a *readable* Byron; for Byron at his best is extraordinarily readable; and yet I believe that there are very few modern readers who have not, at one time or another, lost their time and patience astray in the labyrinths of his collected work. No doubt, my presumptuous attempt will provoke some criticism. I have excluded the interminable poetic dramas, the long Eastern Tales (with the exception of a brief and famous extract from *The Bride of Abydos*) and I have ruthlessly cut down the fourth Canto of *Childe Harold*. Where is *Lara* (a critic may demand), that poem into which Byron asserted that he had poured so much of himself? Where is *Manfred*, the drama that, in cryptic form, has been thought to contain an extremely important secret of his private life? I have omitted both, firstly because the essence of these poems receives full expression elsewhere, secondly because—their biographical interest apart—they cannot be considered interesting or memorable productions. Three quarters of Byron's verse is, at any rate from the modern point of view, quite remarkably bad; yet, as a significant literary figure and as an exceptionally interesting and unusually ill-fated human being, Byron can never cease to command our attention, extorting our sympathy even at moments when we are inclined to like and admire him least. No writer would have been more distressed to feel that he was in danger of becoming the victim of his own celebrity—that he was destined to be often quoted but seldom read—the prisoner of dusty gilt-tooled volumes shut up behind the glass doors of the family book-case. I have done my best, therefore, to separate that part of his poetic achievement which is capable of giving definite aesthetic satisfaction, and to accompany it with a large and catholic selection of his prose writings. For the sake of brevity, I have not printed his prefaces and notes.

Some comments were necessary; but these have been reduced to a bare minimum. They will be found, in decent obscurity, at the end of the book.

My thanks are due to Mr. A. S. B. Glover for his work in proof-reading and correction.

PETER QUENNELL

ENGLISH BARDS, AND SCOTCH REVIEWERS

ENGLISH BARDS, AND SCOTCH REVIEWERS

A SATIRE

'I had rather be a kitten, and cry, mew!
Than one of these same metre ballad-mongers.'
Shakespeare

'Such shameless Bards we have; and yet 'tis true,
There are as mad, abandon'd Critics, too.'
Pope

Still must I hear?—shall hoarse FITZGERALD bawl
His creaking couplets in a tavern hall,
And I not sing, lest, haply, Scotch Reviews
Should dub me scribbler, and denounce my *Muse*?
Prepare for rhyme—I'll publish, right or wrong:
Fools are my theme, let Satire be my song.

Oh! Nature's noblest gift—my grey goose-quill!
Slave of my thoughts, obedient to my will,
Torn from thy parent bird to form a pen,
That mighty instrument of little men!
The pen! foredoomed to aid the mental throes
Of brains that labour, big with Verse or Prose;
Though Nymphs forsake, and Critics may deride,
The Lover's solace, and the Author's pride.
What Wits! what Poets dost thou daily raise!
How frequent is thy use, how small thy praise!
Condemned at length to be forgotten quite,
With all the pages which 'twas thine to write.
But thou, at least, mine own especial pen!
Once laid aside, but now assumed again,
Our task complete, like Hamet's shall be free;
Though spurned by others, yet beloved by me:
Then let us soar to-day; no common theme,

3

No Eastern vision, no distempered dream
Inspires—our path, though full of thorns, is plain;
Smooth be the verse, and easy be the strain.

When Vice triumphant holds her sov'reign sway,
Obeyed by all who nought beside obey;
When Folly, frequent harbinger of crime,
Bedecks her cap with bells of every Clime;
When knaves and fools combined o'er all prevail,
And weigh their Justice in a Golden Scale;
E'en then the boldest start from public sneers,
Afraid of Shame, unknown to other fears,
More darkly sin, by Satire kept in awe,
And shrink from Ridicule, though not from Law.

Such is the force of Wit! but not belong
To me the arrows of satiric song;
The royal vices of our age demand
A keener weapon, and a mightier hand.
Still there are follies, e'en for me to chase,
And yield at least amusement in the race:
Laugh when I laugh, I seek no other fame,
The cry is up, and scribblers are my game:
Speed, Pegasus!—ye strains of great and small,
Ode! Epic! Elegy!—have at you all!
I, too, can scrawl, and once upon a time
I poured along the town a flood of rhyme,
A schoolboy freak, unworthy praise or blame;
I printed—older children do the same.
'Tis pleasant, sure, to see one's name in print;
A Book's a Book, altho' there's nothing in't.
Not that a Title's sounding charm can save
Or scrawl or scribbler from an equal grave:
This LAMB must own, since his patrician name
Failed to preserve the spurious Farce from shame.
No matter, GEORGE continues still to write,
Tho' now the name is veiled from public sight.
Moved by the great example, I pursue

The self-same road, but make my own review:
Not seek great JEFFREY's, yet like him will be
Self-constituted Judge of Poesy.

A man must serve his time to every trade
Save Censure—Critics all are ready made.
Take hackneyed jokes from MILLER, got by rote,
With just enough of learning to misquote;
A mind well skilled to find, or forge a fault;
A turn for punning—call it Attic salt;
To JEFFREY go, be silent and discreet,
His pay is just ten sterling pounds per sheet:
Fear not to lie, 'twill seem a *sharper* hit;
Shrink not from blasphemy, 'twill pass for wit;
Care not for feeling—pass your proper jest,
And stand a Critic, hated yet caressed.

And shall we own such judgment? no—as soon
Seek roses in December—ice in June;
Hope constancy in wind, or corn in chaff,
Believe a woman or an epitaph,
Or any other thing that's false, before
You trust in Critics, who themselves are sore;
Or yield one single thought to be misled
By JEFFREY's heart, or LAMB's Bœotian head.
To these young tyrants, by themselves misplaced,
Combined usurpers on the Throne of Taste;
To these, when Authors bend in humble awe,
And hail their voice as Truth, their word as Law;
While these are Censors, 'twould be sin to spare;
While such are Critics, why should I forbear?
But yet, so near all modern worthies run,
'Tis doubtful whom to seek, or whom to shun;
Nor know we when to spare, or where to strike,
Our Bards and Censors are so much alike.

Then should you ask me, why I venture o'er
The path which POPE and GIFFORD trod before;

If not yet sickened, you can still proceed;
Go on; my rhyme will tell you as you read.
'But hold!' exclaims a friend,—'here's some neglect:
This—that—and t'other line seem incorrect.'
What then? the self-same blunder Pope has got,
And careless Dryden—'Aye, but Pye has not':—
Indeed!—'tis granted, faith!—but what care I?
Better to err with POPE, than shine with PYE.

Time was, ere yet in these degenerate days
Ignoble themes obtained mistaken praise,
When Sense and Wit with Poesy allied,
No fabled Graces, flourished side by side;
From the same fount their inspiration drew,
And, reared by Taste, bloomed fairer as they grew.
Then, in this happy Isle, a POPE'S pure strain
Sought the rapt soul to charm, nor sought in vain;
A polished nation's praise aspired to claim,
And raised the people's, as the poet's fame.
Like him great DRYDEN poured the tide of song,
In stream less smooth, indeed, yet doubly strong.
Then CONGREVE'S scenes could cheer, or OTWAY'S melt;
For Nature then an English audience felt—
But why these names, or greater still, retrace,
When all to feebler Bards resign their place?
Yet to such times our lingering looks are cast,
When taste and reason with those times are past.
Now look around, and turn each trifling page,
Survey the precious works that please the age;
This truth at least let Satire's self allow,
No dearth of Bards can be complained of now.
The loaded Press beneath her labour groans,
And Printers' devils shake their weary bones;
While SOUTHEY'S Epics cram the creaking shelves,
And LITTLE'S Lyrics shine in hot-pressed twelves.
Thus saith the *Preacher*: 'Nought beneath the sun
Is new,' yet still from change to change we run.
What varied wonders tempt us as they pass!

The Cow-pox, Tractors, Galvanism, and Gas,
In turns appear, to make the vulgar stare,
Till the swoln bubble bursts—and all is air!
Nor less new schools of Poetry arise,
Where dull pretenders grapple for the prize:
O'er Taste awhile these Pseudo-bards prevail;
Each country Book-club bows the knee to Baal,
And, hurling lawful Genius from the throne,
Erects a shrine and idol of its own;
Some leaden calf—but whom it matters not,
From soaring SOUTHEY, down to grovelling STOTT.

    Behold! in various throngs the scribbling crew,
For notice eager, pass in long review:
Each spurs his jaded Pegasus apace,
And Rhyme and Blank maintain an equal race;
Sonnets on sonnets crowd, and ode on ode;
And Tales of Terror jostle on the road;
Immeasurable measures move along;
For simpering Folly loves a varied song,
To strange, mysterious Dulness still the friend,
Admires the strain she cannot comprehend.
Thus Lays of Minstrels—may they be the last!—
On half-strung harps whine mournful to the blast,
While mountain spirits prate to river sprites,
That dames may listen to the sound at nights;
And goblin brats, of Gilpin Horner's brood
Decoy young Border-nobles through the wood,
And skip at every step, Lord knows how high,
And frighten foolish babes, the Lord knows why;
While high-born ladies in their magic cell,
Forbidding Knights to read who cannot spell,
Despatch a courier to a wizard's grave,
And fight with honest men to shield a knave.

    Next view in state, proud prancing on his roan,
The golden-crested haughty Marmion,

Now forging scrolls, now foremost in the fight,
Not quite a Felon, yet but half a Knight,
The gibbet or the field prepared to grace—
A mighty mixture of the great and base.
And think'st thou, SCOTT! by vain conceit perchance,
On public taste to foist thy stale romance,
Though MURRAY with his MILLER may combine
To yield thy muse just half-a-crown per line?
No! when the sons of song descend to trade,
Their bays are sear, their former laurels fade,
Let such forego the poet's sacred name,
Who rack their brains for lucre, not for fame:
Still for stern Mammon may they toil in vain!
And sadly gaze on gold they cannot gain!
Such be their meed, such still the just reward
Of prostituted Muse and hireling bard!
For this we spurn Apollo's venal son,
And bid a long 'good night to Marmion.'

These are the themes that claim our plaudits now;
These are the Bards to whom the Muse must bow;
While MILTON, DRYDEN, POPE, alike forgot,
Resign their hallowed Bays to WALTER SCOTT.

The time has been, when yet the Muse was young,
When HOMER swept the lyre, and MARO sung,
An Epic scarce ten centuries could claim,
While awe-struck nations hailed the magic name:
The work of each immortal Bard appears
The single wonder of a thousand years.
Empires have mouldered from the face of earth,
Tongues have expired with those who gave them birth,
Without the glory such a strain can give,
As even in ruin bids the language live.
Not so with us, though minor Bards content,
On one great work a life of labour spent:
With eagle pinion soaring to the skies,
Behold the Ballad-monger SOUTHEY rise!

To him let CAMOENS, MILTON, TASSO yield,
Whose annual strains, like armies, take the field.
First in the ranks see Joan of Arc advance,
The scourge of England and the boast of France!
Though burnt by wicked BEDFORD for a witch,
Behold her statue placed in Glory's niche;
Her fetters burst, and just released from prison,
A virgin Phœnix from her ashes risen.
Next see tremendous Thalaba come on,
Arabia's monstrous, wild, and wondrous son;
Domdaniel's dread destroyer, who o'erthrew
More mad magicians than the world e'er knew.
Immortal Hero! all thy foes o'ercome,
For ever reign—the rival of Tom Thumb!
Since startled Metre fled before thy face,
Well wert thou doomed the last of all thy race!
Well might triumphant Genii bear thee hence,
Illustrious conqueror of common sense!
Now, last and greatest, Madoc spreads his sails,
Cacique in Mexico, and Prince in Wales;
Tells us strange tales, as other travellers do,
More old than Mandeville's, and not so true.
Oh, SOUTHEY! SOUTHEY! cease thy varied song!
A bard may chaunt too often and too long:
As thou art strong in verse, in mercy spare!
A fourth, alas! were more than we could bear.
But if, in spite of all the world can say,
Thou still wilt verseward plod thy weary way;
If still in Berkeley-Ballads most uncivil,
Thou wilt devote old women to the devil,
The babe unborn thy dread intent may rue:
'God help thee,' SOUTHEY, and thy readers too.

Next comes the dull disciple of thy school,
That mild apostate from poetic rule,
The simple WORDSWORTH, framer of a lay
As soft as evening in his favourite May,
Who warns his friend 'to shake off toil and trouble,

And quit his books, for fear of growing double';
Who, both by precept and example, shows
That prose is verse, and verse is merely prose;
Convincing all, by demonstration plain,
Poetic souls delight in prose insane;
And Christmas stories tortured into rhyme
Contain the essence of the true sublime.
Thus, when he tells the tale of Betty Foy,
The idiot mother of 'an idiot Boy';
A moon-struck, silly lad, who lost his way,
And, like his bard, confounded night with day;
So close on each pathetic part he dwells,
And each adventure so sublimely tells,
That all who view the 'idiot in his glory'
Conceive the Bard the hero of the story.

Shall gentle COLERIDGE pass unnoticed here,
To turgid ode and tumid stanza dear?
Though themes of innocence amuse him best,
Yet still Obscurity's a welcome guest.
If Inspiration should her aid refuse
To him who takes a Pixy for a muse,
Yet none in lofty numbers can surpass
The bard who soars to elegize an ass:
So well the subject suits his noble mind,
He brays, the Laureate of the long-eared kind.

Oh! wonder-working LEWIS! Monk, or Bard,
Who fain would make Parnassus a churchyard!
Lo! wreaths of yew, not laurel, bind thy brow,
Thy Muse a Sprite, Apollo's sexton thou!
Whether on ancient tombs thou tak'st thy stand,
By gibb'ring spectres hailed, thy kindred band;
Or tracest chaste descriptions on thy page,
To please the females of our modest age;
All hail, M.P.! from whose infernal brain
Thin-sheeted phantoms glide, a grisly train;
At whose command 'grim women' throng in crowds,

And kings of fire, of water, and of clouds,
With 'small grey men,'—'wild yagers,' and what not,
To crown with honour thee and WALTER SCOTT:
Again, all hail! if tales like thine may please,
St. Luke alone can vanquish the disease:
Even Satan's self with thee might dread to dwell,
And in thy skull discern a deeper Hell.

    Who in soft guise, surrounded by a choir
Of virgins melting, not to Vesta's fire,
With sparkling eyes, and cheek by passion flushed
Strikes his wild lyre, whilst listening dames are hushed?
'Tis LITTLE! young Catullus of his day,
As sweet, but as immoral, in his Lay!
Grieved to condemn, the Muse must still be just,
Nor spare melodious advocates of lust.
Pure is the flame which o'er her altar burns;
From grosser incense with disgust she turns:
Yet, kind to youth, this expiation o'er,
She bids thee, 'mend thy line, and sin no more.'

    For thee, translator of the tinsel song,
To whom such glittering ornaments belong,
Hibernian STRANGFORD! with thine eyes of blue,
And boasted locks of red or auburn hue,
Whose plaintive strain each love-sick Miss admires,
And o'er harmonious fustian half expires,
Learn, if thou canst, to yield thine author's sense,
Nor vend thy sonnets on a false pretence.
Think'st thou to gain thy verse a higher place,
By dressing Camoëns in a suit of lace?
Mend, STRANGFORD! mend thy morals and thy taste;
Be warm, but pure; be amorous, but be chaste:
Cease to deceive; thy pilfered harp restore,
Nor teach the Lusian Bard to copy MOORE.

    Behold—Ye Tarts!—one moment spare the text!
HAYLEY's last work, and worst—until his next;

Whether he spin poor couplets into plays,
Or damn the dead with purgatorial praise,
His style in youth or age is still the same,
For ever feeble and for ever tame.
Triumphant first see 'Temper's Triumphs' shine!
At least I'm sure they triumphed over mine.
Of 'Music's Triumphs,' all who read may swear
That luckless Music never triumphed there.

    Moravians, rise! bestow some meet reward
On dull devotion—Lo! the Sabbath Bard,
Sepulchral GRAHAME, pours his notes sublime
In mangled prose, nor e'en aspires to rhyme;
Breaks into blank the Gospel of St. Luke,
And boldly pilfers from the Pentateuch;
And, undisturbed by conscientious qualms,
Perverts the Prophets, and purloins the Psalms.

    Hail, Sympathy! thy soft idea brings
A thousand visions of a thousand things,
And shows, still whimpering through three-score of years,
The maudlin prince of mournful sonneteers.
And art thou not their prince, harmonious Bowles!
Thou first, great oracle of tender souls?
Whether thou sing'st with equal ease, and grief,
The fall of empires, or a yellow leaf;
Whether thy muse most lamentably tells
What merry sounds proceed from Oxford bells,
Or, still in bells delighting, finds a friend
In every chime that jingled from Ostend;
Ah! how much juster were thy Muse's hap,
If to thy bells thou would'st but add a cap!
Delightful BOWLES! still blessing and still blest,
All love thy strain, but children like it best.
'Tis thine, with gentle LITTLE's moral song,
To soothe the mania of the amorous throng!
With thee our nursery damsels shed their tears,
Ere Miss as yet completes her infant years:

But in her teens thy whining powers are vain;
She quits poor BOWLES for LITTLE's purer strain.
Now to soft themes thou scornest to confine
The lofty numbers of a harp like thine;
'Awake a louder and a loftier strain,'
Such as none heard before, or will again!
Where all discoveries jumbled from the flood,
Since first the leaky ark reposed in mud,
By more or less, are sung in every book,
From Captain Noah down to Captain Cook.
Nor this alone—but, pausing on the road,
The Bard sighs forth a gentle episode,
And gravely tells—attend, each beauteous Miss!—
When first Madeira trembled to a kiss.
Bowles! in thy memory let this precept dwell,
Stick to thy Sonnets, Man!—at least they sell.
But if some new-born whim, or larger bribe,
Prompt thy crude brain, and claim thee for a scribe:
If 'chance some bard, though once by dunces feared,
Now, prone in dust, can only be revered;
If Pope, whose fame and genius, from the first,
Have foiled the best of critics, needs the worst,
Do thou essay: each fault, each failing scan;
The first of poets was, alas! but man.
Rake from each ancient dunghill ev'ry pearl,
Consult Lord Fanny, and confide in CURLL;
Let all the scandals of a former age
Perch on thy pen, and flutter o'er thy page;
Affect a candour which thou canst not feel,
Clothe envy in the garb of honest zeal;
Write, as if St. John's soul could still inspire,
And do from hate what MALLET did for hire.
Oh! hadst thou lived in that congenial time,
To rave with DENNIS, and with RALPH to rhyme—
Thronged with the rest around his living head,
Not raised thy hoof against the lion dead,
A meet reward had crowned thy glorious gains,
And linked thee to the Dunciad for thy pains.

   Another Epic! Who inflicts again
More books of blank upon the sons of men?
Bœotian COTTLE, rich Bristowa's boast,
Imports old stories from the Cambrian coast,
And sends his goods to market—all alive!
Lines forty thousand, Cantos twenty-five!
Fresh fish from Hippocrene! who'll buy? who'll buy?
The precious bargain's cheap—in faith, not I.
Your turtle-feeder's verse must needs be flat,
Though Bristol bloat him with the verdant fat;
If Commerce fills the purse, she clogs the brain,
And AMOS COTTLE strikes the Lyre in vain.
In him an author's luckless lot behold!
Condemned to make the books which once he sold.
Oh, AMOS COTTLE!—Phœbus! what a name
To fill the speaking-trump of future fame!—
Oh, AMOS COTTLE! for a moment think
What meagre profits spring from pen and ink!
When thus devoted to poetic dreams,
Who will peruse thy prostituted reams?
Oh! pen perverted! paper misapplied!
Had COTTLE still adorned the counter's side,
Bent o'er the desk, or, born to useful toils,
Been taught to make the paper which he soils,
Ploughed, delved, or plied the oar with lusty limb,
He had not sung of Wales, nor I of him.

   As Sisyphus against the infernal steep
Rolls the huge rock whose motions ne'er may sleep,
So up thy hill, ambrosial Richmond! heaves
Dull MAURICE all his granite weight of leaves:
Smooth, solid monuments of mental pain!
The petrifactions of a plodding brain,
That, ere they reach the top, fall lumbering back again.

   With broken lyre and cheek serenely pale,
Lo! sad Alcæus wanders down the vale;
Though fair they rose, and might have bloomed at last,

His hopes have perished by the northern blast:
Nipped in the bud by Caledonian gales,
His blossoms wither as the blast prevails!
O'er his lost works let *classic* SHEFFIELD weep;
May no rude hand disturb their early sleep!

    Yet say! why should the Bard, at once, resign
His claim to favour from the sacred Nine?
For ever startled by the mingled howl
Of Northern Wolves, that still in darkness prowl;
A coward Brood, which mangle as they prey,
By hellish instinct, all that cross their way:
Agéd or young, the living or the dead,
No mercy find—these harpies must be fed.
Why do the injured unresisting yield
The calm possession of their native field?
Why tamely thus before their fangs retreat,
Nor hunt the blood-hounds back to Arthur's Seat?

    Health to immortal JEFFREY! once, in name,
England could boast a judge almost the same;
In soul so like, so merciful, yet just,
Some think that Satan has resigned his trust,
And given the Spirit to the world again,
To sentence Letters, as he sentenced men.
With hand less mighty, but with heart as black,
With voice as willing to decree the rack;
Bred in the Courts betimes, though all that law
As yet have taught him is to find a flaw,—
Since well instructed in the patriot school
To rail at party, though a party tool—
Who knows? if chance his patrons should restore
Back to the sway they forfeited before,
His scribbling toils some recompense may meet,
And raise this Daniel to the Judgment-Seat.
Let JEFFREY's shade indulge the pious hope,
And greeting thus, present him with a rope:
Heir to my virtues! man of equal mind!

Skilled to condemn as to traduce mankind,
This cord receive! for thee reserved with care,
To wield in judgment, and at length to wear.'

    Health to great JEFFREY! Heaven preserve his life,
To flourish on the fertile shores of Fife,
And guard it sacred in its future wars,
Since authors sometimes seek the field of Mars!
Can none remember that eventful day,
That ever-glorious, almost fatal fray,
When LITTLE's leadless pistol met his eye,
And Bow-street Myrmidons stood laughing by?
Oh, day disastrous! on her firm-set rock,
Dunedin's castle felt a secret shock;
Dark rolled the sympathetic waves of Forth,
Low groaned the startled whirlwinds of the north;
TWEED ruffled half his waves to form a tear,
The other half pursued his calm career;
ARTHUR's steep summit nodded to its base,
The surly Tolbooth scarcely kept her place.
The Tolbooth felt—for marble sometimes can,
On such occasions, feel as much as man—
The Tolbooth felt defrauded of his charms,
If JEFFREY died, except within her arms:
Nay last, not least, on that portentous morn,
The sixteenth story, where himself was born,
His patrimonial garret, fell to ground,
And pale Edina shuddered at the sound:
Strewed were the streets around with milk-white reams
Flowed all the Canongate with inky streams;
This of his candour seemed the sable dew,
That of his valour showed the bloodless hue;
And all with justice deemed the two combined
The mingled emblems of his mighty mind.
But Caledonia's goddess hovered o'er
The field, and saved him from the wrath of Moore;
From either pistol snatched the vengeful lead,
And straight restored it to her favourite's head;

That head, with greater than magnetic power,
Caught it, as Danäe caught the golden shower,
And, though the thickening dross will scarce refine,
Augments its ore, and is itself a mine.
'My son,' she cried, 'ne'er thirst for gore again,
Resign the pistol and resume the pen;
O'er politics and poesy preside,
Boast of thy country, and Britannia's guide!
For long as Albion's heedless sons submit,
Or Scottish taste decides on English wit,
So long shall last thine unmolested reign,
Nor any dare to take thy name in vain.
Behold, a chosen band shall aid thy plan,
And own thee chieftain of the critic clan.
First in the oat-fed phalanx shall be seen
The travelled Thane, Athenian Aberdeen.
HERBERT shall wield THOR's hammer, and sometimes
In gratitude, thou'lt praise his rugged rhymes.
Smug SYDNEY, too, thy bitter page shall seek,
And classic HALLAM, much renowned for Greek;
SCOTT may perchance his name and influence lend
And paltry PILLANS shall traduce his friend;
While gay Thalia's luckless votary, LAMB,
Damned like the Devil—Devil-like will damn.
Known be thy name! unbounded be thy sway!
Thy HOLLAND's banquets shall each toil repay!
While grateful Britain yields the praise she owes
To HOLLAND's hirelings and to Learning's foes.
Yet mark one caution ere thy next Review
Spread its light wings of Saffron and of Blue,
Beware lest blundering BROUGHAM destroy the sale,
Turn Beef to Bannocks, Cauliflowers to Kail.'
Thus having said, the kilted Goddess kissed
Her son, and vanished in a Scottish mist.

Then prosper, JEFFREY! pertest of the train
Whom Scotland pampers with her fiery grain!
Whatever blessing waits a genuine Scot,

In double portion swells thy glorious lot;
For thee Edina culls her evening sweets,
And showers their odours on thy candid sheets,
Whose Hue and Fragrance to thy work adhere—
This scents its pages, and that gilds its rear.
Lo! blushing Itch, coy nymph, enamoured grown,
Forsakes the rest, and cleaves to thee alone,
And, too unjust to other Pictish men,
Enjoys thy person, and inspires thy pen!

Illustrious HOLLAND! hard would be his lot,
His hirelings mentioned, and himself forgot!
HOLLAND, with HENRY PETTY at his back,
The whipper-in and huntsman of the pack.
Blest be the banquets spread at Holland House,
Where Scotchmen feed, and Critics may carouse!
Long, long beneath that hospitable roof
Shall Grub-street dine, while duns are kept aloof.
See honest HALLAM lay aside his fork,
Resume his pen, review his Lordship's work,
And, grateful for the dainties on his plate,
Declare his landlord can at least translate!
Dunedin! view thy children with delight,
They write for food—and feed because they write:
And lest, when heated with the unusual grape,
Some glowing thoughts should to the press escape,
And tinge with red the female reader's cheek,
My lady skims the cream of each critique;
Breathes o'er the page her purity of soul,
Reforms each error, and refines the whole.

Now to the Drama turn—Oh! motley sight!
What precious scenes the wondering eyes invite:
Puns, and a Prince within a barrel pent,
And Dibdin's nonsense yield complete content.
Though now, thank Heaven! the Rosciomania's o'er,
And full-grown actors are endured once more;
Yet what avail their vain attempts to please,

While British critics suffer scenes like these;
While REYNOLDS vents his '*dammes!*' 'poohs!' and 'zounds!'
And common-place and common-sense confounds?
While KENNEY'S 'World'—ah! where is KENNEY'S wit?—
Tires the sad gallery, lulls the listless Pit;
And BEAUMONT'S pilfered Caratach affords
A tragedy complete in all but words?
Who but must mourn, while these are all the rage,
The degradation of our vaunted stage?
Heavens! is all sense of shame and talent gone?
Have we no living Bard of merit?—none?
Awake, GEORGE COLMAN! CUMBERLAND, awake!
Ring the alarum bell! let folly quake!
Oh! SHERIDAN! if aught can move thy pen,
Let Comedy assume her throne again;
Abjure the mummery of German schools;
Leave new Pizarros to translating fools;
Give, as thy last memorial to the age,
One classic drama, and reform the stage.
Gods! o'er those boards shall Folly rear her head,
Where GARRICK trod, and SIDDONS lives to tread?
On those shall Farce display Buffoonery's mask,
And HOOK conceal his heroes in a cask?
Shall sapient managers new scenes produce
From CHERRY, SKEFFINGTON, and Mother GOOSE?
While SHAKESPEARE, OTWAY, MASSINGER, forgot,
On stalls must moulder, or in closets rot?
Lo! with what pomp the daily prints proclaim
The rival candidates for Attic fame!
In grim array though LEWIS' spectres rise,
Still SKEFFINGTON and GOOSE divide the prize.
And, sure, *great* Skeffington must claim our praise,
For skirtless coats and skeletons of plays
Renowned alike; whose genius ne'er confines
Her flight to garnish Greenwood's gay designs;
Nor sleeps with 'Sleeping Beauties,' but anon
In five facetious acts comes thundering on;
While poor John Bull, bewildered with the scene,

Stares, wondering what the devil it can mean;
But as some hands applaud, a venal few!
Rather than sleep, why, John applauds it too.

Such are we now. Ah! wherefore should we turn
To what our fathers were, unless to mourn?
Degenerate Britons! are ye dead to shame,
Or, kind to dulness, do you fear to blame?
Well may the nobles of our present race
Watch each distortion of a NALDI's face;
Well may they smile on Italy's buffoons,
And worship CATALANI's pantaloons,
Since their own Drama yields no fairer trace
Of wit than puns, of humour than grimace.

Then let Ausonia, skilled in every art
To soften manners, but corrupt the heart,
Pour her exotic follies o'er the town,
To sanction Vice, and hunt Decorum down:
Let wedded strumpets languish o'er DESHAYES,
And bless the promise which his form displays;
While Gayton bounds before th' enraptured looks
Of hoary Marquises, and stripling Dukes:
Let high-born lechers eye the lively Presle
Twirl her light limbs, that spurn the needless veil;
Let Angiolini bare her breast of snow,
Wave the white arm, and point the pliant toe;
Collini trill her love-inspiring song,
Strain her fair neck, and charm the listening throng!
Whet not your scythe, Suppressors of our Vice!
Reforming Saints! too delicately nice!
By whose decrees, our sinful souls to save,
No Sunday tankards foam, no barbers shave;
And beer undrawn, and beards unmown, display
Your holy reverence for the Sabbath-day.

Or hail at once the patron and the pile
Of vice and folly, Greville and Argyle!

Where yon proud palace, Fashion's hallowed fane,
Spreads wide her portals for the motley train,
Behold the new Petronius of the day,
Our arbiter of pleasure and of play!
There the hired eunuch, the Hesperian choir,
The melting lute, the soft lascivious lyre,
The song from Italy, the step from France,
The midnight orgy, and the mazy dance,
The smile of beauty, and the flush of wine,
For fops, fools, gamesters, knaves and Lords combine:
Each to his humour—Comus all allows;
Champagne, dice, music—or your neighbour's spouse.
Talk not to us, ye starving sons of trade!
Of piteous ruin, which ourselves have made;
In Plenty's sunshine Fortune's minions bask,
Nor think of Poverty, except 'en masque,'
When for the night some lately titled ass
Appears the beggar which his grandsire was.
The curtain dropped, the gay Burletta o'er,
The audience take their turn upon the floor:
Now round the room the circling dow'gers sweep,
Now in loose waltz the thin-clad daughters leap;
The first in lengthened line majestic swim,
The last display the free unfettered limb!
Those for Hibernia's lusty sons repair
With art the charms which Nature could not spare;
These after husbands wing their eager flight,
Nor leave much mystery for the nuptial night.

Oh! blest retreats of infamy and ease,
Where, all forgotten but the power to please,
Each maid may give a loose to genial thought,
Each swain may teach new systems, or be taught:
There the blithe youngster, just returned from Spain,
Cuts the light pack, or calls the rattling main;
The jovial Caster's set, and seven's the Nick,
Or—done!—a thousand on the coming trick!
If, mad with loss, existence 'gins to tire,

And all your hope or wish is to expire,
Here's POWELL's pistol ready for your life,
And, kinder still, two PAGETS for your wife:
Fit consummation of an earthly race
Begun in folly, ended in disgrace,
While none but menials o'er the bed of death,
Wash thy red wounds, or watch thy wavering breath:
Traduced by liars, and forgot by all,
The mangled victim of a drunken brawl,
To live like CLODIUS, and like FALKLAND fall.

Truth! rouse some genuine Bard, and guide his hand
To drive this pestilence from out the land.
E'en I—least thinking of a thoughtless throng,
Just skilled to know the right and choose the wrong,
Freed at that age when Reason's shield is lost,
To fight my course through Passion's countless host,
Whom every path of Pleasure's flow'ry way
Has lured in turn, and all have led astray—
E'en I must raise my voice, e'en I must feel
Such scenes, such men, destroy the public weal:
Altho' some kind, censorious friend will say,
'What art thou better, meddling fool, than they?'
And every Brother Rake will smile to see
That miracle, a Moralist in me.
No matter—when some Bard in virtue strong,
Gifford perchance, shall raise the chastening song,
Then sleep my pen for ever! and my voice
Be only heard to hail him, and rejoice,
Rejoice, and yield my feeble praise, though I
May feel the lash that Virtue must apply.

As for the smaller fry, who swarm in shoals
From silly HAFIZ up to simple BOWLES,
Why should we call them from their dark abode,
In broad St. Giles's or in Tottenham-Road?
Or (since some men of fashion nobly dare
To scrawl in verse) from Bond-street or the Square?

If things of Ton their harmless lays indite,
Most wisely doomed to shun the public sight,
What harm? in spite of every critic elf,
Sir T. may read his stanzas to himself;
MILES ANDREWS still his strength in couplets try,
And live in prologues, though his dramas die.
Lords too are Bards: such things at times befall,
And 'tis some praise in Peers to write at all.
Yet, did or Taste or Reason sway the times,
Ah! who would take their titles with their rhymes?
ROSCOMMON! SHEFFIELD! with your spirits fled,
No future laurels deck a noble head;
No Muse will cheer, with renovating smile,
The paralytic puling of CARLISLE.
The puny schoolboy and his early lay
Men pardon, if his follies pass away;
But who forgives the Senior's ceaseless verse,
Whose hairs grow hoary as his rhymes grow worse?
What heterogeneous honours deck the Peer!
Lord, rhymester, petit-maître, pamphleteer!
So dull in youth, so drivelling in his age,
His scenes alone had damned our sinking stage;
But Managers for once cried, 'Hold, enough!'
Nor drugged their audience with the tragic stuff.
Yet at their judgment let his Lordship laugh,
And case his volumes in congenial calf;
Yes! doff that covering, where Morocco shines,
And hang a calf-skin on those recreant lines.

With you, ye Druids! rich in native lead,
Who daily scribble for your daily bread:
With you I war not: GIFFORD's heavy hand
Has crushed, without remorse, your numerous band.
On 'All the Talents' vent your venal spleen;
Want is your plea, let Pity be your screen.
Let Monodies on Fox regale your crew,
And Melville's Mantle prove a Blanket too!
One common Lethe waits each hapless Bard,

And, peace be with you! 'tis your best reward.
Such damning fame as Dunciads only give
Could bid your lines beyond a morning live;
But now at once your fleeting labours close,
With names of greater note in blest repose.
Far be't from me unkindly to upbraid
The lovely ROSA's prose in masquerade,
Whose strains, the faithful echoes of her mind,
Leave wondering comprehension far behind.
Though Crusca's bards no more our journals fill,
Some stragglers skirmish round the columns still;
Last of the howling host which once was Bell's,
Matilda snivels yet, and Hafiz yells;
And Merry's metaphors appear anew,
Chained to the signature of O. P. Q.

When some brisk youth, the tenant of a stall,
Employs a pen less pointed than his awl,
Leaves his snug shop, forsakes his store of shoes,
St. Crispin quits, and cobbles for the Muse,
Heavens! how the vulgar stare! how crowds app'aud!
How ladies read, and Literati laud!
If, 'chance, some wicked wag should pass his jest,
'Tis sheer ill-nature—don't the world know best?
Genius must guide when wits admire the rhyme,
And CAPEL LOFFT declares 'tis quite sublime.
Hear, then, ye happy sons of needless trade!
Swains! quit the plough, resign the useless spade!
Lo! BURNS and BLOOMFIELD, nay, a greater far,
GIFFORD was born beneath an adverse star,
Forsook the labours of a servile state,
Stemmed the rude storm, and triumphed over Fate:
Then why no more? if Phœbus smiled on you,
BLOOMFIELD! why not on brother Nathan too?
Him too the Mania, not the Muse, has seized;
Not inspiration, but a mind diseased:
And now no Boor can seek his last abode,
No common be inclosed without an ode.

Oh! since increased refinement deigns to smile
On Britain's sons, and bless our genial Isle,
Let Poesy go forth, pervade the whole,
Alike the rustic, and mechanic soul!
Ye tuneful cobblers! still your notes prolong,
Compose at once a slipper and a song;
So shall the fair your handywork peruse,
Your sonnets sure shall please—perhaps your shoes.
May Moorland weavers boast Pindaric skill,
And tailors' lays be longer than their bill!
While punctual beaux reward the grateful notes,
And pay for poems—when they pay for coats.

To the famed throng now paid the tribute due,
Neglected Genius! let me turn to you.
Come forth, oh CAMPBELL! give thy talents scope;
Who dares aspire if thou must cease to hope?
And thou, melodious ROGERS! rise at last,
Recall the pleasing memory of the past;
Arise! let blest remembrance still inspire,
And strike to wonted tones thy hallowed lyre;
Restore Apollo to his vacant throne,
Assert thy country's honour and thine own.
What! must deserted Poesy still weep
Where her last hopes with pious COWPER sleep?
Unless, perchance, from his cold bier she turns,
To deck the turf that wraps her minstrel, BURNS!
No! though Contempt hath marked the spurious brood,
The race who rhyme from folly, or for food,
Yet still some genuine sons 'tis hers to boast,
Who, least affecting, still affect the most:
Feel as they write, and write but as they feel—
Bear witness GIFFORD, SOTHEBY, MACNEIL.

'Why slumbers GIFFORD?' once was asked in vain;
Why slumbers GIFFORD? let us ask again.
Are there no follies for his pen to purge?
Are there no fools whose backs demand the scourge?

Are there no sins for Satire's Bard to greet?
Stalks not gigantic Vice in every street?
Shall Peers or Princes tread Pollution's path,
And 'scape alike the Law's, and Muse's wrath,
Nor blaze with guilty glare through future time,
Eternal beacons of consummate crime?
Arouse thee, GIFFORD! be thy promise claimed,
Make bad men better, or at least ashamed.

Unhappy WHITE! while life was in its spring,
And thy young Muse just waved her joyous wing,
The Spoiler swept that soaring Lyre away,
Which else had sounded an immortal lay.
Oh! what a noble heart was here undone,
When Science' self destroyed her favourite son!
Yes, she too much indulged thy fond pursuit,
She showed the seeds, but Death has reaped the fruit.
'Twas thine own Genius gave the final blow,
And helped to plant the wound that laid thee low:
So the struck Eagle, stretched upon the plain, .
No more through rolling clouds to soar again,
Viewed his own feather on the fatal dart,
And winged the shaft that quivered in his heart;
Keen were his pangs, but keener far to feel
He nursed the pinion which impelled the steel;
While the same plumage that had warmed his nest
Drank the last life-drop of his bleeding breast.

There be who say, in these enlightened days,
That splendid lies are all the poet's praise;
That strained Invention, ever on the wing,
Alone impels the modern Bard to sing:
'Tis true, that all who rhyme—nay, all who write,
Shrink from that fatal word to Genius—Trite;
Yet Truth sometimes will lend her noblest fires,
And decorate the verse herself inspires:
This fact in Virtue's name let CRABBE attest:
Though Nature's sternest Painter, yet the best.

And here let SHEE and Genius find a place,
Whose pen and pencil yield an equal grace;
To guide whose hand the sister Arts combine,
And trace the Poet's or the Painter's line;
Whose magic touch can bid the canvas glow,
Or pour the easy rhyme's harmonious flow;
While honours, doubly merited, attend
The Poet's rival, but the Painter's friend.

Blest is the man who dares approach the bower
Where dwelt the Muses at their natal hour;
Whose steps have pressed, whose eye has marked afar,
The clime that nursed the sons of song and war,
The scenes which Glory still must hover o'er,
Her place of birth, her own Achaian shore.
But doubly blest is he whose heart expands
With hallowed feelings for those classic lands;
Who rends the veil of ages long gone by,
And views their remnants with a poet's eye!
WRIGHT! 'twas thy happy lot at once to view
Those shores of glory, and to sing them too;
And, sure, no common Muse inspired thy pen
To hail the land of Gods and Godlike men.

And you, associate Bards! who snatched to light
Those gems too long withheld from modern sight;
Whose mingling taste combined to cull the wreath
While Attic flowers Aonian odours breathe,
And all their renovated fragrance flung,
To grace the beauties of your native tongue;
Now let those minds, that nobly could transfuse
The glorious Spirit of the Grecian Muse,
Though soft the echo, scorn a borrowed tone:
Resign Achaia's lyre, and strike your own.

Let these, or such as these, with just applause,
Restore the Muse's violated laws;
But not in flimsy DARWIN's pompous chime,

That mighty master of unmeaning rhyme,
Whose gilded cymbals, more adorned than clear,
The eye delighted, but fatigued the ear,
In show the simple lyre could once surpass,
But now, worn down, appear in native brass;
While all his train of hovering sylphs around
Evaporate in similes and sound:
Him let them shun, with him let tinsel die:
False glare attracts, but more offends the eye.

Yet let them not to vulgar WORDSWORTH stoop,
The meanest object of the lowly group,
Whose verse, of all but childish prattle void,
Seems blessed harmony to LAMB and LLOYD:
Let them—but hold, my Muse, nor dare to teach
A strain far, far beyond thy humble reach:
The native genius with their being given
Will point the path, and peal their notes to heaven.

And thou, too, SCOTT! resign to minstrels rude
The wilder Slogan of a Border feud:
Let others spin their meagre lines for hire;
Enough for Genius, if itself inspire!
Let SOUTHEY sing, altho' his teeming muse,
Prolific every spring, be too profuse;
Let simple WORDSWORTH chime his childish verse,
And brother COLERIDGE lull the babe at nurse;
Let Spectre-mongering LEWIS aim, at most,
To rouse the Galleries, or to raise a ghost;
Let MOORE still sigh; let STRANGFORD steal from MOORE,
And swear that CAMOËNS sang such notes of yore;
Let HAYLEY hobble on, MONTGOMERY rave,
And godly GRAHAME chant a stupid stave;
Let sonneteering BOWLES his strains refine,
And whine and whimper to the fourteenth line;
Let STOTT, CARLISLE, MATILDA, and the rest
Of Grub Street, and of Grosvenor Place the best,
Scrawl on, till Death release us from the strain,

Or Common Sense assert her rights again;
But Thou, with powers that mock the aid of praise,
Should'st leave to humbler Bards ignoble lays:
Thy country's voice, the voice of all the Nine,
Demand a hallowed harp—that harp is thine.
Say! will not Caledonia's annals yield
The glorious record of some nobler field,
Than the vile foray of a plundering clan,
Whose proudest deeds disgrace the name of man?
Or Marmion's acts of darkness, fitter food
For SHERWOOD's outlaw tales of ROBIN HOOD?
Scotland! still proudly claim thy native Bard,
And be thy praise his first, his best reward!
Yet not with thee alone his name should live
But own the vast renown a world can give;
Be known, perchance, when Albion is no more
And tell the tale of what she was before;
To future times her faded fame recall,
And save her glory, though his country fall.

Yet what avails the sanguine Poet's hope,
To conquer ages, and with time to cope?
New eras spread their wings, new nations rise,
And other Victors fil! th' applauding skies;
A few brief generations fleet along,
Whose sons forget the Poet and his song:
E'en now, what once-loved Minstrels scarce may claim
The transient mention of a dubious name!
When Fame's loud trump hath blown its noblest blast,
Though long the sound, the echo sleeps at last;
And Glory, like the Phœnix midst her fires,
Exhales her odours, blazes, and expires.

Shall hoary Granta call her sable sons,
Expert in science, more expert at puns?
Shall these approach the Muse? ah, no! she flies,
Even from the tempting ore of Seaton's prize;
Though Printers condescend the press to soil

With rhyme by HOARE, and epic blank by HOYLE:—
Not him whose page, if still upheld by whist,
Requires no sacred theme to bid us list.
Ye! who in Granta's honours would surpass,
Must mount her Pegasus, a full-grown ass;
A foal well worthy of her ancient Dam,
Whose Helicon is duller than her Cam.

There CLARKE, still striving piteously 'to please,'
Forgetting doggerel leads not to degrees,
A would-be Satirist, a hired Buffoon,
A monthly scribbler of some low lampoon,
Condemned to drudge, the meanest of the mean,
And furbish falsehoods for a magazine,
Devotes to scandal his congenial mind;
Himself a living libel on mankind.

Oh! dark asylum of a Vandal race!
At once the boast of learning, and disgrace!
So lost to Phœbus, that nor Hodgson's verse
Can make thee better, nor poor Hewson's worse.
But where fair Isis rolls her purer wave,
The partial Muse delighted loves to lave;
On her green banks a greener wreath she wove,
To crown the Bards that haunt her classic grove;
Where RICHARDS wakes a genuine poet's fires,
And modern Britons glory in their Sires.

For me, who, thus unasked, have dared to tell
My country, what her sons should know too well,
Zeal for her honour bade me here engage
The host of idiots that infest her age;
No just applause her honoured name shall lose,
As first in freedom, dearest to the Muse.
Oh! would thy bards but emulate thy fame,
And rise more worthy, Albion, of thy name!
What Athens was in science, Rome in power,
What Tyre appeared in her meridian hour,

'Tis thine at once, fair Albion! to have been—
Earth's chief Dictatress, Ocean's lovely Queen:
But Rome decayed, and Athens strewed the plain,
And Tyre's proud piers lie shattered in the main;
Like these, thy strength may sink in ruin hurled,
And Britain fall, the bulwark of the world.
But let me cease, and dread Cassandra's fate,
With warning ever scoffed at, till too late;
To themes less lofty still my lay confine,
And urge thy Bards to gain a name like thine.

   Then, hapless Britain! be thy rulers blest,
The Senate's oracles, the people's jest!
Still hear thy motley orators dispense
The flowers of rhetoric, though not of sense,
While CANNING's colleagues hate him for his wit,
And old dame PORTLAND fills the place of PITT.

   Yet once again, adieu! ere this the sail
That wafts me hence is shivering in the gale;
And Afric's coast and Calpe's adverse height,
And Stamboul's minarets must greet my sight:
Thence shall I stray through Beauty's native clime,
Where Kaff is clad in rocks, and crowned with snows sublime.
But should I back return, no tempting press
Shall drag my Journal from the desk's recess;
Let coxcombs, printing as they come from far,
Snatch his own wreath of Ridicule from Carr;
Let ABERDEEN and ELGIN still pursue
The shade of fame through regions of Virtù;
Waste useless thousands on their Phidian freaks,
Misshapen monuments and maimed antiques;
And make their grand saloons a general mart
For all the mutilated blocks of art:
Of Dardan tours let Dilettanti tell,
I leave topography to rapid GELL;
And, quite content, no more shall interpose
To stun the public ear—at least with Prose.

Thus far I've held my undisturbed career,
Prepared for rancour, steeled 'gainst selfish fear;
This thing of rhyme I ne'er disdained to own—
Though not obtrusive, yet not quite unknown:
My voice was heard again, though not so loud,
My page, though nameless, never disavowed;
And now at once I tear the veil away:—
Cheer on the pack! the Quarry stands at bay,
Unscared by all the din of MELBOURNE house,
By LAMB's resentment, or by HOLLAND's spouse,
By JEFFREY's harmless pistol, HALLAM's rage,
Edina's brawny sons and brimstone page.
Our men in buckram shall have blows enough,
And feel they too are 'penetrable stuff':
And though I hope not hence unscathed to go,
Who conquers me shall find a stubborn foe.
The time hath been, when no harsh sound would fall
From lips that now may seem imbued with gall;
Nor fools nor follies tempt me to despise
The meanest thing that crawled beneath my eyes:
But now, so callous grown, so changed since youth,
I've learned to think, and sternly speak the truth;
Learned to deride the critic's starch decree,
And break him on the wheel he meant for me;
To spurn the rod a scribbler bids me kiss,
Nor care if courts and crowds applaud or hiss:
Nay more, though all my rival rhymesters frown,
I too can hunt a Poetaster down;
And, armed in proof, the gauntlet cast at once
To Scotch marauder, and to Southern dunce.
Thus much I've dared; if my incondite lay
Hath wronged these righteous times, let others say:
This, let the world, which knows not how to spare,
Yet rarely blames unjustly, now declare.

from

CHILDE HAROLD'S
PILGRIMAGE

from

CHILDE HAROLD'S PILGRIMAGE

A ROMAUNT

TO IANTHE

Not in those climes where I have late been straying,
Though Beauty long hath there been matchless deemed,
Not in those visions to the heart displaying
Forms which it sighs but to have only dreamed,
Hath aught like thee in Truth or Fancy seemed:
Nor, having seen thee, shall I vainly seek
To paint those charms which varied as they beamed—
To such as see thee not my words were weak;
To those who gaze on thee what language could they speak?

Ah! may'st thou ever be what now thou art,
Nor unbeseem the promise of thy Spring—
As fair in form, as warm yet pure in heart,
Love's image upon earth without his wing,
And guileless beyond Hope's imagining!
And surely she who now so fondly rears
Thy youth, in thee, thus hourly brightening,
Beholds the Rainbow of her future years,
Before whose heavenly hues all Sorrow disappears.

Young Peri of the West!—'tis well for me
My years already doubly number thine;
My loveless eye unmoved may gaze on thee,
And safely view thy ripening beauties shine;
Happy, I ne'er shall see them in decline;
Happier, that, while all younger hearts shall bleed,
Mine shall escape the doom thine eyes assign
To those whose admiration shall succeed,
But mixed with pangs to Love's even loveliest hours decreed.

Oh! let that eye, which, wild as the Gazelle's,
Now brightly bold or beautifully shy,
Wins as it wanders, dazzles where it dwells,
Glance o'er this page, nor to my verse deny
That smile for which my breast might vainly sigh
Could I to thee be ever more than friend:
This much, dear Maid, accord; nor question why
To one so young my strain I would commend,
But bid me with my wreath one matchless Lily blend.

Such is thy name with this my verse entwined;
And long as kinder eyes a look shall cast
On Harold's page, Ianthe's here enshrined
Shall thus be *first* beheld, forgotten *last*:
My days once numbered—should this homage past
Attract thy fairy fingers near the Lyre
Of him who hailed thee loveliest, as thou wast—
Such is the most my Memory may desire;
Though more than Hope can claim, could Friendship less
    require?

CANTO THE FIRST

I

Oh, thou! in Hellas deemed of heavenly birth,
Muse! formed or fabled at the Minstrel's will!
Since shamed full oft by later lyres on earth,
Mine dares not call thee from thy sacred Hill:
Yet there I've wandered by thy vaunted rill;
Yes! sighed o'er Delphi's long deserted shrine.
Where, save that feeble fountain, all is still;
Nor mote my shell awake the weary Nine
To grace so plain a tale—this lowly lay of mine.

II

Whilome in Albion's isle there dwelt a youth,
Who ne in Virtue's ways did take delight;
But spent his days in riot most uncouth,

And vexed with mirth the drowsy ear of Night.
Ah me! in sooth he was a shameless wight,
Sore given to revel, and ungodly glee;
Few earthly things found favour in his sight
Save concubines and carnal companie,
And flaunting wassailers of high and low degree.

III

Childe Harold was he hight:—but whence his name
And lineage long, it suits me not to say;
Suffice it, that perchance they were of fame,
And had been glorious in another day:
But one sad losel soils a name for ay,
However mighty in the olden time;
Nor all that heralds rake from coffined clay,
Nor florid prose, nor honied lies of rhyme,
Can blazon evil deeds, or consecrate a crime.

IV

Childe Harold basked him in the Noontíde sun,
Disporting there like any other fly;
Nor deemed before his little day was done
One blast might chill him into misery.
But long ere scarce a third of his passed by,
Worse than Adversity the Childe befell;
He felt the fulness of Satiety:
Then loathed he in his native land to dwell,
Which seemed to him more lone than Eremite's sad cell.

V

For he through Sin's long labyrinth had run,
Nor made atonement when he did amiss,
Had sighed to many though he loved but one,
And that loved one, alas! could ne'er be his.
Ah, happy she! to 'scape from him whose kiss
Had been pollution unto aught so chaste;
Who soon had left her charms for vulgar bliss,
And spoiled her goodly lands to gild his waste,
Nor calm domestic peace had ever deigned to taste.

VI

And now Childe Harold was sore sick at heart,
And from his fellow Bacchanals would flee;
'Tis said, at times the sullen tear would start,
But Pride congealed the drop within his ee:
Apart he stalked in joyless reverie,
And from his native land resolved to go,
And visit scorching climes beyond the sea;
With pleasure drugged, he almost longed for woe,
And e'en for change of scene would seek the shades below.

VII

The Childe departed from his father's hall:
It was a vast and venerable pile;
So old, it seeméd only not to fall,
Yet strength was pillared in each massy aisle.
Monastic dome! condemned to uses vile!
Where Superstition once had made her den
Now Paphian girls were known to sing and smile;
And monks might deem their time was come agen,
If ancient tales say true, nor wrong these holy men.

VIII

Yet oft-times in his maddest mirthful mood
Strange pangs would flash along Childe Harold's brow,
As if the Memory of some deadly feud
Or disappointed passion lurked below:
But this none knew, nor haply cared to know;
For his was not that open, artless soul
That feels relief by bidding sorrow flow,
Nor sought he friend to counsel or condole,
Whate'er this grief mote be, which he could not control.

IX

And none did love him!—though to hall and bower
He gathered revellers from far and near,
He knew them flatterers of the festal hour,
The heartless Parasites of present cheer.
Yea! none did love him—not his lemans dear—

But pomp and power alone are Woman's care,
And where these are light Eros finds a feere;
Maidens, like moths, are ever caught by glare,
And Mammon wins his way where Seraphs might despair.

X

Childe Harold had a mother—not forgot,
Though parting from that mother he did shun;
A sister whom he loved, but saw her not
Before his weary pilgrimage begun:
If friends he had, he bade adieu to none.
Yet deem not thence his breast a breast of steel:
Ye, who have known what 'tis to dote upon
A few dear objects, will in sadness feel
Such partings break the heart they fondly hope to heal.

XI

His house, his home, his heritage, his lands,
The laughing dames in whom he did delight,
Whose large blue eyes, fair locks, and snowy hands,
Might shake the Saintship of an Anchorite,
And long had fed his youthful appetite;
His goblets brimmed with every costly wine,
And all that mote to luxury invite,
Without a sigh he left, to cross the brine,
And traverse Paynim shores, and pass Earth's central line.

XII

The sails were filled, and fair the light winds blew,
As glad to waft him from his native home;
And fast the white rocks faded from his view,
And soon were lost in circumambient foam:
And then, it may be, of his wish to roam
Repented he, but in his bosom slept
The silent thought, nor from his lips did come
One word of wail, whilst others sate and wept,
And to the reckless gales unmanly moaning kept.

XIII

But when the Sun was sinking in the sea
He seized his harp, which he at times could string,
And strike, albeit with untaught melody,
When deemed he no strange ear was listening:
And now his fingers o'er it he did fling,
And tuned his farewell in the dim twilight;
While flew the vessel on her snowy wing,
And fleeting shores receded from his sight,
Thus to the elements he poured his last 'Good Night.'

CHILDE HAROLD'S GOOD NIGHT

1

'Adieu, adieu! my native shore
    Fades o'er the waters blue;
The night-winds sigh, the breakers roar,
    And shrieks the wild sea-mew.
Yon Sun that sets upon the sea
    We follow in his flight;
Farewell awhile to him and thee,
    My native Land—Good Night!

2

'A few short hours and He will rise
    To give the Morrow birth;
And I shall hail the main and skies,
    But not my mother Earth.
Deserted is my own good Hall,
    Its hearth is desolate;
Wild weeds are gathering on the wall;
    My Dog howls at the gate.

3

'Come hither, hither, my little page!
    Why dost thou weep and wail?

Or dost thou dread the billows' rage,
 Or tremble at the gale?
But dash the tear-drop from thine eye;
 Our ship is swift and strong:
Our fleetest falcon scarce can fly
 More merrily along.'

4

'Let winds be shrill, let waves roll high,
 I fear not wave nor wind:
Yet marvel not, Sir Childe, that I
 Am sorrowful in mind;
For I have from my father gone,
 A mother whom I love,
And have no friends, save these alone,
 But thee—and One above.

5

'My father blessed me fervently,
 Yet did not much complain;
But sorely will my mother sigh
 Till I come back again.'—
'Enough, enough, my little lad!
 Such tears become thine eye;
If I thy guileless bosom had,
 Mine own would not be dry.

6

'Come hither, hither, my staunch yeoman,
 Why dost thou look so pale?
Or dost thou dread a French foeman?
 Or shiver at the gale?'—
'Deem'st thou I tremble for my life?
 Sir Childe, I'm not so weak;
But thinking on an absent wife
 Will blanch a faithful cheek.

7

'My spouse and boys dwell near thy hall,
 Along the bordering Lake,

And when they on their father call,
    What answer shall she make?'—
'Enough, enough, my yeoman good,
    Thy grief let none gainsay;
But I, who am of lighter mood,
    Will laugh to flee away.

8

'For who would trust the seeming sighs
    Of wife or paramour?
Fresh feeres will dry the bright blue eyes
    We late saw streaming o'er.
For pleasures past I do not grieve,
    Nor perils gathering near;
My greatest grief is that I leave
    No thing that claims a tear.

9

'And now I'm in the world alone,
    Upon the wide, wide sea:
But why should I for others groan,
    When none will sigh for me?
Perchance my Dog will whine in vain,
    Till fed by stranger hands;
But long ere I come back again,
    He'd tear me where he stands.

10

'With thee, my bark, I'll swiftly go
    Athwart the foaming brine;
Nor care what land thou bear'st me to,
    So not again to mine.
Welcome, welcome, ye dark-blue waves!
    And when you fail my sight,
Welcome, ye deserts, and ye caves!
    My native Land—Good Night!'

XIV

On, on the vessel flies, the land is gone,
And winds are rude in Biscay's sleepless bay.
Four days are sped, but with the fifth, anon,
New shores descried make every bosom gay;
And Cintra's mountain greets them on their way,
And Tagus dashing onward to the Deep,
His fabled golden tribute bent to pay;
And soon on board the Lusian pilots leap,
And steer 'twixt fertile shores where yet few rustics reap.

XV

Oh, Christ! it is a goodly sight to see
What Heaven hath done for this delicious land!
What fruits of fragrance blush on every tree!
What goodly prospects o'er the hills expand!
But man would mar them with an impious hand:
And when the Almighty lifts his fiercest scourge
'Gainst those who most transgress his high command,
With treble vengeance will his hot shafts urge
Gaul's locust host, and earth from fellest foeman purge.

XVI

What beauties doth Lisboa first unfold!
Her image floating on that noble tide,
Which poets vainly pave with sands of gold,
But now whereon a thousand keels did ride
Of mighty strength, since Albion was allied,
And to the Lusians did her aid afford:—
A nation swoln with ignorance and pride,
Who lick yet loathe the hand that waves the sword
To save them from the wrath of Gaul's unsparing Lord.

XVII

But whoso entereth within this town,
That, sheening far, celestial seems to be,
Disconsolate will wander up and down,

'Mid many things unsightly to strange ee;
For hut and palace show like filthily:
The dingy denizens are reared in dirt;
Ne personage of high or mean degree
Doth care for cleanness of surtout or shirt,
Though shent with Egypt's plague, unkempt, unwashed, un-
    hurt.

XVIII

Poor, paltry slaves! yet born 'midst noblest scenes—
Why, Nature, waste thy wonders on such men?
Lo! Cintra's glorious Eden intervenes
In variegated maze of mount and glen.
Ah, me! what hand can pencil guide, or pen,
To follow half on which the eye dilates
Through views more dazzling unto mortal ken
Than those whereof such things the Bard relates,
Who to the awe-struck world unlocked Elysium's gates!

XIX

The horrid crags, by toppling convent crowned,
The cork-trees hoar that clothe the shaggy steep,
The mountain-moss by scorching skies imbrowned,
The sunken glen, whose sunless shrubs must weep,
The tender azure of the unruffled deep,
The orange tints that gild the greenest bough,
The torrents that from cliff to valley leap,
The vine on high, the willow branch below,
Mixed in one mighty scene, with varied beauty glow.

XX

Then slowly climb the many-winding way,
And frequent turn to linger as you go,
From loftier rocks new loveliness survey,
And rest ye at 'Our Lady's house of Woe;'
Where frugal monks their little relics show,
And sundry legends to the stranger tell:

Here impious men have punished been, and lo!
Deep in yon cave Honorius long did dwell,
In hope to merit Heaven by making earth a Hell.

XXI

And here and there, as up the crags you spring,
Mark many rude-carved crosses near the path:
Yet deem not these Devotion's offering—
These are memorials frail of murderous wrath:
For wheresoe'er the shrieking victim hath
Poured forth his blood beneath the assassin's knife,
Some hand erects a cross of mouldering lath;
And grove and glen with thousand such are rife
Throughout this purple land, where Law secures not life.

XXII

On sloping mounds, or in the vale beneath,
Are domes where whilome kings did make repair;
But now the wild flowers round them only breathe:
Yet ruined Splendour still is lingering there.
And yonder towers the Prince's palace fair:
There thou too, Vathek! England's wealthiest son,
Once formed thy Paradise, as not aware
When wanton Wealth her mightiest deeds hath done,
Meek Peace voluptuous lures was ever wont to shun.

XXIII

Here didst thou dwell, here schemes of pleasure plan,
Beneath yon mountain's ever beauteous brow:
But now, as if a thing unblest by Man,
Thy fairy dwelling is as lone as Thou!
Here giant weeds a passage scarce allow
To Halls deserted, portals gaping wide:
Fresh lessons to the thinking bosom, how
Vain are the pleasaunces on earth supplied,
Swept into wrecks anon by Time's ungentle tide!

XXIV

Behold the hall where chiefs were late convened!
Oh! dome displeasing unto British eye!
With diadem hight Foolscap, lo! a Fiend,
A little Fiend that scoffs incessantly,
There sits in parchment robe arrayed, and by
His side is hung a seal and sable scroll,
Where blazoned glare names known to chivalry,
And sundry signatures adorn the roll,
Whereat the Urchin points and laughs with all his soul.

XXV

Convention is the dwarfish demon styled
That foiled the knights in Marialva's dome:
Of brains (if brains they had) he them beguiled,
And turned a nation's shallow joy to gloom.
Here Folly dashed to earth the victor's plume,
And Policy regained what arms had lost:
For chiefs like ours in vain may laurels bloom!
Woe to the conquering, not the conquered host,
Since baffled Triumph droops on Lusitania's coast!

XXVI

And ever since that martial Synod met,
Britannia sickens, Cintra! at thy name;
And folks in office at the mention fret,
And fain would blush, if blush they could, for shame.
How will Posterity the deed proclaim!
Will not our own and fellow-nations sneer,
To view these champions cheated of their fame,
By foes in fight o'erthrown, yet victors here,
Where Scorn her finger points through many a coming year?

XXVII

So deemed the Childe, as o'er the mountains he
Did take his way in solitary guise:
Sweet was the scene, yet soon he thought to flee,
More restless than the swallow in the skies:

Though here awhile he learned to moralise,
For Meditation fixed at times on him;
And conscious Reason whispered to despise
His early youth, misspent in maddest whim;
But as he gazed on truth his aching eyes grew dim.

XXVIII

To horse! to horse! he quits, for ever quits
A scene of peace, though soothing to his soul:
Again he rouses from his moping fits,
But seeks not now the harlot and the bowl.
Onward he flies, nor fixed as yet the goal
Where he shall rest him on his pilgrimage;
And o'er him many changing scenes must roll
Ere toil his thirst for travel can assuage,
Or he shall calm his breast, or learn experience sage.

XXIX

Yet Mafra shall one moment claim delay,
Where dwelt of yore the Lusians' luckless queen;
And Church and Court did mingle their array,
And Mass and revel were alternate seen;
Lordlings and freres—ill-sorted fry I ween!
But here the Babylonian Whore hath built
A dome, where flaunts she in such glorious sheen,
That men forget the blood which she hath spilt,
And bow the knee to Pomp that loves to varnish guilt.

XXX

O'er vales that teem with fruits, romantic hills,
(Oh, that such hills upheld a freeborn race!)
Whereon to gaze the eye with joyaunce fills,
Childe Harold wends through many a pleasant place.
Though sluggards deem it but a foolish chase,
And marvel men should quit their easy chair,
The toilsome way, and long, long league to trace,
Oh! there is sweetness in the mountain air,
And Life, that bloated Ease can never hope to share.

XXXI

More bleak to view the hills at length recede,
And, less luxuriant, smoother vales extend:
Immense horizon-bounded plains succeed!
Far as the eye discerns, withouten end,
Spain's realms appear whereon her shepherds tend
Flocks, whose rich fleece right well the trader knows—
Now must the Pastor's arm his *lambs* defend:
For Spain is compassed by unyielding foes,
And *all* must shield their *all*, or share Subjection's woes.

XXXII

Where Lusitania and her Sister meet,
Deem ye what bounds the rival realms divide?
Or ere the jealous Queens of Nations greet,
Doth Tayo interpose his mighty tide?
Or dark Sierras rise in craggy pride?
Or fence of art, like China's vasty wall?
Ne barrier wall, ne river deep and wide,
Ne horrid crags, nor mountains dark and tall,
Rise like the rocks that part Hispania's land from Gaul:

XXXIII

But these between a silver streamlet glides,
And scarce a name distinguisheth the brook,
Though rival kingdoms press its verdant sides,
Here leans the idle shepherd on his crook,
And vacant on the rippling waves doth look,
That peaceful still 'twixt bitterest foemen flow;
For proud each peasant as the noblest duke:
Well doth the Spanish hind the difference know
'Twixt him and Lusian slave, the lowest of the low.

XXXIV

But ere the mingling bounds have far been passed,
Dark Guadiana rolls his power along
In sullen billows, murmuring and vast,
So noted ancient roundelays among.

Whilome upon his banks did legions throng
Of Moor and Knight, in mailéd splendour drest:
Here ceased the swift their race, here sunk the strong;
The Paynim turban and the Christian crest
Mixed on the bleeding stream, by floating hosts oppressed.

XXXV

Oh, lovely Spain! renowned, romantic Land!
Where is that Standard which Pelagio bore,
When Cava's traitor-sire first called the band
That dyed thy mountain streams with Gothic gore?
Where are those bloody Banners which of yore
Waved o'er thy sons, victorious to the gale,
And drove at last the spoilers to their shore?
Red gleamed the Cross, and waned the Crescent pale,
While Afric's echoes thrilled with Moorish matrons' wail.

XXXVI

Teems not each ditty with the glorious tale?
Ah! such, alas! the hero's amplest fate!
When granite moulders and when records fail,
A peasant's plaint prolongs his dubious date.
Pride! bend thine eye from Heaven to thine estate,
See how the Mighty shrink into a song!
Can Volume, Pillar, Pile preserve thee great?
Or must thou trust Tradition's simple tongue,
When Flattery sleeps with thee, and History does thee wrong?

XXXVII

Awake, ye Sons of Spain! awake! advance!
Lo! Chivalry, your ancient Goddess, cries,
But wields not, as of old, her thirsty lance,
Nor shakes her crimson plumage in the skies:
Now on the smoke of blazing bolts she flies,
And speaks in thunder through yon engine's roar:
In every peal she calls—'Awake! arise!'
Say, is her voice more feeble than of yore,
When her war-song was heard on Andalusia's shore?

C

XXXVIII

Hark!—heard you not those hoofs of dreadful note?
Sounds not the clang of conflict on the heath?
Saw ye not whom the reeking sabre smote,
Nor saved your brethren ere they sank beneath
Tyrants and Tyrants' slaves?—the fires of Death,
The Bale-fires flash on high :—from rock to rock
Each volley tells that thousands cease to breathe;
Death rides upon the sulphury Siroc,
Red Battle stamps his foot, and Nations feel the shock.

XXXIX

Lo! where the Giant on the mountain stands,
His blood-red tresses deepening in the Sun,
With death-shot glowing in his fiery hands,
And eye that scorcheth all it glares upon;
Restless it rolls, now fixed, and now anon
Flashing afar,—and at his iron feet
Destruction cowers, to mark what deeds are done;
For on this morn three potent Nations meet,
To shed before his Shrine the blood he deems most sweet.

XL

By Heaven! it is a splendid sight to see
(For one who hath no friend, no brother there)
Their rival scarfs of mixed embroidery,
Their various arms that glitter in the air!
What gallant War-hounds rouse them from their lair,
And gnash their fangs, loud yelling for the prey!
All join the chase, but few the triumph share;
The Grave shall bear the chiefest prize away,
And Havoc scarce for joy can number their array.

XLI

Three hosts combine to offer sacrifice;
Three tongues prefer strange orisons on high;
Three gaudy standards flout the pale blue skies;
The shouts are France, Spain, Albion, Victory!

The Foe, the Victim, and the fond Ally
That fights for all, but ever fights in vain,
Are met—as if at home they could not die—
To feed the crow on Talavera's plain,
And fertilise the field that each pretends to gain.

XLII

There shall they rot—Ambition's honoured fools!
Yes, Honour decks the turf that wraps their clay!
Vain Sophistry! in these behold the tools,
The broken tools, that Tyrants cast away
By myriads, when they dare to pave their way
With human hearts—to what?—a dream alone.
Can Despots compass aught that hails their sway?
Or call with truth one span of earth their own,
Save that wherein at last they crumble bone by bone?

XLIII

Oh, Albuera! glorious field of grief!
As o'er thy plain the Pilgrim pricked his steed,
Who could foresee thee, in a space so brief,
A scene where mingling foes should boast and bleed!
Peace to the perished! may the warrior's meed
And tears of triumph their reward prolong!
Till others fall where other chieftains lead,
Thy name shall circle round the gaping throng,
And shine in worthless lays, the theme of transient song.

XLIV

Enough of Battle's minions! let them play
Their game of lives, and barter breath for fame:
Fame that will scarce reanimate their clay,
Though thousands fall to deck some single name.
In sooth 'twere sad to thwart their noble aim
Who strike, blest hirelings! for their country's good,
And die, that living might have proved her shame;
Perished, perchance, in some domestic feud,
Or in a narrower sphere wild Rapine's path pursued.

XLV

Full swiftly Harold wends his lonely way
Where proud Sevilla triumphs unsubdued:
Yet is she free? the Spoiler's wished-for prey!
Soon, soon shall Conquest's fiery foot intrude,
Blackening her lovely domes with traces rude.
Inevitable hour! 'Gainst fate to strive
Where Desolation plants her famished brood
Is vain, or Ilion, Tyre might yet survive,
And Virtue vanquish all, and Murder cease to thrive.

XLVI

But all unconscious of the coming doom,
The feast, the song, the revel here abounds;
Strange modes of merriment the hours consume,
Nor bleed these patriots with their country's wounds:
Nor here War's clarion, but Love's rebeck sounds;
Here Folly still his votaries inthralls;
And young-eyed Lewdness walks her midnight rounds:
Girt with the silent crimes of Capitals,
Still to the last kind Vice clings to the tott'ring walls.

XLVII

Not so the rustic—with his trembling mate
He lurks, nor casts his heavy eye afar,
Lest he should view his vineyard desolate,
Blasted below the dun hot breath of War.
No more beneath soft eve's consenting star
Fandango twirls his jocund castanet:
Ah, Monarchs! could ye taste the mirth ye mar,
Not in the toils of Glory would ye fret;
The hoarse dull drum would sleep, and Man be happy yet!

XLVIII

How carols now the lusty muleteer?
Of Love, Romance, Devotion is his lay,
As whilome he was wont the leagues to cheer,
His quick bells wildly jingling on the way?

No! as he speeds, he chants 'Vivā el Rey!'
And checks his song to execrate Godoy,
The royal wittol Charles, and curse the day
When first Spain's queen beheld the black-eyed boy,
And gore-faced Treason sprung from her adulterate joy.

XLIX

On yon long level plain, at distance crowned
With crags, whereon those Moorish turrets rest,
Wide-scattered hoof-marks dint the wounded ground;
And, scathed by fire, the greensward's darkened vest
Tells that the foe was Andalusia's guest:
Here was the camp, the watch-flame, and the host,
Here the bold peasant stormed the Dragon's nest;
Still does he mark it with triumphant boast,
And points to yonder cliffs, which oft were won and lost.

L

And whomsoe'er along the path you meet
Bears in his cap the badge of crimson hue,
Which tells you whom to shun and whom to greet:
Woe to the man that walks in public view
Without of loyalty this token true:
Sharp is the knife, and sudden is the stroke;
And sorely would the Gallic foeman rue,
If subtle poniards, wrapt beneath the cloke
Could blunt the sabre's edge, or clear the cannon's smoke.

LI

At every turn Morena's dusky height
Sustains aloft the battery's iron load;
And, far as mortal eye can compass sight,
The mountain-howitzer, the broken road,
The bristling palisade, the fosse o'erflowed,
The stationed bands, the never-vacant watch,
The magazine in rocky durance stowed,
The holstered steed beneath the shed of thatch,
The ball-piled pyramid, the ever-blazing match

LII

Portend the deeds to come :—but he whose nod
Has tumbled feebler despots from their sway,
A moment pauseth ere he lifts the rod ;
A little moment deigneth to delay :
Soon will his legions sweep through these their way ;
The West must own the Scourger of the world.
Ah! Spain! how sad will be thy reckoning-day,
When soars Gaul's Vulture, with his wings unfurled,
And thou shalt view thy sons in crowds to Hades hurled.

LIII

And must they fall? the young, the proud, the brave,
To swell one bloated Chief's unwholesome reign?
No step between submission and a grave?
The rise of Rapine and the fall of Spain?
And doth the Power that man adores ordain
Their doom, nor heed the suppliant's appeal?
Is all that desperate Valour acts in vain?
And Counsel sage, and patriotic Zeal—
The Veteran's skill—Youth's fire—and Manhood's heart of
    steel?

LIV

Is it for this the Spanish maid, aroused,
Hangs on the willow her unstrung guitar,
And, all unsexed, the Anlace hath espoused,
Sung the loud song, and dared the deed of war?
And she, whom once the semblance of a scar
Appalled, an owlet's 'larum chilled with dread,
Now views the column-scattering bay'net jar,
The falchion flash, and o'er the yet warm dead
Stalks with Minerva's step where Mars might quake to tread.

LV

Ye who shall marvel when you hear her tale,
Oh! had you known her in her softer hour,
Marked her black eye that mocks her coal-black veil,
Heard her light, lively tones in Lady's bower,

Seen her long locks that foil the painter's power,
Her fairy form, with more than female grace,
Scarce would you deem that Saragoza's tower
Beheld her smile in Danger's Gorgon face,
Thin the closed ranks, and lead in Glory's fearful chase.

LVI

Her lover sinks—she sheds no ill-timed tear;
Her Chief is slain—she fills his fatal post;
Her fellows flee—she checks their base career;
The Foe retires—she heads the sallying host:
Who can appease like her a lover's ghost?
Who can avenge so well a leader's fall?
What maid retrieve when man's flushed hope is lost?
Who hang so fiercely on the flying Gaul,
Foiled by a woman's hand, before a battered wall?

LVII

Yet are Spain's maids no race of Amazons,
But formed for all the witching arts of love:
Though thus in arms they emulate her sons,
And in the horrid phalanx dare to move,
'Tis but the tender fierceness of the dove,
Pecking the hand that hovers o'er her mate:
In softness as in firmness far above
Remoter females, famed for sickening prate;
Her mind is nobler sure, her charms perchance as great.

LVIII

The seal Love's dimpling finger hath impressed
Denotes how soft that chin which bears his touch:
Her lips, whose kisses pout to leave their nest
Bid man be valiant ere he merit such:
Her glance how wildly beautiful! how much
Hath Phœbus wooed in vain to spoil her cheek
Which glows yet smoother from his amorous clutch!
Who round the North for paler dames would seek?
How poor their forms appear! how languid, wan, and weak!

LIX

Match me, ye climes! which poets love to laud;
Match me, ye harems of the land! where now
I strike my strain, far distant, to applaud
Beauties that ev'n a cynic must avow;
Match me those Houries, whom ye scarce allow
To taste the gale lest Love should ride the wind,
With Spain's dark-glancing daughters—deign to know
There your wise Prophet's Paradise we find,
His black-eyed maids of Heaven, angelically kind.

LX

Oh, thou Parnassus! whom I now survey,
Not in the phrensy of a dreamer's eye,
Not in the fabled landscape of a lay,
But soaring snow-clad through thy native sky,
In the wild pomp of mountain-majesty!
What marvel if I thus essay to sing?
The humblest of thy pilgrims passing by
Would gladly woo thine Echoes with his string,
Though from thy heights no more one Muse will wave her
    wing.

LXI

Oft have I dreamed of Thee! whose glorious name
Who knows not, knows not man's divinest lore:
And now I view thee—'tis, alas! with shame
That I in feeblest accents must adore.
When I recount thy worshippers of yore
I tremble, and can only bend the knee;
Nor raise my voice, nor vainly dare to soar,
But gaze beneath thy cloudy canopy
In silent joy to think at last I look on Thee!

LXII

Happier in this than mightiest Bards have been,
Whose Fate to distant homes confined their lot,
Shall I unmoved behold the hallowed scene,

Which others rave of, though they know it not?
Though here no more Apollo haunts his Grot,
And thou, the Muses' seat, art now their grave,
Some gentle Spirit still pervades the spot,
Sighs in the gale, keeps silence in the Cave,
And glides with glassy foot o'er yon melodious wave.

LXIII

Of thee hereafter. Ev'n amidst my strain
I turned aside to pay my homage here;
Forgot the land, the sons, the maids of Spain;
Her fate, to every freeborn bosom dear;
And hailed thee, not perchance without a tear.
Now to my theme—but from thy holy haunt
Let me some remnant, some memorial bear;
Yield me one leaf of Daphne's deathless plant,
Nor let thy votary's hope be deemed an idle vaunt.

LXIV

But ne'er didst thou, fair Mount! when Greece was young,
See round thy giant base a brighter choir,
Nor e'er did Delphi, when her Priestess sung
The Pythian hymn with more than mortal fire,
Behold a train more fitting to inspire
The song of love, than Andalusia's maids
Nurst in the glowing lap of soft Desire:
Ah! that to these were given such peaceful shades
As Greece can still bestow, though Glory fly her glades.

LXV

Fair is proud Seville; let her country boast
Her strength, her wealth, her site of ancient days;
But Cadiz, rising on the distant coast,
Calls forth a sweeter, though ignoble praise.
Ah, Vice! how soft are thy voluptuous ways!
While boyish blood is mantling, who can 'scape
The fascination of thy magic gaze?
A Cherub-Hydra round us dost thou gape,
And mould to every taste thy dear delusive shape.

LXVI

When Paphos fell by Time—accursèd Time!
The Queen who conquers all must yield to thee—
The Pleasures fled, but sought as warm a clime;
And Venus, constant to her native Sea,
To nought else constant, hither deigned to flee,
And fixed her shrine within these walls of white:
Though not to one dome circumscribeth She
Her worship, but, devoted to her rite,
A thousand Altars rise, for ever blazing bright.

LXVII

From morn till night, from night till startled Morn
Peeps blushing on the Revel's laughing crew,
The Song is heard, the rosy Garland worn;
Devices quaint, and Frolics ever new,
Tread on each other's kibes. A long adieu
He bids to sober joy that here sojourns:
Nought interrupts the riot, though in lieu
Of true devotion monkish incense burns,
And Love and Prayer unite, or rule the hour by turns.

LXVIII

The Sabbath comes, a day of blessèd rest:
What hallows it upon this Christian shore?
Lo! it is sacred to a solemn Feast:
Hark! heard you not the forest-monarch's roar?
Crashing the lance, he snuffs the spouting gore
Of man and steed, o'erthrown beneath his horn;
The thronged arena shakes with shouts for more;
Yells the mad crowd o'er entrails freshly torn,
Nor shrinks the female eye, nor ev'n affects to mourn.

LXIX

The seventh day this—the Jubilee of man!
London! right well thou know'st the day of prayer:
Then thy spruce citizen, washed artisan,
And smug apprentice gulp their weekly air:

Thy coach of hackney, whiskey, one-horse chair,
And humblest gig through sundry suburbs whirl,
To Hampstead, Brentford, Harrow make repair;
Till the tired jade the wheel forgets to hurl,
Provoking envious gibe from each pedestrian churl.

LXX

Some o'er thy Thamis row the ribboned fair,
Others along the safer turnpike fly;
Some Richmond-hill ascend, some scud to Ware,
And many to the steep of Highgate hie.
Ask ye, Bœotian Shades! the reason why?
'Tis to the worship of the solemn Horn,
Grasped in the holy hand of Mystery,
In whose dread name both men and maids are sworn,
And consecrate the oath with draught, and dance till morn.

LXXI

All have their fooleries—not alike are thine,
Fair Cadiz, rising o'er the dark blue sea!
Soon as the Matin bell proclaimeth nine,
Thy Saint-adorers count the Rosary:
Much is the VIRGIN teased to shrive them free
(Well do I ween the only virgin there)
From crimes as numerous as her beadsmen be;
Then to the crowded circus forth they fare:
Young, old, high, low, at once the same diversion share.

LXXII

The lists are oped, the spacious area cleared,
Thousands on thousands piled are seated round;
Long ere the first loud trumpet's note is heard,
Ne vacant space for lated wight is found:
Here Dons, Grandees, but chiefly Dames abound,
Skilled in the ogle of a roguish eye,
Yet ever well inclined to heal the wound;
None through their cold disdain are doomed to die,
As moon-struck bards complain, by Love's sad archery.

LXXIII

Hushed is the din of tongues—on gallant steeds,
With milk-white crest, gold spur, and light-poised lance,
Four cavaliers prepare for venturous deeds
And lowly-bending to the lists advance;
Rich are their scarfs, their chargers featly prance:
If in the dangerous game they shine to-day,
The crowd's loud shout and ladies' lovely glance,
Best prize of better acts! they bear away;
And all that kings or chiefs e'er gain their toils repay.

LXXIV

In costly sheen and gaudy cloak arrayed,
But all afoot, the light-limbed Matadore
Stands in the centre, eager to invade
The lord of lowing herds; but not before
The ground, with cautious tread, is traversed o'er,
Lest aught unseen should lurk to thwart his speed:
His aims a dart, he fights aloof, nor more
Can Man achieve without the friendly steed—
Alas! too oft condemned for him to bear and bleed.

LXXV

Thrice sounds the Clarion; lo! the signal falls,
The den expands, and Expectation mute
Gapes round the silent circle's peopled walls:
Bounds with one lashing spring the mighty brute,
And, wildly staring, spurns, with sounding foot,
The sand, nor blindly rushes on his foe:
Here, there, he points his threatening front, to suit
His first attack, wide-waving to and fro
His angry tail; red rolls his eye's dilated glow.

LXXVI

Sudden he stops—his eye is fixed—away—
Away, thou heedless boy! prepare the spear;
Now is thy time, to perish, or display
The skill that yet may check his mad career!
With well-timed croupe the nimble coursers veer;

On foams the Bull, but not unscathed he goes;
Streams from his flank the crimson torrent clear:
He flies, he wheels, distracted with his throes;
Dart follows dart—lance, lance—loud bellowings speak his
　　woes.

LXXVII

Again he comes; nor dart nor lance avail,
Nor the wild plunging of the tortured horse;
Though Man and Man's avenging arms assail,
Vain are his weapons, vainer is his force.
One gallant steed is stretched a mangled corse;
Another, hideous sight! unseamed appears,
His gory chest unveils life's panting source;
Though death-struck, still his feeble frame he rears;
Staggering, but stemming all, his Lord unharmed he bears

LXXVIII

Foiled, bleeding, breathless, furious to the last.
Full in the centre stands the Bull at bay,
'Mid wounds, and clinging darts, and lances brast.
And foes disabled in the brutal fray:
And now the Matadores around him play,
Shake the red cloak, and poise the ready brand:
Once more through all he bursts his thundering way—
Vain rage! the mantle quits the conynge hand,
Wraps his fierce eye—'tis past—he sinks upon the sand!

LXXIX

Where his vast neck just mingles with the spine.
Sheathed in his form the deadly weapon lies.
He stops—he starts—disdaining to decline:
Slowly he falls, amidst triumphant cries,
Without a groan, without a struggle dies.
The decorated car appears—on high
The corse is piled—sweet sight for vulgar eyes—
Four steeds that spurn the rein, as swift as shy,
Hurl the dark bulk along, scarce seen in dashing by.

LXXX

Such the ungentle sport that oft invites
The Spanish maid, and cheers the Spanish swain.
Nurtured in blood betimes, his heart delights
In vengeance, gloating on another's pain.
What private feuds the troubled village stain!
Though now one phalanxed host should meet the foe,
Enough, alas! in humble homes remain,
To meditate 'gainst friend the secret blow,
For some slight cause of wrath, whence Life's warm stream
    must flow.

LXXXI

But Jealousy has fled: his bars, his bolts,
His withered Centinel, Duenna sage!
And all whereat the generous soul revolts,
Which the stern dotard deemed he could encage,
Have passed to darkness with the vanished age.
Who late so free as Spanish girls were seen,
(Ere War uprose in his volcanic rage,)
With braided tresses bounding o'er the green,
While on the gay dance shone Night's lover-loving Queen?

LXXXII

Oh! many a time and oft, had Harold loved,
Or dreamed he loved, since Rapture is a dream;
But now his wayward bosom was unmoved,
For not yet had he drunk of Lethe's stream;
And lately had he learned with truth to deem
Love has no gift so grateful as his wings:
How fair, how young, how soft soe'er he seem,
Full from the fount of Joy's delicious springs
Some bitter o'er the flowers its bubbling venom flings.

LXXXIII

Yet to the beauteous form he was not blind,
Though now it moved him as it moves the wise;
Not that Philosophy on such a mind
E'er deigned to bend her chastely-awful eyes:

But Passion raves herself to rest, or flies;
And Vice, that digs her own voluptuous tomb,
Had buried long his hopes, no more to rise:
Pleasure's palled Victim! life-abhorring Gloom
Wrote on his faded brow curst Cain's unresting doom.

LXXXIV

Still he beheld, nor mingled with the throng;
But viewed them not with misanthropic hate:
Fain would he now have joined the dance, the song;
But who may smile that sinks beneath his fate?
Nought that he saw his sadness could abate:
Yet once he struggled 'gainst the Demon's sway,
And as in Beauty's bower he pensive sate,
Poured forth his unpremeditated lay,
To charms as fair as those that soothed his happier day.

TO INEZ

1

Nay, smile not at my sullen brow;
   Alas! I cannot smile again:
Yet Heaven avert that ever thou
   Shouldst weep, and haply weep in vain.

2

And dost thou ask what secret woe
   I bear, corroding Joy and Youth?
And wilt thou vainly seek to know
   A pang, ev'n thou must fail to soothe?

3

It is not love, it is not hate,
   Nor low Ambition's honours lost,
That bids me loathe my present state,
   And fly from all I prized the most:

4

It is that weariness which springs
    From all I meet, or hear, or see:
To me no pleasure Beauty brings;
    Thine eyes have scarce a charm for me

5

It is that settled, ceaseless gloom
    The fabled Hebrew Wanderer bore;
That will not look beyond the tomb,
    But cannot hope for rest before.

6

What Exile from himself can flee?
    To zones though more and more remote,
Still, still pursues, where'er I be,
    The blight of Life—the Demon Thought.

7

Yet others rapt in pleasure seem,
    And taste of all that I forsake;
Oh! may they still of transport dream,
    And ne'er—at least like me—awake!

8

Through many a clime 'tis mine to go,
    With many a retrospection curst;
And all my solace is to know,
    Whate'er betides, I've known the worst.

9

What is that worst? Nay do not ask—
    In pity from the search forbear:
Smile on—nor venture to unmask
    Man's heart, and view the Hell that's there.

LXXXV

Adieu, fair Cadiz! yea, a long adieu!
Who may forget how well thy walls have stood?
When all were changing thou alone wert true,
First to be free and last to be subdued:
And if amidst a scene, a shock so rude,
Some native blood was seen thy streets to dye,
A Traitor only fell beneath the feud:
Here all were noble, save Nobility;
None hugged a Conqueror's chain, save fallen Chivalry!

LXXXVI

Such be the sons of Spain, and strange her Fate!
They fight for Freedom who were never free,
A Kingless people for a nerveless state;
Her vassals combat when their Chieftains flee,
True to the veriest slaves of Treachery:
Fond of a land which gave them nought but life,
Pride points the path that leads to Liberty;
Back to the struggle, baffled in the strife,
War, war is still the cry, 'War even to the knife!'

LXXXVII

Ye, who would more of Spain and Spaniards know
Go, read whate'er is writ of bloodiest strife:
Whate'er keen Vengeance urged on foreign foe
Can act, is acting there against man's life:
From flashing scimitar to secret knife,
War mouldeth there each weapon to his need—
So may he guard the sister and the wife,
So may he make each curst oppressor bleed—
So may such foes deserve the most remorseless deed!

LXXXVIII

Flows there a tear of Pity for the dead?
Look o'er the ravage of the reeking plain;
Look on the hands with female slaughter red;
Then to the dogs resign the unburied slain,

Then to the vulture let each corse remain,
Albeit unworthy of the prey-bird's maw;
Let their bleached bones, and blood's unbleaching stain,
Long mark the battle-field with hideous awe:
Thus only may our sons conceive the scenes we saw!

LXXXIX

Nor yet, alas! the dreadful work is done;
Fresh legions pour adown the Pyrenees:
It deepens still, the work is scarce begun,
Nor mortal eye the distant end foresees.
Fall'n nations gaze on Spain; if freed, she frees
More than her fell Pizarros once enchained:
Strange retribution! now Columbia's ease
Repairs the wrongs that Quito's sons sustained,
While o'er the parent clime prowls Murder unrestrained.

XC

Not all the blood at Talavera shed,
Not all the marvels of Barossa's fight,
Not Albuera lavish of the dead,
Have won for Spain her well asserted right.
When shall her Olive-Branch be free from blight?
When shall she breathe her from the blushing toil?
How many a doubtful day shall sink in night,
Ere the Frank robber turn him from his spoil,
And Freedom's stranger-tree grow native of the soil!

XCI

And thou, my friend!—since unavailing woe
Bursts from my heart, and mingles with the strain—
Had the sword laid thee with the mighty low,
Pride might forbid e'en Friendship to complain:
But thus unlaurelled to descend in vain,
By all forgotten, save the lonely breast,
And mix unbleeding with the boasted slain,
While Glory crowns so many a meaner crest!
What hadst thou done to sink so peacefully to rest?

XCII

Oh, known the earliest, and esteemed the most!
Dear to a heart where nought was left so dear!
Though to my hopeless days for ever lost,
In dreams deny me not to see thee here!
And Morn in secret shall renew the tear
Of Consciousness awaking to her woes,
And Fancy hover o'er thy bloodless bier,
Till my frail frame return to whence it rose,
And mourned and mourner lie united in repose.

XCIII

Here is one fytte of Harold's pilgrimage:
Ye who of him may further seek to know,
Shall find some tidings in a future page,
If he that rhymeth now may scribble moe.
Is this too much? stern Critic! say not so:
Patience! and ye shall hear what he beheld
In other lands, where he was doomed to go:
Lands that contain the monuments of Eld,
Ere Greece and Grecian arts by barbarous hands were quelled.

CANTO THE SECOND

I

Come, blue-eyed Maid of Heaven!—but Thou, alas!
Didst never yet one mortal song inspire—
Goddess of Wisdom! here thy temple was,
And is, despite of War and wasting fire,
And years, that bade thy worship to expire:
But worse than steel, and flame, and ages slow,
Is the dread sceptre and dominion dire
Of men who never felt the sacred glow
That thoughts of thee and thine on polished breasts bestow.

II

Ancient of days! august Athena! where,
Where are thy men of might? thy grand in soul?

Gone—glimmering through the dream of things that were:
First in the race that led to Glory's goal,
They won, and passed away—is this the whole?
A schoolboy's tale, the wonder of an hour!
The Warrior's weapon and the Sophist's stole
Are sought in vain, and o'er each mouldering tower,
Dim with the mist of years, gray flits the shade of power.

III

Son of the Morning, rise! approach you here!
Come—but molest not yon defenceless Urn:
Look on this spot—a Nation's sepulchre!
Abode of Gods, whose shrines no longer burn.
Even Gods must yield—Religions take their turn:
'Twas Jove's—'tis Mahomet's—and other Creeds
Will rise with other years, till Man shall learn
Vainly his incense soars, his victim bleeds;
Poor child of Doubt and Death, whose hope is built on reeds.

IV

Bound to the Earth, he lifts his eye to Heaven—
Is 't not enough, Unhappy Thing! to know
Thou art? Is this a boon so kindly given,
That being, thou would'st be again, and go,
Thou know'st not, reck'st not to what region, so
On Earth no more, but mingled with the skies?
Still wilt thou dream on future Joy and Woe?
Regard and weigh yon dust before it flies:
That little urn saith more than thousand Homilies.

V

Or burst the vanished Hero's lofty mound;
Far on the solitary shore he sleeps:
He fell, and falling nations mourned around;
But now not one of saddening thousands weeps,
Nor warlike worshipper his vigil keeps
Where demi-gods appeared, as records tell.
Remove yon skull from out the scattered heaps:

Is that a Temple where a God may dwell?
Why ev'n the Worm at last disdains her shattered cell!

VI

Look on its broken arch, its ruined wall,
Its chambers desolate, and portals foul:
Yes, this was once Ambition's airy hall,
The Dome of Thought, the Palace of the Soul:
Behold through each lack-lustre, eyeless hole,
The gay recess of Wisdom and of Wit
And Passion's host, that never brooked control:
Can all Saint, Sage, or Sophist ever writ,
People this lonely tower, this tenement refit?

VII

Well didst thou speak, Athena's wisest son!
'All that we know is, nothing can be known.'
Why should we shrink from what we cannot shun?
Each hath its pang, but feeble sufferers groan
With brain-born dreams of Evil all their own.
Pursue what Chance or Fate proclaimeth best—
Peace waits us on the shores of Acheron:
There no forced banquet claims the sated guest,
But Silence spreads the couch of ever welcome Rest.

VIII

Yet if, as holiest men have deemed, there be
A land of Souls beyond that sable shore,
To shame the Doctrine of the Sadducee
And Sophists, madly vain of dubious lore;
How sweet it were in concert to adore
With those who made our mortal labours light!
To hear each voice we feared to hear no more!
Behold each mighty shade revealed to sight,
The Bactrian, Samian sage, and all who taught the Right!

IX

There, Thou!—whose Love and Life together fled,
Have left me here to love and live in vain—

Twined with my heart, and can I deem thee dead
When busy Memory flashes on my brain?
Well—I will dream that we may meet again,
And woo the vision to my vacant breast:
If aught of young Remembrance then remain,
Be as it may Futurity's behest,
For me 'twere bliss enough to know thy spirit blest!

X

Here let me sit upon this massy stone,
The marble column's yet unshaken base;
Here, son of Saturn! was thy favourite throne:
Mightiest of many such! Hence let me trace
The latent grandeur of thy dwelling-place.
It may not be: nor ev'n can Fancy's eye
Restore what Time hath laboured to deface:
Yet these proud Pillars claim no passing sigh;
Unmoved the Moslem sits, the light Greek carols by.

XI

But who, of all the plunderers of yon Fane
On high—where Pallas lingered, loth to flee
The latest relic of her ancient reign—
The last, the worst, dull spoiler, who was he?
Blush, Caledonia! such thy son could be!
England! I joy no child he was of thine:
Thy free-born men should spare what once was free;
Yet they could violate each saddening shrine,
And bear these altars o'er the long-reluctant brine.

XII

But most the modern Pict's ignoble boast,
To rive what Goth, and Turk, and Time hath spared:
Cold as the crags upon his native coast,
His mind as barren and his heart as hard,
Is he whose head conceived, whose hand prepared,
Aught to displace Athena's poor remains:
Her Sons too weak the sacred shrine to guard,

Yet felt some portion of their Mother's pains,
And never knew, till then, the weight of Despot's chains.

XIII

What! shall it e'er be said by British tongue,
Albion was happy in Athena's tears?
Though in thy name the slaves her bosom wrung,
Tell not the deed to blushing Europe's ears;
The Ocean Queen, the free Britannia, bears
The last poor plunder from a bleeding land:
Yes, she, whose generous aid her name endears,
Tore down those remnants with a Harpy's hand,
Which envious Eld forbore, and tyrants left to stand.

XIV

Where was thine Ægis, Pallas! that appalled
Stern Alaric and Havoc on their way?
Where Peleus' son? whom Hell in vain enthralled,
His shade from Hades upon that dread day
Bursting to light in terrible array!
What! could not Pluto spare the Chief once more,
To scare a second robber from his prey?
Idly he wandered on the Stygian shore,
Nor now preserved the walls he loved to shield before.

XV

Cold is the heart, fair Greece! that looks on Thee,
Nor feels as Lovers o'er the dust they loved;
Dull is the eye that will not weep to see
Thy walls defaced, thy mouldering shrines removed
By British hands, which it had best behoved
To guard those relics ne'er to be restored:—
Curst be the hour when from their isle they roved,
And once again thy hapless bosom gored,
And snatched thy shrinking Gods to Northern climes abhorred!

XVI

But where is Harold? shall I then forget
To urge the gloomy Wanderer o'er the wave?

Little recked he of all that Men regret;
No loved-one now in feigned lament could rave;
No friend the parting hand extended gave,
Ere the cold Stranger passed to other climes:
Hard is his heart whom charms may not enslave;
But Harold felt not as in other times,
And left without a sigh the land of War and Crimes.

XVII

He that has sailed upon the dark blue sea
Has viewed at times, I ween, a full fair sight,
When the fresh breeze is fair as breeze may be,
The white sail set, the gallant Frigate tight—
Masts, spires, and strand retiring to the right,
The glorious Main expanding o'er the bow,
The Convoy spread like wild swans in their flight,
The dullest sailer wearing bravely now—
So gaily curl the waves before each dashing prow.

XVIII

And oh, the little warlike world within!
The well-reeved guns, the netted canopy,
The hoarse command, the busy humming din,
When, at a word, the tops are manned on high:
Hark, to the Boatswain's call, the cheering cry!
While through the seaman's hand the tackle glides;
Or schoolboy Midshipman that, standing by,
Strains his shrill pipe as good or ill betides,
And well the docile crew that skilful Urchin guides.

XIX

White is the glassy deck, without a stain,
Where on the watch the staid Lieutenant walks:
Look on that part which sacred doth remain
For the lone Chieftain, who majestic stalks,
Silent and feared by all—not oft he talks
With aught beneath him, if he would preserve
That strict restraint, which broken, ever balks

Conquest and Fame: but Britons rarely swerve
From law, however stern, which tends their strength to nerve

XX

Blow! swiftly blow, thou keel-compelling gale!
Till the broad Sun withdraws his lessening ray;
Then must the Pennant-bearer slacken sail,
That lagging barks may make their lazy way.
Ah! grievance sore, and listless dull delay,
To waste on sluggish hulks the sweetest breeze!
What leagues are lost, before the dawn of day,
Thus loitering pensive on the willing seas,
The flapping sail hauled down to halt for logs like these!

XXI

The Moon is up; by Heaven, a lovely eve!
Long streams of light o'er dancing waves expand;
Now lads on shore may sigh, and maids believe:
Such be our fate when we return to land!
Meantime some rude Arion's restless hand
Wakes the brisk harmony that sailors love;
A circle there of merry listeners stand
Or to some well-known measure featly move,
Thoughtless, as if on shore they still were free to rove.

XXII

Through Calpe's straits survey the steepy shore;
Europe and Afric on each other gaze!
Lands of the dark-eyed Maid and dusky Moor
Alike beheld beneath pale Hecate's blaze:
How softly on the Spanish shore she plays!
Disclosing rock, and slope, and forest brown,
Distinct, though darkening with her waning phase;
But Mauritania's giant-shadows frown,
From mountain-cliff to coast descending sombre down.

XXIII

'Tis night, when Meditation bids us feel
We once have loved, though Love is at an end:

The Heart, lone mourner of its baffled zeal,
Though friendless now, will dream it had a friend.
Who with the weight of years would wish to bend,
When Youth itself survives young Love and Joy?
Alas! when mingling souls forget to blend,
Death hath but little left him to destroy!
Ah! happy years! once more who would not be a boy?

XXIV

Thus bending o'er the vessel's laving side,
To gaze on Dian's wave-reflected sphere,
The Soul forgets her schemes of Hope and Pride,
And flies unconscious o'er each backward year;
None are so desolate but something dear,
Dearer than self, possesses or possessed
A thought, and claims the homage of a tear;
A flashing pang! of which the weary breast
Would still, albeit in vain, the heavy heart divest.

XXV

To sit on rocks—to muse o'er flood and fell—
To slowly trace the forest's shady scene,
Where things that own not Man's dominion dwell,
And mortal foot hath ne'er or rarely been;
To climb the trackless mountain all unseen,
With the wild flock that never needs a fold;
Alone o'er steeps and foaming falls to lean;
This is not Solitude—'tis but to hold
Converse with Nature's charms, and view her stores unrolled.

XXVI

But midst the crowd, the hum, the shock of men,
To hear, to see, to feel, and to possess,
And roam along, the World's tired denizen,
With none who bless us, none whom we can bless;
Minions of Splendour shrinking from distress!
None that, with kindred consciousness endued,
If we were not, would seem to smile the less,

Of all that flattered—followed—sought, and sued;
This is to be alone—This, This is Solitude!

XXVII

More blest the life of godly Eremite,
Such as on lonely Athos may be seen,
Watching at eve upon the Giant Height,
Which looks o'er waves so blue, skies so serene,
That he who there at such an hour hath been
Will wistful linger on that hallowed spot;
Then slowly tear him from the 'witching scene,
Sigh forth one wish that such had been his lot,
Then turn to hate a world he had almost forgot.

XXVIII

Pass we the long unvarying course, the track
Oft trod, that never leaves a trace behind;
Pass we the calm—the gale—the change—the tack,
And each well known caprice of wave and wind;
Pass we the joys and sorrows sailors find,
Cooped in their wingéd sea-girt citadel;
The foul—the fair—the contrary—the kind—
As breezes rise and fall and billows swell,
Till on some jocund morn—lo, Land! and All is well!

XXIX

But not in silence pass Calypso's isles,
The sister tenants of the middle deep;
There for the weary still a Haven smiles,
Though the fair Goddess long hath ceased to weep,
And o'er her cliffs a fruitless watch to keep
For him who dared prefer a mortal bride:
Here, too, his boy essayed the dreadful leap
Stern Mentor urged from high to yonder tide;
While thus of both bereft, the Nymph-Queen doubly sighed.

XXX

Her reign is past, her gentle glories gone:
But trust not this; too easy Youth, beware!

A mortal Sovereign holds her dangerous throne,
And thou may'st find a new Calypso there.
Sweet Florence! could another ever share
This wayward, loveless heart, it would be thine:
But checked by every tie, I may not dare
To cast a worthless offering at thy shrine,
Nor ask so dear a breast to feel one pang for *mine*.

XXXI

Thus Harold deemed, as on that Lady's eye
He looked, and met its beam without a thought,
Save Admiration glancing harmless by:
Love kept aloof, albeit not far remote,
Who knew his Votary often lost and caught,
But knew him as his Worshipper no more,
And ne'er again the Boy his bosom sought:
Since now he vainly urged him to adore,
Well deemed the little God his ancient sway was o'er.

XXXII

Fair Florence found, in sooth with some amaze,
One who, 'twas said, still sighed to all he saw,
Withstand, unmoved, the lustre of her gaze,
Which others hailed with real or mimic awe,
Their hope, their doom, their punishment, their law;
All that gay Beauty from her bondsmen claims:
And much she marvelled that a youth so raw
Nor felt, nor feigned at least, the oft-told flames,
Which, though sometimes they frown, yet rarely anger dames.

XXXIII

Little knew she that seeming marble heart,
Now masked in silence or withheld by Pride,
Was not unskilful in the spoiler's art,
And spread its snares licentious far and wide;
Nor from the base pursuit had turned aside,
As long as aught was worthy to pursue:
But Harold on such arts no more relied;

And had he doted on those eyes so blue,
Yet never would he join the lovers' whining crew.

XXXIV

Not much he kens, I ween, of Woman's breast,
Who thinks that wanton thing is won by sighs;
What careth she for hearts when once possessed?
Do proper homage to thine Idol's eyes,
But not too humbly—or she will despise
Thee and thy suit, though told in moving tropes:
Disguise ev'n tenderness, if thou art wise;
Brisk Confidence still best with woman copes:
Pique her and soothe in turn—soon Passion crowns thy hopes.

XXXV

'Tis an old lesson—Time approves it true,
And those who know it best, deplore it most;
When all is won that all desire to woo,
The paltry prize is hardly worth the cost:
Youth wasted—Minds degraded—Honour lost—
These are thy fruits, successful Passion! these!
If, kindly cruel, early Hope is crost,
Still to the last it rankles, a disease,
Not to be cured when Love itself forgets to please.

XXXVI

Away! nor let me loiter in my song,
For we have many a mountain-path to tread,
And many a varied shore to sail along,
By pensive Sadness, not by Fiction, led—
Climes, fair withal as ever mortal head
Imagined in its little schemes of thought,
Or e'er in new Utopias were ared,
To teach Man what he might be, or he ought—
If that corrupted thing could ever such be taught.

XXXVII

Dear Nature is the kindest mother still!
Though always changing, in her aspect mild;

From her bare bosom let me take my fill,
Her never-weaned, though not her favoured child.
Oh! she is fairest in her features wild,
Where nothing polished dares pollute her path:
To me by day or night she ever smiled,
Though I have marked her when none other hath,
And sought her more and more, and loved her best in wrath.

XXXVIII

Land of Albania! where Iskander rose,
Theme of the young, and beacon of the wise,
And he his namesake, whose oft-baffled foes
Shrunk from his deeds of chivalrous emprize:
Land of Albania! let me bend mine eyes
On thee, thou rugged Nurse of savage men!
The Cross descends, thy Minarets arise,
And the pale Crescent sparkles in the glen,
Through many a cypress-grove within each city's ken.

XXXIX

Childe Harold sailed, and passed the barren spot,
Where sad Penelope o'erlooked the wave;
And onward viewed the mount, not yet forgot,
The Lover's refuge, and the Lesbian's grave.
Dark Sappho! could not Verse immortal save
That breast imbued with such immortal fire?
Could she not live who life eternal gave?
If life eternal may await the lyre,
That only Heaven to which Earth's children may aspire.

XL

'Twas on a Grecian autumn's gentle eve
Childe Harold hailed Leucadia's cape afar;
A spot he longed to see, nor cared to leave:
Oft did he mark the scenes of vanished war,
Actium—Lepanto—fatal Trafalgar;
Mark them unmoved, for he would not delight
(Born beneath some remote inglorious star)

In themes of bloody fray, or gallant fight,
But loathed the bravo's trade, and laughed at martial wight.

XLI

But when he saw the Evening star above
Leucadia's far-projecting rock of woe,
And hailed the last resort of fruitless love,
He felt, or deemed he felt, no common glow:
And as the stately vessel glided slow
Beneath the shadow of that ancient mount,
He watched the billows' melancholy flow,
And, sunk albeit in thought as he was wont,
More placid seemed his eye, and smooth his pallid front.

XLII

Morn dawns; and with it stern Albania's hills,
Dark Suli's rocks, and Pindus' inland peak,
Robed half in mist, bedewed with snowy rills,
Arrayed in many a dun and purple streak,
Arise; and, as the clouds along them break,
Disclose the dwelling of the mountaineer:
Here roams the wolf—the eagle whets his beak—
Birds—beasts of prey—and wilder men appear,
And gathering storms around convulse the closing year.

XLIII

Now Harold felt himself at length alone,
And bade to Christian tongues a long adieu;
Now he adventured on a shore unknown,
Which all admire, but many dread to view:
His breast was armed 'gainst fate, his wants were few;
Peril he sought not, but ne'er shrank to meet:
The scene was savage, but the scene was new;
This made the ceaseless toil of travel sweet,
Beat back keen Winter's blast, and welcomed Summer's heat.

XLIV

Here the red Cross, for still the Cross is here,
Though sadly scoffed at by the circumcised,

Forgets that Pride to pampered priesthood dear,—
Churchman and Votary alike despised.
Foul Superstition! howsoe'er disguised,
Idol—Saint—Virgin—Prophet—Crescent—Cross—
For whatsoever symbol thou art prized,
Thou sacerdotal gain, but general loss!
Who from true Worship's gold can separate thy dross?

XLV

Ambracia's gulf behold, where once was lost
A world for Woman, lovely, harmless thing!
In yonder rippling bay, their naval host
Did many a Roman chief and Asian King
To doubtful conflict, certain slaughter bring:
Look where the second Cæsar's trophies rose!
Now, like the hands that reared them, withering:
Imperial Anarchs, doubling human woes!
GOD! was thy globe ordained for such to win and lose?

XLVI

From the dark barriers of that rugged clime,
Ev'n to the centre of Illyria's vales,
Childe Harold passed o'er many a mount sublime,
Through lands scarce noticed in historic tales:
Yet in famed Attica such lovely dales
Are rarely seen; nor can fair Tempe boast
A charm they know not; loved Parnassus fails,
Though classic ground and consecrated most,
To match some spots that lurk within this lowering coast.

XLVII

He passed bleak Pindus, Acherusia's lake,
And left the primal city of the land,
And onwards did his further journey take
To greet Albania's Chief, whose dread command
Is lawless law; for with a bloody hand
He sways a nation, turbulent and bold:
Yet here and there some daring mountain-band

Disdain his power, and from their rocky hold
Hurl their defiance far, nor yield, unless to gold.

XLVIII

Monastic Zitza! from thy shady brow,
Thou small, but favoured spot of holy ground!
Where'er we gaze—around—above—below,—
What rainbow tints, what magic charms are found!
Rock, river, forest, mountain, all abound,
And bluest skies that harmonise the whole:
Beneath, the distant Torrent's rushing sound
Tells where the volumed Cataract doth roll
Between those hanging rocks, that shock yet please the soul.

XLIX

Amidst the grove that crowns yon tufted hill,
Which, were it not for many a mountain nigh
Rising in lofty ranks and loftier still,
Might well itself be deemed of dignity,
The Convent's white walls glisten fair on high:
Here dwells the caloyer, nor rude is he,
Nor niggard of his cheer; the passer by
Is welcome still; nor heedless will he flee
From hence, if he delight kind Nature's sheen to see.

L

Here in the sultriest season let him rest,
Fresh is the green beneath those agéd trees;
Here winds of gentlest wing will fan his breast,
From Heaven itself he may inhale the breeze:
The plain is far beneath—oh! let him seize
Pure pleasure while he can; the scorching ray
Here pierceth not, impregnate with disease:
Then let his length the loitering pilgrim lay,
And gaze, untired, the Morn—the Noon—the Eve away.

LI

Dusky and huge, enlarging on the sight,
Nature's volcanic Amphitheatre,

D

Chimæra's Alps extend from left to right:
Beneath, a living valley seems to stir;
Flocks play, trees wave, streams flow—the mountain-fir
Nodding above; behold black Acheron!
Once consecrated to the sepulchre.
Pluto! if this be Hell I look upon,
Close shamed Elysium's gates—my shade shall seek for none.

LII

Ne city's towers pollute the lovely view;
Unseen is Yanina, though not remote,
Veiled by the screen of hills: here men are few,
Scanty the hamlet, rare the lonely cot:
But, peering down each precipice, the goat
Browseth; and, pensive o'er his scattered flock,
The little shepherd in his white capote
Doth lean his boyish form along the rock,
Or in his cave awaits the Tempest's short-lived shock.

LIII

Oh! where, Dodona! is thine agéd Grove,
Prophetic Fount, and Oracle divine?
What valley echoed the response of Jove?
What trace remaineth of the Thunderer's shrine?
All, all forgotten—and shall Man repine
That his frail bonds to fleeting life are broke?
Cease, Fool! the fate of Gods may well be thine:
Wouldst thou survive the marble or the oak?
When nations, tongues, and worlds must sink beneath the
    stroke!

LIV

Epirus' bounds recede, and mountains fail;
Tired of up-gazing still, the wearied eye
Reposes gladly on as smooth a vale
As ever Spring yclad in glassy dye:
Ev'n on a plain no humble beauties lie,
Where some bold river breaks the long expanse,

And woods along the banks are waving high,
Whose shadows in the glassy waters dance,
Or with the moonbeam sleep in Midnight's solemn trance.

LV

The Sun had sunk behind vast Tomerit,
And Laos wide and fierce came roaring by;
The shades of wonted night were gathering yet,
When, down the steep banks winding warily,
Childe Harold saw, like meteors in the sky,
The glittering minarets of Tepalen,
Whose walls o'erlook the stream; and drawing nigh,
He heard the busy hum of warrior-men
Swelling the breeze that sighed along the lengthening glen.

LVI

He passed the sacred Haram's silent tower,
And underneath the wide o'erarching gate
Surveyed the dwelling of this Chief of power,
Where all around proclaimed his high estate.
Amidst no common pomp the Despot sate,
While busy preparation shook the court,
Slaves, eunuchs, soldiers, guests, and santons wait:—
Within, a palace, and without, a fort—
Here men of every clime appear to make resort.

LVII

Richly caparisoned, a ready row
Of arméd horse, and many a warlike store,
Circled the wide-extending court below;
Above, strange groups adorned the corridore;
And oft-times through the area's echoing door
Some high-capped Tartar spurred his steed away:
The Turk—the Greek—the Albanian—and the Moor,
Here mingled in their many-hued array,
While the deep war-drum's sound announced the close of day.

LVIII

The wild Albanian kirtled to his knee,
With shawl-girt head and ornamented gun,
And gold-embroidered garments, fair to see;
The crimson-scarféd men of Macedon;
The Delhi with his cap of terror on,
And crooked glaive—the lively, supple Greek,
And swarthy Nubia's mutilated son;
The bearded Turk that rarely deigns to speak,
Master of all around, too potent to be meek,

LIX

Are mixed conspicuous: some recline in groups,
Scanning the motley scene that varies round;
There some grave Moslem to devotion stoops,
And some that smoke, and some that play, are found;
Here the Albanian proudly treads the ground;
Half-whispering there the Greek is heard to prate;
Hark! from the Mosque the nightly solemn sound,
The Muezzin's call doth shake the minaret,
'There is no god but God!—to prayer—lo! God is great!'

LX

Just at this season Ramazani's fast
Through the long day its penance did maintain:
But when the lingering twilight hour was past,
Revel and feast assumed the rule again:
Now all was bustle, and the menial train
Prepared and spread the plenteous board within;
The vacant Gallery now seemed made in vain,
But from the chambers came the mingling din,
As page and slave anon were passing out and in.

LXI

Here woman's voice is never heard: apart,
And scarce permitted—guarded, veiled—to move,
She yields to one her person and her heart,
Tamed to her cage, nor feels a wish to rove:

For, not unhappy in her Master's love,
And joyful in a mother's gentlest cares,
Blest cares! all other feelings far above!
Herself more sweetly rears the babe she bears,
Who never quits the breast—no meaner passion shares.

LXII

In marble-paved pavilion, where a spring
Of living water from the centre rose,
Whose bubbling did a genial freshness fling,
And soft voluptuous couches breathed repose,
ALI reclined, a man of war and woes:
Yet in his lineaments ye cannot trace,
While Gentleness her milder radiance throws
Along that aged venerable face,
The deeds that lurk beneath, and stain him with disgrace.

LXIII

It is not that yon hoary lengthening beard
Ill suits the passions which belong to Youth;
Love conquers Age—so Hafiz hath averred,
So sings the Teian, and he sings in sooth—
But crimes that scorn the tender voice of rúth,
Beseeming all men ill, but most the man
In years, have marked him with a tiger's tooth;
Blood follows blood, and, through their mortal span,
In bloodier acts conclude those who with blood began.

LXIV

'Mid many things most new to ear and eye
The Pilgrim rested here his weary feet,
And gazed around on Moslem luxury,
Till quickly wearied with that spacious seat
Of Wealth and Wantonness, the choice retreat
Of sated Grandeur from the city's noise:
And were it humbler it in sooth were sweet;
But Peace abhorreth artificial joys,
And Pleasure, leagued with Pomp, the zest of both destroys.

LXV

Fierce are Albania's children, yet they lack
Not virtues, were those virtues more mature.
Where is the foe that ever saw their back?
Who can so well the toil of War endure?
Their native fastnesses not more secure
Than they in doubtful time of troublous need:
Their wrath how deadly! but their friendship sure,
When Gratitude or Valour bids them bleed—
Unshaken rushing on where'er their Chief may lead.

LXVI

Childe Harold saw them in their Chieftain's tower
Thronging to War in splendour and success;
And after viewed them, when, within their power,
Himself awhile the victim of distress;
That saddening hour when bad men hotlier press:
But these did shelter him beneath their roof,
When less barbarians would have cheered him less,
And fellow-countrymen have stood aloof—
In aught that tries the heart, how few withstand the proof!

LXVII

It chanced that adverse winds once drove his bark
Full on the coast of Suli's shaggy shore,
When all around was desolate and dark;
To land was perilous, to sojourn more;
Yet for awhile the mariners forbore,
Dubious to trust where Treachery might lurk:
At length they ventured forth, though doubting sore
That those who loathe alike the Frank and Turk
Might once again renew their ancient butcher-work.

LXVIII

Vain fear! the Suliotes stretched the welcome hand,
Led them o'er rocks and past the dangerous swamp,
Kinder than polished slaves though not so bland,
And piled the hearth, and wrung their garments damp,

And filled the bowl, and trimmed the cheerful lamp,
And spread their fare—though homely, all they had:
Such conduct bears Philanthropy's rare stamp:
To rest the weary and to soothe the sad,
Doth lesson happier men, and shames at least the bad.

LXIX

It came to pass, that when he did address
Himself to quit at length this mountain-land,
Combined marauders half-way barred egress,
And wasted far and near with glaive and brand;
And therefore did he take a trusty band
To traverse Acarnania's forest wide,
In war well-seasoned, and with labours tanned,
Till he did greet white Achelous' tide,
And from his further bank Ætolia's wolds espied.

LXX

Where lone Utraikey forms its circling cove,
And weary waves retire to gleam at rest,
How brown the foliage of the green hill's grove,
Nodding at midnight o'er the calm bay's breast,
As winds come lightly whispering from the West,
Kissing, not ruffling, the blue deep's serene:—
Here Harold was received a welcome guest;
Nor did he pass unmoved the gentle scene,
For many a joy could he from Night's soft presence glean.

LXXI

On the smooth shore the night-fires brightly blazed,
The feast was done, the red wine circling fast,
And he that unawares had there ygazed
With gaping wonderment had stared aghast;
For ere night's midmost, stillest hour was past,
The native revels of the troop began;
Each Palikar his sabre from him cast,
And bounding hand in hand, man linked to man,
Yelling their uncouth dirge, long daunced the kirtled clan.

LXXII

Childe Harold at a little distance stood
And viewed, but not displeased, the revelrie,
Nor hated harmless mirth, however rude:
In sooth, it was no vulgar sight to see
Their barbarous, yet their not indecent, glee;
And, as the flames along their faces gleamed,
Their gestures nimble, dark eyes flashing free,
The long wild locks that to their girdles streamed,
While thus in concert they this lay half sang, half screamed:—

1

Tambourgi! Tambourgi! thy 'larum afar
Gives hope to the valiant, and promise of war;
All the Sons of the mountains arise at the note,
Chimariot, Illyrian, and dark Suliote!

2

Oh! who is more brave than a dark Suliote,
In his snowy camese and his shaggy capote?
To the wolf and the vulture he leaves his wild flock,
And descends to the plain like the stream from the rock.

3

Shall the sons of Chimari, who never forgive
The fault of a friend, bid an enemy live?
Let those guns so unerring such vengeance forego?
What mark is so fair as the breast of a foe?

4

Macedonia sends forth her invincible race;
For a time they abandon the cave and the chase;
But those scarfs of blood-red shall be redder, before
The sabre is sheathed and the battle is o'er.

5

Then the Pirates of Parga that dwell by the waves,
And teach the pale Franks what it is to be slaves,

Shall leave on the beach the long galley and oar,
And track to his covert the captive on shore.

6

I ask not the pleasures that riches supply,
My sabre shall win what the feeble must buy;
Shall win the young bride with her long flowing hair,
And many a maid from her mother shall tear.

7

I love the fair face of the maid in her youth,
Her caresses shall lull me, her music shall soothe;
Let her bring from the chamber her many-toned lyre,
And sing us a song on the fall of her Sire.

8

Remember the moment when Previsa fell,
The shrieks of the conquered, the conquerors' yell;
The roofs that we fired, and the plunder we shared,
The wealthy we slaughtered, the lovely we spared.

9

I talk not of mercy, I talk not of fear;
He neither must know who would serve the Vizier:
Since the days of our Prophet the Crescent ne'er saw
A chief ever glorious like Ali Pashaw.

10

Dark Muchtar his son to the Danube is sped,
Let the yellow-haired Giaours view his horse-tail with dread;
When his Delhis come dashing in blood o'er the banks,
How few shall escape from the Muscovite ranks!

11

Selictar! unsheathe then our chief's Scimitar;
Tambourgi! thy 'larum gives promise of War.
Ye mountains, that see us descend to the shore,
Shall view us as Victors, or view us no more!

LXXIII

Fair Greece! sad relic of departed Worth!
Immortal, though no more; though fallen, great'
Who now shall lead thy scattered children forth,
And long accustomed bondage uncreate?
Not such thy sons who whilome did await,
The hopeless warriors of a willing doom,
In bleak Thermopylæ's sepulchral strait—
Oh! who that gallant spirit shall resume,
Leap from Eurotas' banks, and call thee from the tomb?

LXXIV

Spirit of Freedom! when on Phyle's brow
Thou sat'st with Thrasybulus and his train,
Couldst thou forebode the dismal hour which now
Dims the green beauties of thine Attic plain?
Not thirty tyrants now enforce the chain,
But every carle can lord it o'er thy land;
Nor rise thy sons, but idly rail in vain,
Trembling beneath the scourge of Turkish hand,
From birth till death enslaved—in word, in deed, unmanned.

LXXV

In all save form alone, how changed! and who
That marks the fire still sparkling in each eye,
Who but would deem their bosoms burned anew
With thy unquenchéd beam, lost Liberty!
And many dream withal the hour is nigh
That gives them back their fathers' heritage:
For foreign arms and aid they fondly sigh,
Nor solely dare encounter hostile rage,
Or tear their name defiled from Slavery's mournful page.

LXXVI

Hereditary Bondsmen! know ye not
Who would be free *themselves* must strike the blow?
By their right arms the conquest must be wrought?
Will Gaul or Muscovite redress ye? No!

True—they may lay your proud despoilers low,
But not for you will Freedom's Altars flame.
Shades of the Helots! triumph o'er your foe!
Greece! change thy lords, thy state is still the same;
Thy glorious day is o'er, but not thine years of shame.

LXXVII

The city won for Allah from the Giaour
The Giaour from Othman's race again may wrest;
And the Serai's impenetrable tower
Receive the fiery Frank, her former guest;
Or Wahab's rebel brood who dared divest
The Prophet's tomb of all its pious spoil,
May wind their path of blood along the West;
But ne'er will Freedom seek this fated soil,
But slave succeed to slave through years of endless toil.

LXXVIII

Yet mark their mirth—ere Lenten days begin,
That penance which their holy rites prepare
To shrive from Man his weight of mortal sin,
By daily abstinence and nightly prayer;
But ere his sackcloth garb Repentance wear,
Some days of joyaunce are decreed to all,
To take of pleasaunce each his secret share,
In motley robe to dance at masking ball,
And join the mimic train of merry Carnival.

LXXIX

And whose more rife with merriment than thine,
Oh Stamboul! once the Empress of their reign?
Though turbans now pollute Sophia's shrine,
And Greece her very altars eyes in vain:
(Alas! her woes will still pervade my strain!)
Gay were her minstrels once, for free her throng,
All felt the common joy they now must feign,
Nor oft I've seen such sight, nor heard such song,
As wooed the eye, and thrilled the Bosphorus along.

LXXX

Loud was the lightsome tumult on the shore;
Oft Music changed, but never ceased her tone,
And timely echoed back the measured oar,
And rippling waters made a pleasant moan:
The Queen of tides on high consenting shone,
And when a transient breeze swept o'er the wave,
'Twas, as if darting from her heavenly throne,
A brighter glance her form reflected gave,
Till sparkling billows seemed to light the banks they lave.

LXXXI

Glanced many a light Caique along the foam,
Danced on the shore the daughters of the land,
No thought had man or maid of rest or home,
While many a languid eye and thrilling hand
Exchanged the look few bosoms may withstand,
Or gently prest, returned the pressure still:
Oh Love! young Love! bound in thy rosy band,
Let sage or cynic prattle as he will,
These hours, and only these, redeem Life's years of ill!

LXXXII

But, midst the throng in merry masquerade,
Lurk there no hearts that throb with secret pain,
Even through the closest searment half betrayed?
To such the gentle murmurs of the main
Seem to re-echo all they mourn in vain;
To such the gladness of the gamesome crowd
Is source of wayward thought and stern disdain:
How do they loathe the laughter idly loud,
And long to change the robe of revel for the shroud!

LXXXIII

This must he feel, the true-born son of Greece,
If Greece one true-born patriot still can boast:
Not such as prate of War, but skulk in Peace,
The bondsman's peace, who sighs for all he lost,

Yet with smooth smile his Tyrant can accost,
And wield the slavish sickle, not the sword:
Ah! Greece! they love thee least who owe thee most—
Their birth, their blood, and that sublime record
Of hero Sires, who shame thy now degenerate horde!

LXXXIV

When riseth Lacedemon's Hardihood,
When Thebes Epaminondas rears again,
When Athens' children are with hearts endued,
When Grecian mothers shall give birth to men,
Then may'st thou be restored; but not till then.
A thousand years scarce serve to form a state;
An hour may lay it in the dust: and when
Can Man its shattered splendour renovate,
Recall its virtues back, and vanquish Time and Fate?

LXXXV

And yet how lovely in thine age of woe,
Land of lost Gods and godlike men, art thou!
Thy vales of evergreen, thy hills of snow,
Proclaim thee Nature's varied favourite now:
Thy fanes, thy temples to thy surface bow,
Commingling slowly with heroic earth,
Broke by the share of every rustic plough:
So perish monuments of mortal birth,
So perish all in turn, save well-recorded *Worth*:

LXXXVI

Save where some solitary column mourns
Above its prostrate brethren of the cave;
Save where Tritonia's airy shrine adorns
Colonna's cliff, and gleams along the wave;
Save o'er some warrior's half-forgotten grave,
Where the gray stones and unmolested grass
Ages, but not Oblivion, feebly brave;
While strangers, only, not regardless pass,
Lingering like me, perchance, to gaze, and sigh 'Alas!'

LXXXVII

Yet are thy skies as blue, thy crags as wild;
Sweet are thy groves, and verdant are thy fields,
Thine olive ripe as when Minerva smiled,
And still his honied wealth Hymettus yields;
There the blithe Bee his fragrant fortress builds,
The free-born wanderer of thy mountain-air;
Apollo still thy long, long summer gilds,
Still in his beam Mendeli's marbles glare:
Art, Glory, Freedom fail—but Nature still is fair.

LXXXVIII

Where'er we tread 'tis haunted, holy ground;
No earth of thine is lost in vulgar mould,
But one vast realm of Wonder spreads around,
And all the Muse's tales seem truly told,
Till the sense aches with gazing to behold
The scenes our earliest dreams have dwelt upon;
Each hill and dale, each deepening glen and wold
Defies the power which crushed thy temples gone:
Age shakes Athena's tower, but spares gray Marathon.

LXXXIX

The Sun, the soil—but not the slave, the same;
Unchanged in all except its foreign Lord—
Preserves alike its bounds and boundless fame
The Battle-field, where Persia's victim horde
First bowed beneath the brunt of Hellas' sword,
As on the morn to distant Glory dear,
When Marathon became a magic word;
Which uttered, to the hearer's eye appear
The camp, the host, the fight, the Conqueror's career,

XC

The flying Mede, his shaftless broken bow—
The fiery Greek, his red pursuing spear;
Mountains above—Earth's, Ocean's plain below—
Death in the front, Destruction in the rear!

Such was the scene—what now remaineth here?
What sacred Trophy marks the hallowed ground,
Recording Freedom's smile and Asia's tear?
The rifled urn, the violated mound,
The dust thy courser's hoof, rude stranger! spurns around.

XCI

Yet to the remnants of thy Splendour past
Shall pilgrims, pensive, but unwearied, throng;
Long shall the voyager, with th' Ionian blast,
Hail the bright clime of Battle and of Song:
Long shall thine annals and immortal tongue
Fill with thy fame the youth of many a shore;
Boast of the agéd! lesson of the young!
Which Sages venerate and Bards adore,
As Pallas and the Muse unveil their awful lore.

XCII

The parted bosom clings to wonted home,
If aught that's kindred cheer the welcome hearth;
He that is lonely—hither let him roam,
And gaze complacent on congenial earth.
Greece is no lightsome land of social mirth:
But he whom Sadness sootheth may abide,
And scarce regret the region of his birth,
When wandering slow by Delphi's sacred side,
Or gazing o'er the plains where Greek and Persian died.

XCIII

Let such approach this consecrated Land,
And pass in peace along the magic waste;
But spare its relics—let no busy hand
Deface the scenes, already how defaced!
Not for such purpose were these altars placed:
Revere the remnants Nations once revered:
So may our Country's name be undisgraced,
So may'st thou prosper where thy youth was reared,
By every honest joy of Love and Life endeared!

XCIV

For thee, who thus in too protracted song
Hath soothed thine Idlesse with inglorious lays,
Soon shall thy voice be lost amid the throng
Of louder Minstrels in these later days:
To such resign the strife for fading Bays—
Ill may such contest now the spirit move
Which heeds nor keen Reproach nor partial Praise,
Since cold each kinder heart that might approve—
And none are left to please when none are left to love.

XCV

Thou too art gone, thou loved and lovely one!
Whom Youth and Youth's affections bound to me;
Who did for me what none beside have done,
Nor shrank from one albeit unworthy thee.
What is my Being! thou hast ceased to be!
Nor staid to welcome here thy wanderer home,
Who mourns o'er hours which we no more shall see—
Would they had never been, or were to come!
Would he had ne'er returned to find fresh cause to roam!

XCVI

Oh! ever loving, lovely, and beloved!
How selfish Sorrow ponders on the past,
And clings to thoughts now better far removed!
But Time shall tear thy shadow from me last.
All thou couldst have of mine, stern Death! thou hast;
The Parent, Friend, and now the more than friend:
Ne'er yet for one thine arrows flew so fast,
And grief with grief continuing still to blend,
Hath snatched the little joy that Life had yet to lend.

XCVII

Then must I plunge again into the crowd,
And follow all that Peace disdains to seek?
Where Revel calls, and Laughter, vainly loud,
False to the heart, distorts the hollow cheek,

To leave the flagging spirit doubly weak;
Still o'er the features, which perforce they cheer,
To feign the pleasure or conceal the pique:
Smiles form the channel of a future tear,
Or raise the writhing lip with ill-dissembled sneer.

XCVIII

What is the worst of woes that wait on Age?
What stamps the wrinkle deeper on the brow?
To view each loved one blotted from Life's page,
And be alone on earth, as I am now:
Before the Chastener humbly let me bow,
O'er Hearts divided and o'er Hopes destroyed:
Roll on, vain days! full reckless may ye flow,
Since Time hath reft whate'er my soul enjoyed,
And with the ills of Eld mine earlier years alloyed.

CANTO THE THIRD

I

Is thy face like thy mother's, my fair child!
ADA! sole daughter of my house and heart?
When last I saw thy young blue eyes they smiled,
And then we parted,—not as now we part,
But with a hope.—

            Awaking with a start,
The waters heave around me; and on high
The winds lift up their voices: I depart,
Whither I know not; but the hour's gone by,
When Albion's lessening shores could grieve or glad mine eye.

II

Once more upon the waters! yet once more!
And the waves bound beneath me as a steed
That knows his rider. Welcome to their roar!
Swift be their guidance, wheresoe'er it lead!
Though the strained mast should quiver as a reed,

And the rent canvass fluttering strew the gale,
Still must I on; for I am as a weed,
Flung from the rock, on Ocean's foam, to sail
Where'er the surge may sweep, the tempest's breath prevail.

III

In my youth's summer I did sing of One,
The wandering outlaw of his own dark mind;
Again I seize the theme, then but begun,
And bear it with me, as the rushing wind
Bears the cloud onwards: in that Tale I find
The furrows of long thought, and dried-up tears,
Which, ebbing, leave a sterile track behind,
O'er which all heavily the journeying years
Plod the last sands of life,—where not a flower appears.

IV

Since my young days of passion—joy or pain—
Perchance my heart and harp have lost a string—
And both may jar: it may be that in vain
I would essay, as I have sung, to sing:
Yet, though a dreary strain, to this I cling;
So that it wean me from the weary dream
Of selfish grief or gladness—so it fling
Forgetfulness around me—it shall seem
To me, though to none else, a not ungrateful theme.

V

He, who grown agéd in this world of woe,
In deeds, not years, piercing the depths of life,
So that no wonder waits him—nor below
Can Love or Sorrow, Fame, Ambition, Strife,
Cut to his heart again with the keen knife
Of silent, sharp endurance—he can tell
Why Thought seeks refuge in lone caves, yet rife
With airy images, and shapes which dwell
Still unimpaired, though old, in the Soul's haunted cell.

VI

'Tis to create, and in creating live
A being more intense, that we endow
With form our fancy, gaining as we give
The life we image, even as I do now—
What am I? Nothing: but not so art thou,
Soul of my thought! with whom I traverse earth,
Invisible but gazing, as I glow
Mixed with thy spirit, blended with thy birth,
And feeling still with thee in my crushed feelings' dearth.

VII

Yet must I think less wildly:—I *have* thought
Too long and darkly, till my brain became,
In its own eddy boiling and o'erwrought,
A whirling gulf of phantasy and flame:
And thus, untaught in youth my heart to tame,
My springs of life were poisoned. 'Tis too late!
Yet am I changed; though still enough the same
In strength to bear what Time can not abate,
And feed on bitter fruits without accusing Fate.

VIII

Something too much of this:—but now 'tis past,
And the spell closes with its silent seal:
Long absent HAROLD re-appears at last—
He of the breast which fain no more would feel,
Wrung with the wounds which kill not, but ne'er heal;
Yet Time, who changes all, had altered him
In soul and aspect as in age: years steal
Fire from the mind as vigour from the limb;
And Life's enchanted cup but sparkles near the brim.

IX

His had been quaffed too quickly, and he found
The dregs were wormwood; but he filled again,
And from a purer fount, on holier ground,
And deemed its spring perpetual—but in vain!

Still round him clung invisibly a chain
Which galled for ever, fettering though unseen,
And heavy though it clanked not; worn with pain,
Which pined although it spoke not, and grew keen,
Entering with every step he took through many a scene.

X

Secure in guarded coldness, he had mixed
Again in fancied safety with his kind,
And deemed his spirit now so firmly fixed
And sheathed with an invulnerable mind,
That, if no joy, no sorrow lurked behind;
And he, as one, might 'midst the many stand
Unheeded, searching through the crowd to find
Fit speculation—such as in strange land
He found in wonder-works of God and Nature's hand.

XI

But who can view the ripened rose, nor seek
To wear it? who can curiously behold
The smoothness and the sheen of Beauty's cheek,
Nor feel the heart can never all grow old?
Who can contemplate Fame through clouds unfold
The star which rises o'er her steep, nor climb?
Harold, once more within the vortex, rolled
On with the giddy circle, chasing Time,
Yet with a nobler aim than in his Youth's fond prime.

XII

But soon he knew himself the most unfit
Of men to herd with Man, with whom he held
Little in common; untaught to submit
His thoughts to others, though his soul was quelled
In youth by his own thoughts; still uncompelled,
He would not yield dominion of his mind
To Spirits against whom his own rebelled,
Proud though in desolation—which could find
A life within itself, to breathe without mankind.

XIII

Where rose the mountains, there to him were friends;
Where rolled the Ocean, thereon was his home;
Where a blue sky, and glowing clime, extends,
He had the passion and the power to roam;
The desert, forest, cavern, breaker's foam,
Were unto him companionship; they spake
A mutual language, clearer than the tome
Of his land's tongue, which he would oft forsake
For Nature's pages glassed by sunbeams on the lake.

XIV

Like the Chaldean, he could watch the stars,
Till he had peopled them with beings bright
As their own beams; and earth, and earth-born jars,
And human frailties, were forgotten quite:
Could he have kept his spirit to that flight
He had been happy; but this clay will sink
Its spark immortal, envying it the light
To which it mounts, as if to break the link
That keeps us from yon heaven which woos us to its brink.

XV

But in Man's dwellings he became a thing
Restless and worn, and stern and wearisome,
Drooped as a wild-born falcon with clipt wing,
To whom the boundless air alone were home:
Then came his fit again, which to o'ercome,
As eagerly the barred-up bird will beat
His breast and beak against his wiry dome
Till the blood tinge his plumage—so the heat
Of his impeded Soul would through his bosom eat.

XVI

Self-exiled Harold wanders forth again,
With nought of Hope left—but with less of gloom;
The very knowledge that he lived in vain,
That all was over on this side the tomb,

Had made Despair a smilingness assume,
Which, though 'twere wild,—as on the plundered wreck
When mariners would madly meet their doom
With draughts intemperate on the sinking deck,—
Did yet inspire a cheer, which he forbore to check.

XVII

Stop!—for thy tread is on an Empire's dust!
An Earthquake's spoil is sepulchred below!
Is the spot marked with no colossal bust?
Nor column trophied for triumphal show?
None; but *the moral's truth* tells simpler so.
As the ground was before, thus let it be ;—
How that red rain hath made the harvest grow!
And is this all the world has gained by thee,
Thou first and last of Fields! king-making Victory?

XVIII

And Harold stands upon this place of skulls,
The grave of France, the deadly Waterloo!
How in an hour the Power which gave annuls
Its gifts, transferring fame as fleeting too!—
In 'pride of place' here last the Eagle flew,
Then tore with bloody talon the rent plain,
Pierced by the shaft of banded nations through ;
Ambition's life and labours all were vain—
He wears the shattered links of the World's broken chain.

XIX

Fit retribution! Gaul may champ the bit
And foam in fetters ;—but is Earth more free?
Did nations combat to make *One* submit?
Or league to teach all Kings true Sovereignty?
What! shall reviving Thraldom again be
The patched-up Idol of enlightened days?
Shall we, who struck the Lion down, shall we
Pay the Wolf homage? proffering lowly gaze
And servile knees to Thrones? No! *prove* before ye praise!

XX

If not, o'er one fallen Despot boast no more!
In vain fair cheeks were furrowed with hot tears
For Europe's flowers long rooted up before
The trampler of her vineyards; in vain, years
Of death, depopulation, bondage, fears,
Have all been borne, and broken by the accord
Of roused-up millions: all that most endears
Glory, is when the myrtle wreathes a Sword—
Such as Harmodius drew on Athens' tyrant Lord.

XXI

There was a sound of revelry by night,
And Belgium's Capital had gathered then
Her Beauty and her Chivalry—and bright
The lamps shone o'er fair women and brave men;
A thousand hearts beat happily; and when
Music arose with its voluptuous swell,
Soft eyes looked love to eyes which spake again,
And all went merry as a marriage bell;
But hush! hark! a deep sound strikes like a rising knell!

XXII

Did ye not hear it?—No—'twas but the Wind,
Or the car rattling o'er the stony street;
On with the dance! let joy be unconfined;
No sleep till morn, when Youth and Pleasure meet
To chase the glowing Hours with flying feet—
But hark!—that heavy sound breaks in once more,
As if the clouds its echo would repeat;
And nearer—clearer—deadlier than before!
Arm! Arm! it is—it is—the cannon's opening roar!

XXIII

Within a windowed niche of that high hall
Sate Brunswick's fated Chieftain; he did hear
That sound the first amidst the festival,
And caught its tone with Death's prophetic ear;

And when they smiled because he deemed it near,
His heart more truly knew that peal too well
Which stretched his father on a bloody bier,
And roused the vengeance blood alone could quell;
He rushed into the field, and, foremost fighting, fell.

XXIV

Ah! then and there was hurrying to and fro—
And gathering tears, and tremblings of distress,
And cheeks all pale, which but an hour ago
Blushed at the praise of their own loveliness—
And there were sudden partings, such as press
The life from out young hearts, and choking sighs
Which ne'er might be repeated; who could guess
If ever more should meet those mutual eyes,
Since upon night so sweet such awful morn could rise!

XXV

And there was mounting in hot haste—the steed,
The mustering squadron, and the clattering car,
Went pouring forward with impetuous speed,
And swiftly forming in the ranks of war—
And the deep thunder peal on peal afar;
And near, the beat of the alarming drum
Roused up the soldier ere the Morning Star;
While thronged the citizens with terror dumb,
Or whispering, with white lips—'The foe! They come! they
        come!'

XXVI

And wild and high the 'Cameron's Gathering' rose!
The war-note of Lochiel, which Albyn's hills
Have heard, and heard, too, have her Saxon foes:—
How in the noon of night that pibroch thrills,
Savage and shrill! But with the breath which fills
Their mountain pipe, so fill the mountaineers
With the fierce native daring which instils
The stirring memory of a thousand years,
And Evan's—Donald's—fame rings in each clansman's ears!

XXVII

And Ardennes waves above them her green leaves,
Dewy with Nature's tear-drops, as they pass—
Grieving, if aught inanimate e'er grieves,
Over the unreturning brave,—alas!
Ere evening to be trodden like the grass
Which *now* beneath them, but *above* shall grow
In its next verdure, when this fiery mass
Of living Valour, rolling on the foe
And burning with high Hope, shall moulder cold and low.

XXVIII

Last noon beheld them full of lusty life;—
Last eve in Beauty's circle proudly gay;
The Midnight brought the signal-sound of strife,
The Morn the marshalling in arms,—the Day
Battle's magnificently-stern array!
The thunder-clouds close o'er it, which when rent
The earth is covered thick with other clay
Which her own clay shall cover, heaped and pent,
Rider and horse,—friend,—foe—in one red burial blent!

XXIX

Their praise is hymned by loftier harps than mine;
Yet one I would select from that proud throng,
Partly because they blend me with his line,
And partly that I did his Sire some wrong,
And partly that bright names will hallow song;
And his was of the bravest, and when showered
The death-bolts deadliest the thinned files along,
Even where the thickest of War's tempest lowered,
They reached no nobler breast than thine, young, gallant
    Howard!

XXX

There have been tears and breaking hearts for thee,
And mine were nothing, had I such to give;
But when I stood beneath the fresh green tree,
Which living waves where thou didst cease to live,

And saw around me the wide field revive
With fruits and fertile promise, and the Spring
Come forth her work of gladness to contrive, ·
With all her reckless birds upon the wing,
I turned from all she brought to those she could not bring.

XXXI

I turned to thee, to thousands, of whom each
And one as all a ghastly gap did make
In his own kind and kindred, whom to teach
Forgetfulness were mercy for their sake;
The Archangel's trump, not Glory's, must awake
Those whom they thirst for; though the sound of Fame
May for a moment soothe, it cannot slake
The fever of vain longing, and the name
So honoured but assumes a stronger, bitterer claim.

XXXII

They mourn, but smile at length—and, smiling, mourn:
The tree will wither long before it fall;
The hull drives on, though mast and sail be torn;
The roof-tree sinks, but moulders on the hall
In massy hoariness; the ruined wall
Stands when its wind-worn battlements are gone;
The bars survive the captive they enthral;
The day drags through though storms keep out the sun;
And thus the heart will break, yet brokenly live on:

XXXIII

Even as a broken Mirror, which the glass
In every fragment multiplies—and makes
A thousand images of one that was
The same—and still the more, the more it breaks;
And thus the heart will do which not forsakes,
Living in shattered guise; and still, and cold,
And bloodless, with its sleepless sorrow aches,
Yet withers on till all without is old,
Showing no visible sign, for such things are untold.

XXXIV

There is a very life in our despair,
Vitality of poison,—a quick root
Which feeds these deadly branches; for it were
As nothing did we die; but Life will suit
Itself to Sorrow's most detested fruit,
Like to the apples on the Dead Sea's shore,
All ashes to the taste: Did man compute
Existence by enjoyment, and count o'er
Such hours 'gainst years of life,—say, would he name three-
    score?

XXXV

The Psalmist numbered out the years of man:
They are enough; and if thy tale be *true*,
Thou, who didst grudge him even that fleeting span,
More than enough, thou fatal Waterloo!
Millions of tongues record thee, and anew
Their children's lips shall echo them, and say—
'Here, where the sword united nations drew,
Our countrymen were warring on that day!'
And this is much—and all—which will not pass away.

XXXVI

There sunk the greatest, nor the worst of men,
Whose Spirit, antithetically mixed,
One moment of the mightiest, and again
On little objects with like firmness fixed;
Extreme in all things! hadst thou been betwixt,
Thy throne had still been thine, or never been;
For Daring made thy rise as fall: thou seek'st
Even now to re-assume the imperial mien,
And shake again the world, the Thunderer of the scene!

XXXVII

Conqueror and Captive of the Earth art thou!
She trembles at thee still, and thy wild name
Was ne'er more bruited in men's minds than now
That thou art nothing, save the jest of Fame,

Who wooed thee once, thy Vassal, and became
The flatterer of thy fierceness—till thou wert
A God unto thyself; nor less the same
To the astounded kingdoms all inert,
Who deemed thee for a time whate'er thou didst assert.

XXXVIII

Oh, more or less than man—in high or low—
Battling with nations, flying from the field;
Now making monarchs' necks thy footstool, now
More than thy meanest soldier taught to yield;
An Empire thou couldst crush, command, rebuild,
But govern not thy pettiest passion, nor,
However deeply in men's spirits skilled,
Look through thine own, nor curb the lust of War,
Nor learn that tempted Fate will leave the loftiest Star.

XXXIX

Yet well thy soul hath brooked the turning tide
With that untaught innate philosophy,
Which, be it Wisdom, Coldness, or deep Pride,
Is gall and wormwood to an enemy.
When the whole host of hatred stood hard by,
To watch and mock thee shrinking, thou hast smiled
With a sedate and all-enduring eye;—
When Fortune fled her spoiled and favourite child,
He stood unbowed beneath the ills upon him piled.

XL

Sager than in thy fortunes; for in them
Ambition steeled thee on too far to show
That just habitual scorn, which could contemn
Men and their thoughts; 'twas wise to feel, not so
To wear it ever on thy lip and brow,
And spurn the instruments thou wert to use
Till they were turned unto thine overthrow:
'Tis but a worthless world to win or lose;
So hath it proved to thee, and all such lot who choose.

XLI

If, like a tower upon a headlong rock,
Thou hadst been made to stand or fall alone,
Such scorn of man had helped to brave the shock;
But men's thoughts were the steps which paved thy throne,
Their admiration thy best weapon shone;
The part of Philip's son was thine—not then
(Unless aside thy Purple had been thrown)
Like stern Diogenes to mock at men:
For sceptred Cynics Earth were far too wide a den.

XLII

But Quiet to quick bosoms is a Hell,
And *there* hath been thy bane; there is a fire
And motion of the Soul which will not dwell
In its own narrow being, but aspire
Beyond the fitting medium of desire;
And, but once kindled, quenchless evermore,
Preys upon high adventure, nor can tire
Of aught but rest; a fever at the core,
Fatal to him who bears, to all who ever bore.

XLIII

This makes the madmen who have made men mad
By their contagion; Conquerors and Kings,
Founders of sects and systems, to whom add
Sophists, Bards, Statesmen, all unquiet things
Which stir too strongly the soul's secret springs,
And are themselves the fools to those they fool;
Envied, yet how unenviable! what stings
Are theirs! One breast laid open were a school
Which would unteach Mankind the lust to shine or rule:

XLIV

Their breath is agitation, and their life
A storm whereon they ride, to sink at last,
And yet so nursed and bigoted to strife,
That should their days, surviving perils past,

Melt to calm twilight, they feel overcast
With sorrow and supineness, and so die;
Even as a flame unfed, which runs to waste
With its own flickering, or a sword laid by,
Which eats into itself, and rusts ingloriously.

XLV

He who ascends to mountain tops, shall find
The loftiest peaks most wrapt in clouds and snow;
He who surpasses or subdues mankind,
Must look down on the hate of those below.
Though high *above* the Sun of Glory glow,
And far *beneath* the Earth and Ocean spread,
Round him are icy rocks, and loudly blow
Contending tempests on his naked head,
And thus reward the toils which to those summits led.

XLVI

Away with these! true Wisdom's world will be
Within its own creation, or in thine,
Maternal Nature! for who teems like thee,
Thus on the banks of thy majestic Rhine?
There Harold gazes on a work divine,
A blending of all beauties; streams and dells,
Fruit, foliage, crag, wood, cornfield, mountain, vine,
And chiefless castles breathing stern farewells
From gray but leafy walls, where Ruin greenly dwells.

XLVII

And there they stand, as stands a lofty mind,
Worn, but unstooping to the baser crowd,
All tenantless, save to the crannying Wind,
Or holding dark communion with the Cloud.
There was a day when they were young and proud;
Banners on high, and battles passed below;
But they who fought are in a bloody shroud,
And those which waved are shredless dust ere now,
And the bleak battlements shall bear no future blow.

XLVIII

Beneath these battlements, within those walls,
Power dwelt amidst her passions; in proud state
Each robber chief upheld his arméd halls,
Doing his evil will, nor less elate
Than mightier heroes of a longer date.
What want these outlaws conquerors should have,
But History's purchased page to call them great?
A wider space—an ornamented grave?
Their hopes were not less warm, their souls were full as brave.

XLIX

In their baronial feuds and single fields,
What deeds of prowess unrecorded died!
And Love, which lent a blazon to their shields,
With emblems well devised by amorous pride,
Through all the mail of iron hearts would glide;
But still their flame was fierceness, and drew on
Keen contest and destruction near allied,
And many a tower for some fair mischief won,
Saw the discoloured Rhine beneath its ruin run.

L

But Thou, exulting and abounding river!
Making thy waves a blessing as they flow
Through banks whose beauty would endure for ever
Could man but leave thy bright creation so,
Nor its fair promise from the surface mow
With the sharp scythe of conflict,—then to see
Thy valley of sweet waters, were to know
Earth paved like Heaven—and to seem such to me,
Even now what wants thy stream?—that it should Lethe be.

LI

A thousand battles have assailed thy banks,
But these and half their fame have passed away,
And Slaughter heaped on high his weltering ranks:
Their very graves are gone, and what are they?

Thy tide washed down the blood of yesterday,
And all was stainless, and on thy clear stream
Glassed, with its dancing light, the sunny ray;
But o'er the blackened Memory's blighting dream
Thy waves would vainly roll, all sweeping as they seem.

LII

Thus Harold inly said, and passed along,
Yet not insensible to all which here
Awoke the jocund birds to early song
In glens which might have made even exile dear:
Though on his brow were graven lines austere,
And tranquil sternness, which had ta'en the place
Of feelings fierier far but less severe—
Joy was not always absent from his face,
But o'er it in such scenes would steal with transient trace.

LIII

Nor was all Love shut from him, though his days
Of Passion had consumed themselves to dust.
It is in vain that we would coldly gaze
On such as smile upon us; the heart must
Leap kindly back to kindness, though Disgust
Hath weaned it from all worldlings: thus he felt,
For there was soft Remembrance, and sweet Trust
In one fond breast, to which his own would melt,
And in its tenderer hour on that his bosom dwelt.

LIV

And he had learned to love,—I know not why,
For this in such as him seems strange of mood,—
The helpless looks of blooming Infancy,
Even in its earliest nurture; what subdued,
To change like this, a mind so far imbued
With scorn of man, it little boots to know;
But thus it was; and though in solitude
Small power the nipped affections have to grow,
In him this glowed when all beside had ceased to glow.

LV

And there was one soft breast, as hath been said,
Which unto his was bound by stronger ties
Than the church links withal; and,—though unwed,
That love was pure—and, far above disguise,
Had stood the test of mortal enmities,
Still undivided, and cemented more
By peril, dreaded most in female eyes;
But this was firm, and from a foreign shore
Well to that heart might his these absent greetings pour!

1

The castled Crag of Drachenfels
Frowns o'er the wide and winding Rhine,
Whose breast of waters broadly swells
Between the banks which bear the vine;
And hills all rich with blossomed trees,
And fields which promise corn and wine,
And scattered cities crowning these,
Whose far white walls along them shine,
Have strewed a scene, which I should see
With double joy wert *thou* with me.

2

And peasant girls, with deep blue eyes,
And hands which offer early flowers,
Walk smiling o'er this Paradise;
Above, the frequent feudal towers
Through green leaves lift their walls of gray;
And many a rock which steeply lowers,
And noble arch in proud decay,
Look o'er this vale of vintage-bowers;
But one thing want these banks of Rhine,—
Thy gentle hand to clasp in mine!

3

I send the lilies given to me—
Though long before thy hand they touch,

E

I know that they must withered be,
But yet reject them not as such;
For I have cherished them as dear,
Because they yet may meet thine eye,
And guide thy soul to mine even here,—
When thou behold'st them drooping nigh,
And know'st them gathered by the Rhine,
And offered from my heart to thine!

4

The river nobly foams and flows—
The charm of this enchanted ground,
And all its thousand turns disclose
Some fresher beauty's varying round:
The haughtiest breast its wish might bound
Through life to dwell delighted here;
Nor could on earth a spot be found
To Nature and to me so dear—
Could thy dear eyes in following mine
Still sweeten more these banks of Rhine!

LVI

By Coblentz, on a rise of gentle ground,
There is a small and simple Pyramid,
Crowning the summit of the verdant mound;
Beneath its base are Heroes' ashes hid—
Our enemy's—but let not that forbid
Honour to Marceau! o'er whose early tomb
Tears, big tears, gushed from the rough soldier's lid,
Lamenting and yet envying such a doom,
Falling for France, whose rights he battled to resume.

LVII

Brief, brave, and glorious was his young career,—
His mourners were two hosts, his friends and foes;
And fitly may the stranger lingering here
Pray for his gallant Spirit's bright repose;—

For he was Freedom's Champion, one of those
The few in number, who had not o'erstept
The charter to chastise which she bestows
On such as wield her weapons; he had kept
The whiteness of his soul—and thus men o'er him wept.

LVIII

Here Ehrenbreitstein, with her shattered wall
Black with the miner's blast, upon her height
Yet shows of what she was, when shell and ball
Rebounding idly on her strength did light:—
A Tower of Victory! from whence the flight
Of baffled foes was watched along the plain:
But Peace destroyed what War could never blight,
And laid those proud roofs bare to Summer's rain—
On which the iron shower for years had poured in vain.

LIX

Adieu to thee, fair Rhine! How long delighted
The stranger fain would linger on his way!
Thine is a scene alike where souls united,
Or lonely Contemplation thus might stray;
And could the ceaseless vultures cease to prey
On self-condemning bosoms, it were here,
Where Nature, nor too sombre nor too gay,
Wild but not rude, awful yet not austere,
Is to the mellow Earth as Autumn to the year.

LX

Adieu to thee again! a vain adieu!
There can be no farewell to scene like thine;
The mind is coloured by thy every hue;
And if reluctantly the eyes resign
Their cherished gaze upon thee, lovely Rhine!
'Tis with the thankful glance of parting praise;
More mighty spots may rise—more glaring shine,
But none unite, in one attaching maze,
The brilliant, fair, and soft,—the glories of old days.

LXI

The negligently grand, the fruitful bloom
Of coming ripeness, the white city's sheen,
The rolling stream, the precipice's gloom,
The forest's growth, and Gothic walls between,—
The wild rocks shaped, as they had turrets been,
In mockery of man's art; and these withal
A race of faces happy as the scene,
Whose fertile bounties here extend to all,
Still springing o'er thy banks, though Empires near them fall.

LXII

But these recede. Above me are the Alps,
The Palaces of Nature, whose vast walls
Have pinnacled in clouds their snowy scalps,
And throned Eternity in icy halls
Of cold Sublimity, where forms and falls
The Avalanche—the thunderbolt of snow!
All that expands the spirit, yet appals,
Gather around these summits, as to show
How Earth may pierce to Heaven, yet leave vain man below.

LXIII

But ere these matchless heights I dare to scan,
There is a spot should not be passed in vain,—
Morat! the proud, the patriot field! where man
May gaze on ghastly trophies of the slain,
Nor blush for those who conquered on that plain;
Here Burgundy bequeathed his tombless host,
A bony heap, through ages to remain,
Themselves their monument;—the Stygian coast
Unsepulchred they roamed, and shrieked each wandering
      ghost.

LXIV

While Waterloo with Cannæ's carnage vies,
Morat and Marathon twin names shall stand;
They were true Glory's stainless victories,
Won by the unambitious heart and hand

Of a proud, brotherly, and civic band,
All unbought champions in no princely cause
Of vice-entailed Corruption; they no land
Doomed to bewail the blasphemy of laws
Making Kings' rights divine, by some Draconic clause.

LXV

By a lone wall a lonelier column rears
A gray and grief-worn aspect of old days;
'Tis the last remnant of the wreck of years,
And looks as with the wild-bewildered gaze
Of one to stone converted by amaze,
Yet still with consciousness; and there it stands
Making a marvel that it not decays,
When the coeval pride of human hands,
Levelled Aventicum, hath strewed her subject lands.

LXVI

And there—oh! sweet and sacred be the name!
Julia—the daughter—the devoted—gave
Her youth to Heaven; her heart, beneath a claim
Nearest to Heaven's, broke o'er a father's grave.
Justice is sworn 'gainst tears, and hers would crave
The life she lived in—but the Judge was just—
And then she died on him she could not save.
Their tomb was simple, and without a bust,
And held within their urn one mind—one heart—one dust.

LXVII

But these are deeds which should not pass away,
And names that must not wither, though the Earth
Forgets her empires with a just decay,
The enslavers and the enslaved—their death and birth;
The high, the mountain-majesty of Worth
Should be—and shall, survivor of its woe,
And from its immortality, look forth
In the Sun's face, like yonder Alpine snow,
Imperishably pure beyond all things below.

LXVIII

Lake Leman woos me with its crystal face,
The mirror where the stars and mountains view
The stillness of their aspect in each trace
Its clear depth yields of their far height and hue:
There is too much of Man here, to look through
With a fit mind the might which I behold;
But soon in me shall Loneliness renew
Thoughts hid, but not less cherished than of old,
Ere mingling with the herd had penned me in their fold.

LXIX

To fly from, need not be to hate, mankind:
All are not fit with them to stir and toil,
Nor is it discontent to keep the mind
Deep in its fountain, lest it overboil
In the hot throng, where we become the spoil
Of our infection, till, too late and long,
We may deplore and struggle with the coil,
In wretched interchange of wrong for wrong
Midst a contentious world, striving where none are strong.

LXX

There, in a moment, we may plunge our years
In fatal penitence, and in the blight
Of our own Soul turn all our blood to tears,
And colour things to come with hues of Night;
The race of life becomes a hopeless flight
To those that walk in darkness: on the sea
The boldest steer but where their ports invite—
But there are wanderers o'er Eternity,
Whose bark drives on and on, and anchored ne'er shall be.

LXXI

Is it not better, then, to be alone,
And love Earth only for its earthly sake?
By the blue rushing of the arrowy Rhone,
Or the pure bosom of its nursing Lake,

Which feeds it as a mother who doth make
A fair but froward infant her own care,
Kissing its cries away as these awake;—
Is it not better thus our lives to wear,
Than join the crushing crowd, doomed to inflict or bear?

LXXII

I live not in myself, but I become
Portion of that around me; and to me
High mountains are a feeling, but the hum
Of human cities torture: I can see
Nothing to loathe in Nature, save to be
A link reluctant in a fleshly chain,
Classed among creatures, when the soul can flee,
And with the sky—the peak—the heaving plain
Of ocean, or the stars, mingle—and not in vain.

LXXIII

And thus I am absorbed, and this is life:—
I look upon the peopled desert past,
As on a place of agony and strife,
Where, for some sin, to Sorrow I was cast,
To act and suffer, but remount at last
With a fresh pinion; which I feel to spring,
Though young, yet waxing vigorous as the Blast
Which it would cope with, on delighted wing,
Spurning the clay-cold bonds which round our being cling.

LXXIV

And when, at length, the mind shall be all free
From what it hates in this degraded form,
Reft of its carnal life, save what shall be
Existent happier in the fly and worm,—
When Elements to Elements conform,
And dust is as it should be, shall I not
Feel all I see less dazzling but more warm?
The bodiless thought? the Spirit of each spot?
Of which, even now, I share at times the immortal lot?

LXXV

Are not the mountains, waves, and skies, a part
Of me and of my Soul, as I of them?
Is not the love of these deep in my heart
With a pure passion? should I not contemn
All objects, if compared with these? and stem
A tide of suffering, rather than forego
Such feelings for the hard and worldly phlegm
Of those whose eyes are only turned below,
Gazing upon the ground, with thoughts which dare not glow?

LXXVI

But this is not my theme; and I return
To that which is immediate, and require
Those who find contemplation in the urn,
To look on One, whose dust was once all fire,—
A native of the land where I respire
The clear air for a while—a passing guest,
Where he became a being,—whose desire
Was to be glorious; 'twas a foolish quest,
The which to gain and keep, he sacrificed all rest.

LXXVII

Here the self-torturing sophist, wild Rousseau,
The apostle of Affliction, he who threw
Enchantment over Passion, and from Woe
Wrung overwhelming eloquence, first drew
The breath which made him wretched; yet he knew
How to make Madness beautiful, and cast
O'er erring deeds and thoughts, a heavenly hue
Of words, like sunbeams, dazzling as they past
The eyes, which o'er them shed tears feelingly and fast.

LXXVIII

His love was Passion's essence—as a tree
On fire by lightning; with ethereal flame
Kindled he was, and blasted; for to be
Thus and enamoured, were in him the same.

But his was not the love of living dame,
Nor of the dead who rise upon our dreams,
But of ideal Beauty, which became
In him existence, and o'erflowing teems
Along his burning page, distempered though it seems.

LXXIX

This breathed itself to life in Julie, *this*
Invested her with all that's wild and sweet;
This hallowed, too, the memorable kiss
Which every morn his fevered lip would greet,
From hers, who but with friendship his would meet;
But to that gentle touch, through brain and breast
Flashed the thrilled Spirit's love-devouring heat;
In that absorbing sigh perchance more blest
Than vulgar minds may be with all they seek possest.

LXXX

His life was one long war with self-fought foes,
Or friends by him self-banished; for his mind
Had grown Suspicion's sanctuary, and chose,
For its own cruel sacrifice, the kind,
'Gainst whom he raged with fury strange and blind.
But he was phrensied,—wherefore, who may know?
Since cause might be which Skill could never find;
But he was phrensied by disease or woe,
To that worst pitch of all, which wears a reasoning show.

LXXXI

For then he was inspired, and from him came,
As from the Pythian's mystic cave of yore,
Those oracles which set the world in flame,
Nor ceased to burn till kingdoms were no more:
Did he not this for France? which lay, before,
Bowed to the inborn tyranny of years,
Broken and trembling to the yoke she bore,
Till by the voice of him and his compeers,
Rouscd up to too much wrath which follows o'ergrown fears?

LXXXII

They made themselves a fearful monument!
The wreck of old opinions—things which grew,
Breathed from the birth of Time: the veil they rent,
And what behind it lay, all earth shall view;
But good with ill they also overthrew,
Leaving but ruins, wherewith to rebuild
Upon the same foundation, and renew
Dungeons and thrones, which the same hour refilled,
As heretofore, because Ambition was self-willed.

LXXXIII

But this will not endure, nor be endured!
Mankind have felt their strength, and made it felt.
They might have used it better, but, allured
By their new vigour, sternly have they dealt
On one another; Pity ceased to melt
With her once natural charities. But they,
Who in Oppression's darkness caved had dwelt,
They were not eagles, nourished with the day;
What marvel then, at times, if they mistook their prey?

LXXXIV

What deep wounds ever closed without a scar?
The heart's bleed longest, and but heal to wear
That which disfigures it; and they who war
With their own hopes, and have been vanquished, bear
Silence, but not submission: in his lair
Fixed Passion holds his breath, until the hour
Which shall atone for years; none need despair:
It came—it cometh—and will come,—the power
To punish or forgive—in *one* we shall be slower.

LXXXV

Clear, placid Leman! thy contrasted lake,
With the wild world I dwelt in, is a thing
Which warns me, with its stillness, to forsake
Earth's troubled waters for a purer spring.

This quiet sail is as a noiseless wing
To waft me from distraction; once I loved
Torn Ocean's roar, but thy soft murmuring
Sounds sweet as if a Sister's voice reproved,
That I with stern delights should e'er have been so moved.

LXXXVI

It is the hush of night, and all between
Thy margin and the mountains, dusk, yet clear,
Mellowed and mingling, yet distinctly seen,
Save darkened Jura, whose capt heights appear
Precipitously steep; and drawing near,
There breathes a living fragrance from the shore,
Of flowers yet fresh with childhood; on the ear
Drops the light drip of the suspended oar,
Or chirps the grasshopper one good-night carol more.

LXXXVII

He is an evening reveller, who makes
His life an infancy, and sings his fill;
At intervals, some bird from out the brakes
Starts into voice a moment, then is still.
There seems a floating whisper on the hill,
But that is fancy—for the Starlight dews
All silently their tears of Love instil,
Weeping themselves away, till they infuse
Deep into Nature's breast the spirit of her hues.

LXXXVIII

Ye Stars! which are the poetry of Heaven!
If in your bright leaves we would read the fate
Of men and empires,—'tis to be forgiven,
That in our aspirations to be great,
Our destinies o'erleap their mortal state,
And claim a kindred with you; for ye are
A Beauty and a Mystery, and create
In us such love and reverence from afar,
That Fortune,—Fame,—Power,—Life, have named them-
selves a Star.

LXXXIX

All Heaven and Earth are still—though not in sleep,
But breathless, as we grow when feeling most;
And silent, as we stand in thoughts too deep:—
All Heaven and Earth are still: From the high host
Of stars, to the lulled lake and mountain-coast,
All is concentered in a life intense,
Where not a beam, nor air, nor leaf is lost,
But hath a part of Being, and a sense
Of that which is of all Creator and Defence.

XC

Then stirs the feeling infinite, so felt
In solitude, where we are *least* alone;
A truth, which through our being then doth melt,
And purifies from self: it is a tone,
The soul and source of Music, which makes known
Eternal harmony, and sheds a charm
Like to the fabled Cytherea's zone,
Binding all things with beauty;—'twould disarm
The spectre Death, had he substantial power to harm.

XCI

Not vainly did the early Persian make
His altar the high places, and the peak
Of earth-o'ergazing mountains, and thus take
A fit and unwalled temple, there to seek
The Spirit, in whose honour shrines are weak,
Upreared of human hands. Come, and compare
Columns and idol-dwellings—Goth or Greek—
With Nature's realms of worship, earth and air—
Nor fix on fond abodes to circumscribe thy prayer!

XCII

The sky is changed!—and such a change! Oh Night,
And Storm, and Darkness, ye are wondrous strong,
Yet lovely in your strength, as is the light
Of a dark eye in Woman! Far along,

From peak to peak, the rattling crags among
Leaps the live thunder! Not from one lone cloud,
But every mountain now hath found a tongue,
And Jura answers, through her misty shroud,
Back to the joyous Alps, who call to her aloud!

XCIII

And this is in the Night:—Most glorious Night!
Thou wert not sent for slumber! let me be
A sharer in thy fierce and far delight,—
A portion of the tempest and of thee!
How the lit lake shines, a phosphoric sea,
And the big rain comes dancing to the earth!
And now again 'tis black,—and now, the glee
Of the loud hills shakes with its mountain-mirth,
As if they did rejoice o'er a young Earthquake's birth.

XCIV

Now, where the swift Rhone cleaves his way between
Heights which appear as lovers who have parted
In hate, whose mining depths so intervene,
That they can meet no more, though broken-hearted:
Though in their souls, which thus each other thwarted,
Love was the very root of the fond rage
Which blighted their life's bloom, and then departed:—
Itself expired, but leaving them an age
Of years all winters,—war within themselves to wage:

XCV

Now, where the quick Rhone thus hath cleft his way,
The mightiest of the storms hath ta'en his stand:
For here, not one, but many, make their play
And fling their thunder-bolts from hand to hand,
Flashing and cast around: of all the band,
The brightest through these parted hills hath forked
His lightnings,—as if he did understand,
That in such gaps as Desolation worked,
There the hot shaft should blast whatever therein lurked.

XCVI

Sky—Mountains—River—Winds—Lake—Lightnings! ye!
With night, and clouds, and thunder—and a Soul
To make these felt and feeling, well may be
Things that have made me watchful; the far roll
Of your departing voices, is the knoll
Of what in me is sleepless,—if I rest.
But where of ye, O Tempests! is the goal?
Are ye like those within the human breast?
Or do ye find, at length, like eagles, some high nest?

XCVII

Could I embody and unbosom now
That which is most within me,—could I wreak
My thoughts upon expression, and thus throw
Soul—heart—mind—passions—feelings—strong or weak–
All that I would have sought, and all I seek,
Bear, know, feel—and yet breathe—into *one* word,
And that one word were Lightning, I would speak;
But as it is, I live and die unheard,
With a most voiceless thought, sheathing it as a sword.

XCVIII

The Morn is up again, the dewy Morn,
With breath all incense, and with cheek all bloom—
Laughing the clouds away with playful scorn,
And living as if earth contained no tomb,—
And glowing into day: we may resume
The march of our existence: and thus I,
Still on thy shores, fair Leman! may find room
And food for meditation, nor pass by
Much, that may give us pause, if pondered fittingly.

XCIX

Clarens! sweet Clarens, birthplace of deep Love!
Thine air is the young breath of passionate Thought;
Thy trees take root in Love; the snows above,
The very Glaciers have his colours caught,

And Sun-set into rose-hues sees them wrought
By rays which sleep there lovingly : the rocks,
The permanent crags, tell here of Love, who sought
In them a refuge from the worldly shocks,
Which stir and sting the Soul with Hope that woos, then mocks.

C

Clarens! by heavenly feet thy paths are trod,—
Undying Love's, who here ascends a throne
To which the steps are mountains ; where the God
Is a pervading Life and Light,—so shown
Not on those summits solely, nor alone
In the still cave and forest ; o'er the flower
His eye is sparkling, and his breath hath blown,
His soft and summer breath, whose tender power
Passes the strength of storms in their most desolate hour.

CI

All things are here of *Him*; from the black pines,
Which are his shade on high, and the loud roar
Of torrents, where he listeneth, to the vines
Which slope his green path downward to the shore,
Where the bowed Waters meet him, and adore,
Kissing his feet with murmurs ; and the Wood,
The covert of old trees, with trunks all hoar,
But light leaves, young as joy, stands where it stood,
Offering to him, and his, a populous solitude.

CII

A populous solitude of bees and birds,
And fairy-formed and many-coloured things,
Who worship him with notes more sweet than words,
And innocently open their glad wings,
Fearless and full of life : the gush of springs,
And fall of lofty fountains, and the bend
Of stirring branches, and the bud which brings
The swiftest thought of Beauty, here extend
Mingling—and made by Love—unto one mighty end.

CIII

He who hath loved not, here would learn that lore,
And make his heart a spirit; he who knows
That tender mystery, will love the more;
For this is Love's recess, where vain men's woes,
And the world's waste, have driven him far from those,
For 'tis his nature to advance or die;
He stands not still, but or decays, or grows
Into a boundless blessing, which may vie
With the immortal lights, in its eternity!

CIV

'Twas not for fiction chose Rousseau the spot,
Peopling it with affections; but he found
It was the scene which Passion must allot
To the Mind's purified beings; 'twas the ground
Where early Love his Psyche's zone unbound,
And hallowed it with loveliness: 'tis lone,
And wonderful, and deep, and hath a sound,
And sense, and sight of sweetness; here the Rhone
Hath spread himself a couch, the Alps have reared a throne.

CV

Lausanne! and Ferney! ye have been the abodes
Of Names which unto you bequeathed a name;
Mortals, who sought and found, by dangerous roads,
A path to perpetuity of Fame:
They were gigantic minds, and their steep aim
Was, Titan-like, on daring doubts to pile
Thoughts which should call down thunder, and the flame
Of Heaven again assailed—if Heaven, the while,
On man and man's research could deign do more than smile.

CVI

The one was fire and fickleness, a child
Most mutable in wishes, but in mind
A wit as various,—gay, grave, sage, or wild,—
Historian, bard, philosopher, combined;

He multiplied himself among mankind,
The Proteus of their talents: But his own
Breathed most in ridicule,—which, as the wind,
Blew where it listed, laying all things prone,—
Now to o'erthrow a fool, and now to shake a throne.

CVII

The other, deep and slow, exhausting thought,
And hiving wisdom with each studious year,
In meditation dwelt—with learning wrought,
And shaped his weapon with an edge severe,
Sapping a solemn creed with solemn sneer;
The lord of irony,—that master spell,
Which stung his foes to wrath, which grew from fear,
And doomed him to the zealot's ready Hell,
Which answers to all doubts so eloquently well.

CVIII

Yet, peace be with their ashes,—for by them
If merited, the penalty is paid;
It is not ours to judge,—far less condemn;
The hour must come when such things shall be made
Known unto all,—or hope and dread allayed
By slumber, on one pillow, in the dust,
Which, thus much we are sure, must lie decayed;
And when it shall revive, as is our trust,
'Twill be to be forgiven—or suffer what is just.

CIX

But let me quit Man's works, again to read
His Maker's, spread around me, and suspend
This page, which from my reveries I feed,
Until it seems prolonging without end.
The clouds above me to the white Alps tend,
And I must pierce them, and survey whate'er
May be permitted, as my steps I bend
To their most great and growing region, where
The earth to her embrace compels the powers of air.

CX

Italia, too! Italia! looking on thee,
Full flashes on the Soul the light of ages,
Since the fierce Carthaginian almost won thee,
To the last halo of the Chiefs and Sages
Who glorify thy consecrated pages;
Thou wert the throne and grave of empires—still,
The fount at which the panting Mind assuages
Her thirst of knowledge, quaffing there her fill,
Flows from the eternal source of Rome's imperial hill.

CXI

Thus far have I proceeded in a theme
Renewed with no kind auspices:—to feel
We are not what we have been, and to deem
We are not what we should be,—and to steel
The heart against itself; and to conceal,
With a proud caution, love, or hate, or aught,—
Passion or feeling, purpose, grief, or zeal,
Which is the tyrant Spirit of our thought,—
Is a stern task of soul:—No matter,—it is taught.

CXII

And for these words, thus woven into song,
It may be that they are a harmless wile,—
The colouring of the scenes which fleet along,
Which I would seize, in passing, to beguile
My breast, or that of others, for a while.
Fame is the thirst of youth,—but I am not
So young as to regard men's frown or smile,
As loss or guerdon of a glorious lot;—
I stood and stand alone,—remembered or forgot.

CXIII

I have not loved the World, nor the World me;
I have not flattered its rank breath, nor bowed
To its idolatries a patient knee,
Nor coined my cheek to smiles,—nor cried aloud

In worship of an echo : in the crowd
They could not deem me one of such—I stood
Among them, but not of them—in a shroud
Of thoughts which were not their thoughts, and still could,
Had I not filed my mind, which thus itself subdued.

CXIV

I have not loved the World, nor the World me,—
But let us part fair foes ; I do believe,
Though I have found them not, that there may be
Words which are things,—hopes which will not deceive,
And Virtues which are merciful, nor weave
Snares for the failing : I would also deem
O'er others' griefs that some sincerely grieve—
That two, or one, are almost what they seem,—
That Goodness is no name—and Happiness no dream.

CXV

My daughter! with thy name this song begun!
My daughter! with thy name thus much shall end!—
I see thee not—I hear thee not—but none
Can be so wrapt in thee ; Thou art the Friend
To whom the shadows of far years extend :
Albeit my brow thou never should'st behold,
My voice shall with thy future visions blend,
And reach into thy heart,—when mine is cold,—
A token and a tone, even from thy father's mould.

CXVI

To aid thy mind's development,—to watch
Thy dawn of little joys,—to sit and see
Almost thy very growth,—to view thee catch
Knowledge of objects,—wonders yet to thee!
To hold thee lightly on a gentle knee,
And print on thy soft cheek a parent's kiss,—
This, it should seem, was not reserved for me—
Yet this was in my nature :—as it is,
I know not what is there, yet something like to this.

CXVII

Yet, though dull Hate as duty should be taught,
I know that thou wilt love me,—though my name
Should be shut from thee, as a spell still fraught
With desolation, and a broken claim:
Though the grave closed between us,—'twere the same—
I know that thou wilt love me—though to drain
My blood from out thy being were an aim,
And an attainment,—all would be in vain,—
Still thou would'st love me, still that more than life retain.

CXVIII

The child of Love! though born in bitterness,
And nurtured in Convulsion! Of thy sire
These were the elements,—and thine no less.
As yet such are around thee,—but thy fire
Shall be more tempered, and thy hope far higher.
Sweet be thy cradled slumbers! O'er the sea
And from the mountains where I now respire,
Fain would I waft such blessing upon thee,
As—with a sigh—I deem thou might'st have been to me!

CANTO THE FOURTH

I

I stood in Venice, on the 'Bridge of Sighs';
A Palace and a prison on each hand:
I saw from out the wave her structures rise
As from the stroke of the Enchanter's wand:
A thousand Years their cloudy wings expand
Around me, and a dying Glory smiles
O'er the far times, when many a subject land
Looked to the wingéd Lion's marble piles,
Where Venice sate in state, throned on her hundred isles!

II

She looks a sea Cybele, fresh from Ocean,
Rising with her tiara of proud towers

At airy distance, with majestic motion,
A Ruler of the waters and their powers:
And such she was;—her daughters had their dowers
From spoils of nations, and the exhaustless East
Poured in her lap all gems in sparkling showers:
In purple was she robed, and of her feast
Monarchs partook, and deemed their dignity increased.

III

In Venice Tasso's echoes are no more,
And silent rows the songless Gondolier;
Her palaces are crumbling to the shore,
And Music meets not always now the ear:
Those days are gone—but Beauty still is here.
States fall—Arts fade—but Nature doth not die,
Nor yet forget how Venice once was dear,
The pleasant place of all festivity,
The Revel of the earth—the Masque of Italy!

IV

But unto us she hath a spell beyond
Her name in story, and her long array
Of mighty shadows, whose dim forms despond
Above the Dogeless city's vanished sway;
Ours is a trophy which will not decay
With the Rialto; Shylock and the Moor,
And Pierre, can not be swept or worn away—
The keystones of the Arch! though all were o'er,
For us repeopled were the solitary shore.

V

The Beings of the Mind are not of clay:
Essentially immortal, they create
And multiply in us a brighter ray
And more beloved existence: that which Fate
Prohibits to dull life in this our state
Of mortal bondage, by these Spirits supplied,
First exiles, then replaces what we hate;

Watering the heart whose early flowers have died,
And with a fresher growth replenishing the void.

VI

Such is the refuge of our youth and age—
The first from Hope, the last from Vacancy;
And this wan feeling peoples many a page—
And, may be, that which grows beneath mine eye:
Yet there are things whose strong reality
Outshines our fairy-land; in shape and hues
More beautiful than our fantastic sky,
And the strange constellations which the Muse
O'er her wild universe is skilful to diffuse:

VII

I saw or dreamed of such,—but let them go,—
They came like Truth—and disappeared like dreams;
And whatsoe'er they were—are now but so:
I could replace them if I would; still teems
My mind with many a form which aptly seems
Such as I sought for, and at moments found;
Let these too go—for waking Reason deems
Such over-weening phantasies unsound,
And other voices speak, and other sights surround.

VIII

I've taught me other tongues—and in strange eyes
Have made me not a stranger; to the mind
Which is itself, no changes bring surprise;
Nor is it harsh to make, nor hard to find
A country with—aye, or without mankind;
Yet was I born where men are proud to be,—
Not without cause; and should I leave behind
The inviolate Island of the sage and free,
And seek me out a home by a remoter sea,

IX

Perhaps I loved it well; and should I lay
My ashes in a soil which is not mine,

My Spirit shall resume it—if we may
Unbodied choose a sanctuary. I twine
My hopes of being remembered in my line
With my land's language: if too fond and far
These aspirations in their scope incline,—
If my Fame should be, as my fortunes are,
Of hasty growth and blight, and dull Oblivion bar

X

My name from out the temple where the dead
Are honoured by the Nations—let it be—
And light the Laurels on a loftier head!
And be the Spartan's epitaph on me—
'Sparta hath many a worthier son than he.'
Meantime I seek no sympathies, nor need—
The thorns which I have reaped are of the tree
I planted,—they have torn me,—and I bleed:
I should have known what fruit would spring from such a seed.

XI

The spouseless Adriatic mourns her Lord,
And annual marriage now no more renewed—
The Bucentaur lies rotting unrestored,
Neglected garment of her widowhood!
St. Mark yet sees his Lion where he stood
Stand, but in mockery of his withered power,
Over the proud Place where an Emperor sued,
And monarchs gazed and envied in the hour
When Venice was a Queen with an unequalled dower.

XII

The Suabian sued, and now the Austrian reigns—
An Emperor tramples where an Emperor knelt;
Kingdoms are shrunk to provinces, and chains
Clank over sceptred cities; Nations melt
From Power's high pinnacle, when they have felt
The sunshine for a while, and downward go
Like Lauwine loosened from the mountain's belt;

Oh for one hour of blind old Dandolo!
Th' octogenarian chief, Byzantium's conquering foe.

XIII

Before St. Mark still glow his Steeds of brass,
Their gilded collars glittering in the sun;
But is not Doria's menace come to pass?
Are they not bridled?—Venice, lost and won,
Her thirteen hundred years of freedom done,
Sinks, like a sea-weed, unto whence she rose!
Better be whelmed beneath the waves, and shun,
Even in Destruction's depth, her foreign foes,
From whom Submission wrings an infamous repose.

XIV

In youth She was all glory,—a new Tyre,—
Her very by-word sprung from Victory,
The 'Planter of the Lion,' which through fire
And blood she bore o'er subject Earth and Sea;
Though making many slaves, Herself still free,
And Europe's bulwark 'gainst the Ottomite;
Witness Troy's rival, Candia! Vouch it, ye
Immortal waves that saw Lepanto's fight!
For ye are names no Time nor Tyranny can blight.

XV

Statues of glass—all shivered—the long file
Of her dead Doges are declined to dust;
But where they dwelt, the vast and sumptuous pile
Bespeaks the pageant of their splendid trust;
Their sceptre broken, and their sword in rust,
Have yielded to the stranger: empty halls,
Thin streets, and foreign aspects, such as must
Too oft remind her who and what enthrals,
Have flung a desolate cloud o'er Venice' lovely walls.

XVI

When Athens' armies fell at Syracuse,
And fettered thousands bore the yoke of war,

Redemption rose up in the Attic Muse,
Her voice their only ransom from afar:
See! as they chant the tragic hymn, the car
Of the o'ermastered Victor stops—the reins
Fall from his hands—his idle scimitar
Starts from its belt—he rends his captive's chains,
And bids him thank the Bard for Freedom and his strains.

XVII

Thus, Venice! if no stronger claim were thine,
Were all thy proud historic deeds forgot—
Thy choral memory of the Bard divine,
Thy love of Tasso, should have cut the knot
Which ties thee to thy tyrants; and thy lot
Is shameful to the nations,—most of all,
Albion! to thee: the Ocean queen should not
Abandon Ocean's children; in the fall
Of Venice think of thine, despite thy watery wall.

XVIII

I loved her from my boyhood—she to me
Was as a fairy city of the heart,
Rising like water-columns from the sea—
Of Joy the sojourn, and of Wealth the mart;
And Otway, Radcliffe, Schiller, Shakespeare's art,
Had stamped her image in me, and even so,
Although I found her thus, we did not part;
Perchance even dearer in her day of woe,
Than when she was a boast, a marvel, and a show.

XIX

I can repeople with the past—and of
The present there is still for eye and thought,
And meditation chastened down, enough;
And more, it may be, than I hoped or sought;
And of the happiest moments which were wrought
Within the web of my existence, some
From thee, fair Venice! have their colours caught:

There are some feelings Time can not benumb,
Nor Torture shake, or mine would now be cold and dumb.

*　　*　　*　　*

XXVII

The Moon is up, and yet it is not night—
Sunset divides the sky with her—a sea
Of glory streams along the Alpine height
Of blue Friuli's mountains; Heaven is free
From clouds, but of all colours seems to be,—
Melted to one vast Iris of the West,—
Where the Day joins the past Eternity;
While, on the other hand, meek Dian's crest
Floats through the azure air—an island of the blest!

XXVIII

A single star is at her side, and reigns
With her o'er half the lovely heaven; but still
Yon sunny Sea heaves brightly, and remains
Rolled o'er the peak of the far Rhætian hill,
As Day and Night contending were, until
Nature reclaimed her order:—gently flows
The deep-dyed Brenta, where their hues instil
The odorous purple of a new-born rose,
Which streams upon her stream, and glassed within it glows,

XXIX

Filled with the face of heaven, which, from afar,
Comes down upon the waters! all its hues,
From the rich sunset to the rising star,
Their magical variety diffuse:
And now they change—a paler Shadow strews
Its mantle o'er the mountains; parting Day
Dies like the Dolphin, whom each pang imbues
With a new colour as it gasps away—
The last still loveliest, till—'tis gone—and all is gray.

XXX

There is a tomb in Arqua;—reared in air,
Pillared in their sarcophagus, repose

The bones of Laura's lover: here repair
Many familiar with his well-sung woes,
The Pilgrims of his Genius. He arose
To raise a language, and his land reclaim
From the dull yoke of her barbaric foes:
Watering the tree which bears his Lady's name
With his melodious tears, he gave himself to Fame.

XXXI

They keep his dust in Arqua, where he died—
The mountain-village where his latter days
Went down the vale of years; and 'tis their pride—•
An honest pride—and let it be their praise,
To offer to the passing stranger's gaze
His mansion and his sepulchre—both plain
And venerably simple—such as raise
A feeling more accordant with his strain
Than if a Pyramid formed his monumental fane.

XXXII

And the soft quiet hamlet where he dwelt
Is one of that complexion which seems made
For those who their mortality have felt,
And sought a refuge from their hopes decayed
In the deep umbrage of a green hill's shade,
Which shows a distant prospect far away
Of busy cities, now in vain displayed,
For they can lure no further; and the ray
Of a bright Sun can make sufficient holiday.

*   *   *   *

XLVIII

But Arno wins us to the fair white walls,
Where the Etrurian Athens claims and keeps
A softer feeling for her fairy halls:
Girt by her theatre of hills, she reaps
Her corn, and wine, and oil—and Plenty leaps

To laughing life, with her redundant Horn.
Along the banks where smiling Arno sweeps
Was modern Luxury of Commerce born,
And buried Learning rose, redeemed to a new Morn.

XLIX

There, too, the Goddess loves in stone, and fills
The air around with Beauty—we inhale
The ambrosial aspect, which, beheld, instils
Part of its immortality—the veil
Of heaven is half undrawn—within the pale
We stand, and in that form and face behold
What Mind can make, when Nature's self would fail;
And to the fond Idolaters of old
Envy the innate flash which such a Soul could mould:

L

We gaze and turn away, and know not where,
Dazzled and drunk with Beauty, till the heart
Reels with its fulness; there—for ever there—
Chained to the chariot of triumphal Art,
We stand as captives, and would not depart.
Away!—there need no words, nor terms precise,
The paltry jargon of the marble mart,
Where Pedantry gulls Folly—we have eyes:
Blood—pulse—and breast confirm the Dardan Shepherd's
prize.

LI

Appear'dst thou not to Paris in this guise?
Or to more deeply blest Anchises? or,
In all thy perfect Goddess-ship, when lies
Before thee thy own vanquished Lord of War?
And gazing in thy face as toward a star,
Laid on thy lap, his eyes to thee upturn,
Feeding on thy sweet cheek! while thy lips are
With lava kisses melting while they burn,
Showered on his eyelids, brow, and mouth, as from an urn!

LII

Glowing, and circumfused in speechless love—
Their full divinity inadequate
That feeling to express, or to improve—
The Gods become as mortals—and man's fate
Has moments like their brightest; but the weight
Of earth recoils upon us;—let it go!
We can recall such visions, and create,
From what has been, or might be, things which grow
Into thy statue's form, and look like gods below.

* * * *

LXXVIII

Oh, Rome! my Country! City of the Soul!
The orphans of the heart must turn to thee,
Lone Mother of dead Empires! and control
In their shut breasts their petty misery.
What are our woes and sufferance? Come and see
The cypress—hear the owl—and plod your way
O'er steps of broken thrones and temples—Ye!
Whose agonies are evils of a day—
A world is at our feet as fragile as our clay.

LXXIX

The Niobe of nations! there she stands,
Childless and crownless, in her voiceless woe;
An empty urn within her withered hands,
Whose holy dust was scattered long ago;
The Scipios' tomb contains no ashes now;
The very sepulchres lie tenantless
Of their heroic dwellers: dost thou flow,
Old Tiber! through a marble wilderness?
Rise, with thy yellow waves, and mantle her distress.

LXXX

The Goth, the Christian—Time—War—Flood, and Fire,
Have dealt upon the seven-hilled City's pride;

She saw her glories star by star expire,
And up the steep barbarian Monarchs ride,
Where the car climbed the Capitol; far and wide
Temple and tower went down, nor left a site:—
Chaos of ruins! who shall trace the void,
O'er the dim fragments cast a lunar light,
And say, 'here was, or is,' where all is doubly night?

LXXXI

The double night of ages, and of her,
Night's daughter, Ignorance, hath wrapt and wrap
All round us; we but feel our way to err:
The Ocean hath his chart, the Stars their map,
And Knowledge spreads them on her ample lap;
But Rome is as the desert—where we steer
Stumbling o'er recollections; now we clap
Our hands, and cry 'Eureka!' 'it is clear'—
When but some false Mirage of ruin rises near.

LXXXII

Alas! the lofty city! and, alas,
The trebly hundred triumphs! and the day
When Brutus made the dagger's edge surpass
The Conqueror's sword in bearing fame away!
Alas, for Tully's voice, and Virgil's lay,
And Livy's pictured page!—but these shall be
Her resurrection; all beside—decay.
Alas, for Earth, for never shall we see
That brightness in her eye she bore when Rome was free!

*   *   *   *

XCIX

There is a stern round tower of other days,
Firm as a fortress, with its fence of stone,
Such as an army's baffled strength delays,
Standing with half its battlements alone.
And with two thousand years of ivy grown,

The garland of Eternity, where wave
The green leaves over all by Time o'erthrown;—
What was this tower of strength? within its cave
What treasure lay so locked, so hid?—A woman's grave.

C

But who was she, the Lady of the dead,
Tombed in a palace? Was she chaste and fair?
Worthy a king's—or more—a Roman's bed?
What race of Chiefs and Heroes did she bear?
What daughter of her beauties was the heir?
How lived—how loved—how died she? Was she not
So honoured—and conspicuously there,
Where meaner relics must not dare to rot,
Placed to commemorate a more than mortal lot?

CI

Was she as those who love their lords, or they
Who love the lords of others? such have been
Even in the olden time, Rome's annals say.
Was she a matron of Cornelia's mien,
Or the light air of Egypt's graceful Queen,
Profuse of joy—or 'gainst it did she war,
Inveterate in virtue? Did she lean
To the soft side of the heart, or wisely bar
Love from amongst her griefs?—for such the affections are.

CII

Perchance she died in youth—it may be, bowed
With woes far heavier than the ponderous tomb
That weighed upon her gentle dust: a cloud
Might gather o'er her beauty, and a gloom
In her dark eye, prophetic of the doom
Heaven gives its favourites—early death—yet shed
A sunset charm around her, and illume
With hectic light, the Hesperus of the dead,
Of her consuming cheek the autumnal leaf-like red.

CIII

Perchance she died in age—surviving all,
Charms—kindred—children—with the silver gray
On her long tresses, which might yet recall,
It may be, still a something of the day
When they were braided, and her proud array
And lovely form were envied, praised, and eyed
By Rome—But whither would Conjecture stray?
Thus much alone we know—Metella died,
The wealthiest Roman's wife: Behold his love or pride!

* * * *

CXV

Egeria! sweet creation of some heart
Which found no mortal resting-place so fair
As thine ideal breast; whate'er thou art
Or wert,—a young Aurora of the air,
The nympholepsy of some fond despair—
Or—it might be—a Beauty of the earth,
Who found a more than common Votary there
Too much adoring—whatsoe'er thy birth,
Thou wert a beautiful Thought, and softly bodied forth.

CXVI

The mosses of thy Fountain still are sprinkled
With thine Elysian water-drops; the face
Of thy cave-guarded Spring, with years unwrinkled,
Reflects the meek-eyed Genius of the place,
Whose green, wild margin now no more erase
Art's works; nor must the delicate waters sleep
Prisoned in marble—bubbling from the base
Of the cleft statue, with a gentle leap
The rill runs o'er—and, round—fern, flowers, and ivy, creep,

CXVII

Fantastically tangled: the green hills
Are clothed with early blossoms—through the grass

The quick-eyed lizard rustles—and the bills
Of summer-birds sing welcome as ye pass;
Flowers fresh in hue, and many in their class,
Implore the pausing step, and with their dyes
Dance in the soft breeze in a fairy mass;
The sweetness of the Violet's deep blue eyes,
Kissed by the breath of heaven, seems coloured by its skies.

CXVIII

Here didst thou dwell, in this enchanted cover,
Egeria! thy all heavenly bosom beating
For the far footsteps of thy mortal lover;
The purple Midnight veiled that mystic meeting
With her most starry canopy—and seating
Thyself by thine adorer, what befel?
This cave was surely shaped out for the greeting
Of an enamoured Goddess, and the cell
Haunted by holy Love—the earliest Oracle!

CXIX

And didst thou not, thy breast to his replying,
Blend a celestial with a human heart;
And Love, which dies as it was born, in sighing,
Share with immortal transports? could thine art
Make them indeed immortal, and impart
The purity of Heaven to earthly joys,
Expel the venom and not blunt the dart—
The dull satiety which all destroys—
And root from out the soul the deadly weed which cloys?

CXX

Alas! our young affections run to waste,
Or water but the desert! whence arise
But weeds of dark luxuriance, tares of haste,
Rank at the core, though tempting to the eyes,
Flowers whose wild odours breathe but agonies,
And trees whose gums are poison; such the plants
Which spring beneath her steps as Passion flies

F

O'er the World's wilderness, and vainly pants
For some celestial fruit forbidden to our wants.

CXXI

Oh, Love! no habitant of earth thou art—
An unseen Seraph, we believe in thee,—
A faith whose martyrs are the broken heart,—
But never yet hath seen, nor e'er shall see
The naked eye, thy form, as it should be;
The mind hath made thee, as it peopled Heaven,
Even with its own desiring phantasy,
And to a thought such shape and image given,
As haunts the unquenched soul—parched—wearied—wrung
    —and riven.

CXXII

Of its own beauty is the mind diseased,
And fevers into false creation:—where,
Where are the forms the sculptor's soul hath seized?
In him alone. Can Nature show so fair?
Where are the charms and virtues which we dare
Conceive in boyhood and pursue as men,
The unreached Paradise of our despair,
Which o'er-informs the pencil and the pen,
And overpowers the page where it would bloom again?

CXXIII

Who loves, raves—'tis youth's frenzy—but the cure
Is bitterer still, as charm by charm unwinds
Which robed our idols, and we see too sure
Nor Worth nor Beauty dwells from out the mind's
Ideal shape of such; yet still it binds—
The fatal spell, and still it draws us on,
Reaping the whirlwind from the oft-sown winds;
The stubborn heart, its alchemy begun,
Seems ever near the prize—wealthiest when most undone.

CXXIV

We wither from our youth, we gasp away—
Sick—sick ; unfound the boon—unslaked the thirst,
Though to the last, in verge of our decay,
Some phantom lures, such as we sought at first—
But all too late,—so are we doubly curst.
Love, Fame, Ambition, Avarice—'tis the same,
Each idle—and all ill—and none the worst—
For all are meteors with a different name,
And Death the sable smoke where vanishes the flame.

CXXV

Few—none—find what they love or could have loved,
Though accident, blind contact, and the strong
Necessity of loving, have removed
Antipathies—but to recur, ere long,
Envenomed with irrevocable wrong ;
And Circumstance, that unspiritual God
And Miscreator, makes and helps along
Our coming evils with a crutch-like rod,
Whose touch turns Hope to dust,—the dust we all have trod.

CXXVI

Our life is a false nature—'tis not in
The harmony of things,—this hard decree,
This uneradicable taint of Sin,
This boundless Upas, this all-blasting tree,
Whose root is Earth—whose leaves and branches be
The skies which rain their plagues on men like dew—
Disease, death, bondage—all the woes we see,
And worse, the woes we see not—which throb through
The immedicable soul, with heart-aches ever new.

CXXVII

Yet let us ponder boldly—'tis a base
Abandonment of reason to resign
Our right of thought—our last and only place
Of refuge ; this, at least, shall still be mine :

Though from our birth the faculty divine
Is chained and tortured—cabined, cribbed, confined,
And bred in darkness, lest the Truth should shine
Too brightly on the unpreparéd mind,
The beam pours in—for Time and Skill will couch the blind.

CXXVIII

Arches on arches! as it were that Rome,
Collecting the chief trophies of her line,
Would build up all her triumphs in one dome,
Her Coliseum stands; the moonbeams shine
As 'twere its natural torches—for divine
Should be the light which streams here,—to illume
This long-explored but still exhaustless mine
Of Contemplation; and the azure gloom
Of an Italian night, where the deep skies assume

CXXIX

Hues which have words and speak to ye of Heaven,
Floats o'er this vast and wondrous monument,
And shadows forth its glory. There is given
Unto the things of earth, which Time hath bent,
A Spirit's feeling, and where he hath leant
His hand, but broke his scythe, there is a power
And magic in the ruined battlement,
For which the Palace of the present hour
Must yield its pomp, and wait till Ages are its dower.

CXXX

Oh, Time! the Beautifier of the dead,
Adorner of the ruin—Comforter
And only Healer when the heart hath bled;—
Time! the Corrector where our judgments err,
The test of Truth, Love—sole philosopher,
For all beside are sophists—from thy thrift,
Which never loses though it doth defer—
Time, the Avenger! unto thee I lift
My hands, and eyes, and heart, and crave of thee a gift:

CXXXI

Amidst this wreck, where thou hast made a shrine
And temple more divinely desolate—
Among thy mightier offerings here are mine,
Ruins of years—though few, yet full of fate :—
If thou hast ever seen me too elate,
Hear me not; but if calmly I have borne
Good, and reserved my pride against the hate
Which shall not whelm me, let me not have worn
This iron in my soul in vain—shall *they* not mourn?

CXXXII

And Thou, who never yet of human wrong
Left the unbalanced scale, great Nemesis!
Here, where the ancient paid thee homage long—
Thou, who didst call the Furies from the abyss,
And round Orestes bade them howl and hiss
For that unnatural retribution—just,
Had it but been from hands less near—in this
Thy former realm, I call thee from the dust!
Dost thou not hear my heart?—Awake! thou shalt, and must.

CXXXIII

It is not that I may not have incurred,
For my ancestral faults or mine, the wound
I bleed withal; and, had it been conferred
With a just weapon, it had flowed unbound;
But now my blood shall not sink in the ground—
To thee I do devote it—*Thou* shalt take
The vengeance, which shall yet be sought and found—
Which if *I* have not taken for the sake——
But let that pass—I sleep—but Thou shalt yet awake.

CXXXIV

And if my voice break forth, 'tis not that now
I shrink from what is suffered : let him speak
Who hath beheld decline, upon my brow,
Or seen my mind's convulsion leave it weak;

But in this page a record will I seek.
Not in the air shall these my words disperse,
Though I be ashes; a far hour shall wreak
The deep prophetic fulness of this verse,
And pile on human heads the mountain of my curse!

CXXXV

That curse shall be Forgiveness.—Have I not—
Hear me, my mother Earth! behold it, Heaven!—
Have I not had to wrestle with my lot?
Have I not suffered things to be forgiven?
Have I not had my brain seared, my heart riven,
Hopes sapped, name blighted, Life's life lied away?
And only not to desperation driven,
Because not altogether of such clay
As rots into the souls of those whom I survey.

CXXXVI

From mighty wrongs to petty perfidy
Have I not seen what human things could do?
From the loud roar of foaming calumny
To the small whisper of the as paltry few—
And subtler venom of the reptile crew,
The Janus glance of whose significant eye,
Learning to lie with silence, would *seem* true—
And without utterance, save the shrug or sigh,
Deal round to happy fools its speechless obloquy.

CXXXVII

But I have lived, and have not lived in vain:
My mind may lose its force, my blood its fire,
And my frame perish even in conquering pain;
But there is that within me which shall tire
Torture and Time, and breathe when I expire;
Something unearthly, which they deem not of,
Like the remembered tone of a mute lyre,
Shall on their softened spirits sink, and move
In hearts all rocky now the late remorse of Love.

CXXXVIII

The seal is set.—Now welcome, thou dread Power
Nameless, yet thus omnipotent, which here
Walk'st in the shadow of the midnight hour
With a deep awe, yet all distinct from fear;
Thy haunts are ever where the dead walls rear
Their ivy mantles, and the solemn scene
Derives from thee a sense so deep and clear
That we become a part of what has been,
And grow upon the spot—all-seeing but unseen.

CXXXIX

And here the buzz of eager nations ran,
In murmured pity, or loud-roared applause,
As man was slaughtered by his fellow man.
And wherefore slaughtered? wherefore, but because
Such were the bloody Circus' genial laws,
And the imperial pleasure.—Wherefore not?
What matters where we fall to fill the maws
Of worms—on battle-plains or listed spot?
Both are but theatres—where the chief actors rot.

CXL

I see before me the Gladiator lie:
He leans upon his hand—his manly brow
Consents to death, but conquers agony,
And his drooped head sinks gradually low—
And through his side the last drops, ebbing slow
From the red gash, fall heavy, one by one,
Like the first of a thunder-shower; and now
The arena swims around him—he is gone,
Ere ceased the inhuman shout which hailed the wretch who
    won.

CXLI

He heard it, but he heeded not—his eyes
Were with his heart—and that was far away;
He recked not of the life he lost nor prize,
But where his rude hut by the Danube lay—

There were his young barbarians all at play,
There was their Dacian mother—he, their sire,
Butchered to make a Roman holiday—
All this rushed with his blood—Shall he expire
And unavenged?—Arise! ye Goths, and glut your ire!

CXLII

But here, where Murder breathed her bloody steam;—
And here, where buzzing nations choked the ways,
And roared or murmured like a mountain stream
Dashing or winding as its torrent strays;
Here, where the Roman million's blame or praise
Was Death or Life—the playthings of a crowd—
My voice sounds much—and fall the stars' faint rays
On the arena void—seats crushed—walls bowed—
And galleries, where my steps seem echoes strangely loud.

CXLIII

A Ruin—yet what Ruin! from its mass
Walls—palaces—half-cities, have been reared;
Yet oft the enormous skeleton ye pass,
And marvel where the spoil could have appeared.
Hath it indeed been plundered, or but cleared?
Alas! developed, opens the decay,
When the colossal fabric's form is neared:
It will not bear the brightness of the day,
Which streams too much on all—years—man—have reft
        away.

CXLIV

But when the rising moon begins to climb
Its topmost arch, and gently pauses there—
When the stars twinkle through the loops of Time,
And the low night-breeze waves along the air
The garland-forest, which the gray walls wear,
Like laurels on the bald first Cæsar's head—
When the light shines serene but doth not glare—
Then in this magic circle raise the dead;—
Heroes have trod this spot—'tis on their dust ye tread.

CXLV

'While stands the Coliseum, Rome shall stand:
'When falls the Coliseum, Rome shall fall;
'And when Rome falls—the World.' From our own land
Thus spake the pilgrims o'er this mighty wall
In Saxon times, which we are wont to call
Ancient; and these three mortal things are still
On their foundations, and unaltered all—
Rome and her Ruin past Redemption's skill—
The World—the same wide den—of thieves, or what ye will.

* * * *

CLXXV

But I forget.—My Pilgrim's shrine is won,
And he and I must part,—so let it be,—
His task and mine alike are nearly done;
Yet once more let us look upon the Sea;
The Midland Ocean breaks on him and me,
And from the Alban Mount we now behold
Our friend of youth, that Ocean, which when we
Beheld it last by Calpe's rock unfold
Those waves, we followed on till the dark Euxine rolled

CLXXVI

Upon the blue Symplegades: long years—
Long, though not very many—since have done
Their work on both; some suffering and some tears
Have left us nearly where we had begun:
Yet not in vain our mortal race hath run—
We have had our reward—and it is here,
That we can yet feel gladdened by the Sun,
And reap from Earth—Sea—joy almost as dear
As if there were no Man to trouble what is clear.

CLXXVII

Oh! that the Desert were my dwelling-place,
With one fair Spirit for my minister,

That I might all forget the human race,
And, hating no one, love but only her!
Ye elements!—in whose ennobling stir
I feel myself exalted—Can ye not
Accord me such a Being? Do I err
In deeming such inhabit many a spot?
Though with them to converse can rarely be our lot.

CLXXVIII

There is a pleasure in the pathless woods,
There is a rapture on the lonely shore,
There is society, where none intrudes,
By the deep Sea, and Music in its roar:
I love not Man the less, but Nature more,
From these our interviews, in which I steal
From all I may be, or have been before,
To mingle with the Universe, and feel
What I can ne'er express—yet can not all conceal.

CLXXIX

Roll on, thou deep and dark blue Ocean—roll!
Ten thousand fleets sweep over thee in vain;
Man marks the earth with ruin—his control
Stops with the shore;—upon the watery plain
The wrecks are all thy deed, nor doth remain
A shadow of man's ravage, save his own,
When, for a moment, like a drop of rain,
He sinks into thy depths with bubbling groan—
Without a grave—unknelled, uncoffined, and unknown.

CLXXX

His steps are not upon thy paths,—thy fields
Are not a spoil for him,—thou dost arise
And shake him from thee; the vile strength he wields
For Earth's destruction thou dost all despise,
Spurning him from thy bosom to the skies—
And send'st him, shivering in thy playful spray
And howling, to his Gods, where haply lies

His petty hope in some near port or bay,
And dashest him again to Earth :—there let him lay.

CLXXXI

The armaments which thunderstrike the walls
Of rock-built cities, bidding nations quake,
And Monarchs tremble in their Capitals,
The oak Leviathans, whose huge ribs make
Their clay creator the vain title take
Of Lord of thee, and Arbiter of War—
These are thy toys, and, as the snowy flake,
They melt into thy yeast of waves, which mar
Alike the Armada's pride, or spoils of Trafalgar.

CLXXXII

Thy shores are empires, changed in all save thee—
Assyria—Greece—Rome—Carthage—what are they?
Thy waters washed them power while they were free,
And many a tyrant since ; their shores obey
The stranger, slave, or savage ; their decay
Has dried up realms to deserts :—not so thou,
Unchangeable save to thy wild waves' play ;
Time writes no wrinkle on thine azure brow—
Such as Creation's dawn beheld, thou rollest now.

CLXXXIII

Thou glorious mirror, where the Almighty's form
Glasses itself in tempests ; in all time,
Calm or convulsed—in breeze, or gale, or storm—
Icing the Pole, or in the torrid clime
Dark-heaving—boundless, endless, and sublime—
The image of Eternity—the throne
Of the Invisible ; even from out thy slime
The monsters of the deep are made—each Zone
Obeys thee—thou goest forth, dread, fathomless, alone.

CLXXXIV

And I have loved thee, Ocean! and my joy
Of youthful sports was on thy breast to be

Borne, like thy bubbles, onward: from a boy
I wantoned with thy breakers—they to me
Were a delight; and if the freshening sea
Made them a terror—'twas a pleasing fear,
For I was as it were a Child of thee,
And trusted to thy billows far and near,
And laid my hand upon thy mane—as I do here.

CLXXXV

My task is done—my song hath ceased—my theme
Has died into an echo; it is fit
The spell should break of this protracted dream.
The torch shall be extinguished which hath lit
My midnight lamp—and what is writ, is writ,—
Would it were worthier! but I am not now
That which I have been—and my visions flit
Less palpably before me—and the glow
Which in my Spirit dwelt is fluttering, faint, and low.

CLXXXVI

Farewell! a word that must be, and hath been—
A sound which makes us linger;—yet—farewell!
Ye! who have traced the Pilgrim to the scene
Which is his last—if in your memories dwell
A thought which once was his—if on ye swell
A single recollection—not in vain
He wore his sandal-shoon, and scallop-shell;
Farewell! with *him* alone may rest the pain,
If such there were—with *you*, the Moral of his Strain.

SHORTER POEMS

SHORTER POEMS

REMEMBER THEE! REMEMBER THEE!

1

Remember thee! remember thee!
 Till Lethe quench Life's burning stream
Remorse and Shame shall cling to thee,
 And haunt thee like a feverish dream!

2

Remember thee! Aye, doubt it not.
 Thy husband too shall think of thee:
By neither shalt thou be forgot,
 Thou *false* to him, thou *fiend* to me!

REMEMBER HIM, WHOM PASSION'S POWER

1

Remember him, whom Passion's power
 Severely—deeply—vainly proved:
Remember thou that dangerous hour,
 When neither fell, though both were loved.

2

That yielding breast, that melting eye,
 Too much invited to be blessed:
That gentle prayer, that pleading sigh,
 The wilder wish reproved, repressed.

3

Oh! let me feel that all I lost
 But saved thee all that Conscience fears;
And blush for every pang it cost
 To spare the vain remorse of years.

4

Yet think of this when many a tongue,
 Whose busy accents whisper blame,

Would do the heart that loved thee wrong,
  And brand a nearly blighted name.

5

Think that, whate'er to others, thou
  Hast seen each selfish thought subdued:
I bless thy purer soul even now,
  Even now, in midnight solitude.

6

Oh, God! that we had met in time,
  Our hearts as fond, thy hand more free;
When thou hadst loved without a crime,
  And I been less unworthy thee!

7

Far may thy days, as heretofore,
  From this our gaudy world be past!
And that too bitter moment o'er,
  Oh! may such trial be thy last.

8

This heart, alas! perverted long,
  Itself destroyed might there destroy;
To meet thee in the glittering throng,
  Would wake Presumption's hope of joy.

9

Then to the things whose bliss or woe,
  Like mine, is wild and worthless all,
That world resign—such scenes forego,
  Where those who feel must surely fall.

10

Thy youth, thy charms, thy tenderness—
  Thy soul from long seclusion pure;
From what even here hath passed, may guess
  What there thy bosom must endure.

11

Oh! pardon that imploring tear,
   Since not by Virtue shed in vain,
My frenzy drew from eyes so dear;
   For me they shall not weep again.

12

Though long and mournful must it be,
   The thought that we no more may meet;
Yet I deserve the stern decree,
   And almost deem the sentence sweet.

13

Still—had I loved thee less—my heart
   Had then less sacrificed to thine;
It felt not half so much to part
   As if its guilt had made thee mine.

from THE BRIDE OF ABYDOS

XXVIII

Within the place of thousand tombs
   That shine beneath, while dark above
The sad but living cypress glooms
   And withers not, though branch and leaf
Are stamped with an eternal grief,
   Like early unrequited Love,
One spot exists, which ever blooms,
   Ev'n in that deadly grove—
A single rose is shedding there
   Its lonely lustre, meek and pale:
It looks as planted by Despair—
   So white—so faint—the slightest gale
Might whirl the leaves on high;
   And yet, though storms and blight assail,
And hands more rude than wintry sky
   May wring it from the stem—in vain—
   To-morrow sees it bloom again!

The stalk some Spirit gently rears,
And waters with celestial tears;
   For well may maids of Helle deem
That this can be no earthly flower,
Which mocks the tempest's withering hour,
And buds unsheltered by a bower;
Nor droops, though Spring refuse her shower,
   Nor woos the Summer beam:
To it the livelong night there sings
   A Bird unseen—but not remote:
Invisible his airy wings,
But soft as harp that Houri strings
   His long entrancing note!
It were the Bulbul; but his throat,
   Though mournful, pours not such a strain:
For they who listen cannot leave
The spot, but linger there and grieve,
   As if they loved in vain!
And yet so sweet the tears they shed,
'Tis sorrow so unmixed with dread,
They scarce can bear the morn to break
   That melancholy spell,
And longer yet would weep and wake,
   He sings so wild and well!
But when the day-blush bursts from high
   Expires that magic melody.
And some have been who could believe,
(So fondly youthful dreams deceive,
   Yet harsh be they that blame,)
That note so piercing and profound
Will shape and syllable its sound
   Into Zuleika's name.
'Tis from her cypress summit heard,
That melts in air the liquid word:
'Tis from her lowly virgin earth
That white rose takes its tender birth.
There late was laid a marble stone;
Eve saw it placed—the Morrow gone!

It was no mortal arm that bore
That deep fixed pillar to the shore;
For there, as Helle's legends tell,
Next morn 'twas found where Selim fell;
Lashed by the tumbling tide, whose wave
Denied his bones a holier grave:
And there by night, reclined, 'tis said,
Is seen a ghastly turbaned head:
　　And hence extended by the billow,
　　'Tis named the 'Pirate-phantom's pillow!'
　　Where first it lay that mourning flower
　　Hath flourished; flourisheth this hour,
Alone and dewy—coldly pure and pale;
As weeping Beauty's cheek at Sorrow's tale!

SHE WALKS IN BEAUTY

I

She walks in Beauty, like the night
　　Of cloudless climes and starry skies;
And all that's best of dark and bright
　　Meet in her aspect and her eyes:
Thus mellowed to that tender light
　　Which Heaven to gaudy day denies.

II

One shade the more, one ray the less,
　　Had half impaired the nameless grace
Which waves in every raven tress,
　　Or softly lightens o'er her face;
Where thoughts serenely sweet express,
　　How pure, how dear their dwelling-place.

III

And on that cheek, and o'er that brow,
　　So soft, so calm, yet eloquent,

The smiles that win, the tints that glow,
    But tell of days in goodness spent,
A mind at peace with all below,
    A heart whose love is innocent!

IF THAT HIGH WORLD

I

If that high world, which lies beyond
    Our own, surviving Love endears;
If there the cherished heart be fond,
    The eye the same, except in tears—
How welcome those untrodden spheres!
    How sweet this very hour to die!
To soar from earth and find all fears
    Lost in thy light—Eternity!

II

It must be so: 'tis not for self
    That we so tremble on the brink;
And striving to o'erleap the gulf,
    Yet cling to Being's severing link.
Oh! in that future let us think
    To hold, each heart, the heart that shares;
With them the immortal waters drink,
    And, soul in soul, grow deathless theirs!

OH! SNATCHED AWAY IN BEAUTY'S BLOOM

I

Oh! snatched away in Beauty's bloom,
On thee shall press no ponderous tomb;
    But on thy turf shall roses rear
    Their leaves, the earliest of the year;
And the wild cypress wave in tender gloom:

II

And oft by yon blue gushing stream
  Shall Sorrow lean her drooping head,
And feed deep thought with many a dream,
  And lingering pause and lightly tread;
Fond wretch! as if her step disturbed the dead!

III

Away! we know that tears are vain,
  That Death nor heeds nor hears distress:
Will this unteach us to complain?
  Or make one mourner weep the less?
And thou—who tell'st me to forget—
Thy looks are wan, thine eyes are wet.

SUN OF THE SLEEPLESS!

Sun of the sleepless! melancholy star!
Whose tearful beam glows tremulously far,
That show'st the darkness thou canst not dispel,
How like art thou to Joy remembered well!
So gleams the past, the light of other days,
Which shines, but warms not with its powerless rays:
A night-beam, Sorrow watcheth to behold,
Distinct, but distant—clear—but, oh how cold!

STANZAS FOR MUSIC

1

I speak not, I trace not, I breathe not thy name,
There is grief in the sound, there is guilt in the fame:
But the tear which now burns on my cheek may impart
The deep thoughts that dwell in that silence of heart.

2

Too brief for our passion, too long for our peace,
Were those hours—can their joy or their bitterness cease?
We repent, we abjure, we will break from our chain,—
We will part, we will fly to—unite it again!

3

Oh! thine be the gladness, and mine be the guilt!
Forgive me, adored one!—forsake, if thou wilt;—
But the heart which is thine shall expire undebased,
And *man* shall not break it—whatever *thou* mayst.

4

And stern to the haughty, but humble to thee,
This soul, in its bitterest blackness, shall be:
And our days seem as swift, and our moments more sweet,
With thee by my side, than with worlds at our feet.

5

One sigh of thy sorrow, one look of thy love,
Shall turn me or fix, shall reward or reprove;
And the heartless may wonder at all I resign—
Thy lip shall reply, not to them, but to *mine*.

STANZAS FOR MUSIC

1

There be none of Beauty's daughters
   With a magic like thee;
And like music on the waters
   Is thy sweet voice to me:
When, as if its sound were causing
The charméd Ocean's pausing
The waves lie still and gleaming,
And the lulled winds seem dreaming:

2

And the Midnight Moon is weaving
   Her bright chain o'er the deep;
Whose breast is gently heaving,
   As an infant's asleep:
So the spirit bows before thee,
To listen and adore thee;
With a full but soft emotion,
Like the swell of Summer's ocean.

A SKETCH

'Honest—honest Iago!
If that thou be'st a devil, I cannot kill thee.'
—SHAKESPEARE.

Born in the garret, in the kitchen bred,
Promoted thence to deck her mistress' head;
Next—for some gracious service unexpressed,
And from its wages only to be guessed—
Raised from the toilet to the table,—where
Her wondering betters wait behind her chair.
With eye unmoved, and forehead unabashed,
She dines from off the plate she lately washed.
Quick with the tale, and ready with the lie,
The genial confidante and general spy—
Who could, ye gods! her next employment guess—
An only infant's earliest governess!
She taught the child to read, and taught so well,
That she herself, by teaching, learned to spell.
An adept next in penmanship she grows,
As many a nameless slander deftly shows:
What she had made the pupil of her art,
None know—but that high Soul secured the heart,
And panted for the truth it could not hear,
With longing breast and undeluded ear.
Foiled was perversion by that youthful mind,
Which Flattery fooled not, Baseness could not blind,
Deceit infect not, near Contagion soil,
Indulgence weaken, nor Example spoil,
Nor mastered Science tempt her to look down
On humbler talents with a pitying frown,
Nor Genius swell, nor Beauty render vain,
Nor Envy ruffle to retaliate pain,
Nor Fortune change, Pride raise, nor Passion bow,
Nor Virtue teach austerity—till now.
Serenely purest of her sex that live,
But wanting one sweet weakness—to forgive;

Too shocked at faults her soul can never know,
She deems that all could be like her below:
Foe to all vice, yet hardly Virtue's friend—
For Virtue pardons those she would amend.
But to the theme, now laid aside too long,
The baleful burthen of this honest song,
Though all her former functions are no more,
She rules the circle which she served before.
If mothers—none know why—before her quake;
If daughters dread her for the mother's sake;
If early habits—those false links, which bind
At times the loftiest to the meanest mind—
Have given her power too deeply to instil
The angry essence of her deadly will;
If like a snake she steal within your walls,
Till the black slime betray her as she crawls;
If like a viper to the heart she wind,
And leave the venom there she did not find;
What marvel that this hag of hatred works
Eternal evil latent as she lurks,
To make a Pandemonium where she dwells,
And reign the Hecate of domestic hells?
Skilled by a touch to deepen Scandal's tints
With all the kind mendacity of hints,
While mingling truth with falsehood—sneers with smiles—
A thread of candour with a web of wiles;
A plain blunt show of briefly-spoken seeming,
To hide her bloodless heart's soul-hardened scheming;
A lip of lies; a face formed to conceal,
And, without feeling, mock at all who feel:
With a vile mask the Gorgon would disown,—
A cheek of parchment, and an eye of stone.
Mark, how the channels of her yellow blood
Ooze to her skin, and stagnate there to mud,
Cased like the centipede in saffron mail,
Or darker greenness of the scorpion's scale—
(For drawn from reptiles only may we trace
Congenial colours in that soul or face)—

Look on her features! and behold her mind
As in a mirror of itself defined:
Look on the picture! deem it not o'ercharged—
There is no trait which might not be enlarged:
Yet true to 'Nature's journeymen,' who made
This monster when their mistress left off trade—
This female dog-star of her little sky,
Where all beneath her influence droop or die.

Oh! wretch without a tear—without a thought,
Save joy above the ruin thou hast wrought—
The time shall come, nor long remote, when thou
Shalt feel far more than thou inflictest now;
Feel for thy vile self-loving self in vain,
And turn thee howling in unpitied pain.
May the strong curse of crushed affections light
Back on thy bosom with reflected blight!
And make thee in thy leprosy of mind
As loathsome to thyself as to mankind!
Till all thy self-thoughts curdle into hate,
Black—as thy will for others would create:
Till thy hard heart be calcined into dust,
And thy soul welter in its hideous crust.
Oh, may thy grave be sleepless as the bed,
The widowed couch of fire, that thou hast spread!
Then, when thou fain wouldst weary Heaven with prayer,
Look on thine earthly victims—and despair!
Down to the dust!—and, as thou rott'st away,
Even worms shall perish on thy poisonous clay.
But for the love I bore, and still must bear,
To her thy malice from all ties would tear—
Thy name—thy human name—to every eye
The climax of all scorn should hang on high,
Exalted o'er thy less abhorred compeers—
And festering in the infamy of years.

THE DREAM

I

Our life is twofold: Sleep hath its own world,
A boundary between the things misnamed
Death and existence: Sleep hath its own world,
And a wide realm of wild reality,
And dreams in their development have breath,
And tears, and tortures, and the touch of Joy;
They leave a weight upon our waking thoughts,
They take a weight from off our waking toils,
They do divide our being; they become
A portion of ourselves as of our time,
And look like heralds of Eternity;
They pass like spirits of the past,—they speak
Like Sibyls of the future; they have power—
The tyranny of pleasure and of pain;
They make us what we were not—what they will,
And shake us with the vision that's gone by,
The dread of vanished shadows—Are they so?
Is not the past all shadow—What are they?
Creations of the mind?—The mind can make
Substance, and people planets of its own
With beings brighter than have been, and give
A breath to forms which can outlive all flesh.
I would recall a vision which I dreamed
Perchance in sleep—for, in itself, a thought,
A slumbering thought, is capable of years,
And curdles a long life into one hour.

II

I saw two beings in the hues of youth
Standing upon a hill, a gentle hill,
Green and of mild declivity, the last
As 'twere the cape of a long ridge of such,
Save that there was no sea to lave its base,

But a most living landscape, and the wave
Of woods and cornfields, and the abodes of men
Scattered at intervals, and wreathing smoke
Arising from such rustic roofs ;—the hill
Was crowned with a peculiar diadem
Of trees, in circular array, so fixed,
Not by the sport of nature, but of man :
These two, a maiden and a youth, were there
Gazing—the one on all that was beneath
Fair as herself—but the Boy gazed on her ;
And both were young, and one was beautiful :
And both were young—yet not alike in youth.
As the sweet moon on the horizon's verge,
The Maid was on the eve of Womanhood ;
The Boy had fewer summers, but his heart
Had far outgrown his years, and to his eye
There was but one belovéd face on earth,
And that was shining on him : he had looked
Upon it till it could not pass away ;
He had no breath, no being, but in hers ;
She was his voice ; he did not speak to her,
But trembled on her words ; she was his sight,
For his eye followed hers, and saw with hers,
Which coloured all his objects :—he had ceased
To live within himself ; she was his life,
The ocean to the river of his thoughts,
Which terminated all : upon a tone,
A touch of hers, his blood would ebb and flow,
And his cheek change tempestuously—his heart
Unknowing of its cause of agony.
But she in these fond feelings had no share :
Her sighs were not for him ; to her he was
Even as a brother—but no more ; 'twas much,
For brotherless she was, save in the name
Her infant friendship had bestowed on him ;
Herself the solitary scion left
Of a time-honoured race.—It was a name
Which pleased him, and yet pleased him not—and why?

Time taught him a deep answer—when she loved
Another: even *now* she loved another,
And on the summit of that hill she stood
Looking afar if yet her lover's steed
Kept pace with her expectancy, and flew.

III

A change came o'er the spirit of my dream.
There was an ancient mansion, and before
Its walls there was a steed caparisoned:
Within an antique Oratory stood
The Boy of whom I spake;—he was alone,
And pale, and pacing to and fro: anon
He sate him down, and seized a pen, and traced
Words which I could not guess of; then he leaned
His bowed head on his hands, and shook as 'twere
With a convulsion—then arose again,
And with his teeth and quivering hands did tear
What he had written, but he shed no tears.
And he did calm himself, and fix his brow
Into a kind of quiet: as he paused,
The Lady of his love re-entered there;
She was serene and smiling then, and yet
She knew she was by him beloved—she knew,
For quickly comes such knowledge, that his heart
Was darkened with her shadow, and she saw
That he was wretched, but she saw not all.
He rose, and with a cold and gentle grasp
He took her hand; a moment o'er his face
A tablet of unutterable thoughts
Was traced, and then it faded, as it came;
He dropped the hand he held, and with slow steps
Retired, but not as bidding her adieu,
For they did part with mutual smiles; he passed
From out the massy gate of that old Hall,
And mounting on his steed he went his way;
And ne'er repassed that hoary threshold more.

IV

A change came o'er the spirit of my dream.
The Boy was sprung to manhood: in the wilds
Of fiery climes he made himself a home,
And his Soul drank their sunbeams: he was girt
With strange and dusky aspects; he was not
Himself like what he had been; on the sea
And on the shore he was a wanderer;
There was a mass of many images
Crowded like waves upon me, but he was
A part of all; and in the last he lay
Reposing from the noontide sultriness,
Couched among fallen columns, in the shade
Of ruined walls that had survived the names
Of those who reared them; by his sleeping side
Stood camels grazing, and some goodly steeds
Were fastened near a fountain; and a man
Clad in a flowing garb did watch the while,
While many of his tribe slumbered around:
And they were canopied by the blue sky,
So cloudless, clear, and purely beautiful,
That God alone was to be seen in Heaven.

V

A change came o'er the spirit of my dream.
The Lady of his love was wed with One
Who did not love her better:—in her home,
A thousand leagues from his,—her native home,
She dwelt, begirt with growing Infancy,
Daughters and sons of Beauty,—but behold!
Upon her face there was the tint of grief,
The settled shadow of an inward strife,
And an unquiet drooping of the eye,
As if its lid were charged with unshed tears.
What could her grief be?—she had all she loved,
And he who had so loved her was not there
To trouble with bad hopes, or evil wish,
Or ill-repressed affliction, her pure thoughts.

What could her grief be?—she had loved him not,
Nor given him cause to deem himself beloved,
Nor could he be a part of that which preyed
Upon her mind—a spectre of the past.

VI

A change came o'er the spirit of my dream.
The Wanderer was returned.—I saw him stand
Before an Altar—with a gentle bride;
Her face was fair, but was not that which made
The Starlight of his Boyhood;—as he stood
Even at the altar, o'er his brow there came
The self-same aspect, and the quivering shock
That in the antique Oratory shook
His bosom in its solitude; and then—
As in that hour—a moment o'er his face
The tablet of unutterable thoughts
Was traced,—and then it faded as it came,
And he stood calm and quiet, and he spoke
The fitting vows, but heard not his own words,
And all things reeled around him; he could see
Not that which was, nor that which should have been—
But the old mansion, and the accustomed hall,
And the remembered chambers, and the place,
The day, the hour, the sunshine, and the shade,
All things pertaining to that place and hour,
And her who was his destiny, came back
And thrust themselves between him and the light:
What business had they there at such a time?

VII

A change came o'er the spirit of my dream.
The Lady of his love;—Oh! she was changed
As by the sickness of the soul; her mind
Had wandered from its dwelling, and her eyes
They had not their own lustre, but the look
Which is not of the earth; she was become
The Queen of a fantastic realm; her thoughts

Were combinations of disjointed things;
And forms, impalpable and unperceived
Of others' sight, familiar were to hers.
And this the world calls frenzy; but the wise
Have a far deeper madness—and the glance
Of melancholy is a fearful gift;
What is it but the telescope of truth?
Which strips the distance of its fantasies,
And brings life near in utter nakedness,
Making the cold reality too real!

VIII

A change came o'er the spirit of my dream.
The Wanderer was alone as heretofore,
The beings which surrounded him were gone,
Or were at war with him; he was a mark
For blight and desolation, compassed round
With Hatred and Contention; Pain was mixed
In all which was served up to him, until,
Like to the Pontic monarch of old days,
He fed on poisons, and they had no power,
But were a kind of nutriment; he lived
Through that which had been death to many men,
And made him friends of mountains: with the stars
And the quick Spirit of the Universe
He held his dialogues; and they did teach
To him the magic of their mysteries;
To him the book of Night was opened wide,
And voices from the deep abyss revealed
A marvel and a secret—Be it so.

IX

My dream was past; it had no further change.
It was of a strange order, that the doom
Of these two creatures should be thus traced out
Almost like a reality—the one
To end in madness—both in misery.

CHURCHILL'S GRAVE

A FACT LITERALLY RENDERED

I stood beside the grave of him who blazed
    The Comet of a season, and I saw
The humblest of all sepulchres, and gazed
    With not the less of sorrow and of awe
On that neglected turf and quiet stone,
With name no clearer than the names unknown,
Which lay unread around it; and I asked
    The Gardener of that ground, why it might be
That for this plant strangers his memory tasked,
    Through the thick deaths of half a century;
And thus he answered—'Well, I do not know
Why frequent travellers turn to pilgrims so;
He died before my day of Sextonship,
    And I had not the digging of this grave.'
And is this all? I thought,—and do we rip
    The veil of Immortality, and crave
I know not what of honour and of light
Through unborn ages, to endure this blight?
So soon, and so successless? As I said,
The Architect of all on which we tread,
For Earth is but a tombstone, did essay
To extricate remembrance from the clay,
Whose minglings might confuse a Newton's thought,
    Were it not that all life must end in one,
Of which we are but dreamers;—as he caught
    As 'twere the twilight of a former Sun,
Thus spoke he,—'I believe the man of whom
You wot, who lies in this selected tomb,
Was a most famous writer in his day,
And therefore travellers step from out their way
To pay him honour,—and myself whate'er
    Your honour pleases:'—then most pleased I shook
    From out my pocket's avaricious nook
Some certain coins of silver, which as 'twere

Perforce I gave this man, though I could spare
So much but inconveniently :—Ye smile,
I see ye, ye profane ones! all the while,
Because my homely phrase the truth would tell.
You are the fools, not I—for I did dwell
With a deep thought, and with a softened eye,
On that old Sexton's natural homily,
In which there was Obscurity and Fame,—
The Glory and the Nothing of a Name.

EPISTLE TO AUGUSTA

I

My Sister! my sweet Sister! if a name
Dearer and purer were, it should be thine.
Mountains and seas divide us, but I claim
No tears, but tenderness to answer mine :
Go where I will, to me thou art the same—
A loved regret which I would not resign.
There yet are two things in my destiny,—
A world to roam through, and a home with thee.

II

The first were nothing—had I still the last,
It were the haven of my happiness ;
But other claims and other ties thou hast,
And mine is not the wish to make them less.
A strange doom is thy father's son's, and past
Recalling, as it lies beyond redress ;
Reversed for him our grandsire's fate of yore,—
He had no rest at sea, nor I on shore.

III

If my inheritance of storms hath been
In other elements, and on the rocks
Of perils, overlooked or unforeseen,
I have sustained my share of worldly shocks,

G

The fault was mine; nor do I seek to screen
My errors with defensive paradox;
I have been cunning in mine overthrow,
The careful pilot of my proper woe.

IV

Mine were my faults, and mine be their reward.
My whole life was a contest, since the day
That gave me being, gave me that which marred
The gift,—a fate, or will, that walked astray;
And I at times have found the struggle hard,
And thought of shaking off my bonds of clay:
But now I fain would for a time survive,
If but to see what next can well arrive.

V

Kingdoms and Empires in my little day
I have outlived, and yet I am not old;
And when I look on this, the petty spray
Of my own years of trouble, which have rolled
Like a wild bay of breakers, melts away:
Something—I know not what—does still uphold
A spirit of slight patience;—not in vain,
Even for its own sake, do we purchase Pain.

VI

Perhaps the workings of defiance stir
Within me—or, perhaps, a cold despair
Brought on when ills habitually recur,—
Perhaps a kinder clime, or purer air,
(For even to this may change of soul refer,
And with light armour we may learn to bear,)
Have taught me a strange quiet, which was not
The chief companion of a calmer lot.

VII

I feel almost at times as I have felt
In happy childhood; trees, and flowers, and brooks,

Which do remember me of where I dwelt,
Ere my young mind was sacrificed to books,
Come as of yore upon me, and can melt
My heart with recognition of their looks;
And even at moments I could think I see
Some living thing to love—but none like thee.

VIII

Here are the Alpine landscapes which create
A fund for contemplation;—to admire
Is a brief feeling of a trivial date;
But something worthier do such scenes inspire:
Here to be lonely is not desolate,
For much I view which I could most desire,
And, above all, a Lake I can behold
Lovelier, not dearer, than our own of old.

IX

Oh that thou wert but with me!—but I grow
The fool of my own wishes, and forget
The solitude which I have vaunted so
Has lost its praise in this but one regret;
There may be others which I less may show;—
I am not of the plaintive mood, and yet
I feel an ebb in my philosophy,
And the tide rising in my altered eye.

X

I did remind thee of our own dear Lake,
By the old Hall which may be mine no more.
Leman's is fair; but think not I forsake
The sweet remembrance of a dearer shore:
Sad havoc Time must with my memory make,
Ere that or thou can fade these eyes before;
Though, like all things which I have loved, they are
Resigned for ever, or divided far.

XI

The world is all before me; I but ask
Of Nature that with which she will comply—
It is but in her Summer's sun to bask,
To mingle with the quiet of her sky,
To see her gentle face without a mask,
And never gaze on it with apathy.
She was my early friend, and now shall be
My sister—till I look again on thee.

XII

I can reduce all feelings but this one,—
And that I would not;—for at length I see
Such scenes as those wherein my life begun—
The earliest—even the only paths for me—
Had I but sooner learnt the crowd to shun,
I had been better than I now can be;
The Passions which have torn me would have slept—
I had not suffered, and *thou* hadst not wept.

XIII

With false Ambition what had I to do?
Little with Love, and least of all with Fame;
And yet they came unsought, and with me grew,
And made me all which they can make—a Name.
Yet this was not the end I did pursue;
Surely I once beheld a nobler aim.
But all is over—I am one the more
To baffled millions which have gone before.

XIV

And for the future, this world's future may
From me demand but little of my care:
I have outlived myself by many a day,
Having survived so many things that were;
My years have been no slumber, but the prey
Of ceaseless vigils; for I had the share
Of life which might have filled a century,
Before its fourth in time had passed me by.

XV

And for the remnant which may be to come
I am content; and for the past I feel
Not thankless,—for within the crowded sum
Of struggles, Happiness at times would steal,
And, for the present, I would not benumb
My feelings farther.—Nor shall I conceal
That with all this I still can look around,
And worship Nature with a thought profound.

XVI

For thee, my own sweet sister, in thy heart
I know myself secure, as thou in mine;
We were and are—I am, even as thou art—
Beings who ne'er each other can resign;
It is the same, together or apart—
From Life's commencement to its slow decline
We are entwined—let Death come slow or fast,
The tie which bound the first endures the last!

SO WE'LL GO NO MORE A-ROVING

1

So we'll go no more a-roving
  So late into the night,
Though the heart be still as loving,
  And the moon be still as bright.

2

For the sword outwears its sheath,
  And the soul wears out the breast,
And the heart must pause to breathe,
  And Love itself have rest.

3

Though the night was made for loving,
  And the day returns too soon,
Yet we'll go no more a-roving
  By the light of the moon.

STANZAS TO THE PO

1

River, that rollest by the ancient walls,
    Where dwells the Lady of my love, when she
Walks by thy brink, and there, perchance, recalls
    A faint and fleeting memory of me:

2

What if thy deep and ample stream should be
    A mirror of my heart, where she may read
The thousand thoughts I now betray to thee,
    Wild as thy wave, and headlong as thy speed!

3

What do I say—a mirror of my heart?
    Are not thy waters sweeping, dark, and strong?
Such as my feelings were and are, thou art;
    And such as thou art were my passions long.

4

Time may have somewhat tamed them,—not for ever;
    Thou overflow'st thy banks, and not for aye
Thy bosom overboils, congenial river!
    Thy floods subside, and mine have sunk away:

5

But left long wrecks behind, and now again,
    Borne in our old unchanged career, we move;
Thou tendest wildly onwards to the main,
    And I—to loving *one* I should not love.

6

The current I behold will sweep beneath
    Her native walls, and murmur at her feet;
Her eyes will look on thee, when she shall breathe
    The twilight air, unharmed by summer's heat.

7

She will look on thee,—I have looked on thee,
   Full of that thought: and, from that moment, ne'er
Thy waters could I dream of, name, or see,
   Without the inseparable sigh for her!

8

Her bright eyes will be imaged in thy stream,—
   Yes! they will meet the wave I gaze on now:
Mine cannot witness, even in a dream,
   That happy wave repass me in its flow!

9

The wave that bears my tears returns no more:
   Will she return by whom that wave shall sweep?—
Both tread thy banks, both wander on thy shore,
   I by thy source, she by the dark-blue deep.

10

But that which keepeth us apart is not
   Distance, nor depth of wave, nor space of earth,
But the distraction of a various lot,
   As various as the climates of our birth.

11

A stranger loves the Lady of the land,
   Born far beyond the mountains, but his blood
Is all meridian, as if never fanned
   By the black wind that chills the polar flood.

12

My blood is all meridian; were it not,
   I had not left my clime, nor should I be,
In spite of tortures, ne'er to be forgot,
   A slave again of love,—at least of thee.

13

'Tis vain to struggle—let me perish young—
   Live as I lived, and love as I have loved;
To dust if I return, from dust I sprung,
   And then, at least, my heart can ne'er be moved.

ON THIS DAY I COMPLETE MY THIRTY-SIXTH YEAR

1

'T is time this heart should be unmoved,
    Since others it hath ceased to move:
Yet, though I cannot be beloved,
        Still let me love!

2

My days are in the yellow leaf;
    The flowers and fruits of Love are gone;
The worm, the canker, and the grief
        Are mine alone!

3

The fire that on my bosom preys
    Is lone as some Volcanic isle;
No torch is kindled at its blaze—
        A funeral pile.

4

The hope, the fear, the zealous care,
    The exalted portion of the pain
And power of love, I cannot share,
        But wear the chain.

5

But 't is not *thus*—and 't is not *here*—
    Such thoughts should shake my soul, nor *now*
Where Glory decks the hero's bier,
        Or binds his brow.

6

The Sword, the Banner, and the Field,
    Glory and Greece, around me see!
The Spartan, borne upon his shield,
        Was not more free.

7

Awake! (not Greece—she *is* awake!)
   Awake, my spirit! Think through *whom*
Thy life-blood tracks its parent lake,
      And then strike home!

8

Tread those reviving passions down,
   Unworthy manhood!—unto thee
Indifferent should the smile or frown
      Of Beauty be.

9

If thou regret'st thy youth, *why live?*
   The land of honourable death
Is here :—up to the Field, and give
      Away thy breath!

10

Seek out—less often sought than found—
   A soldier's grave, for thee the best ;
Then look around, and choose thy ground,
      And take thy Rest.

THE VISION OF
JUDGMENT

THE VISION OF JUDGMENT

by

QUEVEDO REDIVIVUS

(Suggested by the composition so entitled by the
author of *Wat Tyler*)

'A Daniel come to judgment! yea, a Daniel!
I thank thee, Jew, for teaching me that word.'
Merchant of Venice,
Act IV, sc. I, lines 218, 336

I

Saint Peter sat by the celestial gate:
　His keys were rusty, and the lock was dull,
So little trouble had been given of late;
　Not that the place by any means was full,
But since the Gallic era 'eighty-eight'
　The Devils had ta'en a longer, stronger pull,
And 'a pull altogether,' as they say
At sea—which drew most souls another way.

II

The Angels all were singing out of tune,
　And hoarse with having little else to do,
Excepting to wind up the sun and moon,
　Or curb a runaway young star or two,
Or wild colt of a comet, which too soon
　Broke out of bounds o'er the ethereal blue,
Splitting some planet with its playful tail,
As boats are sometimes by a wanton whale.

III

The Guardian Seraphs had retired on high,
　Finding their charges past all care below;
Terrestrial business filled nought in the sky
　Save the Recording Angel's black bureau;

189

Who found, indeed, the facts to multiply
    With such rapidity of vice and woe,
That he had stripped off both his wings in quills,
And yet was in arrear of human ills.

IV

His business so augmented of late years,
    That he was forced, against his will, no doubt,
(Just like those cherubs, earthly ministers,)
    For some resource to turn himself about,
And claim the help of his celestial peers,
    To aid him ere he should be quite worn out
By the increased demand for his remarks:
Six Angels and twelve Saints were named his clerks.

V

This was a handsome board—at least for Heaven;
    And yet they had even then enough to do,
So many Conquerors' cars were daily driven,
    So many kingdoms fitted up anew;
Each day, too, slew its thousands six or seven,
    Till at the crowning carnage, Waterloo,
They threw their pens down in divine disgust—
The page was so besmeared with blood and dust.

VI

This by the way; 'tis not mine to record
    What Angels shrink from: even the very Devil
On this occasion his own work abhorred,
    So surfeited with the infernal revel:
Though he himself had sharpened every sword,
    It almost quenched his innate thirst of evil.
(Here Satan's sole good work deserves insertion—
'Tis, that he has both Generals in reversion.)

VII

Let's skip a few short years of hollow peace,
    Which peopled earth no better, Hell as wont,

And Heaven none—they form the tyrant's lease,
   With nothing but new names subscribed upon 't;
'Twill one day finish: meantime they increase,
   'With seven heads and ten horns,' and all in front,
Like Saint John's foretold beast; but ours are born
Less formidable in the head than horn.

VIII

In the first year of Freedom's second dawn
   Died George the Third; although no tyrant, one
Who shielded tyrants, till each sense withdrawn
   Left him nor mental nor external sun:
A better farmer ne'er brushed dew from lawn,
   A worse king never left a realm undone!
He died—but left his subjects still behind,
One half as mad—and t'other no less blind.

IX

He died! his death made no great stir on earth:
   His burial made some pomp; there was profusion
Of velvet—gilding—brass—and no great dearth
   Of aught but tears—save those shed by collusion:
For these things may be bought at their true worth;
   Of elegy there was the due infusion—
Bought also; and the torches, cloaks and banners,
Heralds, and relics of old Gothic manners,

X

Formed a sepulchral melodrame. Of all
   The fools who flocked to swell or see the show,
Who cared about the corpse? The funeral
   Made the attraction, and the black the woe.
There throbbed not there a thought which pierced the pall
   And when the gorgeous coffin was laid low,
It seemed the mockery of hell to fold
The rottenness of eighty years in gold.

XI

So mix his body with the dust! It might
    Return to what it *must* far sooner, were
The natural compound left alone to fight
    Its way back into earth, and fire, and air;
But the unnatural balsams merely blight
    What Nature made him at his birth, as bare
As the mere million's base unmummied clay—
Yet all his spices but prolong decay.

XII

He's dead—and upper earth with him has done;
    He's buried; save the undertaker's bill,
Or lapidary scrawl, the world is gone
    For him, unless he left a German will:
But where's the proctor who will ask his son?
    In whom his qualities are reigning still,
Except that household virtue, most uncommon,
Of constancy to a bad, ugly woman.

XIII

'God save the king!' It is a large economy
    In God to save the like; but if he will
Be saving, all the better; for not one am I
    Of those who think damnation better still:
I hardly know too if not quite alone am I
    In this small hope of bettering future ill
By circumscribing, with some slight restriction,
The eternity of Hell's hot jurisdiction.

XIV

I know this is unpopular; I know
    'Tis blasphemous; I know one may be damned
For hoping no one else may e'er be so;
    I know my catechism; I know we're crammed
With the best doctrines till we quite o'erflow;
    I know that all save England's Church have shammed,
And that the other twice two hundred churches
And synagogues have made a *damned* bad purchase.

XV

God help us all! God help me too! I am,
    God knows, as helpless as the Devil can wish,
And not a whit more difficult to damn,
    Than is to bring to land a late-hooked fish,
Or to the butcher to purvey the lamb;
    Not that I'm fit for such a noble dish,
As one day will be that immortal fry
Of almost every body born to die.

XVI

Saint Peter sat by the celestial gate,
    And nodded o'er his keys: when, lo! there came
A wondrous noise he had not heard of late—
    A rushing sound of wind, and stream, and flame;
In short, a roar of things extremely great,
    Which would have made aught save a Saint exclaim;
But he, with first a start and then a wink,
Said, 'There's another star gone out, I think!'

XVII

But ere he could return to his repose,
    A Cherub flapped his right wing o'er his eyes—
At which Saint Peter yawned, and rubbed his nose:
    'Saint porter,' said the angel, 'prithee rise!'
Waving a goodly wing, which glowed, as glows
    An earthly peacock's tail, with heavenly dyes:
To which the saint replied, 'Well, what's the matter?
Is Lucifer come back with all this clatter?'

XVIII

'No,' quoth the Cherub: 'George the Third is dead.'
    'And who *is* George the Third?' replied the apostle:
'*What George? What Third?*' 'The King of England,' said
    The angel. 'Well! he won't find kings to jostle
Him on his way; but does he wear his head?
    Because the last we saw here had a tustle,
And ne'er would have got into Heaven's good graces
Had he not flung his head in all our faces.

XIX

'He was—if I remember—King of France;
    That head of his, which could not keep a crown
On earth, yet ventured in my face to advance
    A claim to those of martyrs—like my own:
If I had had my sword, as I had once
    When I cut ears off, I had cut him down;
But having but my *keys*, and not my brand,
I only knocked his head from out his hand.

XX

'And then he set up such a headless howl,
    That all the Saints came out and took him in;
And there he sits by Saint Paul, cheek by jowl;
    That fellow Paul—the parvenù! The skin
Of Saint Bartholomew, which makes his cowl
    In heaven, and upon earth redeemed his sin,
So as to make a martyr, never sped
Better than did this weak and wooden head.

XXI

'But had it come up here upon its shoulders,
    There would have been a different tale to tell:
The fellow-feeling in the Saint's beholders
    Seems to have acted on them like a spell;
And so this very foolish head Heaven solders
    Back on its trunk: it may be very well,
And seems the custom here to overthrow
Whatever has been wisely done below.'

XXII

The Angel answered, 'Peter! do not pout:
    The King who comes has head and all entire,
And never knew much what it was about—
    He did as doth the puppet—by its wire,
And will be judged like all the rest, no doubt:
    My business and your own is not to inquire
Into such matters, but to mind our cue—
Which is to act as we are bid to do.'

XXIII

While thus they spake, the angelic caravan,
  Arriving like a rush of mighty wind,
Cleaving the fields of space, as doth the swan
  Some silver stream (say Ganges, Nile, or Inde,
Or Thames, or Tweed), and midst them an old man
  With an old soul, and both extremely blind,
Halted before the gate, and, in his shroud,
Seated their fellow-traveller on a cloud.

XXIV

But bringing up the rear of this bright host
  A Spirit of a different aspect waved
His wings, like thunder-clouds above some coast
  Whose barren beach with frequent wrecks is paved;
His brow was like the deep when tempest-tossed;
  Fierce and unfathomable thoughts engraved
Eternal wrath on his immortal face,
And *where* he gazed a gloom pervaded space.

XXV

As he drew near, he gazed upon the gate
  Ne'er to be entered more by him or Sin,
With such a glance of supernatural hate,
  As made Saint Peter wish himself within;
He pottered with his keys at a great rate,
  And sweated through his Apostolic skin:
Of course his perspiration was but ichor,
Or some such other spiritual liquor.

XXVI

The very Cherubs huddled all together,
  Like birds when soars the falcon; and they felt
A tingling to the tip of every feather,
  And formed a circle like Orion's belt
Around their poor old charge; who scarce knew whither
  His guards had led him, though they gently dealt
With Royal Manes (for by many stories,
And true, we learn the Angels all are Tories).

XXVII

As things were in this posture, the gate flew
   Asunder, and the flashing of its hinges
Flung over space an universal hue
   Of many-coloured flame, until its tinges
Reached even our speck of earth, and made a new
   Aurora borealis spread its fringes
O'er the North Pole; the same seen, when ice-bound,
By Captain Parry's crew, in 'Melville's Sound.'

XXVIII

And from the gate thrown open issued beaming
   A beautiful and mighty Thing of Light,
Radiant with glory, like a banner streaming
   Victorious from some world-o'erthrowing fight:
My poor comparisons must needs be teeming
   With earthly likenesses, for here the night
Of clay obscures our best conceptions, saving
Johanna Southcote, or Bob Southey raving.

XXIX

'Twas the Archangel Michael: all men know
   The make of Angels and Archangels, since
There's scarce a scribbler has not one to show,
   From the fiends' leader to the Angels' Prince.
There also are some altar-pieces, though
   I really can't say that they much evince
One's inner notions of immortal spirits;
But let the connoisseurs explain *their* merits.

XXX

Michael flew forth in glory and in good;
   A goodly work of him from whom all Glory
And Good arise; the portal past—he stood;
   Before him the young Cherubs and Saints hoary—
(I say *young*, begging to be understood
   By looks, not years; and should be very sorry
To state, they were not older than Saint Peter,
But merely that they seemed a little sweeter).

XXXI

The Cherubs and the Saints bowed down before
　　That arch-angelic Hierarch, the first
Of Essences angelical who wore
　　The aspect of a god; but this ne'er nursed
Pride in his heavenly bosom, in whose core
　　No thought, save for his Maker's service, durst
Intrude—however glorified and high,
He knew him but the Viceroy of the sky.

XXXII

He and the sombre, silent Spirit met—
　　They knew each other both for good and ill;
Such was their power, that neither could forget
　　His former friend and future foe; but still
There was a high, immortal, proud regret
　　In either's eye, as if 'twere less their will
Than destiny to make the eternal years
Their date of war, and their 'Champ Clos' the spheres.

XXXIII

But here they were in neutral space: we know
　　From Job, that Satan hath the power to pay
A heavenly visit thrice a-year or so;
　　And that the 'Sons of God,' like those of clay,
Must keep him company; and we might show
　　From the same book, in how polite a way
The dialogue is held between the Powers
Of Good and Evil—but 'twould take up hours.

XXXIV

And this is not a theologic tract,
　　To prove with Hebrew and with Arabic,
If Job be allegory or a fact,
　　But a true narrative; and thus I pick
From out the whole but such and such an act
　　As sets aside the slightest thought of trick.
'Tis every tittle true, beyond suspicion,
And accurate as any other vision.

XXXV

The spirits were in neutral space, before
   The gate of Heaven; like eastern thresholds is
The place where Death's grand cause is argued o'er,
   And souls despatched to that world or to this;
And therefore Michael and the other wore
   A civil aspect: though they did not kiss,
Yet still between his Darkness and his Brightness
There passed a mutual glance of great politeness.

XXXVI

The Archangel bowed, not like a modern beau,
   But with a graceful oriental bend,
Pressing one radiant arm just where below
   The heart in good men is supposed to tend;
He turned as to an equal, not too low,
   But kindly; Satan met his ancient friend
With more hauteur, as might an old Castilian
Poor Noble meet a mushroom rich civilian.

XXXVII

He merely bent his diabolic brow
   An instant; and then raising it, he stood
In act to assert his right or wrong, and show
   Cause why King George by no means could or should
Make out a case to be exempt from woe
   Eternal, more than other kings, endued
With better sense and hearts, whom History mentions,
Who long have 'paved Hell with their good intentions.'

XXXVIII

Michael began: 'What wouldst thou with this man,
   Now dead, and brought before the Lord? What ill
Hath he wrought since his mortal race began,
   That thou canst claim him? Speak! and do thy will,
If it be just: if in this earthly span
   He hath been greatly failing to fulfil
His duties as a king and mortal, say,
And he is thine; if not—let him have way.'

XXXIX

'Michael!' replied the Prince of Air, 'even here
Before the gate of Him thou servest, must
I claim my subject: and will make appear
    That as he was my worshipper in dust,
So shall he be in spirit, although dear
    To thee and thine, because nor wine nor lust
Were of his weaknesses; yet on the throne
He reigned o'er millions to serve me alone.

XL

'Look to *our* earth, or rather *mine*; it was,
    Once, more thy master's: but I triumph not
In this poor planet's conquest; nor, alas!
    Need he thou servest envy me my lot:
With all the myriads of bright worlds which pass
    In worship round him, he may have forgot
Yon weak creation of such paltry things:
I think few worth damnation save their kings,

XLI

'And these but as a kind of quit-rent, to
    Assert my right as Lord: and even had
I such an inclination, 'twere (as you
    Well know) superfluous; they are grown so bad,
That Hell has nothing better left to do
    Than leave them to themselves: so much more mad
And evil by their own internal curse,
Heaven cannot make them better, nor I worse.

XLII

'Look to the earth, I said, and say again:
    When this old, blind, mad, helpless, weak, poor worm
Began in youth's first bloom and flush to reign,
    The world and he both wore a different form,
And much of earth and all the watery plain
    Of Ocean called him king: through many a storm
His isles had floated on the abyss of Time;
For the rough virtues chose them for their clime.

XLIII

'He came to his sceptre young; he leaves it old:
    Look to the state in which he found his realm,
And left it; and his annals too behold,
    How to a minion first he gave the helm;
How grew upon his heart a thirst for gold,
    The beggar's vice, which can but overwhelm
The meanest hearts; and for the rest, but glance
Thine eye along America and France.

XLIV

' 'Tis true, he was a tool from first to last
    (I have the workmen safe); but as a tool
So let him be consumed. From out the past
    Of ages, since mankind have known the rule
Of monarchs—from the bloody rolls amassed
    Of Sin and Slaughter—from the Cæsars' school,
Take the worst pupil; and produce a reign
More drenched with gore, more cumbered with the slain.

XLV

'He ever warred with freedom and the free:
    Nations as men, home subjects, foreign foes,
So that they uttered the word 'Liberty!'
    Found George the Third their first opponent. Whose
History was ever stained as his will be
    With national and individual woes?
I grant his household abstinence; I grant
His neutral virtues, which most monarchs want;

XLVI

'I know he was a constant consort; own
    He was a decent sire, and middling lord.
All this is much, and most upon a throne;
    As temperance, if at Apicius' board,
Is more than at an anchorite's supper shown.
    I grant him all the kindest can accord;
And this was well for him, but not for those
Millions who found him what Oppression chose.

XLVII

'The New World shook him off; the Old yet groans
  Beneath what he and his prepared, if not
Completed: he leaves heirs on many thrones
  To all his vices, without what begot
Compassion for him—his tame virtues; drones
  Who sleep, or despots who have now forgot
A lesson which shall be retaught them, wake
Upon the thrones of earth; but let them quake!

XLVIII

'Five millions of the primitive, who hold
  The faith which makes ye great on earth, implored
A *part* of that vast *all* they held of old,—
  Freedom to worship—not alone your Lord,
Michael, but you, and you, Saint Peter! Cold
  Must be your souls, if you have not abhorred
The foe to Catholic participation
In all the license of a Christian nation.

XLIX

'True! he allowed them to pray God; but as
  A consequence of prayer, refused the law
Which would have placed them upon the same base
  With those who did not hold the Saints in awe.'
But here Saint Peter started from his place
  And cried, 'You may the prisoner withdraw:
Ere Heaven shall ope her portals to this Guelph,
While I am guard, may I be damned myself!

L

'Sooner will I with Cerberus exchange
  My office (and *his* is no sinecure)
Than see this royal Bedlam-bigot range
  The azure fields of Heaven, of that be sure!'
'Saint!' replied Satan, 'you do well to avenge
  The wrongs he made your satellites endure;
And if to this exchange you should be given,
I'll try to coax *our* Cerberus up to Heaven!'

LI

Here Michael interposed: 'Good Saint! and Devil!
　　Pray, not so fast; you both outrun discretion.
Saint Peter! you were wont to be more civil:
　　Satan! excuse this warmth of his expression,
And condescension to the vulgar's level:
　　Even Saints sometimes forget themselves in session.
Have you got more to say?'—'No.'—'If you please,
I'll trouble you to call your witnesses.'

LII

Then Satan turned and waved his swarthy hand,
　　Which stirred with its electric qualities
Clouds farther off than we can understand,
　　Although we find him sometimes in our skies;
Infernal thunder shook both sea and land
　　In all the planets—and Hell's batteries
Let off the artillery, which Milton mentions
As one of Satan's most sublime inventions.

LIII

This was a signal unto such damned souls
　　As have the privilege of their damnation
Extended far beyond the mere controls
　　Of worlds past, present, or to come; no station
Is theirs particularly in the rolls
　　Of Hell assigned; but where their inclination
Or business carries them in search of game,
They may range freely—being damned the same.

LIV

They are proud of this—as very well they may,
　　It being a sort of knighthood, or gilt key
Stuck in their loins; or like to an 'entré'
　　Up the back stairs, or such free-masonry.
I borrow my comparisons from clay,
　　Being clay myself. Let not those spirits be
Offended with such base low likenesses;
We know their posts are nobler far than these.

LV

When the great signal ran from Heaven to Hell—
  About ten million times the distance reckoned
From our sun to its earth, as we can tell
  How much time it takes up, even to a second,
For every ray that travels to dispel
  The fogs of London, through which, dimly beaconed,
The weathercocks are gilt some thrice a year,
If that the *summer* is not too severe:

LVI

I say that I can tell—'twas half a minute;
  I know the solar beams take up more time
Ere, packed up for their journey, they begin it;
  But then their Telegraph is less sublime,
And if they ran a race, they would not win it
  'Gainst Satan's couriers bound for their own clime.
The sun takes up some years for every ray
To reach its goal—the Devil not half a day.

LVII

Upon the verge of space, about the size
  Of half-a-crown, a little speck appeared
(I've seen a something like it in the skies
  In the Ægean, ere a squall); it neared,
And, growing bigger, took another guise;
  Like an aërial ship it tacked, and steered,
Or *was* steered (I am doubtful of the grammar
Of the last phrase, which makes the stanza stammer;

LVIII

But take your choice): and then it grew a cloud;
  And so it was—a cloud of witnesses.
But such a cloud! No land ere saw a crowd
  Of locusts numerous as the heavens saw these;
They shadowed with their myriads Space; their loud
  And varied cries were like those of wild geese,
(If nations may be likened to a goose),
And realised the phrase of 'Hell broke loose.'

LIX

Here crashed a sturdy oath of stout John Bull,
　　Who damned away his eyes as heretofore:
There Paddy brogued 'By Jasus!'—'What's your wull?'
　　The temperate Scot exclaimed: the French ghost swore
In certain terms I shan't translate in full,
　　As the first coachman will; and 'midst the war,
The voice of Jonathan was heard to express,
'*Our* President is going to war, I guess.'

LX

Besides there were the Spaniard, Dutch, and Dane;
　　In short, an universal shoal of shades
From Otaheite's isle to Salisbury Plain,
　　Of all climes and professions, years and trades,
Ready to swear against the good king's reign,
　　Bitter as clubs in cards are against spades:
All summoned by this grand 'subpœna,' to
Try if kings mayn't be damned like me or you.

LXI

When Michael saw this host, he first grew pale,
　　As Angels can; next, like Italian twilight,
He turned all colours—as a peacock's tail,
　　Or sunset streaming through a Gothic skylight
In some old abbey, or a trout not stale,
　　Or distant lightning on the horizon *by* night,
Or a fresh rainbow, or a grand review
Of thirty regiments in red, green, and blue.

LXII

Then he addressed himself to Satan: 'Why—
　　My good old friend, for such I deem you, though
Our different parties make us fight so shy,
　　I ne'er mistake you for a *personal* foe;
Our difference is *political*, and I
　　Trust that, whatever may occur below,
You know my great respect for you: and this
Makes me regret whate'er you do amiss—

LXIII

'Why, my dear Lucifer, would you abuse
   My call for witnesses? I did not mean
That you should half of Earth and Hell produce;
   'Tis even superfluous, since two honest, clean,
True testimonies are enough: we lose
   Our Time, nay, our Eternity, between
The accusation and defence: if we
Hear both, 'twill stretch our immortality.'

LXIV

Satan replied, 'To me the matter is
   Indifferent, in a personal point of view:
I can have fifty better souls than this
   With far less trouble than we have gone through
Already; and I merely argued his
   Late Majesty of Britain's case with you
Upon a point of form: you may dispose
Of him; I've kings enough below, God knows!'

LXV

Thus spoke the Demon (late called 'multi-faced'
   By multo-scribbling Southey). 'Then we'll call
One or two persons of the myriads placed
   Around our congress, and dispense with all
The rest,' quoth Michael: 'Who may be so graced
   As to speak first? there's choice enough—who shall
It be?' Then Satan answered, 'There are many;
But you may choose Jack Wilkes as well as any.'

LXVI

A merry, cock-eyed, curious-looking Sprite
   Upon the instant started from the throng,
Dressed in a fashion now forgotten quite;
   For all the fashions of the flesh stick long
By people in the next world; where unite
   All the costumes since Adam's, right or wrong,
From Eve's fig-leaf down to the petticoat,
Almost as scanty, of days less remote.

LXVII

The Spirit looked around upon the crowds
 Assembled, and exclaimed, 'My friends of all
The spheres, we shall catch cold amongst these clouds;
 So let's to business: why this general call?
If those are freeholders I see in shrouds,
 And 'tis for an election that they bawl,
Behold a candidate with unturned coat!
Saint Peter, may I count upon your vote?'

LXVIII

'Sir,' replied Michael, 'you mistake; these things
 Are of a former life, and what we do
Above is more august; to judge of kings
 Is the tribunal met: so now you know.'
'Then I presume those gentlemen with wings,'
 Said Wilkes, 'are Cherubs; and that soul below
Looks much like George the Third, but to my mind
A good deal older—bless me! is he blind?'

LXIX

'He is what you behold him, and his doom
 Depends upon his deeds,' the Angel said;
'If you have aught to arraign in him, the tomb
 Gives licence to the humblest beggar's head
To lift itself against the loftiest.'—'Some,'
 Said Wilkes, 'don't wait to see them laid in lead,
For such a liberty—and I, for one,
Have told them what I thought beneath the sun.'

LXX

'*Above* the sun repeat, then, what thou hast
 To urge against him,' said the Archangel. 'Why,'
Replied the spirit, 'since old scores are past,
 Must I turn evidence? In faith, not I.
Besides, I beat him hollow at the last,
 With all his Lords and Commons: in the sky
I don't like ripping up old stories, since
His conduct was but natural in a prince.

LXXI

'Foolish, no doubt, and wicked, to oppress
  A poor unlucky devil without a shilling;
But then I blame the man himself much less
  Than Bute and Grafton, and shall be unwilling
To see him punished here for their excess,
  Since they were both damned long ago, and still in
Their place below: for me, I have forgiven,
And vote his *habeas corpus* into Heaven.'

LXXII

'Wilkes,' said the Devil, 'I understand all this;
  You turned to half a courtier ere you died,
And seem to think it would not be amiss
  To grow a whole one on the other side
Of Charon's ferry; you forget that *his*
  Reign is concluded; whatsoe'er betide,
He won't be sovereign more: you've lost your labour,
For at the best he will but be your neighbour.

LXXIII

'However, I knew what to think of it,
  When I beheld you in your jesting way,
Flitting and whispering round about the spit
  Where Belial, upon duty for the day,
With Fox's lard was basting William Pitt,
  His pupil; I knew what to think, I say:
That fellow even in Hell breeds farther ills;
I'll have him *gagged*—'twas one of his own Bills.

LXXIV

'Call Junius!' From the crowd a shadow stalked,
  And at the name there was a general squeeze,
So that the very ghosts no longer walked
  In comfort, at their own aërial ease,
But were all rammed, and jammed (but to be balked,
  As we shall see), and jostled hands and knees,
Like wind compressed and pent within a bladder,
Or like a human colic, which is sadder.

LXXV

The shadow came—a tall, thin, grey-haired figure,
    That looked as it had been a shade on earth;
Quick in its motions, with an air of vigour,
    But nought to mark its breeding or its birth;
Now it waxed little, then again grew bigger,
    With now an air of gloom, or savage mirth;
But as you gazed upon its features, they
Changed every instant—to *what*, none could say,

LXXVI

The more intently the ghosts gazed, the less
    Could they distinguish whose the features were;
The Devil himself seemed puzzled even to guess;
    They varied like a dream—now here, now there;
And several people swore from out the press,
    They knew him perfectly; and one could swear
He was his father; upon which another
Was sure he was his mother's cousin's brother:

LXXVII

Another, that he was a duke, or knight,
    An orator, a lawyer, or a priest,
A nabob, a man-midwife; but the wight
    Mysterious changed his countenance at east
As oft as they their minds: though in full sight
    He stood, the puzzle only was increased;
The man was a phantasmagoria in
Himself—he was so volatile and thin.

LXXVIII

The moment that you had pronounced him *one*,
    Presto! his face changed, and he was another;
And when that change was hardly well put on,
    It varied, till I don't think his own mother
(If that he had a mother) would her son
    Have known, he shifted so from one to t'other;
Till guessing from a pleasure grew a task,
At this epistolary 'Iron Mask'.

LXXIX

For sometimes he like Cerberus would seem—
    'Three gentlemen at once' (as sagely says
Good Mrs. Malaprop); then you might deem
    That he was not even *one*; now many rays
Were flashing round him; and now a thick steam
    Hid him from sight—like fogs on London days:
Now Burke, now Tooke, he grew to people's fancies,
And certes often like Sir Philip Francis.

LXXX

I've an hypothesis—'tis quite my own;
    I never let it out till now, for fear
Of doing people harm about the throne,
    And injuring some minister or peer,
On whom the stigma might perhaps be blown;
    It is—my gentle public, lend thine ear!
'Tis, that what Junius we are wont to call,
Was *really—truly*—nobody at all.

LXXXI

I don't see wherefore letters should not be
    Written without hands, since we daily view
Them written without heads; and books, we see,
    Are filled as well without the latter too:
And really till we fix on somebody
    For certain sure to claim them as his due,
Their author, like the Niger's mouth, will bother
The world to say if *there* be mouth or author.

LXXXII

'And who and what art thou?' the Archangel said.
    'For *that* you may consult my title-page,'
Replied this mighty shadow of a shade:
    'If I have kept my secret half an age,
I scarce shall tell it now.'—'Canst thou upbraid,'
    Continued Michael, 'George Rex, or allege
Aught further?' Junius answered, 'You had better
First ask him for *his* answer to my letter:

H

LXXXIII

'My charges upon record will outlast
   The brass of both his epitaph and tomb.'
'Repent'st thou not,' said Michael, 'of some past
   Exaggeration? something which may doom
Thyself if false, as him if true? Thou wast
   Too bitter—is it not so?—in thy gloom
Of passion?'—'Passion!' cried the phantom dim,
'I loved my country, and I hated him.

LXXXIV

'What I have written, I have written : let
   The rest be on his head or mine!' So spoke
Old '*Nominis Umbra*' ; and while speaking yet,
   Away he melted in celestial smoke.
Then Satan said to Michael, 'Don't forget
   To call George Washington, and John Horne Tooke,
And Franklin ;'—but at this time there was heard
A cry for room, though not a phantom stirred.

LXXXV

At length with jostling, elbowing, and the aid
   Of Cherubim appointed to that post,
The devil Asmodeus to the circle made
   His way, and looked as if his journey cost
Some trouble. When his burden down he laid,
   'What's this?' cried Michael ; 'why, 'tis not a ghost?'
'I know it,' quoth the Incubus ; 'but he
Shall be one, if you leave the affair to me.

LXXXVI

'Confound the renegado! I have sprained
   My left wing, he's so heavy ; one would think
Some of his works about his neck were chained.
   But to the point ; while hovering o'er the brink
Of Skiddaw (where as usual it still rained),
   I saw a taper, far below me, wink,
And stooping, caught this fellow at a libel—
No less on History—than the Holy Bible.

LXXXVII

'The former is the Devil's scripture, and
     The latter yours, good Michael: so the affair
Belongs to all of us, you understand.

     I snatched him up just as you see him there,
And brought him off for sentence out of hand:

     I've scarcely been ten minutes in the air—
At least a quarter it can hardly be:
I dare say that his wife is still at tea.'

LXXXVIII

Here Satan said, 'I know this man of old,
     And have expected him for some time here;
A sillier fellow you will scarce behold,
     Or more conceited in his petty sphere:
But surely it was not worth while to fold
     Such trash below your wing, Asmodeus dear:
We had the poor wretch safe (without being bored
With carriage) coming of his own accord.

LXXXIX

'But since he's here, let's see what he has done.'
     'Done!' cried Asmodeus, 'he anticipates
The very business you are now upon,
     And scribbles as if head clerk to the Fates.
Who knows to what his ribaldry may run,
     When such an ass as this, like Balaam's, prates?'
'Let's hear,' quoth Michael, 'what he has to say:
You know we're bound to that in every way.'

XC

Now the Bard, glad to get an audience, which
     By no means often was his case below,
Began to cough, and hawk, and hem, and pitch
     His voice into that awful note of woe
To all unhappy hearers within reach
     Of poets when the tide of rhyme's in flow;
But stuck fast with his first hexameter,
Not one of all whose gouty feet would stir.

XCI

But ere the spavined dactyls could be spurred
   Into recitative, in great dismay
Both Cherubim and Seraphim were heard
   To murmur loudly through their long array;
And Michael rose ere he could get a word
   Of all his foundered verses under way,
And cried, 'For God's sake stop, my friend! 'twere best—
"*Non Di, non homines*"—you know the rest.'

XCII

A general bustle spread throughout the throng,
   Which seemed to hold all verse in detestation;
The Angels had of course enough of song
   When upon service; and the generation
Of ghosts had heard too much in life, not long
   Before, to profit by a new occasion:
The Monarch, mute till then, exclaimed, 'What! what!
Pye come again? No more—no more of that!'

XCIII

The tumult grew; an universal cough
   Convulsed the skies, as during a debate,
When Castlereagh has been up long enough
   (Before he was first minister of state,
I mean—the *slaves hear now*); some cried 'Off, off!'
   As at a farce; till, grown quite desperate.
The Bard Saint Peter prayed to interpose
(Himself an author) only for his prose.

XCIV

The varlet was not an ill-favoured knave;
   A good deal like a vulture in the face,
With a hook nose and a hawk's eye, which gave
   A smart and sharper-looking sort of grace
To his whole aspect, which, though rather grave,
   Was by no means so ugly as his case;
But that, indeed, was hopeless as can be,
Quite a poetic felony '*de se*'.

XCV

Then Michael blew his trump, and stilled the noise
  With one still greater, as is yet the mode
On earth besides; except some grumbling voice,
  Which now and then will make a slight inroad
Upon decorous silence, few will twice
  Lift up their lungs when fairly overcrowed;
And now the Bard could plead his own bad cause,
With all the attitudes of self-applause.

XCVI

He said—(I only give the heads)—he said,
  He meant no harm in scribbling; 'twas his way
Upon all topics; 'twas, besides, his bread,
  Of which he buttered both sides; 'twould delay
Too long the assembly (he was pleased to dread),
  And take up rather more time than a day,
To name his works—he would but cite a few—
'Wat Tyler'—'Rhymes on Blenheim'—'Waterloo.'

XCVII

He had written praises of a Regicide;
  He had written praises of all kings whatever;
He had written for republics far and wide,
  And then against them bitterer than ever;
For pantisocracy he once had cried
  Aloud, a scheme less moral than 'twas clever;
Then grew a hearty anti-jacobin—
Had turned his coat—and would have turned his skin.

XCVIII

He had sung against all battles, and again
  In their high praise and glory; he had called
Reviewing 'the ungentle craft,' and then
  Became as base a critic as e'er crawled—
Fed, paid, and pampered by the very men
  By whom his muse and morals had been mauled:
He had written much blank verse, and blanker prose,
And more of both than any body knows.

XCIX

He had written Wesley's life :—here turning round
   To Satan, 'Sir, I'm ready to write yours,
In two octavo volumes, nicely bound,
   With notes and preface, all that most allures
The pious purchaser ; and there's no ground
   For fear, for I can chose my own reviewers :
So let me have the proper documents,
That I may add you to my other saints.'

C

Satan bowed, and was silent. 'Well, if you,
   With amiable modesty, decline
My offer, what says Michael? There are few
   Whose memoirs could be rendered more divine.
Mine is a pen of all work ; not so new
   As it was once, but I would make you shine
Like your own trumpet. By the way, my own
Has more of brass in it, and is as well blown.

CI

'But talking about trumpets, here's my "Vision"!
   Now you shall judge, all people—yes—you shall
Judge with my judgment! and by my decision
   Be guided who shall enter heaven or fall.
I settle all these things by intuition,
   Times present, past, to come—Heaven—Hell—and all,
Like King Alfonso. When I thus see double,
I save the Deity some worlds of trouble.'

CII

He ceased, and drew forth an MS. ; and no
   Persuasion on the part of Devils, Saints,
Or Angels, now could stop the torrent ; so
   He read the first three lines of the contents ;
But at the fourth, the whole spiritual show
   Had vanished, with variety of scents,
Ambrosial and sulphureous, as they sprang,
Like lightning, off from his 'melodious twang'.

CIII

Those grand heroics acted as a spell;
   The Angels stopped their ears and plied their pinions;
The Devils ran howling, deafened, down to Hell;
   The ghosts fled, gibbering, for their own dominions—
(For 'tis not yet decided where they dwell,
   And I leave every man to his opinions);
Michael took refuge in his trump—but, lo!
His teeth were set on edge, he could not blow!

CIV

Saint Peter, who has hitherto been known
   For an impetuous saint, upraised his keys,
And at the fifth line knocked the poet down;
   Who fell like Phaeton, but more at ease,
Into his lake, for there he did not drown;
   A different web being by the Destinies
Woven for the Laureate's final wreath, whene'er
Reform shall happen either here or there.

CV

He first sank to the bottom—like his works,
   But soon rose to the surface—like himself;
For all corrupted things are buoyed like corks,
   By their own rottenness, light as an elf,
Or wisp that flits o'er a morass: he lurks,
   It may be, still, like dull books on a shelf,
In his own den, to scrawl some 'Life' or 'Vision,'
As Welborn says—'the Devil turned precisian.'

CVI

As for the rest, to come to the conclusion
   Of this true dream, the telescope is gone
Which kept my optics free from all delusion,
   And showed me what I in my turn have shown;
All I saw farther, in the last confusion,
   Was, that King George slipped into Heaven for one;
And when the tumult dwindled to a calm,
I left him practising the hundredth psalm.

from

DON JUAN

from

DON JUAN

FRAGMENT

ON THE BACK OF THE MS. OF CANTO I

I would to Heaven that I were so much clay,
    As I am blood, bone, marrow, passion, feeling—
Because at least the past were passed away,
    And for the future—(but I write this reeling,
Having got drunk exceedingly to-day,
    So that I seem to stand upon the ceiling)
I say—the future is a serious matter—
And so—for God's sake—hock and soda-water!

DEDICATION

I

Bob Southey! You're a poet—Poet-laureate,
    And representative of all the race;
Although 't is true that you turned out a Tory at
    Last,—yours has lately been a common case;
And now, my Epic Renegade! what are ye at?
    With all the Lakers, in and out of place?
A nest of tuneful persons, to my eye
Like 'four and twenty Blackbirds in a pye;

II

'Which pye being opened they began to sing,'
    (This old song and new simile holds good),
'A dainty dish to set before the King,'
    Or Regent, who admires such kind of food;—
And Coleridge, too, has lately taken wing,
    But like a hawk encumbered with his hood,—
Explaining Metaphysics to the nation—
I wish he would explain his Explanation.

III

You, Bob! are rather insolent, you know,
　　At being disappointed in your wish
To supersede all warblers here below,
　　And be the only Blackbird in the dish;
And then you overstrain yourself, or so,
　　And tumble downward like the flying fish
Gasping on deck, because you soar too high, Bob,
And fall, for lack of moisture, quite a-dry, Bob!

IV

And Wordsworth, in a rather long 'Excursion,'
　　(I think the quarto holds five hundred pages),
Has given a sample from the vasty version
　　Of his new system to perplex the sages;
'T is poetry—at least by his assertion,
　　And may appear so when the dog-star rages—
And he who understands it would be able
To add a story to the Tower of Babel.

V

You—Gentlemen! by dint of long seclusion
　　From better company, have kept your own
At Keswick, and, through still continued fusion
　　Of one another's minds, at last have grown
To deem as a most logical conclusion,
　　That Poesy has wreaths for you alone:
There is a narrowness in such a notion,
Which makes me wish you'd change your lakes for Ocean.

VI

I would not imitate the petty thought,
　　Nor coin my self-love to so base a vice,
For all the glory your conversion brought,
　　Since gold alone should not have been its price.
You have your salary; was 't for that you wrought?
　　And Wordsworth has his place in the Excise.
You 're shabby fellows—true—but poets still,
And duly seated on the Immortal Hill.

VII

Your bays may hide the baldness of your brows—
    Perhaps some virtuous blushes;—let them go—
To you I envy neither fruit nor boughs—
    And for the fame you would engross below,
The field is universal, and allows
    Scope to all such as feel the inherent glow:
Scott, Rogers, Campbell, Moore, and Crabbe, will try
'Gainst you the question with posterity.

VIII

For me, who, wandering with pedestrian Muses,
    Contend not with you on the wingéd steed,
I wish your fate may yield ye, when she chooses,
    The fame you envy, and the skill you need;
And, recollect, a poet nothing loses
    In giving to his brethren their full meed
Of merit—and complaint of present days
Is not the certain path to future praise.

IX

He that reserves his laurels for posterity
    (Who does not often claim the bright reversion)
Has generally no great crop to spare it, he
    Being only injured by his own assertion;
And although here and there some glorious rarity
    Arise like Titan from the sea's immersion,
The major part of such appellants go
To—God knows where—for no one else can know.

X

If, fallen in evil days on evil tongues,
    Milton appealed to the Avenger, Time,
If Time, the Avenger, execrates his wrongs,
    And makes the word 'Miltonic' mean '*Sublime*',
He deigned not to belie his soul in songs,
    Nor turn his very talent to a crime;
He did not loathe the Sire to laud the Son,
But closed the tyrant-hater he begun.

XI

Think'st thou, could he—the blind Old Man—arise
    Like Samuel from the grave, to freeze once more
The blood of monarchs with his prophecies,
    Or be alive again—again all hoar
With time and trials, and those helpless eyes,
    And heartless daughters—worn—and pale—and poor;
Would *he* adore a sultan? *he* obey
The intellectual eunuch Castlereagh?

XII

Cold-blooded, smooth-faced, placid miscreant!
    Dabbling its sleek young hands in Erin's gore,
And thus for wider carnage taught to pant,
    Transferred to gorge upon a sister shore,
The vulgarest tool that Tyranny could want,
    With just enough of talent, and no more,
To lengthen fetters by another fixed,
And offer poison long already mixed.

XIII

An orator of such set trash of phrase
    Ineffably—legitimately vile,
That even its grossest flatterers dare not praise,
    Nor foes—all nations—condescend to smile,—
Nor even a sprightly blunder's spark can blaze
    From that Ixion grindstone's ceaseless toil,
That turns and turns to give the world a notion
Of endless torments and perpetual motion.

XIV

A bungler even in its disgusting trade,
    And botching, patching, leaving still behind
Something of which its masters are afraid—
    States to be curbed, and thoughts to be confined,
Conspiracy or Congress to be made—
    Cobbling at manacles for all mankind—
A tinkering slave-maker, who mends old chains,
With God and Man's abhorrence for its gains.

XV

If we may judge of matter by the mind,
  Emasculated to the marrow *It*
Hath but two objects, how to serve, and bind,
  Deeming the chain it wears even men may fit,
Eutropius of its many masters,—blind
  To worth as freedom, wisdom as to wit,
Fearless—because *no* feeling dwells in ice,
Its very courage stagnates to a vice.

XVI

Where shall I turn me not to *view* its bonds,
  For I will never *feel* them?—Italy!
Thy late reviving Roman soul desponds
  Beneath the lie this State-thing breathed o'er thee—
Thy clanking chain, and Erin's yet green wounds,
  Have voices—tongues to cry aloud for me.
Europe has slaves—allies—kings—armies still—
And Southey lives to sing them very ill.

XVII

Meantime, Sir Laureate, I proceed to dedicate,
  In honest simple verse, this song to you,
And, if in flattering strains I do not predicate,
  'T is that I still retain my 'buff and blue';
My politics as yet are all to educate:
  Apostasy's so fashionable, too,
To keep *one* creed 's a task grown quite Herculean;
Is it not so, my Tory, ultra-Julian?

CANTO THE FIRST

I

I want a hero: an uncommon want,
  When every year and month sends forth a new one,
Till, after cloying the gazettes with cant,
  The age discovers he is not the true one;

Of such as these I should not care to vaunt,
   I'll therefore take our ancient friend Don Juan—
We all have seen him, in the pantomime,
Sent to the Devil somewhat ere his time.

II

Vernon, the butcher Cumberland, Wolfe, Hawke,
   Prince Ferdinand, Granby, Burgoyne, Keppel, Howe,
Evil and good, have had their tithe of talk,
   And filled their sign-posts then, like Wellesley now;
Each in their turn like Banquo's monarchs stalk,
   Followers of Fame, 'nine farrow' of that sow:
France, too, had Buonaparté and Dumourier
Recorded in the Moniteur and Courier.

III

Barnave, Brissot, Condorcet, Mirabeau,
   Petion, Clootz, Danton, Marat, La Fayette
Were French, and famous people, as we know;
   And there were others, scarce forgotten yet,
Joubert, Hoche, Marceau, Lannes, Desaix, Moreau,
   With many of the military set,
Exceedingly remarkable at times,
But not at all adapted to my rhymes.

IV

Nelson was once Britannia's god of War,
   And still should be so, but the tide is turned;
There's no more to be said of Trafalgar,
   'Tis with our hero quietly inurned;
Because the army's grown more popular,
   At which the naval people are concerned;
Besides, the Prince is all for the land-service,
Forgetting Duncan, Nelson, Howe, and Jervis.

V

Brave men were living before Agamemnon
   And since, exceeding valorous and sage,

A good deal like him too, though quite the same none;
   But then they shone not on the poet's page,
And so have been forgotten:—I condemn none,
   But can't find any in the present age
Fit for my poem (that is, for my new one);
So, as I said, I'll take my friend Don Juan.

VI

Most epic poets plunge '*in medias res*'
   (Horace makes this the heroic turnpike road),
And then your hero tells, whene'er you please,
   What went before—by way of episode,
While seated after dinner at his ease,
   Beside his mistress in some soft abode,
Palace, or garden, paradise, or cavern,
Which serves the happy couple for a tavern.

VII

That is the usual method, but not mine—
   My way is to begin with the beginning;
The regularity of my design
   Forbids all wandering as the worst of sinning,
And therefore I shall open with a line
   (Although it cost me half an hour in spinning),
Narrating somewhat of Don Juan's father,
And also of his mother, if you'd rather.

VIII

In Seville was he born, a pleasant city,
   Famous for oranges and women,—he
Who has not seen it will be much to pity,
   So says the proverb—and I quite agree;
Of all the Spanish towns is none more pretty,
   Cadiz perhaps—but that you soon may see;—
Don Juan's parents lived beside the river,
A noble stream, and called the Guadalquivir.

IX

His father's name was José—*Don*, of course—
　　A true Hidalgo, free from every stain
Of Moor or Hebrew blood, he traced his source
　　Through the most Gothic gentleman of Spain;
A better cavalier ne'er mounted horse,
　　Or, being mounted, e'er got down again,
Than José, who begot our hero, who
Begot—but that's to come——Well, to renew:

X

His mother was a learnéd lady, famed
　　For every branch of every science known—
In every Christian language ever named,
　　With virtues equalled by her wit alone:
She made the cleverest people quite ashamed,
　　And even the good with inward envy groan,
Finding themselves so very much exceeded,
In their own way, by all the things that she did.

XI

Her memory was a mine: she knew by heart
　　All Calderon and greater part of Lopé,
So, that if any actor missed his part,
　　She could have served him for the prompter's copy;
For her Feinagle's were a useless art,
　　And he himself obliged to shut up shop—he
Could never make a memory so fine as
That which adorned the brain of Donna Inez.

XII

Her favourite science was the mathematical,
　　Her noblest virtue was her magnanimity,
Her wit (she sometimes tried at wit) was Attic all,
　　Her serious sayings darkened to sublimity;
In short, in all things she was fairly what I call
　　A prodigy—her morning dress was dimity,
Her evening silk, or, in the summer, muslin,
And other stuffs, with which I won't stay puzzling.

XIII

She knew the Latin—that is, 'the Lord's prayer,'
  And Greek—the alphabet—I'm nearly sure;
She read some French romances here and there,
  Although her mode of speaking was not pure;
For native Spanish she had no great care,
  At least her conversation was obscure;
Her thoughts were theorems, her words a problem,
As if she deemed that mystery would ennoble 'em.

XIV

She liked the English and the Hebrew tongue,
  And said there was analogy between 'em;
She proved it somehow out of sacred song,
  But I must leave the proofs to those who've seen 'em;
But this I heard her say, and can't be wrong,
  And all may think which way their judgments lean 'em,
'T is strange—the Hebrew noun which means "I am",
The English always use to govern d—n.'

XV

Some women use their tongues—she *looked* a lecture,
  Each eye a sermon, and her brow a homily,
An all-in-all sufficient self-director,
  Like the lamented late Sir Samuel Romilly,
The Law's expounder, and the State's corrector
  Whose suicide was almost an anomaly—
One sad example more, that 'All is vanity,'—
(The jury brought their verdict in 'Insanity'!)

XVI

In short, she was a walking calculation,
  Miss Edgeworth's novels stepping from their covers,
Or Mrs. Trimmer's books on education,
  Or 'Cœlebs' Wife' set out in quest of lovers,
Morality's prim personification,
  In which not Envy's self a flaw discovers;
To others' share let 'female errors fall,'
For she had not even one—the worst of all.

XVII

Oh! she was perfect past all parallel—
    Of any modern female saint's comparison;
So far above the cunning powers of Hell,
    Her Guardian Angel had given up his garrison;
Even her minutest motions went as well
    As those of the best time-piece made by Harrison:
In virtues nothing earthly could surpass her,
Save thine 'incomparable oil,' Macassar!

XVIII

Perfect she was, but as perfection is
    Insipid in this naughty world of ours,
Where our first parents never learned to kiss
    Till they were exiled from their earlier bowers,
Where all was peace, and innocence, and bliss,
    (I wonder how they got through the twelve hours),
Don José, like a lineal son of Eve,
Went plucking various fruit without her leave.

XIX

He was a mortal of the careless kind,
    With no great love for learning, or the learned,
Who chose to go where'er he had a mind,
    And never dreamed his lady was concerned;
The world, as usual, wickedly inclined
    To see a kingdom or a house o'erturned,
Whispered he had a mistress, some said *two*.
But for domestic quarrels *one* will do.

XX

Now Donna Inez had, with all her merit,
    A great opinion of her own good qualities;
Neglect, indeed, requires a saint to bear it,
    And such, indeed, she was in her moralities;
But then she had a devil of a spirit,
    And sometimes mixed up fancies with realities,
And let few opportunities escape
Of getting her liege lord into a scrape.

XXI

This was an easy matter with a man
    Oft in the wrong, and never on his guard,
And even the wisest, do the best they can,
    Have moments, hours, and days, so unprepared,
That you might 'brain them with their lady's fan';
    And sometimes ladies hit exceeding hard,
And fans turn into falchions in fair hands,
And why and wherefore no one understands.

XXII

'T is pity learnéd virgins ever wed
    With persons of no sort of education,
Or gentlemen, who, though well born and bred,
    Grow tired of scientific conversation:
I don't choose to say much upon this head,
    I'm a plain man, and in a single station,
But—Oh! ye lords of ladies intellectual,
Inform us truly, have they not hen-pecked you all?

XXIII

Don José and his lady quarrelled—*why*,
    Not any of the many could divine,
Though several thousand people chose to try,
    'T was surely no concern of theirs nor mine;
I loathe that low vice—curiosity;
    But if there's anything in which I shine,
'T is in arranging all my friends' affairs,
Not having, of my own, domestic cares.

XXIV

And so I interfered, and with the best
    Intentions, but their treatment was not kind;
I think the foolish people were possessed,
    For neither of them could I ever find,
Although their porter afterwards confessed—
    But that 's no matter, and the worst 's behind,
For little Juan o'er me threw, down stairs,
A pail of housemaid's water unawares.

XXV

A little curly-headed, good-for-nothing,
 And mischief-making monkey from his birth;
His parents ne'er agreed except in doting
 Upon the most unquiet imp on earth;
Instead of quarrelling, had they been but both in
 Their senses, they'd have sent young master forth
To school, or had him soundly whipped at home,
To teach him manners for the time to come.

XXVI

Don José and the Donna Inez led
 For some time an unhappy sort of life,
Wishing each other, not divorced, but dead;
 They lived respectably as man and wife,
Their conduct was exceedingly well-bred,
 And gave no outward signs of inward strife,
Until at length the smothered fire broke out,
And put the business past all kind of doubt.

XXVII

For Inez called some druggists and physicians,
 And tried to prove her loving lord was *mad*,
But as he had some lucid intermissions,
 She next decided he was only *bad*;
Yet when they asked her for her depositions,
 No sort of explanation could be had,
Save that her duty both to man and God
Required this conduct—which seemed very odd.

XXVIII

She kept a journal, where his faults were noted,
 And opened certain trunks of books and letters,
All which might, if occasion served, be quoted;
 And then she had all Seville for abettors,
Besides her good old grandmother (who doted);
 The hearers of her case became repeaters,
Then advocates, inquisitors, and judges,
Some for amusement, others for old grudges.

XXIX

And then this best and meekest woman bore
  With such serenity her husband's woes,
Just as the Spartan ladies did of yore,
  Who saw their spouses killed, and nobly chose
Never to say a word about them more—
  Calmly she heard each calumny that rose,
And saw *his* agonies with such sublimity,
That all the world exclaimed, 'What magnanimity!'

XXX

No doubt this patience, when the world is damning us,
  Is philosophic in our former friends;
'T is also pleasant to be deemed magnanimous,
  The more so in obtaining our own ends;
And what the lawyers call a '*malus animus*'
  Conduct like this by no means comprehends:
Revenge in person's certainly no virtue,
But then 't is not *my* fault, if *others* hurt you.

XXXI

And if our quarrels should rip up old stories,
  And help them with a lie or two additional,
I'm not to blame, as you well know—no more is
  Any one else—they were become traditional;
Besides, their resurrection aids our glories
  By contrast, which is what we just were wishing all:
And Science profits by this resurrection—
Dead scandals form good subjects for dissection.

XXXII

Their friends had tried at reconciliation,
  Then their relations, who made matters worse.
('T were hard to tell upon a like occasion
  To whom it may be best to have recourse—
I can't say much for friend or yet relation):
  The lawyers did their utmost for divorce,
But scarce a fee was paid on either side
Before, unluckily, Don José died.

XXXIII

He died: and most unluckily, because,
  According to all hints I could collect
From Counsel learnéd in those kinds of laws,
  (Although their talk 's obscure and circumspect)
His death contrived to spoil a charming cause;
  A thousand pities also with respect
To public feeling, which on this occasion
Was manifested in a great sensation.

XXXIV

But ah! he died; and buried with him lay
  The public feeling and the lawyers' fees:
His house was sold, his servants sent away,
  A Jew took one of his two mistresses,
A priest the other—at least so they say:
  I asked the doctors after his disease—
He died of the slow fever called the tertian,
And left his widow to her own aversion.

XXXV

Yet José was an honourable man,
  That I must say, who knew him very well;
Therefore his frailties I'll no further scan,
  Indeed there were not many more to tell:
And if his passions now and then outran
  Discretion, and were not so peaceable
As Numa's (who was also named Pompilius),
He had been ill brought up, and was born bilious.

XXXVI

Whate'er might be his worthlessness or worth,
  Poor fellow! he had many things to wound him.
Let's own—since it can do no good on earth—
  It was a trying moment that which found him
Standing alone beside his desolate hearth,
  Where all his household gods lay shivered round him:
No choice was left his feelings or his pride,
Save Death or Doctors' Commons—so he died.

XXXVII

Dying intestate, Juan was sole heir
　　To a chancery suit, and messuages, and lands,
Which, with a long minority and care,
　　Promised to turn out well in proper hands:
Inez became sole guardian, which was fair,
　　And answered but to Nature's just demands;
An only son left with an only mother
Is brought up much more wisely than another.

XXXVIII

Sagest of women, even of widows, she
　　Resolved that Juan should be quite a paragon,
And worthy of the noblest pedigree,
　　(His Sire was of Castile, his Dam from Aragon):
Then, for accomplishments of chivalry,
　　In case our Lord the King should go to war again,
He learned the arts of riding, fencing, gunnery,
And how to scale a fortress—or a nunnery.

XXXIX

But that which Donna Inez most desired,
　　And saw into herself each day before all
The learnéd tutors whom for him she hired,
　　Was, that his breeding should be strictly moral:
Much into all his studies she inquired,
　　And so they were submitted first to her, all,
Arts, sciences—no branch was made a mystery
To Juan's eyes, excepting natural history.

XL

The languages, especially the dead,
　　The sciences, and most of all the abstruse,
The arts, at least all such as could be said
　　To be the most remote from common use,
In all these he was much and deeply read:
　　But not a page of anything that's loose,
Or hints continuation of the species,
Was ever suffered, lest he should grow vicious.

XLI

His classic studies made a little puzzle,
    Because of filthy loves of gods and goddesses,
Who in the earlier ages raised a bustle,
    But never put on pantaloons or bodices;
His reverend tutors had at times a tussle,
    And for their Æneids, Iliads, and Odysseys
Were forced to make an odd sort of apology
For Donna Inez dreaded the Mythology.

XLII

Ovid's a rake, as half his verses show him,
    Anacreon's morals are a still worse sample,
Catullus scarcely has a decent poem,
    I don't think Sappho's Ode a good example,
Although Longinus tells us there is no hymn
    Where the Sublime soars forth on wings more ample:
But Virgil's songs are pure, except that horrid one
Beginning with '*Formosum Pastor Corydon.*'

XLIII

Lucretius' irreligion is too strong
    For early stomachs, to prove wholesome food;
I can't help thinking Juvenal was wrong,
    Although no doubt his real intent was good,
For speaking out so plainly in his song,
    So much indeed as to be downright rude;
And then what proper person can be partial
To all those nauseous epigrams of Martial?

XLIV

Juan was taught from out the best edition,
    Expurgated by learnéd men, who place,
Judiciously, from out the schoolboy's vision,
    The grosser parts; but, fearful to deface
Too much their modest bard by this omission,
    And pitying sore his mutilated case,
They only add them all in an appendix,
Which saves, in fact, the trouble of an index;

XLV

For there we have them all 'at one fell swoop,'
  Instead of being scattered through the pages;
They stand forth marshalled in a handsome troop,
  To meet the ingenuous youth of future ages,
Till some less rigid editor shall stoop
  To call them back into their separate cages,
Instead of standing staring all together,
Like garden gods—and not so decent either.

XLVI

The Missal too (it was the family Missal)
  Was ornamented in a sort of way
Which ancient mass-books often are, and this all
  Kinds of grotesques illumined; and how they,
Who saw those figures on the margin kiss all,
  Could turn their optics to the text and pray,
Is more than I know—But Don Juan's mother
Kept this herself, and gave her son another.

XLVII

Sermons he read, and lectures he endured,
  And homilies, and lives of all the saints;
To Jerome and to Chrysostom inured,
  He did not take such studies for restraints;
But how Faith is acquired, and then insured,
  So well not one of the aforesaid paints
As Saint Augustine in his fine Confessions,
Which make the reader envy his transgressions.

XLVIII

This, too, was a sealed book to little Juan—
  I can't but say that his mamma was right,
If such an education was the true one.
  She scarcely trusted him from out her sight;
Her maids were old, and if she took a new one,
  You might be sure she was a perfect fright;
She did this during even her husband's life—
I recommend as much to every wife.

XLIX

Young Juan waxed in goodliness and grace;
    At six a charming child, and at eleven
With all the promise of as fine a face
    As e'er to Man's maturer growth was given:
He studied steadily, and grew apace,
    And seemed, at least, in the right road to Heaven,
For half his days were passed at church, the other
Between his tutors, confessor, and mother.

L

At six, I said, he was a charming child,
    At twelve he was a fine, but quiet boy;
Although in infancy a little wild,
    They tamed him down amongst them: to destroy
His natural spirit not in vain they toiled,
    At least it seemed so; and his mother's joy
Was to declare how sage, and still, and steady,
Her young philosopher was grown already.

LI

I had my doubts, perhaps I have them still,
    But what I say is neither here nor there:
I knew his father well, and have some skill
    In character—but it would not be fair
From sire to son to augur good or ill:
    He and his wife were an ill-sorted pair—
But scandal's my aversion—I protest
Against all evil speaking, even in jest.

LII

For my part I say nothing—nothing—but
    This I will say—my reasons are my own—
That if I had an only son to put
    To school (as God be praised that I have none),
'T is not with Donna Inez I would shut
    Him up to learn his catechism alone,
No—no—I'd send him out betimes to college,
For there it was I picked up my own knowledge.

LIII

For there one learns—'t is not for me to boast,
  Though I acquired—but I pass over *that*,
As well as all the Greek I since have lost:—
  I say that there's the place—but '*Verbum sat*,'
I think I picked up too, as well as most,
  Knowledge of matters—but no matter *what*—
I never married—but, I think, I know
That sons should not be educated so.

LIV

Young Juan now was sixteen years of age,
  Tall, handsome, slender, but well knit: he seemed
Active, though not so sprightly, as a page;
  And everybody but his mother deemed
Him almost man; but she flew in a rage
  And bit her lips (for else she might have screamed)
If any said so—for to be precocious
Was in her eyes a thing the most atrocious.

LV

Amongst her numerous acquaintance, all
  Selected for discretion and devotion,
There was the Donna Julia, whom to call
  Pretty were but to give a feeble notion
Of many charms in her as natural
  As sweetness to the flower, or salt to Ocean,
Her zone to Venus, or his bow to Cupid,
(But this last simile is trite and stupid.)

LVI

The darkness of her Oriental eye
  Accorded with her Moorish origin;
(Her blood was not all Spanish; by the by,
  In Spain, you know, this is a sort of sin:)
When proud Granada fell, and, forced to fly,
  Boabdil wept: of Donna Julia's kin
Some went to Africa, some stayed in Spain—
Her great great grandmamma chose to remain.

LVII

She married (I forget the pedigree)
     With an Hidalgo, who transmitted down
His blood less noble than such blood should be;
     At such alliances his sires would frown,
In that point so precise in each degree
     That they bred *in and in*, as might be shown,
Marrying their cousins—nay, their aunts, and nieces,
Which always spoils the breed, if it increases.

LVIII

This heathenish cross restored the breed again,
     Ruined its blood, but much improved its flesh;
For from a root the ugliest in Old Spain
     Sprung up a branch as beautiful as fresh;
The sons no more were short, the daughters plain:
     But there's a rumour which I fain would hush,
'T is said that Donna Julia's grandmamma
Produced her Don more heirs at love than law.

LIX

However this might be, the race went on
     Improving still through every generation,
Until it centred in an only son,
     Who left an only daughter; my narration
May have suggested that this single one
     Could be but Julia (whom on this occasion
I shall have much to speak about), and she
Was married, charming, chaste, and twenty-three.

LX

Her eye (I'm very fond of handsome eyes)
     Was large and dark, suppressing half its fire
Until she spoke, then through its soft disguise
     Flashed an expression more of pride than ire,
And love than either; and there would arise
     A something in them which was not desire,
But would have been, perhaps, but for the soul
Which struggled through and chastened down the whole.

LXI

Her glossy hair was clustered o'er a brow
  Bright with intelligence, and fair, and smooth;
Her eyebrow's shape was like the aërial bow,
  Her cheek all purple with the beam of youth,
Mounting, at times, to a transparent glow,
  As if her veins ran lightning; she, in sooth,
Possessed an air and grace by no means common:
Her stature tall—I hate a dumpy woman.

LXII

Wedded she was some years, and to a man
  Of fifty, and such husbands are in plenty;
And yet, I think, instead of such a ONE
  'T were better to have TWO of five-and-twenty,
Especially in countries near the sun:
  And now I think on 't, '*mi vien in mente*,'
Ladies even of the most uneasy virtue
Prefer a spouse whose age is short of thirty.

LXIII

'T is a sad thing, I cannot choose but say,
  And all the fault of that indecent sun,
Who cannot leave alone our helpless clay,
  But will keep baking, broiling, burning on,
That howsoever people fast and pray,
  The flesh is frail, and so the soul undone:
What men call gallantry, and gods adultery,
Is much more common where the climate's sultry.

LXIV

Happy the nations of the moral North!
  Where all is virtue, and the winter season
Sends sin, without a rag on, shivering forth
  ('T was snow that brought St. Anthony to reason);
Where juries cast up what a wife is worth,
  By laying whate'er sum, in mulct, they please on
The lover, who must pay a handsome price,
Because it is a marketable vice.

LXV

Alfonso was the name of Julia's lord,
　A man well looking for his years, and who
Was neither much beloved nor yet abhorred:
　They lived together as most people do,
Suffering each other's foibles by accord,
　And not exactly either *one* or *two*;
Yet he was jealous, though he did not show it,
For Jealousy dislikes the world to know it.

LXVI

Julia was—yet I never could see why—
　With Donna Inez quite a favourite friend;
Between their tastes there was small sympathy,
　For not a line had Julia ever penned:
Some people whisper (but, no doubt, they lie,
　For Malice still imputes some private end)
That Inez had, ere Don Alfonso's marriage,
Forgot with him her very prudent carriage;

LXVII

And that still keeping up the old connection,
　Which Time had lately rendered much more chaste,
She took his lady also in affection,
　And certainly this course was much the best:
She flattered Julia with her sage protection,
　And complimented Don Alfonso's taste;
And if she could not (who can?) silence scandal,
At least she left it a more slender handle.

LXVIII

I can't tell whether Julia saw the affair
　With other people's eyes, or if her own
Discoveries made, but none could be aware
　Of this, at least no symptom e'er was shown;
Perhaps she did not know, or did not care,
　Indifferent from the first, or callous grown:
I'm really puzzled what to think or say,
She kept her counsel in so close a way.

LXIX

Juan she saw, and, as a pretty child,
   Caressed him often—such a thing might be
Quite innocently done, and harmless styled,
   When she had twenty years, and thirteen he;
But I am not so sure I should have smiled
   When he was sixteen, Julia twenty-three;
These few short years make wondrous alterations,
Particularly amongst sun-burnt nations.

LXX

Whate'er the cause might be, they had become
   Changed; for the dame grew distant, the youth shy,
Their looks cast down, their greetings almost dumb,
   And much embarrassment in either eye;
There surely will be little doubt with some
   That Donna Julia knew the reason why,
But as for Juan, he had no more notion
Than he who never saw the sea of Ocean.

LXXI

Yet Julia's very coldness still was kind,
   And tremulously gentle her small hand
Withdrew itself from his, but left behind
   A little pressure, thrilling, and so bland
And slight, so very slight, that to the mind
   'T was but a doubt; but ne'er magician's wand
Wrought change with all Armida's fairy art
Like what this light touch left on Juan's heart.

LXXII

And if she met him, though she smiled no more,
   She looked a sadness sweeter than her smile,
As if her heart had deeper thoughts in store
   She must not own, but cherished more the while
For that compression in its burning core;
   Even Innocence itself has many a wile,
And will not dare to trust itself with truth,
And Love is taught hypocrisy from youth.

I

LXXIII

But Passion most dissembles, yet betrays
  Even by its darkness; as the blackest sky
Foretells the heaviest tempest, it displays
  Its workings through the vainly guarded eye,
And in whatever aspect it arrays
  Itself, 't is still the same hypocrisy;
Coldness or Anger, even Disdain or Hate,
Are masks it often wears, and still too late.

LXXIV

Then there were sighs, the deeper for suppression,
  And stolen glances, sweeter for the theft,
And burning blushes, though for no transgression,
  Tremblings when met, and restlessness when left;
All these are little preludes to possession,
  Of which young Passion cannot be bereft,
And merely tend to show how greatly Love is
Embarrassed at first starting with a novice.

LXXV

Poor Julia's heart was in an awkward state;
  She felt it going, and resolved to make
The noblest efforts for herself and mate,
  For Honour's, Pride's, Religion's, Virtue's sake:
Her resolutions were most truly great,
  And almost might have made a Tarquin quake:
She prayed the Virgin Mary for her grace,
As being the best judge of a lady's case.

LXXVI

She vowed she never would see Juan more,
  And next day paid a visit to his mother,
And looked extremely at the opening door,
  Which, by the Virgin's grace, let in another;
Grateful she was, and yet a little sore—
  Again it opens, it can be no other,
'T is surely Juan now—No! I'm afraid
That night the Virgin was no further prayed.

LXXVII

She now determined that a virtuous woman
  Should rather face and overcome temptation,
That flight was base and dastardly, and no man
  Should ever give her heart the least sensation,
That is to say, a thought beyond the common
  Preference, that we must feel, upon occasion,
For people who are pleasanter than others,
But then they only seem so many brothers.

LXXVIII

And even if by chance—and who can tell?
  The Devil's so very sly—she should discover
That all within was not so very well,
  And, if still free, that such or such a lover
Might please perhaps, a virtuous wife can quell
  Such thoughts, and be the better when they're over;
And if the man should ask, 't is but denial:
I recommend young ladies to make trial.

LXXIX

And, then, there are such things as Love divine,
  Bright and immaculate, unmixed and pure,
Such as the angels think so very fine,
  And matrons, who would be no less secure,
Platonic, perfect, 'just such love as mine;'
  Thus Julia said—and thought so, to be sure;
And so I'd have her think, were *I* the man
On whom her reveries celestial ran.

LXXX

Such love is innocent, and may exist
  Between young persons without any danger.
A hand may first, and then a lip be kissed;
  For my part, to such doings I'm a stranger,
But *hear* these freedoms form the utmost list
  Of all o'er which such love may be a ranger:
If people go beyond, 't is quite a crime,
But not my fault—I tell them all in time.

LXXXI

Love, then, but Love within its proper limits,
  Was Julia's innocent determination
In young Don Juan's favour, and to him its
  Exertion might be useful on occasion;
And, lighted at too pure a shrine to dim its
  Ethereal lustre, with what sweet persuasion
He might be taught, by Love and her together—
I really don't know what, nor Julia either.

LXXXII

Fraught with this fine intention, and well fenced
  In mail of proof—her purity of soul—
She, for the future, of her strength convinced,
  And that her honour was a rock, or mole,
Exceeding sagely from that hour dispensed
  With any kind of troublesome control;
But whether Julia to the task was equal
Is that which must be mentioned in the sequel.

LXXXIII

Her plan she deemed both innocent and feasible,
  And, surely, with a stripling of sixteen
Not Scandal's fangs could fix on much that's seizable,
  Or if they did so, satisfied to mean
Nothing but what was good, her breast was peaceable—
  A quiet conscience makes one so serene!
Christians have burnt each other, quite persuaded
That all the Apostles would have done as they did.

LXXXIV

And if in the mean time her husband died,
  But Heaven forbid that such a thought should cross
Her brain, though in a dream! (and then she sighed)
  Never could she survive that common loss;
But just suppose that moment should betide,
  I only say suppose it—*inter nos*:
(This should be *entre nous*, for Julia thought
In French, but then the rhyme would go for nought.)

LXXXV

I only say, suppose this supposition:
  Juan being then grown up to man's estate
Would fully suit a widow of condition,
  Even seven years hence it would not be too late;
And in the interim (to pursue this vision)
  The mischief, after all, could not be great,
For he would learn the rudiments of Love,
I mean the *seraph* way of those above.

LXXXVI

So much for Julia! Now we'll turn to Juan.
  Poor little fellow! he had no idea
Of his own case, and never hit the true one;
  In feelings quick as Ovid's Miss Medea,
He puzzled over what he found a new one,
  But not as yet imagined it could be a
Thing quite in course, and not at all alarming,
Which, with a little patience, might grow charming.

LXXXVII

Silent and pensive, idle, restless, slow,
  His home deserted for the lonely wood,
Tormented with a wound he could not know,
  His, like all deep grief, plunged in solitude:
I'm fond myself of solitude or so,
  But then, I beg it may be understood,
By solitude I mean a Sultan's (not
A Hermit's), with a haram for a grot.

LXXXVIII

'Oh Love! in such a wilderness as this,
  Where Transport and Security entwine,
Here is the Empire of thy perfect bliss,
  And here thou art a God indeed divine.'
The bard I quote from does not sing amiss,
  With the exception of the second line,
For that same twining 'Transport and Security'
Are twisted to a phrase of some obscurity.

LXXXIX

The Poet meant, no doubt, and thus appeals
  To the good sense and senses of mankind,
The very thing which everybody feels,
  As all have found on trial, or may find,
That no one likes to be disturbed at meals
  Or love.—I won't say more about 'entwined'
Or 'Transport,' as we knew all that before,
But beg 'Security' will bolt the door.

XC

Young Juan wandered by the glassy brooks,
  Thinking unutterable things; he threw
Himself at length within the leafy nooks
  Where the wild branch of the cork forest grew;
There poets find materials for their books,
  And every now and then we read them through,
So that their plan and prosody are eligible,
Unless, like Wordsworth, they prove unintelligible.

XCI

He, Juan (and not Wordsworth), so pursued
  His self-communion with his own high soul,
Until his mighty heart, in its great mood,
  Had mitigated part, though not the whole
Of its disease; he did the best he could
  With things not very subject to control,
And turned, without perceiving his condition,
Like Coleridge, into a metaphysician.

XCII

He thought about himself, and the whole earth,
  Of man the wonderful, and of the stars,
And how the deuce they ever could have birth;
  And then he thought of earthquakes, and of wars,
How many miles the moon might have in girth,
  Of air-balloons, and of the many bars
To perfect knowledge of the boundless skies;—
And then he thought of Donna Julia's eyes.

XCIII

In thoughts like these true Wisdom may discern
  Longings sublime, and aspirations high,
Which some are born with, but the most part learn
  To plague themselves withal, they know not why:
'T was strange that one so young should thus concern
  His brain about the action of the sky;
If *you* think 't was Philosophy that this did,
I can't help thinking puberty assisted.

XCIV

He pored upon the leaves, and on the flowers,
  And heard a voice in all the winds; and then
He thought of wood-nymphs and immortal bowers,
  And how the goddesses came down to men:
He missed the pathway, he forgot the hours,
  And when he looked upon his watch again,
He found how much old Time had been a winner—
He also found that he had lost his dinner.

XCV

Sometimes he turned to gaze upon his book,
  Boscan, or Garcilasso;—by the wind
Even as the page is rustled while we look,
  So by the poesy of his own mind
Over the mystic leaf his soul was shook,
  As if 't were one whereon magicians bind
Their spells, and give them to the passing gale,
According to some good old woman's tale.

XCVI

Thus would he while his lonely hours away
  Dissatisfied, not knowing what he wanted;
Nor glowing reverie, nor poet's lay,
  Could yield his spirit that for which it panted,
A bosom whereon he his head might lay,
  And hear the heart beat with the love it granted,
With—several other things, which I forget,
Or which, at least, I need not mention yet.

XCVII

Those lonely walks, and lengthening reveries,
   Could not escape the gentle Julia's eyes;
She saw that Juan was not at his ease;
   But that which chiefly may, and must surprise,
Is, that the Donna Inez did not tease
   Her only son with question or surmise;
Whether it was she did not see, or would not,
Or, like all very clever people, could not.

XCVIII

This may seem strange, but yet 't is very common;
   For instance—gentlemen, whose ladies take
Leave to o'erstep the written rights of Woman,
   And break the——Which commandment is't they break?
(I have forgot the number, and think no man
   Should rashly quote, for fear of a mistake;)
I say, when these same gentlemen are jealous,
They make some blunder, which their ladies tell us.

XCIX

A real husband always is suspicious,
   But still no less suspects in the wrong place,
Jealous of some one who had no such wishes,
   Or pandering blindly to his own disgrace,
By harbouring some dear friend extremely vicious;
   The last indeed 's infallibly the case:
And when the spouse and friend are gone off wholly,
He wonders at their vice, and not his folly.

C

Thus parents also are at times short-sighted:
   Though watchful as the lynx, they ne'er discover,
The while the wicked world beholds delighted,
   Young Hopeful's mistress, or Miss Fanny's lover,
Till some confounded escapade has blighted
   The plan of twenty years, and all is over;
And then the mother cries, the father swears
And wonders why the devil he got heirs.

CI

But Inez was so anxious, and so clear
  Of sight, that I must think, on this occasion,
She had some other motive much more near
  For leaving Juan to this new temptation,
But what that motive was, I shan't say here;
  Perhaps to finish Juan's education,
Perhaps to open Don Alfonso's eyes,
In case he thought his wife too great a prize.

CII

It was upon a day, a summer's day;—
  Summer 's indeed a very dangerous season,
And so is spring about the end of May;
  The sun, no doubt, is the prevailing reason;
But whatsoe'er the cause is, one may say,
  And stand convicted of more truth than treason,
That there are months which nature grows more merry in,—
March has its hares, and May must have its heroine.

CIII

'T was on a summer's day—the sixth of June:
  I like to be particular in dates,
Not only of the age, and year, but moon;
  They are a sort of post-house, where the Fates
Change horses, making History change its tune,
  Then spur away o'er empires and o'er states,
Leaving at last not much besides chronology,
Excepting the post-obits of theology.

CIV

'T was on the sixth of June, about the hour
  Of half-past six—perhaps still nearer seven—
When Julia sate within as pretty a bower
  As e'er held houri in that heathenish heaven
Described by Mahomet, and Anacreon Moore,
  To whom the lyre and laurels have been given,
With all the trophies of triumphant song—
He won them well, and may he wear them long!

CV

She sate, but not alone; I know not well
    How this same interview had taken place,
And even if I knew, I shall not tell—
    People should hold their tongues in any case;
No matter how or why the thing befell,
    But there were she and Juan, face to face—
When two such faces are so, 't would be wise,
But very difficult, to shut their eyes.

CVI

How beautiful she looked! her conscious heart
    Glowed in her cheek, and yet she felt no wrong:
Oh Love! how perfect is thy mystic art,
    Strengthening the weak, and trampling on the strong!
How self-deceitful is the sagest part
    Of mortals whom thy lure hath led along!—
The precipice she stood on was immense,
So was her creed in her own innocence.

CVII

She thought of her own strength, and Juan's youth,
    And of the folly of all prudish fears,
Victorious Virtue, and domestic Truth,
    And then of Don Alfonso's fifty years:
I wish these last had not occurred, in sooth,
    Because that number rarely much endears,
And through all climes, the snowy and the sunny,
Sounds ill in love, whate'er it may in money.

CVIII

When people say, 'I've told you *fifty* times,'
    They mean to scold, and very often do;
When poets say, 'I've written *fifty* rhymes,'
    They make you dread that they'll recite them too;
In gangs of *fifty*, thieves commit their crimes;
    At *fifty* love for love is rare, 't is true,
But then, no doubt, it equally as true is,
A good deal may be bought for *fifty* Louis.

CIX

Julia had honour, virtue, truth, and love
  For Don Alfonso; and she inly swore,
By all the vows below to Powers above,
  She never would disgrace the ring she wore,
Nor leave a wish which wisdom might reprove;
  And while she pondered this, besides much more,
One hand on Juan's carelessly was thrown,
Quite by mistake—she thought it was her own;

CX

Unconsciously she leaned upon the other,
  Which played within the tangles of her hair;
And to contend with thoughts she could not smother
  She seemed by the distraction of her air.
'T was surely very wrong in Juan's mother
  To leave together this imprudent pair,
She who for many years had watched her son so—
I'm very certain *mine* would not have done so.

CXI

The hand which still held Juan's, by degrees
  Gently, but palpably confirmed its grasp,
As if it said, 'Detain me, if you please;'
  Yet there's no doubt she only meant to clasp
His fingers with a pure Platonic squeeze;
  She would have shrunk as from a toad, or asp,
Had she imagined such a thing could rouse
A feeling dangerous to a prudent spouse.

CXII

I cannot know what Juan thought of this,
  But what he did, is much what you would do;
His young lip thanked it with a grateful kiss,
  And then, abashed at its own joy, withdrew
In deep despair, lest he had done amiss,—
  Love is so very timid when 't is new:
She blushed, and frowned not, but she strove to speak,
And held her tongue, her voice was grown so weak.

CXIII

The sun set, and up rose the yellow moon:
  The Devil's in the moon for mischief; they
Who called her CHASTE, methinks, began too soon
  Their nomenclature; there is not a day,
The longest, not the twenty-first of June,
  Sees half the business in a wicked way,
On which three single hours of moonshine smile—
And then she looks so modest all the while!

CXIV

There is a dangerous silence in that hour,
  A stillness, which leaves room for the full soul
To open all itself, without the power
  Of calling wholly back its self-control;
The silver light which, hallowing tree and tower,
  Sheds beauty and deep softness o'er the whole,
Breathes also to the heart, and o'er it throws
A loving languor, which is not repose.

CXV

And Julia sate with Juan, half embraced
  And half retiring from the glowing arm,
Which trembled like the bosom where 't was placed;
  Yet still she must have thought there was no harm
Or else 't were easy to withdraw her waist;
  But then the situation had its charm,
And then—God knows what next—I can't go on;
I'm almost sorry that I e'er begun.

CXVI

Oh Plato! Plato! you have paved the way,
  With your confounded fantasies, to more
Immoral conduct by the fancied sway
  Your system feigns o'er the controlless core
Of human hearts, than all the long array
  Of poets and romancers:—You're a bore,
A charlatan, a coxcomb—and have been,
At best, no better than a go-between.

CXVII

And Julia's voice was lost, except in sighs,
  Until too late for useful conversation;
The tears were gushing from her gentle eyes,
  I wish, indeed, they had not had occasion;
But who, alas! can love, and then be wise?
  Not that Remorse did not oppose Temptation;
A little still she strove, and much repented,
And whispering 'I will ne'er consent'—consented.

CXVIII

'T is said that Xerxes offered a reward
  To those who could invent him a new pleasure:
Methinks the requisition's rather hard,
  And must have cost his Majesty a treasure:
For my part, I'm a moderate-minded bard,
  Fond of a little love (which I call leisure);
I care not for new pleasures, as the old
Are quite enough for me, so they but hold.

CXIX

Oh Pleasure! you're indeed a pleasant thing,
  Although one must be damned for you, no doubt:
I make a resolution every spring
  Of reformation, ere the year run out,
But somehow, this my vestal vow takes wing,
  Yet still, I trust, it may be kept throughout:
I'm very sorry, very much ashamed,
And mean, next winter, to be quite reclaimed.

CXX

Here my chaste Muse a liberty must take—
  Start not! still chaster reader—she'll be nice hence—
Forward, and there is no great cause to quake;
  This liberty is a poetic licence,
Which some irregularity may make
  In the design, and as I have a high sense
Of Aristotle and the Rules, 't is fit
To beg his pardon when I err a bit.

CXXI

This licence is to hope the reader will
　　Suppose from June the sixth (the fatal day,
Without whose epoch my poetic skill
　　For want of facts would all be thrown away),
But keeping Julia and Don Juan still
　　In sight, that several months have passed; we'll say
'T was in November, but I'm not so sure
About the day—the era's more obscure.

CXXII

We'll talk of that anon.—'T is sweet to hear
　　At midnight on the blue and moonlit deep
The song and oar of Adria's gondolier,
　　By distance mellowed, o'er the waters sweep;
'T is sweet to see the evening star appear;
　　'T is sweet to listen as the night-winds creep
From leaf to leaf; 't is sweet to view on high
The rainbow, based on ocean, span the sky.

CXXIII

'T is sweet to hear the watch-dog's honest bark
　　Bay deep-mouthed welcome as we draw near home;
'T is sweet to know there is an eye will mark
　　Our coming, and look brighter when we come;
'T is sweet to be awakened by the lark,
　　Or lulled by falling waters; sweet the hum
Of bees, the voice of girls, the song of birds,
The lisp of children, and their earliest words.

CXXIV

Sweet is the vintage, when the showering grapes
　　In Bacchanal profusion reel to earth,
Purple and gushing: sweet are our escapes
　　From civic revelry to rural mirth;
Sweet to the miser are his glittering heaps,
　　Sweet to the father is his first-born's birth,
Sweet is revenge—especially to women—
Pillage to soldiers, prize-money to seamen.

CXXV

Sweet is a legacy, and passing sweet
   The unexpected death of some old lady,
Or gentleman of seventy years complete,
   Who 've made 'us youth' wait too—too long already,
For an estate, or cash, or country seat,
   Still breaking, but with stamina so steady,
That all the Israelites are fit to mob its
Next owner for their double-damned post-obits.

CXXVI

'T is sweet to win, no matter how, one's laurels,
   By blood or ink; 't is sweet to put an end
To strife; 't is sometimes sweet to have our quarrels,
   Particularly with a tiresome friend:
Sweet is old wine in bottles, ale in barrels;
   Dear is the helpless creature we defend
Against the world; and dear the schoolboy spot
We ne'er forget, though there we are forgot.

CXXVII

But sweeter still than this, than these, than all,
   Is first and passionate Love—it stands alone,
Like Adam's recollection of his fall;
   The Tree of Knowledge has been plucked—all's known—
And Life yields nothing further to recall
   Worthy of this ambrosial sin, so shown,
No doubt in fable, as the unforgiven
Fire which Prometheus filched for us from Heaven.

CXXVIII

Man's a strange animal, and makes strange use
   Of his own nature, and the various arts,
And likes particularly to produce
   Some new experiment to show his parts;
This is the age of oddities let loose,
   Where different talents find their different marts;
You 'd best begin with truth, and when you've lost your
Labour, there's a sure market for imposture.

CXXIX

What opposite discoveries we have seen!
    (Signs of true genius, and of empty pockets.)
One makes new noses, one a guillotine,
    One breaks your bones, one sets them in their sockets;
But Vaccination certainly has been
    A kind antithesis to Congreve's rockets,
With which the Doctor paid off an old pox,
By borrowing a new one from an ox.

CXXX

Bread has been made (indifferent) from potatoes:
    And Galvanism has set some corpses grinning,
But has not answered like the apparatus
    Of the Humane Society's beginning,
By which men are unsuffocated gratis:
    What wondrous new machines have late been spinning!
I said the small-pox has gone out of late;
Perhaps it may be followed by the great.

CXXXI

'T is said the great came from America;
    Perhaps it may set out on its return,—
The population there so spreads, they say
    'T is grown high time to thin it in its turn,
With war, or plague, or famine—any way,
    So that civilisation they may learn;
And which in ravage the more loathsome evil is—
Their real *lues*, or our pseudo-syphilis?

CXXXII

This is the patent age of new inventions
    For killing bodies, and for saving souls,
All propagated with the best intentions;
    Sir Humphry Davy's lantern, by which coals
Are safely mined for in the mode he mentions,
    Tombuctoo travels, voyages to the Poles
Are ways to benefit mankind, as true,
Perhaps, as shooting them at Waterloo.

CXXXIII

Man 's a phenomenon, one knows not what,
   And wonderful beyond all wondrous measure;
'T is pity though, in this sublime world, that
   Pleasure 's a sin, and sometimes Sin 's a pleasure;
Few mortals know what end they would be at,
   But whether Glory, Power, or Love, or Treasure,
The path is through perplexing ways, and when
The goal is gained, we die, you know—and then——

CXXXIV

What then?—I do not know, no more do you—
   And so good night.—Return we to our story:
'T was in November, when fine days are few,
   And the far mountains wax a little hoary,
And clap a white cape on their mantles blue;
   And the sea dashes round the promontory,
And the loud breaker boils against the rock,
And sober suns must set at five o'clock.

CXXXV

'T was, as the watchmen say, a cloudy night;
   No moon, no stars, the wind was low or loud
By gusts, and many a sparkling hearth was bright
   With the piled wood, round which the family crowd;
There 's something cheerful in that sort of light,
   Even as a summer sky's without a cloud:
I'm fond of fire, and crickets, and all that,
A lobster salad, and champagne, and chat.

CXXXVI

'T was midnight—Donna Julia was in bed,
   Sleeping, most probably,—when at her door
Arose a clatter might awake the dead,
   If they had never been awoke before,
And that they have been so we all have read,
   And are to be so, at the least, once more;—
The door was fastened, but with voice and fist
First knocks were heard, then 'Madam—Madam—hist!

CXXXVII

'For God's sake, Madam—Madam—here's my master,
    With more than half the city at his back—
Was ever heard of such a curst disaster!
    'T is not my fault—I kept good watch—Alack!
Do pray undo the bolt a little faster—
    They're on the stair just now, and in a crack
Will all be here; perhaps he yet may fly—
Surely the window's not so *very* high!'

CXXXVIII

By this time Don Alfonso was arrived,
    With torches, friends, and servants in great number
The major part of them had long been wived,
    And therefore paused not to disturb the slumber
Of any wicked woman, who contrived
    By stealth her husband's temples to encumber:
Examples of this kind are so contagious,
Were *one* not punished, *all* would be outrageous.

CXXXIX

I can't tell how, or why, or what suspicion
    Could enter into Don Alfonso's head;
But for a cavalier of his condition
    It surely was exceedingly ill-bred,
Without a word of previous admonition,
    To hold a levee round his lady's bed,
And summon lackeys, armed with fire and sword,
To prove himself the thing he most abhorred.

CXL

Poor Donna Julia! starting as from sleep,
    (Mind—that I do not say—she had not slept),
Began at once to scream, and yawn, and weep;
    Her maid, Antonia, who was an adept,
Contrived to fling the bed-clothes in a heap,
    As if she had just now from out them crept:
I can't tell why she should take all this trouble
To prove her mistress had been sleeping double.

CXLI

But Julia mistress, and Antonia maid,
   Appeared like two poor harmless women who
Of goblins, but still more of men afraid,
   Had thought one man might be deterred by two,
And therefore side by side were gently laid,
   Until the hours of absence should run through,
And truant husband should return, and say,
'My dear,—I was the first who came away.'

CXLII

Now Julia found at length a voice, and cried,
   'In Heaven's name, Don Alfonso, what d' ye mean?
Has madness seized you? would that I had died
   Ere such a monster's victim I had been!
What may this midnight violence betide,
   A sudden fit of drunkenness or spleen?
Dare you suspect me, whom the thought would kill?
Search, then, the room!'—Alfonso said, 'I will.'

CXLIII

He searched, *they* searched, and rummaged everywhere,
   Closet and clothes' press, chest and window-seat,
And found much linen, lace, and several pair
   Of stockings, slippers, brushes, combs, complete
With other articles of ladies fair,
   To keep them beautiful, or leave them neat:
Arras they pricked and curtains with their swords,
And wounded several shutters, and some boards.

CXLIV

Under the bed they searched, and there they found—
   No matter what—it was not that they sought;
They opened windows, gazing if the ground
   Had signs of footmarks, but the earth said nought;
And then they stared each others' faces round:
   'T is odd, not one of all these seekers thought,
And seems to me almost a sort of blunder,
Of looking *in* the bed as well as under.

CXLV

During this inquisition Julia's tongue
    Was not asleep—'Yes, search and search,' she cried,
'Insult on insult heap, and wrong on wrong!
    It was for this that I became a bride!
For this in silence I have suffered long
    A husband like Alfonso at my side;
But now I'll bear no more, nor here remain,
If there be law or lawyers in all Spain.

CXLVI

'Yes, Don Alfonso! husband now no more,
    If ever you indeed deserved the name,
Is 't worthy of your years?—you have threescore—
    Fifty, or sixty, it is all the same—
Is 't wise or fitting, causeless to explore
    For facts against a virtuous woman's fame?
Ungrateful, perjured, barbarous Don Alfonso,
How dare you think your lady would go on so?

CXLVII

'Is it for this I have disdained to hold
    The common privileges of my sex?
That I have chosen a confessor so old
    And deaf, that any other it would vex,
And never once he has had cause to scold,
    But found my very innocence perplex
So much, he always doubted I was married—
How sorry you will be when I've miscarried!

CXLVIII

'Was it for this that no Cortejo e'er
    I yet have chosen from out the youth of Seville?
Is it for this I scarce went anywhere,
    Except to bull-fights, mass, play, rout, and revel?
Is it for this, whate'er my suitors were,
    I favoured none—nay, was almost uncivil?
Is it for this that General Count O'Reilly,
Who took Algiers, declares I used him vilely?

CXLIX

'Did not the Italian *Musico* Cazzani
  Sing at my heart six months at least in vain?
Did not his countryman, Count Corniani,
  Call me the only virtuous wife in Spain?
Were there not also Russians, English, many?
  The Count Strongstroganoff I put in pain,
And Lord Mount Coffeehouse, the Irish peer,
Who killed himself for love (with wine) last year.

CL

'Have I not had two bishops at my feet?
  The Duke of Ichar, and Don Fernan Nunez;
And is it thus a faithful wife you treat?
  I wonder in what quarter now the moon is:
I praise your vast forbearance not to beat
  Me also, since the time so opportune is—
Oh, valiant man! with sword drawn and cocked trigger,
Now, tell me, don't you cut a pretty figure?

CLI

'Was it for this you took your sudden journey,
  Under pretence of business indispensable
With that sublime of rascals your attorney,
  Whom I see standing there, and looking sensible
Of having played the fool? though both I spurn, he
  Deserves the worst, his conduct 's less defensible,
Because, no doubt, 't was for his dirty fee,
And not from any love to you nor me.

CLII

'If he comes here to take a deposition,
  By all means let the gentleman proceed;
You 've made the apartment in a fit condition:—
  There 's pen and ink for you, sir, when you need—
Let everything be noted with precision,
  I would not you for nothing should be fee'd—
But, as my maid's undressed, pray turn your spies out.'
'Oh!' sobbed Antonia, 'I could tear their eyes out.'

CLIII

'There is the closet, there the toilet, there
    The antechamber—search them under, over;
There is the sofa, there the great arm-chair,
    The chimney—which would really hold a lover.
I wish to sleep, and beg you will take care
    And make no further noise, till you discover
The secret cavern of this lurking treasure—
And when 't is found, let me, too, have that pleasure.

CLIV

'And now, Hidalgo! now that you have thrown
    Doubt upon me, confusion over all,
Pray have the courtesy to make it known
    Who is the man you search for? how d' ye call
Him? what's his lineage? let him but be shown—
    I hope he's young and handsome—is he tall?
Tell me—and be assured, that since you stain
My honour thus, it shall not be in vain.

CLV

'At least, perhaps, he has not sixty years,
    At that age he would be too old for slaughter,
Or for so young a husband's jealous fears—
    (Antonia! let me have a glass of water.)
I am ashamed of having shed these tears,
    They are unworthy of my father's daughter;
My mother dreamed not in my natal hour,
That I should fall into a monster's power.

CLVI

'Perhaps 't is of Antonia you are jealous,
    You saw that she was sleeping by my side,
When you broke in upon us with your fellows:
    Look where you please—we've nothing, sir, to hide;
Only another time, I trust you 'll tell us,
    Or for the sake of decency abide
A moment at the door, that we may be
Dressed to receive so much good company.

CLVII

'And now, sir, I have done, and say no more;
    The little I have said may serve to show
The guileless heart in silence may grieve o'er
    The wrongs to whose exposure it is slow:—
I leave you to your conscience as before,
    'T will one day ask you *why* you used me so?
God grant you feel not then the bitterest grief!—
Antonia! where's my pocket-handkerchief?'

CLVIII

She ceased, and turned upon her pillow; pale
    She lay, her dark eyes flashing through their tears,
Like skies that rain and lighten; as a veil,
    Waved and o'ershading her wan cheek, appears
Her streaming hair; the black curls strive, but fail
    To hide the glossy shoulder, which uprears
Its snow through all;—her soft lips lie apart,
And louder than her breathing beats her heart.

CLIX

The Senhor Don Alfonso stood confused;
    Antonia bustled round the ransacked room,
And, turning up her nose, with looks abused
    Her master, and his myrmidons, of whom
Not one, except the attorney, was amused;
    He, like Achates, faithful to the tomb,
So there were quarrels, cared not for the cause,
Knowing they must be settled by the laws.

CLX

With prying snub-nose, and small eyes, he stood,
    Following Antonia's motions here and there,
With much suspicion in his attitude;
    For reputations he had little care;
So that a suit or action were made good,
    Small pity had he for the young and fair,
And ne'er believed in negatives, till these
Were proved by competent false witnesses.

CLXI

But Don Alfonso stood with downcast looks,
   And, truth to say, he made a foolish figure;
When, after searching in five hundred nooks,
   And treating a young wife with so much rigour,
He gained no point, except some self-rebukes,
   Added to those his lady with such vigour
Had poured upon him for the last half-hour,
Quick, thick, and heavy—as a thunder-shower.

CLXII

At first he tried to hammer an excuse,
   To which the sole reply was tears, and sobs,
And indications of hysterics, whose
   Prologue is always certain throes, and throbs,
Gasps, and whatever else the owners choose;
   Alfonso saw his wife, and thought of Job's;
He saw too, in perspective, her relations,
And then he tried to muster all his patience.

CLXIII

He stood in act to speak, or rather stammer,
   But sage Antonia cut him short before
The anvil of his speech received the hammer,
   With 'Pray, sir, leave the room, and say no more,
Or madam dies.'—Alfonso muttered, 'D—n her,'
   But nothing else, the time of words was o'er;
He cast a rueful look or two, and did,
He knew not wherefore, that which he was bid.

CLXIV

With him retired his '*posse comitatus*,'
   The attorney last, who lingered near the door
Reluctantly, still tarrying there as late as
   Antonia let him—not a little sore
At this most strange and unexplained '*hiatus*'
   In Don Alfonso's facts, which just now wore
An awkward look; as he revolved the case,
The door was fastened in his legal face.

CLXV

No sooner was it bolted, than—Oh Shame!
  Oh Sin! Oh Sorrow! and Oh Womankind!
How can you do such things and keep your fame,
  Unless this world, and t' other too, be blind?
Nothing so dear as an unfilched good name!
  But to proceed—for there is more behind:
With much heartfelt reluctance be it said,
Young Juan slipped, half-smothered, from the bed.

CLXVI

He had been hid—I don't pretend to say
  How, nor can I indeed describe the where—
Young, slender, and packed easily, he lay,
  No doubt, in little compass, round or square;
But pity him I neither must nor may
  His suffocation by that pretty pair;
'T were better, sure, to die so, than be shut
With maudlin Clarence in his Malmsey butt.

CLXVII

And, secondly, I pity not, because
  He had no business to commit a sin,
Forbid by heavenly, fined by human laws;—
  At least 't was rather early to begin,
But at sixteen the conscience rarely gnaws
  So much as when we call our old debts in
At sixty years, and draw the accompts of evil,
And find a deuced balance with the Devil.

CLXVIII

Of his position I can give no notion:
  'T is written in the Hebrew Chronicle,
How the physicians, leaving pill and potion,
  Prescribed, by way of blister, a young belle,
When old King David's blood grew dull in motion,
  And that the medicine answered very well;
Perhaps 't was in a different way applied,
For David lived, but Juan nearly died.

CLXIX

What 's to be done? Alfonso will be back
  The moment he has sent his fools away.
Antonia's skill was put upon the rack,
  But no device could be brought into play—
And how to parry the renewed attack?
  Besides, it wanted but few hours of day:
Antonia puzzled; Julia did not speak,
But pressed her bloodless lip to Juan's cheek.

CLXX

He turned his lip to hers, and with his hand
  Called back the tangles of her wandering hair;
Even then their love they could not all command,
  And half forgot their danger and despair:
Antonia's patience now was at a stand—
  'Come, come, 't is no time now for fooling there,'
She whispered, in great wrath—'I must deposit
This pretty gentleman within the closet:

CLXXI

'Pray, keep your nonsense for some luckier night—
  Who can have put my master in this mood?
What will become on 't—I'm in such a fright,
  The Devil 's in the urchin, and no good—
Is this a time for giggling? this a plight?
  Why don't you know that it may end in blood?
You'll lose your life, and I shall lose my place,
My mistress all, for that half-girlish face.

CLXXII

'Had it but been for a stout cavalier
  Of twenty-five or thirty—(come, make haste)
But for a child, what piece of work is here!
  I really, madam, wonder at your taste—
(Come, sir, get in)—my master must be near:
  There, for the present, at the least, he's fast,
And if we can but till the morning keep
Our counsel—(Juan, mind, you must not sleep.)'

CLXXIII

Now, Don Alfonso entering, but alone,
  Closed the oration of the trusty maid:
She loitered, and he told her to be gone,
  An order somewhat sullenly obeyed;
However, present remedy was none,
  And no great good seemed answered if she staid:
Regarding both with slow and sidelong view,
She snuffed the candle, curtsied, and withdrew.

CLXXIV

Alfonso paused a minute—then begun
  Some strange excuses for his late proceeding;
He would not justify what he had done,
  To say the best, it was extreme ill-breeding;
But there were ample reasons for it, none
  Of which he specified in this his pleading:
His speech was a fine sample, on the whole,
Of rhetoric, which the learned call '*rigmarole*.'

CLXXV

Julia said nought; though all the while there rose
  A ready answer, which at once enables
A matron, who her husband's foible knows,
  By a few timely words to turn the tables,
Which, if it does not silence, still must pose,—
  Even if it should comprise a pack of fables;
'T is to retort with firmness, and when he
Suspects with *one*, do you reproach with *three*.

CLXXVI

Julia, in fact, had tolerable grounds,—
  Alfonso's loves with Inez were well known;
But whether 't was that one's own guilt confounds—
  But that can't be, as has been often shown,
A lady with apologies abounds;—
  It might be that her silence sprang alone
From delicacy to Don Juan's ear,
To whom she knew his mother's fame was dear.

CLXXVII

There might be one more motive, which makes two;
  Alfonso ne'er to Juan had alluded,—
Mentioned his jealousy, but never who
  Had been the happy lover, he concluded,
Concealed amongst his premises; 't is true,
  His mind the more o'er this its mystery brooded;
To speak of Inez now were, one may say,
Like throwing Juan in Alfonso's way.

CLXXVIII

A hint, in tender cases, is enough;
  Silence is best: besides, there is a *tact*—
(That modern phrase appears to me sad stuff,
  But it will serve to keep my verse compact)—
Which keeps, when pushed by questions rather rough,
  A lady always distant from the fact:
The charming creatures lie with such a grace,
There 's nothing so becoming to the face.

CLXXIX

They blush, and we believe them; at least I
  Have always done so; 't is of no great use,
In any case, attempting a reply,
  For then their eloquence grows quite profuse;
And when at length they 're out of breath, they sigh,
  And cast their languid eyes down, and let loose
A tear or two, and then we make it up;
And then—and then—and then—sit down and sup.

CLXXX

Alfonso closed his speech, and begged her pardon,
  Which Julia half withheld, and then half granted,
And laid conditions he thought very hard on,
  Denying several little things he wanted:
He stood like Adam lingering near his garden,
  With useless penitence perplexed and haunted;
Beseeching she no further would refuse,
When, lo! he stumbled o'er a pair of shoes.

CLXXXI

A pair of shoes!—what then? not much, if they
    Are such as fit with ladies' feet, but these
(No one can tell how much I grieve to say)
    Were masculine; to see them, and to seize,
Was but a moment's act.—Ah! well-a-day!
    My teeth begin to chatter, my veins freeze!
Alfonso first examined well their fashion,
And then flew out into another passion.

CLXXXII

He left the room for his relinquished sword,
    And Julia instant to the closet flew.
'Fly, Juan, fly! for Heaven's sake—not a word—
    The door is open—you may yet slip through
The passage you so often have explored—
    Here is the garden-key—Fly—fly—Adieu!
Haste—haste! I hear Alfonso's hurrying feet—
Day has not broke—there 's no one in the street.'

CLXXXIII

None can say that this was not good advice,
    The only mischief was, it came too late;
Of all experience 't is the usual price,
    A sort of income-tax laid on by fate:
Juan had reached the room-door in a trice,
    And might have done so by the garden-gate,
But met Alfonso in his dressing-gown,
Who threatened death—so Juan knocked him down.

CLXXXIV

Dire was the scuffle, and out went the light;
    Antonia cried out 'Rape!' and Julia 'Fire!'
But not a servant stirred to aid the fight.
    Alfonso, pommelled to his heart's desire,
Swore lustily he'd be revenged this night;
    And Juan, too, blasphemed an octave higher;
His blood was up: though young, he was a Tartar,
And not at all disposed to prove a martyr.

CLXXXV

Alfonso's sword had dropped ere he could draw it,
  And they continued battling hand to hand,
For Juan very luckily ne'er saw it;
  His temper not being under great command,
If at that moment he had chanced to claw it,
  Alfonso's days had not been in the land
Much longer.—Think of husbands', lovers' lives!
And how ye may be doubly widows—wives!

CLXXXVI

Alfonso grappled to detain the foe,
  And Juan throttled him to get away,
And blood ('t was from the nose) began to flow;
  At last, as they more faintly wrestling lay,
Juan contrived to give an awkward blow,
  And then his only garment quite gave way;
He fled, like Joseph, leaving it; but there,
I doubt, all likeness ends between the pair.

CLXXXVII

Lights came at length, and men, and maids, who found
  An awkward spectacle their eyes before;
Antonia in hysterics, Julia swooned,
  Alfonso leaning, breathless by the door;
Some half-torn drapery scattered on the ground,
  Some blood, and several footsteps, but no more:
Juan the gate gained, turned the key about,
And liking not the inside, locked the out.

CLXXXVIII

Here ends this canto.—Need I sing, or say,
  How Juan, naked, favoured by the night,
Who favours what she should not, found his way,
  And reached his home in an unseemly plight?
The pleasant scandal which arose next day,
  The nine days' wonder which was brought to light,
And how Alfonso sued for a divorce,
Were in the English newspapers, of course.

CLXXXIX

If you would like to see the whole proceedings,
　The depositions, and the Cause at full,
The names of all the witnesses, the pleadings
　Of Counsel to nonsuit, or to annul,
There's more than one edition, and the readings
　Are various, but they none of them are dull :·
The best is that in short-hand ta'en by Gurney,
Who to Madrid on purpose made a journey.

CXC

But Donna Inez, to divert the train
　Of one of the most circulating scandals
That had for centuries been known in Spain,
　At least since the retirement of the Vandals,
First vowed (and never had she vowed in vain)
　To Virgin Mary several pounds of candles ;
And then, by the advice of some old ladies,
She sent her son to be shipped off from Cadiz.

CXCI

She had resolved that he should travel through
　All European climes, by land or sea,
To mend his former morals, and get new,
　Especially in France and Italy—
(At least this is the thing most people do.)
　Julia was sent into a convent—she
Grieved—but, perhaps, her feelings may be better
Shown in the following copy of her Letter :—

CXCII

'They tell me 't is decided you depart :
　'T is wise—'t is well, but not the less a pain ;
I have no further claim on your young heart,
　Mine is the victim, and would be again :
To love too much has been the only art
　I used ;—I write in haste, and if a stain
Be on this sheet, 't is not what it appears ;
My eyeballs burn and throb, but have no tears.

CXCIII

'I loved, I love you, for this love have lost
   State, station, Heaven, Mankind's, my own esteem,
And yet can not regret what it hath cost,
   So dear is still the memory of that dream;
Yet, if I name my guilt, 't is not to boast,
   None can deem harshlier of me than I deem:
I trace this scrawl because I cannot rest—
I've nothing to reproach, or to request.

CXCIV

'Man's love is of man's life a thing apart,
   'T is Woman's whole existence; Man may range
The Court, Camp, Church, the Vessel, and the Mart;
   Sword, Gown, Gain, Glory offer, in exchange
Pride, Fame, Ambition, to fill up his heart,
   And few there are whom these can not estrange;
Men have all these resources, We but one—
To love again, and be again undone.

CXCV

'You will proceed in pleasure, and in pride,
   Beloved and loving many; all is o'er
For me on earth, except some years to hide
   My shame and sorrow deep in my heart's core:
These I could bear, but cannot cast aside
   The passion which still rages as before,—
And so farewell—forgive me, love me—No,
That word is idle now—but let it go.

CXCVI

'My breast has been all weakness, is so yet;
   But still I think I can collect my mind;
My blood still rushes where my spirit's set,
   As roll the waves before the settled wind;
My heart is feminine, nor can forget—
   To all, except one image, madly blind;
So shakes the needle, and so stands the pole,
As vibrates my fond heart to my fixed soul.

CXCVII

'I have no more to say, but linger still,
    And dare not set my seal upon this sheet,
And yet I may as well the task fulfil,
    My misery can scarce be more complete;
I had not lived till now, could sorrow kill;
    Death shuns the wretch who fain the blow would meet,
And I must even survive this last adieu,
And bear with life, to love and pray for you!'

CXCVIII

This note was written upon gilt-edged paper
    With a neat little crow-quill, slight and new;
Her small white hand could hardly reach the taper,
    It trembled as magnetic needles do,
And yet she did not let one tear escape her;
    The seal a sun-flower; '*Elle vous suit partout,*'
The motto cut upon a white cornelian;
The wax was superfine, its hue vermilion.

CXCIX

This was Don Juan's earliest scrape; but whether
    I shall proceed with his adventures is
Dependent on the public altogether;
    We'll see, however, what they say to this:
Their favour in an author's cap 's a feather,
    And no great mischief 's done by their caprice;
And if their approbation we experience,
Perhaps they'll have some more about a year hence.

CC

My poem 's epic, and is meant to be
    Divided in twelve books; each book containing,
With Love, and War, a heavy gale at sea,
    A list of ships, and captains, and kings reigning,
New characters; the episodes are three:
    A panoramic view of Hell 's in training,
After the style of Virgil and of Homer,
So that my name of Epic's no misnomer.

K

CCI

All these things will be specified in time,
    With strict regard to Aristotle's rules,
The *Vade Mecum* of the true sublime,
    Which makes so many poets, and some fools:
Prose poets like blank-verse, I 'm fond of rhyme,
    Good workmen never quarrel with their tools;
I 've got new mythological machinery,
And very handsome supernatural scenery.

CCII

There 's only one slight difference between
    Me and my epic brethren gone before,
And here the advantage is my own, I ween,
    (Not that I have not several merits more,
But this will more peculiarly be seen);
    They so embellish, that 't is quite a bore
Their labyrinth of fables to thread through,
Whereas this story 's actually true.

CCIII

If any person doubt it, I appeal
    To History, Tradition, and to Facts,
To newspapers, whose truth all know and feel,
    To plays in five, and operas in three acts;
All these confirm my statement a good deal,
    But that which more completely faith exacts
Is, that myself, and several now in Seville,
Saw Juan's last elopement with the Devil.

CCIV

If ever I should condescend to prose,
    I 'll write poetical commandments, which
Shall supersede beyond all doubt all those
    That went before; in these I shall enrich
My text with many things that no one knows,
    And carry precept to the highest pitch:
I 'll call the work 'Longinus o'er a Bottle,
Or, Every Poet his *own* Aristotle.'

CCV

Thou shalt believe in Milton, Dryden, Pope;
   Thou shalt not set up Wordsworth, Coleridge, Southey;
Because the first is crazed beyond all hope,
   The second drunk, the third so quaint and mouthy:
With Crabbe it may be difficult to cope,
   And Campbell's Hippocrene is somewhat drouthy:
Thou shalt not steal from Samuel Rogers, nor
Commit—flirtation with the muse of Moore.

CCVI

Thou shalt not covet Mr. Sotheby's Muse,
   His Pegasus, nor anything that's his;
Thou shalt not bear false witness like 'the Blues'—
   (There's *one*, at least, is very fond of this);
Thou shalt not write, in short, but what I choose:
   This is true criticism, and you may kiss—
Exactly as you please, or not,—the rod;
But if you don't, I'll lay it on, by G—d!

CCVII

If any person should presume to assert
   This story is not moral, first, I pray,
That they will not cry out before they're hurt,
   Then that they'll read it o'er again, and say
(But, doubtless, nobody will be so pert),
   That this is not a moral tale, though gay:
Besides, in Canto Twelfth, I mean to show
The very place where wicked people go.

CCVIII

If, after all, there should be some so blind
   To their own good this warning to despise,
Led by some tortuosity of mind,
   Not to believe my verse and their own eyes,
And cry that they 'the moral cannot find,'
   I tell him, if a clergyman, he lies;
Should captains the remark, or critics, make,
They also lie too—under a mistake.

CCIX

The public approbation I expect,
    And beg they 'll take my word about the moral,
Which I with their amusement will connect
    (So children cutting teeth receive a coral);
Meantime they 'll doubtless please to recollect
    My epical pretensions to the laurel:
For fear some prudish readers should grow skittish,
I 've bribed my Grandmother's Review—the British.

CCX

I sent it in a letter to the Editor,
    Who thanked me duly by return of post—
I 'm for a handsome article his creditor;
    Yet, if my gentle Muse he please to roast,
And break a promise after having made it her,
    Denying the receipt of what it cost,
And smear his page with gall instead of honey,
All I can say is—that he had the money.

CCXI

I think that with this holy *new* alliance
    I may ensure the public, and defy
All other magazines of art or science,
    Daily, or monthly, or three monthly; I
Have not essayed to multiply their clients,
    Because they tell me 't were in vain to try,
And that the Edinburgh Review and Quarterly
Treat a dissenting author very martyrly.

CCXII

'*Non ego hoc ferrem calidus juventâ*
    Consule Planco,' Horace said, and so
Say I; by which quotation there is meant a
    Hint that some six or seven good years ago
(Long ere I dreamt of dating from the Brenta)
    I was most ready to return a blow,
And would not brook at all this sort of thing
In my hot youth—when George the Third was King.

CCXIII

But now at thirty years my hair is grey—
   (I wonder what it will be like at forty?
I thought of a peruke the other day—)
   My heart is not much greener; and, in short, I
Have squandered my whole summer while 't was May,
   And feel no more the spirit to retort; I
Have spent my life, both interest and principal,
And deem not, what I deemed—my soul invincible.

CCXIV

No more—no more—Oh! never more on me
   The freshness of the heart can fall like dew,
Which out of all the lovely things we see
   Extracts emotions beautiful and new,
Hived in our bosoms like the bag o' the bee.
   Think'st thou the honey with those objects grew?
Alas! 't was not in them, but in thy power
To double even the sweetness of a flower.

CCXV

No more—no more—Oh! never more, my heart,
   Canst thou be my sole world, my universe!
Once all in all, but now a thing apart,
   Thou canst not be my blessing or my curse:
The illusion's gone for ever, and thou art
   Insensible, I trust, but none the worse,
And in thy stead I 've got a deal of judgment,
Though Heaven knows how it ever found a lodgment.

CCXVI

My days of love are over; me no more
   The charms of maid, wife, and still less of widow,
Can make the fool of which they made before,—
   In short, I must not lead the life I did do;
The credulous hope of mutual minds is o'er,
   The copious use of claret is forbid too,
So for a good old-gentlemanly vice,
I think I must take up with avarice.

CCXVII

Ambition was my idol, which was broken
    Before the shrines of Sorrow, and of Pleasure;
And the two last have left me many a token
    O'er which reflection may be made at leisure:
Now, like Friar Bacon's Brazen Head, I 've spoken,
    'Time is, Time was, Time 's past:'—a chymic treasure
Is glittering Youth, which I have spent betimes—
My heart in passion, and my head on rhymes.

CCXVIII

What is the end of fame? 't is but to fill
    A certain portion of uncertain paper:
Some liken it to climbing up a hill,
    Whose summit, like all hills, is lost in vapour;
For this men write, speak, preach, and heroes kill,
    And bards burn what they call their 'midnight taper,'
To have, when the original is dust,
A name, a wretched picture and worse bust.

CCXIX

What are the hopes of man? Old Egypt's King
    Cheops erected the first Pyramid
And largest, thinking it was just the thing
    To keep his memory whole, and mummy hid;
But somebody or other rummaging,
    Burglariously broke his coffin's lid:
Let not a monument give you or me hopes,
Since not a pinch of dust remains of Cheops.

CCXX

But I, being fond of true philosophy,
    Say very often to myself, 'Alas!
All things that have been born were born to die,
    And flesh (which Death mows down to hay) is grass;
You 've passed your youth not so unpleasantly,
    And if you had it o'er again—'t would pass—
So thank your stars that matters are no worse,
And read your Bible, Sir, and mind your purse.'

CCXXI

But for the present, gentle reader! and
   Still gentler purchaser! the Bard—that's I—
Must, with permission, shake you by the hand,
   And so—'your humble servant, and Good-bye!'
We meet again, if we should understand
   Each other; and if not, I shall not try
Your patience further than by this short sample—
'T were well if others followed my example.

CCXXII

'Go, little Book, from this my solitude!
   I cast thee on the waters—go thy ways!
And if—as I believe, thy vein be good,
   The World will find thee after many days.'
When Southey 's read, and Wordsworth understood,
   I can't help putting in my claim to praise—
The four first rhymes are Southey's every line:
For God's sake, reader! take them not for mine.

CANTO THE SECOND

I

Oh ye! who teach the ingenuous youth of nations,
   Holland, France, England, Germany, or Spain,
I pray ye flog them upon all occasions—
   It mends their morals, never mind the pain:
The best of mothers and of educations
   In Juan's case were but employed in vain,
Since, in a way that's rather of the oddest, he
Became divested of his native modesty.

II

Had he but been placed at a public school
   In the third form, or even in the fourth,
His daily task had kept his fancy cool,
   At least, had he been nurtured in the North;
Spain may prove an exception to the rule,

But then exceptions always prove its worth—
A lad of sixteen causing a divorce
Puzzled his tutors very much, of course.

III

I can't say that it puzzles me at all,
　　If all things be considered : first, there was
His lady-mother, mathematical,
　　A——never mind ;—his tutor, an old ass ;
A pretty woman—(that 's quite natural,
　　Or else the thing had hardly come to pass)
A husband rather old, not much in unity
With his young wife—a time, and opportunity.

IV

Well—well ; the World must turn upon its axis,
　　And all Mankind turn with it, heads or tails,
And live and die, make love and pay our taxes,
　　And as the veering wind shifts, shift our sails ;
The King commands us, and the Doctor quacks us,
　　The Priest instructs, and so our life exhales,
A little breath, love, wine, ambition, fame,
Fighting, devotion, dust,—perhaps a name.

V

I said that Juan had been sent to Cadiz—
　　A pretty town, I recollect it well—
'T is there the mart of the colonial trade is,
　　(Or was, before Peru learned to rebel),
And such sweet girls!—I mean, such graceful ladies,
　　Their very walk would make your bosom swell ;
I can't describe it, though so much it strike,
Nor liken it—I never saw the like :

VI

An Arab horse, a stately stag, a barb
　　New broke, a camelopard, a gazelle,

No—none of these will do;—and then their garb,
    Their veil and petticoat—Alas! to dwell
Upon such things would very near absorb
    A canto—then their feet and ankles,—well,
Thank Heaven I've got no metaphor quite ready,
(And so, my sober Muse—come, let's be steady—

VII

Chaste Muse!—well,—if you must, you must)—the veil
    Thrown back a moment with the glancing hand,
While the o'erpowering eye, that turns you pale,
    Flashes into the heart:—All sunny land
Of Love! when I forget you, may I fail
    To——say my prayers—but never was there planned
A dress through which the eyes give such a volley,
Excepting the Venetian Fazzioli.

VIII

But to our tale: the Donna Inez sent
    Her son to Cadiz only to embark;
To stay there had not answered her intent,
    But why?—we leave the reader in the dark—
'T was for a voyage the young man was meant,
    As if a Spanish ship were Noah's ark,
To wean him from the wickedness of earth,
And send him like a Dove of Promise forth.

IX

Don Juan bade his valet pack his things
    According to directions, then received
A lecture and some money: for four springs
    He was to travel; and though Inez grieved
(As every kind of parting has its stings),
    She hoped he would improve—perhaps believed:
A letter, too, she gave (he never read it)
Of good advice—and two or three of credit.

X

In the mean time, to pass her hours away,
    Brave Inez now set up a Sunday school
For naughty children, who would rather play
    (Like truant rogues) the devil, or the fool;
Infants of three years old were taught that day,
    Dunces were whipped, or set upon a stool:
The great success of Juan's education
Spurred her to teach another generation.

XI

Juan embarked—the ship got under way,
    The wind was fair, the water passing rough;
A devil of a sea rolls in that bay,
    As I, who 've crossed it oft, know well enough;
And, standing on the deck, the dashing spray
    Flies in one's face, and makes it weather-tough:
And there he stood to take, and take again,
His first—perhaps his last—farewell of Spain.

XII

I can't but say it is an awkward sight
    To see one's native land receding through
The growing waters; it unmans one quite,
    Especially when life is rather new:
I recollect Great Britain's coast looks white,
    But almost every other country's blue,
When gazing on them, mystified by distance,
We enter on our nautical existence.

XIII

So Juan stood, bewildered on the deck:
    The wind sung, cordage strained, and sailors swore,
And the ship creaked, the town became a speck,
    From which away so fair and fast they bore.
The best of remedies is a beef-steak
    Against sea-sickness: try it, Sir, before
You sneer, and I assure you this is true,
For I have found it answer—so may you.

XIV

Don Juan stood, and, gazing from the stern,
  Beheld his native Spain receding far:
First partings form a lesson hard to learn,
  Even nations feel this when they go to war;
There is a sort of unexpressed concern,
  A kind of shock that sets one's heart ajar,
At leaving even the most unpleasant people
And places—one keeps looking at the steeple.

XV

But Juan had got many things to leave,
  His mother, and a mistress, and no wife,
So that he had much better cause to grieve
  Than many persons more advanced in life:
And if we now and then a sigh must heave
  At quitting even those we quit in strife,
No doubt we weep for those the heart endears—
That is, till deeper griefs congeal our tears.

XVI

So Juan wept, as wept the captive Jews
  By Babel's waters, still remembering Sion:
I'd weep,—but mine is not a weeping Muse,
  And such light griefs are not a thing to die on;
Young men should travel, if but to amuse
  Themselves; and the next time their servants tie on
Behind their carriages their new portmanteau,
Perhaps it may be lined with this my canto.

XVII

And Juan wept, and much he sighed and thought,
  While his salt tears dropped into the salt sea,
'Sweets to the sweet;' (I like so much to quote;
  You must excuse this extract,—'t is where she,
The Queen of Denmark, for Ophelia brought
  Flowers to the grave;) and, sobbing, often, he
Reflected on his present situation,
And seriously resolved on reformation.

XVIII

'Farewell, my Spain! a long farewell!' he cried,
　　'Perhaps I may revisit thee no more,
But die, as many an exiled heart hath died,
　　Of its own thirst to see again thy shore:
Farewell, where Guadalquivir's waters glide!
　　Farewell, my mother! and, since all is o'er,
Farewell, too, dearest Julia!—(here he drew
Her letter out again, and read it through.)

XIX

'And oh! if e'er I should forget, I swear—
　　But that's impossible, and cannot be—
Sooner shall this blue Ocean melt to air,
　　Sooner shall Earth resolve itself to sea,
Than I resign thine image, oh, my fair!
　　Or think of anything, excepting thee;
A mind diseased no remedy can physic—
(Here the ship gave a lurch, and he grew sea-sick.)

XX

'Sooner shall Heaven kiss earth—(here he fell sicker)
　　Oh, Julia! what is every other woe?—
(For God's sake let me have a glass of liquor;
　　Pedro, Battista, help me down below.)
Julia, my love!—(you rascal, Pedro, quicker)—
　　Oh, Julia!—(this curst vessel pitches so)—
Belovéd Julia, hear me still beseeching!'
(Here he grew inarticulate with retching.)

XXI

He felt that chilling heaviness of heart,
　　Or rather stomach, which, alas! attends,
Beyond the best apothecary's art,
　　The loss of Love, the treachery of friends,
Or death of those we dote on, when a part
　　Of us dies with them as each fond hope ends:
No doubt he would have been much more pathetic,
But the sea acted as a strong emetic.

XXII

Love's a capricious power: I 've known it hold
    Out through a fever caused by its own heat,
But be much puzzled by a cough and cold,
    And find a quinsy very hard to treat;
Against all noble maladies he's bold,
    But vulgar illnesses don't like to meet,
Nor that a sneeze should interrupt his sigh,
Nor inflammation redden his blind eye.

XXIII

But worst of all is nausea, or a pain
    About the lower region of the bowels;
Love, who heroically breathes a vein,
    Shrinks from the application of hot towels,
And purgatives are dangerous to his reign,
    Sea-sickness death: his love was perfect, how else
Could Juan's passion, while the billows roar,
Resist his stomach, ne'er at sea before?

XXIV

The ship, called the most holy 'Trinidada,'
    Was steering duly for the port Leghorn;
For there the Spanish family Moncada
    Were settled long ere Juan's sire was born:
They were relations, and for them he had a
    Letter of introduction, which the morn
Of his departure had been sent him by
His Spanish friends for those in Italy.

XXV

His suite consisted of three servants and
    A tutor, the licentiate Pedrillo,
Who several languages did understand,
    But now lay sick and speechless on his pillow,
And, rocking in his hammock, longed for land,
    His headache being increased by every billow;
And the waves oozing through the port-hole made
His berth a little damp, and him afraid.

XXVI

'T was not without some reason, for the wind
    Increased at night, until it blew a gale;
And though 't was not much to a naval mind,
    Some landsmen would have looked a little pale,
For sailors are, in fact, a different kind:
    At sunset they began to take in sail,
    For the sky showed it would come on to blow,
And carry away, perhaps, a mast or so.

XXVII

At one o'clock the wind with sudden shift
    Threw the ship right into the trough of the sea,
Which struck her aft, and made an awkward rift,
    Started the stern-post, also shattered the
Whole of her stern-frame, and, ere she could lift
    Herself from out her present jeopardy,
    The rudder tore away: 't was time to sound
The pumps, and there were four feet water found.

XXVIII

One gang of people instantly was put
    Upon the pumps, and the remainder set
To get up part of the cargo, and what not;
    But they could not come at the leak as yet;
At last they did get at it really, but
    Still their salvation was an even bet:
    The water rushed through in a way quite puzzling,
While they thrust sheets, shirts, jackets, bales of muslin,

XXIX

Into the opening; but all such ingredients
    Would have been in vain, and they must have gone down,
Despite of all their efforts and expedients,
    But for the pumps: I 'm glad to make them known
To all the brother tars who may have need hence,
    For fifty tons of water were upthrown
    By them per hour, and they had all been undone,
But for the maker, Mr. Mann, of London.

XXX

As day advanced the weather seemed to abate,
    And then the leak they reckoned to reduce,
And keep the ship afloat, though three feet yet
    Kept two hand and one chain-pump still in use.
The wind blew fresh again: as it grew late
    A squall came on, and while some guns broke loose,
A gust—which all descriptive power transcends—
Laid with one blast the ship on her beam ends.

XXXI

There she lay, motionless, and seemed upset;
    The water left the hold, and washed the decks,
And made a scene men do not soon forget;
    For they remember battles, fires, and wrecks,
Or any other thing that brings regret,
    Or breaks their hopes, or hearts, or heads, or necks:
Thus drownings are much talked of by the divers,
And swimmers, who may chance to be survivors.

XXXII

Immediately the masts were cut away,
    Both main and mizen; first the mizen went,
The main-mast followed: but the ship still lay
    Like a mere log, and baffled our intent.
Foremast and bowsprit were cut down, and they
    Eased her at last (although we never meant
To part with all till every hope was blighted),
And then with violence the old ship righted.

XXXIII

It may be easily supposed, while this
    Was going on, some people were unquiet,
That passengers would find it much amiss
    To lose their lives, as well as spoil their diet;
That even the able seaman, deeming his
    Days nearly o'er, might be disposed to riot,
As upon such occasions tars will ask
For grog, and sometimes drink rum from the cask.

XXXIV

There 's nought, no doubt, so much the spirit calms
    As rum and true religion : thus it was,
Some plundered, some drank spirits, some sung psalms,
    The high wind made the treble, and as bass
The hoarse harsh waves kept time ; fright cured the qualms
    Of all the luckless landsmen's sea-sick maws :
Strange sounds of wailing, blasphemy, devotion,
Clamoured in chorus to the roaring Ocean.

XXXV

Perhaps more mischief had been done, but for
    Our Juan, who, with sense beyond his years,
Got to the spirit-room, and stood before
    It with a pair of pistols ; and their fears,
As if Death were more dreadful by his door
    Of fire than water, spite of oaths and tears,
Kept still aloof the crew, who, ere they sunk,
Thought it would be becoming to die drunk.

XXXVI

'Give us more grog,' they cried, 'for it will be
    All one an hour hence.' Juan answered, 'No!
'T is true that Death awaits both you and me,
    But let us die like men, not sink below
Like brutes :'—and thus his dangerous post kept he,
    And none liked to anticipate the blow ;
And even Pedrillo, his most reverend tutor,
Was for some rum a disappointed suitor.

XXXVII

The good old gentleman was quite aghast,
    And made a loud and pious lamentation ;
Repented all his sins, and made a last
    Irrevocable vow of reformation ;
Nothing should tempt him more (this peril past)
    To quit his academic occupation,
In cloisters of the classic Salamanca,
To follow Juan's wake, like Sancho Panca.

XXXVIII

But now there came a flash of hope once more;
　　Day broke, and the wind lulled: the masts were gone,
The leak increased; shoals round her, but no shore,
　　The vessel swam, yet still she held her own.
They tried the pumps again, and though, before,
　　Their desperate efforts seemed all useless grown,
A glimpse of sunshine set some hands to bale—
The stronger pumped, the weaker thrummed a sail.

XXXIX

Under the vessel's keel the sail was passed,
　　And for the moment it had some effect;
But with a leak, and not a stick of mast,
　　Nor rag of canvas, what could they expect?
But still 't is best to struggle to the last,
　　'T is never too late to be wholly wrecked:
And though 't is true that man can only die once,
'T is not so pleasant in the Gulf of Lyons.

XL

There winds and waves had hurled them, and from thence,
　　Without their will, they carried them away;
For they were forced with steering to dispense,
　　And never had as yet a quiet day
On which they might repose, or even commence
　　A jurymast or rudder, or could say
The ship would swim an hour, which, by good luck,
Still swam—though not exactly like a duck.

XLI

The wind, in fact, perhaps, was rather less,
　　But the ship laboured so, they scarce could hope
To weather out much longer; the distress
　　Was also great with which they had to cope
For want of water, and their solid mess
　　Was scant enough: in vain the telescope
Was used—nor sail nor shore appeared in sight,
Nought but the heavy sea, and coming night.

XLII

Again the weather threatened,—again blew
　　A gale, and in the fore and after hold
Water appeared; yet, though the people knew
　　All this, the most were patient, and some bold,
Until the chains and leathers were worn through
　　Of all our pumps:—a wreck complete she rolled,
At mercy of the waves, whose mercies are
Like human beings during civil war.

XLIII

Then came the carpenter, at last, with tears
　　In his rough eyes, and told the captain, he
Could do no more: he was a man in years,
　　And long had voyaged through many a stormy sea,
And if he wept at length, they were not fears
　　That made his eyelids as a woman's be,
But he, poor fellow, had a wife and children,—
Two things for dying people quite bewildering.

XLIV

The ship was evidently settling now
　　Fast by the head; and, all distinction gone,
Some went to prayers again, and made a vow
　　Of candles to their saints—but there were none
To pay them with; and some looked o'er the bow;
　　Some hoisted out the boats; and there was one
That begged Pedrillo for an absolution,
Who told him to be damned—in his confusion.

XLV

Some lashed them in their hammocks; some put on
　　Their best clothes, as if going to a fair;
Some cursed the day on which they saw the Sun,
　　And gnashed their teeth, and, howling, tore their hair;
And others went on as they had begun,
　　Getting the boats out, being well aware
That a tight boat will live in a rough sea,
Unless with breakers close beneath her lee.

XLVI

The worst of all was, that in their condition,
　Having been several days in great distress,
'T was difficult to get out such provision
　As now might render their long suffering less:
Men, even when dying, dislike inanition;
　Their stock was damaged by the weather's stress:
Two casks of biscuit, and a keg of butter,
Were all that could be thrown into the cutter.

XLVII

But in the long-boat they contrived to stow
　Some pounds of bread, though injured by the wet;
Water, a twenty-gallon cask or so;
　Six flasks of wine; and they contrived to get
A portion of their beef up from below,
　And with a piece of pork, moreover, met,
But scarce enough to serve them for a luncheon—
Then there was rum, eight gallons in a puncheon.

XLVIII

The other boats, the yawl and pinnace, had
　Been stove in the beginning of the gale;
And the long-boat's condition was but bad,
　As there were but two blankets for a sail,
And one oar for a mast, which a young lad
　Threw in by good luck over the ship's rail;
And two boats could not hold, far less be stored,
To save one half the people then on board.

XLIX

'T was twilight, and the sunless day went down
　Over the waste of waters; like a veil,
Which, if withdrawn, would but disclose the frown
　Of one whose hate is masked but to assail.
Thus to their hopeless eyes the night was shown,
　And grimly darkled o'er the faces pale,
And the dim desolate deep: twelve days had Fear
Been their familiar, and now Death was here.

L

Some trial had been making at a raft,
   With little hope in such a rolling sea,
A sort of thing at which one would have laughed,
   If any laughter at such times could be,
Unless with people who too much have quaffed,
   And have a kind of wild and horrid glee,
Half epileptical, and half hysterical :—
Their preservation would have been a miracle.

LI

At half-past eight o'clock, booms, hencoops, spars,
   And all things, for a chance, had been cast loose,
That still could keep afloat the struggling tars,
   For yet they strove, although of no great use :
There was no light in heaven but a few stars,
   The boats put off o'ercrowded with their crews ;
She gave a heel, and then a lurch to port,
And, going down head foremost—sunk, in short.

LII

Then rose from sea to sky the wild farewell—
   Then shrieked the timid, and stood still the brave,—
Then some leaped overboard with dreadful yell,
   As eager to anticipate their grave ;
And the sea yawned around her like a hell,
   And down she sucked with her the whirling wave,
Like one who grapples with his enemy,
And strives to strangle him before he die.

LIII

And first one universal shriek there rushed,
   Louder than the loud Ocean, like a crash
Of echoing thunder ; and then all was hushed,
   Save the wild wind and the remorseless dash
Of billows ; but at intervals there gushed,
   Accompanied by a convulsive splash,
A solitary shriek, the bubbling cry
Of some strong swimmer in his agony.

LIV

The boats, as stated, had got off before,
    And in them crowded several of the crew;
And yet their present hope was hardly more
    Than what it had been, for so strong it blew
There was slight chance of reaching any shore;
    And then they were too many, though so few—
Nine in the cutter, thirty in the boat,
Were counted in them when they got afloat.

LV

All the rest perished; near two hundred souls
    Had left their bodies; and what's worse, alas!
When over Catholics the Ocean rolls,
    They must wait several weeks before a mass
Takes off one peck of purgatorial coals,
    Because, till people know what 's come to pass,
They won't lay out their money on the dead—
It costs three francs for every mass that 's said.

LVI

Juan got into the long-boat, and there
    Contrived to help Pedrillo to a place;
It seemed as if they had exchanged their care,
    For Juan wore the magisterial face
Which courage gives, while poor Pedrillo's pair
    Of eyes were crying for their owner's case:
Battista, though, (a name called shortly Tita),
Was lost by getting at some aqua-vita.

LVII

Pedro, his valet, too, he tried to save,
    But the same cause, conducive to his loss,
Left him so drunk, he jumped into the wave,
    As o'er the cutter's edge he tried to cross,
And so he found a wine-and-watery grave;
    They could not rescue him although so close,
Because the sea ran higher every minute,
And for the boat—the crew kept crowding in it.

LVIII

A small old spaniel,—which had been Don José's,
    His father's, whom he loved, as ye may think,
For on such things the memory reposes
    With tenderness—stood howling on the brink,
Knowing, (dogs have such intellectual noses!)
    No doubt, the vessel was about to sink;
And Juan caught him up, and ere he stepped
Off threw him in, then after him he leaped.

LIX

He also stuffed his money where he could
    About his person, and Pedrillo's too,
Who let him do, in fact, whate'er he would,
    Not knowing what himself to say, or do,
As every rising wave his dread renewed;
    But Juan, trusting they might still get through,
And deeming there were remedies for any ill,
Thus re-embarked his tutor and his spaniel.

LX

'T was a rough night, and blew so stiffly yet,
    That the sail was becalmed between the seas,
Though on the wave's high top too much to set,
    They dared not take it in for all the breeze:
Each sea curled o'er the stern, and kept them wet,
    And made them bale without a moment's ease,
So that themselves as well as hopes were damped,
And the poor little cutter quickly swamped.

LXI

Nine souls more went in her: the long-boat still
    Kept above water, with an oar for mast,
Two blankets stitched together, answering ill
    Instead of sail, were to the oar made fast;
Though every wave rolled menacing to fill,
    And present peril all before surpassed,
They grieved for those who perished with the cutter,
And also for the biscuit-casks and butter,

LXII

The sun rose red and fiery, a sure sign
  Of the continuance of the gale : to run
Before the sea until it should grow fine,
  Was all that for the present could be done:
A few tea-spoonfuls of their rum and wine
  Were served out to the people, who begun
To faint, and damaged bread wet through the bags,
And most of them had little clothes but rags.

LXIII

They counted thirty, crowded in a space
  Which left scarce room for motion or exertion;
They did their best to modify their case,
  One half sate up, though numbed with the immersion,
While t' other half were laid down in their place,
  At watch and watch; thus, shivering like the tertian
Ague in its cold fit, they filled their boat,
With nothing but the sky for a great coat.

LXIV

'T is very certain the desire of life
  Prolongs it : this is obvious to physicians,
When patients, neither plagued with friends nor wife,
  Survive through very desperate conditions,
Because they still can hope, nor shines the knife
  Nor shears of Atropos before their visions:
Despair of all recovery spoils longevity,
And makes men's misery of alarming brevity.

LXV

'T is said that persons living on annuities
  Are longer lived than others,—God knows why,
Unless to plague the grantors,—yet so true it is,
  That some, I really think, *do* never die:
Of any creditors the worst a Jew it is,
  And *that's* their mode of furnishing supply:
In my young days they lent me cash that way,
Which I found very troublesome to pay.

LXVI

'T is thus with people in an open boat,
    They live upon the love of Life, and bear
More than can be believed, or even thought,
    And stand like rocks the tempest's wear and tear;
And hardship still has been the sailor's lot,
    Since Noah's ark went cruising here and there;
She had a curious crew as well as cargo,
Like the first old Greek privateer, the Argo.

LXVII

But man is a carnivorous production,
    And must have meals, at least one meal a day;
He cannot live, like woodcocks, upon suction,
    But, like the shark and tiger, must have prey;
Although his anatomical construction
    Bears vegetables, in a grumbling way,
Your labouring people think, beyond all question,
Beef, veal, and mutton, better for digestion.

LXVIII

And thus it was with this our hapless crew;
    For on the third day there came on a calm,
And though at first their strength it might renew,
    And lying on their weariness like balm,
Lulled them like turtles sleeping on the blue
    Of Ocean, when they woke they felt a qualm,
And fell all ravenously on their provision,
Instead of hoarding it with due precision.

LXIX

The consequence was easily foreseen—
    They ate up all they had, and drank their wine,
In spite of all remonstrances, and then
    On what, in fact, next day were they to dine?
They hoped the wind would rise, these foolish men!
    And carry them to shore; these hopes were fine,
But as they had but one oar, and that brittle,
It would have been more wise to save their victual.

LXX

The fourth day came, but not a breath of air,
   And Ocean slumbered like an unweaned child:
The fifth day, and their boat lay floating there,
   The sea and sky were blue, and clear, and mild—
With their one oar (I wish they had had a pair)
   What could they do? and Hunger's rage grew wild:
So Juan's spaniel, spite of his entreating,
Was killed, and portioned out for present eating.

LXXI

On the sixth day they fed upon his hide,
   And Juan, who had still refused, because
The creature was his father's dog that died,
   Now feeling all the vulture in his jaws,
With some remorse received (though first denied)
   As a great favour one of the fore-paws,
Which he divided with Pedrillo, who
Devoured it, longing for the other too.

LXXII

The seventh day, and no wind—the burning sun
   Blistered and scorched, and, stagnant on the sea,
They lay like carcasses; and hope was none,
   Save in the breeze that came not: savagely
They glared upon each other—all was done,
   Water, and wine, and food,—and you might see
The longings of the cannibal arise
(Although they spoke not) in their wolfish eyes.

LXXIII

At length one whispered his companion, who
   Whispered another, and thus it went round
And then into a hoarser murmur grew,
   An ominous, and wild, and desperate sound;
And when his comrade's thought each sufferer knew,
   'T was but his own, suppressed till now, he found:
And out they spoke of lots for flesh and blood,
And who should die to be his fellow's food.

LXXIV

But ere they came to this, they that day shared
    Some leathern caps, and what remained of shoes;
And then they looked around them, and despaired,
    And none to be the sacrifice would choose;
At length the lots were torn up, and prepared,
    But of materials that must shock the Muse—
Having no paper, for the want of better,
They took by force from Juan Julia's letter.

LXXV

The lots were made, and marked, and mixed, and handed,
    In silent horror, and their distribution
Lulled even the savage hunger which demanded,
    Like the Promethean vulture, this pollution.
None in particular had sought or planned it,
    'T was Nature gnawed them to this resolution,
By which none were permitted to be neuter—
And the lot fell on Juan's luckless tutor.

LXXVI

He but requested to be bled to death:
    The surgeon had his instruments, and bled
Pedrillo, and so gently ebbed his breath,
    You hardly could perceive when he was dead.
He died as born, a Catholic in faith,
    Like most in the belief in which they 're bred,
And first a little crucifix he kissed,
And then held out his jugular and wrist.

LXXVII

The surgeon, as there was no other fee,
    Had his first choice of morsels for his pains;
But being thirstiest at the moment, he
    Preferred a draught from the fast-flowing veins:
Part was divided, part thrown in the sea,
    And such things as the entrails and the brains
Regaled two sharks, who followed o'er the billow—
The sailors ate the rest of poor Pedrillo.

LXXVIII

The sailors ate him, all save three or four,
  Who were not quite so fond of animal food;
To these was added Juan, who, before
  Refusing his own spaniel, hardly could
Feel now his appetite increased much more;
  'T was not to be expected that he should,
Even in extremity of their disaster,
Dine with them on his pastor and his master.

LXXIX

'T was better that he did not; for, in fact,
  The consequence was awful in the extreme;
For they, who were most ravenous in the act,
  Went raging mad—Lord! how they did blaspheme!
And foam, and roll, with strange convulsions racked,
  Drinking salt-water like a mountain-stream,
Tearing, and grinning, howling, screeching, swearing,
And, with hyæna-laughter, died despairing.

LXXX

Their numbers were much thinned by this infliction,
  And all the rest were thin enough, Heaven knows;
And some of them had lost their recollection,
  Happier than they who still perceived their woes;
But others pondered on a new dissection,
  As if not warned sufficiently by those
Who had already perished, suffering madly,
For having used their appetites so sadly.

LXXXI

And next they thought upon the master's mate,
  As fattest; but he saved himself, because,
Besides being much averse from such a fate,
  There were some other reasons: the first was,
He had been rather indisposed of late;
  And—that which chiefly proved his saving clause—
Was a small present made to him at Cadiz,
By general subscription of the ladies.

LXXXII

Of poor Pedrillo something still remained,
    But was used sparingly,—some were afraid,
And others still their appetites constrained,
    Or but at times a little supper made;
All except Juan, who throughout abstained,
    Chewing a piece of bamboo, and some lead:
At length they caught two Boobies, and a Noddy,
And then they left off eating the dead body.

LXXXIII

And if Pedrillo's fate should shocking be,
    Remember Ugolino condescends
To eat the head of his arch-enemy
    The moment after he politely ends
His tale: if foes be food in Hell, at sea
    'T is surely fair to dine upon our friends,
When Shipwreck's short allowance grows too scanty,
Without being much more horrible than Dante.

LXXXIV

And the same night there fell a shower of rain,
    For which their mouths gaped, like the cracks of earth
When dried to summer dust; till taught by pain,
    Men really know not what good water 's worth;
If you had been in Turkey or in Spain,
    Or with a famished boat's-crew had your berth,
Or in the desert heard the camel's bell,
You 'd wish yourself where Truth is—in a well.

LXXXV

It poured down torrents, but they were no richer
    Until they found a ragged piece of sheet,
Which served them as a sort of spongy pitcher,
    And when they deemed its moisture was complete,
They wrung it out, and though a thirsty ditcher
    Might not have thought the scanty draught so sweet
As a full pot of porter, to their thinking
They ne'er till now had known the joys of drinking.

LXXXVI

And their baked lips, with many a bloody crack,
   Sucked in the moisture, which like nectar streamed;
Their throats were ovens, their swoln tongues were black,
   As the rich man's in Hell, who vainly screamed
To beg the beggar, who could not rain back
   A drop of dew, when every drop had seemed
To taste of Heaven—If this be true, indeed,
Some Christians have a comfortable creed.

LXXXVII

There were two fathers in this ghastly crew,
   And with them their two sons, of whom the one
Was more robust and hardy to the view,
   But he died early; and when he was gone,
His nearest messmate told his sire, who threw
   One glance at him, and said, 'Heaven's will be done!
I can do nothing,' and he saw him thrown
Into the deep without a tear or groan.

LXXXVIII

The other father had a weaklier child,
   Of a soft cheek, and aspect delicate;
But the boy bore up long, and with a mild
   And patient spirit held aloof his fate;
Little he said, and now and then he smiled,
   As if to win a part from off the weight
He saw increasing on his father's heart,
With the deep deadly thought, that they must part.

LXXXIX

And o'er him bent his sire, and never raised
   His eyes from off his face, but wiped the foam
From his pale lips, and ever on him gazed,
   And when the wished-for shower at length was come,
And the boy's eyes, which the dull film half glazed,
   Brightened, and for a moment seemed to roam,
He squeezed from out a rag some drops of rain
Into his dying child's mouth—but in vain.

XC

The boy expired—the father held the clay,
      And looked upon it long, and when at last
Death left no doubt, and the dead burthen lay
      Stiff on his heart, and pulse and hope were past,
He watched it wistfully, until away
      'T was borne by the rude wave wherein 't was cast;
Then he himself sunk down all dumb and shivering,
And gave no sign of life, save his limbs quivering.

XCI

Now overhead a rainbow, bursting through
      The scattering clouds, shone, spanning the dark sea,
Resting its bright base on the quivering blue;
      And all within its arch appeared to be
Clearer than that without, and its wide hue
      Waxed broad and waving, like a banner free,
Then changed like to a bow that's bent, and then
Forsook the dim eyes of these shipwrecked men.

XCII

It changed, of course; a heavenly Chameleon,
      The airy child of vapour and the sun,
Brought forth in purple, cradled in vermilion,
      Baptized in molten gold, and swathed in dun,
Glittering like crescents o'er a Turk's pavilion,
      And blending every colour into one,
Just like a black eye in a recent scuffle
(For sometimes we must box without the muffle).

XCIII

Our shipwrecked seamen thought it a good omen—
      It is as well to think so, now and then;
'T was an old custom of the Greek and Roman,
      And may become of great advantage when
Folks are discouraged; and most surely no men
      Had greater need to nerve themselves again
Than these, and so this rainbow looked like Hope—
Quite a celestial Kaleidoscope.

XCIV

About this time a beautiful white bird,
　　Webfooted, not unlike a dove in size
And plumage (probably it might have erred
　　Upon its course), passed oft before their eyes,
And tried to perch, although it saw and heard
　　The men within the boat, and in this guise
It came and went, and fluttered round them till
Night fell :—this seemed a better omen still.

XCV

But in this case I also must remark,
　　'T was well this bird of promise did not perch,
Because the tackle of our shattered bark
　　Was not so safe for roosting as a church ;
And had it been the dove from Noah's ark,
　　Returning there from her successful search,
Which in their way that moment chanced to fall,
They would have eat her, olive-branch and all.

XCVI

With twilight it again came on to blow,
　　But not with violence ; the stars shone out,
The boat made way ; yet now they were so low,
　　They knew not where or what they were about ;
Some fancied they saw land, and some said 'No!'
　　The frequent fog-banks gave them cause to doubt—
Some swore that they heard breakers, others guns,
And all mistook about the latter once.

XCVII

As morning broke, the light wind died away,
　　When he who had the watch sung out and swore,
If 't was not land that rose with the Sun's ray,
　　He wished that land he never might see more ;
And the rest rubbed their eyes and saw a bay,
　　Or thought they saw, and shaped their course for shore ;
For shore it was, and gradually grew
Distinct, and high, and palpable to view.

XCVIII

And then of these some part burst into tears,
　　And others, looking with a stupid stare,
Could not yet separate their hopes from fears,
　　And seemed as if they had no further care;
While a few prayed—(the first time for some years)—
　　And at the bottom of the boat three were
Asleep: they shook them by the hand and head,
And tried to awaken them, but found them dead.

XCIX

The day before, fast sleeping on the water,
　　They found a turtle of the hawk's-bill kind,
And by good fortune, gliding softly, caught her,
　　Which yielded a day's life, and to their mind
Proved even still a more nutritious matter,
　　Because it left encouragement behind:
They thought that in such perils, more than chance
Had sent them this for their deliverance.

C

The land appeared a high and rocky coast,
　　And higher grew the mountains as they drew,
Set by a current, toward it: they were lost
　　In various conjectures, for none knew
To what part of the earth they had been tost,
　　So changeable had been the winds that blew;
Some thought it was Mount Ætna, some the highlands
Of Candia, Cyprus, Rhodes, or other islands.

CI

Meantime the current, with a rising gale,
　　Still set them onwards to the welcome shore,
Like Charon's bark of spectres, dull and pale:
　　Their living freight was now reduced to four,
And three dead, whom their strength could not avail
　　To heave into the deep with those before,
Though the two sharks still followed them, and dashed
The spray into their faces as they splashed.

CII

Famine—despair—cold—thirst and heat, had done
   Their work on them by turns, and thinned them to
Such things a mother had not known her son
   Amidst the skeletons of that gaunt crew;
By night chilled, by day scorched, thus one by one
   They perished, until withered to these few,
But chiefly by a species of self-slaughter,
In washing down Pedrillo with salt water.

CIII

As they drew nigh the land, which now was seen
   Unequal in its aspect here and there,
They felt the freshness of its growing green,
   That waved in forest-tops, and smoothed the air,
And fell upon their glazed eyes like a screen
   From glistening waves, and skies so hot and bare—
Lovely seemed any object that should sweep
Away the vast—salt—dread—eternal Deep.

CIV

The shore looked wild, without a trace of man,
   And girt by formidable waves; but they
Were mad for land, and thus their course they ran,
   Though right ahead the roaring breakers lay:
A reef between them also now began
   To show its boiling surf and bounding spray,
But finding no place for their landing better,
They ran the boat for shore,—and overset her.

CV

But in his native stream, the Guadalquivir,
   Juan to lave his youthful limbs was wont;
And having learnt to swim in that sweet river,
   Had often turned the art to some account:
A better swimmer you could scarce see ever,
   He could, perhaps, have passed the Hellespont,
As once (a feat on which ourselves we prided)
Leander, Mr. Ekenhead, and I did.

L

CVI

So here, though faint, emaciated, and stark,
    He buoyed his boyish limbs, and strove to ply
With the quick wave, and gain, ere it was dark,
    The beach which lay before him, high and dry:
The greatest danger here was from a shark,
    That carried off his neighbour by the thigh;
As for the other two, they could not swim,
So nobody arrived on shore but him.

CVII

Nor yet had he arrived but for the oar,
    Which, providentially for him, was washed
Just as his feeble arms could strike no more,
    And the hard wave o'erwhelmed him as 't was dashed
Within his grasp; he clung to it, and sore
    The waters beat while he thereto was lashed;
At last, with swimming, wading, scrambling, he
Rolled on the beach, half-senseless, from the sea:

CVIII

There, breathless, with his digging nails he clung
    Fast to the sand, lest the returning wave,
From whose reluctant roar his life he wrung,
    Should suck him back to her insatiate grave:
And there he lay, full length, where he was flung,
    Before the entrance of a cliff-worn cave,
With just enough of life to feel its pain,
And deem that it was saved, perhaps, in vain.

CIX

With slow and staggering effort he arose,
    But sunk again upon his bleeding knee
And quivering hand; and then he looked for those
    Who long had been his mates upon the sea;
But none of them appeared to share his woes,
    Save one, a corpse, from out the famished three,
Who died two days before, and now had found
An unknown barren beach for burial ground.

CX

And as he gazed, his dizzy brain spun fast,
 And down he sunk; and as he sunk, the sand
Swam round and round, and all his senses passed:
 He fell upon his side, and his stretched hand
Drooped dripping on the oar (their jury-mast),
 And, like a withered lily, on the land
His slender frame and pallid aspect lay,
As fair a thing as e'er was formed of clay.

CXI

How long in his damp trance young Juan lay
 He knew not, for the earth was gone for him,
And Time had nothing more of night nor day
 For his congealing blood, and senses dim;
And how this heavy faintness passed away
 He knew not, till each painful pulse and limb,
And tingling vein, seemed throbbing back to life,
For Death, though vanquished, still retired with strife.

CXII

His eyes he opened, shut, again unclosed,
 For all was doubt and dizziness; he thought
He still was in the boat, and had but dozed,
 And felt again with his despair o'erwrought,
And wished it Death in which he had reposed,
 And then once more his feelings back were brought,
And slowly by his swimming eyes was seen
A lovely female face of seventeen.

CXIII

'T was bending close o'er his, and the small mouth
 Seemed almost prying into his for breath;
And chafing him, the soft warm hand of youth
 Recalled his answering spirits back from Death:
And, bathing his chill temples, tried to soothe
 Each pulse to animation, till beneath
Its gentle touch and trembling care, a sigh
To these kind efforts made a low reply.

CXIV

Then was the cordial poured, and mantle flung
    Around his scarce-clad limbs; and the fair arm
Raised higher the faint head which o'er it hung;
    And her transparent cheek, all pure and warm,
Pillowed his death-like forehead; then she wrung
    His dewy curls, long drenched by every storm;
And watched with eagerness each throb that drew
A sigh from his heaved bosom—and hers, too.

CXV

And lifting him with care into the cave,
    The gentle girl, and her attendant,—one
Young, yet her elder, and of brow less grave,
    And more robust of figure,—then begun
To kindle fire, and as the new flames gave
    Light to the rocks that roofed them, which the sun
Had never seen, the maid, or whatsoe'er
She was, appeared distinct, and tall, and fair.

CXVI

Her brow was overhung with coins of gold,
    That sparkled o'er the auburn of her hair—
Her clustering hair, whose longer locks were rolled
    In braids behind; and though her stature were
Even of the highest for a female mould,
    They nearly reached her heel; and in her air
There was a something which bespoke command,
As one who was a Lady in the land.

CXVII

Her hair, I said, was auburn; but her eyes
    Were black as Death, their lashes the same hue,
Of downcast length, in whose silk shadow lies
    Deepest attraction; for when to the view
Forth from its raven fringe the full glance flies,
    Ne'er with such force the swiftest arrow flew;
'T is as the snake late coiled, who pours his length,
And hurls at once his venom and his strength.

CXVIII

Her brow was white and low, her cheek's pure dye
　　Like twilight rosy still with the set sun;
Short upper lip—sweet lips! that make us sigh
　　Ever to have seen such; for she was one
Fit for the model of a statuary,
　　(A race of mere impostors, when all's done—
I 've seen much finer women, ripe and real,
Than all the nonsense of their stone ideal).

CXIX

I 'll tell you why I say so, for 't is just
　　One should not rail without a decent cause:
There was an Irish lady, to whose bust
　　I ne'er saw justice done, and yet she was
A frequent model; and if e'er she must
　　Yield to stern Time and Nature's wrinkling laws,
They will destroy a face which mortal thought
Ne'er compassed, nor less mortal chisel wrought.

CXX

And such was she, the lady of the cave:
　　Her dress was very different from the Spanish,
Simpler, and yet of colours not so grave;
　　For, as you know, the Spanish women banish
Bright hues when out of doors, and yet, while wave
　　Around them (what I hope will never vanish)
The basquiña and the mantilla, they
Seem at the same time mystical and gay.

CXXI

But with our damsel this was not the case:
　　Her dress was many-coloured, finely spun;
Her locks curled negligently round her face,
　　But through them gold and gems profusely shone:
Her girdle sparkled, and the richest lace
　　Flowed in her veil, and many a precious stone
Flashed on her little hand; but, what was shocking,
Her small snow feet had slippers, but no stocking.

CXXII

The other female's dress was not unlike,
　　But of inferior materials : she
Had not so many ornaments to strike,
　　Her hair had silver only, bound to be
Her dowry ; and her veil, in form alike,
　　Was coarser ; and her air, though firm, less free ;
Her hair was thicker, but less long ; her eyes
As black, but quicker, and of smaller size.

CXXIII

And these two tended him, and cheered him both
　　With food and raiment, and those soft attentions,
Which are—as I must own—of female growth,
　　And have ten thousand delicate inventions :
They made a most superior mess of broth,
　　A thing which poesy but seldom mentions,
But the best dish that e'er was cooked since Homer's
Achilles ordered dinner for new comers.

CXXIV

I'll tell you who they were, this female pair,
　　Lest they should seem Princesses in disguise ;
Besides, I hate all mystery, and that air
　　Of clap-trap, which your recent poets prize ;
And so, in short, the girls they really were
　　They shall appear before your curious eyes,
Mistress and maid ; the first was only daughter
Of an old man, who lived upon the water.

CXXV

A fisherman he had been in his youth,
　　And still a sort of fisherman was he ;
But other speculations were, in sooth,
　　Added to his connection with the sea,
Perhaps not so respectable, in truth :
　　A little smuggling, and some piracy,
Left him, at last, the sole of many masters
Of an ill-gotten million of piastres.

CXXVI

A fisher, therefore, was he,—though of men,
  Like Peter the Apostle, and he fished
For wandering merchant-vessels, now and then,
  And sometimes caught as many as he wished;
The cargoes he confiscated, and gain
  He sought in the slave-market too, and dished
Full many a morsel for that Turkish trade,
By which, no doubt, a good deal may be made.

CXXVII

He was a Greek, and on his isle had built
  (One of the wild and smaller Cyclades)
A very handsome house from out his guilt,
  And there he lived exceedingly at ease;
Heaven knows what cash he got, or blood he spilt,
  A sad old fellow was he, if you please;
But this I know, it was a spacious building,
Full of barbaric carving, paint, and gilding.

CXXVIII

He had an only daughter, called Haidée,
  The greatest heiress of the Eastern Isles;
Besides, so very beautiful was she,
  Her dowry was as nothing to her smiles:
Still in her teens, and like a lovely tree
  She grew to womanhood, and between whiles
Rejected several suitors, just to learn
How to accept a better in his turn.

CXXIX

And walking out upon the beach, below
  The cliff, towards sunset, on that day she found,
Insensible,—not dead, but nearly so,—
  Don Juan, almost famished, and half drowned;
But being naked, she was shocked, you know,
  Yet deemed herself in common pity bound,
As far as in her lay, 'to take him in,
A stranger' dying—with so white a skin.

CXXX

But taking him into her father's house
   Was not exactly the best way to save,
But like conveying to the cat the mouse,
   Or people in a trance into their grave;
Because the good old man had so much 'νοῦς,'
   Unlike the honest Arab thieves so brave,
He would have hospitably cured the stranger,
And sold him instantly when out of danger.

CXXXI

And therefore, with her maid, she thought it best
   (A virgin always on her maid relies)
To place him in the cave for present rest:
   And when, at last, he opened his black eyes,
Their charity increased about their guest;
   And their compassion grew to such a size,
It opened half the turnpike-gates to Heaven—
(St. Paul says, 't is the toll which must be given).

CXXXII

They made a fire,—but such a fire as they
   Upon the moment could contrive with such
Materials as were cast up round the bay,—
   Some broken planks, and oars, that to the touch
Were nearly tinder, since, so long they lay,
   A mast was almost crumbled to a crutch;
But, by God's grace, here wrecks were in such plenty,
That there was fuel to have furnished twenty.

CXXXIII

He had a bed of furs, and a pelisse,
   For Haidée stripped her sables off to make
His couch; and, that he might be more at ease,
   And warm, in case by chance he should awake,
They also gave a petticoat apiece,
   She and her maid,—and promised by daybreak
To pay him a fresh visit, with a dish
For breakfast, of eggs, coffee, bread, and fish.

CXXXIV

And thus they left him to his lone repose:
   Juan slept like a top, or like the dead,
Who sleep at last, perhaps (God only knows),
   Just for the present: and in his lulled head
Not even a vision of his former woes
   Throbbed in accurséd dreams, which sometimes spread
Unwelcome visions of our former years,
Till the eye, cheated, opens thick with tears.

CXXXV

Young Juan slept all dreamless:—but the maid,
   Who smoothed his pillow, as she left the den
Looked back upon him, and a moment stayed
   And turned, believing that he called again.
He slumbered; yet she thought, at least she said
   (The heart will slip, even as the tongue and pen),
He had pronounced her name—but she forgot
That at this moment Juan knew it not.

CXXXVI

And pensive to her father's house she went,
   Enjoining silence strict to Zoe, who
Better than her knew what, in fact, she meant,
   She being wiser by a year or two:
A year or two's an age when rightly spent,
   And Zoe spent hers, as most women do,
In gaining all that useful sort of knowledge
Which is acquired in Nature's good old college.

CXXXVII

The morn broke, and found Juan slumbering still
   Fast in his cave, and nothing clashed upon
His rest; the rushing of the neighbouring rill,
   And the young beams of the excluded Sun,
Troubled him not, and he might sleep his fill;
   And need he had of slumber yet, for none
Had suffered more—his hardships were comparative
To those related in my grand-dad's 'Narrative.'

CXXXVIII

Not so Haidée : she sadly tossed and tumbled,
    And started from her sleep, and, turning o'er,
Dreamed of a thousand wrecks, o'er which she stumbled,
    And handsome corpses strewed upon the shore ;
And woke her maid so early that she grumbled,
    And called her father's old slaves up, who swore
In several oaths—Armenian, Turk, and Greek—
They knew not what to think of such a freak.

CXXXIX

But up she got, and up she made them get,
    With some pretence about the Sun, that makes
Sweet skies just when he rises, or is set ;
    And 't is, no doubt, a sight to see when breaks
Bright Phœbus, while the mountains still are wet
    With mist, and every bird with him awakes,
And night is flung off like a mourning suit
Worn for a husband,—or some other brute.

CXL

I say, the Sun is a most glorious sight,
    I 've seen him rise full oft, indeed of late
I have sat up on purpose all the night,
    Which hastens, as physicians say, one's fate ;
And so all ye, who would be in the right
    In health and purse, begin your day to date
From daybreak, and when coffined at four-score,
Engrave upon the plate, you rose at four.

CXLI

And Haidée met the morning face to face ;
    Her own was freshest, though a feverish flush
Had dyed it with the headlong blood, whose race
    From heart to cheek is curbed into a blush,
Like to a torrent which a mountain's base,
    That overpowers some Alpine river's rush,
Checks to a lake, whose waves in circles spread ;
Or the Red Sea—but the sea is not red.

CXLII

And down the cliff the island virgin came,
    And near the cave her quick light footsteps drew,
While the Sun smiled on her with his first flame,
    And young Aurora kissed her lips with dew,
Taking her for a sister; just the same
    Mistake you would have made on seeing the two,
Although the mortal, quite as fresh and fair,
Had all the advantage, too, of not being air.

CXLIII

And when into the cavern Haidée stepped
    All timidly, yet rapidly, she saw
That like an infant Juan sweetly slept;
    And then she stopped, and stood as if in awe
(For sleep is awful), and on tiptoe crept
    And wrapped him closer, lest the air, too raw,
Should reach his blood, then o'er him still as Death
Bent, with hushed lips, that drank his scarce-drawn breath.

CXLIV

And thus like to an Angel o'er the dying
    Who die in righteousness, she leaned; and there
All tranquilly the shipwrecked boy was lying,
    As o'er him lay the calm and stirless air:
But Zoe the meantime some eggs was frying,
    Since, after all, no doubt the youthful pair
Must breakfast—and, betimes, lest they should ask it,
She drew out her provision from the basket.

CXLV

She knew that the best feelings must have victual,
    And that a shipwrecked youth would hungry be;
Besides, being less in love, she yawned a little,
    And felt her veins chilled by the neighbouring sea;
And so, she cooked their breakfast to a tittle;
    I can't say that she gave them any tea,
But there were eggs, fruit, coffee, bread, fish, honey,
With Scio wine,—and all for love, not money.

CXLVI

And Zoe, when the eggs were ready, and
    The coffee made, would fain have wakened Juan;
But Haidée stopped her with her quick small hand,
    And without word, a sign her finger drew on
Her lip, which Zoe needs must understand;
    And, the first breakfast spoilt, prepared a new one,
Because her mistress would not let her break
That sleep which seemed as it would ne'er awake.

CXLVII

For still he lay, and on his thin worn cheek
    A purple hectic played like dying day
On the snow-tops of distant hills; the streak
    Of sufferance yet upon his forehead lay,
Where the blue veins looked shadowy, shrunk, and weak;
    And his black curls were dewy with the spray,
Which weighed upon them yet, all damp and salt,
Mixed with the stony vapours of the vault.

CXLVIII

And she bent o'er him, and he lay beneath,
    Hushed as a babe upon its mother's breast,
Drooped as the willow when no winds can breathe,
    Lulled like the depth of Ocean when at rest,
Fair as the crowning rose of the whole wreath,
    Soft as the callow cygnet in its nest;
In short, he was a very pretty fellow,
Although his woes had turned him rather yellow.

CXLIX

He woke and gazed, and would have slept again,
    But the fair face which met his eyes forbade
Those eyes to close, though weariness and pain
    Had further sleep a further pleasure made:
For Woman's face was never formed in vain
    For Juan, so that even when he prayed
He turned from grisly saints, and martyrs hairy,
To the sweet portraits of the Virgin Mary.

CL

And thus upon his elbow he arose,
    And looked upon the lady, in whose cheek
The pale contended with the purple rose,
    As with an effort she began to speak;
Her eyes were eloquent, her words would pose,
    Although she told him, in good modern Greek,
With an Ionian accent, low and sweet,
That he was faint, and must not talk, but eat.

CLI

Now Juan could not understand a word,
    Being no Grecian; but he had an ear,
And her voice was the warble of a bird,
    So soft, so sweet, so delicately clear,
That finer, simpler music ne'er was heard;
    The sort of sound we echo with a tear,
Without knowing why—an overpowering tone,
Whence Melody descends as from a throne.

CLII

And Juan gazed as one who is awoke
    By a distant organ, doubting if he be
Not yet a dreamer, till the spell is broke
    By the watchman, or some such reality,
Or by one's early valet's curséd knock;
    At least it is a heavy sound to me,
Who like a morning slumber—for the night
Shows stars and women in a better light.

CLIII

And Juan, too, was helped out from his dream,
    Or sleep, or whatsoe'er it was, by feeling
A most prodigious appetite; the steam
    Of Zoe's cookery no doubt was stealing
Upon his senses, and the kindling beam
    Of the new fire, which Zoe kept up, kneeling,
To stir her viands, made him quite awake
And long for food, but chiefly a beef-steak.

CLIV

But beef is rare within these oxless isles;
   Goat's flesh there is, no doubt, and kid, and mutton,
And, when a holiday upon them smiles,
   A joint upon their barbarous spits they put on:
But this occurs but seldom, between whiles,
   For some of these are rocks with scarce a hut on;
Others are fair and fertile, among which
This, though not large, was one of the most rich.

CLV

I say that beef is rare, and can't help thinking
   That the old fable of the Minotaur—
From which our modern morals, rightly shrinking,
   Condemn the royal lady's taste who wore
A cow's shape for a mask—was only (sinking
   The allegory) a mere type, no more,
That Pasiphae promoted breeding cattle,
To make the Cretans bloodier in battle.

CLVI

For we all know that English people are
   Fed upon beef—I won't say much of beer,
Because 't is liquor only, and being far
   From this my subject, has no business here;
We know, too, they are very fond of war,
   A pleasure—like all pleasures—rather dear;
So were the Cretans—from which I infer,
That beef and battles both were owing to her.

CLVII

But to resume. The languid Juan raised
   His head upon his elbow, and he saw
A sight on which he had not lately gazed,
   As all his latter meals had been quite raw,
Three or four things, for which the Lord he praised,
   And, feeling still the famished vulture gnaw,
He fell upon whate'er was offered, like
A priest, a shark, an alderman, or pike.

CLVIII

He ate, and he was well supplied ; and she,
   Who watched him like a mother, would have fed
Him past all bounds, because she smiled to see
   Such appetite in one she had deemed dead :
But Zoe, being older than Haidée,
   Knew (by tradition, for she ne'er had read)
That famished people must be slowly nurst,
And fed by spoonfuls, else they always burst.

CLIX

And so she took the liberty to state,
   Rather by deeds than words, because the case
Was urgent, that the gentleman, whose fate
   Had made her mistress quit her bed to trace
The sea-shore at this hour, must leave his plate,
   Unless he wished to die upon the place—
She snatched it, and refused another morsel,
Saying, he had gorged enough to make a horse ill.

CLX

Next they—he being naked, save a tattered
   Pair of scarce decent trousers—went to work,
And in the fire his recent rags they scattered,
   And dressed him, for the present, like a Turk,
Or Greek—that is, although it not much mattered,
   Omitting turban, slippers, pistol, dirk,—
They furnished him, entire, except some stitches,
With a clean shirt, and very spacious breeches.

CLXI

And then fair Haidée tried her tongue at speaking,
   But not a word could Juan comprehend,
Although he listened so that the young Greek in
   Her earnestness would ne'er have made an end ;
And, as he interrupted not, went eking
   Her speech out to her protégé and friend,
Till pausing at the last her breath to take,
She saw he did not understand Romaic.

CLXII

And then she had recourse to nods, and signs,
    And smiles, and sparkles of the speaking eye,
And read (the only book she could) the lines
    Of his fair face, and found, by sympathy,
The answer eloquent, where the Soul shines
    And darts in one quick glance a long reply;
And thus in every look she saw expressed
A world of words, and things at which she guessed.

CLXIII

And now, by dint of fingers and of eyes,
    And words repeated after her, he took
A lesson in her tongue; but by surmise,
    No doubt, less of her language than her look:
As he who studies fervently the skies
    Turns oftener to the stars than to his book,
Thus Juan learned his *alpha beta* better
From Haidée's glance than any graven letter.

CLXIV

'T is pleasing to be schooled in a strange tongue
    By female lips and eyes—that is, I mean,
When both the teacher and the taught are young,
    As was the case, at least, where I have been;
They smile so when one 's right, and when one 's wrong
    They smile still more, and then there intervene
Pressure of hands, perhaps even a chaste kiss;—
I learned the little that I know by this:

CLXV

That is, some words of Spanish, Turk and Greek,
    Italian not at all, having no teachers;
Much English I cannot pretend to speak,
    Learning that language chiefly from its preachers,
Barrow, South, Tillotson, whom every week
    I study, also Blair—the highest reachers
Of eloquence in piety and prose—
I hate your poets, so read none of those.

CLXVI

As for the ladies, I have nought to say,
  A wanderer from the British world of Fashion,
Where I, like other 'dogs, have had my day,'
  Like other men, too, may have had my passion—
But that, like other things, has passed away,
  And all her fools whom I *could* lay the lash on:
Foes, friends, men, women, now are nought to me
But dreams of what has been, no more to be.

CLXVII

Return we to Don Juan. He begun
  To hear new words, and to repeat them; but
Some feelings, universal as the Sun,
  Were such as could not in his breast be shut
More than within the bosom of a nun:
  He was in love,—as you would be, no doubt,
With a young benefactress,—so was she,
Just in the way we very often see.

CLXVIII

And every day by daybreak—rather early
  For Juan, who was somewhat fond of rest—
She came into the cave, but it was merely
  To see her bird reposing in his nest;
And she would softly stir his locks so curly,
  Without disturbing her yet slumbering guest,
Breathing all gently o'er his cheek and mouth,
As o'er a bed of roses the sweet South.

CLXIX

And every morn his colour freshlier came,
  And every day helped on his convalescence;
'T was well, because health in the human frame
  Is pleasant, besides being true Love's essence,
For health and idleness to Passion's flame
  Are oil and gunpowder; and some good lessons
Are also learnt from Ceres and from Bacchus,
Without whom Venus will not long attack us.

CLXX

While Venus fills the heart, (without heart, really,
  Love, though good always, is not quite so good,)
Ceres presents a plate of vermicelli,—
  For Love must be sustained like flesh and blood,—
While Bacchus pours out wine, or hands a jelly:
  Eggs, oysters, too, are amatory food;
But who is their purveyor from above
Heaven knows,—it may be Neptune, Pan, or Jove.

CLXXI

When Juan woke he found some good things ready,
  A bath, a breakfast, and the finest eyes
That ever made a youthful heart less steady,
  Besides her maid's, as pretty for their size;
But I have spoken of all this already—
  A repetition 's tiresome and unwise,—
Well—Juan, after bathing in the sea,
Came always back to coffee and Haidée.

CLXXII

Both were so young, and one so innocent,
  That bathing passed for nothing; Juan seemed
To her, as 't were, the kind of being sent,
  Of whom these two years she had nightly dreamed,
A something to be loved, a creature meant
  To be her happiness, and whom she deemed
To render happy; all who joy would win
Must share it,—Happiness was born a Twin.

CLXXIII

It was such pleasure to behold him, such
  Enlargement of existence to partake
Nature with him, to thrill beneath his touch,
  To watch him slumbering, and to see him wake:
To live with him for ever were too much;
  But then the thought of parting made her quake;
He was her own, her ocean-treasure, cast
Like a rich wreck—her first love, and her last.

CLXXIV

And thus a moon rolled on, and fair Haidée
    Paid daily visits to her boy, and took
Such plentiful precautions, that still he
    Remained unknown within his craggy nook;
At last her father's prows put out to sea,
    For certain merchantmen upon the look,
Not as of yore to carry off an Io,
But three Ragusan vessels, bound for Scio.

CLXXV

Then came her freedom, for she had no mother,
    So that, her father being at sea, she was
Free as a married woman, or such other
    Female, as where she likes may freely pass,
Without even the encumbrance of a brother,
    The freest she that ever gazed on glass:
I speak of Christian lands in this comparison,
Where wives, at least, are seldom kept in garrison.

CLXXVI

Now she prolonged her visits and her talk
    (For they must talk), and he had learnt to say
So much as to propose to take a walk,—
    For little had he wandered since the day
On which, like a young flower snapped from the stalk,
    Drooping and dewy on the beach he lay,—
And thus they walked out in the afternoon,
And saw the sun set opposite the moon.

CLXXVII

It was a wild and breaker-beaten coast,
    With cliffs above, and a broad sandy shore,
Guarded by shoals and rocks as by an host,
    With here and there a creek, whose aspect wore
A better welcome to the tempest-tost;
    And rarely ceased the haughty billow's roar,
Save on the dead long summer days, which make
The outstretched Ocean glitter like a lake.

CLXXVIII

And the small ripple spilt upon the beach
    Scarcely o'erpassed the cream of your champagne,
When o'er the brim the sparkling bumpers reach,
    That spring-dew of the spirit! the heart's rain!
Few things surpass old wine; and they may preach
    Who please,—the more because they preach in vain,—
Let us have Wine and Woman, Mirth and Laughter,
Sermons and soda-water the day after.

CLXXIX

Man, being reasonable, must get drunk;
    The best of Life is but intoxication:
Glory, the Grape, Love, Gold, in these are sunk
    The hopes of all men, and of every nation;
Without their sap, how branchless were the trunk
    Of Life's strange tree, so fruitful on occasion!
But to return,—Get very drunk, and when
You wake with headache—you shall see what then!

CLXXX

Ring for your valet—bid him quickly bring
    Some hock and soda-water, then you 'll know
A pleasure worthy Xerxes the great king;
    For not the blest sherbet, sublimed with snow,
Nor the first sparkle of the desert-spring,
    Nor Burgundy in all its sunset glow,
After long travel, Ennui, Love, or Slaughter,
Vie with that draught of hock and soda-water!

CLXXXI

The coast—I think it was the coast that I
    Was just describing—Yes, it *was* the coast—
Lay at this period quiet as the sky,
    The sands untumbled, the blue waves untossed,
And all was stillness, save the sea-bird's cry,
    And dolphin's leap, and little billow crossed
By some low rock or shelve, that made it fret
Against the boundary it scarcely wet.

CLXXXII

And forth they wandered, her sire being gone,
  As I have said, upon an expedition;
And mother, brother, guardian, she had none,
  Save Zoe, who, although with due precision
She waited on her lady with the Sun,
  Thought daily service was her only mission,
Bringing warm water, wreathing her long tresses,
And asking now and then for cast-off dresses.

CLXXXIII

It was the cooling hour, just when the rounded
  Red sun sinks down behind the azure hill,
Which then seems as if the whole earth it bounded,
  Circling all Nature, hushed, and dim, and still,
With the far mountain-crescent half surrounded
  On one side, and the deep sea calm and chill
Upon the other, and the rosy sky
With one star sparkling through it like an eye.

CLXXXIV

And thus they wandered forth, and hand in hand,
  Over the shining pebbles and the shells,
Glided along the smooth and hardened sand,
  And in the worn and wild receptacles
Worked by the storms, yet worked as it were planned—
  In hollow halls, with sparry roofs and cells,
They turned to rest; and, each clasped by an arm,
Yielded to the deep Twilight's purple charm.

CLXXXV

They looked up to the sky, whose floating glow
  Spread like a rosy Ocean, vast and bright;
They gazed upon the glittering sea below,
  Whence the broad Moon rose circling into sight;
They heard the waves' splash, and the wind so low,
  And saw each other's dark eyes darting light
Into each other—and, beholding this,
Their lips drew near, and clung into a kiss;

CLXXXVI

A long, long kiss, a kiss of Youth, and Love,
     And Beauty, all concentrating like rays
Into one focus, kindled from above;
     Such kisses as belong to early days,
Where Heart, and Soul, and Sense, in concert move,
     And the blood's lava, and the pulse a blaze,
Each kiss a heart-quake,—for a kiss's strength,
I think, it must be reckoned by its length.

CLXXXVII

By length I mean duration; theirs endured
     Heaven knows how long—no doubt they never reckoned;
And if they had, they could not have secured
     The sum of their sensations to a second:
They had not spoken, but they felt allured,
     As if their souls and lips each other beckoned,
Which, being joined, like swarming bees they clung—
Their hearts the flowers from whence the honey sprung.

CLXXXVIII

They were alone, but not alone as they
     Who shut in chambers think it loneliness;
The silent Ocean, and the starlight bay,
     The twilight glow, which momently grew less,
The voiceless sands, and dropping caves, that lay
     Around them, made them to each other press,
As if there were no life beneath the sky
Save theirs, and that their life could never die.

CLXXXIX

They feared no eyes nor ears on that lone beach;
     They felt no terrors from the night; they were
All in all to each other: though their speech
     Was broken words, they *thought* a language there,—
And all the burning tongues the Passions teach
     Found in one sigh the best interpreter
Of Nature's oracle—first love,—that all
Which Eve has left her daughters since her fall.

CXC

Haidée spoke not of scruples, asked no vows,
    Nor offered any; she had never heard
Of plight and promises to be a spouse,
    Or perils by a loving maid incurred;
She was all which pure Ignorance allows,
    And flew to her young mate like a young bird;
And, never having dreamt of falsehood, she
Had not one word to say of constancy.

CXCI

She loved, and was belovéd—she adored,
    And she was worshipped after Nature's fashion—
Their intense souls, into each other poured,
    If souls could die, had perished in that passion,—
But by degrees their senses were restored,
    Again to be o'ercome, again to dash on;
And, beating 'gainst *his* bosom, Haidée's heart
Felt as if never more to beat apart.

CXCII

Alas! they were so young, so beautiful,
    So lonely, loving, helpless, and the hour
Was that in which the Heart is always full,
    And, having o'er itself no further power,
Prompts deeds Eternity can not annul,
    But pays off moments in an endless shower
Of hell-fire—all prepared for people giving
Pleasure or pain to one another living.

CXCIII

Alas! for Juan and Haidée! they were
    So loving and so lovely—till then never,
Excepting our first parents, such a pair
    Had run the risk of being damned for ever:
And Haidée, being devout as well as fair,
    Had, doubtless, heard about the Stygian river,
And Hell and Purgatory—but forgot
Just in the very crisis she should not.

CXCIV

They look upon each other, and their eyes
    Gleam in the moonlight; and her white arm clasps
Round Juan's head, and his around her lies
    Half buried in the tresses which it grasps;
She sits upon his knee, and drinks his sighs,
    He hers, until they end in broken gasps;
And thus they form a group that's quite antique,
Half naked, loving, natural, and Greek.

CXCV

And when those deep and burning moments passed,
    And Juan sunk to sleep within her arms,
She slept not, but all tenderly, though fast,
    Sustained his head upon her bosom's charms;
And now and then her eye to Heaven is cast,
    And then on the pale cheek her breast now warms,
Pillowed on her o'erflowing heart, which pants
With all it granted, and with all it grants.

CXCVI

An infant when it gazes on a light,
    A child the moment when it drains the breast,
A devotee when soars the Host in sight,
    An Arab with a stranger for a guest,
A sailor when the prize has struck in fight,
    A miser filling his most hoarded chest,
Feel rapture; but not such true joy are reaping
As they who watch o'er what they love while sleeping.

CXCVII

For there it lies so tranquil, so beloved,
    All that it hath of Life with us is living;
So gentle, stirless, helpless, and unmoved,
    And all unconscious of the joy 't is giving;
All it hath felt, inflicted, passed, and proved,
    Hushed into depths beyond the watcher's diving:
There lies the thing we love with all its errors
And all its charms—like Death without its terrors.

CXCVIII

The Lady watched her lover—and that hour
  Of Love's, and Night's, and Ocean's solitude,
O'erflowed her soul with their united power;
  Amidst the barren sand and rocks so rude
She and her wave-worn love had made their bower,
  Where nought upon their passion could intrude,
And all the stars that crowded the blue space
Saw nothing happier than her glowing face.

CXCIX

Alas! the love of Women! it is known
  To be a lovely and a fearful thing;
For all of theirs upon that die is thrown,
  And if 't is lost, Life hath no more to bring
To them but mockeries of the past alone,
  And their revenge is as the tiger's spring,
Deadly, and quick, and crushing; yet, as real
Torture is theirs—what they inflict they feel.

CC

They are right; for Man, to man so oft unjust,
  Is always so to Women: one sole bond
Awaits them—treachery is all their trust;
  Taught to conceal, their bursting hearts despond
Over their idol, till some wealthier lust
  Buys them in marriage—and what rests beyond?
A thankless husband—next, a faithless lover—
Then dressing, nursing, praying—and all 's over.

CCI

Some take a lover, some take drams or prayers,
  Some mind their household, others dissipation,
Some run away, and but exchange their cares,
  Losing the advantage of a virtuous station;
Few changes e'er can better their affairs,
  Theirs being an unnatural situation,
From the dull palace to the dirty hovel:
Some play the devil, and then write a novel.

CCII

Haidée was Nature's bride, and knew not this;
　　Haidée was Passion's child, born where the Sun
Showers triple light, and scorches even the kiss
　　Of his gazelle-eyed daughters; she was one
Made but to love, to feel that she was his
　　Who was her chosen: what was said or done
Elsewhere was nothing. She had nought to fear,
Hope, care, nor love, beyond,—her heart beat *here*.

CCIII

And oh! that quickening of the heart, that beat!
　　How much it costs us! yet each rising throb
Is in its cause as its effect so sweet,
　　That Wisdom, ever on the watch to rob
Joy of its alchemy, and to repeat
　　Fine truths; even Conscience, too, has a tough job
To make us understand each good old maxim,
So good—I wonder Castlereagh don't tax 'em.

CCIV

And now 't was done—on the lone shore were plighted
　　Their hearts; the stars, their nuptial torches, shed
Beauty upon the beautiful they lighted:
　　Ocean their witness, and the cave their bed,
By their own feelings hallowed and united,
　　Their priest was Solitude, and they were wed:
And they were happy—for to their young eyes
Each was an angel, and earth Paradise.

CCV

Oh, Love! of whom great Cæsar was the suitor,
　　Titus the master, Antony the slave,
Horace, Catullus, scholars—Ovid tutor—
　　Sappho the sage blue-stocking, in whose grave
All those may leap who rather would be neuter—
　　(Leucadia's rock still overlooks the wave)—
Oh, Love! thou art the very God of evil,
For, after all, we cannot call thee Devil.

CCVI

Thou mak'st the chaste connubial state precarious,
    And jestest with the brows of mightiest men:
Cæsar and Pompey, Mahomet, Belisarius,
    Have much employed the Muse of History's pen:
Their lives and fortunes were extremely various,
    Such worthies Time will never see again;
Yet to these four in three things the same luck holds,
They all were heroes, conquerors, and cuckolds.

CCVII

Thou mak'st philosophers; there 's Epicurus
    And Aristippus, a material crew!
Who to immoral courses would allure us
    By theories quite practicable too;
If only from the Devil they would insure us,
    How pleasant were the maxim (not quite new),
'Eat, drink, and love, what can the rest avail us?'
So said the royal sage Sardanapalus.

CCVIII

But Juan! had he quite forgotten Julia?
    And should he have forgotten her so soon?
I can't but say it seems to me most truly a
    Perplexing question; but, no doubt, the moon
Does these things for us, and whenever newly a
    Strong palpitation rises, 't is her boon,
Else how the devil is it that fresh features
Have such a charm for us poor human creatures?

CCIX

I hate inconstancy—I loathe, detest,
    Abhor, condemn, abjure the mortal made
Of such quicksilver clay that in his breast
    No permanent foundation can be laid;
Love, constant love, has been my constant guest,
    And yet last night, being at a masquerade,
I saw the prettiest creature, fresh from Milan,
Which gave me some sensations like a villain.

CCX

But soon Philosophy came to my aid,
    And whispered, 'Think of every sacred tie!'
'I will, my dear Philosophy!' I said,
    'But then her teeth, and then, oh, Heaven! her eye!
I 'll just inquire if she be wife or maid,
    Or neither—out of curiosity.'
'Stop!' cried Philosophy, with air so Grecian,
(Though she was masqued then as a fair Venetian;)

CCXI

'Stop!' so I stopped.—But to return: that which
    Men call inconstancy is nothing more
Than admiration due where Nature's rich
    Profusion with young beauty covers o'er
Some favoured object; and as in the niche
    A lovely statue we almost adore,
This sort of adoration of the real
Is but a heightening of the *beau ideal*.

CCXII

'T is the perception of the Beautiful,
    A fine extension of the faculties,
Platonic, universal, wonderful,
    Drawn from the stars, and filtered through the skies,
Without which Life would be extremely dull;
    In short, it is the use of our own eyes,
With one or two small senses added, just
To hint that flesh is formed of fiery dust.

CCXIII

Yet 't is a painful feeling, and unwilling,
    For surely if we always could perceive
In the same object graces quite as killing
    As when she rose upon us like an Eve,
'T would save us many a heartache, many a shilling,
    (For we must get them anyhow, or grieve),
Whereas if one sole lady pleased for ever,
How pleasant for the heart, as well as liver!

CCXIV

The Heart is like the sky, a part of Heaven,
  But changes night and day, too, like the sky;
Now o'er it clouds and thunder must be driven,
  And Darkness and Destruction as on high:
But when it hath been scorched, and pierced, and riven,
  Its storms expire in water-drops; the eye
Pours forth at last the Heart's blood turned to tears,
Which make the English climate of our years.

CCXV

The liver is the lazaret of bile,
  But very rarely executes its function,
For the first passion stays there such a while,
  That all the rest creep in and form a junction,
Like knots of vipers on a dunghill's soil—
  Rage, fear, hate, jealousy, revenge, compunction—
So that all mischiefs spring up from this entrail,
Like Earthquakes from the hidden fire called 'central.'

CCXVI

In the mean time, without proceeding more
  In this anatomy, I 've finished now
Two hundred and odd stanzas as before,
  That being about the number I 'll allow
Each canto of the twelve, or twenty-four;
  And, laying down my pen, I make my bow,
Leaving Don Juan and Haidée to plead
For them and theirs with all who deign to read.

CANTO THE THIRD

I

Hail, Muse! *et cetera.*—We left Juan sleeping,
  Pillowed upon a fair and happy breast,
And watched by eyes that never yet knew weeping,
  And loved by a young heart, too deeply blest
To feel the poison through her spirit creeping,
  Or know who rested there, a foe to rest,

Had soiled the current of her sinless years,
And turned her pure heart's purest blood to tears!

II

Oh, Love! what is it in this world of ours
   Which makes it fatal to be loved? Ah why
With cypress branches hast thou wreathed thy bowers,
   And made thy best interpreter a sigh?
As those who dote on odours pluck the flowers,
   And place them on their breast—but place to die—
Thus the frail beings we would fondly cherish
Are laid within our bosoms but to perish.

III

In her first passion Woman loves her lover,
   In all the others all she loves is Love,
Which grows a habit she can ne'er get over,
   And fits her loosely—like an easy glove,
As you may find, whene'er you like to prove her:
   One man alone at first her heart can move;
She then prefers him in the plural number,
Not finding that the additions much encumber.

IV

I know not if the fault be men's or theirs;
   But one thing 's pretty sure; a woman planted
(Unless at once she plunge for life in prayers)—
   After a decent time must be gallanted;
Although, no doubt, her first of love affairs
   Is that to which her heart is wholly granted;
Yet there are some, they say, who have had *none*,
But those who have ne'er end with only *one*.

V

'T is melancholy, and a fearful sign
   Of human frailty, folly, also crime,
That Love and Marriage rarely can combine,
   Although they both are born in the same clime;

Marriage from Love, like vinegar from wine—
    A sad, sour, sober beverage—by Time
Is sharpened from its high celestial flavour
Down to a very homely household savour.

VI

There 's something of antipathy, as 't were,
    Between their present and their future state;
A kind of flattery that 's hardly fair
    Is used until the truth arrives too late—
Yet what can people do, except despair?
    The same things change their names at such a rate;
For instance—Passion in a lover 's glorious,
But in a husband is pronounced uxorious.

VII

Men grow ashamed of being so very fond;
    They sometimes also get a little tired
(But that, of course, is rare), and then despond:
    The same things cannot always be admired,
Yet 't is 'so nominated in the bond,'
    That both are tied till one shall have expired.
Sad thought! to lose the spouse that was adorning
Our days, and put one's servants into mourning.

VIII

There 's doubtless something in domestic doings
    Which forms, in fact, true Love's antithesis;
Romances paint at full length people's wooings,
    But only give a bust of marriages;
For no one cares for matrimonial cooings,
    There 's nothing wrong in a connubial kiss:
Think you, if Laura had been Petrarch's wife,
He would have written sonnets all his life?

IX

All tragedies are finished by a death,
    All comedies are ended by a marriage;

The future states of both are left to faith,
    For authors fear description might disparage
The worlds to come of both, or fall beneath,
    And then both worlds would punish their miscarriage;
So leaving each their priest and prayer-book ready,
They say no more of Death or of the Lady.

X

The only two that in my recollection,
    Have sung of Heaven and Hell, or marriage, are
Dante and Milton, and of both the affection
    Was hapless in their nuptials, for some bar
Of fault or temper ruined the connection
    (Such things, in fact, it don't ask much to mar);
But Dante's Beatrice and Milton's Eve
Were not drawn from their spouses, you conceive.

XI

Some persons say that Dante meant Theology
    By Beatrice, and not a mistress—I,
Although my opinion may require apology,
    Deem this a commentator's phantasy,
Unless indeed it was from his own knowledge he
    Decided thus, and showed good reason why;
I think that Dante's more abstruse ecstatics
Meant to personify the Mathematics.

XII

Haidée and Juan were not married, but
    The fault was theirs, not mine: it is not fair,
Chaste reader, then, in any way to put
    The blame on me, unless you wish they were;
Then if you'd have them wedded, please to shut
    The book which treats of this erroneous pair,
Before the consequences grow too awful;
'T is dangerous to read of loves unlawful.

XIII

Yet they were happy,—happy in the illicit
   Indulgence of their innocent desires;
But more imprudent grown with every visit,
   Haidée forgot the island was her Sire's;
When we have what we like 't is hard to miss it,
   At least in the beginning, ere one tires;
Thus she came often, not a moment losing,
Whilst her piratical papa was cruising.

XIV

Let not his mode of raising cash seem strange,
   Although he fleeced the flags of every nation,
For into a Prime Minister but change
   His title, and 't is nothing but taxation;
But he, more modest, took an humbler range
   Of Life, and in an honester vocation
Pursued o'er the high seas his watery journey,
And merely practised as a sea-attorney.

XV

The good old gentleman had been detained
   By winds and waves, and some important captures;
And, in the hope of more, at sea remained,
   Although a squall or two had damped his raptures,
By swamping one of the prizes; he had chained
   His prisoners, dividing them like chapters
In numbered lots; they all had cuffs and collars,
And averaged each from ten to a hundred dollars.

XVI

Some he disposed of off Cape Matapan,
   Among his friends the Mainots; some he sold
To his Tunis correspondents, save one man
   Tossed overboard unsaleable (being old);
The rest—save here and there some richer one,
   Reserved for future ransom—in the hold,
Were linked alike, as, for the common people, he
Had a large order from the Dey of Tripoli.

M

XVII

The merchandise was served in the same way,
    Pieced out for different marts in the Levant,
Except some certain portions of the prey,
    Like classic articles of female want,
French stuffs, lace, tweezers, toothpicks, teapot, tray,
    Guitars and castanets from Alicant,
All which selected from the spoil he gathers,
Robbed for his daughter by the best of fathers.

XVIII

A monkey, a Dutch mastiff, a mackaw,
    Two parrots, with a Persian cat and kittens,
He chose from several animals he saw—
    A terrier, too, which once had been a Briton's,
Who dying on the coast of Ithaca,
    The peasants gave the poor dumb thing a pittance:
These to secure in this strong blowing weather,
He caged in one huge hamper altogether.

XIX

Then, having settled his marine affairs,
    Despatching single cruisers here and there,
His vessel having need of some repairs,
    He shaped his course to where his daughter fair
Continued still her hospitable cares;
    But that part of the coast being shoal and bare,
And rough with reefs which ran out many a mile,
His port lay on the other side o' the isle.

XX

And there he went ashore without delay,
    Having no custom-house nor quarantine
To ask him awkward questions on the way,
    About the time and place where he had been:
He left his ship to be hove down next day,
    With orders to the people to careen;
So that all hands were busy beyond measure,
In getting out goods, ballast, guns, and treasure.

XXI

Arriving at the summit of a hill
　　Which overlooked the white walls of his home,
He stopped.—What singular emotions fill
　　Their bosoms who have been induced to roam!
With fluttering doubts if all be well or ill—
　　With love for many, and with fears for some;
All feelings which o'erleap the years long lost,
And bring our hearts back to their starting-post.

XXII

The approach of home to husbands and to sires,
　　After long travelling by land or water,
Most naturally some small doubt inspires—
　　A female family 's a serious matter,
(None trusts the sex more, or so much admires—
　　But they hate flattery, so I never flatter);
Wives in their husbands' absences grow subtler,
And daughters sometimes run off with the butler.

XXIII

An honest gentleman at his return
　　May not have the good fortune of Ulysses;
Not all lone matrons for their husbands mourn,
　　Or show the same dislike to suitors' kisses;
The odds are that he finds a handsome urn
　　To his memory—and two or three young misses
Born to some friend, who holds his wife and riches—
And that *his* Argus—bites him by the breeches.

XXIV

If single, probably his plighted Fair
　　Has in his absence wedded some rich miser;
But all the better, for the happy pair
　　May quarrel, and, the lady growing wiser,
He may resume his amatory care
　　As *cavalier servente*, or despise her;
And that his sorrow may not be a dumb one,
Writes odes on the Inconstancy of Woman.

XXV

And oh! ye gentlemen who have already
  Some chaste *liaison* of the kind—I mean
An honest friendship with a married lady—
  The only thing of this sort ever seen
To last—of all connections the most steady,
  And the true Hymen, (the first 's but a screen)—
Yet, for all that, keep not too long away—
I 've known the absent wronged four times a day.

XXVI

Lambro, our sea-solicitor, who had
  Much less experience of dry land than Ocean,
On seeing his own chimney-smoke, felt glad;
  But not knowing metaphysics, had no notion
Of the true reason of his not being sad,
  Or that of any other strong emotion;
He loved his child, and would have wept the loss of her,
But knew the cause no more than a philosopher.

XXVII

He saw his white walls shining in the sun,
  His garden trees all shadowy and green;
He heard his rivulet's light bubbling run,
  The distant dog-bark; and perceived between
The umbrage of the wood, so cool and dun,
  The moving figures, and the sparkling sheen
Of arms (in the East all arm)—and various dyes
Of coloured garbs, as bright as butterflies.

XXVIII

And as the spot where they appear he nears,
  Surprised at these unwonted signs of idling,
He hears—alas! no music of the spheres,
  But an unhallowed, earthly sound of fiddling!
A melody which made him doubt his ears,
  The cause being past his guessing or unriddling;
A pipe, too, and a drum, and shortly after—
A most unoriental roar of laughter.

XXIX

And still more nearly to the place advancing,
  Descending rather quickly the declivity,
Through the waved branches o'er the greensward glancing,
  'Midst other indications of festivity,
Seeing a troop of his domestics dancing
  Like Dervises, who turn as on a pivot, he
Perceived it was the Pyrrhic dance so martial,
To which the Levantines are very partial.

XXX

And further on a troop of Grecian girls,
  The first and tallest her white kerchief waving,
Were strung together like a row of pearls,
  Linked hand in hand, and dancing; each too having
Down her white neck long floating auburn curls—
  (The least of which would set ten poets raving);
Their leader sang—and bounded to her song
With choral step and voice the virgin throng.

XXXI

And here, assembled cross-legged round their trays,
  Small social parties just begun to dine;
Pilaus and meats of all sorts met the gaze,
  And flasks of Samian and of Chian wine,
And sherbet cooling in the porous vase;
  Above them their dessert grew on its vine;—
The orange and pomegranate nodding o'er,
Dropped in their laps, scarce plucked, their mellow store.

XXXII

A band of children, round a snow-white ram,
  There wreathe his venerable horns with flowers;
While peaceful as if still an unweaned lamb,
  The patriarch of the flock all gently cowers
His sober head, majestically tame,
  Or eats from out the palm, or playful lowers
His brow, as if in act to butt, and then
Yièlding to their small hands, draws back again.

XXXIII

Their classical profiles, and glittering dresses,
    Their large black eyes, and soft seraphic cheeks,
Crimson as cleft pomegranates, their long tresses,
    The gesture which enchants, the eye that speaks,
The innocence which happy childhood blesses,
    Made quite a picture of these little Greeks;
So that the philosophical beholder
Sighed for their sakes—that they should e'er grow older.

XXXIV

Afar, a dwarf buffoon stood telling tales
    To a sedate grey circle of old smokers,
Of secret treasures found in hidden vales,
    Of wonderful replies from Arab jokers,
Of charms to make good gold and cure bad ails,
    Of rocks bewitched that open to the knockers,
Of magic ladies who, by one sole act,
Transformed their lords to beasts (but that 's a fact).

XXXV

Here was no lack of innocent diversion
    For the imagination or the senses,
Song, dance, wine, music, stories from the Persian,
    All pretty pastimes in which no offence is;
But Lambro saw all these things with aversion,
    Perceiving in his absence such expenses,
Dreading that climax of all human ills,
The inflammation of his weekly bills.

XXXVI

Ah! what is man? what perils still environ
    The happiest mortals even after dinner!
A day of gold from out an age of iron
    Is all that Life allows the luckiest sinner;
Pleasure (whene'er she sings, at least) 's a Siren,
    That lures, to flay alive, the young beginner;
Lambro's reception at his people's banquet
Was such as fire accords to a wet blanket.

XXXVII

He—being a man who seldom used a word
    Too much, and wishing gladly to surprise
(In general he surprised men with the sword)
    His daughter—had not sent before to advise
Of his arrival, so that no one stirred;
    And long he paused to re-assure his eyes,
In fact much more astonished than delighted,
To find so much good company invited.

XXXVIII

He did not know (alas! how men will lie)
    That a report (especially to the Greeks)
Avouched his death (such people never die),
    And put his house in mourning several weeks,—
But now their eyes and also lips were dry;
    The bloom, too, had returned to Haidée's cheeks:
Her tears, too, being returned into their fount,
She now kept house upon her own account.

XXXIX

Hence all this rice, meat, dancing, wine, and fiddling,
    Which turned the isle into a place of pleasure;
The servants all were getting drunk or idling,
    A life which made them happy beyond measure.
Her father's hospitality seemed middling,
    Compared with what Haidée did with his treasure;
'T was wonderful how things went on improving,
While she had not one hour to spare from loving.

XL

Perhaps you think, in stumbling on this feast,
    He flew into a passion, and in fact
There was no mighty reason to be pleased;
    Perhaps you prophesy some sudden act,
The whip, the rack, or dungeon at the least,
    To teach his people to be more exact,
And that, proceeding at a very high rate,
He showed the royal *penchants* of a pirate.

XLI

You're wrong.—He was the mildest mannered man
　　That ever scuttled ship or cut a throat;
With such true breeding of a gentleman,
　　You never could divine his real thought;
No courtier could, and scarcely woman can
　　Gird more deceit within a petticoat;
Pity he loved adventurous life's variety,
He was so great a loss to good society.

XLII

Advancing to the nearest dinner tray,
　　Tapping the shoulder of the nighest guest,
With a peculiar smile, which, by the way,
　　Boded no good, whatever it expressed,
He asked the meaning of this holiday;
　　The vinous Greek to whom he had addressed
His question, much too merry to divine
The questioner, filled up a glass of wine,

XLIII

And without turning his facetious head,
　　Over his shoulder, with a Bacchant air,
Presented the o'erflowing cup, and said,
　　'Talking 's dry work, I have no time to spare.'
A second hiccuped, 'Our old Master 's dead,
　　You'd better ask our Mistress who 's his heir.'
'Our Mistress!' quoth a third: 'Our Mistress!—pooh!—
You mean our Master—not the old, but new.'

XLIV

These rascals, being new comers, knew not whom
　　They thus addressed—and Lambro's visage fell—
And o'er his eye a momentary gloom
　　Passed, but he strove quite courteously to quell
The expression, and endeavouring to resume
　　His smile, requested one of them to tell
The name and quality of his new patron,
Who seemed to have turned Haidée into a matron.

XLV

'I know not,' quoth the fellow, 'who or what
   He is, nor whence he came—and little care;
But this I know, that this roast capon's fat,
   And that good wine ne'er washed down better fare;
And if you are not satisfied with that,
   Direct your questions to my neighbour there;
He 'll answer all for better or for worse,
For none likes more to hear himself converse.'

XLVI

I said that Lambro was a man of patience,
   And certainly he showed the best of breeding,
Which scarce even France, the Paragon of nations,
   E'er saw her most polite of sons exceeding;
He bore these sneers against his near relations,
   His own anxiety, his heart, too, bleeding,
The insults, too, of every servile glutton,
Who all the time was eating up his mutton.

XLVII

Now in a person used to much command—
   To bid men come, and go, and come again—
To see his orders done, too, out of hand—
   Whether the word was death, or but the chain—
It may seem strange to find his manners bland;
   Yet such things are, which I cannot explain,
Though doubtless, he who can command himself
Is good to govern—almost as a Guelf.

XLVIII

Not that he was not sometimes rash or so,
   But never in his real and serious mood;
Then calm, concentrated, and still, and slow,
   He lay coiled like the Boa in the wood;
With him it never was a word and blow,
   His angry word once o'er, he shed no blood,
But in his silence there was much to rue,
And his *one* blow left little work for *two*.

XLIX

He asked no further questions, and proceeded
 On to the house, but by a private way,
So that the few who met him hardly heeded,
 So little they expected him that day;
If love paternal in his bosom pleaded
 For Haidée's sake, is more than I can say,
But certainly to one deemed dead returning,
This revel seemed a curious mode of mourning.

L

If all the dead could now return to life,
 (Which God forbid!) or some, or a great many,
For instance, if a husband or his wife
 (Nuptial examples are as good as any),
No doubt whate'er might be their former strife,
 The present weather would be much more rainy—
Tears shed into the grave of the connection
Would share most probably its resurrection.

LI

He entered in the house no more his home,
 A thing to human feelings the most trying,
And harder for the heart to overcome,
 Perhaps, than even the mental pangs of dying;
To find our hearthstone turned into a tomb,
 And round its once warm precincts palely lying
The ashes of our hopes, is a deep grief,
Beyond a *single gentleman's* belief.

LII

He entered in the house—his home no more,
 For without hearts there is no home;—and felt
The solitude of passing his own door
 Without a welcome: *there* he long had dwelt,
There his few peaceful days Time had swept o'er,
 There his worn bosom and keen eye would melt
Over the innocence of that sweet child,
His only shrine of feelings undefiled.

LIII

He was a man of a strange temperament,
  Of mild demeanour though of savage mood,
Moderate in all his habits, and content
  With temperance in pleasure, as in food,
Quick to perceive, and strong to bear, and meant
  For something better, if not wholly good;
His Country's wrongs and his despair to save her
  Had stung him from a slave to an enslaver.

LIV

The love of power, and rapid gain of gold,
  The hardness by long habitude produced,
The dangerous life in which he had grown old,
  The mercy he had granted oft abused,
The sights he was accustomed to behold,
  The wild seas, and wild men with whom he cruised,
Had cost his enemies a long repentance,
And made him a good friend, but bad acquaintance.

LV

But something of the spirit of old Greece
  Flashed o'er his soul a few heroic rays,
Such as lit onward to the Golden Fleece
  His predecessors in the Colchian days;
'T is true he had no ardent love for peace—
  Alas! his country showed no path to praise:
Hate to the world and war with every nation
He waged, in vengeance of her degradation.

LVI

Still o'er his mind the influence of the clime
  Shed its Ionian elegance, which showed
Its power unconsciously full many a time,—
  A taste seen in the choice of his abode,
A love of music and of scenes sublime,
  A pleasure in the gentle stream that flowed
Past him in crystal, and a joy in flowers,
Bedewed his spirit in his calmer hours.

LVII

But whatsoe'er he had of love reposed
　　On that belovéd daughter; she had been
The only thing which kept his heart unclosed
　　Amidst the savage deeds he had done and seen,
A lonely pure affection unopposed:
　　There wanted but the loss of this to wean
His feelings from all milk of human kindness,
And turn him like the Cyclops mad with blindness.

LVIII

The cubless tigress in her jungle raging
　　Is dreadful to the shepherd and the flock;
The Ocean when its yeasty war is waging
　　Is awful to the vessel near the rock;
But violent things will sooner bear assuaging,
　　Their fury being spent by its own shock,
Than the stern, single, deep, and wordless ire
Of a strong human heart, and in a Sire.

LIX

It is a hard although a common case
　　To find our children running restive—they
In whom our brightest days we would retrace,
　　Our little selves re-formed in finer clay,
Just as old age is creeping on apace,
　　And clouds come o'er the sunset of our day,
They kindly leave us, though not quite alone,
But in good company—the gout or stone.

LX

Yet a fine family is a fine thing
　　(Provided they don't come in after dinner);
'T is beautiful to see a matron bring
　　Her children up (if nursing them don't thin her):
Like cherubs round an altar-piece they cling
　　To the fire-side (a sight to touch a sinner).
A lady with her daughters or her nieces
Shine like a guinea and seven-shilling pieces.

LXI

Old Lambro passed unseen a private gate,
　　And stood within his hall at eventide;
Meantime the lady and her lover sate
　　At wassail in their beauty and their pride:
An ivory inlaid table spread with state
　　Before them, and fair slaves on every side;
Gems, gold, and silver, formed the service mostly,
Mother of pearl and coral the less costly.

LXII

The dinner made about a hundred dishes;
　　Lamb and pistachio nuts—in short, all meats
And saffron soups, and sweetbreads; and the fishes
　　Were of the finest that e'er flounced in nets,
Dressed to a Sybarite's most pampered wishes;
　　The beverage was various sherbets
Of raisin, orange, and pomegranate juice,
Squeezed through the rind, which makes it best for use.

LXIII

These were ranged round, each in its crystal ewer,
　　And fruits, and date-bread loaves closed the repast,
And Mocha's berry, from Arabia pure,
　　In small fine China cups, came in at last;
Gold cups of filigree, made to secure
　　The hand from burning, underneath them placed;
Cloves, cinnamon, and saffron too were boiled
Up with the coffee, which (I think) they spoiled.

LXIV

The hangings of the room were tapestry, made
　　Of velvet panels, each of different hue,
And thick with damask flowers of silk inlaid;
　　And round them ran a yellow border too;
The upper border, richly wrought, displayed,
　　Embroidered delicately o'er with blue,
Soft Persian sentences, in lilac letters,
From poets, or the moralists their betters.

LXV

These Oriental writings on the wall,
    Quite common in those countries, are a kind
Of monitors adapted to recall,
    Like skulls at Memphian banquets, to the mind,
The words which shook Belshazzar in his hall,
    And took his kingdom from him: You will find,
Though sages may pour out their wisdom's treasure,
There is no sterner moralist than Pleasure.

LXVI

A Beauty at the season's close grown hectic,
    A Genius who has drunk himself to death,
A Rake turned methodistic, or Eclectic—
    (For that 's the name they like to pray beneath)—
But most, an Alderman struck apoplectic,
    Are things that really take away the breath,—
And show that late hours, wine, and love are able
To do not much less damage than the table.

LXVII

Haidée and Juan carpeted their feet
    On crimson satin, bordered with pale blue;
Their sofa occupied three parts complete
    Of the apartment—and appeared quite new;
The velvet cushions (for a throne more meet)
    Were scarlet, from whose glowing centre grew
A sun embossed in gold, whose rays of tissue,
Meridian-like, were seen all light to issue.

LXVIII

Crystal and marble, plate and porcelain,
    Had done their work of splendour; Indian mats
And Persian carpets, which the heart bled to stain,
    Over the floors were spread; gazelles and cats,
And dwarfs and blacks, and such like things, that gain
    Their bread as ministers and favourites (that 's
To say, by degradation) mingled there
As plentiful as in a court, or fair.

LXIX

There was no want of lofty mirrors, and
　　The tables, most of ebony inlaid
With mother of pearl or ivory, stood at hand;
　　Or were of tortoise-shell or rare woods made,
Fretted with gold or silver:—by command
　　The greater part of these were ready spread
With viands and sherbets in ice—and wine—
Kept for all comers at all hours to dine.

LXX

Of all the dresses I select Haidée's;
　　She wore two jelicks—one was of pale yellow;
Of azure, pink, and white was her chemise—
　　'Neath which her breast heaved like a little billow:
With buttons formed of pearls as large as peas,
　　All gold and crimson shone her jelick's fellow,
And the striped white gauze baracan that bound her,
Like fleecy clouds about the moon, flowed round her.

LXXI

One large gold bracelet clasped each lovely arm,
　　Lockless—so pliable from the pure gold
That the hand stretched and shut it without harm,
　　The limb which it adorned its only mould;
So beautiful—its very shape would charm,
　　And clinging, as if loath to lose its hold,
The purest ore enclosed the whitest skin
That e'er by precious metal was held in.

LXXII

Around, as Princess of her father's land,
　　A like gold bar above her instep rolled
Announced her rank; twelve rings were on her hand;
　　Her hair was starred with gems; her veil's fine fold
Below her breast was fastened with a band
　　Of lavish pearls, whose worth could scarce be told;
Her orange silk full Turkish trousers furled
About the prettiest ankle in the world.

LXXIII

Her hair's long auburn waves down to her heel
    Flowed like an Alpine torrent which the sun
Dyes with his morning light,—and would conceal
    Her person if allowed at large to run,
And still they seemed resentfully to feel
    The silken fillet's curb, and sought to shun
Their bonds whene'er some Zephyr caught began
To offer his young pinion as her fan.

LXXIV

Round her she made an atmosphere of life,
    The very air seemed lighter from her eyes,
They were so soft and beautiful, and rife
    With all we can imagine of the skies,
And pure as Psyche ere she grew a wife—
    Too pure even for the purest human ties;
Her overpowering presence made you feel
It would not be idolatry to kneel.

LXXV

Her eyelashes, though dark as night, were tinged
    (It is the country's custom, but in vain),
For those large black eyes were so blackly fringed,
    The glossy rebels mocked the jetty stain,
And in their native beauty stood avenged:
    Her nails were touched with henna; but, again,
The power of Art was turned to nothing, for
They could not look more rosy than before.

LXXVI

The henna should be deeply dyed to make
    The skin relieved appear more fairly fair;
She had no need of this, day ne'er will break
    On mountain tops more heavenly white than her:
The eye might doubt if it were well awake,
    She was so like a vision; I might err,
But Shakespeare also says, 't is very silly
'To gild refinéd gold, or paint the lily.'

LXXVII

Juan had on a shawl of black and gold,
    But a white baracan, and so transparent
The sparkling gems beneath you might behold,
    Like small stars through the milky way apparent;
His turban, furled in many a graceful fold,
    An emerald aigrette, with Haidée's hair in 't,
Surmounted, as its clasp, a glowing crescent,
Whose rays shone ever trembling, but incessant.

LXXVIII

And now they were diverted by their suite,
    Dwarfs, dancing girls, black eunuchs, and a poet,
Which made their new establishment complete;
    The last was of great fame, and liked to show it;
His verses rarely wanted their due feet—
    And for his theme—he seldom sung below it,
He being paid to satirise or flatter,
As the Psalm says, 'inditing a good matter.'

LXXIX

He praised the present, and abused the past,
    Reversing the good custom of old days,
An Eastern anti-jacobin at last
    He turned, preferring pudding to *no* praise—
For some few years his lot had been o'ercast
    By his seeming independent in his lays,
But now he sung the Sultan and the Pacha—
With truth like Southey, and with verse like Crashaw.

LXXX

He was a man who had seen many changes,
    And always changed as true as any needle;
His Polar Star being one which rather ranges,
    And not the fixed—he knew the way to wheedle:
So vile he 'scaped the doom which oft avenges;
    And being fluent (save indeed when fee'd ill),
He lied with such a fervour of intention—
There was no doubt he earned his laureate pension.

LXXXI

But *he* had genius,—when a turncoat has it,
   The *Vates irritabilis* takes care
That without notice few full moons shall pass it;
   Even good men like to make the public stare:—
But to my subject—let me see—what was it?—
   Oh!—the third canto—and the pretty pair—
Their loves, and feasts, and house, and dress, and mode
Of living in their insular abode.

LXXXII

Their poet, a sad trimmer, but, no less,
   In company a very pleasant fellow,
Had been the favourite of full many a mess
   Of men, and made them speeches when half mellow;
And though his meaning they could rarely guess,
   Yet still they deigned to hiccup or to bellow
The glorious meed of popular applause,
Of which the first ne'er knows the second cause.

LXXXIII

But now being lifted into high society,
   And having picked up several odds and ends
Of free thoughts in his travels for variety,
   He deemed, being in a lone isle, among friends,
That, without any danger of a riot, he
   Might for long lying make himself amends;
And, singing as he sung in his warm youth,
Agree to a short armistice with Truth.

LXXXIV

He had travelled 'mongst the Arabs, Turks and Franks,
   And knew the self-loves of the different nations;
And having lived with people of all ranks,
   Had something ready upon most occasions—
Which got him a few presents and some thanks.
   He varied with some skill his adulations;
To 'do at Rome as Romans do,' a piece
Of conduct was which *he* observed in Greece.

LXXXV

Thus, usually, when *he* was asked to sing,
  He gave the different nations something national;
'T was all the same to him—'God save the King,'
  Or 'Ça ira,' according to the fashion all:
His Muse made increment of anything,
  From the high lyric down to the low rational;
If Pindar sang horse-races, what should hinder
Himself from being as pliable as Pindar?

LXXXVI

In France, for instance, he would write a chanson;
  In England a six canto quarto tale;
In Spain he'd make a ballad or romance on
  The last war—much the same in Portugal;
In Germany, the Pegasus he'd prance on
  Would be old Goethe's—(see what says De Staël);
In Italy he 'd ape the 'Trecentisti';
In Greece, he 'd sing some sort of hymn like this t' ye:

1

The Isles of Greece, the Isles of Greece!
  Where burning Sappho loved and sung,
Where grew the arts of War and Peace,
  Where Delos rose, and Phœbus sprung!
Eternal summer gilds them yet,
But all, except their Sun, is set.

2

The Scian and the Teian muse,
  The Hero's harp, the Lover's lute,
Have found the fame your shores refuse:
  Their place of birth alone is mute
To sounds which echo further west
Than your Sires' 'Islands of the Blest.'

3

The mountains look on Marathon—
  And Marathon looks on the sea;

And musing there an hour alone,
   I dreamed that Greece might still be free;
For standing on the Persians' grave,
I could not deem myself a slave.

4

A King sate on the rocky brow
   Which looks o'er sea-born Salamis;
And ships, by thousands, lay below,
   And men in nations;—all were his!
He counted them at break of day—
And, when the Sun set, where were they?

5

And where are they? and where art thou,
   My country? On thy voiceless shore
The heroic lay is tuneless now—
   The heroic bosom beats no more!
And must thy Lyre, so long divine,
Degenerate into hands like mine?

6

'T is something, in the dearth of Fame,
   Though linked among a fettered race,
To feel at least a patriot's shame,
   Even as I sing, suffuse my face;
For what is left the poet here?
For Greeks a blush—for Greece a tear.

7

Must *we* but weep o'er days more blest?
   Must *we* but blush?—Our fathers bled.
Earth! render back from out thy breast
   A remnant of our Spartan dead!
Of the three hundred grant but three,
To make a new Thermopylæ!

8

What, silent still? and silent all?
    Ah! no ;—the voices of the dead
Sound like a distant torrent's fall,
    And answer, 'Let one living head,
But one arise,— we come, we come!'
'T is but the living who are dumb.

9

In vain—in vain: strike other chords;
    Fill high the cup with Samian wine!
Leave battles to the Turkish hordes,
    And shed the blood of Scio's vine!
Hark! rising to the ignoble call—
How answers each bold Bacchanal!

10

You have the Pyrrhic dance as yet,
    Where is the Pyrrhic phalanx gone?
Of two such lessons, why forget
    The nobler and the manlier one?
You have the letters Cadmus gave—
Think ye he meant them for a slave?

11

Fill high the bowl with Samian wine!
    We will not think of themes like these!
It made Anacreon's song divine:
    He served—but served Polycrates—
A Tyrant; but our masters then
Were still, at least, our countrymen.

12

The Tyrant of the Chersonese
    Was Freedom's best and bravest friend;
That tyrant was Miltiades!
    Oh! that the present hour would lend
Another despot of the kind!
Such chains as his were sure to bind.

13

Fill high the bowl with Samian wine!
  On Suli's rock, and Parga's shore,
Exists the remnant of a line
  Such as the Doric mothers bore;
And there perhaps some seed is sown,
The Heracleidan blood might own.

14

Trust not for freedom to the Franks—
  They have a king who buys and sells;
In native swords and native ranks,
  The only hope of courage dwells;
But Turkish force, and Latin fraud,
Would break your shield, however broad.

15

Fill high the bowl with Samian wine!
  Our virgins dance beneath the shade—
I see their glorious black eyes shine;
  But gazing on each glowing maid,
My own the burning tear-drop laves,
To think such breasts must suckle slaves.

16

Place me on Sunium's marbled steep,
  Where nothing, save the waves and I,
May hear our mutual murmurs sweep;
  There, swan-like, let me sing and die:
A land of slaves shall ne'er be mine—
Dash down yon cup of Samian wine!

LXXXVII

Thus sung, or would, or could, or should have sung,
  The modern Greek, in tolerable verse;
If not like Orpheus quite, when Greece was young,
  Yet in these times he might have done much worse:

His strain displayed some feeling—right or wrong;
    And feeling, in a poet, is the source
Of others' feeling; but they are such liars,
And take all colours—like the hands of dyers.

LXXXVIII

But words are things, and a small drop of ink,
    Falling like dew, upon a thought, produces
That which makes thousands, perhaps millions, think;
    'T is strange, the shortest letter which man uses
Instead of speech, may form a lasting link
    Of ages; to what straits old Time reduces
Frail man, when paper—even a rag like this,
Survives himself, his tomb, and all that 's his!

LXXXIX

And when his bones are dust, his grave a blank,
    His station, generation, even his nation,
Become a thing, or nothing, save to rank
    In chronological commemoration,
Some dull MS. Oblivion long has sank,
    Or graven stone found in a barrack's station
In digging the foundation of a closet,
May turn his name up, as a rare deposit.

XC

And Glory long has made the sages smile;
    'T is something, nothing, words, illusion, wind—
Depending more upon the historian's style
    Than on the name a person leaves behind:
Troy owns to Homer what whist owes to Hoyle:
    The present century was growing blind
To the great Marlborough's skill in giving knocks,
Until his late Life by Archdeacon Coxe.

XCI

Milton 's the Prince of poets—so we say;
    A little heavy, but no less divine:

An independent being in his day—
 Learned, pious, temperate in love and wine;
But, his life falling into Johnson's way,
 We 're told this great High Priest of all the Nine
Was whipped at college—a harsh sire—odd spouse,
For the first Mrs. Milton left his house.

XCII

All these are, *certes*, entertaining facts,
 Like Shakespeare's stealing deer, Lord Bacon's bribes;
Like Titus' youth, and Cæsar's earliest acts;
 Like Burns (whom Doctor Currie well describes);
Like Cromwell's pranks;—but although Truth exacts
 These amiable descriptions from the scribes,
As most essential to their hero's story,
They do not much contribute to his glory.

XCIII

All are not moralists, like Southey, when
 He prated to the world of 'Pantisocracy';
Or Wordsworth unexcised, unhired, who then
 Seasoned his pedlar poems with Democracy;
Or Coleridge long before his flighty pen
 Let to the Morning Post its aristocracy;
When he and Southey, following the same path,
Espoused two partners (milliners of Bath).

XCIV

Such names at present cut a convict figure,
 The very Botany Bay in moral geography;
Their loyal treason, renegado rigour,
 Are good manure for their more bare biography;
Wordsworth's last quarto, by the way, is bigger
 Than any since the birthday of typography;
A drowsy, frowzy poem, called the 'Excursion,'
Writ in a manner which is my aversion.

XCV

He there builds up a formidable dyke
    Between his own and others' intellect;
But Wordsworth's poem, and his followers, like
    Joanna Southcote's Shiloh and her sect,
Are things which in this century don't strike
    The public mind,—so few are the elect;
And the new births of both their stale Virginities
Have proved but Dropsies, taken for Divinities.

XCVI

But let me to my story: I must own,
    If I have any fault, it is digression,
Leaving my people to proceed alone,
    While I soliloquise beyond expression;
But these are my addresses from the throne,
    Which put off business to the ensuing session:—
Forgetting each omission is a loss to
The world, not quite so great as Ariosto.

XCVII

I know that what our neighbours call '*longueurs*,'
    (We've not so good a *word*, but have the *thing*,
In that complete perfection which insures
    An epic from Bob Southey every spring—)
Form not the true temptation which allures
    The reader; but 't would not be hard to bring
Some fine examples of the *Epopée*,
To prove its grand ingredient is *Ennui*.

XCVIII

We learn from Horace, 'Homer sometimes sleeps';
    We feel without him,—Wordsworth sometimes wakes,—
To show with what complacency he creeps,
    With his dear '*Waggoners*,' around his lakes.
He wishes for 'a boat' to sail the deeps—
    Of Ocean?—No, of air; and then he makes
Another outcry for 'a little boat,'
And drivels seas to set it well afloat.

XCIX

If he must fain sweep o'er the ethereal plain,
    And Pegasus runs restive in his 'Waggon,'
Could he not beg the loan of Charles's Wain?
    Or pray Medea for a single dragon?
Or if, too classic for his vulgar brain,
    He feared his neck to venture such a nag on,
And he must needs mount nearer to the moon,
Could not the blockhead ask for a balloon?

C

'Pedlars,' and 'Boats,' and 'Waggons!' Oh! ye shades
    Of Pope and Dryden, are we come to this?
That trash of such sort not alone evades
    Contempt, but from the bathos' vast abyss
Floats scumlike uppermost, and these Jack Cades
    Of sense and song above your graves may hiss—
The 'little boatman' and his *Peter Bell*
Can sneer at him who drew 'Achitophel'!

CI

T' our tale.—The feast was over, the slaves gone,
    The dwarfs and dancing girls had all retired;
The Arab lore and Poet's song were done,
    And every sound of revelry expired;
The lady and her lover, left alone,
    The rosy flood of Twilight's sky admired;—
Ave Maria! o'er the earth and sea,
That heavenliest hour of Heaven is worthiest thee!

CII

Ave Maria! blessèd be the hour!
    The time, the clime, the spot, where I so oft
Have felt that moment in its fullest power
    Sink o'er the earth—so beautiful and soft—
While swung the deep bell in the distant tower,
    Or the faint dying day-hymn stole aloft,
And not a breath crept through the rosy air,
And yet the forest leaves seemed stirred with prayer.

CIII

Ave Maria! 't is the hour of prayer!
   Ave Maria! 't is the hour of Love!
Ave Maria! may our spirits dare
   Look up to thine and to thy Son's above!
Ave Maria! oh that face so fair!
   Those downcast eyes beneath the Almighty Dove—
What though 't is but a pictured image?—strike—
That painting is no idol,—'t is too like.

CIV

Some kinder casuists are pleased to say,
   In nameless print—that I have no devotion;
But set those persons down with me to pray,
   And you shall see who has the properest notion
Of getting into Heaven the shortest way;
   My altars are the mountains and the Ocean,
Earth—air—stars,—all that springs from the great Whole,
Who hath produced, and will receive the Soul.

CV

Sweet Hour of Twilight!—in the solitude
   Of the pine forest, and the silent shore
Which bounds Ravenna's immemorial wood,
   Rooted where once the Adrian wave flowed o'er,
To where the last Cæsarean fortress stood,
   Evergreen forest! which Boccaccio's lore
And Dryden's lay made haunted ground to me,
How have I loved the twilight hour and thee!

CVI

The shrill cicalas, people of the pine,
   Making their summer lives one ceaseless song,
Were the sole echoes, save my steed's and mine,
   And Vesper bell's that rose the boughs along;
The spectre huntsman of Onesti's line,
   His hell-dogs, and their chase, and the fair throng
Which learned from this example not to fly
From a true lover,—shadowed my mind's eye.

CVII

Oh, Hesperus! thou bringest all good things—
    Home to the weary, to the hungry cheer,
To the young bird the parent's brooding wings;
    The welcome stall to the o'erlaboured steer;
Whate'er of peace about our hearthstone clings,
    Whate'er our household gods protect of dear,
Are gathered round us by thy look of rest;
Thou bring'st the child, too, to the mother's breast.

CVIII

Soft Hour! which wakes the wish and melts the heart
    Of those who sail the seas, on the first day
When they from their sweet friends are torn apart;
    Or fills with love the pilgrim on his way
As the far bell of Vesper makes him start,
    Seeming to weep the dying day's decay;
Is this a fancy which our reason scorns?
Ah! surely Nothing dies but Something mourns!

CIX

When Nero perished by the justest doom
    Which ever the Destroyer yet destroyed,
Amidst the roar of liberated Rome,
    Of nations freed, and the world overjoyed,
Some hands unseen strewed flowers upon his tomb:
    Perhaps the weakness of a heart not void
Of feeling for some kindness done, when Power
Had left the wretch an uncorrupted hour.

CX

But I'm digressing; what on earth has Nero,
    Or any such like sovereign buffoons,
To do with the transactions of my hero,
    More than such madmen's fellow man—the moon's?
Sure my invention must be down at zero,
    And I grown one of many 'Wooden Spoons'
Of verse, (the name with which we Cantabs please
To dub the last of honours in degrees).

CXI

I feel this tediousness will never do—
    'T is being *too* epic, and I must cut down
(In copying) this long canto into two;
    They'll never find it out, unless I own
The fact, excepting some experienced few;
    And then as an improvement 't will be shown:
I 'll prove that such the opinion of the critic is
From Aristotle *passim.*—See *ΠΟΙΗΤΙΚΗΣ.*

*   *   *   *

CANTO THE ELEVENTH

I

When Bishop Berkeley said 'there was no matter,'
    And proved it—'t was no matter what he said:
They say his system 't is in vain to batter,
    Too subtle for the airiest human head;
And yet who can believe it? I would shatter
    Gladly all matters down to stone or lead,
Or adamant, to find the World a spirit,
And wear my head, denying that I wear it.

II

What a sublime discovery 't was to make the
    Universe universal egotism,
That all 's ideal—*all ourselves!*—I 'll stake the
    World (be it what you will) that *that 's* no schism.
Oh Doubt!—if thou be'st Doubt, for which some take thee,
    But which I doubt extremely—thou sole prism
Of the Truth's rays, spoil not my draught of spirit!
Heaven's brandy, though our brain can hardly bear it.

III

For ever and anon comes Indigestion
    (Not the most 'dainty Ariel'), and perplexes
Our soarings with another sort of question:
    And that which after all my spirit vexes,

Is, that I find no spot where Man can rest eye on,
    Without confusion of the sorts and sexes,
Of Beings, Stars, and this unriddled wonder,
The World, which at the worst 's a *glorious* blunder—

IV

If it be chance—or, if it be according
    To the old text, still better:—lest it should
Turn out so, we 'll say nothing 'gainst the wording,
    As several people think such hazards rude.
They 're right; our days are too brief for affording
    Space to dispute what *no one* ever could
Decide, and *everybody one day* will
Know very clearly—or at least lie still.

V

And therefore will I leave off metaphysical
    Discussion, which is neither here nor there:
If I agree that what is, is;—then this I call
    Being quite perspicuous and extremely fair;
The truth is, I 've grown lately rather phthisical:
    I don't know what the reason is—the air
Perhaps; but as I suffer from the shocks
Of illness, I grow much more orthodox.

VI

The first attack at once proved the Divinity
    (But *that* I never doubted, nor the Devil);
The next, the Virgin's mystical virginity;
    The third, the usual Origin of Evil;
The fourth at once established the whole Trinity
    On so uncontrovertible a level,
That I devoutly wished the three were four—
On purpose to believe so much the more.

VII

To our theme.—The man who has stood on the Acropolis,
    And looked down over Attica; or he

Who has sailed where picturesque Constantinople is,
    Or seen Timbuctoo, or hath taken tea
In small-eyed China's crockery-ware metropolis,
    Or sat amidst the bricks of Nineveh,
May not think much of London's first appearance—
But ask him what he thinks of it a year hence!

VIII

Don Juan had got out on Shooter's Hill;
    Sunset the time, the place the same declivity
Which looks along that vale of Good and Ill
    Where London streets ferment in full activity,
While everything around was calm and still,
    Except the creak of wheels, which on their pivot he
Heard,—and that bee-like, bubbling, busy hum
Of cities, that boil over with their scum :—

IX

I say, Don Juan, wrapped in contemplation,
    Walked on behind his carriage, o'er the summit,
And lost in wonder of so great a nation,
    Gave way to 't, since he could not overcome it.
'And here,' he cried, 'is Freedom's chosen station;
    Here peals the People's voice nor can entomb it
Racks—prisons—inquisitions; Resurrection
Awaits it, each new meeting or election.

X

'Here are chaste wives, pure lives; here people pay
    But what they please; and if that things be dear,
'T is only that they love to throw away
    Their cash, to show how much they have a-year.
Here laws are all inviolate—none lay
    Traps for the traveller—every highway 's clear—
Here'—he was interrupted by a knife,
With—'Damn your eyes! your money or your life!'—

XI

These free-born sounds proceeded from four pads
    In ambush laid, who had perceived him loiter
Behind his carriage; and, like handy lads,
    Had seized the lucky hour to reconnoitre,
In which the heedless gentleman who gads
    Upon the road, unless he prove a fighter,
May find himself within that isle of riches
Exposed to lose his life as well as breeches.

XII

Juan, who did not understand a word
    Of English, save their shibboleth, 'God damn!'
And even that he had so rarely heard,
    He sometimes thought 't was only their 'Salām,'
Or 'God be with you!'—and 't is not absurd
    To think so,—for half English as I am
(To my misfortune), never can I say
I heard them wish 'God with you,' save that way;—

XIII

Juan yet quickly understood their gesture,
    And being somewhat choleric and sudden,
Drew forth a pocket pistol from his vesture,
    And fired it into one assailant's pudding—
Who fell, as rolls an ox o'er in his pasture,
    And roared out, as he writhed his native mud in,
Unto his nearest follower or henchman,
'Oh Jack! I 'm floored by that 'ere bloody Frenchman!'

XIV

On which Jack and his train set off at speed,
    And Juan's suite, late scattered at a distance,
Came up, all marvelling at such a deed,
    And offering, as usual, late assistance.
Juan, who saw the moon's late minion bleed
    As if his veins would pour out his existence,
Stood calling out for bandages and lint,
And wished he had been less hasty with his flint.

XV

'Perhaps,' thought he, 'it is the country's wont
    To welcome foreigners in this way: now
I recollect some innkeepers who don't
    Differ, except in robbing with a bow,
In lieu of a bare blade and brazen front—
    But what is to be done? I can't allow
The fellow to lie groaning on the road:
So take him up—I'll help you with the load.'

XVI

But ere they could perform this pious duty,
    The dying man cried, 'Hold! I 've got my gruel!
Oh! for a glass of *max*! We 've missed our booty;
    Let me die where I am!' And as the fuel
Of Life shrunk in his heart, and thick and sooty
    The drops fell from his death-wound, and he drew ill
His breath,—he from his swelling throat untied
A kerchief, crying, 'Give Sal that!'—and died.

XVII

The cravat stained with bloody drops fell down
    Before Don Juan's feet: he could not tell
Exactly why it was before him thrown,
    Nor what the meaning of the man's farewell.
Poor Tom was once a kiddy upon town,
    A thorough varmint, and a *real* swell,
Full flash, all fancy, until fairly diddled,
His pockets first and then his body riddled.

XVIII

Don Juan, having done the best he could
    In all the circumstances of the case,
As soon as 'Crowner's quest' allowed, pursued
    His travels to the capital apace;—
Esteeming it a little hard he should
    In twelve hours' time, and very little space,
Have been obliged to slay a free-born native
In self-defence: this made him meditative.

N

XIX

He from the world had cut off a great man,
　Who in his time had made heroic bustle.
Who in a row like Tom could lead the van,
　Booze in the ken, or at the spellken hustle?
Who queer a flat? Who (spite of Bow-street's ban)
　On the high toby-spice so flash the muzzle?
Who on a lark with black-eyed Sal (his blowing),
So prime—so swell—so nutty—and so knowing?

XX

But Tom 's no more—and so no more of Tom.
　Heroes must die; and by God's blessing 't is
Not long before the most of them go home.
　Hail! Thamis, hail! Upon thy verge it is
That Juan's chariot, rolling like a drum
　In thunder, holds the way it can't well miss,
Through Kennington and all the other 'tons,'
Which make us wish ourselves in town at once;—

XXI

Through Groves, so called as being void of trees,
　(Like *lucus* from *no* light); through prospects named
Mount Pleasant, as containing nought to please,
　Nor much to climb; through little boxes framed
Of bricks, to let the dust in at your ease,
　With 'To be let,' upon their doors proclaimed;
Through 'Rows' most modestly called 'Paradise,'
Which Eve might quit without much sacrifice;—

XXII

Through coaches, drays, choked turnpikes, and a whirl
　Of wheels, and roar of voices, and confusion;
Here taverns wooing to a pint of 'purl,'
　There mails fast flying off like a delusion;
There barbers' blocks with periwigs in curl
　In windows; here the lamplighter's infusion
Slowly distilled into the glimmering glass
(For in those days we had not got to gas—);

XXIII

Through this, and much, and more, is the approach
    Of travellers to mighty Babylon:
Whether they come by horse, or chaise, or coach,
    With slight exceptions, all the ways seem one.
I could say more, but do not choose to encroach
    Upon the Guide-book's privilege. The Sun
Had set some time, and night was on the ridge
Of twilight, as the party crossed the bridge.

XXIV

That 's rather fine, the gentle sound of Thamis—
    Who vindicates a moment, too, his stream—
Though hardly heard through multifarious 'damme's:'
    The lamps of Westminster's more regular gleam,
The breadth of pavement, and yon shrine where Fame is
    A spectral resident—whose pallid beam
In shape of moonshine hovers o'er the pile—
Make this a sacred part of Albion's isle.

XXV

The Druids' groves are gone—so much the better:
    Stonehenge is not—but what the devil is it?—
But Bedlam still exists with its sage fetter,
    That madmen may not bite you on a visit;
The Bench too seats or suits full many a debtor;
    The Mansion House, too (though some people quiz it),
To me appears a stiff yet grand erection;
But then the Abbey 's worth the whole collection.

XXVI

The line of lights, too, up to Charing Cross,
    Pall Mall, and so forth, have a coruscation
Like gold as in comparison to dross,
    Matched with the Continent's illumination,
Whose cities Night by no means deigns to gloss.
    The French were not yet a lamp-lighting nation,
And when they grew so—on their new-found lantern,
Instead of wicks, they made a wicked man turn.

XXVII

A row of Gentlemen along the streets
   Suspended may illuminate mankind,
As also bonfires made of country seats;
   But the old way is best for the purblind:
The other looks like phosphorus on sheets,
   A sort of *ignis fatuus* to the mind,
Which, though 't is certain to perplex and frighten,
Must burn more mildly ere it can enlighten.

XXVIII

But London 's so well lit, that if Diogenes
   Could recommence to hunt his *honest man*,
And found him not amidst the various progenies
   Of this enormous City's spreading span,
'T were not for want of lamps to aid his dodging his
   Yet undiscovered treasure. What *I* can,
I 've done to find the same throughout Life's journey,
But see the World is only one attorney.

XXIX

Over the stones still rattling, up Pall Mall,
   Through crowds and carriages, but waxing thinner
As thundered knockers broke the long sealed spell
   Of doors 'gainst duns, and to an early dinner
Admitted a small party as night fell,—
   Don Juan, our young diplomatic sinner,
Pursued his path, and drove past some hotels,
St. James's Palace, and St. James's 'Hells.'

XXX

They reached the hotel: forth streamed from the front door
   A tide of well-clad waiters, and around
The mob stood, and as usual several score
   Of those pedestrian Paphians who abound
In decent London when the daylight 's o'er;
   Commodious but immoral, they are found
Useful, like Malthus, in promoting marriage.—
But Juan now is stepping from his carriage

XXXI

Into one of the sweetest of hotels,
  Especially for foreigners—and mostly
For those whom favour or whom Fortune swells,
  And cannot find a bill's small items costly.
There many an envoy either dwelt or dwells
  (The den of many a diplomatic lost lie),
Until to some conspicuous square they pass,
And blazon o'er the door their names in brass.

XXXII

Juan, whose was a delicate commission,
  Private, though publicly important, bore
No title to point out with due precision
  The exact affair on which he was sent o'er.
'T was merely known, that on a secret mission
  A foreigner of rank had graced our shore,
Young, handsome, and accomplished, who was said
(In whispers) to have turned his Sovereign's head.

XXXIII

Some rumour also of some strange adventures
  Had gone before him, and his wars and loves;
And as romantic heads are pretty painters,
  And, above all, an Englishwoman's roves
Into the excursive, breaking the indentures
  Of sober reason, wheresoe'er it moves,
He found himself extremely in the fashion,
Which serves our thinking people for a passion.

XXXIV

I don't mean that they are passionless, but quite
  The contrary; but then 't is in the head;
Yet as the consequences are as bright
  As if they acted with the heart instead,
What after all can signify the site
  Of ladies' lucubrations? So they lead
In safety to the place for which you start,
What matters if the road be head or heart?

XXXV

Juan presented in the proper place,
  To proper placement, every Russ credential;
And was received with all the due grimace
  By those who govern in the mood potential,
Who, seeing a handsome stripling with smooth face,
  Thought (what in state affairs is most essential),
That they as easily might *do* the youngster,
As hawks may pounce upon a woodland songster.

XXXVI

They erred, as agéd men will do; but by
  And by we 'll talk of that; and if we don't,
'T will be because our notion is not high
  Of politicians and their double front,
Who live by lies, yet dare not boldly lie:—
  Now, what I love in women is, they won't
Or can't do otherwise than lie—but do it
So well, the very Truth seems falsehood to it.

XXXVII

And, after all, what is a lie? 'T is but
  The truth in masquerade; and I defy
Historians—heroes—lawyers—priests, to put
  A fact without some leaven of a lie.
The very shadow of true Truth would shut
  Up annals—revelations—poesy,
And prophecy—except it should be dated
Some years before the incidents related.

XXXVIII

Praised be all liars and all lies! Who now
  Can tax my mild Muse with misanthropy?
She rings the World's 'Te Deum,' and her brow
  Blushes for those who will not:—but to sigh
Is idle; let us like most others bow,
  Kiss hands—feet—any part of Majesty,
After the good example of 'Green Erin,'
Whose shamrock now seems rather worse for Wearing.

XXXIX

Don Juan was presented, and his dress
    And mien excited general admiration—
I don't know which was more admired or less:
    One monstrous diamond drew much observation,
Which Catherine in a moment of '*ivresse*'
    (In Love or Brandy's fervent fermentation),
Bestowed upon him, as the public learned;
And, to say truth, it had been fairly earned.

XL

Besides the ministers and underlings,
    Who must be courteous to the accredited
Diplomatists of rather wavering Kings,
    Until their royal riddle 's fully read,
The very clerks,—those somewhat dirty springs
    Of Office, or the House of Office, fed
By foul corruption into streams,—even they
Were hardly rude enough to earn their pay:

XLI

And insolence no doubt is what they are
    Employed for, since it is their daily labour,
In the dear offices of Peace or War;
    And should you doubt, pray ask of your next neighbour,
When for a passport, or some other bar
    To freedom, he applied (a grief and a bore),
If he found not this spawn of tax-born riches,
Like lap-dogs, the least civil sons of b——s.

XLII

But Juan was received with much '*empressement*':—
    These phrases of refinement I must borrow
From our next neighbours' land, where, like a chessman,
    There is a move set down for joy or sorrow,
Not only in mere talking, but the press. Man
    In Islands is, it seems, downright and thorough,
More than on Continents—as if the Sea
(See Billingsgate) made even the tongue more free.

XLIII

And yet the British 'Damme' 's rather Attic,
    Your continental oaths are but incontinent,
And turn on things which no aristocratic
    Spirit would name, and therefore even I won't anent
This subject quote; as it would be schismatic
    In *politesse*, and have a sound affronting in 't;—
But 'Damme' 's quite ethereal, though too daring—
Platonic blasphemy—the soul of swearing.

XLIV

For downright rudeness, ye may stay at home;
    For true or false politeness (and scarce *that*
Now) you may cross the blue deep and white foam—
    The first the emblem (rarely though) of what
You leave behind, the next of much you come
    To meet. However, 't is no time to chat
On general topics: poems must confine
Themselves to unity, like this of mine.

XLV

In the great world,—which, being interpreted,
    Meaneth the West or worst end of a city,
And about twice two thousand people bred
    By no means to be very wise or witty,
But to sit up while others lie in bed,
    And look down on the Universe with pity,—
Juan, as an inveterate patrician,
Was well received by persons of condition.

XLVI

He was a bachelor, which is a matter
    Of import both to virgin and to bride,
The former's hymeneal hopes to flatter;
    And (should she not hold fast by Love or Pride)
'T is also of some moment to the latter:
    A rib 's a thorn in a wed gallant's side,
Requires decorum, and is apt to double
The horrid sin—and what 's still worse, the trouble.

XLVII

But Juan was a bachelor—of arts,
 And parts,—and hearts: he danced and sung, and had
An air as sentimental as Mozart's
 Softest of melodies; and could be sad
Or cheerful, without any 'flaws or starts,'
 Just at the proper time: and though a lad,
Had seen the world—which is a curious sight,
And very much unlike what people write.

XLVIII

Fair virgins blushed upon him; wedded dames
 Bloomed also in less transitory hues;
For both commodities dwell by the Thames
 The painting and the painted; Youth, Ceruse,
Against his heart preferred their usual claims,
 Such as no gentleman can quite refuse:
Daughters admired his dress, and pious mothers
Inquired his income, and if he had brothers.

XLIX

The milliners who furnish 'drapery Misses'
 Throughout the season, upon speculation
Of payment ere the Honeymoon's last kisses
 Have waned into a crescent's coruscation,
Thought such an opportunity as this is,
 Of a rich foreigner's initiation,
Not to be overlooked—and gave such credit,
That future bridegrooms swore, and sighed, and paid it.

L

The Blues, that tender tribe, who sigh o'er sonnets,
 And with the pages of the last Review
Line the interior of their heads or bonnets,
 Advanced in all their azure's highest hue:
They talked bad French or Spanish, and upon its
 Late authors asked him for a hint or two;
And which was softest, Russian or Castilian?
And whether in his travels he saw Ilion?

LI

Juan, who was a little superficial,
    And not in literature a great Drawcansir,
Examined by this learnéd and especial
    Jury of matrons, scarce knew what to answer:
His duties warlike, loving or official,
    His steady application as a dancer,
Had kept him from the brink of Hippocrene,
Which now he found was blue instead of green.

LII

However, he replied at hazard, with
    A modest confidence and calm assurance,
Which lent his learnéd lucubrations pith,
    And passed for arguments of good endurance.
That prodigy, Miss Araminta Smith
    (Who at sixteen translated 'Hercules Furens'
Into as furious English), with her best look,
Set down his sayings in her common-place book.

LIII

Juan knew several languages—as well
    He might—and brought them up with skill, in time
To save his fame with each accomplished belle,
    Who still regretted that he did not rhyme.
There wanted but this requisite to swell
    His qualities (with them) into sublime:
Lady Fitz-Frisky, and Miss Mævia Mannish,
Both longed extremely to be sung in Spanish.

LIV

However, he did pretty well, and was
    Admitted as an aspirant to all
The coteries, and, as in Banquo's glass,
    At great assemblies or in parties small,
He saw ten thousand living authors pass,
    That being about their average numeral;
Also the eighty 'greatest living poets,'
As every paltry magazine can show *it's*.

LV

In twice five years the 'greatest living poet,'
    Like to the champion in the fisty ring,
Is called on to support his claim, or show it,
    Although 't is an imaginary thing.
Even I—albeit I 'm sure I did not know it,
    Nor sought of foolscap subjects to be king,—
Was reckoned, a considerable time,
The grand Napoleon of the realms of rhyme.

LVI

But Juan was my Moscow, and Faliero
    My Leipsic, and my Mont Saint Jean seems Cain:
La Belle Alliance of dunces down at zero,
    Now that the Lion 's fallen, may rise again:
But I will fall at least as fell my Hero;
    Nor reign at all, or as a *monarch* reign;
Or to some lonely isle of gaolers go,
With turncoat Southey for my turnkey Lowe.

LVII

Sir Walter reigned before me; Moore and Campbell
    Before and after; but now grown more holy,
The Muses upon Sion's hill must ramble
    With poets almost clergymen, or wholly;
And Pegasus has a psalmodic amble
    Beneath the very Reverend Rowley Powley,
Who shoes the glorious animal with stilts,
A modern Ancient Pistol—'by these hilts!'

LVIII

Still he excels that artificial hard
    Labourer in the same vineyard, though the vine
Yields him but vinegar for his reward,—
    That neutralised dull Dorus of the Nine;
That swarthy Sporus, neither man nor bard;
    That ox of verse, who *ploughs* for every line:—
Cambyses' roaring Romans beat at least
The howling Hebrews of Cybele's priest.—

LIX

Then there 's my gentle Euphues,— who, they say,
　　Sets up for being a sort of *moral me*;
He 'll find it rather difficult some day
　　To turn out both, or either, it may be.
Some persons think that Coleridge hath the sway;
　　And Wordsworth has supporters, two or three;
And that deep-mouthed Bœotian 'Savage Landor'
Has taken for a swan rogue Southey's gander.

LX

John Keats, who was killed off by one critique,
　　Just as he really promised something great,
If not intelligible, without Greek
　　Contrived to talk about the gods of late,
Much as they might have been supposed to speak.
　　Poor fellow! His was an untoward fate;
'T is strange the mind, that very fiery particle,
Should let itself be snuffed out by an article.

LXI

The list grows long of live and dead pretenders
　　To that which none will gain—or none will know
The conqueror at least; who ere time renders
　　His last award, will have the long grass grow
Above his burnt-out brain, and sapless cinders.
　　If I might augur, I should rate but low
Their chances;—they 're too numerous, like the thirty
Mock tyrants, when Rome's annals waxed but dirty.

LXII

This is the literary *lower* empire,
　　Where the prætorian bands take up the matter;—
A 'dreadful trade,' like his who 'gathers samphire,'
　　The insolent soldiery to soothe and flatter,
With the same feelings as you 'd coax a vampire.
　　Now, were I once at home, and in good satire,
I 'd try conclusions with those Janizaries,
And show them *what* an intellectual war is.

LXIII

I think I know a trick or two, would turn
    Their flanks;—but it is hardly worth my while,
With such small gear to give myself concern:
    Indeed I 've not the necessary bile;
My natural temper 's really aught but stern,
    And even my Muse's worst reproof 's a smile;
And then she drops a brief and modern curtsy,
And glides away, assured she never hurts ye.

LXIV

My Juan, whom I left in deadly peril
    Amongst live poets and *blue* ladies, passed
With some small profit through that field so sterile,
    Being tired in time—and, neither least nor last,
Left it before he had been treated very ill;
    And henceforth found himself more gaily classed
Amongst the higher spirits of the day,
The Sun's true son, no vapour, but a ray.

LXV

His morns he passed in business—which dissected,
    Was, like all business, a laborious nothing
That leads to lassitude, the most infected
    And Centaur Nessus garb of mortal clothing,
And on our sofas makes us lie dejected,
    And talk in tender horrors of our loathing
All kinds of toil, save for our country's good—
Which grows no better, though 't is time it should.

LXVI

His afternoons he passed in visits, luncheons,
    Lounging and boxing; and the twilight hour
In riding round those vegetable puncheons
    Called 'Parks,' where there is neither fruit nor flower
Enough to gratify a bee's slight munchings;
    But after all it is the only 'bower'
(In Moore's phrase) where the fashionable fair
Can form a slight acquaintance with fresh air.

LXVII

Then dress, then dinner, then awakes the world!
  Then glare the lamps, then whirl the wheels, then roar
Through street and square fast flushing chariots hurled
  Like harnessed meteors; then along the floor
Chalk mimics painting; then festoons are twirled;
  Then roll the brazen thunders of the door,
Which opens to the thousand happy few
An earthly Paradise of *Or Molu*.

LXVIII

There stands the noble hostess, nor shall sink
  With the three-thousandth curtsy; there the waltz,
The only dance which teaches girls to think,
  Makes one in love even with its very faults.
Saloon, room, hall, o'erflow beyond their brink,
  And long the latest of arrivals halts,
'Midst royal dukes and dames condemned to climb,
And gain an inch of staircase at a time.

LXIX

Thrice happy he who, after a survey
  Of the good company, can win a corner,
A door that's *in* or boudoir *out* of the way,
  Where he may fix himself like small 'Jack Horner,'
And let the Babel round run as it may,
  And look on as a mourner, or a scorner,
Or an approver, or a mere spectator,
Yawning a little as the night grows later.

LXX

But this won't do, save by and by; and he
  Who, like Don Juan, takes an active share,
Must steer with care through all that glittering sea
  Of gems and plumes and pearls and silks, to where
He deems it is his proper place to be;
  Dissolving in the waltz to some soft air,
Or proudlier prancing with mercurial skill,
Where Science marshals forth her own quadrille.

LXXI

Or, if he dance not, but hath higher views
　　Upon an heiress or his neighbour's bride,
Let him take care that that which he pursues
　　Is not at once too palpably descried:
Full many an eager gentleman oft rues
　　His haste; Impatience is a blundering guide
Amongst a people famous for reflection,
Who like to play the fool with circumspection.

LXXII

But, if you can contrive, get next at supper;
　　Or, if forestalled, get opposite and ogle:—
Oh, ye ambrosial moments! always upper
　　In mind, a sort of sentimental bogle,
Which sits for ever upon Memory's crupper,
　　The ghost of vanished pleasures once in vogue! Ill
Can tender souls relate the rise and fall
Of hopes and fears which shake a single ball.

LXXIII

But these precautionary hints can touch
　　Only the common run, who must pursue,
And watch and ward; whose plans a word too much
　　Or little overturns; and not the few
Or many (for the number 's sometimes such)
　　Whom a good mien, especially if new,
Or fame—or name—for Wit, War, Sense, or Nonsense,
Permits whate'er they please,—or *did* not long since.

LXXIV

Our Hero—as a hero—young and handsome,
　　Noble, rich, celebrated, and a stranger,
Like other slaves of course must pay his ransom,
　　Before he can escape from so much danger
As will environ a conspicuous man. Some
　　Talk about poetry, and 'rack and manger,'
And ugliness, disease, as toil and trouble;—
I wish they knew the life of a young noble.

LXXV

They are young, but know not Youth—it is anticipated;
   Handsome but wasted, rich without a sou;
Their vigour in a thousand arms is dissipated;
   Their cash comes *from*, their wealth goes *to* a Jew;
Both senates see their nightly votes participated
   Between the Tyrant's and the Tribunes' crew;
And having voted, dined, drunk, gamed and whored,
The family vault receives another Lord.

LXXVI

'Where is the World?' cries Young, 'at *eighty*'—'Where
   The World in which a man was born?' Alas!
Where is the world of *eight* years past? *'T was there*—
   I look for it—'t is gone, a globe of glass!
Cracked, shivered, vanished, scarcely gazed on, ere
   A silent change dissolves the glittering mass.
Statesmen, Chiefs, Orators, Queens, Patriots, Kings,
And Dandies—all are gone on the Wind's wings.

LXXVII

Where is Napoleon the Grand? God knows!
   Where little Castlereagh? The devil can tell!
Where Grattan, Curran, Sheridan—all those
   Who bound the Bar or Senate in their spell?
Where is the unhappy Queen, with all her woes?
   And where the Daughter, whom the Isles loved well?
Where are those martyred saints the Five per Cents?
And where—oh, where the devil are the Rents?

LXXVIII

Where 's Brummell? Dished. Where 's Long Pole Wellesley?
     Diddled.
   Where 's Whitbread? Romilly? Where 's George the Third?
Where is his will? (That 's not so soon unriddled.)
   And where is 'Fum' the Fourth, our 'royal bird'?
Gone down, it seems, to Scotland to be fiddled
   Unto by Sawney's violin, we have heard:

'Caw me, caw thee'—for six months hath been hatching
This scene of royal itch and loyal scratching.

LXXIX

Where is Lord This? And where my Lady That?
   The Honourable Mistresses and Misses?
Some laid aside like an old Opera hat,
   Married, unmarried, and remarried: (this is
An evolution oft performed of late).
   Where are the Dublin shouts—and London hisses?
Where are the Grenvilles? Turned as usual. Where
My friends the Whigs? Exactly where they were.

LXXX

Where are the Lady Carolines and Franceses?
   Divorced or doing thereanent. Ye annals
So brilliant, where the list of routs and dances is,—
   Thou Morning Post, sole record of the panels
Broken in carriages, and all the phantasies
   Of fashion,—say what streams now fill those channels?
Some die, some fly, some languish on the Continent,
Because the times have hardly left them *one* tenant.

LXXXI

Some who once set their caps at cautious dukes,
   Have taken up at length with younger brothers:
Some heiresses have bit at sharper's hooks:
   Some maids have been made wives, some merely mothers:
Others have lost their fresh and fairy looks:
   In short, the list of alterations bothers.
There 's little strange in this, but something strange is
The unusual quickness of these common changes.

LXXXII

Talk not of seventy years as age; in seven
   I have seen more changes, down from monarchs to
The humblest individuals under Heaven,
   Than might suffice a moderate century through.

I knew that nought was lasting, but now even
 Change grows too changeable, without being new:
Nought 's permanent among the human race,
Except the Whigs *not* getting into place.

LXXXIII

I have seen Napoleon, who seemed quite a Jupiter,
 Shrink to a Saturn. I have seen a Duke
(No matter which) turn politician stupider,
 If that can well be, than his wooden look.
But it is time that I should hoist my 'blue Peter,'
 And sail for a new theme:—I have seen—and shook
To see it—the King hissed, and then caressed;
But don't pretend to settle which was best.

LXXXIV

I have seen the Landholders without a rap—
 I have seen Joanna Southcote—I have seen
The House of Commons turned to a tax-trap—
 I have seen that sad affair of the late Queen—
I have seen crowns worn instead of a fool's cap—
 I have seen a Congress doing all that 's mean—
I have seen some nations, like o'erloaded asses,
Kick off their burthens—meaning the high classes.

LXXXV

I have seen small poets, and great prosers, and
 Interminable—*not eternal*—speakers—
I have seen the funds at war with house and land—
 I have seen the country gentlemen turn squeakers—
I have seen the people ridden o'er like sand
 By slaves on horseback—I have seen malt liquors
Exchanged for 'thin potations' by John Bull—
I have seen John half detect himself a fool.—

LXXXVI

But '*carpe diem*,' Juan, '*carpe, carpe!*'
 To-morrow sees another race as gay

And transient, and devoured by the same harpy.
  'Life 's a poor player,'—then 'play out the play,
Ye villains!' and above all keep a sharp eye
  Much less on what you do than what you say:
Be hypocritical, be cautious, be
Not what you *seem*, but always what you *see*.

LXXXVII

But how shall I relate in other cantos
  Of what befell our hero in the land,
Which 't is the common cry and lie to vaunt as
  A moral country? But I hold my hand—
For I disdain to write an Atalantis;
  But 't is as well at once to understand,
You are *not* a moral people, and you know it,
Without the aid of too sincere a poet.

LXXXVIII

What Juan saw and underwent shall be
  My topic, with of course the due restriction
Which is required by proper courtesy;
  And recollect the work is only fiction,
And that I sing of neither mine nor me,
  Though every scribe, in some slight turn of diction,
Will hint allusions never *meant*. Ne'er doubt
This—when I speak, I *don't hint*, but *speak out*.

LXXXIX

Whether he married with the third or fourth
  Offspring of some sage husband-hunting countess,
Or whether with some virgin of more worth
  (I mean in Fortune's matrimonial bounties),
He took to regularly peopling Earth,
  Of which your lawful, awful wedlock fount is,—
Or whether he was taken in for damages,
For being too excursive in his homages,—

XC

Is yet within the unread events of Time.
    Thus far, go forth, thou Lay, which I will back
Against the same given quantity of rhyme,
    For being as much the subject of attack
As ever yet was any work sublime,
    By those who love to say that white is black.
So much the better!—I may stand alone,
But would not change my free thoughts for a throne.

CANTO THE TWELFTH

I

Of all the barbarous middle ages, that
    Which is most barbarous is the middle age
Of man! it is—I really scarce know what;
    But when we hover between fool and sage,
And don't know justly what we would be at—
    A period something like a printed page,
Black letter upon foolscap, while our hair
Grows grizzled, and we are not what we were;—

II

Too old for Youth,—too young, at thirty-five,
    To herd with boys, or hoard with good threescore,—
I wonder people should be left alive;
    But since they are, that epoch is a bore:
Love lingers still, although 't were late to wive:
    And as for other love, the illusion 's o'er;
And Money, that most pure imagination,
Gleams only through the dawn of its creation.

III

O Gold! Why call we misers miserable?
    Theirs is the pleasure that can never pall;
Theirs is the best bower anchor, the chain cable
    Which holds fast other pleasures great and small.

Ye who but see the saving man at table,
    And scorn his temperate board, as none at all,
And wonder how the wealthy can be sparing,
Know not what visions spring from each cheese-paring.

IV

Love or lust makes Man sick, and wine much sicker;
    Ambition rends, and gaming gains a loss;
But making money, slowly first, then quicker,
    And adding still a little through each cross
(Which *will* come over things), beats Love or liquor,
    The gamester's counter, or the statesman's *dross*.
O Gold! I still prefer thee unto paper,
Which makes bank credit like a bank of *vapour*.

V

Who hold the balance of the World? Who reign
    O'er congress, whether royalist or liberal?
Who rouse the shirtless patriots of Spain?
    (That make old Europe's journals 'squeak and gibber' all)
Who keep the World, both old and new, in pain
    Or pleasure? Who make politics run glibber all?
The shade of Buonaparte's noble daring?—
Jew Rothschild, and his fellow-Christian, Baring.

VI

Those, and the truly liberal Lafitte,
    Are the true Lords of Europe. Every loan
Is not a merely speculative hit,
    But seats a Nation or upsets a Throne.
Republics also get involved a bit;
    Columbia's stock hath holders not unknown
On 'Change; and even thy silver soil, Peru,
Must get itself discounted by a Jew.

VII

Why call the miser miserable? as
    I said before: the frugal life is his,

Which in a saint or cynic ever was
    The theme of praise: a hermit would not miss
Canonization for the self-same cause,
    And wherefore blame gaunt Wealth's austerities?
Because, you 'll say, nought calls for such a trial;—
Then there 's more merit in his self-denial.

VIII

He is your only poet;—Passion, pure
    And sparkling on from heap to heap, displays,
Possessed, the ore, of which *mere hopes* allure
    Nations athwart the deep: the golden rays
Flash up in ingots from the mine obscure:
    On him the Diamond pours its brilliant blaze,
While the mild Emerald's beam shades down the dies
Of other stones, to soothe the miser's eyes.

IX

The lands on either side are his; the ship
    From Ceylon, Inde, or far Cathay, unloads
For him the fragrant produce of each trip;
    Beneath his cars of Ceres groan the roads,
And the vine blushes like Aurora's lip;
    His very cellars might be King's abodes;
While he, despising every sensual call,
Commands—the intellectual Lord of *all*.

X

Perhaps he hath great projects in his mind,
    To build a college, or to found a race,
A hospital, a church,—and leave behind
    Some dome surmounted by his meagre face:
Perhaps he fain would liberate Mankind
    Even with the very ore which makes them base;
Perhaps he would be wealthiest of his nation,
Or revel in the joys of calculation.

XI

But whether all, or each, or none of these
  May be the hoarder's principle of action,
The fool will call such mania a disease:—
  What is his *own*? Go—look at each transaction,
Wars, revels, loves—do these bring men more ease
  Than the mere plodding through each 'vulgar fraction'?
Or do they benefit Mankind? Lean Miser!
Let spendthrifts' heirs inquire of yours—who 's wiser?

XII

How beauteous are rouleaus! how charming chests
  Containing ingots, bags of dollars, coins
(Not of old victors, all whose heads and crests
  Weigh not the thin ore where their visage shines,
But) of fine unclipped gold, where dully rests
  Some likeness, which the glittering cirque confines,
Of modern, reigning, sterling, stupid stamp!—
Yes! ready money *is* Aladdin's lamp.

XIII

'Love rules the Camp, the Court, the Grove, —for Love
  Is Heaven, and Heaven is Love:'—so sings the bard;
Which it were rather difficult to prove
  (A thing with poetry in general hard).
Perhaps there may be something in 'the Grove,'
  At least it rhymes to 'Love': but I 'm prepared
To doubt (no less than landlords of their rental)
If 'Courts' and 'Camps' be quite so sentimental.

XIV

But if Love don't, *Cash* does, and Cash alone:
  Cash rules the Grove, and fells it too besides;
Without cash, camps were thin, and courts were none;
  Without cash, Malthus tells you—'take no brides.'
So Cash rules Love the ruler, on his own
  High ground, as virgin Cynthia sways the tides:
And as for 'Heaven being Love,' why not say honey
Is wax? Heaven is not Love, 't is Matrimony.

XV

Is not all Love prohibited whatever,
    Excepting Marriage? which is Love, no doubt,
After a sort; but somehow people never
    With the same thought the two words have helped out.
Love may exist *with* Marriage, and *should* ever,
    And Marriage also may exist without;
But Love *sans* banns is both a sin and shame,
And ought to go by quite another name.

XVI

Now if the 'Court,' and 'Camp,' and 'Grove,' be not
    Recruited all with constant married men,
Who never coveted their neighbour's lot,
    I say *that* line 's a lapsus of the pen;—
Strange too in my *buon camerado* Scott,
    So celebrated for his morals, when
My Jeffrey held him up as an example
To me;—of whom these morals are a sample.

XVII

Well, if I don't succeed, I *have* succeeded,
    And that 's enough;—succeeded in my youth,
The only time when much success is needed:
    And my success produced what I, in sooth,
Cared most about; it need not now be pleaded—
    Whate'er it was, 'twas mine; I 've paid, in truth,
Of late, the penalty of such success,
But have not learned to wish it any less.

XVIII

That suit in Chancery,—which some persons plead
    In an appeal to the unborn, whom they,
In the faith of their procreative creed,
    Baptize Posterity, or future clay,—
To me seems but a dubious kind of reed
    To lean on for support in any way;
Since odds are that Posterity will know
No more of them, than they of her, I trow.

XIX

Why, I 'm Posterity—and so are you;
   And whom do we remember? Not a hundred.
Were every memory written down all true,
   The tenth or twentieth name would be but blundered;
Even Plutarch's Lives have but picked out a few,
   And 'gainst those few your annalists have thundered;
And Mitford in the nineteenth century
Gives, with Greek truth, the good old Greek the lie.

XX

Good people all, of every degree,
   Ye gentle readers and ungentle writers,
In this twelfth Canto 't is my wish to be
   As serious as if I had for inditers
Malthus and Wilberforce:—the last set free
   The Negroes, and is worth a million fighters;
While Wellington has but enslaved the Whites,
And Malthus does the thing 'gainst which he writes.

XXI

I 'm serious—so are all men upon paper;
   And why should I not form my speculation,
And hold up to the Sun my little taper?
   Mankind just now seem wrapped in meditation
On constitutions and steam-boats of vapour;
   While sages write against all procreation,
Unless a man can calculate his means
Of feeding brats the moment his wife weans.

XXII

That 's noble! That 's romantic! For my part,
   I think that 'Philo-genitiveness' is—
(Now here's a word quite after my own heart,
   Though there 's a shorter a good deal than this,
If that politeness set it not apart;
   But I 'm resolved to say nought that 's amiss)—
I say, methinks that 'Philo-genitiveness'
Might meet from men a little more forgiveness.

XXIII

And now to business.—O my gentle Juan!
    Thou art in London—in that pleasant place,
Where every kind of mischief 's daily brewing,
    Which can await warm Youth in its wild race.
'T is true, that thy career is not a new one;
    Thou art no novice in the headlong chase
Of early life; but this is a new land,
Which foreigners can never understand.

XXIV

What with a small diversity of climate,
    Of hot or cold, mercurial or sedate,
I could send forth my mandate like a Primate
    Upon the rest of Europe's social state;
But thou art the most difficult to rhyme at,
    Great Britain, which the Muse may penetrate.
All countries have their 'Lions,' but in thee
There is but one superb menagerie.

XXV

But I am sick of politics. Begin—
    '*Paulo Majora.*' Juan, undecided
Amongst the paths of being 'taken in,'
    Above the ice had like a skater glided:
When tired of play, he flirted without sin
    With some of those fair creatures who have prided
Themselves on innocent tantalisation,
And hate all vice except its reputation.

XXVI

But these are few, and in the end they make
    Some devilish escapade or stir, which shows
That even the purest people may mistake
    Their way through Virtue's primrose paths of snows;
And then men stare, as if a new ass spake
    To Balaam, and from tongue to ear o'erflows
Quicksilver small talk, ending (if you note it)
With the kind World's Amen—'Who would have thought it?'

XXVII

The little Leila, with her Orient eyes,
    And taciturn Asiatic disposition,
(Which saw all Western things with small surprise,
    To the surprise of people of condition,
Who think that novelties are butterflies
    To be pursued as food for inanition,)
Her charming figure and romantic history
Became a kind of fashionable mystery.

XXVIII

The women much divided—as is usual
    Amongst the sex in little things or great—
Think not, fair creatures, that I mean to abuse you all,
    I have always liked you better than I state—
Since I 've grown moral, still I must accuse you all
    Of being apt to talk at a great rate;
And now there was a general sensation
Amongst you, about Leila's education.

XXIX

In one point only were you settled—and
    You had reason; 't was that a young child of grace,
As beautiful as her own native land,
    And far away, the last bud of her race,
Howe'er our friend Don Juan might command
    Himself for five, four, three, or two years' space,
Would be much better taught beneath the eye
Of peeresses whose follies had run dry.

XXX

So first there was a generous emulation,
    And then there was a general competition,
To undertake the orphan's education:
    As Juan was a person of condition,
It had been an affront on this occasion
    To talk of a subscription or petition;
But sixteen dowagers, ten unwed she sages
Whose tale belongs to 'Hallam's Middle Ages,'

XXXI

And one or two sad, separate wives, without
    A fruit to bloom upon their withering bough—
Begged to bring *up* the little girl, and '*out*,'—
    For that 's the phrase that settles all things now,
Meaning a virgin's first blush at a rout,
    And all her points as thorough-bred to show:
And I assure you, that like virgin honey
Tastes their first season (mostly if they have money).

XXXII

How all the needy honourable misters,
    Each out-at-elbow peer, or desperate dandy,
The watchful mothers, and the careful sisters,
    (Who, by the by, when clever, are more handy
At making matches, where ' 't is gold that glisters,'
    Than their *he* relatives), like flies o'er candy
Buzz round 'the Fortune' with their busy battery,
To turn her head with waltzing and with flattery!

XXXIII

Each aunt, each cousin, hath her speculation;
    Nay, married dames will now and then discover
Such pure disinterestedness of passion,
    I 've known them court an heiress for their lover.
'*Tantæne!*' Such the virtues of high station,
    Even in the hopeful Isle, whose outlet 's 'Dover'!
While the poor rich wretch, object of these cares,
Has cause to wish her sire had had male heirs.

XXXIV

Some are soon bagged, and some reject three dozen:
    'T is fine to see them scattering refusals
And wild dismay o'er every angry cousin
    (Friends of the party), who begin accusals,
Such as—'Unless Miss Blank meant to have chosen
    Poor Frederick, why did she accord perusals
To his billets? *Why* waltz with him? Why, I pray,
Look '*Yes*' last night, and yet say '*No*' to-day?

XXXV

'Why?—Why?—Besides, Fred really was *attached*;
　'T was not her fortune—he has enough without;
The time will come she 'll wish that she had snatched
　So good an opportunity, no doubt:—
But the old Marchioness some plan had hatched,
　As I 'll tell Aurea at to-morrow's rout:
And after all poor Frederick may do better—
Pray did you see her answer to his letter?'

XXXVI

Smart uniforms and sparkling coronets
　Are spurned in turn, until her turn arrives,
After male loss of time, and hearts, and bets
　Upon the sweepstakes for substantial wives;
And when at last the pretty creature gets
　Some gentleman, who fights, or writes, or drives,
It soothes the awkward squad of the rejected
To find how very badly she selected.

XXXVII

For sometimes they accept some long pursuer,
　Worn out with importunity; or fall
(But here perhaps the instances are fewer)
　To the lot of him who scarce pursued at all.
A hazy widower turned of forty 's sure
　(If 't is not vain examples to recall)
To draw a high prize: now, howe'er he got her, I
See nought more strange in this than 't other lottery.

XXXVIII

I, for my part—(one 'modern instance' more,
　'True, 't is a pity—pity 't is, 't is true')—
Was chosen from out an amatory score,
　Albeit my years were less discreet than few;
But though I also had reformed before
　Those became one who soon were to be two,
I 'll not gainsay the generous public's voice,
That the young lady made a monstrous choice.

XXXIX

Oh, pardon my digression—or at least
  Peruse! 'T is always with a moral end
That I dissert, like grace before a feast:
  For like an agéd aunt, or tiresome friend,
A rigid guardian, or a zealous priest,
  My Muse by exhortation means to mend
All people, at all times, and in most places,
Which puts my Pegasus to these grave paces.

XL

But now I'm going to be immoral; now
  I mean to show things really as they are,
Not as they ought to be: for I avow,
  That till we see what's what in fact, we're far
From much improvement with that virtuous plough
  Which skims the surface, leaving scarce a scar
Upon the black loam long manured by Vice,
Only to keep its corn at the old price.

XLI

But first of little Leila we'll dispose,
  For like a day-dawn she was young and pure—
Or like the old comparison of snows,
  (Which are more pure than pleasant, to be sure,
Like many people everybody knows),—
  Don Juan was delighted to secure
A goodly guardian for his infant charge,
Who might not profit much by being at large.

XLII

Besides, he had found out he was no tutor
  (I wish that others would find out the same),
And rather wished in such things to stand neuter,
  For silly wards will bring their guardians blame:
So when he saw each ancient dame a suitor
  To make his little wild Asiatic tame,
Consulting 'the Society for Vice
Suppression,' Lady Pinchbeck was his choice.

XLIII

Olden she was—but had been very young;
   Virtuous she was—and had been, I believe;
Although the World has such an evil tongue
   That—but my chaster ear will not receive
An echo of a syllable that 's wrong:
   In fact, there 's nothing makes me so much grieve,
As that abominable tittle-tattle,
Which is the cud eschewed by human cattle.

XLIV

Moreover I 've remarked (and I was once
   A slight observer in a modest way),
And so may every one except a dunce,
   That ladies in their youth a little gay,
Besides their knowledge of the World, and sense
   Of the sad consequence of going astray,
Are wiser in their warnings 'gainst the woe
Which the mere passionless can never know.

XLV

While the harsh prude indemnifies her virtue
   By railing at the unknown and envied passion,
Seeking far less to save you than to hurt you,
   Or, what 's still worse, to put you out of fashion,—
The kinder veteran with calm words will court you,
   Entreating you to pause before you dash on;
Expounding and illustrating the riddle
Of epic Love's beginning—end—and middle.

XLVI

Now whether it be thus, or that they are stricter,
   As better knowing why they should be so,
I think you 'll find from many a family picture
   That daughters of such mothers as may know
The World by experience rather than by lecture,
   Turn out much better for the Smithfield Show
Of vestals brought into the marriage mart,
Than those bred up by prudes without a heart.

XLVII

I said that Lady Pinchbeck had been talked about—
  As who has not, if female, young, and pretty?
But now no more the ghost of Scandal stalked about;
  She merely was deemed amiable and witty,
And several of her best *bons-mots* were hawked about:
  Then she was given to charity and pity,
And passed (at least the latter years of life)
For being a most exemplary wife.

XLVIII

High in high circles, gentle in her own,
  She was the mild reprover of the young,
Whenever—which means every day—they 'd shown
  An awkward inclination to go wrong.
The quantity of good she did 's unknown,
  Or at the least would lengthen out my song:
In brief, the little orphan of the East
Had raised an interest in her,—which increased.

XLIX

Juan, too, was a sort of favourite with her,
  Because she thought him a good heart at bottom,
A little spoiled, but not so altogether;
  Which was a wonder, if you think who got him,
And how he had been tossed, he scarce knew whither:
  Though this might ruin others, it did *not* him,
At least entirely—for he had seen too many
Changes in Youth, to be surprised at any.

L

And these vicissitudes tell best in youth;
  For when they happen at a riper age,
People are apt to blame the Fates, forsooth,
  And wonder Providence is not more sage.
Adversity is the first path to Truth:
  He who hath proved War—Storm—or Woman's rage,
Whether his winters be eighteen or eighty,
Hath won the experience which is deemed so weighty.

LI

How far it profits is another matter.—
    Our hero gladly saw his little charge
Safe with a lady, whose last grown-up daughter
    Being long married, and thus set at large,
Had left all the accomplishments she taught her
    To be transmitted, like the Lord Mayor's barge,
To the next comer ; or—as it will tell
More Muse-like—like to Cytherea's shell.

LII

I call such things transmission ; for there is
    A floating balance of accomplishment,
Which forms a pedigree from Miss to Miss,
    According as their minds or backs are bent.
Some waltz—some draw—some fathom the abyss
    Of Metaphysics ; others are content
With Music ; the most moderate shine as wits ;—
While others have a genius turned for fits.

LIII

But whether fits, or wits, or harpsichords—
    Theology—fine arts—or finer stays,
May be the baits for Gentlemen or Lords
    With regular descent, in these our days,
The last year to the new transfers its hoards ;
    New vestals claim men's eyes with the same praise
Of 'elegant' *et cætera*, in fresh batches—
All matchless creatures—and yet bent on matches.

LIV

But now I will begin my poem. 'Tis
    Perhaps a little strange, if not quite new,
That from the first of Cantos up to this
    I 've not begun what we have to go through.
These first twelve books are merely flourishes,
    Preludios, trying just a string or two
Upon my lyre, or making the pegs sure ;
And when so, you shall have the overture.

o

LV

My Muses do not care a pinch of rosin
    About what 's called success, or not succeeding:
Such thoughts are quite below the strain they have chosen;
    'T is a 'great moral lesson' they are reading.
I thought, at setting off, about two dozen
    Cantos would do; but at Apollo's pleading,
If that my Pegasus should not be foundered,
I think to canter gently through a hundred.

LVI

Don Juan saw that Microcosm on stilts,
    Yclept the Great World; for it is the least,
Although the highest: but as swords have hilts
    By which their power of mischief is increased,
When Man in battle or in quarrel tilts,
    Thus the low world, north, south, or west, or east,
Must still obey the high—which is their handle,
Their Moon, their Sun, their gas, their farthing candle.

LVII

He had many friends who had many wives, and was
    Well looked upon by both, to that extent
Of friendship which you may accept or pass,
    It does nor good nor harm; being merely meant
To keep the wheels going of the higher class,
    And draw them nightly when a ticket 's sent;
And what with masquerades, and fêtes, and balls,
For the first season such a life scarce palls.

LVIII

A young unmarried man, with a good name
    And fortune, has an awkward part to play;
For good society is but a game,
    'The royal game of Goose,' as I may say,
Where everybody has some separate aim,
    An end to answer, or a plan to lay—
The single ladies wishing to be double,
The married ones to save the virgins trouble.

LIX

I don't mean this as general, but particular
   Examples may be found of such pursuits:
Though several also keep their perpendicular
   Like poplars, with good principles for roots;
Yet many have a method more *reticular*—
   'Fishers for men,' like Sirens with soft lutes:
For talk six times with the same single lady,
And you may get the wedding-dresses ready.

LX

Perhaps you 'll have a letter from the mother,
   To say her daughter's feelings are trepanned;
Perhaps you 'll have a visit from the brother,
   All strut, and stays, and whiskers, to demand
What 'your intentions are'?—One way or other
   It seems the virgin's heart expects your hand:
And between pity for her case and yours,
You 'll add to Matrimony's list of cures.

LXI

I 've known a dozen weddings made even *thus*,
   And some of them high names: I have also known
Young men who—though they hated to discuss
   Pretensions which they never dreamed to have shown—
Yet neither frightened by a female fuss,
   Nor by mustachios moved, were let alone,
And lived, as did the broken-hearted fair,
In happier plight than if they formed a pair.

LXII

There 's also nightly, to the uninitiated,
   A peril—not indeed like Love or Marriage,
But not the less for this to be depreciated:
   It is—I meant and mean not to disparage
The show of Virtue even in the vitiated—
   It adds an outward grace unto their carriage—
But to denounce the amphibious sort of harlot,
Couleur de rose, who 's neither white nor scarlet.

LXIII

Such is your cold coquette, who can't say 'No,'
    And won't say 'Yes,' and keeps you on and off-ing
On a lee-shore, till it begins to blow—
    Then sees your heart wrecked, with an inward scoffing.
This works a world of sentimental woe,
    And sends new Werters yearly to their coffin;
But yet is merely innocent flirtation,
Not quite adultery, but adulteration.

LXIV

'Ye gods, I grow a talker!' Let us prate.
    The next of perils, though I place it *stern*est,
Is when, without regard to Church or State,
    A wife makes or takes love in upright earnest.
Abroad, such things decide few women's fate—
    (Such, early Traveller! is the truth thou learnest)—
But in old England, when a young bride errs,
Poor thing! Eve's was a trifling case to hers.

LXV

For 't is a low, newspaper, humdrum lawsuit
    Country, where a young couple of the same ages
Can't form a friendship, but the world o'erawes it.
    Then there 's the vulgar trick of those d—d damages!
A verdict—grievous foe to those who cause it!—
    Forms a sad climax to romantic homages;
Besides those soothing speeches of the pleaders,
And evidences which regale all readers.

LXVI

But they who blunder thus are raw beginners;
    A little genial sprinkling of hypocrisy
Has saved the fame of thousand splendid sinners,
    The loveliest oligarchs of our Gynocracy;
You may see such at all the balls and dinners,
    Among the proudest of our aristocracy,
So gentle, charming, charitable, chaste—
And all by having *tact* as well as taste.

LXVII

Juan, who did not stand in the predicament
　　Of a mere novice, had one safeguard more;
For he was sick——no, 't was not the word *sick* I meant—
　　But he had seen so much good love before,
That he was not in heart so very weak;—I meant
　　But thus much, and no sneer against the shore
Of white cliffs, white necks, blue eyes, bluer stockings—
Tithes, taxes, duns—and doors with double knockings.

LXVIII

But coming young from lands and scenes romantic,
　　Where lives, not lawsuits, must be risked for Passion,
And Passion's self must have a spice of frantic,
　　Into a country where 't is half a fashion,
Seemed to him half commercial, half pedantic,
　　Howe'er he might esteem this moral nation:
Besides (alas! his taste—forgive and pity!)
At *first* he did not think the women pretty.

LXIX

I say at *first*—for he found out at *last*,
　　But by degrees, that they were fairer far
Than the more glowing dames whose lot is cast
　　Beneath the influence of the Eastern Star.
A further proof we should not judge in haste;
　　Yet inexperience could not be his bar
To taste:—the truth is, if men would confess,
That novelties *please* less than they *impress*.

LXX

Though travelled, I have never had the luck to
　　Trace up those shuffling negroes, Nile or Niger,
To that impracticable place Timbuctoo,
　　Where Geography finds no one to oblige her
With such a chart as may be safely stuck to—
　　For Europe ploughs in Afric like '*bos piger*':
But if I *had been* at Timbuctoo, there
No doubt I should be told that black is fair.

LXXI

It is. I will not swear that black is white,
  But I suspect in fact that white is black,
And the whole matter rests upon eye-sight :—
  Ask a blind man, the best judge. You 'll attack
Perhaps this new position—but I 'm right ;
  Or if I 'm wrong, I 'll not be ta'en aback :—
He hath no morn nor night, but all is dark
Within—and what seest thou? A dubious spark!

LXXII

But I 'm relapsing into Metaphysics,
  That labyrinth, whose clue is of the same
Construction as your cures for hectic phthisics,
  Those bright moths fluttering round a dying flame :
And this reflection brings me to plain Physics,
  And to the beauties of a foreign dame,
Compared with those of our pure pearls of price,
Those polar summers, *all* Sun, and some ice.

LXXIII

Or say they are like virtuous mermaids, whose
  Beginnings are fair faces, ends mere fishes ;—
Not that there 's not a quantity of those
  Who have a due respect for their own wishes.
Like Russians rushing from hot baths to snows
  Are they, at bottom virtuous even when vicious :
They warm into a scrape, but keep of course,
As a reserve, a plunge into remorse.

LXXIV

But this has nought to do with their outsides.
  I said that Juan did not think them pretty
At the first blush ; for a fair Briton hides
  Half her attractions—probably from pity—
And rather calmly into the heart glides,
  Than storms it as a foe would take a city ;
But once *there* (if you doubt this, prithee try)
She keeps it for you like a true ally.

LXXV

She cannot step as does an Arab barb,
  Or Andalusian girl from mass returning,
Nor wear as gracefully as Gauls her garb,
  Nor in her eye Ausonia's glance is burning;
Her voice, though sweet, is not so fit to warb-
  le those *bravuras* (which I still am learning
To like, though I have been seven years in Italy,
And have, or had, an ear that served me prettily);—

LXXVI

She cannot do these things, nor one or two
  Others, in that off-hand and dashing style
Which takes so much—to give the Devil his due;
  Nor is she quite so ready with her smile,
Nor settles all things in one interview,
  (A thing approved as saving time and toil);—
But though the soil may give you time and trouble,
Well cultivated, it will render double.

LXXVII

And if in fact she takes to a *grande passion*,
  It is a very serious thing indeed:
Nine times in ten 't is but caprice or fashion,
  Coquetry, or a wish to take the lead,
The pride of a mere child with a new sash on,
  Or wish to make a rival's bosom bleed:
But the *tenth* instance will be a tornado,
For there 's no saying what they will or may do.

LXXVIII

The reason is obvious: if there 's an *éclat*,
  They lose their caste at once, as do the Parias;
And when the delicacies of the Law
  Have filled their papers with their comments various,
Society, that china without flaw,
  (The Hypocrite!) will banish them like Marius,
To sit amidst the ruins of their guilt:
For Fame 's a Carthage not so soon rebuilt.

LXXIX

Perhaps this is as it should be ;—it is
   A comment on the Gospel's 'Sin no more,
And be thy sins forgiven :'—but upon this
   I leave the Saints to settle their own score.
Abroad, though doubtless they do much amiss,
   An erring woman finds an opener door
For her return to Virtue—as they call
That Lady, who should be at home to all.

LXXX

For me, I leave the matter where I find it,
   Knowing that such uneasy virtue leads
People some ten times less in fact to mind it,
   And care but for discoveries, and not deeds.
And as for Chastity, you 'll never bind it
   By all the laws the strictest lawyer pleads,
But aggravate the crime you have not prevented,
By rendering desperate those who had else repented.

LXXXI

But Juan was no casuist, nor had pondered
   Upon the moral lessons of mankind :
Besides, he had not seen of several hundred
   A lady altogether to his mind.
A little *blasé*—'t is not to be wondered
   At, that his heart had got a tougher rind :
And though not vainer from his past success,
No doubt his sensibilities were less.

LXXXII

He also had been busy seeing sights—
   The Parliament and all the other houses ;
Had sat beneath the Gallery at nights,
   To hear debates whose thunder *roused* (not *rouses*)
The World to gaze upon those Northern Lights,
   Which flashed as far as where the musk-bull browses ;
He had also stood at times behind the Throne—
But Grey was not arrived, and Chatham gone.

LXXXIII

He saw, however, at the closing session,
  That noble sight, when *really* free the nation,
A King in constitutional possession
  Of such a Throne as is the proudest station,
Though Despots know it not—till the progression
  Of Freedom shall complete their education.
'T is not mere Splendour makes the show august
To eye or heart—it is the People's trust.

LXXXIV

There, too, he saw (whate'er he may be now)
  A Prince, the Prince of Princes at the time,
With fascination in his very bow,
  And full of promise, as the spring of prime.
Though Royalty was written on his brow,
  He had *then* the grace, too, rare in every clime,
Of being, without alloy of fop or beau,
A finished Gentleman from top to toe.

LXXXV

And Juan was received, as hath been said,
  Into the best society; and there
Occurred what often happens, I 'm afraid,
  However disciplined and debonnaire:—
The talent and good humour he displayed,
  Besides the marked distinction of his air,
Exposed him, as was natural, to temptation,
Even though himself avoided the occasion.

LXXXVI

But what, and where, with whom, and when, and why,
  Is not to be put hastily together;
And as my object is Morality
  (Whatever people say), I don't know whether
I 'll leave a single reader's eyelid dry,
  But harrow up his feelings till they wither,
And hew out a huge monument of pathos,
As Philip's son proposed to do with Athos.

LXXXVII

Here the twelfth canto of our Introduction
    Ends. When the body of the Book 's begun,
You 'll find it of a different construction
    From what some people say 't will be when done;
The plan at present 's simple in concoction.
    I can't oblige you, reader, to read on;
That 's your affair, not mine: a real spirit
Should neither court neglect, nor dread to bear it.

LXXXVIII

And if my thunderbolt not always rattles,
    Remember, reader! you have had before,
The worst of tempests and the best of battles,
    That e'er were brewed from elements or gore,
Besides the most sublime of—Heaven knows what else;
    An usurer could scarce expect much more—
But my best canto—save one on astronomy—
Will turn upon 'Political Economy.'

LXXXIX

That is your present theme for popularity:
    Now that the public hedge hath scarce a stake,
It grows an act of patriotic charity,
    To show the people the best way to break.
My plan (but I, if but for singularity,
    Reserve it) will be very sure to take.
Meantime, read all the National-Debt sinkers,
And tell me what you think of our great thinkers.

CANTO THE THIRTEENTH

I

I now mean to be serious;—it is time,
    Since Laughter now-a-days is deemed too serious;
A jest at Vice by Virtue 's called a crime,
    And critically held as deleterious:

Besides, the sad 's a source of the sublime,
    Although, when long, a little apt to weary us;
And therefore shall my lay soar high and solemn,
As an old temple dwindled to a column.

II

The Lady Adeline Amundeville
    ('T is an old Norman name, and to be found
In pedigrees, by those who wander still
    Along the last fields of that Gothic ground)
Was high-born, wealthy by her father's will,
    And beauteous, even where beauties most abound,
In Britain,—which, of course, true patriots find
The goodliest soil of Body and of Mind.

III

I 'll not gainsay them; it is not my cue;
    I'll leave them to their taste, no doubt the best;
An eye 's an eye, and whether black or blue,
    Is no great matter, so 't is in request;
'T is nonsense to dispute about a hue—
    The kindest may be taken as a test.
The fair sex should be always fair; and no man,
Till thirty, should perceive there 's a plain woman.

IV

And after that serene and somewhat dull
    Epoch, that awkward corner turned for days
More quiet, when our moon 's no more at full,
    We may presume to criticise or praise;
Because Indifference begins to lull
    Our passions, and we walk in Wisdom's ways;
Also because the figure and the face
Hint that 't is time to give the younger place.

V

I know that some would fain postpone this era,
    Reluctant as all placemen to resign

Their post; but theirs is merely a chimera,
    For they have passed Life's equinoctial line:
But then they have their claret and Madeira,
    To irrigate the dryness of decline;
And County meetings, and the Parliament,
And debt—and what not, for their solace sent.

VI

And is there not Religion and Reform,
    Peace, War, the taxes, and what 's called the 'Nation'?
The struggle to be pilots in a storm?
    The landed and the monied speculation?
The joys of mutual hate to keep them warm,
    Instead of Love, that mere hallucination?
Now Hatred is by far the longest pleasure;
Men love in haste, but they detest at leisure.

VII

Rough Johnson, the great moralist, professed,
    Right honestly, 'he liked an honest hater'!
The only truth that yet has been confessed
    Within these latest thousand years or later.
Perhaps the fine old fellow spoke in jest:—
    For my part, I am but a mere spectator,
And gaze where'er the palace or the hovel is,
Much in the mode of Goethe's Mephistopheles;

VIII

But neither love nor hate in much excess;
    Though 't was not once so. If I sneer sometimes,
It is because I cannot well do less,
    And now and then it also suits my rhymes.
I should be very willing to redress
    Men's wrongs, and rather check than punish crimes,
Had not Cervantes, in that too true tale
Of Quixote, shown how all such efforts fail.

IX

Of all tales 't is the saddest—and more sad,
  Because it makes us smile: his hero 's right,
And still pursues the right;—to curb the bad
  His only object, and 'gainst odds to fight
His guerdon: 't is his virtue makes him mad!
  But his adventures form a sorry sight;—
A sorrier still is the great moral taught
By that real Epic unto all who have thought.

X

Redressing injury, revenging wrong,
  To aid the damsel and destroy the caitiff;
Opposing singly the united strong,
  From foreign yoke to free the helpless native:—
Alas! must noblest views, like an old song,
  Be for mere Fancy's sport a theme creative,
A jest, a riddle, Fame through thin and thick sought!
And Socrates himself but Wisdom's Quixote?

XI

Cervantes smiled Spain's chivalry away;
  A single laugh demolished the right arm
Of his own country;—seldom since that day
  Has Spain had heroes. While Romance could charm,
The World gave ground before her bright array;
  And therefore have his volumes done such harm,
That all their glory, as a composition,
Was dearly purchased by his land's perdition.

XII

I 'm 'at my old lunes'—digression, and forget
  The lady Adeline Amundeville;
The fair most fatal Juan ever met,
  Although she was not evil nor meant ill;
But Destiny and Passion spread the net
  (Fate is a good excuse for our own will),
And caught them;—what do they *not* catch, methinks?
But I 'm not Œdipus, and Life 's a Sphinx.

XIII

I tell the tale as it is told, nor dare
  To venture a solution: '*Davus sum!*'
And now I will proceed upon the pair.
  Sweet Adeline, amidst the gay World's hum,
Was the Queen-Bee, the glass of all that 's fair;
  Whose charms made all men speak, and women dumb.
The last 's a miracle, and such was reckoned,
And since that time there has not been a second.

XIV

Chaste was she, to Detraction's desperation,
  And wedded unto one she had loved well—
A man known in the councils of the Nation,
  Cool, and quite English, imperturbable,
Though apt to act with fire upon occasion,
  Proud of himself and her: the World could tell
Nought against either, and both seemed secure—
She in her virtue, he in his hauteur.

XV

It chanced some diplomatical relations,
  Arising out of business, often brought
Himself and Juan in their mutual stations
  Into close contact. Though reserved, nor caught
By specious seeming, Juan's youth, and patience,
  And talent, on his haughty spirit wrought,
And formed a basis of esteem, which ends
In making men what Courtesy calls friends,

XVI

And thus Lord Henry, who was cautious as
  Reserve and Pride could make him, and full slow
In judging men—when once his judgment was
  Determined, right or wrong, on friend or foe,
Had all the pertinacity Pride has,
  Which knows no ebb to its imperious flow,
And loves or hates, disdaining to be guided,
Because its own good pleasure hath decided.

XVII

His friendships, therefore, and no less aversions,
    Though oft well founded, which confirmed but more
His prepossessions, like the laws of Persians
    And Medes, would ne'er revoke what went before.
His feelings had not those strange fits, like tertians,
    Of common likings, which make some deplore
What they should laugh at—the mere ague still
Of men's regard, the fever or the chill.

XVIII

'Tis not in mortals to command success:'
    But *do you more*, Sempronius—*don't* deserve it,
And take my word, you won't have any less.
    Be wary, watch the time, and always serve it;
Give gently way, when there 's too great a press;
    And for your conscience, only learn to nerve it;
For, like a racer, or a boxer training,
'T will make, if proved, vast efforts without paining.

XIX

Lord Henry also liked to be superior,
    As most men do, the little or the great;
The very lowest find out an inferior,
    At least they think so, to exert their state
Upon: for there are very few things wearier
    Than solitary Pride's oppressive weight,
Which mortals generously would divide,
By bidding others carry while they ride.

XX

In birth, in rank, in fortune likewise equal,
    O'er Juan he could no distinction claim;
In years he had the advantage of Time's sequel;
    And, as he thought, in country much the same—
Because bold Britons have a tongue and free quill,
    At which all modern nations vainly aim;
And the Lord Henry was a great debater,
So that few Members kept the House up later.

XXI

These were advantages: and then he thought—
    It was his foible, but by no means sinister—
That few or none more than himself had caught
    Court mysteries, having been himself a minister:
He liked to teach that which he had been taught,
    And greatly shone whenever there had been a stir;
And reconciled all qualities which grace man,
Always a patriot—and, sometimes, a placeman.

XXII

He liked the gentle Spaniard for his gravity;
    He almost honoured him for his docility;
Because, though young, he acquiesced with suavity,
    Or contradicted but with proud humility.
He knew the World, and would not see depravity
    In faults which sometimes show the soil's fertility,
If that the weeds o'erlive not the first crop—
For then they are very difficult to stop.

XXIII

And then he talked with him about Madrid,
    Constantinople, and such distant places;
Where people always did as they were bid,
    Or did what they should not with foreign graces.
Of coursers also spake they: Henry rid
    Well, like most Englishmen, and loved the races;
And Juan, like a true-born Andalusian,
Could back a horse, as Despots ride a Russian.

XXIV

And thus acquaintance grew, at noble routs,
    And diplomatic dinners, or at other—
For Juan stood well both with Ins and Outs,
    As in freemasonry a higher brother.
Upon his talent Henry had no doubts;
    His manner showed him sprung from a high mother,
And all men like to show their hospitality
To him whose breeding matches with his quality.

XXV

At Blank-Blank Square;—for we will break no squares
  By naming streets: since men are so censorious
And apt to sow an author's wheat with tares,
  Reaping allusions private and inglorious,
Where none were dreamt of, unto Love's affairs,
  Which were, or are, or are to be notorious,
That therefore do I previously declare,
Lord Henry's mansion was in Blank-Blank Square.

XXVI

Also there bin another pious reason
  For making squares and streets anonymous;
Which is, that there is scarce a single season
  Which doth not shake some very splendid house
With some slight heart-quake of domestic treason—
  A topic Scandal doth delight to rouse:
Such I might stumble over unawares,
Unless I knew the very chastest squares.

XXVII

'T is true, I might have chosen Piccadilly,
  A place where peccadillos are unknown;
But I have motives, whether wise or silly,
  For letting that pure sanctuary alone.
Therefore I name not square, street, place, until I
  Find one where nothing naughty can be shown,
A vestal shrine of Innocence of Heart:
Such are——but I have lost the London Chart.

XXVIII

At Henry's mansion then, in Blank-Blank Square,
  Was Juan a *recherché*, welcome guest,
As many other noble scions were;
  And some who had but Talent for their crest;
Or Wealth, which is a passport everywhere;
  Or even mere Fashion, which indeed 's the best
Recommendation; and to be well dressed
Will very often supersede the rest.

XXIX

And since 'there 's safety in a multitude
   Of counsellors,' as Solomon has said,
Or some one for him, in some sage, grave mood ;—
   Indeed we see the daily proof displayed
In Senates, at the Bar, in wordy feud,
   Where'er collective wisdom can parade,
Which is the only cause that we can guess
Of Britain's present wealth and happiness ;—

XXX

But as 'there 's safety' grafted in the number
   'Of counsellors,' for men,—thus for the sex
A large acquaintance lets not Virtue slumber ;
   Or should it shake, the choice will more perplex—
Variety itself will more encumber.
   'Midst many rocks we guard more against wrecks—
And thus with women : howsoe'er it shocks some's
Self-love, there 's safety in a crowd of coxcombs.

XXXI

But Adeline had not the least occasion
   For such a shield, which leaves but little merit
To Virtue proper, or good education.
   Her chief resource was in her own high spirit,
Which judged Mankind at their due estimation ;
   And for coquetry, she disdained to wear it—
Secure of admiration : its impression
Was faint—as of an every-day possession.

XXXII

To all she was polite without parade ;
   To some she showed attention of that kind
Which flatters, but is flattery conveyed
   In such a sort as cannot leave behind
A trace unworthy either wife or maid ;—
   A gentle, genial courtesy of mind,
To those who were, or passed for meritorious,
Just to console sad Glory for being glorious ;

XXXIII

Which is in all respects, save now and then,
 A dull and desolate appendage. Gaze
Upon the shades of those distinguished men
 Who were or are the puppet-shows of praise,
The praise of persecution. Gaze again
 On the most favoured; and amidst the blaze
Of sunset halos o'er the laurel-browed,
What can ye recognise?—a gilded cloud.

XXXIV

There also was of course in Adeline
 That calm patrician polish in the address,
Which ne'er can pass the equinoctial line
 Of anything which Nature would express;
Just as a Mandarin finds nothing fine,—
 At least his manner suffers not to guess,
That anything he views can greatly please:
Perhaps we have borrowed this from the Chinese—

XXXV

Perhaps from Horace: his 'Nil admirari'
 Was what he called the 'Art of Happiness'—
An art on which the artists greatly vary,
 And have not yet attained to much success.
However, 't is expedient to be wary:
 Indifference, certes, don't produce distress;
And rash Enthusiasm in good society
Were nothing but a moral inebriety.

XXXVI

But Adeline was not indifferent: for
 (*Now* for a common-place!) beneath the snow,
As a Volcano holds the lava more
 Within—*et cœtera*. Shall I go on?—No!
I hate to hunt down a tired metaphor,
 So let the often-used Volcano go.
Poor thing! How frequently, by me and others,
It hath been stirred up till its smoke quite smothers!

XXXVII

I 'll have another figure in a trice :—
 What say you to a bottle of champagne?
Frozen into a very vinous ice,
 Which leaves few drops of that immortal rain,
Yet in the very centre, past all price,
 About a liquid glassful will remain ;
And this is stronger than the strongest grape
Could e'er express in its expanded shape :

XXXVIII

'T is the whole spirit brought to a quintessence ;
 And thus the chilliest aspects may concentre
A hidden nectar under a cold presence.
 And such are many—though I only meant her
From whom I now deduce these moral lessons,
 On which the Muse has always sought to enter.
And your cold people are beyond all price,
When once you've broken their confounded ice.

XXXIX

But after all they are a North-West Passage
 Unto the glowing India of the soul ;
And as the good ships sent upon that message
 Have not exactly ascertained the Pole
(Though Parry's efforts look a lucky presage),
 Thus gentlemen may run upon a shoal ;
For if the Pole 's not open, but all frost
(A chance still), 't is a voyage or vessel lost.

XL

And young beginners may as well commence
 With quiet cruising o'er the ocean, Woman ;
While those who are not beginners should have sense
 Enough to make for port, ere Time shall summon
With his grey signal-flag ; and the past tense,
 The dreary *Fuimus* of all things human,
Must be declined, while Life's thin thread 's spun out
Between the gaping heir and gnawing gout.

XLI

But Heaven must be diverted; its diversion
  Is sometimes truculent—but never mind:
The World upon the whole is worth the assertion
  (If but for comfort) that all things are kind:
And that same devilish doctrine of the Persian,
  Of the 'Two Principles,' but leaves behind
As many doubts as any other doctrine
Has ever puzzled Faith withal, or yoked her in.

XLII

The English winter—ending in July,
  To recommence in August—now was done.
'T is the postilion's paradise: wheels fly;
  On roads, East, South, North, West, there is a run.
But for post-horses who finds sympathy?
  Man's pity 's for himself, or for his son,
Always premising that said son at college
Has not contracted much more debt than knowledge.

XLIII

The London winter 's ended in July—
  Sometimes a little later. I don't err
In this: whatever other blunders lie
  Upon my shoulders, here I must aver
My Muse a glass of *Weatherology*;
  For Parliament is our barometer:
Let Radicals its other acts attack,
Its sessions form our only almanack.

XLIV

When its quicksilver 's down at zero,—lo!
  Coach, chariot, luggage, baggage, equipage!
Wheels whirl from Carlton Palace to Soho,
  And happiest they who horses can engage;
The turnpikes glow with dust; and Rotten Row
  Sleeps from the Chivalry of this bright age;
And tradesmen, with long bills and longer faces,
Sigh—as the postboys fasten on the traces.

XLV

They and their bills, 'Arcadians both,' are left
  To the Greek Kalends of another session.
Alas! to them of ready cash bereft,
  What hope remains? Of *hope* the full possession,
Or generous draft, conceded as a gift,
  At a long date—till they can get a fresh one—
Hawked about at a discount, small or large;
Also the solace of an overcharge.

XLVI

But these are trifles. Downward flies my Lord,
  Nodding beside my Lady in his carriage.
Away! away! 'Fresh horses!' are the word,
  And changed as quickly as hearts after marriage;
The obsequious landlord hath the change restored;
  The postboys have no reason to disparage
Their fee; but ere the watered wheels may hiss hence,
The ostler pleads too for a reminiscence.

XLVII

'T is granted; and the valet mounts the dickey—
  That gentleman of Lords and Gentlemen;
Also my Lady's gentlewoman, tricky,
  Tricked out, but modest more than poet's pen
Can paint,—'*Cosi viaggino i Ricchi!*'
  (Excuse a foreign slipslop now and then,
If but to show I 've travelled: and what 's Travel,
Unless it teaches one to quote and cavil?)

XLVIII

The London winter and the country summer
  Were well nigh over. 'T is perhaps a pity,
When Nature wears the gown that doth become her,
  To lose those best months in a sweaty city,
And wait until the nightingale grows dumber,
  Listening debates not very wise or witty,
Ere patriots their true *country* can remember;—
But there 's no shooting (save grouse) till September.

XLIX

I 've done with my tirade. The World was gone;
   The twice two thousand, for whom Earth was made,
Were vanished to be what they call alone—
   That is, with thirty servants for parade,
As many guests, or more; before whom groan
   As many covers, duly, daily laid.
Let none accuse old England's hospitality—
Its quantity is but condensed to quality.

L

Lord Henry and the Lady Adeline
   Departed like the rest of their compeers,
The peerage, to a mansion very fine—
   The Gothic Babel of a thousand years.
None than themselves could boast a longer line,
   Where Time through heroes and through beauties steers;
And oaks as olden as their pedigree
Told of their Sires—a tomb in every tree.

LI

A paragraph in every paper told
   Of their departure—such is modern fame:
'T is pity that it takes no further hold
   Than an advertisement, or much the same;
When, ere the ink be dry, the sound grows cold.
   The Morning Post was foremost to proclaim—
'Departure, for his country seat, to-day,
Lord H. Amundeville and Lady A.

LII

'We understand the splendid host intends
   To entertain, this autumn, a select
And numerous party of his noble friends;
   'Midst whom we have heard, from sources quite correct,
The Duke of D—— the shooting season spends,
   With many more by rank and fashion decked;
Also a foreigner of high condition,
The envoy of the secret Russian mission.'

LIII

And thus we see—who doubts the Morning Post?
    (Whose articles are like the 'Thirty-nine,'
Which those most swear to who believe them most)—
    Our gay Russ Spaniard was ordained to shine,
Decked by the rays reflected from his host,
    With those who, Pope says, 'Greatly daring dine.'—
'T is odd, but true,—last war the News abounded
More with these dinners than the killed or wounded;—

LIV

As thus: 'On Thursday there was a grand dinner;
    Present, Lords A. B. C.' Earls, dukes, by name
Announced with no less pomp than Victory's winner:
    Then underneath, and in the very same
Column: date, 'Falmouth. There has lately been here
    The Slap-dash regiment, so well known to Fame,
Whose loss in the late action we regret:
The vacancies are filled up—see Gazette.'

LV

To Norman Abbey whirled the noble pair,—
    An old, old Monastery once, and now
Still older mansion—of a rich and rare
    Mixed Gothic, such as artists all allow
Few specimens yet left us can compare
    Withal: it lies, perhaps, a little low,
Because the monks preferred a hill behind,
To shelter their devotion from the wind.

LVI

It stood embosomed in a happy valley,
    Crowned by high woodlands, where the Druid oak
Stood like Caractacus, in act to rally
    His host, with broad arms 'gainst the thunder-stroke;
And from beneath his boughs were seen to sally
    The dappled foresters; as Day awoke,
The branching stag swept down with all his herd,
To quaff a brook which murmured like a bird.

LVII

Before the mansion lay a lucid Lake,
  Broad as transparent, deep, and freshly fed
By a river, which its softened way did take
  In currents through the calmer water spread
Around : the wildfowl nestled in the brake
  And sedges, brooding in their liquid bed :
The woods sloped downwards to its brink, and stood
With their green faces fixed upon the flood.

LVIII

Its outlet dashed into a deep cascade,
  Sparkling with foam, until again subsiding,
Its shriller echoes—like an infant made
  Quiet—sank into softer ripples, gliding
Into a rivulet ; and thus allayed,
  Pursued its course, now gleaming, and now hiding
Its windings through the woods ; now clear, now blue,
According as the skies their shadows threw.

LIX

A glorious remnant of the Gothic pile
  (While yet the Church was Rome's) stood half apart
In a grand Arch, which once screened many an aisle.
  These last had disappeared—a loss to Art :
The first yet frowned superbly o'er the soil,
  And kindled feelings in the roughest heart,
Which mourned the power of Time's or Tempest's march,
In gazing on that venerable Arch.

LX

Within a niche, nigh to its pinnacle,
  Twelve Saints had once stood sanctified in stone ;
But these had fallen, not when the friars fell,
  But in the war which struck Charles from his throne,
When each house was a fortalice—as tell
  The annals of full many a line undone,—
The gallant Cavaliers, who fought in vain
For those who knew not to resign or reign.

LXI

But in a higher niche, alone, but crowned,
  The Virgin-Mother of the God-born Child,
With her Son in her blesséd arms, looked round,
  Spared by some chance when all beside was spoiled:
She made the earth below seem holy ground.
  This may be superstition, weak or wild;
But even the faintest relics of a shrine
Of any worship wake some thoughts divine.

LXII

A mighty window, hollow in the centre,
  Shorn of its glass of thousand colourings,
Through which the deepened glories once could enter,
  Streaming from off the Sun like Seraph's wings,
Now yawns all desolate: now loud, now fainter,
  The gale sweeps through its fretwork, and oft sings
The owl his anthem, where the silenced quire
Lie with their Hallelujahs quenched like fire.

LXIII

But in the noontide of the moon, and when
  The wind is wingéd from one point of heaven,
There moans a strange unearthly sound, which then
  Is musical—a dying accent driven
Through the huge Arch, which soars and sinks again.
  Some deem it but the distant echo given
Back to the night wind by the waterfall,
And harmonized by the old choral wall:

LXIV

Others, that some original shape, or form
  Shaped by decay perchance, hath given the power
(Though less than that of Memnon's statue, warm
  In Egypt's rays, to harp at a fixed hour)
To this grey ruin: with a voice to charm,
  Sad, but serene, it sweeps o'er tree or tower;
The cause I know not, nor can solve; but such
The fact:—I 've heard it,—once perhaps too much.

LXV

Amidst the court a Gothic fountain played,
  Symmetrical, but decked with carvings quaint—
Strange faces, like to men in masquerade,
  And here perhaps a monster, there a saint:
The spring gushed through grim mouths of granite made,
  And sparkled into basins, where it spent
Its little torrent in a thousand bubbles,
Like man's vain glory, and his vainer troubles.

LXVI

The Mansion's self was vast and venerable,
  With more of the monastic than has been
Elsewhere preserved: the cloisters still were stable,
  The cells, too, and Refectory, I ween:
An exquisite small chapel had been able,
  Still unimpaired, to decorate the scene;
The rest had been reformed, replaced, or sunk,
And spoke more of the baron than the monk.

LXVII

Huge halls, long galleries, spacious chambers, joined
  By no quite lawful marriage of the arts,
Might shock a connoisseur; but when combined,
  Formed a whole which, irregular in parts,
Yet left a grand impression on the mind,
  At least of those whose eyes are in their hearts:
We gaze upon a giant for his stature,
Nor judge at first if all be true to nature.

LXVIII

Steel Barons, molten the next generation
  To silken rows of gay and gartered Earls,
Glanced from the walls in goodly preservation:
  And Lady Marys blooming into girls,
With fair long locks, had also kept their station:
  And Countesses mature in robes and pearls:
Also some beauties of Sir Peter Lely,
Whose drapery hints we may admire them freely.

LXIX

Judges in very formidable ermine
    Were there, with brows that did not much invite
The accused to think their lordships would determine
    His cause by leaning much from might to right:
Bishops, who had not left a single sermon;
    Attorneys-general, awful to the sight,
As hinting more (unless our judgments warp us)
Of the 'Star Chamber' than of 'Habeas Corpus.'

LXX

Generals, some all in armour, of the old
    And iron time, ere lead had ta'en the lead;
Others in wigs of Marlborough's martial fold,
    Huger than twelve of our degenerate breed:
Lordlings, with staves of white or keys of gold:
    Nimrods, whose canvas scarce contained the steed;
And, here and there, some stern high patriot stood,
Who could not get the place for which he sued.

LXXI

But ever and anon, to soothe your vision,
    Fatigued with these hereditary glories,
There rose a Carlo Dolce or a Titian,
    Or wilder group of savage Salvatore's:
Here danced Albano's boys, and here the sea shone
    In Vernet's ocean lights; and there the stories
Of martyrs awed, as Spagnoletto tainted
His brush with all the blood of all the sainted.

LXXII

Here sweetly spread a landscape of Lorraine;
    There Rembrandt made his darkness equal light,
Or gloomy Caravaggio's gloomier stain
    Bronzed o'er some lean and stoic anchorite:—
But, lo! a Teniers woos, and not in vain,
    Your eyes to revel in a livelier sight:
His bell-mouthed goblet makes me feel quite Danish
Or Dutch with thirst—What, ho! a flask of Rhenish.

LXXIII

Oh, reader! if that thou canst read,—and know,
　　'T is not enough to spell, or even to read,
To constitute a reader—there must go
　　Virtues of which both you and I have need ;—
Firstly, begin with the beginning—(though
　　That clause is hard) ; and secondly, proceed :
Thirdly, commence not with the end—or sinning
In this sort, end at last with the beginning.

LXXIV

But, reader, thou hast patient been of late,
　　While I, without remorse of rhyme, or fear,
Have built and laid out ground at such a rate,
　　Dan Phœbus takes me for an auctioneer.
That Poets were so from their earliest date,
　　By Homer's 'Catalogue of ships' is clear ;
But a mere modern must be moderate—
I spare you then the furniture and plate.

LXXV

The mellow Autumn came, and with it came
　　The promised party, to enjoy its sweets.
The corn is cut, the manor full of game ;
　　The pointer ranges, and the sportsman beats
In russet jacket :—lynx-like in his aim ;
　　Full grows his bag, and wonder*ful* his feats.
Ah, nutbrown partridges! Ah, brilliant pheasants!
And ah, ye poachers!—'T is no sport for peasants.

LXXVI

An English Autumn, though it hath no vines,
　　Blushing with Bacchant coronals along
The paths o'er which the far festoon entwines
　　The red grape in the sunny lands of song,
Hath yet a purchased choice of choicest wines ;
　　The Claret light, and the Madeira strong.
If Britain mourn her bleakness, we can tell her,
The very best of vineyards is the cellar.

LXXVII

Then, if she hath not that serene decline
　　Which makes the southern Autumn's day appear
As if 't would to a second Spring resign
　　The season, rather than to Winter drear,—
Of in-door comforts still she hath a mine,—
　　The sea-coal fires, the 'earliest of the year';
Without doors, too, she may compete in mellow,
As what is lost in green is gained in yellow.

LXXVIII

And for the effeminate *villeggiatura*—
　　Rife with more horns than hounds—she hath the chase,
So animated that it might allure a
　　Saint from his beads to join the jocund race:
Even Nimrod's self might leave the plains of Dura,
　　And wear the Melton jacket for a space:
If she hath no wild boars, she hath a tame
Preserve of bores, who ought to be made game.

LXXIX

The noble guests, assembled at the Abbey,
　　Consisted of—we give the sex the *pas*—
The Duchess of Fitz-Fulke; the Countess Crabby;
　　The Ladies Scilly, Busey;—Miss Eclat,
Miss Bombazeen, Miss Mackstay, Miss O'Tabby,
　　And Mrs. Rabbi, the rich banker's squaw;
Also the honourable Mrs. Sleep,
Who looked a white lamb, yet was a black sheep:

LXXX

With other Countesses of Blank—but rank;
　　At once the 'lie' and the *élite* of crowds;
Who pass like water filtered in a tank,
　　All purged and pious from their native clouds;
Or paper turned to money by the Bank:
　　No matter how or why, the passport shrouds
The *passée* and the past; for good society
　　no less famed for tolerance than piety,—

LXXXI

That is, up to a certain point; which point
  Forms the most difficult in punctuation.
Appearances appear to form the joint
  On which it hinges in a higher station;
And so that no explosion cry Aroint
  Thee, witch!' or each Medea has her Jason;
Or (to the point with Horace and with Pulci)
'*Omne tulit punctum, quæ miscuit utile dulci.*'

LXXXII

I can't exactly trace their rule of right,
  Which hath a little leaning to a lottery:
I 've seen a virtuous woman put down quite
  By the mere combination of a coterie;
Also a so-so matron boldly fight
  Her way back to the world by dint of plottery,
And shine the very *Siria* of the spheres,
Escaping with a few slight, scarless sneers.

LXXXIII

I have seen more than I 'll say:—but we will see
  How our '*villeggiatura*' will get on.
The party might consist of thirty-three
  Of highest caste—the Brahmins of the *ton*.
I have named a few, not foremost in degree,
  But ta'en at hazard as the rhyme may run.
By way of sprinkling, scattered amongst these,
There also were some Irish absentees.

LXXXIV

There was Parolles, too, the legal bully,
  Who limits all his battles to the Bar
And Senate: when invited elsewhere, truly,
  He shows more appetite for words than war.
There was the young bard Rackrhyme, who had newly
  Come out and glimmered as a six weeks' star.
There was Lord Pyrrho, too, the great freethinker;
And Sir John Pottledeep, the mighty drinker.

LXXXV

There was the Duke of Dash, who was a—duke,
   'Aye, every inch a' duke; there were twelve peers
Like Charlemagne's—and all such peers in *look*
   And *intellect*, that neither eyes nor ears
For commoners had ever them mistook.
   There were the six Miss Rawbolds—pretty dears!
All song and sentiment; whose hearts were set
Less on a convent than a coronet.

LXXXVI

There were four Honourable Misters, whose
   Honour was more before their names than after;
There was the *preux Chevalier de la Ruse*,
   Whom France and Fortune lately deigned to waft here,
Whose chiefly harmless talent was to amuse;
   But the clubs found it rather serious laughter,
Because—such was his magic power to please—
The dice seemed charmed, too, with his repartees.

LXXXVII

There was Dick Dubious, the metaphysician,
   Who loved philosophy and a good dinner;
Angle, the *soi-disant* mathematician;
   Sir Henry Silvercup, the great race-winner.
There was the Reverend Rodomont Precisian,
   Who did not hate so much the sin as sinner:
And Lord Augustus Fitz-Plantagenet,
Good at all things, but better at a bet.

LXXXVIII

There was Jack Jargon, the gigantic guardsman;
   And General Fireface, famous in the field,
A great tactician, and no less a swordsman,
   Who ate, last war, more Yankees than he killed.
There was the waggish Welsh Judge, Jefferies Hardsman,
   In his grave office so completely skilled,
That when a culprit came for condemnation,
He had his Judge's joke for consolation.

LXXXIX

Good company 's a chess-board—there are kings,
    Queens, bishops, knights, rooks, pawns ; the World 's a game ;
Save that the puppets pull at their own strings,
    Methinks gay Punch hath something of the same.
My Muse, the butterfly hath but her wings,
    Not stings, and flits through ether without aim,
Alighting rarely :—were she but a hornet,
Perhaps there might be vices which would mourn it.

XC

I had forgotten—but must not forget—
    An orator, the latest of the session,
Who had delivered well a very set
    Smooth speech, his first and maidenly transgression
Upon debate : the papers echoed yet
    With his *début*, which made a strong impression,
And ranked with what is every day displayed—
'The best first speech that ever yet was made.'

XCI

Proud of his 'Hear hims!' proud, too, of his vote,
    And lost virginity of oratory,
Proud of his learning (just enough to quote),
    He revelled in his Ciceronian glory :
With memory excellent to get by rote,
    With wit to hatch a pun or tell a story,
Graced with some merit, and with more effrontery,
'His country's pride,' he came down to the country.

XCII

There also were two wits by acclamation,
    Longbow from Ireland, Strongbow from the Tweed—
Both lawyers and both men of education—
    But Strongbow's wit was of more polished breed ;
Longbow was rich in an imagination
    As beautiful and bounding as a steed,
But sometimes stumbling over a potato,—
While Strongbow's best things might have come from Cato.

P

XCIII

Strongbow was like a new-tuned harpsichord;
  But Longbow wild as an Æolian harp,
With which the winds of heaven can claim accord,
  And make a music, whether flat or sharp.
Of Strongbow's talk you would not change a word:
  At Longbow's phrases you might sometimes carp:
Both wits—one born so, and the other bred—
This by his heart—his rival by his head.

XCIV

If all these seem an heterogeneous mass
  To be assembled at a country seat,
Yet think, a specimen of every class
  Is better than a humdrum tête-à-tête.
The days of Comedy are gone, alas!
  When Congreve's fool could vie with Molière's *bête*:
Society is smoothed to that excess,
That manners hardly differ more than dress.

XCV

Our ridicules are kept in the back-ground—
  Ridiculous enough, but also dull;
Professions, too, are no more to be found
  Professional; and there is nought to cull
Of Folly's fruit; for though your fools abound,
  They 're barren, and not worth the pains to pull.
Society is now one polished horde,
Formed of two mighty tribes, the *Bores* and *Bored*.

XCVI

But from being farmers, we turn gleaners, gleaning
  The scanty but right-well threshed ears of Truth;
And, gentle reader! when you gather meaning,
  You may be Boaz, and I—modest Ruth.
Further I 'd quote, but Scripture intervening
  Forbids. A great impression in my youth
Was made by Mrs. Adams, where she cries,
'That Scriptures out of church are blasphemies.'

XCVII

But what we can we glean in this vile age
   Of chaff, although our gleanings be not grist.
I must not quite omit the talking sage,
   Kit-Cat, the famous Conversationist,
Who, in his common-place book, had a page
   Prepared each morn for evenings. 'List, oh list!'
'Alas, poor ghost!'—What unexpected woes
Await those who have studied their *bons-mots*!

XCVIII

Firstly, they must allure the conversation,
   By many windings to their clever clinch;
And secondly, must let slip no occasion,
   Nor *bate* (abate) their hearers of an *inch*,
But take an ell—and make a great sensation,
   If possible; and thirdly, never flinch
When some smart talker puts them to the test,
But seize the last word, which no doubt 's the best.

XCIX

Lord Henry and his lady were the hosts;
   The party we have touched on were the guests.
Their table was a board to tempt even ghosts
   To pass the Styx for more substantial feasts.
I will not dwell upon *ragoûts* or roasts,
   Albeit all human history attests
That happiness for Man—the hungry sinner!—
Since Eve ate apples, much depends on dinner.

C

Witness the lands which 'flowed with milk and honey,'
   Held out unto the hungry Israelites:
To this we have added since, the love of money,
   The only sort of pleasure which requites.
Youth fades, and leaves our days no longer sunny;
   We tire of mistresses and parasites;
But oh, ambrosial cash! Ah! who would lose thee?
When we no more can use, or even abuse thee!

CI

The gentlemen got up betimes to shoot,
    Or hunt: the young, because they liked the sport—
The first thing boys like after play and fruit;
    The middle-aged, to make the day more short;
For *ennui* is a growth of English root,
    Though nameless in our language:—we retort
The fact for words, and let the French translate
That awful yawn which sleep can not abate.

CII

The elderly walked through the library,
    And tumbled books, or criticized the pictures,
Or sauntered through the gardens piteously,
    And made upon the hot-house several strictures,
Or rode a nag which trotted not too high,
    Or on the morning papers read their lectures,
Or on the watch their longing eyes would fix,
Longing at sixty for the hour of six.

CIII

But none were *gêné*: the great hour of union
    Was rung by dinner's knell; till then all were
Masters of their own time—or in communion,
    Or solitary, as they chose to bear
The hours, which how to pass is but to few known.
    Each rose up at his own, and had to spare
What time he chose for dress, and broke his fast
When, where, and how he chose for that repast.

CIV

The ladies—some rouged, some a little pale—
    Met the morn as they might. If fine, they rode,
Or walked; if foul, they read, or told a tale,
    Sung, or rehearsed the last dance from abroad;
Discussed the fashion which might next prevail,
    And settled bonnets by the newest code,
Or crammed twelve sheets into one little letter,
To make each correspondent a new debtor.

CV

For some had absent lovers, all had friends;
   The earth has nothing like a she epistle,
And hardly Heaven—because it never ends.
   I love the mystery of a female missal,
Which, like a creed, ne'er says all it intends,
   But full of cunning as Ulysses' whistle,
When he allured poor Dolon:—you had better
Take care what you reply to such a letter.

CVI

Then there were billiards; cards, too, but *no* dice;—
   Save in the clubs no man of honour plays;—
Boats when 't was water, skating when 't was ice,
   And the hard frost destroyed the scenting days:
And angling, too, that solitary vice,
   Whatever Izaak Walton sings or says:
The quaint, old, cruel coxcomb, in his gullet
Should have a hook, and a small trout to pull it.

CVII

With evening came the banquet and the wine;
   The conversazione—the duet
Attuned by voices more or less divine
   (My heart or head aches with the memory yet).
The four Miss Rawbolds in a glee would shine;
   But the two youngest loved more to be set
Down to the harp—because to Music's charms
They added graceful necks, white hands and arms.

CVIII

Sometimes a dance (though rarely on field days,
   For then the gentlemen were rather tired)
Displayed some sylph-like figures in its maze;
   Then there was small-talk ready when required;
Flirtation—but decorous; the mere praise
   Of charms that should or should not be admired.
The hunters fought their fox-hunt o'er again,
And then retreated soberly—at ten.

CIX

The politicians, in a nook apart,
  Discussed the World, and settled all the spheres:
The wits watched every loophole for their art,
  To introduce a *bon-mot* head and ears;
Small is the rest of those who would be smart,
  A moment's good thing may have cost them years
Before they find an hour to introduce it;
And then, even *then*, some bore may make them lose it.

CX

But all was gentle and aristocratic
  In this our party; polished, smooth, and cold,
As Phidian forms cut out of marble Attic.
  There now are no Squire Westerns, as of old;
And our Sophias are not so emphatic,
  But fair as then, or fairer to behold:
We have no accomplished blackguards, like Tom Jones,
But gentlemen in stays, as stiff as stones.

CXI

They separated at an early hour;
  That is, ere midnight—which is London's noon:
But in the country ladies seek their bower
  A little earlier than the waning moon.
Peace to the slumbers of each folded flower—
  May the rose call back its true colour soon!
Good hours of fair cheeks are the fairest tinters,
And lower the price of rouge—at least some winters.

CANTO THE FOURTEENTH

I

If from great Nature's or our own abyss
  Of Thought we could but snatch a certainty,
Perhaps Mankind might find the path they miss—
  But then 't would spoil much good philosophy.

One system eats another up, and this
    Much as old Saturn ate his progeny;
For when his pious consort gave him stones
In lieu of sons, of these he made no bones.

II

But System doth reverse the Titan's breakfast,
    And eats her parents, albeit the digestion
Is difficult. Pray tell me, can you make fast,
    After due search, your faith to any question?
Look back o'er ages, ere unto the stake fast
    You bind yourself, and call some mode the best one.
Nothing more true than *not* to trust your senses;
And yet what are your other evidences?

III

For me, I know nought; nothing I deny,
    Admit—reject—contemn: and what know *you*,
Except perhaps that you were born to die?
    And both may after all turn out untrue.
An age may come, Font of Eternity,
    When nothing shall be either old or new.
Death, so called, is a thing which makes men weep,
And yet a third of Life is passed in sleep.

IV

A sleep without dreams, after a rough day
    Of toil, is what we covet most; and yet
How clay shrinks back from more quiescent clay!
    The very Suicide that pays his debt
At once without instalments (an old way
    Of paying debts, which creditors regret),
Lets out impatiently his rushing breath,
Less from disgust of Life than dread of Death.

V

'T is round him—near him—here—there—everywhere—
    And there 's a courage which grows out of fear,

Perhaps of all most desperate, which will dare
   The worst to *know* it:—when the mountains rear
Their peaks beneath your human foot, and there
   You look down o'er the precipice, and drear
The gulf of rock yawns,—you can't gaze a minute,
Without an awful wish to plunge within it.

VI

'T is true, you don't—but, pale and struck with terror,
   Retire: but look into your past impression!
And you will find, though shuddering at the mirror
   Of your own thoughts, in all their self-confession,
The lurking bias, be it truth or error,
   To the *unknown*; a secret prepossession,
To plunge with all your fears—but where? You know not,
And that 's the reason why you do—or do not.

VII

But what 's this to the purpose? you will say.
   Gent. reader, nothing; a mere speculation,
For which my sole excuse is—'t is my way;
   Sometimes *with* and sometimes without occasion,
I write what 's uppermost, without delay;
   This narrative is not meant for narration,
But a mere airy and fantastic basis,
To build up common things with common places.

VIII

You know, or don't know, that great Bacon saith,
   'Fling up a straw, 't will show the way the wind blows;'
And such a straw, borne on by human breath,
   Is Poesy, according as the Mind glows;
A paper kite which flies 'twixt Life and Death,
   A shadow which the onward Soul behind throws:
And mine 's a bubble, not blown up for praise,
But just to play with, as an infant plays.

IX

The World is all before me—or behind;
　For I have seen a portion of that same,
And quite enough for me to keep in mind;—
　Of passions, too, I have proved enough to blame,
To the great pleasure of our friends, Mankind,
　Who like to mix some slight alloy with fame;
For I was rather famous in my time,
Until I fairly knocked it up with rhyme.

X

I have brought this world about my ears, and eke
　The other; that 's to say, the Clergy—who
Upon my head have bid their thunders break
　In pious libels by no means a few.
And yet I can't help scribbling once a week,
　Tiring old readers, nor discovering new.
In Youth I wrote because my mind was full,
And *now* because I feel it growing dull.

XI

But 'why then publish?'—There are no rewards
　Of fame or profit when the World grows weary.
I ask in turn,—Why do you play at cards?
　Why drink? Why read?—To make some hour less dreary.
It occupies me to turn back regards
　On what I 've seen or pondered, sad or cheery;
And what I write I cast upon the stream,
To swim or sink—I have had at least my dream.

XII

I think that were I *certain* of success,
　I hardly could compose another line:
So long I 've battled either more or less,
　That no defeat can drive me from the Nine.
This feeling 't is not easy to express,
　And yet 't is not affected, I opine.
In play, there are two pleasures for your choosing—
The one is winning, and the other losing.

XIII

Besides, my Muse by no means deals in fiction:
　　She gathers a repertory of facts,
Of course with some reserve and slight restriction,
　　But mostly sings of human things and acts—
And that 's one cause she meets with contradiction;
　　For too much truth, at first sight, ne'er attracts;
And were her object only what 's called Glory,
With more ease, too, she 'd tell a different story.

XIV

Love—War—a tempest—surely there 's variety;
　　Also a seasoning slight of lucubration;
A bird's-eye view, too, of that wild, Society;
　　A slight glance thrown on men of every station.
If you have nought else, here 's at least satiety,
　　Both in performance and in preparation;
And though these lines should only line portmanteaus,
Trade will be all the better for these Cantos.

XV

The portion of this World which I at present
　　Have taken up to fill the following sermon,
Is one of which there 's no description recent:
　　The reason why is easy to determine:
Although it seems both prominent and pleasant,
　　There is a sameness in its gems and ermine,
A dull and family likeness through all ages,
Of no great promise for poetic pages.

XVI

With much to excite, there 's little to exalt;
　　Nothing that speaks to all men and all times;
A sort of varnish over every fault,
　　A kind of common-place, even in their crimes;
Factitious passions—Wit without much salt—
　　A want of that true nature which sublimes
Whate'er it shows with Truth; a smooth monotony
Of character, in those at least who have got any.

XVII

Sometimes, indeed, like soldiers off parade
  They break their ranks and gladly leave the drill;
But then the roll-call draws them back afraid,
  And they must be or seem what they were: still
Doubtless it is a brilliant masquerade:
  But when of the first sight you have had your fill,
It palls—at least it did so upon me,
This paradise of Pleasure and *Ennui*.

XVIII

When we have made our love, and gamed our gaming,
  Dressed, voted, shone, and, may be, something more—
With dandies dined—heard senators declaiming—
  Seen beauties brought to market by the score,
Sad rakes to sadder husbands chastely taming—
  There's little left but to be bored or bore:
Witness those *ci-devant jeunes hommes* who stem
The stream, nor leave the world which leaveth them.

XIX

'T is said—indeed a general complaint—
  That no one has succeeded in describing
The *monde*, exactly as they ought to paint:
  Some say, that authors only snatch, by bribing
The porter, some slight scandals strange and quaint,
  To furnish matter for their moral gibing;
And that their books have but one style in common—
My Lady's prattle, filtered through her woman.

XX

But this can't well be true, just now; for writers
  Are grown of the *beau monde* a part potential:
I've seen them balance even the scale with fighters,
  Especially when young, for that's essential.
Why do their sketches fail them as inditers
  Of what they deem themselves most consequential,
The *real* portrait of the highest tribe?
'T is that—in fact—there's little to describe.

XXI

'*Haud ignara loquor*'; these are *Nugæ*, '*quarum
  Pars* parva *fui*,' but still art and part.
Now I could much more easily sketch a harem,
  A battle, wreck, or history of the heart,
Than these things; and besides, I wish to spare 'em,
  For reasons which I choose to keep apart.
'*Vetabo Cereris sacrum qui vulgarit*'—
Which means, that vulgar people must not share it.

XXII

And therefore what I throw off is ideal—
  Lowered, leavened, like a history of Freemasons,
Which bears the same relation to the real,
  As Captain Parry's Voyage may do to Jason's.
The grand *Arcanum* 's not for men to see all;
  My music has some mystic diapasons;
And there is much which could not be appreciated
In any manner by the uninitiated.

XXIII

Alas! worlds fall—and Woman, since she felled
  The World (as, since that history, less polite
Than true, hath been a creed so strictly held),
  Has not yet given up the practice quite.
Poor Thing of Usages! coerced, compelled,
  Victim when wrong, and martyr oft when right,
Condemned to child-bed, as men for their sins
Have shaving, too, entailed upon their chins.—

XXIV

A daily plague, which in the aggregate
  May average on the whole with parturition.—
But as to women—who can penetrate
  The real sufferings of their she condition?
Man's very sympathy with their estate
  Has much of selfishness, and more suspicion.
Their love, their virtue, beauty, education,
But form good housekeepers—to breed a nation.

XXV

All this were very well, and can't be better;
    But even this is difficult, Heaven knows,
So many troubles from her birth beset her,
    Such small distinction between friends and foes;
The gilding wears so soon from off her fetter,
    That——but ask any woman if she 'd choose
(Take her at thirty, that is) to have been
Female or male? a schoolboy or a Queen?

XXVI

'Petticoat Influence' is a great reproach,
    Which even those who obey would fain be thought
To fly from, as from hungry pikes a roach;
    But since beneath it upon earth we are brought,
By various joltings of Life's hackney coach,
    I for one venerate a petticoat—
A garment of a mystical sublimity,
No matter whether russet, silk, or dimity.

XXVII

Much I respect, and much I have adored,
    In my young days, that chaste and goodly veil,
Which holds a treasure, like a miser's hoard,
    And more attracts by all it doth conceal—
A golden scabbard on a Damasque sword,
    A loving letter with a mystic seal,
A cure for grief—for what can ever rankle
Before a petticoat and peeping ankle?

XXVIII

And when upon a silent, sullen day,
    With a Sirocco, for example, blowing,
When even the sea looks dim with all its spray,
    And sulkily the river's ripple 's flowing,
And the sky shows that very ancient gray,
    The sober, sad antithesis to glowing,—
'T is pleasant, if *then* anything is pleasant,
To catch a glimpse even of a pretty peasant.

XXIX

We left our heroes and our heroines
  In that fair clime which don't depend on climate,
Quite independent of the Zodiac's signs,
  Though certainly more difficult to rhyme at,
Because the Sun, and stars, and aught that shines,
  Mountains, and all we can be most sublime at,
Are there oft dull and dreary as a *dun*—
Whether a sky's or tradesman's is all one.

XXX

An in-door life is less poetical;
  And out-of-door hath showers, and mists, and sleet,
With which I could not brew a pastoral:
  But be it as it may, a bard must meet
All difficulties, whether great or small,
  To spoil his undertaking, or complete—
And work away—like Spirit upon Matter—
Embarrassed somewhat both with fire and water.

XXXI

Juan—in this respect, at least, like saints—
  Was all things unto people of all sorts,
And lived contentedly, without complaints,
  In camps, in ships, in cottages, or courts—
Born with that happy soul which seldom faints,
  And mingling modestly in toils or sports.
He likewise could be most things to all women,
Without the coxcombry of certain *she* men.

XXXII

A fox-hunt to a foreigner is strange;
  'T is also subject to the double danger
Of tumbling first, and having in exchange
  Some pleasant jesting at the awkward stranger:
But Juan had been early taught to range
  The wilds, as doth an Arab turned avenger,
So that his horse, or charger, hunter, hack,
Knew that he had a rider on his back.

XXXIII

And now in this new field, with some applause,
   He cleared hedge, ditch, and double post, and rail,
And never *craned*, and made but few '*faux pas*,'
   And only fretted when the scent 'gan fail.
He broke, 't is true, some statutes of the laws
   Of hunting—for the sagest youth is frail;
Rode o'er the hounds, it may be, now and then,
And once o'er several Country Gentlemen.

XXXIV

But on the whole, to general admiration,
   He acquitted both himself and horse: the Squires
Marvelled at merit of another nation;
   The boors cried 'Dang it! who 'd have thought it?'—Sires,
The Nestors of the sporting generation,
   Swore praises, and recalled their former fires;
The Huntsman's self relented to a grin,
And rated him almost a whipper-in.

XXXV

Such were his trophies—not of spear and shield,
   But leaps, and bursts, and sometimes foxes' brushes;
Yet I must own,—although in this I yield
   To patriot sympathy a Briton's blushes,—
He thought at heart like courtly Chesterfield,
   Who, after a long chase o'er hills, dales, bushes,
And what not, though he rode beyond all price,
Asked next day, 'If men ever hunted *twice*?'

XXXVI

He also had a quality uncommon
   To early risers after a long chase,
Who wake in winter ere the cock can summon
   December's drowsy day to his dull race,—
A quality agreeable to Woman,
   When her soft, liquid words run on apace,
Who likes a listener, whether Saint or Sinner,—
He did not fall asleep just after dinner;

XXXVII

But, light and airy, stood on the alert,
　　And shone in the best part of dialogue,
By humouring always what they might assert,
　　And listening to the topics most in vogue,—
Now grave, now gay, but never dull or pert;
　　And smiling but in secret—cunning rogue!
He ne'er presumed to make an error clearer;—
In short, there never was a better hearer.

XXXVIII

And then he danced;—all foreigners excel
　　The serious Angles in the eloquence
Of pantomime!—he danced, I say, right well,
　　With emphasis, and also with good sense—
A thing in footing indispensable;
　　He danced without theatrical pretence,
Not like a ballet-master in the van
Of his drilled nymphs, but like a gentleman.

XXXIX

Chaste were his steps, each kept within due bound,
　　And Elegance was sprinkled o'er his figure;
Like swift Camilla, he scarce skimmed the ground,
　　And rather held in than put forth his vigour;
And then he had an ear for Music's sound,
　　Which might defy a crotchet critic's rigour.
Such classic *pas—sans* flaws—set off our hero,
He glanced like a personified Bolero;

XL

Or like a flying Hour before Aurora,
　　In Guido's famous fresco (which alone
Is worth a tour to Rome, although no more a
　　Remnant were there of the old World's sole throne)
The *tout ensemble* of his movements wore a
　　Grace of the soft Ideal, seldom shown,
And ne'er to be described; for to the dolour
Of bards and prosers, words are void of colour.

XLI

No marvel then he was a favourite;
    A full-grown Cupid, very much admired;
A little spoilt, but by no means so quite;
    At least he kept his vanity retired.
Such was his tact, he could alike delight
    The chaste, and those who are not so much inspired.
The Duchess of Fitz-Fulke, who loved *tracasserie*,
Began to treat him with some small *agacerie*.

XLII

She was a fine and somewhat full-blown blonde,
    Desirable, distinguished, celebrated
For several winters in the grand, *grand Monde*:
    I'd rather not say what might be related
Of her exploits, for this were ticklish ground;
    Besides there might be falsehood in what's stated:
Her late performance had been a dead set
At Lord Augustus Fitz-Plantagenet.

XLIII

This noble personage began to look
    A little black upon this new flirtation;
But such small licences must lovers brook,
    Mere freedoms of the female corporation.
Woe to the man who ventures a rebuke!
    'T will but precipitate a situation
Extremely disagreeable, but common
To calculators when they count on Woman.

XLIV

The circle smiled, then whispered, and then sneered;
    The misses bridled, and the matrons frowned;
Some hoped things might not turn out as they feared;
    Some would not deem such women could be found;
Some ne'er believed one half of what they heard;
    Some looked perplexed, and others looked profound:
And several pitied with sincere regret
Poor Lord Augustus Fitz-Plantagenet.

XLV

But what is odd, none ever named the Duke,
    Who, one might think, was something in the affair:
True, he was absent, and, 't was rumoured, took
    But small concern about the when, or where,
Or what his consort did: if he could brook
    Her gaieties, none had a right to stare:
Theirs was that best of unions, past all doubt,
Which never meets, and therefore can't fall out.

XLVI

But, oh! that I should ever pen so sad a line!
    Fired with an abstract love of Virtue, she,
My Dian of the Ephesians, Lady Adeline,
    Began to think the Duchess' conduct free;
Regretting much that she had chosen so bad a line,
    And waxing chiller in her courtesy,
Looked grave and pale to see her friend's fragility,
For which most friends reserve their sensibility.

XLVII

There 's nought in this bad world like sympathy:
    'T is so becoming to the soul and face,
Sets to soft music the harmonious sigh,
    And robes sweet Friendship in a Brussels lace.
Without a friend, what were Humanity,
    To hunt our errors up with a good grace?
Consoling us with—'Would you had thought twice!
Ah! if you had but followed my advice!'

XLVIII

O Job! you had two friends: one 's quite enough,
    Especially when we are ill at ease;
They 're but bad pilots when the weather 's rough,
    Doctors less famous for their cures than fees.
Let no man grumble when his friends fall off,
    As they will do like leaves at the first breeze:
When your affairs come round, one way or t 'other,
Go to the coffee-house, and take another.

XLIX

But this is not my maxim: had it been,
   Some heart-aches had been spared me: yet I care not—
I would not be a tortoise in his screen
   Of stubborn shell, which waves and weather wear not:
'T is better on the whole to have felt and seen
   That which Humanity may bear, or bear not:
'T will teach discernment to the sensitive,
And not to pour their Ocean in a sieve.

L

Of all the horrid, hideous notes of woe,
   Sadder than owl-songs or the midnight blast,
Is that portentous phrase, 'I told you so,'
   Uttered by friends, those prophets of the *past*,
Who, 'stead of saying what you *now* should do,
   Own they foresaw that you would fall at last,
And solace your slight lapse 'gainst *bonos mores*,
With a long memorandum of old stories.

LI

The Lady Adeline's serene severity
   Was not confined to feeling for her friend,
Whose fame she rather doubted with posterity,
   Unless her habits should begin to mend:
But Juan also shared in her austerity,
   But mixed with pity, pure as e'er was penned:
His Inexperience moved her gentle ruth,
And (as her junior by six weeks) his Youth.

LII

These forty days' advantage of her years—
   And hers were those which can face calculation,
Boldly referring to the list of Peers
   And noble births, nor dread the enumeration—
Gave her a right to have maternal fears
   For a young gentleman's fit education,
Though she was far from that leap year, whose leap,
In female dates, strikes Time all of a heap.

LIII

This may be fixed at somewhere before thirty—
    Say seven-and-twenty; for I never knew
The strictest in chronology and virtue
    Advance beyond, while they could pass for new.
O Time! why dost not pause? Thy scythe, so dirty
    With rust, should surely cease to hack and hew:
Reset it—shave more smoothly, also slower,
If but to keep thy credit as a mower.

LIV

But Adeline was far from that ripe age,
    Whose ripeness is but bitter at the best:
'T was rather her Experience made her sage,
    For she had seen the World and stood its test,
As I have said in—I forget what page;
    My Muse despises reference, as you have guessed
By this time;—but strike six from seven-and-twenty,
And you will find her sum of years in plenty.

LV

At sixteen she came out; presented, vaunted,
    She put all coronets into commotion:
At seventeen, too, the World was still enchanted
    With the new Venus of their brilliant Ocean:
At eighteen, though below her feet still panted
    A Hecatomb of suitors with devotion,
She had consented to create again
That Adam, called 'The happiest of men.'

LVI

Since then she had sparkled through three glowing winters,
    Admired, adored; but also so correct,
That she had puzzled all the acutest hinters,
    Without the apparel of being circumspect:
They could not even glean the slightest splinters
    From off the marble, which had no defect.
She had also snatched a moment since her marriage
To bear a son and heir—and one miscarriage.

LVII

Fondly the wheeling fire-flies flew around her,
    Those little glitterers of the London night;
But none of these possessed a sting to wound her—
    She was a pitch beyond a coxcomb's flight.
Perhaps she wished an aspirant profounder;
    But whatsoe'er she wished, she acted right;
And whether Coldness, Pride, or Virtue dignify
A Woman—so she's good—what *does* it signify?

LVIII

I hate a motive, like a lingering bottle
    Which with the landlord makes too long a stand,
Leaving all-claretless the unmoistened throttle,
    Especially with politics on hand;
I hate it, as I hate a drove of cattle,
    Who whirl the dust as Simooms whirl the sand;
I hate it as I hate an argument,
A Laureate's Ode, or servile Peer's 'Content.'

LIX

'T is sad to hack into the roots of things,
    They are so much intertwisted with the earth;
So that the branch a goodly verdure flings,
    I reck not if an acorn gave it birth.
To trace all actions to their secret springs
    Would make indeed some melancholy mirth:
But this is not at present my concern,
And I refer you to wise Oxenstiern.

LX

With the kind view of saving an *éclat*,
    Both to the Duchess and Diplomatist,
The Lady Adeline, as soon's she saw
    That Juan was unlikely to resist—
(For foreigners don't know that a *faux pas*
    In England ranks quite on a different list
From those of other lands unblest with juries,
Whose verdict for such sin a certain cure is;—)

LXI

The Lady Adeline resolved to take
  Such measures as she thought might best impede
The farther progress of this sad mistake.
  She thought with some simplicity indeed;
But Innocence is bold even at the stake,
  And simple in the World, and doth not need
Nor use those palisades by dames erected,
Whose virtue lies in never being detected.

LXII

It was not that she feared the very worst:
  His Grace was an enduring, married man,
And was not likely all at once to burst
  Into a scene, and swell the clients' clan
Of Doctors' Commons; but she dreaded first
  The magic of her Grace's talisman,
And next a quarrel (as he seemed to fret)
With Lord Augustus Fitz-Plantagenet.

LXIII

Her Grace, too, passed for being an *intrigante*,
  And somewhat *méchante* in her amorous sphere;
One of those pretty, precious plagues, which haunt
  A lover with caprices soft and dear,
That like to *make* a quarrel, when they can't
  Find one, each day of the delightful year:
Bewitching, torturing, as they freeze or glow,
And—what is worst of all—won't let you go:

LXIV

The sort of thing to turn a young man's head,
  Or make a Werter of him in the end.
No wonder then a purer soul should dread
  This sort of chaste *liaison* for a friend;
It were much better to be wed or dead,
  Than wear a heart a Woman loves to rend.
'T is best to pause, and think, ere you rush on,
If that a *bonne fortune* be really *bonne*.

LXV

And first, in the overflowing of her heart,
   Which really knew or thought it knew no guile,
She called her husband now and then apart,
   And bade him counsel Juan. With a smile
Lord Henry heard her plans of artless art
   To wean Don Juan from the Siren's wile;
And answered, like a statesman or a prophet,
In such guise that she could make nothing of it.

LXVI

Firstly, he said, 'he never interfered
   In anybody's business but the King's':
Next, that 'he never judged from what appeared,
   Without strong reason, of those sort of things':
Thirdly, that 'Juan had more brain than beard,
   And was not to be held in leading strings';
And fourthly, what need hardly be said twice,
'That good but rarely came from good advice.'

LXVII

And, therefore, doubtless to approve the truth
   Of the last axiom, he advised his spouse
To leave the parties to themselves, forsooth—
   At least as far as *bienséance* allows:
That time would temper Juan's faults of youth;
   That young men rarely made monastic vows
That Opposition only more attaches—
But here a messenger brought in despatches:

LXVIII

And being of the council called 'the Privy,'
   Lord Henry walked into his cabinet,
To furnish matter for some future Livy
   To tell how he reduced the Nation's debt;
And if their full contents I do not give ye,
   It is because I do not know them yet;
But I shall add them in a brief appendix,
To come between mine Epic and its index.

LXIX

But ere he went, he added a slight hint,
  Another gentle common-place or two,
Such as are coined in Conversation's mint,
  And pass, for want of better, though not new:
Then broke his packet, to see what was in 't,
  And having casually glanced it through,
Retired: and, as he went out, calmly kissed her,
Less like a young wife than an agéd sister.

LXX

He was a cold, good, honourable man,
  Proud of his birth, and proud of everything;
A goodly spirit for a state Divan,
  A figure fit to walk before a King;
Tall, stately, formed to lead the courtly van
  On birthdays, glorious with a star and string;
The very model of a chamberlain—
And such I mean to make him when I reign.

LXXI

But there was something wanting on the whole—
  I don't know what, and therefore cannot tell—
Which pretty women—the sweet souls!—call *soul*.
  Certes it was not body; he was well
Proportioned, as a poplar or a pole,
  A handsome man, that human miracle;
And in each circumstance of Love or War
Had still preserved his perpendicular.

LXXII

Still there was something wanting, as I 've said—
  That undefinable '*Je ne sçais quoi*,'
Which, for what I know, may of yore have led
  To Homer's Iliad, since it drew to Troy
The Greek Eve, Helen, from the Spartan's bed;
  Though on the whole, no doubt, the Dardan boy
Was much inferior to King Menelaüs:—
But thus it is some women will betray us.

LXXIII

There is an awkward thing which much perplexes,
  Unless like wise Tiresias we had proved
By turns the difference of the several sexes;
  Neither can show quite *how* they would be loved.
The Sensual for a short time but connects us—
  The Sentimental boasts to be unmoved;
But both together form a kind of Centaur,
Upon whose back 't is better not to venture.

LXXIV

A something all-sufficient for the *heart*
  Is that for which the sex are always seeking:
But how to fill up that same vacant part?
  There lies the rub—and this they are but weak in.
Frail mariners afloat without a chart,
  They run before the wind through high seas breaking;
And when they have made the shore through every shock,
'T is odd—or odds—it may turn out a rock.

LXXV

There is a flower called 'Love in Idleness,'
  For which see Shakespeare's ever-blooming garden;—
I will not make his great description less,
  And beg his British godship's humble pardon,
If, in my extremity of rhyme's distress,
  I touch a single leaf where he is warden;—
But, though the flower is different, with the French
Or Swiss Rousseau—cry '*Voilà la Pervenche!*'

LXXVI

Eureka! I have found it! What I mean
  To say is, not that Love is Idleness,
But that in Love such idleness has been
  An accessory, as I have cause to guess.
Hard Labour 's an indifferent go-between;
  Your men of business are not apt to express
Much passion, since the merchant-ship, the Argo,
Conveyed Medea as her supercargo.

LXXVII

'*Beatus ille procul!*' from '*negotiis*,'
  Saith Horace; the great little poet 's wrong;
His other maxim, '*Noscitur a sociis*,'
  Is much more to the purpose of his song;
Though even that were sometimes too ferocious,
  Unless good company be kept too long;
But, in his teeth, whate'er their state or station,
Thrice happy they who *have* an occupation!

LXXVIII

Adam exchanged his Paradise for ploughing,
  Eve made up millinery with fig leaves—
The earliest knowledge from the Tree so knowing,
  As far as I know, that the Church receives:
And since that time it need not cost much showing,
  That many of the ills o'er which Man grieves,
And still more Women, spring from not employing
Some hours to make the remnant worth enjoying.

LXXIX

And hence high life is oft a dreary void,
  A rack of pleasures, where we must invent
A something wherewithal to be annoyed.
  Bards may sing what they please about *Content*;
Contented, when translated, means but cloyed;
  And hence arise the woes of Sentiment,
Blue-devils—and Blue-stockings—and Romances
Reduced to practice, and performed like dances.

LXXX

I do declare, upon an affidavit,
  Romances I ne'er read like those I have seen;
Nor, if unto the World I ever gave it,
  Would some believe that such a tale had been:
But such intent I never had, nor have it;
  Some truths are better kept behind a screen,
Especially when they would look like lies;
I therefore deal in generalities.

LXXXI

'An oyster may be crossed in love'—and why?
  Because he mopeth idly in his shell,
And heaves a lonely subterraqueous sigh,
  Much as a monk may do within his cell:
And *à-propos* of monks, their Piety
  With Sloth hath found it difficult to dwell:
Those vegetables of the Catholic creed
Are apt exceedingly to run to seed.

LXXXII

O Wilberforce! thou man of black renown,
  Whose merit none enough can sing or say,
Thou hast struck one immense Colossus down,
  Thou moral Washington of Africa!
But there's another little thing, I own,
  Which you should perpetrate some summer's day,
And set the other half of Earth to rights;
You have freed the *blacks*—now pray shut up the whites.

LXXXIII

Shut up the bald-coot bully Alexander!
  Ship off the Holy Three to Senegal;
Teach them that 'sauce for goose is sauce for gander,'
  And ask them how *they* like to be in thrall!
Shut up each high heroic Salamander,
  Who eats fire gratis (since the pay's but small);
Shut up—no, *not* the King, but the Pavilion,
Or else 't will cost us all another million.

LXXXIV

Shut up the World at large, let Bedlam out;
  And you will be perhaps surprised to find
All things pursue exactly the same route,
  As now with those of *soi-disant* sound mind.
This I could prove beyond a single doubt,
  Were there a jot of sense among Mankind;
But till that *point d' appui* is found, alas!
Like Archimedes, I leave Earth as 't was.

LXXXV

Our gentle Adeline had one defect—
    Her heart was vacant, though a splendid mansion;
Her conduct had been perfectly correct,
    As she had seen nought claiming its expansion.
A wavering spirit may be easier wrecked,
    Because 't is frailer, doubtless, than a staunch one;
But when the latter works its own undoing,
Its inner crash is like an Earthquake's ruin.

LXXXVI

She loved her Lord, or thought so; but *that* love
    Cost her an effort, which is a sad toil,
The stone of Sisyphus, if once we move
    Our feelings 'gainst the nature of the soil.
She had nothing to complain of, or reprove,
    No bickerings, no connubial turmoil:
Their union was a model to behold,
Serene and noble,—conjugal, but cold.

LXXXVII

There was no great disparity of years,
    Though much in temper; but they never clashed:
They moved like stars united in their spheres,
    Or like the Rhone by Leman's waters washed,
Where mingled and yet separate appears
    The River from the Lake, all bluely dashed
Through the serene placid and glassy deep,
Which fain would lull its river-child to sleep.

LXXXVIII

Now when she once had ta'en an interest
    In anything, however she might flatter
Herself that her intentions were the best,
    Intense intentions are a dangerous matter:
Impressions were much stronger than she guessed,
    And gathered as they run like growing water
Upon her mind; the more so, as her breast
Was not at first too readily impressed.

LXXXIX

But when it was, she had that lurking Demon
　　Of double nature, and thus doubly named—
Firmness yclept in Heroes, Kings, and seamen,
　　That is, when they succeed; but greatly blamed
As *Obstinacy*, both in Men and Women,
　　Whene'er their triumph pales, or star is tamed:—
And 't will perplex the casuist in morality
To fix the due bounds of this dangerous quality.

XC

Had Buonaparte won at Waterloo,
　　It had been firmness; now 't is pertinacity:
Must the event decide between the two?
　　I leave it to your people of sagacity
To draw the line between the false and true,
　　If such can e'er be drawn by Man's capacity:
My business is with Lady Adeline,
Who in her way too was a heroine.

XCI

She knew not her own heart; then how should I?
　　I think not she was *then* in love with Juan:
If so, she would have had the strength to fly
　　The wild sensation, unto her a new one:
She merely felt a common sympathy
　　(I will not say it was a false or true one)
In him, because she thought he was in danger,—
Her husband's friend—her own—young—and a stranger.

XCII

She was, or thought she was, his friend—and this
　　Without the farce of Friendship, or romance
Of Platonism, which leads so oft amiss
　　Ladies who have studied Friendship but in France
Or Germany, where people *purely* kiss.
　　To thus much Adeline would not advance;
But of such friendship as Man's may to Man be
She was as capable as Woman can be.

XCIII

No doubt the secret influence of the Sex
    Will there, as also in the ties of blood,
An innocent predominance annex,
    And tune the concord to a finer mood.
If free from Passion, which all Friendship checks,
    And your true feelings fully understood,
No friend like to a woman Earth discovers,
So that you have not been nor will be lovers.

XCIV

Love bears within its breast the very germ
    Of Change ; and how should this be otherwise?
That violent things more quickly find a term
    Is shown through Nature's whole analogies ;
And how should the most fierce of all be firm?
    Would you have endless lightning in the skies?
Methinks Love's very title says enough :
How should 'the *tender* passion' e'er be *tough*?

XCV

Alas! by all experience, seldom yet
    (I merely quote what I have heard from many)
Had lovers not some reason to regret
    The passion which made Solomon a zany.
I've also seen some wives (not to forget
    The marriage state, the best or worst of any)
Who were the very paragons of wives,
Yet made the misery of at least two lives.

XCVI

I've also seen some female *friends* ('t is odd,
    But true—as, if expedient, I could prove)
That faithful were through thick and thin, abroad,
    At home, far more than ever yet was Love—
Who did not quit me when Oppression trod
    Upon me ; whom no scandal could remove ;
Who fought, and fight, in absence, too, my battles,
Despite the snake Society's loud rattles.

XCVII

Whether Don Juan and chaste Adeline
   Grew friends in this or any other sense,
Will be discussed hereafter, I opine:
   At present I am glad of a pretence
To leave them hovering, as the effect is fine,
   And keeps the atrocious reader in *suspense*:
The surest way—for ladies and for books—
To bait their tender—or their tenter—hooks.

XCVIII

Whether they rode, or walked, or studied Spanish,
   To read Don Quixote in the original,
A pleasure before which all others vanish;
   Whether their talk was of the kind called 'small,'
Or serious, are the topics I must banish
   To the next Canto; where perhaps I shall
Say something to the purpose, and display
Considerable talent in my way.

XCIX

Above all, I beg all men to forbear
   Anticipating aught about the matter:
They 'll only make mistakes about the fair,
   And Juan, too, especially the latter.
And I shall take a much more serious air
   Than I have yet done, in this Epic Satire.
It is not clear that Adeline and Juan
Will fall; but if they do, 't will be their ruin.

C

But great things spring from little:—Would you think,
   That in our youth, as dangerous a passion
As e'er brought Man and Woman to the brink
   Of ruin, rose from such a slight occasion,
As few would ever dream could form the link
   Of such a sentimental situation?
You 'll never guess, I 'll bet you millions, milliards—
It all sprung from a harmless game at billiards.

CI

'T is strange,—but true; for Truth is always strange—
   Stranger than fiction: if it could be told,
How much would novels gain by the exchange!
   How differently the World would men behold!
How oft would Vice and Virtue places change!
   The new world would be nothing to the old,
If some Columbus of the moral seas
Would show mankind their Souls' antipodes.

CII

What 'antres vast and deserts idle,' then,
   Would be discovered in the human soul!
What icebergs in the hearts of mighty men,
   With self-love in the centre as their Pole!
What Anthropophagi are nine of ten
   Of those who hold the kingdoms in control!
Were things but only called by their right name,
Cæsar himself would be ashamed of Fame.

CANTO THE FIFTEENTH

I

Ah!—What should follow slips from my reflection;
   Whatever follows ne'ertheless may be
As *à-propos* of Hope or Retrospection,
   As though the lurking thought had followed free.
All present life is but an Interjection,
   An 'Oh!' or 'Ah!' of Joy or Misery,
Or a 'Ha! ha!' or 'Bah!'—a yawn, or 'Pooh!'
Of which perhaps the latter is most true.

II

But, more or less, the whole 's a Syncopé
   Or a *Singultus*—emblems of Emotion,
The grand Antithesis to great *Ennui*,
   Wherewith we break our bubbles on the Ocean—

That Watery Outline of Eternity,
    Or miniature, at least, as is my notion—
Which ministers unto the Soul's delight,
In seeing matters which are out of sight.

III

But all are better than the sigh suppressed,
    Corroding in the cavern of the heart,
Making the countenance a masque of rest
    And turning Human Nature to an art.
Few men dare show their thoughts of worst or best;
    Dissimulation always sets apart
A corner for herself; and, therefore, Fiction
Is that which passes with least contradiction.

IV

Ah! who can tell? Or rather, who can not
    Remember, without telling, Passion's errors?
The drainer of Oblivion, even the sot,
    Hath got *blue devils* for his morning mirrors:
What though on Lethe's stream he seem to float,
    He cannot sink his tremors or his terrors;
The ruby glass that shakes within his hand
Leaves a sad sediment of Time's worst sand.

V

And as for Love—O Love!——We will proceed:—
    The Lady Adeline Amundeville,
A pretty name as one would wish to read,
    Must perch harmonious on my tuneful quill.
There 's Music in the sighing of a reed;
    There 's Music in the gushing of a rill;
There 's Music in all things, if men had ears:
Their Earth is but an echo of the Spheres.

VI

The Lady Adeline, Right Honourable,
    And honoured, ran a risk of growing less so;

Q

For few of the soft sex are very stable
　　In their resolves—alas! that I should say so:
They differ as wine differs from its label,
　　When once decanted;—I presume to guess so
But will not swear: yet both upon occasion,
Till old, may undergo adulteration.

VII

But Adeline was of the purest vintage,
　　The unmingled essence of the grape; and yet
Bright as a new napoleon from its mintage,
　　Or glorious as a diamond richly set;
A page where Time should hesitate to print age,
　　And for which Nature might forego her debt—
Sole creditor whose process doth involve in 't
The luck of finding everybody solvent.

VIII

O Death! thou dunnest of all duns! thou daily
　　Knockest at doors, at first with modest tap,
Like a meek tradesman when approaching palely
　　Some splendid debtor he would take by sap:
But oft denied, as Patience 'gins to fail, he
　　Advances with exasperated rap,
And (if let in) insists, in terms unhandsome,
On ready money, or 'a draft on Ransom.'

IX

Whate'er thou takest, spare awhile poor Beauty!
　　She is so rare, and thou hast so much prey.
What though she now and then may slip from duty,
　　The more 's the reason why you ought to stay;
Gaunt Gourmand, with whole nations for your booty,
　　You should be civil in a modest way:
Suppress, then, some slight feminine diseases,
And take as many heroes as Heaven pleases.

X

Fair Adeline, the more ingenuous
   Where she was interested (as was said),
Because she was not apt, like some of us,
   To like too readily, or too high bred
To show it—(points we need not now discuss)—
   Would give up artlessly both Heart and Head
Unto such feelings as seemed innocent,
For objects worthy of the sentiment.

XI

Some parts of Juan's history, which Rumour,
   That live Gazette, had scattered to disfigure,
She had heard; but women hear with more good humour
   Such aberrations than we men of rigour:
Besides, his conduct, since in England, grew more
   Strict, and his mind assumed a manlier vigour:
Because he had, like Alcibiades,
The art of living in all climes with ease.

XII

His manner was perhaps the more seductive,
   Because he ne'er seemed anxious to seduce;
Nothing affected, studied, or constructive
   Of coxcombry or conquest: no abuse
Of his attractions marred the fair perspective,
   To indicate a Cupidon broke loose,
And seem to say, 'Resist us if you can'—
Which makes a Dandy while it spoils a Man.

XIII

They are wrong—that 's not the way to set about it;
   As, if they told the truth, could well be shown.
But right, or wrong, Don Juan was without it;
   In fact, his manner was his own alone:
Sincere he was—at least you could not doubt it,
   In listening merely to his voice's tone.
The Devil hath not in all his quiver's choice
An arrow for the Heart like a sweet voice.

XIV

By nature soft, his whole address held off
    Suspicion : though not timid, his regard
Was such as rather seemed to keep aloof,
    To shield himself than put you on your guard :
Perhaps 't was hardly quite assured enough,
    But Modesty 's at times its own reward,
Like Virtue ; and the absence of pretension
Will go much farther than there 's need to mention.

XV

Serene, accomplished, cheerful but not loud ;
    Insinuating without insinuation ;
Observant of the foibles of the crowd,
    Yet ne'er betraying this in conversation ;
Proud with the proud, yet courteously proud,
    So as to make them feel he knew his station
And theirs :—without a struggle for priority,
He neither brooked nor claimed superiority—

XVI

That is, with Men : with Women he was what
    They pleased to make or take him for ; and their
Imagination 's quite enough for that :
    So that the outline 's tolerably fair,
They fill the canvas up—and '*verbum sat.*'
    If once their phantasies be brought to bear
Upon an object, whether sad or playful,
They can transfigure brighter than a Raphael.

XVII

Adeline, no deep judge of character,
    Was apt to add a colouring from her own :
'T is thus the Good will amiably err,
    And eke the Wise, as has been often shown.
Experience is the chief philosopher,
    But saddest when his science is well known :
And persecuted Sages teach the Schools
Their folly in forgetting there are fools.

XVIII

Was it not so, great Locke? and greater Bacon?
    Great Socrates? And thou, Diviner still,
Whose lot it is by Man to be mistaken,
    And thy pure creed made sanction of all ill?
Redeeming Worlds to be by bigots shaken,
    How was thy toil rewarded? We might fill
Volumes with similar sad illustrations,
But leave them to the conscience of the nations.

XIX

I perch upon an humbler promontory,
    Amidst Life's infinite variety:
With no great care for what is nicknamed Glory,
    But speculating as I cast mine eye
On what may suit or may not suit my story,
    And never straining hard to versify,
I rattle on exactly as I 'd talk
With anybody in a ride or walk.

XX

I don't know that there may be much ability
    Shown in this sort of desultory rhyme;
But there 's a conversational facility,
    Which may round off an hour upon a time.
Of this I 'm sure at least, there 's no servility
    In mine irregularity of chime,
Which rings what 's uppermost of new or hoary,
Just as I feel the *Improvvisatore*.

XXI

'*Omnia vult* belle *Matho dicere—dic aliquando*
    Et bene, *dic* neutrum, *dic aliquando* male.'
The first is rather more than mortal can do;
    The second may be sadly done or gaily;
The third is still more difficult to stand to;
    The fourth we hear, and see, and say too, daily:
The whole together is what I could wish
To serve in this conundrum of a dish.

XXII

A modest hope—but Modesty 's my forte,
　　And Pride my feeble :—let us ramble on.
I meant to make this poem very short,
　　But now I can't tell where it may not run.
No doubt, if I had wished to pay my court
　　To critics, or to hail the *setting* sun
Of Tyranny of all kinds, my concision
Were more ;—but I was born for opposition.

XXIII

But then 't is mostly on the weaker side ;
　　So that I verily believe if they
Who now are basking in their full-blown pride
　　Were shaken down, and 'dogs had had their day,'
Though at the first I might perchance deride
　　Their tumble, I should turn the other way,
And wax an ultra-royalist in Loyalty,
Because I hate even democratic Royalty.

XXIV

I think I should have made a decent spouse,
　　If I had never proved the soft condition ;
I think I should have made monastic vows
　　But for my own peculiar superstition :
'Gainst rhyme I never should have knocked my brows,
　　Nor broken my own head, nor that of Priscian,
Nor worn the motley mantle of a poet,
If some one had not told me to forego it.

XXV

But *laissez aller*—Knights and Dames I sing,
　　Such as the times may furnish. 'T is a flight
Which seems at first to need no lofty wing,
　　Plumed by Longinus or the Stagyrite :
The difficulty lies in colouring
　　(Keeping the due proportions still in sight)
With Nature manners which are artificial,
And rend'ring general that which is especial.

XXVI

The difference is, that in the days of old
　Men made the Manners; Manners now make men—
Pinned like a flock, and fleeced too in their fold,
　At least nine, and a ninth beside of ten.
Now this at all events must render cold
　Your writers, who must either draw again
Days better drawn before, or else assume
The present, with their common-place costume.

XXVII

We 'll do our best to make the best on 't:—March!
　March, my Muse! If you cannot fly, yet flutter;
And when you may not be sublime, be arch,
　Or starch, as are the edicts statesmen utter.
We surely may find something worth research:
　Columbus found a new world in a cutter,
Or brigantine, or pink, of no great tonnage,
While yet America was in her non-age.

XXVIII

When Adeline, in all her growing sense
　Of Juan's merits and his situation,
Felt on the whole an interest intense,—
　Partly perhaps because a fresh sensation,
Or that he had an air of innocence,
　Which is for Innocence a sad temptation,—
As Women hate half measures, on the whole,
She 'gan to ponder how to save his soul.

XXIX

She had a good opinion of Advice,
　Like all who give and eke receive it gratis,
For which small thanks are still the market price,
　Even where the article at highest rate is:
She thought upon the subject twice or thrice,
　And morally decided—the best state is
For Morals—Marriage; and, this question carried,
She seriously advised him to get married.

XXX

Juan replied, with all becoming deference,
  He had a predilection for that tie;
But that, at present, with immediate reference
  To his own circumstances, there might lie
Some difficulties, as in his own preference,
  Or that of her to whom he might apply:
That still he 'd wed with such or such a lady,
If that they were not married all already.

XXXI

Next to the making matches for herself,
  And daughters, brothers, sisters, kith or kin,
Arranging them like books on the same shelf,
  There 's nothing women love to dabble in
More (like a stock-holder in growing pelf)
  Than match-making in general: 't is no sin
Certes, but a preventative, and therefore
That is, no doubt, the only reason wherefore.

XXXII

But never yet (except of course a miss
  Unwed, or mistress never to be wed,
Or wed already, who object to this)
  Was there chaste dame who had not in her head
Some drama of the marriage Unities,
  Observed as strictly both at board and bed,
As those of Aristotle, though sometimes
They turn out Melodrames or Pantomimes.

XXXIII

They generally have some only son,
  Some heir to a large property, some friend
Of an old family, some gay Sir John,
  Or grave Lord George, with whom perhaps might end
A line, and leave Posterity undone,
  Unless a marriage was applied to mend
The prospect and their morals: and besides,
They have at hand a blooming glut of brides.

XXXIV

From these they will be careful to select,
  For this an heiress, and for that a beauty;
For one, a songstress who hath no defect,
  For t' other, one who promises much duty;
For this a lady no one can reject,
  Whose sole accomplishments were quite a booty;
A second for her excellent connections;
A third, because there can be no objections.

XXXV

When Rapp the Harmonist embargoed Marriage
  In his harmonious settlement—(which flourishes
Strangely enough as yet without miscarriage,
  Because it breeds no more mouths than it nourishes,
Without those sad expenses which disparage
  What Nature naturally most encourages)—
Why called he 'Harmony' a state *sans* wedlock?
Now here I 've got the preacher at a dead lock.

XXXVI

Because he either meant to sneer at Harmony
  Or Marriage, by divorcing them thus oddly.
But whether reverend Rapp learned this in Germany
  Or no, 't is said his sect is rich and godly,
Pious and pure, beyond what I can term any
  Of ours, although they propagate more broadly.
My objection 's to his title, not his ritual,
Although I wonder how it grew habitual.

XXXVII

But Rapp is the reverse of zealous matrons,
  Who favour, *malgré* Malthus, Generation—
Professors of that genial art, and patrons
  Of all the modest part of Propagation;
Which after all at such a desperate rate runs,
  That half its produce tends to Emigration,
That sad result of passions and potatoes—
Two weeds which pose our economic Catos.

XXXVIII

Had Adeline read Malthus? I can't tell;
    I wish she had: his book 's the eleventh commandment,
Which says, 'Thou shalt not marry,' unless *well*:
    This he (as far as I can understand) meant.
'T is not my purpose on his views to dwell,
    Nor canvass what 'so eminent a hand' meant;
But, certes, it conducts to lives ascetic,
Or turning Marriage into Arithmetic.

XXXIX

But Adeline, who probably presumed
    That Juan had enough of maintenance,
Or *separate* maintenance, in case 't was doomed—
    As on the whole it is an even chance
That bridegrooms, after they are fairly *groomed*,
    May retrograde a little in the Dance
Of Marriage—(which might form a painter's fame,
Like Holbein's 'Dance of Death'—but 't is the same)—

XL

But Adeline determined Juan's wedding
    In her own mind, and that 's enough for Woman:
But then, with whom? There was the sage Miss Reading,
    Miss Raw, Miss Flaw, Miss Showman, and Miss Knowman,
And the two fair co-heiresses Giltbedding.
    She deemed his merits something more than common:
All these were unobjectionable matches,
And might go on, if well wound up, like watches.

XLI

There was Miss Millpond, smooth as summer's sea,
    That usual paragon, an only daughter,
Who seemed the cream of Equanimity,
    Till skimmed—and then there was some milk and water,
With a slight shade of blue too, it might be,
    Beneath the surface; but what did it matter?
Love 's riotous, but Marriage should have quiet,
And being consumptive, live on a milk diet.

XLII

And then there was the Miss Audacia Shoe-string,
    A dashing *demoiselle* of good estate,
Whose heart was fixed upon a star or blue string;
    But whether English Dukes grew rare of late,
Or that she had not harped upon the true string,
    By which such Sirens can attract our great,
She took up with some foreign younger brother,
A Russ or Turk—the one 's as good as t' other.

XLIII

And then there was—but why should I go on,
    Unless the ladies should go off?—there was
Indeed a certain fair and fairy one,
    Of the best class, and better than her class,—
Aurora Raby, a young star who shone
    O'er Life, too sweet an image for such glass,
A lovely being, scarcely formed or moulded,
A rose with all its sweetest leaves yet folded;

XLIV

Rich, noble, but an orphan—left an only
    Child to the care of guardians good and kind—
But still her aspect had an air so lonely;
    Blood is not water; and where shall we find
Feelings of Youth like those which overthrown lie
    By Death, when we are left, alas! behind,
To feel, in friendless palaces, a home
Is wanting, and our best ties in the tomb?

XLV

Early in years, and yet more infantine
    In figure, she had something of Sublime
In eyes which sadly shone, as Seraphs' shine.
    All Youth—but with an aspect beyond Time;
Radiant and grave—as pitying Man's decline;
    Mournful—but mournful of another's crime,
She looked as if she sat by Eden's door,
And grieved for those who could return no more.

XLVI

She was a Catholic, too, sincere, austere,
　　As far as her own gentle heart allowed,
And deemed that fallen worship far more dear
　　Perhaps because 't was fallen : her Sires were proud
Of deeds and days when they had filled the ear
　　Of nations, and had never bent or bowed
To novel power; and as she was the last,
She held their old faith and old feelings fast.

XLVII

She gazed upon a World she scarcely knew,
　　As seeking not to know it; silent, lone,
As grows a flower, thus quietly she grew,
　　And kept her heart serene within its zone.
There was awe in the homage which she drew;
　　Her Spirit seemed as seated on a throne
Apart from the surrounding world, and strong
In its own strength—most strange in one so young!

XLVIII

Now it so happened, in the catalogue
　　Of Adeline, Aurora was omitted,
Although her birth and wealth had given her vogue,
　　Beyond the charmers we have already cited;
Her beauty also seemed to form no clog
　　Against her being mentioned as well fitted,
By many virtues, to be worth the trouble
Of single gentlemen who would be double.

XLIX

And this omission, like that of the bust
　　Of Brutus at the pageant of Tiberius,
Made Juan wonder, as no doubt he must.
　　This he expressed half smiling and half serious;
When Adeline replied with some disgust,
　　And with an air, to say the least, imperious,
She marvelled 'what he saw in such a baby
As that prim, silent, cold Aurora Raby?'

L

Juan rejoined—'She was a Catholic,
   And therefore fittest, as of his persuasion;
Since he was sure his mother would fall sick,
   And the Pope thunder excommunication,
If——' But here Adeline, who seemed to pique
   Herself extremely on the inoculation
Of others with her own opinions, stated—
As usual—the same reason which she late did.

LI

And wherefore not? A reasonable reason,
   If good, is none the worse for repetition;
If bad, the best way 's certainly to tease on,
   And amplify: you lose much by concision,
Whereas insisting in or out of season
   Convinces all men, even a politician;
Or—what is just the same—it wearies out.
So the end 's gained, what signifies the route?

LII

Why Adeline had this slight prejudice—
   For prejudice it was—against a creature
As pure, as Sanctity itself from Vice,—
   With all the added charm of form and feature,—
For me appears a question far too nice,
   Since Adeline was liberal by nature;
But Nature 's Nature, and has more caprices
Than I have time, or will, to take to pieces.

LIII

Perhaps she did not like the quiet way
   With which Aurora on those baubles looked,
Which charm most people in their earlier day:
   For there are few things by Mankind less brooked,
And Womankind too, if we so may say,
   Than finding thus their genius stand rebuked,
Like 'Antony's by Cæsar,' by the few
Who look upon them as they ought to do.

LIV

It was not envy—Adeline had none;
  Her place was far beyond it, and her mind:
It was not scorn—which could not light on one
  Whose greatest *fault* was leaving few to find:
It was not jealousy, I think—but shun
  Following the *ignes fatui* of Mankind:
It was not——but 't is easier far, alas!
To say what it was *not* than what it was.

LV

Little Aurora deemed she was the theme
  Of such discussion. She was there a guest;
A beauteous ripple of the brilliant stream
  Of Rank and Youth, though purer than the rest,
Which flowed on for a moment in the beam
  Time sheds a moment o'er each sparkling crest.
Had she known this, she would have calmly smiled—
She had so much, or little, of the child.

LVI

The dashing and proud air of Adeline
  Imposed not upon her; she saw her blaze
Much as she would have seen a glow-worm shine,
  Then turned unto the stars for loftier rays.
Juan was something she could not divine,
  Being no Sibyl in the new world's ways;
Yet she was nothing dazzled by the meteor,
Because she did not pin her faith on feature.

LVII

His fame too,—for he had that kind of fame
  Which sometimes plays the deuce with Womankind,
A heterogeneous mass of glorious blame,
  Half virtues and whole vices being combined;
Faults which attract because they are not tame;
  Follies tricked out so brightly that they blind:—
These seals upon her wax made no impression,
Such was her coldness or her self-possession.

LVIII

Juan knew nought of such a character—
   High, yet resembling not his lost Haidée;
Yet each was radiant in her proper sphere:
   The island girl, bred up by the lone sea,
More warm, as lovely, and not less sincere,
   Was Nature's all: Aurora could not be,
Nor would be thus:—the difference in them
Was such as lies between a flower and gem.

LIX

Having wound up with this sublime comparison,
   Methinks we may proceed upon our narrative,
And, as my friend Scott says, 'I sound my warison;'
   Scott, the superlative of my comparative—
Scott, who can paint your Christian knight or Saracen,
   Serf—Lord—Man, with such skill as none would share it, if
There had not been one Shakespeare and Voltaire,
Of one or both of whom he seems the heir.

LX

I say, in my slight way I may proceed
   To play upon the surface of Humanity.
I write the World, nor care if the World read,
   At least for this I cannot spare its vanity.
My Muse hath bred, and still perhaps may breed
   More foes by this same scroll: when I began it, I
Thought that it might turn out so—*now* I *know* it,
But still I am, or was, a pretty poet.

LXI

The conference or congress (for it ended
   As Congresses of late do) of the Lady
Adeline and Don Juan rather blended
   Some acids with the sweets—for she was heady;
But, ere the matter could be marred or mended,
   The silvery bell rang, not for 'dinner ready,'
But for that hour, called *half-hour*, given to dress,
Though ladies' robes seem scant enough for less.

LXII

Great things were now to be achieved at table,
  With massy plate for armour, knives and forks
For weapons; but what Muse since Homer 's able
  (His feasts are not the worst part of his works)
To draw up in array a single day-bill
  Of modern dinners? where more mystery lurks,
In soups or sauces, or a sole *ragoût*,
Than witches, b—ches, or physicians, brew.

LXIII

There was a goodly 'soupe à la *bonne femme*,'
  Though God knows whence it came from; there was, too,
A turbot for relief of those who cram,
  Relieved with 'dindon à la Périgeux';
There also was——the sinner that I am!
  How shall I get this gourmand stanza through?—
'Soupe à la Beauveau,' whose relief was dory,
Relieved itself by pork, for greater glory.

LXIV

But I must crowd all into one grand mess
  Or mass; for should I stretch into detail,
My Muse would run much more into excess,
  Than when some squeamish people deem her frail;
But though a *bonne vivante*, I must confess
  Her stomach 's not her peccant part; this tale
However doth require some slight refection,
Just to relieve her spirits from dejection.

LXV

Fowls 'à la Condé,' slices eke of salmon,
  With 'sauces Génévoises,' and haunch of venison;
Wines too, which might again have slain young Ammon—
  A man like whom I hope we sha'n't see many soon;
They also set a glazed Westphalian ham on,
  Whereon Apicius would bestow his benison;
And then there was champagne with foaming whirls,
As white as Cleopatra's melted pearls.

LXVI

Then there was God knows what 'à l'Allemande,'
   'A l'Espagnole,' 'timballe,' and 'salpicon'—
With things I can't withstand or understand,
   Though swallowed with much zest upon the whole;
And '*entremets*' to piddle with at hand,
   Gently to lull down the subsiding soul;
While great Lucullus' *Robe triumphal* muffles—
(*There's fame*)—young partridge fillets, decked with truffles.

LXVII

What are the *fillets* on the Victor's brow
   To these? They are rags or dust. Where is the arch
Which nodded to the nation's spoils below?
   Where the triumphal chariots' haughty march?
Gone to where Victories must like dinners go.
   Farther I shall not follow the research:
But oh! ye modern Heroes with your cartridges,
When will your names lend lustre e'en to partridges?

LXVIII

Those truffles too are no bad accessories,
   Followed by 'petits puits d'amour'—a dish
Of which perhaps the cookery rather varies,
   So every one may dress it to his wish,
According to the best of dictionaries,
   Which encyclopedize both flesh and fish;
But even, sans *confitures*, it no less true is,
There's pretty picking in those *petits puits*.

LXIX

The mind is lost in mighty contemplation
   Of intellect expanded on two courses;
And Indigestion's grand multiplication
   Requires arithmetic beyond my forces.
Who would suppose, from Adam's simple ration,
   That cookery could have called forth such resources,
As form a science and a nomenclature
From out the commonest demands of Nature?

LXX

The glasses jingled, and the palates tingled;
  The diners of celebrity dined well;
The ladies with more moderation mingled
  In the feast, pecking less than I can tell;
Also the younger men too: for a springald
  Can't, like ripe Age, in *gourmandise* excel,
But thinks less of good eating than the whisper
(When seated next him) of some pretty lisper.

LXXI

Alas! I must leave undescribed the *gibier*,
  The *salmi*, the *consommé*, the *purée*,
All which I use to make my rhymes run glibber
  Than could roast beef in our rough John Bull way:
I must not introduce even a spare rib here,
  'Bubble and squeak' would spoil my liquid lay:
But I have dined, and must forego, alas!
The chaste description even of a 'bécasse';

LXXII

And fruits, and ice, and all that Art refines
  From Nature for the service of the *goût*—
Taste or the *gout*,—pronounce it as inclines
  Your stomach! Ere you dine, the French will do;
But *after*, there are sometimes certain signs
  Which prove plain English truer of the two.
Hast ever *had* the gout? I have not had it—
But I may have, and you too, reader, dread it.

LXXIII

The simple olives, best allies of wine,
  Must I pass over in my bill of fare?
I must, although a favourite *plat* of mine
  In Spain, and Lucca, Athens, everywhere:
On them and bread 't was oft my luck to dine—
  The grass my table-cloth, in open air,
On Sunium or Hymettus, like Diogenes,
Of whom half my philosophy the progeny is.

LXXIV

Amidst this tumult of fish, flesh, and fowl,
    And vegetables, all in masquerade,
The guests were placed according to their roll,
    But various as the various meats displayed :
Don Juan sat next an 'à l'Espagnole'—
    No damsel, but a dish, as hath been said ;
But so far like a lady, that 't was drest
Superbly, and contained a world of zest.

LXXV

By some odd chance too, he was placed between
    Aurora and the Lady Adeline—
A situation difficult, I ween,
    For man therein, with eyes and heart, to dine.
Also the conference which we have seen
    Was not such as to encourage him to shine,
For Adeline, addressing few words to him,
With two transcendent eyes seemed to look through him.

LXXVI

I sometimes almost think that eyes have ears :
    This much is sure, that, out of earshot, things
Are somehow echoed to the pretty dears,
    Of which I can't tell whence their knowledge springs.
Like that same mystic music of the spheres,
    Which no one hears, so loudly though it rings,
'T is wonderful how oft the sex have heard
Long dialogues—which passed without a word!

LXXVII

Aurora sat with that indifference
    Which piques a *preux chevalier*—as it ought :
Of all offences that 's the worst offence,
    Which seems to hint you are not worth a thought.
Now Juan, though no coxcomb in pretence,
    Was not exactly pleased to be so caught,
Like a good ship entangled among ice—
And after so much excellent advice.

LXXVIII

To his gay nothings, nothing was replied,
  Or something which was nothing, as Urbanity
Required. Aurora scarcely looked aside,
  Nor even smiled enough for any vanity.
The Devil was in the girl! Could it be pride?
  Or modesty, or absence, or inanity?
Heaven knows! But Adeline's malicious eyes
Sparkled with her successful prophecies,

LXXIX

And looked as much as if to say, 'I said it;'
  A kind of triumph I 'll not recommend,
Because it sometimes, as I have seen or read it,
  Both in the case of lover and of friend,
Will pique a gentleman, for his own credit,
  To bring what was a jest to a serious end:
For all men prophesy what *is* or *was*,
And hate those who won't let them come to pass.

LXXX

Juan was drawn thus into some attentions,
  Slight but select, and just enough to express,
To females of perspicuous comprehensions,
  That he would rather make them more than less.
Aurora at the last (so history mentions,
  Though probably much less a fact than guess)
So far relaxed her thoughts from their sweet prison,
As once or twice to smile, if not to listen.

LXXXI

From answering she began to question: this
  With her was rare; and Adeline, who as yet
Thought her predictions went not much amiss,
  Began to dread she 'd thaw to a coquette—
So very difficult, they say, it is
  To keep extremes from meeting, when once set
In motion; but she here too much refined—
Aurora's spirit was not of that kind.

LXXXII

But Juan had a sort of winning way,
   A proud humility, if such there be,
Which showed such deference to what females say,
   As if each charming word were a decree.
His tact, too, tempered him from grave to gay,
   And taught him when to be reserved or free:
He had the art of drawing people out,
Without their seeing what he was about.

LXXXIII

Aurora, who in her indifference
   Confounded him in common with the crowd
Of flatterers, though she deemed he had more sense
   Than whispering foplings, or than witlings loud—
Commenced (from such slight things will great commence)
   To feel that flattery which attracts the proud
Rather by deference than compliment,
And wins even by a delicate dissent.

LXXXIV

And then he had good looks;—that point was carried
   Nem. con. amongst the women, which I grieve
To say leads oft to *crim. con.* with the married—
   A case which to the juries we may leave,
Since with digressions we too long have tarried.
   Now though we know of old that looks deceive,
And always have done,—somehow these good looks
Make more impression than the best of books.

LXXXV

Aurora, who looked more on books than faces,
   Was very young, although so very sage,
Admiring more Minerva than the Graces,
   Especially upon a printed page.
But Virtue's self, with all her tightest laces,
   Has not the natural stays of strict old age;
And Socrates, that model of all duty,
Owned to a *penchant*, though discreet, for beauty.

LXXXVI

And girls of sixteen are thus far Socratic,
    But innocently so, as Socrates;
And really, if the Sage sublime and Attic
    At seventy years had phantasies like these,
Which Plato in his dialogues dramatic
    Has shown, I know not why they should displease
In virgins—always in a modest way,
Observe,—for that with me 's a *sine quâ.*

LXXXVII

Also observe, that, like the great Lord Coke
    (See Littleton), whene'er I have expressed
Opinions two, which at first sight may look
    Twin opposites, the second is the best.
Perhaps I have a third too, in a nook,
    Or none at all—which seems a sorry jest:
But if a writer should be quite consistent,
How could he possibly show things existent?

LXXXVIII

If people contradict themselves, can I
    Help contradicting them, and everybody,
Even my veracious self?—But that 's a lie:
    I never did so, never will—how should I?
He who doubts all things nothing can deny:
    Truth's fountains may be clear—her streams are muddy,
And cut through such canals of contradiction,
That she must often navigate o'er fiction.

LXXXIX

Apologue, Fable, Poesy, and Parable,
    Are false, but may be rendered also true,
By those who sow them in a land that 's arable:
    'T is wonderful what Fable will not do!
'T is said it makes Reality more bearable:
    But what 's Reality? Who has its clue?
Philosophy? No; she too much rejects.
Religion? *Yes*; but which of all her sects?

XC

Some millions must be wrong, that's pretty clear;
  Perhaps it may turn out that all were right.
God help us! Since we have need on our career
  To keep our holy beacons always bright,
'T is time that some new prophet should appear,
  Or *old* indulge man with a second sight.
Opinions wear out in some thousand years,
Without a small refreshment from the spheres.

XCI

But here again, why will I thus entangle
  Myself with Metaphysics? None can hate
So much as I do any kind of wrangle;
  And yet, such is my folly, or my fate,
I always knock my head against some angle
  About the present, past, or future state:
Yet I wish well to Trojan and to Tyrian,
For I was bred a moderate Presbyterian.

XCII

But though I am a temperate theologian,
  And also meek as a metaphysician,
Impartial between Tyrian and Trojan,
  As Eldon on a lunatic commission,—
In politics my duty is to show John
  Bull something of the lower world's condition.
It makes my blood boil like the springs of Hecla,
To see men let these scoundrel Sovereigns break law.

XCIII

But Politics, and Policy, and Piety,
  Are topics which I sometimes introduce,
Not only for the sake of their variety,
  But as subservient to a moral use;
Because my business is to *dress* society,
  And stuff with *sage* that very verdant goose.
And now, that we may furnish with some matter all
Tastes, we are going to try the Supernatural.

XCIV

And now I will give up all argument;
    And positively, henceforth, no temptation
Shall 'fool me to the top up of my bent' :—
    Yes, I 'll begin a thorough reformation.
Indeed, I never knew what people meant
    By deeming that my Muse's conversation
Was dangerous;—I think she is as harmless
As some who labour more and yet may charm less.

XCV

Grim reader! did you ever see a ghost?
    No; but you have heard—I understand—be dumb!
And don't regret the time you may have lost,
    For you have got that pleasure still to come:
And do not think I mean to sneer at most
    Of these things, or by ridicule benumb
That source of the Sublime and the Mysterious:—
For certain reasons my belief is serious.

XCVI

Serious? You laugh;—you may: that will I not;
    My smiles must be sincere or not at all.
I say I do believe a haunted spot
    Exists—and where? That shall I not recall,
Because I 'd rather it should be forgot,
    'Shadows the soul of Richard' may appal.
In short, upon that subject I 've some qualms very
Like those of the philosopher of Malmsbury.

XCVII

The night—(I sing by night—sometimes an owl,
    And now and then a nightingale)—is dim,
And the loud shriek of sage Minerva's fowl
    Rattles around me her discordant hymn:
Old portraits from old walls upon me scowl—
    I wish to Heaven they would not look so grim;
The dying embers dwindle in the grate—
I think too that I have sat up too late:

XCVIII

And therefore, though 't is by no means my way
  To rhyme at noon—when I have other things
To think of, if I ever think—I say
  I feel some chilly midnight shudderings,
And prudently postpone, until mid-day,
  Treating a topic which, alas! but brings
Shadows;—but you must be in my condition,
Before you learn to call this superstition.

XCIX

Between two worlds Life hovers like a star,
  'Twixt Night and Morn, upon the horizon's verge.
How little do we know that which we are!
  How less what we may be! The eternal surge
Of Time and Tide rolls on and bears afar
  Our bubbles; as the old burst, new emerge,
Lashed from the foam of ages; while the graves
Of Empires heave but like some passing waves.

CANTO THE SIXTEENTH

I

The antique Persians taught three useful things,
  To draw the bow, to ride, and speak the truth.
This was the mode of Cyrus, best of kings—
  A mode adopted since by modern youth.
Bows have they, generally with two strings;
  Horses they ride without remorse or ruth;
At speaking truth perhaps they are less clever,
But draw the long bow better now than ever.

II

The cause of this effect, or this defect,—
  'For this effect defective comes by cause,'—
Is what I have not leisure to inspect;
  But this I must say in my own applause,

Of all the Muses that I recollect,
　　Whate'er may be her follies or her flaws
In some things, mine 's beyond all contradiction
The most sincere that ever dealt in fiction.

III

And as she treats all things, and ne'er retreats
　　From anything, this Epic will contain
A wilderness of the most rare conceits,
　　Which you might elsewhere hope to find in vain.
T is true there be some bitters with the sweets,
　　Yet mixed so slightly, that you can't complain,
But wonder they so few are, since my tale is
'*De rebus cunctis et quibusdam aliis.*'

IV

But of all truths which she has told, the most
　　True is that which she is about to tell.
I said it was a story of a ghost—
　　What then? I only know it so befell.
Have you explored the limits of the coast,
　　Where all the dwellers of the earth must dwell?
'T is time to strike such puny doubters dumb as
The sceptics who would not believe Columbus.

V

Some people would impose now with authority,
　　Turpin's or Monmouth Geoffry's Chronicle;
Men whose historical superiority
　　Is always greatest at a miracle.
But Saint Augustine has the great priority,
　　Who bids all men believe the impossible,
Because 't is so. Who nibble, scribble, quibble, he
Quiets at once with 'quia *impossibile.*'

VI

And therefore, mortals, cavil not at all;
　　Believe:—if 't is improbable, you *must,*

And if it is impossible, you *shall*:
   'T is always best to take things upon trust.
I do not speak profanely to recall
   Those holier Mysteries which the wise and just
Receive as Gospel, and which grow more rooted,
As all truths must, the more they are disputed:

VII

I merely mean to say what Johnson said,
   That in the course of some six thousand years,
All nations have believed that from the dead
   A visitant at intervals appears:
And what is strangest upon this strange head
   Is, that whatever bar the reason rears
'Gainst such belief, there 's something stronger still
In its behalf—let those deny who will.

VIII

The dinner and the *soirée* too were done,
   The supper too discussed, the dames admired,
The banqueteers had dropped off one by one—
   The song was silent, and the dance expired:
The last thin petticoats were vanished, gone
   Like fleecy clouds into the sky retired,
And nothing brighter gleamed through the saloon
Than dying tapers—and the peeping moon.

IX

The evaporation of a joyous day
   Is like the last glass of champagne, without
The foam which made its virgin bumper gay;
   Or like a system coupled with a doubt;
Or like a soda bottle when its spray
   Has sparkled and let half its spirit out;
Or like a billow left by storms behind,
Without the animation of the wind;

X

Or like an opiate, which brings troubled rest,
    Or none; or like—like nothing that I know
Except itself;—such is the human breast;
    A thing, of which similitudes can show
No real likeness,—like the old Tyrian vest
    Dyed purple, none at present can tell how,
If from a shell-fish or from cochineal.
So perish every Tyrant's robe piece-meal!

XI

But next to dressing for a rout or ball,
    Undressing is a woe; our *robe de chambre*
May sit like that of Nessus, and recall
    Thoughts quite as yellow, but less clear than amber.
Titus exclaimed, 'I 've a lost a day!' Of all
    The nights and days most people can remember,
(I have had of both, some not to be disdained,)
I wish they 'd state how many they have gained.

XII

And Juan, on retiring for the night,
    Felt restless, and perplexed, and compromised:
He thought Aurora Raby's eyes more bright
    Than Adeline (such is advice) advised;
If he had known exactly his own plight,
    He probably would have philosophised:
A great resource to all, and ne'er denied
Till wanted; therefore Juan only sighed.

XIII

He sighed;—the next resource is the full moon,
    Where all sighs are deposited; and now
It happened luckily, the chaste orb shone
    As clear as such a climate will allow;
And Juan's mind was in the proper tone
    To hail her with the apostrophe—'O thou!'
Of amatory egotism the *Tuism*,
Which further to explain would be a truism.

XIV

But Lover, Poet, or Astronomer—
    Shepherd, or swain—whoever may behold,
Feel some abstraction when they gaze on her;
    Great thoughts we catch from thence (besides a cold
Sometimes, unless my feelings rather err);
    Deep secrets to her rolling light are told;
The Ocean's tides and mortals' brains she sways,
And also hearts—if there be truth in lays.

XV

Juan felt somewhat pensive, and disposed
    For contemplation rather than his pillow:
The Gothic chamber, where he was enclosed,
    Let in the rippling sound of the lake's billow,
With all the mystery by midnight caused:
    Below his window waved (of course) a willow;
And he stood gazing out on the cascade
That flashed and after darkened in the shade.

XVI

Upon his table or his toilet,—*which*
    Of these is not exactly ascertained,—
(I state this, for I am cautious to a pitch
    Of nicety, where a fact is to be gained,)
A lamp burned high, while he leant from a niche,
    Where many a Gothic ornament remained,
In chiselled stone and painted glass, and all
That Time has left our fathers of their Hall.

XVII

Then, as the night was clear though cold, he threw
    His chamber door wide open—and went forth
Into a gallery, of a sombre hue,
    Long, furnished with old pictures of great worth,
Of knights and dames heroic and chaste too,
    As doubtless should be people of high birth;
But by dim lights the portraits of the dead
Have something ghastly, desolate, and dread.

XVIII

The forms of the grim Knight and pictured Saint
 Look living in the moon; and as you turn
Backward and forward to the echoes faint
 Of your own footsteps—voices from the Urn
Appear to wake, and shadows wild and quaint
 Start from the frames which fence their aspects stern,
As if to ask how you can dare to keep
A vigil there, where all but Death should sleep.

XIX

And the pale smile of Beauties in the grave,
 The charms of other days, in starlight gleams,
Glimmer on high; their buried locks still wave
 Along the canvas; their eyes glance like dreams
On ours, or spars within some dusky cave,
 But Death is imaged in their shadowy beams.
A picture is the past; even ere its frame
Be gilt, who sate hath ceased to be the same.

XX

As Juan mused on Mutability,
 Or on his Mistress—terms synonymous—
No sound except the echo of his sigh
 Or step ran sadly through that antique house;
When suddenly he heard, or thought so, nigh,
 A supernatural agent—or a mouse,
Whose little nibbling rustle will embarrass
Most people as it plays along the arras.

XXI

It was no mouse—but lo! a monk, arrayed
 In cowl and beads, and dusky garb, appeared,
Now in the moonlight, and now lapsed in shade,
 With steps that trod as heavy, yet unheard;
His garments only a slight murmur made;
 He moved as shadowy as the Sisters weird,
But slowly; and as he passed Juan by,
Glanced, without pausing, on him a bright eye.

XXII

Juan was petrified; he had heard a hint
  Of such a Spirit in these halls of old,
But thought, like most men, there was nothing in 't
  Beyond the rumour which such spots unfold,
Coined from surviving Superstition's mint,
  Which passes ghosts in currency like gold,
But rarely seen, like gold compared with paper.
And did he see this? or was it a vapour?

XXIII

Once, twice, thrice passed, repassed—the thing of air,
  Or earth beneath, or Heaven, or t' other place;
And Juan gazed upon it with a stare,
  Yet could not speak or move; but, on its base
As stands a statue, stood: he felt his hair
  Twine like a knot of snakes around his face;
He taxed his tongue for words, which were not granted,
To ask the reverend person what he wanted.

XXIV

The third time, after a still longer pause,
  The shadow passed away—but where? the hall
Was long, and thus far there was no great cause
  To think his vanishing unnatural:
Doors there were many, through which, by the laws
  Of physics, bodies whether short or tall
Might come or go; but Juan could not state
Through which the Spectre seemed to evaporate.

XXV

He stood—how long he knew not, but it seemed
  An age—expectant, powerless, with his eyes
Strained on the spot where first the figure gleamed;
  Then by degrees recalled his energies,
And would have passed the whole off as a dream,
  But could not wake; he was, he did surmise,
Waking already, and returned at length
Back to his chamber, shorn of half his strength.

XXVI

All there was as he left it : still his taper
    Burned, and not *blue*, as modest tapers use,
Receiving sprites with sympathetic vapour ;
    He rubbed his eyes, and they did not refuse
Their office : he took up an old newspaper ;
    The paper was right easy to peruse ;
He read an article the King attacking,
And a long eulogy of 'Patent Blacking.'

XXVII

This savoured of this world ; but his hand shook :
    He shut his door, and after having read
A paragraph, I think about Horne Tooke,
    Undressed, and rather slowly went to bed.
There, couched all snugly on his pillow's nook,
    With what he had seen his phantasy he fed ;
And though it was no opiate, slumber crept
Upon him by degrees, and so he slept.

XXVIII

He woke betimes ; and, as may be supposed,
    Pondered upon his visitant or vision,
And whether it ought not to be disclosed,
    At risk of being quizzed for superstition.
The more he thought, the more his mind was posed :
    In the mean time, his valet, whose precision
Was great, because his master brooked no less,
Knocked to inform him it was time to dress.

XXIX

He dressed ; and like young people he was wont
    To take some trouble with his toilet, but
This morning rather spent less time upon 't ;
    Aside his very mirror soon was put ;
His curls fell negligently o'er his front,
    His clothes were not curbed to their usual cut,
His very neckcloth's Gordian knot was tied
Almost an hair's breadth too much on one side.

XXX

And when he walked down into the Saloon,
  He sate him pensive o'er a dish of tea,
Which he perhaps had not discovered soon,
  Had it not happened scalding hot to be,
Which made him have recourse unto his spoon;
  So much *distrait* he was, that all could see
That something was the matter—Adeline
The first—but *what* she could not well divine.

XXXI

She looked, and saw him pale, and turned as pale
  Herself; then hastily looked down, and muttered
Something, but what's not stated in my tale.
  Lord Henry said, his muffin was ill buttered;
The Duchess of Fitz-Fulke played with her veil,
  And looked at Juan hard, but nothing uttered.
Aurora Raby with her large dark eyes
Surveyed him with a kind of calm surprise.

XXXII

But seeing him all cold and silent still,
  And everybody wondering more or less,
Fair Adeline inquired, 'If he were ill?'
  He started, and said, 'Yes—no—rather—yes.'
The family physician had great skill,
  And being present, now began to express
His readiness to feel his pulse and tell
The cause, but Juan said, he was 'quite well.'

XXXIII

'Quite well; yes,—no.'—These answers were mysterious,
  And yet his looks appeared to sanction both,
However they might savour of delirious;
  Something like illness of a sudden growth
Weighed on his spirit, though by no means serious:
  But for the rest, as he himself seemed loth
To state the case, it might be ta'en for granted
It was not the physician that he wanted.

R

XXXIV

Lord Henry, who had now discussed his chocolate,
    Also the muffin whereof he complained,
Said, Juan had not got his usual look elate,
    At which he marvelled, since it had not rained;
Then asked her Grace what news were of the Duke of late?
    Her Grace replied, *his* Grace was rather pained
With some slight, light, hereditary twinges
Of gout, which rusts aristocratic hinges.

XXXV

Then Henry turned to Juan, and addressed
    A few words of condolence on his state:
'You look,' quoth he, 'as if you had had your rest
    Broke in upon by the Black Friar of late.'
'What Friar?' said Juan; and he did his best
    To put the question with an air sedate,
Or careless; but the effort was not valid
To hinder him from growing still more pallid.

XXXVI

'Oh! have you never heard of the Black Friar?
    The Spirit of these walls?'—'In truth not I.'
'Why Fame—but Fame you know 's sometimes a liar—
    Tells an odd story, of which by and by:
Whether with time the Spectre has grown shyer,
    Or that our Sires had a more gifted eye
For such sights, though the tale is half believed,
The Friar of late has not been oft perceived.

XXXVII

'The last time was——'—'I pray,' said Adeline—
    (Who watched the changes of Don Juan's brow,
And from its context thought she could divine
    Connections stronger than he chose to avow
With this same legend)—'if you but design
    To jest, you 'll choose some other theme just now,
Because the present tale has oft been told,
And is not much improved by growing old.'

XXXVIII

'Jest!' quoth Milor; 'why, Adeline, you know
   That we ourselves—'t was in the honey moon—
Saw——'—'Well, no matter, 't was so long ago;
   But, come, I 'll set your story to a tune.'
Graceful as Dian when she draws her bow,
   She seized her harp, whose strings were kindled soon
As touched, and plaintively began to play
The air of ''T was a Friar of Orders Gray.'

XXXIX

'But add the words,' cried Henry, 'which you made;
   For Adeline is half a poetess,'
Turning round to the rest, he smiling said.
   Of course the others could not but express
In courtesy their wish to see displayed
   By one *three* talents, for there were no less—
The voice, the words, the harper's skill, at once,
Could hardly be united by a dunce.

XL

After some fascinating hesitation,—
   The charming of these charmers, who seem bound,
I can't tell why, to this dissimulation,—
   Fair Adeline, with eyes fixed on the ground
At first, then kindling into animation,
   Added her sweet voice to the lyric sound,
And sang with much simplicity,—a merit
Not the less precious, that we seldom hear it.

1

Beware! beware! of the Black Friar,
   Who sitteth by Norman stone,
For he mutters his prayer in the midnight air,
   And his mass of the days that are gone.
When the Lord of the Hill, Amundeville,
   Made Norman Church his prey,
And expelled the friars, one friar still
   Would not be driven away.

2

Though he came in his might, with King Henry's right,
 To turn church lands to lay,
With sword in hand, and torch to light
 Their walls, if they said nay;
A monk remained, unchased, unchained,
 And he did not seem formed of clay,
For he 's seen in the porch, and he 's seen in the church,
 Though he is not seen by day.

3

And whether for good, or whether for ill,
 It is not mine to say;
But still with the house of Amundeville
 He abideth night and day.
By the marriage-bed of their lords, 't is said,
 He flits on the bridal eve;
And 't is held as faith, to their bed of Death
 He comes—but not to grieve.

4

When an heir is born, he 's heard to mourn,
 And when aught is to befall
That ancient line, in the pale moonshine
 He walks from hall to hall.
His form you may trace, but not his face,
 'T is shadowed by his cowl;
But his eyes may be seen from the fold between,
 And they seem of a parted soul.

5

But beware! beware! of the Black Friar,
 He still retains his sway,
For he is yet the Church's heir,
 Whoever may be the lay.
Amundeville is Lord by day,
 But the monk is Lord by night;
Nor wine nor wassail could raise a vassal
 To question that Friar's right.

6

Say nought to him as he walks the Hall,
    And he'll say nought to you;
He sweeps along in his dusky pall,
    As o'er the grass the dew.
Then grammercy! for the Black Friar;
    Heaven sain him! fair or foul,—
And whatsoe'er may be his prayer,
    Let ours be for his soul.

XLI

The lady's voice ceased, and the thrilling wires
    Died from the touch that kindled them to sound;
And the pause followed, which when song expires
    Pervades a moment those who listen round;
And then of course the circle much admires,
    Nor less applauds, as in politeness bound,
The tones, the feeling, and the execution,
To the performer's diffident confusion.

XLII

Fair Adeline, though in a careless way,
    As if she rated such accomplishment
As the mere pastime of an idle day,
    Pursued an instant for her own content,
Would now and then as 't were *without* display,
    Yet *with* display in fact, at times relent
To such performances with haughty smile,
To show she *could*, if it were worth her while.

XLIII

Now this (but we will whisper it aside)
    Was—pardon the pedantic illustration—
Trampling on Plato's pride with greater pride,
    As did the Cynic on some like occasion;
Deeming the sage would be much mortified,
    Or thrown into a philosophic passion,
For a spoilt carpet—but the 'Attic Bee'
Was much consoled by his own repartee.

XLIV

Thus Adeline would throw into the shade
 (By doing easily, whene'er she chose,
What dilettanti do with vast parade)
 Their sort of *half profession*; for it grows
To something like this when too oft displayed;
 And that it is so, everybody knows,
Who have heard Miss That or This, or Lady T' other,
Show off—to please their company or mother.

XLV

Oh! the long evenings of duets and trios!
 The admirations and the speculations;
The 'Mamma Mia's!' and the 'Amor Mio's!'
 The 'Tanti palpiti's' on such occasions:
The 'Lasciami's,' and quavering 'Addio's,'
 Amongst our own most musical of nations!
With 'Tu mi chamas's' from Portingale,
To soothe our ears, lest Italy should fail.

XLVI

In Babylon's *bravuras*—as the Home-
 Heart-Ballads of Green Erin or Grey Highlands,
That bring Lochaber back to eyes that roam
 O'er far Atlantic continents or islands,
The calentures of music which o'ercome
 All mountaineers with dreams that they are nigh lands,
No more to be beheld but in such visions—
Was Adeline well versed, as compositions.

XLVII

She also had a twilight tinge of '*Blue*,'
 Could write rhymes, and compose more than she wrote,
Made epigrams occasionally too
 Upon her friends, as everybody ought.
But still from that sublimer azure hue,
 So much the present dye, she was remote;
Was weak enough to deem Pope a great poet,
And what was worse, was not ashamed to show it.

XLVIII

Aurora—since we are touching upon taste,
    Which now-a-days is the thermometer
By whose degrees all characters are classed—
    Was more Shakespearian, if I do not err.
The worlds beyond this World's perplexing waste
    Had more of her existence, for in her
There was a depth of feeling to embrace
Thoughts, boundless, deep, but silent too as Space.

XLIX

Not so her gracious, graceful, graceless Grace,
    The full-grown Hebe of Fitz-Fulke, whose mind,
If she had any, was upon her face,
    And that was of a fascinating kind.
A little turn for mischief you might trace
    Also thereon,—but that 's not much ; we find
Few females without some such gentle leaven,
For fear we should suppose us quite in Heaven.

L

I have not heard she was at all poetic,
    Though once she was seen reading the *Bath Guide*,
And Hayley's *Triumphs*, which she deemed pathetic,
    Because she said *her temper* had been tried
So much, the bard had really been prophetic
    Of what she had gone through with—since a bride.
But of all verse, what most ensured her praise
Were sonnets to herself, or *bouts rimés*.

LI

'T were difficult to say what was the object
    Of Adeline, in bringing this same lay
To bear on what appeared to her the subject
    Of Juan's nervous feelings on that day.
Perhaps she merely had the simple project
    To laugh him out of his supposed dismay ;
Perhaps she might wish to confirm him in it,
Though why I cannot say—at least this minute.

LII

But so far the immediate effect
    Was to restore him to his self-propriety,
A thing quite necessary to the elect,
    Who wish to take the tone of their society:
In which you cannot be too circumspect,
    Whether the mode be persiflage or piety,
But wear the newest mantle of hypocrisy,
On pain of much displeasing the gynocracy.

LIII

And therefore Juan now began to rally
    His spirits, and without more explanation
To jest upon such themes in many a sally.
    Her Grace, too, also seized the same occasion,
With various similar remarks to tally,
    But wished for a still more detailed narration
Of this same mystic friar's curious doings,
About the present family's deaths and wooings.

LIV

Of these few could say more than has been said;
    They passed as such things do, for superstition
With some, while others, who had more in dread
    The theme, half credited the strange tradition;
And much was talked on all sides on that head:
    But Juan, when cross-questioned on the vision,
Which some supposed (though he had not avowed it)
Had stirred him, answered in a way to cloud it.

LV

And then, the mid-day having worn to one,
    The company prepared to separate;
Some to their several pastimes, or to none,
    Some wondering 't was so early, some so late.
There was a goodly match, too, to be run
    Between some greyhounds on my Lord's estate,
And a young race-horse of old pedigree,
Matched for the spring, whom several went to see.

LVI

There was a picture-dealer who had brought
 A special Titian, warranted original,
So precious that it was not to be bought,
 Though Princes the possessor were besieging all—
The King himself had cheapened it, but thought
 The civil list he deigns to accept (obliging all
His subjects by his gracious acceptation)—
Too scanty, in these times of low taxation.

LVII

But as Lord Henry was a connoisseur,—
 The friend of Artists, if not Arts,—the owner,
With motives the most classical and pure,
 So that he would have been the very donor,
Rather than seller, had his wants been fewer,
 So much he deemed his patronage an honour,
Had brought the *capo d'opera*, not for sale,
But for his judgment—never known to fail.

LVIII

There was a modern Goth, I mean a Gothic
 Bricklayer of Babel, called an architect,
Brought to survey these grey walls which, though so thick,
 Might have from Time acquired some slight defect;
Who, after rummaging the Abbey through thick
 And thin, produced a plan whereby to erect
New buildings of correctest conformation,
And throw down old—which he called *restoration*.

LIX

The cost would be a trifle—an 'old song,'
 Set to some thousands ('t is the usual burden
Of that same tune, when people hum it long)—
 The price would speedily repay its worth in
An edifice no less sublime than strong,
 By which Lord Henry's good taste would go forth in
Its glory, through all ages shining sunny,
For Gothic daring shown in English money.

LX

There were two lawyers busy on a mortgage
    Lord Henry wished to raise for a new purchase;
Also a lawsuit upon tenures burgage,
    And one on tithes, which sure are Discord's torches,
Kindling Religion till she throws down *her* gage,
    'Untying' squires 'to fight against the churches';
There was a prize ox, a prize pig, and ploughman,
For Henry was a sort of Sabine showman.

LXI

There were two poachers caught in a steel trap,
    Ready for gaol, their place of convalescence;
There was a country girl in a close cap
    And scarlet cloak (I hate the sight to see, since—
Since—since—in youth, I had the sad mishap—
    But luckily I have paid few parish fees since):
That scarlet cloak, alas! unclosed with rigour,
Presents the problem of a double figure.

LXII

A reel within a bottle is a mystery,
    One can't tell how it e'er got in or out;
Therefore the present piece of natural history
    I leave to those who are fond of solving doubt;
And merely state, though not for the Consistory,
    Lord Henry was a Justice, and that Scout
The constable, beneath a warrant's banner,
Had bagged this poacher upon Nature's manor.

LXIII

Now Justices of Peace must judge all pieces
    Of mischief of all kinds, and keep the game
And morals of the country from caprices
    Of those who have not a licence for the same;
And of all things, excepting tithes and leases,
    Perhaps these are most difficult to tame:
Preserving partridges and pretty wenches
Are puzzles to the most precautious benches.

LXIV

The present culprit was extremely pale,
  Pale as if painted so ; her cheek being red
By nature, as in higher dames less hale
  'T is white, at least when they just rise from bed.
Perhaps she was ashamed of seeming frail,
  Poor soul! for she was country born and bred,
And knew no better in her immorality
Than to wax white—for blushes are for quality.

LXV

Her black, bright, downcast, yet *espiègle* eye,
  Had gathered a large tear into its corner,
Which the poor thing at times essayed to dry,
  For she was not a sentimental mourner
Parading all her sensibility,
  Nor insolent enough to scorn the scorner,
But stood in trembling, patient tribulation,
To be called up for her examination.

LXVI

Of course these groups were scattered here and there,
  Not nigh the gay saloon of ladies gent.
The lawyers in the study ; and in air
  The prize pig, ploughman, poachers : the men sent
From town, viz. architect and dealer, were
  Both busy (as a General in his tent
Writing despatches) in their several stations,
Exulting in their brilliant lucubrations.

LXVII

But this poor girl was left in the great hall,
  While Scout, the parish guardian of the frail,
Discussed (he hated beer yclept the 'small')
  A mighty mug of *moral* double ale.
She waited until Justice could recall
  Its kind attentions to their proper pale,
To name a thing in nomenclature rather
Perplexing for most virgins—a child's father.

LXVIII

You see here was enough of occupation
    For the Lord Henry, linked with dogs and horses.
There was much bustle too, and preparation
    Below stairs on the score of second courses;
Because as suits their rank and situation,
    Those who in counties have great land resources
Have 'public days,' when all men may carouse,
Though not exactly what 's called 'open house.'

LXIX

But once a week or fortnight, *un*invited
    (Thus we translate a *general invitation*)
All country gentlemen, esquired or knighted,
    May drop in without cards, and take their station
At the full board, and sit alike delighted
    With fashionable wines and conversation;
And, as the isthmus of the grand connection,
Talk o'er themselves, the past and next election.

LXX

Lord Henry was a great electioneerer,
    Burrowing for boroughs like a rat or rabbit.
But county contests cost him rather dearer,
    Because the neighbouring Scotch Earl of Giftgabbit
Had English influence, in the self-same sphere here;
    His son, the Honourable Dick Dicedrabbit,
Was member for the 'other interest' (meaning
The same self-interest, with a different leaning).

LXXI

Courteous and cautious therefore in his county,
    He was all things to all men, and dispensed
To some civility, to others bounty,
    And promises to all—which last commenced
To gather to a somewhat large amount, he
    Not calculating how much they condensed;
But what with keeping some, and breaking others,
His word had the same value as another's.

LXXII

A friend to Freedom and freeholders—yet
  No less a friend to Government—he held,
That he exactly the just medium hit
  'Twixt Place and Patriotism—albeit compelled,
Such was his Sovereign's pleasure, (though unfit,
  He added modestly, when rebels railed,)
To hold some sinecures he wished abolished,
But that with them all Law would be demolished.

LXXIII

He was 'free to confess'—(whence comes this phrase?
  Is 't English? No—'tis only parliamentary)
That Innovation's spirit now-a-days
  Had made more progress than for the last century.
He would not tread a factious path to praise,
  Though for the public weal disposed to venture high;
As for his place, he could but say this of it,
That the fatigue was greater than the profit.

LXXIV

Heaven, and his friends, knew that a private life
  Had ever been his sole and whole ambition;
But could he quit his King in times of strife,
  Which threatened the whole country with perdition?
When demagogues would with a butcher's knife
  Cut through and through (oh! damnable incision!)
The Gordian or the Geordi-an knot, whose strings
Have tied together Commons, Lords, and Kings.

LXXV

Sooner 'come Place into the Civil List
  And champion him to the utmost—' he would keep it,
Till duly disappointed or dismissed:
  Profit he cared not for, let others reap it;
But should the day come when Place ceased to exist,
  The country would have far more cause to weep it:
For how could it go on? Explain who can!
He gloried in the name of Englishman.

LXXVI

He was as independent—aye, much more—
  Than those who were not paid for independence,
As common soldiers, or a common——shore,
  Have in their several arts or parts ascendance
O'er the irregulars in lust or gore,
  Who do not give professional attendance.
Thus on the mob all statesmen are as eager
To prove their pride, as footmen to a beggar.

LXXVII

All this (save the last stanza) Henry said,
  And thought. I say no more—I've said too much;
For all of us have either heard or read—
  Off—or *upon* the hustings—some slight such
Hints from the independent heart or head
  Of the official candidate. I 'll touch
No more on this—the dinner-bell hath rung,
And grace is said; the grace I *should* have *sung*—

LXXVIII

But I'm too late, and therefore must make play.
  'T was a great banquet, such as Albion old
Was wont to boast—as if a glutton's tray
  Were something very glorious to behold.
But 't was a public feast and public day,—
  Quite full—right dull—guests hot, and dishes cold,—
Great plenty, much formality, small cheer,—
And everybody out of their own sphere.

LXXIX

The squires familiarly formal, and
  My Lords and Ladies proudly condescending;
The very servants puzzling how to hand
  Their plates—without it might be too much bending
From their high places by the sideboard's stand—
  Yet, like their masters, fearful of offending;
For any deviation from the graces
Might cost both man and master too—their *places*.

LXXX

There were some hunters bold, and coursers keen,
    Whose hounds ne'er erred, nor greyhounds deigned to lurch;
Some deadly shots too, Septembrizers, seen
    Earliest to rise, and last to quit the search
Of the poor partridge through his stubble screen.
    There were some massy members of the church,
Takers of tithes, and makers of good matches,
And several who sung fewer psalms than catches.

LXXXI

There were some country wags too—and, alas!
    Some exiles from the Town, who had been driven
To gaze, instead of pavement, upon grass,
    And rise at nine in lieu of long eleven.
And lo! upon that day it came to pass
    I sate next that o'erwhelming son of Heaven,
The very powerful parson, Peter Pith,
The loudest wit I e'er was deafened with.

LXXXII

I knew him in his livelier London days,
    A brilliant diner-out, though but a curate,
And not a joke he cut but earned its praise,
    Until Preferment, coming at a sure rate,
(O Providence! how wondrous are thy ways!
    Who would suppose thy gifts sometimes obdurate?)
Gave him, to lay the Devil who looks o'er Lincoln,
A fat fen vicarage, and nought to think on.

LXXXIII

His jokes were sermons, and his sermons jokes;
    But both were thrown away amongst the fens;
For Wit hath no great friend in aguish folks.
    No longer ready ears and short-hand pens
Imbibed the gay *bon-mot*, or happy hoax:
    The poor priest was reduced to common sense,
Or to coarse efforts very loud and long,
To hammer a hoarse laugh from the thick throng.

LXXXIV.

There *is* a difference, says the song, 'between
    A beggar and a Queen,' or *was* (of late
The latter worse used of the two we 've seen—
    But we 'll say nothing of affairs of state);
A difference ''twixt a Bishop and a Dean,'
    A difference between crockery ware and plate,
As between English beef and Spartan broth—
And yet great heroes have been bred by both.

LXXXV

But of all Nature's discrepancies, none
    Upon the whole is greater than the difference
Beheld between the Country and the Town,
    Of which the latter merits every preference
From those who have few resources of their own,
    And only think, or act, or feel, with reference
To some small plan of interest or ambition—
Both which are limited to no condition.

LXXXVI

But *En avant*! The light loves languish o'er
    Long banquets and too many guests, although
A slight repast makes people love much more,
    Bacchus and Ceres being, as we know,
Even from our grammar upwards, friends of yore
    With vivifying Venus, who doth owe
To these the invention of champagne and truffles:
Temperance delights her, but long fasting ruffles.

LXXXVII

Dully passed o'er the dinner of the day;
    And Juan took his place, he knew not where,
Confused, in the confusion, and *distrait*,
    And sitting as if nailed upon his chair:
Though knives and forks clanked round as in a fray,
    He seemed unconscious of all passing there,
Till some one, with a groan, expressed a wish
(Unheeded twice) to have a fin of fish.

LXXXVIII

On which, at the *third* asking of the banns,
　He started; and perceiving smiles around
Broadening to grins, he coloured more than once,
　And hastily—as nothing can confound
A wise man more than laughter from a dunce—
　Inflicted on the dish a deadly wound,
And with such hurry, that, ere he could curb it,
He had paid his neighbour's prayer with half a turbot.

LXXXIX

This was no bad mistake, as it occurred,
　The supplicator being an amateur;
But others, who were left with scarce a third,
　Were angry—as they well might, to be sure.
They wondered how a young man so absurd
　Lord Henry at his table should endure;
And this, and his not knowing how much oats
Had fallen last market, cost his host three votes.

XC

They little knew, or might have sympathized,
　That he the night before had seen a ghost,
A prologue which but slightly harmonized
　With the substantial company engrossed
By matter, and so much materialised,
　That one scarce knew at what to marvel most
Of two things—*how* (the question rather odd is)
Such bodies could have souls, or souls such bodies!

XCI

But what confused him more than smile or stare
　From all the 'squires and 'squiresses around,
Who wondered at the abstraction of his air,
　Especially as he had been renowned
For some vivacity among the fair,
　Even in the country circle's narrow bound—
(For little things upon my Lord's estate
Were good small talk for others still less great)—

XCII

Was, that he caught Aurora's eye on his,
    And something like a smile upon her cheek.
Now this he really rather took amiss;
    In those who rarely smile, their smile bespeaks
A strong external motive; and in this
    Smile of Aurora's there was nought to pique,
Or Hope, or Love—with any of the wiles
Which some pretend to trace in ladies' smiles.

XCIII

'T was a mere quiet smile of contemplation,
    Indicative of some surprise and pity;
And Juan grew carnation with vexation,
    Which was not very wise, and still less witty,
Since he had gained at least her observation,
    A most important outwork of the city—
As Juan should have known, had not his senses
By last night's Ghost been driven from their defences.

XCIV

But what was bad, she did not blush in turn,
    Nor seem embarrassed—quite the contrary;
Her aspect was as usual, still—*not* stern—
    And she withdrew, but cast not down, her eye,
Yet grew a little pale—with what? concern?
    I know not; but her colour ne'er was high—
Though sometimes faintly flushed—and always clear,
As deep seas in a sunny atmosphere.

XCV

But Adeline was occupied by fame
    This day; and watching, witching, condescending
To the consumers of fish, fowl, and game,
    And dignity with courtesy so blending,
As all must blend whose part it is to aim
    (Especially as the sixth year is ending)
At their lord's, son's, or similar connection's
Safe conduct through the rocks of re-elections.

XCVI

Though this was most expedient on the whole
  And usual—Juan, when he cast a glance
On Adeline while playing her grand *rôle*,
  Which she went through as though it were a dance,
Betraying only now and then her soul
  By a look scarce perceptibly askance
(Of weariness or scorn), began to feel
Some doubt how much of Adeline was *real*;

XCVII

So well she acted all and every part
  By turns—with that vivacious versatility,
Which many people take for want of heart.
  They err—'t is merely what is called mobility,
A thing of temperament and not of art,
  Though seeming so, from its supposed facility;
And false—though true; for, surely, they 're sincerest
Who are strongly acted on by what is nearest.

XCVIII

This makes your actors, artists, and romancers,
  Heroes sometimes, though seldom—sages never:
But speakers, bards, diplomatists, and dancers,
  Little that 's great, but much of what is clever;
Most orators, but very few financiers,
  Though all Exchequer Chancellors endeavour,
Of late years, to dispense with Cocker's rigours,
And grow quite figurative with their figures.

XCIX

The poets of Arithmetic are they
  Who, though they prove not two and two to be
Five, as they might do in a modest way,
  Have plainly made it out that four are three,
Judging by what they take, and what they pay:
  The Sinking Fund's unfathomable sea,
That most unliquidating liquid, leaves
The debt unsunk, yet sinks all it receives.

C

While Adeline dispensed her airs and graces,
    The fair Fitz-Fulke seemed very much at ease;
Though too well bred to quiz men to their faces,
    Her laughing blue eyes with a glance could seize
The ridicules of people in all places—
    That honey of your fashionable bees—
And store it up for mischievous enjoyment;
And this at present was her kind employment.

CI

However, the day closed, as days must close;
    The evening also waned—and coffee came.
Each carriage was announced, and ladies rose,
    And curtsying off, as curtsies country dame,
Retired: with most unfashionable bows
    Their docile Esquires also did the same,
Delighted with their dinner and their Host,
But with the Lady Adeline the most.

CII

Some praised her beauty: others her great grace;
    The warmth of her politeness, whose sincerity
Was obvious in each feature of her face,
    Whose traits were radiant with the rays of verity.
Yes; *she* was truly worthy *her* high place!
    No one could envy her deserved prosperity.
And then her dress—what beautiful simplicity
Draperied her form with curious felicity!

CIII

Meanwhile sweet Adeline deserved their praises,
    By an impartial indemnification
For all her past exertion and soft phrases,
    In a most edifying conversation,
Which turned upon their late guests' miens and faces,
    Their families, even to the last relation;
Their hideous wives, their horrid selves and dresses,
And truculent distortion of their tresses.

CIV

True, *she* said little—'t was the rest that broke
    Forth into universal epigram;
But then 't was to the purpose what she spoke:
    Like Addison's 'faint praise,' so wont to damn,
Her own but served to set off every joke,
    As music chimes in with a melodrame.
How sweet the task to shield an absent friend!
I ask but this of mine, to——*not* defend.

CV

There were but two exceptions to this keen
    Skirmish of wits o'er the departed; one,
Aurora, with her pure and placid mien;
    And Juan, too, in general behind none
In gay remark on what he had heard or seen,
    Sate silent now, his usual spirits gone:
In vain he heard the others rail or rally,
He would not join them in a single sally.

CVI

'T is true he saw Aurora look as though
    She approved his silence; she perhaps mistook
Its motive for that charity we owe
    But seldom pay the absent, nor would look
Farther—it might or it might not be so.
    But Juan, sitting silent in his nook,
Observing little in his reverie,
Yet saw this much, which he was glad to see.

CVII

The Ghost at least had done him this much good,
    In making him as silent as a ghost,
If in the circumstances which ensued
    He gained esteem where it was worth the most:
And, certainly, Aurora had renewed
    In him some feelings he had lately lost,
Or hardened; feelings which, perhaps ideal,
Are so divine, that I must deem them real:—

CVIII

The love of higher things and better days;
  The unbounded hope, and heavenly ignorance
Of what is called the World, and the World's ways;
  The moments when we gather from a glance
More joy than from all future pride or praise,
  Which kindle manhood, but can ne'er entrance
The Heart in an existence of its own,
Of which another's bosom is the zone.

CIX

Who would not sigh *Aἴ aἴ τὰν Κυθέρειαν*
  That *hath* a memory, or that *had* a heart?
Alas! *her* star must fade like that of Dian:
  Ray fades on ray, as years on years depart.
Anacreon only had the soul to tie an
  Unwithering myrtle round the unblunted dart
Of Eros: but though thou hast played us many tricks,
Still we respect thee, '*Alma Venus Genetrix!*'

CX

And full of sentiments, sublime as billows
  Heaving between this World and Worlds beyond,
Don Juan, when the midnight hour of pillows
  Arrived, retired to his; but to despond
Rather than rest. Instead of poppies, willows
  Waved o'er his couch; he meditated, fond
Of those sweet bitter thoughts which banish sleep,
And make the worldling sneer, the youngling weep.

CXI

The night was as before: he was undrest,
  Saving his night-gown, which is an undress;
Completely *sans culotte*, and without vest;
  In short, he hardly could be clothed with less:
But apprehensive of his spectral guest,
  He sate with feelings awkward to express
(By those who have not had such visitations),
Expectant of the Ghost's fresh operations.

CXII

And not in vain he listened;—Hush! what's that?
　　I see—I see—Ah, no!—'t is not—yet 't is—
Ye powers! it is the—the—the—Pooh! the cat!
　　The Devil may take that stealthy pace of his!
So like a spiritual pit-a-pat,
　　Or tiptoe of an amatory Miss,
Gliding the first time to a *rendezvous*,
And dreading the chaste echoes of her shoe.

CXIII

Again—what is 't? The wind? No, no,—this time
　　It is the sable Friar as before,
With awful footsteps regular as rhyme,
　　Or (as rhymes may be in these days) much more.
Again through shadows of the night sublime,
　　When deep sleep fell on men, and the World wore
The starry darkness round her like a girdle
Spangled with gems—the Monk made his blood curdle.

CXIV

A noise like to wet fingers drawn on glass,
　　Which sets the teeth on edge; and a slight clatter,
Like showers which on the midnight gusts will pass,
　　Sounding like very supernatural water,
Came over Juan's ear, which throbbed, alas!
　　For Immaterialism 's a serious matter;
So that even those whose faith is the most great
In Souls immortal, shun them *tête-à-tête*.

CXV

Were his eyes open?—Yes! and his mouth too.
　　Surprise has this effect—to make one dumb,
Yet leave the gate which Eloquence slips through
　　As wide as if a long speech were to come.
Nigh and more nigh the awful echoes drew,
　　Tremendous to a mortal tympanum:
His eyes were open, and (as was before
Stated) his mouth. What opened next?—the door.

CXVI

It opened with a most infernal creak,
    Like that of Hell. 'Lasciate ogni speranza,
Voi, ch' entrate!' The hinge seemed to speak,
    Dreadful as Dante's *rima*, or this stanza;
Or—but all words upon such themes are weak:
    A single shade's sufficient to entrance a
Hero—for what is Substance to a Spirit?
Or how is 't *Matter* trembles to come near it?

CXVII

The door flew wide, not swiftly,—but, as fly
    The sea-gulls, with a steady, sober flight—
And then swung back; nor close—but stood awry,
    Half letting in long shadows on the light,
Which still in Juan's candlesticks burned high,
    For he had two, both tolerably bright,
And in the doorway, darkening darkness, stood
The sable Friar in his solemn hood.

CXVIII

Don Juan shook, as erst he had been shaken
    The night before; but being sick of shaking,
He first inclined to think he had been mistaken;
    And then to be ashamed of such mistaking;
His own internal ghost began to awaken
    Within him, and to quell his corporal quaking—
Hinting that Soul and Body on the whole
Were odds against a disembodied Soul.

CXIX

And then his dread grew wrath, and his wrath fierce,
    And he arose, advanced—the Shade retreated;
But Juan, eager now the truth to pierce,
    Followed, his veins no longer cold, but heated,
Resolved to thrust the mystery *carte* and *tierce*,
    At whatsoever risk of being defeated:
The Ghost stopped, menaced, then retired, until
He reached the ancient wall, then stood stone still.

CXX

Juan put forth one arm—Eternal powers!
  It touched no soul, nor body, but the wall,
On which the moonbeams fell in silvery showers,
  Chequered with all the tracery of the Hall;
He shuddered, as no doubt the bravest cowers
  When he can't tell what 't is that doth appal.
How odd, a single hobgoblin's nonentity
Should cause more fear than a whole host's identity!

CXXI

But still the Shade remained : the blue eyes glared,
  And rather variably for stony death;
Yet one thing rather good the grave had spared,
  The Ghost had a remarkably sweet breath:
A straggling curl showed he had been fair-haired;
  A red lip, with two rows of pearls beneath,
Gleamed forth, as through the casement's ivy shroud
The Moon peeped, just escaped from a grey cloud.

CXXII

And Juan, puzzled, but still curious, thrust
  His other arm forth—Wonder upon wonder!
It pressed upon a hard but glowing bust,
  Which beat as if there was a warm heart under.
He found, as people on most trials must,
  That he had made at first a silly blunder,
And that in his confusion he had caught
Only the wall, instead of what he sought.

CXXIII

The Ghost, if Ghost it were, seemed a sweet soul
  As ever lurked beneath a holy hood:
A dimpled chin, a neck of ivory, stole
  Forth into something much like flesh and blood;
Back fell the sable frock and dreary cowl,
  And they revealed—alas! that e'er they should!
In full, voluptuous, but *not o'er*grown bulk,
The phantom of her frolic Grace—Fitz-Fulke!

CANTO THE SEVENTEENTH

I

The world is full of orphans: firstly, those
　　Who are so in the strict sense of the phrase;
But many a lonely tree the loftier grows
　　Than others crowded in the Forest's maze—
The next are such as are not doomed to lose
　　Their tender parents, in their budding days,
But, merely, their parental tenderness,
Which leaves them orphans of the heart no less.

II

The next are '*only* Children,' as they are styled,
　　Who grow up *Children* only, since th' old saw
Pronounces that an 'only's' a spoilt child—
　　But not to go too far, I hold it law,
That where their education, harsh or mild,
　　Transgresses the great bounds of love or awe,
The sufferers—be 't in heart or intellect—
Whate'er the *cause*, are orphans in *effect*.

III

But to return unto the stricter rule—
　　As far as words make rules—our common notion
Of orphan paints at once a parish school,
　　A half-starved babe, a wreck upon Life's ocean,
A human (what the Italians nickname) 'Mule'!
　　A theme for Pity or some worse emotion;
Yet, if examined, it might be admitted
The wealthiest orphans are to be more pitied.

IV

Too soon they are Parents to themselves: for what
　　Are Tutors, Guardians, and so forth, compared
With Nature's genial Genitors? so that
　　A child of Chancery, that Star-Chamber ward,

(I'll take the likeness I can first come at,)
    Is like—a duckling by Dame Partlett reared,
And frights—especially if 't is a daughter,
Th' old Hen—by running headlong to the water.

V

There is a common-place book argument,
    Which glibly glides from every tongue;
When any dare a new light to present,
    'If you are right, then everybody 's wrong'!
Suppose the converse of this precedent
    So often urged, so loudly and so long;
'If you are wrong, then everybody 's right'!
Was ever everybody yet so quite?

VI

Therefore I would solicit free discussion
    Upon all points—no matter what, or whose—
Because as Ages upon Ages push on,
    The last is apt the former to accuse
Of pillowing its head on a pin-cushion,
    Heedless of pricks because it was obtuse;
What was a paradox becomes a truth or
A something like it—witness Luther!

VII

The Sacraments have been reduced to two,
    And Witches unto none, though somewhat late
Since burning agéd women (save a few—
    Not witches only b—ches—who create
Mischief in families, as some know or knew,
    Should still be singed, but lightly, let me state,)
Has been declared an act of inurbanity,
Malgré Sir Matthew Hales's great humanity.

VIII

Great Galileo was debarred the Sun,
    Because he fixed it; and, to stop his talking

How Earth could round the solar orbit run,
    Found his own legs embargoed from mere walking:
The man was well-nigh dead, ere men begun
    To think his skull had not some need of caulking;
But now, it seems, he's right—his notion just:
No doubt a consolation to his dust.

IX

Pythagoras, Locke, Socrates—but pages
    Might be filled up, as vainly as before,
With the sad usage of all sorts of sages,
    Who in his life-time, each, was deemed a Bore!
The loftiest minds outrun their tardy ages:
    This they must bear with and, perhaps, much more;
The wise man 's sure when he no more can share it, he
Will have a firm Post Obit on posterity.

X

If such doom waits each intellectual Giant,
    We little people in our lesser way,
In Life's small rubs should surely be more pliant,
    And so for one will I—as well I may—
Would that I were less bilious—but, oh, fie on 't!
    Just as I make my mind up every day,
To be a '*totus*, *teres*,' Stoic, Sage,
The wind shifts and I fly into a rage.

XI

Temperate I am—yet never had a temper;
    Modest I am—yet with some slight assurance;
Changeable too—yet somehow '*Idem semper*':
    Patient—but not enamoured of endurance;
Cheerful—but sometimes, rather apt to whimper:,
    Mild—but at times a sort of '*Hercules furens*':
So that I almost think that the same skin,
For one without—has two or three within.

XII

Our Hero was, in Canto the Sixteenth,
    Left in a tender moonlight situation,
Such as enables Man to show his strength
    Moral or physical : on this occasion
Whether his virtue triumphed—or, at length,
    His vice—for he was of a kindling nation—
Is more than I shall venture to describe ;—
Unless some Beauty with a kiss should bribe.

XIII

I leave the thing a problem, like all things :—
    The morning came—and breakfast, tea and toast,
Of which most men partake, but no one sings.
    The company whose birth, wealth, worth, has cost
My trembling Lyre already several strings,
    Assembled with our hostess, and mine host ;
The guests dropped in—the last but one, Her Grace,
The latest, Juan, with his virgin face.

XIV

Which best it is to encounter—Ghost, or none,
    'Twere difficult to say—but Juan looked
As if he had combated with more than one,
    Being wan and worn, with eyes that hardly brooked
The light, that through the Gothic window shone :
    Her Grace, too, had a sort of air rebuked—
Seemed pale and shivered, as if she had kept
A vigil, or dreamt rather more than slept.

from
LETTERS AND
JOURNALS

from

LETTERS AND JOURNALS

TO ELIZABETH BRIDGET PIGOT

Burgage Manor, August 29, 1804

I received the arms, my dear Miss Pigot, and am very much obliged to you for the trouble you have taken. It is impossible I should have any fault to find with them. The sight of the drawings gives me great pleasure for a double reason,—in the first place, they will ornament my books, in the next, they convince me that *you* have not entirely *forgot* me. I am, however, sorry you do not return sooner—you have already been gone an *age*. I perhaps may have taken my departure for London before you come back; but, however, I will hope not. Do not overlook my watch-riband and purse, as I wish to carry them with me. Your note was given me by Harry, at the play, whither I attended Miss Leacroft, and Dr. S———; and now I have sat down to answer it before I go to bed. If I am at Southwell when you return,—and I sincerely hope you will soon, for I very much regret your absence,—I shall be happy to hear you sing my favourite, 'The Maid of Lodi.' My mother, together with myself, desires to be affectionately remembered to Mrs. Pigot, and, believe me, my dear Miss Pigot, I remain, your affectionate friend,

BYRON

P.S. If you think proper to send me any answer to this, I shall be extremely happy to receive it. Adieu.

P.S. 2d. As you say you are a novice in the art of knitting, I hope it don't give you too much trouble. Go on *slowly*, but surely. Once more, adieu.

TO JOHN PIGOT

16 Piccadilly, August 9, 1806

My dear Pigot,

Many thanks for your amusing narrative of the last proceedings of my amiable Alecto, who now begins to feel the effects of her folly. I have just received a penitential epistle, to which, apprehensive of pursuit, I have despatched a moderate answer, with a *kind* of promise to return in a fortnight;—this, however (*entre nous*), I never mean to fulfil. Her soft warblings must have delighted her auditors, her higher notes being particularly musical, and on a calm moonlight evening would be heard to great advantage. Had I been present as a spectator, nothing would have pleased me more; but to have come forward as one of the *dramatis personæ*—St. Dominic defend me from such a scene! Seriously, your mother has laid me under great obligations, and you, with the rest of your family, merit my warmest thanks for your kind connivance at my escape from 'Mrs. Byron *furiosa*.'

Oh! for the pen of Ariosto to rehearse, in epic, the scolding of that momentous eve,—or rather, let me invoke the shade of Dante to inspire me, for none but the author of the Inferno could properly preside over such an attempt. But, perhaps, where the pen might fail, the pencil would succeed. What a group!—Mrs. B. the principal figure; you cramming your ears with cotton, as the only antidote to total deafness; Mrs. ——— in vain endeavouring to mitigate the wrath of the lioness robbed of her whelp; and last, though not least, Elizabeth and *Wousky*,—wonderful to relate!—both deprived of their parts of speech, and bringing up the rear in mute astonishment. How did S. B. receive the intelligence? How many *puns* did he utter on so *facetious* an event? In your next inform me on this point, and what excuse you made to A. You are probably, by this time, tired of deciphering this hieroglyphical letter;—like Tony Lumpkin, you will pronounce mine to be 'a damned up and down hand.' All Southwell, without doubt, is involved in amazement. *Apropos*, how does my blue-eyed nun, the fair —— ? Is she '*robed in sable garb of woe?*'

Here I remain at least a week or ten days; previous to my departure you shall receive my address, but what it will be I have not determined. My lodgings must be kept secret from Mrs. B. You may present my compliments to her, and say any attempt to pursue me will fail, as I have taken measures to retreat immediately to Portsmouth, on the first intimation of her removal from Southwell. You may add, I have proceeded to a friend's house in the country, there to remain a fortnight.

I have now *blotted* (I must not say written) a complete double letter, and in return shall expect a *monstrous budget.* Without doubt, the dames of Southwell reprobate the pernicious example I have shown, and tremble lest their *babes* should disobey their mandates, and quit, in dudgeon, their mammas on any grievance. Adieu. When you begin your next, drop the 'lordship,' and put 'Byron' in its place. Believe me yours, etc.

BYRON

TO JOHN PIGOT

London, August 18, 1806

I am just on the point of setting off for Worthing, and write merely to request you will send that *idle scoundrel Charles* with my horses immediately; tell him I am excessively provoked he has not made his appearance before, or written to inform me of the cause of his delay, particularly as I supplied him with money for his journey. On *no* pretext is he to postpone his *march* one day longer; and if, in obedience to the caprices of Mrs. B. (who, I presume, is again spreading desolation through her little monarchy), he thinks proper to disregard my positive orders, I shall not, in future, consider him as my servant. He must bring the surgeon's bill with him, which I will discharge immediately on receiving it. Nor can I conceive the reason of his not acquainting Frank with the state of my unfortunate quadrupeds. Dear Pigot, forgive this *petulant* effusion, and attribute it to the idle conduct of that *precious* rascal, who, instead of obeying my injunctions, is sauntering through the streets of that *political Pandemonium,* Nottingham. Present my remembrance to your family and the Leacrofts, and believe me, &c.

P.S. I delegate to *you* the unpleasant task of despatching him on his journey—Mrs. B.'s orders to the contrary are not to be attended to : he is to proceed first to London, and then to Worthing, without delay. Every thing I have *left* must be sent to London. My *Poetics you* will *pack up* for the same place, and not even reserve a copy for yourself and sister, as I am about to give them an *entire new form:* when they are complete, you shall have the *first fruits*. Mrs. B. on no account is to *see* or touch them. Adieu.

TO JOHN PIGOT

Little Hampton, August 26, 1806

I this morning received your epistle, which I was obliged to send for to Worthing, whence I have removed to this place, on the same coast, about eight miles distant from the former. You will probably not be displeased with this letter, when it informs you that I am 30,000*l*. richer than I was at our parting, having just received intelligence from my lawyer that a cause has been gained at Lancaster assizes, which will be worth that sum by the time I come of age. Mrs. B. is, doubtless, acquainted of this acquisition, though not apprised of its exact *value,* of which she had better be ignorant ; for her behaviour under any sudden piece of favourable intelligence, is, if possible, more ridiculous than her detestable conduct on the most trifling circumstances of an unpleasant nature. You may give my compliments to her, and say that her detaining my servant's things shall only lengthen my absence : for unless they are immediately despatched to 16 Piccadilly, together with those which have been so long delayed, belonging to myself, she shall never again behold my *radiant countenance* illuminating her gloomy mansion. If they are sent, I may probably appear in less than two years from the date of my present epistle.

Metrical compliment is an ample reward for my strains: you are one of the few votaries of Apollo who unite the sciences over which that deity presides. I wish you to send my poems to my lodgings in London immediately, as I have several alterations and some additions to make; *every* copy must be sent, as I am about to *amend* them, and you shall soon behold them in all their glory. I hope you have kept them from that upas tree, that antidote to the arts, Mrs. B. *Entre nous,*—you may expect to see me soon. Adieu. Yours ever.

TO JOHN PIGOT

Southwell, Jan. 13, 1807

I ought to begin with *sundry* apologies, for my own negligence, but the variety of my avocations in *prose* and *verse* must plead my excuse. With this epistle you will receive a volume of all my *Juvenilia*, published since your departure: it is of considerably greater size than the *copy* in your possession, which I beg you will destroy, as the present is much more complete. That *unlucky* poem to my poor Mary has been the cause of some animadversion from *ladies in years*. I have not printed it in this collection, in consequence of my being pronounced a most *profligate sinner*, in short, a '*young Moore,*' by —————, your —— friend. I believe, in general, they have been favourably received, and surely the age of their author will preclude *severe* criticism. The adventures of my life from sixteen to nineteen, and the dissipation into which I have been thrown in London, have given a voluptuous tint to my ideas; but the occasions which called forth my muse could hardly admit any other colouring. This volume is *vastly* correct and miraculously chaste. Apropos, talking of love, ...

If you can find leisure to answer this farrago of unconnected nonsense, you need not doubt what gratification will accrue from your reply to yours ever, etc.

TO THE EARL OF CLARE

Southwell, Notts, February 6, 1807

My dearest Clare,

Were I to make all the apologies necessary to atone for my late negligence, you would justly say you had received a petition instead of a letter, as it would be filled with prayers for forgiveness; but instead of this, I will acknowledge my *sins* at once, and I trust to your friendship and generosity rather than to my own excuses. Though my health is not perfectly re-established, I am out of all danger, and have recovered every thing but my spirits, which are subject to depression. You will be astonished to hear I have lately written to Delawarr, for the purpose of explaining (as far as possible without involving some *old friends* of mine in the business) the cause of my behaviour to him during my last residence at Harrow (nearly two years ago), which you will recollect was rather *'en cavalier.'* Since that period, I have discovered he was treated with injustice both by those who misrepresented his conduct, and by me in consequence of their suggestions. I have therefore made all the reparation in my power, by apologising for my mistake, though with very faint hopes of success; indeed I never expected any answer, but desired one for form's sake; *that* has not yet arrived, and most probably never will. However, I have *eased* my own *conscience* by the atonement, which is humiliating enough to one of my disposition; yet I could not have slept satisfied with the reflection of having, *even unintentionally*, injured any individual. I have done all that could be done to repair the injury, and there the affair must end. Whether we renew our intimacy or not is of very trivial consequence.

My time has lately been much occupied with very different pursuits. I have been *transporting* a servant, who cheated me, —rather a disagreeable event;—performing in private theatricals;—publishing a volume of poems (at the request of my friends, for their perusal);—making love,—and taking physic. The two last amusements have not had the best effect in the world; for my attentions have been divided amongst so many fair damsels, and the drugs I swallow are of such variety in their composition, that between Venus and Æsculapius I am harassed to death. However, I have still leisure to devote some hours to the recollections of past, regretted friendships, and in the interval to take the advantage of the moment, to assure you how much I am, and ever will be, my dearest Clare,

Your truly attached and sincere

BYRON

TO MISS PIGOT

Cambridge, June 30, 1807

'Better late than never, Pal,' is a saying of which you know the origin, and as it is applicable on the present occasion, you will excuse its conspicuous place in the front of my epistle. I am almost superannuated here. My old friends (with the exception of a very few) all departed, and I am preparing to follow them, but remain till Monday to be present at three *Oratorios*, two *Concerts*, a *Fair*, and a *Ball*. I find I am not only *thinner* but *taller* by an inch since my last visit. I was obliged to tell every body my *name*, nobody having the least recollection of my *visage*, or person. Even the hero of *my Cornelian* (who is now sitting *vis-à-vis* reading a volume of my *Poetics*) passed me in Trinity walks without recognising me in the least, and was thunderstruck at the alteration which had taken place in my countenance, etc., etc. Some say I look *better*, others *worse*, but all agree I am *thinner*,—more I do not require. I have lost two pounds in my weight since I left your *cursed, detestable,* and *abhorred* abode of *scandal*, where, excepting yourself and John Becher, I care not if the whole race were consigned to the *Pit* of *Acheron*, which I would visit in person rather than contaminate my *sandals* with the polluted dust of Southwell. *Seriously,* unless obliged by the *emptiness* of my purse to revisit Mrs. B., you will see me no more.

On Monday I depart for London. I quit Cambridge with little regret, because our *set* are *vanished*, and my *musical protégé* before mentioned has left the choir, and is stationed in a mercantile house of considerable eminence in the metropolis. You may have heard me observe he is exactly to an hour two years younger than myself. I found him grown considerably, and as you will suppose, very glad to see his former *Patron*. He is nearly my height, very *thin*, very fair complexion, dark eyes, and light locks. My opinion of his mind you already know;—I hope I shall never have occasion to change it. Every body here conceives me to be an *invalid*. The University at present is very gay from the fêtes of divers kinds. I supped out last night, but eat (or ate) nothing, sipped a bottle of claret, went to bed at two, and rose at eight. I have commenced early rising, and find it agrees with me. The Masters and the Fellows all very *polite*, but look a little *askance*—don't much admire *lampoons*—truth always disagreeable.

Write, and tell me how the inhabitants of your *Menagerie* go *on*, and if my publication goes *off* well: do the quadrupeds *growl*? Apropos, my bull-dog is deceased—'Flesh both of cur and man is grass.' Address your answer to Cambridge. If I am gone, it will be forwarded. Sad news just arrived—Russians beat—a bad set, eat nothing but *oil*, consequently must melt before a *hard fire*. I get awkward in my academic habiliments for want of practice. Got up in a window to hear the oratorio at St. Mary's, popped down in the middle of the *Messiah*, tore a *woeful* rent in the back of my best black silk gown, and damaged an egregious pair of breeches. Mem.—never tumble from a church window during service. Adieu, dear —— ! do not remember me to any body:—to *forget* and be forgotten by the people of Southwell is all I aspire to.

TO MISS PIGOT

Trin. Coll., Camb., July 5, 1807

Since my last letter I have determined to reside *another year* at Granta, as my rooms, etc., etc., are finished in great style, several old friends come up again, and many new acquaintances made; consequently my inclination leads me forward, and I shall return to college in October if still *alive*. My life here has been one continued routine of dissipation—out at different places every day, engaged to more dinners, etc., etc., than my *stay* would permit me to fulfil. At this moment I write with a bottle of claret in my *head* and *tears* in my *eyes*; for I have just parted with my '*Cornelian*,' who spent the evening with me. As it was our last interview, I postponed my engagement to devote the hours of the *Sabbath* to friendship: —Edleston and I have separated for the present, and my mind is a chaos of hope and sorrow. To-morrow I set out for London: you will address your answer to 'Gordon's Hotel, Albemarle Street,' where I *sojourn* during my visit to the metropolis.

I rejoice to hear you are interested in my *protégé*; he has been my *almost constant* associate since October, 1805, when I entered Trinity College. His *voice* first attracted my attention, his *countenance* fixed it, and his *manners* attached me to him for ever. He departs for a *mercantile house* in *town* in October, and we shall probably not meet till the expiration of my minority, when I shall leave to his decision either entering as a *partner* through my interest, or residing with me altogether. Of course he would in his present frame of mind prefer the *latter*, but he may alter his opinion previous to that period;— however, he shall have his choice. I certainly love him more than any human being, and neither time nor distance have had the least effect on my (in general) changeable disposition. In short, we shall put *Lady E. Butler* and *Miss Ponsonby* to the blush, *Pylades* and *Orestes* out of countenance, and want nothing but a catastrophe like *Nisus* and *Euryalus*, to give *Jonathan* and *David* the 'go by.' He certainly is perhaps more attached to *me* than even I am in return. During the whole of my residence at Cambridge we met every day, summer and winter, without passing *one* tiresome moment, and separated each time with increasing reluctance. I hope you will one day see us together. He is the only being I esteem, though I *like* many.

The Marquis of Tavistock was down the other day; I supped with him at his tutor's—entirely a Whig party. The opposition muster strong here now, and Lord Hartington, the Duke of Leinster, etc., etc., are to join us in October, so every thing will be *splendid*. The *music* is all over at present. Met with another '*accidency*'—upset a butter-boat in the lap of a lady—look'd very *blue*—*spectators* grinned—'curse 'em!' Apropos, sorry to say, been *drunk* every day, and not quite *sober* yet—however, touch no meat, nothing but fish, soup, and vegetables, consequently it does me no harm—sad dogs all the *Cantabs*. Mem.—*we mean* to reform next January. This place is a *monotony of endless variety*—like it—hate Southwell. Has Ridge sold well? or do the ancients demur? What ladies have bought?

Saw a girl at St. Mary's the image of Anne ——, thought it was her—all in the wrong—the lady stared, so did I—I *blushed*, so did *not* the lady,—sad thing—wish women had *more modesty*. Talking of women, puts me in mind of my terrier Fanny—how is she? Got a headach, must go to bed, up early in the morning to travel. My *protégé* breakfasts with me; parting spoils my appetite—excepting from Southwell. Mem. *I hate Southwell*. Yours, etc.

TO MISS PIGOT

Gordon's Hotel, July 13, 1807

You write most excellent epistles—a fig for other correspondents, with their nonsensical apologies for '*knowing nought about it*,'—you send me a delightful budget. I am here in a perpetual vortex of dissipation (very pleasant for all that), and, strange to tell, I get thinner, being now below eleven stone considerably. Stay in town a *month*, perhaps six weeks, trip into Essex, and then, as a favour, *irradiate* Southwell for three days with the light of my countenance; but nothing shall ever make me *reside* there again. I positively return to Cambridge in October; we are to be uncommonly gay, or in truth I should *cut* the University. An extraordinary circumstance occurred to me at Cambridge; a girl so very like —— made her appearance, that nothing but the most *minute inspection* could have undeceived me. I wish I had asked if *she* had ever been at H——.

What the devil would Ridge have? is not fifty in a fortnight, before the advertisements, a sufficient sale? I hear many of the London booksellers have them, and Crosby has sent copies to the principal watering places. Are they liked or not in South-well? . . . I wish Boatswain had *swallowed* Damon! How is Bran? by the immortal gods, Bran ought to be a *Count* of the *Holy Roman Empire*.

The intelligence of London cannot be interesting to you, who have rusticated all your life—the annals of routs, riots, balls and boxing-matches, cards and crim. cons., parliamentary discussion, political details, masquerades, mechanics, Argyle Street Institution and aquatic races, love and lotteries, Brookes's and Buonaparte, opera-singers and oratorios, wine, women, wax-work, and weathercocks, can't accord with your *insulated* ideas of decorum and other *silly expressions* not inserted in *our vocabulary*.

Oh! Southwell, Southwell, how I rejoice to have left thee, and how I curse the heavy hours I dragged along, for so many months, among the Mohawks who inhabit your kraals!— However, one thing I do not regret, which is having *pared off* a sufficient quantity of flesh to enable me to slip into 'an eel-skin,' and vie with the *slim* beaux of modern times; though I am sorry to say, it seems to be the mode amongst *gentlemen* to grow *fat*, and I am told I am at least fourteen pound below the fashion. However, I *decrease* instead of enlarging, which is extraordinary, as *violent* exercise in London is impracticable; but I attribute the *phenomenon* to our *evening squeezes* at public and private parties. I heard from Ridge this morning (the 14th, my letter was begun yesterday): he says the poems go on as well as can be wished; the seventy-five sent to town are circulated, and a demand for fifty more complied with, the day he dated his epistle, though the advertisements are not yet half published. Adieu.

P.S. Lord Carlisle, on receiving my poems, sent, before he opened the book, a tolerably handsome letter:—I have not heard from him since. His opinions I neither know nor care about: if he is the least insolent, I shall enrol him with *Butler* and the other worthies. He is in Yorkshire, poor man! and very ill! He said he had not had time to read the contents, but thought it necessary to acknowledge the receipt of the volume immediately. Perhaps the Earl '*bears no brother near the throne,*' —*if so*, I will make his *sceptre* totter *in his hands*.—Adieu!

TO MISS PIGOT

Trinity College, Cambridge, October 26, 1807

My dear Elizabeth,

Fatigued with sitting up till four in the morning for the last two days at hazard, I take up my pen to inquire how your highness and the rest of my female acquaintance at the seat of archiepiscopal grandeur go on. I know I deserve a scolding for my negligence in not writing more frequently; but racing up and down the country for these last three months, how was it possible to fulfil the duties of a correspondent? Fixed at last for six weeks, I write, as *thin* as ever (not having gained an ounce since my reduction), and rather in better humour;— but, after all, Southwell was a detestable residence. Thank St. Dominica, I have done with it: I have been twice within eight miles of it, but could not prevail on myself to *suffocate* in its heavy atmosphere. This place is wretched enough—a villanous chaos of din and drunkenness, nothing but hazard and burgundy, hunting, mathematics, and Newmarket, riot and racing. Yet it is a paradise compared with the eternal dulness of Southwell. Oh! the misery of doing nothing but make *love, enemies,* and *verses.*

Next January, (but this is *entre nous only*, and pray let it be so, or my maternal persecutor will be throwing her tomahawk at any of my curious projects,) I am going to *sea* for four or five months, with my cousin Captain Bettesworth, who commands the *Tartar*, the finest frigate in the navy. I have seen most scenes, and wish to look at a naval life. We are going probably to the Mediterranean, or to the West Indies, or—to the devil; and if there is a possibility of taking me to the latter, Bettesworth will do it; for he has received four and twenty wounds in different places, and at this moment possesses a letter from the late Lord Nelson, stating Bettesworth as the only officer in the navy who had more wounds than himself.

I have got a new friend, the finest in the world, a *tame bear*. When I brought him here, they asked me what I meant to do with him, and my reply was, 'he should *sit for a fellowship*.' Sherard will explain the meaning of the sentence, if it is ambiguous. This answer delighted them not. We have several parties here, and this evening a large assortment of jockeys, gamblers, boxers, authors, parsons, and poets, sup with me,— a precious mixture, but they go on well together; and for me, I am a *spice* of every thing except a jockey; by the bye, I was dismounted again the other day.

Thank your brother in my name for his treatise. I have written 214 pages of a novel,—one poem of 380 lines, to be published (without my name) in a few weeks, with notes,— 560 lines of Bosworth Field, and 250 lines of another poem in rhyme, besides half a dozen smaller pieces. The poem to be published is a Satire. *Apropos*, I have been praised to the skies in the *Critical Review*, and abused greatly in another publication. So much the better, they tell me, for the sale of the book: it keeps up controversy, and prevents it being forgotten. Besides, the first men of all ages have had their share, nor do the humblest escape;—so I bear it like a philosopher. It is odd two opposite critiques came out on the same day, and out of five pages o f abuse, my censor only quotes *two lines* from different poems, in support of his opinion. Now, the proper way to *cut up*, is to quote long passages, and make them appear absurd, because simple allegation is no proof. On the other hand, there are seven pages of praise, and more than *my modesty* will allow said on the subject. Adieu.

P.S. Write, write, write!!!

TO JOHN JACKSON

N. A., Notts. September 18, 1808

Dear Jack,

I wish you would inform me what has been done by Jekyll, at No. 40 Sloane Square, concerning the pony I returned as unsound.

I have also to request you will call on Louch at Brompton,

and inquire what the devil he meant by sending such an insolent letter to me at Brighton; and at the same time tell him I by no means can comply with the charge he has made for things pretended to be damaged.

Ambrose behaved most scandalously about the pony. You may tell Jekyll if he does not refund the money, I shall put the affair into my lawyer's hands. Five and twenty guineas is a sound price for a pony, and by God, if it costs me five hundred pounds, I will make an example of Mr. Jekyll, and that immediately, unless the cash is returned.

Believe me, dear Jack, etc.

TO THE HONOURABLE MRS. BYRON

Newstead Abbey, Notts. October 7, 1808

Dear Madam,

I have no beds for the Hansons or any body else at present. The Hansons sleep at Mansfield. I do not know that I resemble Jean Jacques Rousseau. I have no ambition to be like so illustrious a madman—but this I know, that I shall live in my own manner, and as much alone as possible. When my rooms are ready I shall be glad to see you: at present it would be improper, and uncomfortable to both parties. You can hardly object to my rendering my mansion habitable, notwithstanding my departure for Persia in March (or May at farthest), since *you* will be *tenant* till my return; and in case of any accident (for I have already arranged my will to be drawn up the moment I am twenty-one), I have taken care you shall have the house and manor for *life*, besides a sufficient income. So you see my improvements are not entirely selfish. As I have a friend here, we will go to the Infirmary Ball on the 12th; we will drink tea with Mrs. Byron at eight o'clock, and expect to see you at the ball. If that lady will allow us a couple of rooms to dress in, we shall be highly obliged:—if we are at the ball by ten or eleven, it will be time enough, and we shall return to Newstead about three or four. Adieu.

Believe me, yours very truly,

BYRON

TO MRS. BYRON

8 St. James's Street, March 6, 1809

Dear Mother,

My last letter was written under great depression of spirits from poor Falkland's death, who has left without a shilling four children and his wife. I have been endeavouring to assist them, which, God knows, I cannot do as I could wish, for my own embarrassments and the many claims upon me from other quarters.

What you say is all very true: come what may, *Newstead* and I *stand* or fall together. I have now lived on the spot, I have fixed my heart upon it, and no pressure, present or future, shall induce me to barter the last vestige of our inheritance. I have that pride within me which will enable me to support difficulties. I can endure privations; but could I obtain in exchange for Newstead Abbey the first fortune in the country, I would reject the proposition. Set your mind at ease on that score; Mr. Hanson talks like a man of business on the subject,—I feel like a man of honour, and I will not sell Newstead.

I shall get my seat on the return of the affidavits from Carhais, in Cornwall, and will do something in the House soon: I must dash, or it is all over. My Satire must be kept secret for a *month*; after that you may say what you please on the subject. Lord Carlisle has used me infamously, and refused to state any particulars of my family to the Chancellor. I have *lashed* him in my rhymes, and perhaps his lordship may regret not being more conciliatory. They tell me it will have a sale; I hope so, for the bookseller has behaved well, as far as publishing well goes.

Believe me, etc.

P.S.—You shall have a mortgage on one of the farms.

TO WILLIAM HARNESS

8 St. James's Street, March 18, 1809

There was no necessity for your excuses: if you have time and inclination to write, 'for what we receive, the Lord make us thankful,'—if I do not hear from you, I console myself with the idea that you are much more agreeably employed.

I send down to you by this post a certain Satire lately published, and in return for the three and sixpence expenditure upon it, only beg that if you should guess the author, you will keep his name secret; at least for the present. London is full of the Duke's business. The Commons have been at it these last three nights, and are not yet come to a decision. I do not know if the affair will be brought before our House, unless in the shape of an impeachment. If it makes its appearance in a debatable form, I believe I shall be tempted to say something on the subject.—I am glad to hear you like Cambridge: firstly, because, to know that you are happy is pleasant to one who wishes you all possible sublunary enjoyment; and, secondly, I admire the morality of the sentiment. *Alma Mater* was to me *injusta noverca*; and the old beldam only gave me my M. A. degree because she could not avoid it.—You know what a farce a noble Cantab. must perform.

I am going abroad, if possible, in the spring, and before I depart I am collecting the pictures of my most intimate schoolfellows; I have already a few, and shall want yours, or my cabinet will be incomplete. I have employed one of the first miniature painters of the day to take them, of course, at my own expense, as I never allow my acquaintance to incur the least expenditure to gratify a whim of mine. To mention this may seem indelicate; but when I tell you a friend of ours first refused to sit, under the idea that he was to disburse on the occasion, you will see that it is necessary to state these preliminaries to prevent the recurrence of any similar mistake. I shall see you in time, and will carry you to the *limner*. It will be a tax on your patience for a week; but pray excuse it, as it is possible the resemblance may be the sole trace I shall be able to preserve of our past friendship and acquaintance. Just now it seems foolish enough; but in a few years, when some of us are dead, and others are separated by inevitable circumstances, it will be a kind of satisfaction to retain in these images of the living the idea of our former selves, and to contemplate, in the resemblances of the dead, all that remains of judgment,

feeling, and a host of passions. But all this will be dull enough
for you, and so good night; and to end my chapter, or rather
my homily, believe me, my dear H., yours most affectionately.

TO MRS. BYRON

Falmouth, June 22, 1809

Dear Mother,

I am about to sail in a few days; probably before this reaches
you. Fletcher begged so hard, that I have continued him in my
service. If he does not behave well abroad, I will send him
back in a *transport*. I have a German servant, (who has been
with Mr. Wilbraham in Persia before, and was strongly
recommended to me by Dr. Butler, of Harrow,) Robert and
William; they constitute my whole suite. I have letters in
plenty:—you shall hear from me at the different ports I touch
upon; but you must not be alarmed if my letters miscarry.
The Continent is in a fine state—an insurrection has broken
out at Paris, and the Austrians are beating Buonaparte—the
Tyrolese have risen.

There is a picture of me in oil, to be sent down to Newstead
soon.—I wish the Miss Pigots had something better to do than
carry my miniatures to Nottingham to copy. Now they have
done it, you may ask them to copy the others, which are
greater favourites than my own. As to money matters, I am
ruined—at least till Rochdale is sold; and if that does not turn
out well, I shall enter into the Austrian or Russian service—
perhaps the Turkish, if I like their manners. The world is all
before me, and I leave England without regret, and without
a wish to revisit any thing it contains, except *yourself*, and
your present residence.

Believe me, yours ever sincerely.

P.S.—Pray tell Mr. Rushton his son is well, and doing well;
so is Murray, indeed better than I ever saw him; he will be
back in about a month. I ought to add the leaving Murray to
my few regrets, as his age perhaps will prevent my seeing him
again. Robert I take with me; I like him, because, like myself,
he seems a friendless animal.

TO FRANCIS HODGSON

Falmouth, June 25, 1809

My dear Hodgson,

Before this reaches you, Hobhouse, two officers' wives, three children, two waiting-maids, ditto subalterns for the troops, three Portuguese esquires and domestics, in all nine-teen souls, will have sailed in the Lisbon packet, with the noble Captain Kidd, a gallant commander as ever smuggled an anker of right Nantz.

We are going to Lisbon first, because the Malta packet has sailed, d'ye see?—from Lisbon to Gibraltar, Malta, Constanti-nople, and 'all that,' as Orator Henley said, when he put the Church, and 'all that,' in danger.

This town of Falmouth, as you will partly conjecture, is no great ways from the sea. It is defended on the sea-side by tway castles, St. Maws and Pendennis, extremely well calcu-lated for annoying every body except an enemy. St. Maws is garrisoned by an able-bodied person of fourscore, a widower. He has the whole command and sole management of six most unmanageable pieces of ordnance, admirably adapted for the destruction of Pendennis, a like tower of strength on the opposite side of the Channel. We have seen St. Maws, but Pendennis they will not let us behold, save at a distance, because Hobhouse and I are suspected of having already taken St. Maws by a coup de main.

The town contains many Quakers and salt fish—the oysters have a taste of copper, owing to the soil of a mining country—the women (blessed be the Corporation therefor!) are flogged at the cart's tail when they pick and steal, as happened to one of the fair sex yesterday noon. She was pertinacious in her behaviour, and damned the mayor. . . .

I don't know when I can write again, because it depends on that experienced navigator, Captain Kidd, and the 'stormy winds that (don't) blow' at this season. I leave England with-out regret—I shall return to it without pleasure. I am like Adam, the first convict sentenced to transportation, but I

have no Eve, and have eaten no apple but what was sour as a
crab;—and thus ends my first chapter. Adieu.

Yours, etc.

TO FRANCIS HODGSON

Lisbon, July 16, 1809

Thus far have we pursued our route, and seen all sorts of
marvellous sights, palaces, convents, etc. ;—which, being to be
heard in my friend Hobhouse's forthcoming Book of Travels,
I shall not anticipate by smuggling any account whatsoever to
you in a private and clandestine manner. I must just observe,
that the village of Cintra in Estremadura is the most beautiful,
perhaps, in the world.

I am very happy here, because I loves oranges, and talks bad
Latin to the monks, who understand it, as it is like their own,
—and I goes into society (with my pocket-pistols), and I
swims in the Tagus all across at once, and I rides on an ass or a
mule, and swears Portuguese, and have got a diarrhœa and
bites from the mosquitoes. But what of that? Comfort must
not be expected by folks that go a pleasuring.

When the Portuguese are pertinacious, I say, *Carracho!*—
the great oath of the grandees, that very well supplies the place
of 'Damme,'—and, when dissatisfied with my neighbour, I
pronounce him *Ambra di merdo*. With these two phrases,
and a third, *Avra bouro*, which signifieth 'Get an ass,' I am
universally understood to be a person of degree and a master
of languages. How merrily we lives that travellers be!—if we
had food and raiment. But, in sober sadness, any thing is
better than England, and I am infinitely amused with my
pilgrimage as far as it has gone.

To-morrow we start to ride post near 400 miles as far as
Gibraltar, where we embark for Melita and Byzantium. A
letter to Malta will find me, or to be forwarded, if I am absent.
Pray embrace the Drury and Dwyer, and all the Ephesians you
encounter. I am writing with Butler's donative pencil, which
makes my bad hand worse. Excuse illegibility.

Hodgson! send me the news, and the deaths and defeats and

capital crimes and the misfortunes of one's friends; and let us hear of literary matters, and the controversies and the criticisms. All this will be pleasant—*Suave mari magno*, etc. Talking of that, I have been sea-sick, and sick of the sea.

Adieu. Yours faithfully, etc.

TO MRS. BYRON

Aug. 11, 1809

... We lodged in the house of two Spanish unmarried ladies, who possess *six* houses in Seville, and gave me a curious specimen of Spanish manners. They are women of character, and the eldest a fine woman, the youngest pretty, but not so good a figure as Donna Josepha. The freedom of manner, which is general here, astonished me not a little; and in the course of further observation, I find that reserve is not the characteristic of the Spanish belles, who are, in general, very handsome, with large black eyes, and very fine forms. The eldest honoured your *unworthy* son with very particular attention, embracing him with great tenderness at parting (I was there but three days), after cutting off a lock of his hair, and presenting him with one of her own, about three feet in length, which I send, and beg you will retain till my return. Her last words were, *Adios, tu hermoso! me gusto mucho.*—'Adieu, you pretty fellow! you please me much.' She offered me a share of her apartment, which my *virtue* induced me to decline; she laughed, and said I had some English *amante* (lover), and added that she was going to be married to an officer in the Spanish army.

TO MRS. BYRON

Prevesa, November 12, 1809

My dear Mother,

I have now been some time in Turkey: this place is on the coast, but I have traversed the interior of the province of Albania on a visit to the Pacha. I left Malta in the *Spider*, a brig of war, on the 21st of September, and arrived in eight days at Prevesa. I thence have been about 150 miles, as far as Tepaleen, his Highness's country palace, where I stayed three days. The name of the Pacha is *Ali*, and he is considered a man of the first abilities: he governs the whole of Albania (the ancient Illyricum), Epirus, and part of Macedonia. His son, Vely Pacha, to whom he has given me letters, governs the Morea, and has great influence in Egypt; in short, he is one of the most powerful men in the Ottoman empire. When I reached Yanina, the capital, after a journey of three days over the mountains, through a country of the most picturesque beauty, I found that Ali Pacha was with his army in Illyricum, besieging Ibrahim Pacha in the castle of Berat. He had heard that an Englishman of rank was in his dominions, and had left orders in Yanina with the commandant to provide a house, and supply me with every kind of necessary *gratis*; and, though I have been allowed to make presents to the slaves, etc., I have not been permitted to pay for a single article of household consumption.

I rode out on the vizier's horses, and saw the palaces of himself and grandsons: they are splendid, but too much ornamented with silk and gold. I then went over the mountains through Zitza, a village with a Greek monastery (where I slept on my return), in the most beautiful situation (always excepting Cintra, in Portugal) I ever beheld. In nine days I reached Tepaleen. Our journey was much prolonged by the torrents that had fallen from the mountains, and intersected the roads. I shall never forget the singular scene on entering Tepaleen at five in the afternoon, as the sun was going down. It brought to my mind (with some change of *dress*, however) Scott's description of Branksome Castle in his *Lay*, and the feudal system. The Albanians, in their dresses, (the most magnificent in the world, consisting of a long *white kilt*, gold-worked cloak, crimson velvet gold-laced jacket and waistcoat, silver-mounted pistols and daggers,) the Tartars with their high caps, the Turks in their vast pelisses and turbans, the soldiers and black slaves with the horses, the former in groups in an immense large open gallery in front of the palace, the latter placed in a kind of cloister below it, two hundred steeds ready caparisoned to move in a moment, couriers entering or passing out with the despatches, the kettle-drums beating, boys calling the hour from the minaret of the mosque, altogether, with the singular appearance of the building itself, formed a new and delightful spectacle to a stranger. I was conducted to a very handsome apartment, and my health inquired after by the vizier's secretary, *à-la-mode Turque!*

The next day I was introduced to Ali Pacha. I was dressed in a full suit of staff uniform, with a very magnificent sabre, etc. The vizier received me in a large room paved with marble; a fountain was playing in the centre; the apartment was surrounded by scarlet ottomans. He received me standing, a wonderful compliment from a Mussulman, and made me sit down on his right hand. I have a Greek interpreter for general use, but a physician of Ali's named Femlario, who understands Latin, acted for me on this occasion. His first question was, why, at so early an age, I left my country?—(the Turks have no idea of travelling for amusement). He then said, the English minister, Captain Leake, had told him I was of a great family, and desired his respects to my mother; which I now, in the name of Ali Pacha, present to you. He said he was certain I was a man of birth, because I had small ears, curling hair, and little white hands, and expressed himself pleased with my appearance and garb. He told me to consider him as a father whilst I was in Turkey, and said he looked on me as his son. Indeed, he treated me like a child, sending me almonds and sugared sherbet, fruit and sweetmeats, twenty times a day. He begged me to visit him often, and at night, when he was at leisure. I then, after coffee and pipes, retired for the first time. I saw him thrice afterwards. It is singular, that the Turks, who have no hereditary dignities, and few great families, except the Sultans, pay so much respect to birth; for I found my pedigree more regarded than my title.

To-day I saw the remains of the town of Actium, near which Antony lost the world, in a small bay, where two frigates could hardly manœuvre: a broken wall is the sole remnant. On another part of the gulf stand the ruins of Nicopolis, built by Augustus in honour of his victory. Last night I was at a Greek marriage; but this and a thousand things more I have neither time nor *space* to describe. . . .

I am going to-morrow, with a guard of fifty men, to Patras in the Morea, and thence to Athens, where I shall winter. Two days ago I was nearly lost in a Turkish ship of war, owing to the ignorance of the captain and crew, though the storm was not violent. Fletcher yelled after his wife, the Greeks called on all the saints, the Mussulmans on Alla; the captain burst into tears and ran below deck, telling us to call on God; the sails were split, the main-yard shivered, the wind blowing fresh, the night setting in, and all our chance was to make Corfu, which is in possession of the French, or (as Fletcher pathetically termed it) 'a watery grave.' I did what I could to console Fletcher, but finding him incorrigible, wrapped myself up in my Albanian capote (an immense cloak), and lay down on deck to wait the worst. I have learnt to philosophise in my travels; and if I had not, complaint was useless. Luckily the wind abated, and only drove us on the coast of Suli, on the main land, where we landed, and proceeded, by the help of the natives, to Prevesa again; but I shall not trust Turkish sailors in future, though the Pacha had ordered one of his own galliots to take me to Patras. I am therefore going as far as Missolonghi by land, and there have only to cross a small gulf to get to Patras.

Fletcher's next epistle will be full of marvels. We were one night lost for nine hours in the mountains in a thunderstorm, and since nearly wrecked. In both cases Fletcher was sorely bewildered, from apprehensions of famine and banditti in the first, and drowning in the second instance. His eyes were a little hurt by the lightning, or crying (I don't know which), but are now recovered. When you write, address to me at Mr. Strané's, English consul, Patras, Morea.

I could tell you I know not how many incidents that I think would amuse you, but they crowd on my mind as much as they would swell my paper, and I can neither arrange them in the one, nor put them down on the other, except in the greatest confusion. I like the Albanians much; they are not all Turks; some tribes are Christians. But their religion makes little difference in their manner or conduct. They are esteemed the best troops in the Turkish service. I lived on my route, two days at once, and three days again, in a barrack at Salora, and never found soldiers so tolerable, though I have been in the garrisons of Gibraltar and Malta, and seen Spanish, French, Sicilian, and British troops in abundance. I have had nothing stolen, and was always welcome to their provision and milk. Not a week ago an Albanian chief, (every village has its chief, who is called Primate,) after helping us out of the Turkish galley in her distress, feeding us, and lodging my suite, consisting of Fletcher, a Greek, two Athenians, a Greek priest, and my companion, Mr. Hobhouse, refused any compensation but a written paper stating that I was well received; and when I pressed him to accept a few sequins, 'No,' he replied; 'I wish you to love me, not to pay me.' These are his words.

It is astonishing how far money goes in this country. While I was in the capital I had nothing to pay by the vizier's order; but since, though I have generally had sixteen horses, and generally six or seven men, the expense has not been *half* as much as staying only three weeks in Malta, though Sir A. Ball, the governor, gave me a house for nothing, and I had only *one* servant. By the by, I expect Hanson to remit regularly; for I am not about to stay in this province for ever. Let him write to me at Mr. Strané's, English consul, Patras. The fact is, the fertility of the plains is wonderful, and specie is scarce, which makes this remarkable cheapness. I am going to Athens, to study modern Greek, which differs much from the ancient, though radically similar. I have no desire to return to England, nor shall I, unless compelled by absolute want, and Hanson's neglect; but I shall not enter into Asia for a year or two, as I have much to see in Greece, and I may perhaps cross into Africa, at least the Egyptian part. Fletcher, like all Englishmen, is very much dissatisfied, though a little reconciled to the Turks by a present of eighty piastres from the vizier, which, if you consider every thing, and the value of specie here, is nearly worth ten guineas English. He has suffered nothing but from cold, heat, and vermin, which those who lie in cottages and cross mountains in a cold country must undergo, and of which I have equally partaken with himself; but he is not valiant, and is afraid of robbers and tempests. I have no one to be remembered to in England, and wish to hear nothing from it, but that you are well, and a letter or two on business from Hanson, whom you may tell to write. I will write when I can, and beg you to believe me,

Your affectionate son,

BYRON

TO MRS. BYRON

Smyrna, March 19, 1810

Dear Mother,

I cannot write you a long letter; but as I know you will not be sorry to receive any intelligence of my movements, pray accept what I can give. I have traversed the greatest part of Greece, besides Epirus, etc., etc., resided ten weeks at Athens, and am now on the Asiatic side on my way to Constantinople. I have just returned from viewing the ruins of Ephesus, a day's journey from Smyrna. I presume you have received a long letter I wrote from Albania, with an account of my reception by the Pacha of the province.

When I arrive at Constantinople, I shall determine whether to proceed into Persia or return, which latter I do not wish, if I can avoid it. But I have no intelligence from Mr. Hanson, and but one letter from yourself. I shall stand in need of remittances whether I proceed or return. I have written to him repeatedly, that he may not plead ignorance of my situation for neglect. I can give you no account of any thing, for I have not time or opportunity, the frigate sailing immediately. Indeed the further I go the more my laziness increases, and my aversion to letter-writing becomes more confirmed. I have written to no one but to yourself and Mr. Hanson, and these are communications of business and duty rather than of inclination.

Fletcher is very much disgusted with his fatigues, though he has undergone nothing that I have not shared. He is a poor creature; indeed English servants are detestable travellers. I have, besides him, two Albanian soldiers and a Greek interpreter; all excellent in their way. Greece, particularly in the vicinity of Athens, is delightful;—cloudless skies and lovely landscapes. But I must reserve all account of my adventures till we meet. I keep no journal, but my friend Hobhouse scribbles incessantly. Pray take care of Murray and Robert, and tell the boy it is the most fortunate thing for him that he did not accompany me to Turkey. Consider this as merely a notice of my safety, and believe me,

Yours, etc., etc.,

BYRON

TO FRANCIS HODGSON

Salsette frigate, in the Dardanelles, off Abydos,
May 5, 1810

I am on my way to Constantinople, after a tour through Greece, Epirus, etc., and part of Asia Minor, some particulars of which I have just communicated to our friend and host, H. Drury. With these, then, I shall not trouble you; but as you will perhaps be pleased to hear that I am well, etc., I take the opportunity of our ambassador's return to forward the few lines I have time to despatch. We have undergone some inconveniences, and incurred partial perils, but no events worthy of communication, unless you will deem it one that two days ago I swam from Sestos to Abydos. This, with a few alarms from robbers, and some danger of shipwreck in a Turkish galliot six months ago, a visit to a Pacha, a passion for a married woman at Malta, a challenge to an officer, an attachment to three Greek girls at Athens, with a great deal of buffoonery and fine prospects, form all that has distinguished my progress since my departure from Spain.

Hobhouse rhymes and journalises; I stare and do nothing— unless smoking can be deemed an active amusement. The Turks take too much care of their women to permit them to be scrutinised; but I have lived a good deal with the Greeks, whose modern dialect can I converse in enough for my purposes. With the Turks I have also some male acquaintances—female society is out of the question. I have been very well treated by the Pachas and Governors, and have no complaint to make of any kind. Hobhouse will one day inform you of all our adventures—were I to attempt the recital, neither *my* paper nor *your* patience would hold out during the operation.

Nobody, save yourself, has written to me since I left England; but indeed I did not request it. I except my relations, who write quite as often as I wish. Of Hobhouse's volume I know nothing, except that it is out; and of my second edition I do not even know *that*, and certainly do not, at this distance, interest myself in the matter. I hope you and Bland roll down the stream of sale with rapidity.

Of my return I cannot positively speak, but think it probable Hobhouse will precede me in that respect. We have been very nearly one year abroad. I should wish to gaze away another, at least, in these evergreen climates; but I fear business, law business, the worst of employments, will recall me previous to that period, if not very quickly. If so, you shall have due notice.

I hope you will find me an altered personage,—I do not mean in body, but in manner, for I begin to find out that nothing but virtue will do in this damned world. I am tolerably sick of vice, which I have tried in its agreeable varieties, and mean, on my return, to cut all my dissolute acquaintance, leave off wine and carnal company, and betake myself to politics and decorum. I am very serious and cynical, and a good deal disposed to moralise; but fortunately for you the coming homily is cut off by default of pen and defection of paper.

Good morrow! If you write, address to me at Malta, whence your letters will be forwarded. You need not remember me to any body, but believe me,

Yours with all faith,

BYRON

TO MRS. BYRON

Athens, July 25, 1810

Dear Mother,

I have arrived here in four days from Constantinople, which is considered as singularly quick, particularly for the season of the year. . . . Your northern gentry can have no conception of a Greek summer; which, however, is a perfect frost compared with Malta and Gibraltar, where I reposed myself in the shade last year, after a gentle gallop of four hundred miles, without intermission, through Portugal and Spain. You see, by my date, that I am at Athens again, a place which I think I prefer, upon the whole, to any I have seen.

My next movement is to-morrow into the Morea, where I shall probably remain a month or two, and then return to winter here, if I do not change my plans, which, however, are very variable, as you may suppose; but none of them verge to England.

The Marquis of Sligo, my old fellow-collegian, is here, and wishes to accompany me into the Morea. We shall go together for that purpose; but I am woefully sick of travelling companions, after a year's experience of Mr. Hobhouse, who is on his way to Great Britain. Lord S. will afterwards pursue his way to the capital; and Lord B., having seen all the wonders in that quarter, will let you know what he does next, of which at present he is not quite certain. Malta is my perpetual post-office, from which my letters are forwarded to all parts of the habitable globe:—by the bye, I have now been in Asia, Africa, and the east of Europe, and, indeed, made the most of my time, without hurrying over the most interesting scenes of the ancient world. Fletcher, after having been toasted and roasted, and baked, and grilled, and eaten by all sorts of creeping things, begins to philosophise, is grown a refined as well as a resigned character, and promises at his return to become an ornament to his own parish, and a very prominent person in the future family pedigree of the Fletchers, who I take to be Goths by their accomplishments, Greeks by their acuteness,

and ancient Saxons by their appetite. He (Fletcher) begs leave
to send half-a-dozen sighs to Sally his spouse, and wonders
(though I do not) that his ill-written and worse spelt letters
have never come to hand; as for that matter, there is no great
loss in either of our letters, saving and except that I wish you
to know we are well, and warm enough at this present writing,
God knows. You must not expect long letters at present, for
they are written with the sweat of my brow, I assure you. It is
rather singular that Mr. Hanson has not written a syllable
since my departure. Your letters I have mostly received as
well as others; from which I conjecture that the man of law is
either angry or busy.

I trust you like Newstead, and agree with your neighbours;
but you know *you* are a *vixen*—is not that a dutiful appella-
tion? Pray, take care of my books and several boxes of papers
in the hands of Joseph; and pray leave me a few bottles of
champagne to drink, for I am very thirsty;—but I do not
insist on the last article, without you like it. I suppose you have
your house full of silly women, prating scandalous things.
Have you ever received my picture in oil from Sanders, London? It has been paid for these sixteen months: why do you
not get it? My suite, consisting of two Turks, two Greeks, a
Lutheran, and the nondescript, Fletcher, are making so much
noise, that I am glad to sign myself,

> Yours, etc., etc.,
>
> BYRON

TO MRS. BYRON

Athens, January 14, 1811

My dear Madam,

I seize an occasion to write as usual, shortly, but frequently,
as the arrival of letters, where there exists no regular communication, is, of course, very precarious. I have lately made
several small tours of some hundred or two miles about the
Morea, Attica, etc., as I have finished my grand giro by the
Troad, Constantinople, etc., and am returned down again to
Athens. I believe I have mentioned to you more than once that

I swam (in imitation of Leander, though without his lady) across the Hellespont, from Sestos to Abydos. Of this, and all other particulars, Fletcher, whom I have sent home with papers, etc., will apprise you. I cannot find that he is any loss; being tolerably master of the Italian and modern Greek languages, which last I am also studying with a master, I can order and discourse more than enough for a reasonable man. Besides, the perpetual lamentations after beef and beer, the stupid, bigoted contempt for every thing foreign, and insurmountable incapacity of acquiring even a few words of any language, rendered him, like all other English servants, an incumbrance. I do assure you, the plague of speaking for him, the comforts he required (more than myself by far), the pilaws (a Turkish dish of rice and meat) which he could not eat, the wines which he could not drink, the beds where he could not sleep, and the long list of calamities, such as stumbling horses, want of *tea!!!* etc., which assailed him, would have made a lasting source of laughter to a spectator, and inconvenience to a master. After all, the man is honest enough, and, in Christendom, capable enough; but in Turkey, Lord forgive me! my Albanian soldiers, my Tartars and Janissary, worked for him and us too, as my friend Hobhouse can testify.

It is probable I may steer homewards in spring; but to enable me to do that, I must have remittances. My own funds would have lasted me very well; but I was obliged to assist a friend, who, I know, will pay me; but, in the mean time, I am out of pocket. At present, I do not care to venture a winter's voyage, even if I were otherwise tired of travelling; but I am so convinced of the advantages of looking at mankind instead of reading about them, and the bitter effects of staying at home with all the narrow prejudices of an islander, that I think there should be a law amongst us, to set our young men abroad, for a term, among the few allies our wars have left us.

Here I see and have conversed with French, Italians, Germans, Danes, Greeks, Turks, Americans, etc., etc., etc.; and without losing sight of my own, I can judge of the countries and manners of others. Where I see the superiority of England (which, by the by, we are a good deal mistaken about in many things), I am pleased, and where I find her inferior, I am at least enlightened. Now, I might have stayed, smoked in your towns, or fogged in your country, a century, without being sure of this, and without acquiring any thing more useful or amusing at home. I keep no journal, nor have I any intention of scribbling my travels. I have done with authorship, and if, in my last production, I have convinced the critics or the world I was something more than they took me for, I am satisfied; nor will I hazard *that reputation* by a future effort. It is true I have some others in manuscript, but I leave them for those who come after me; and, if deemed worth publishing, they may serve to prolong my memory when I myself shall cease to remember. I have a famous Bavarian artist taking some views of Athens, etc., etc., for me. This will be better than scribbling, a disease I hope myself cured of. I hope, on my return, to lead a quiet, recluse life, but God knows and does best for us all; at least, so they say, and I have nothing to object, as, on the whole, I have no reason to complain of my lot. I am convinced, however, that men do more harm to themselves than ever the devil could do to them. I trust this will find you well, and as happy as we can be; you will, at least, be pleased to hear I am so, and yours ever.

TO FRANCIS HODGSON

Volage Frigate, at sea, June 29, 1811

In a week, with a fair wind, we shall be at Portsmouth, and on the 2d of July I shall have completed (to a day) two years of peregrination, from which I am returning with as little emotion as I set out. I think, upon the whole, I was more grieved at leaving Greece than England, which I am impatient to see, simply because I am tired of a long voyage.

Indeed, my prospects are not very pleasant. Embarrassed in my private affairs, indifferent to public, solitary without the wish to be social, with a body a little enfeebled by a succession of fevers, but a spirit I trust, yet unbroken, I am returning *home* without a hope, and almost without a desire. The first thing I shall have to encounter will be a lawyer, the next a creditor, then colliers, farmers, surveyors, and all the agreeable attachments to estates out of repair, and contested coal-pits. In short, I am sick and sorry, and when I have a little repaired my irreparable affairs, away I shall march, either to campaign in Spain, or back again to the East, where I can at least have cloudless skies and a cessation from impertinence.

I trust to meet, or see you, in town, or at Newstead, whenever you can make it convenient—I suppose you are in love and in poetry as usual. That husband, H. Drury, has never written to me, albeit I have sent him more than one letter;—but I dare say the poor man has a family, and of course all his cares are confined to his circle.

> *For children fresh expenses yet,*
> *And Dicky now for school is fit.*
>
> WARTON

If you see him, tell him I have a letter for him from Tucker, a regimental chirurgeon and friend of his, who prescribed for me, . . . and is a very worthy man, but too fond of hard words. I should be too late for a speech-day, or I should probably go down to Harrow. I regretted very much in Greece having omitted to carry the *Anthology* with me—I mean Bland and Merivale's.—What has *Sir Edgar* done? And the *Imitations and Translations*—where are they? I suppose you don't mean to let the public off so easily, but charge them home with a quarto. For me, I am 'sick of fops, and poesy, and prate,' and shall leave the 'whole Castalian state' to Bufo, or any body else. But you are a sentimental and sensibilitous person, and will rhyme to the end of the chapter. Howbeit, I have written some 4000 lines, of one kind or another, on my travels.

I need not repeat that I shall be happy to see you. I shall be in town about the 8th, at Dorant's Hotel, in Albemarle Street, and proceed in a few days to Notts., and thence to Rochdale on business.

I am, here and there, yours, etc.

TO MRS. BYRON

Reddish's Hotel, St. James's Street, London,
July 23, 1811

My dear Madam,

I am only detained by Mr. Hanson to sign some copyhold papers, and will give you timely notice of my approach. It is with great reluctance I remain in town. I shall pay a short visit as we go on to Lancashire on Rochdale business. I shall attend to your directions, of course, and am, with great respect, yours ever,

BYRON

P.S.—You will consider Newstead as your house, not mine; and me only as a visiter.

TO JOHN PIGOT

Newport Pagnell, August 2, 1811

My dear Doctor,

My poor mother died yesterday! and I am on my way from town to attend her to the family vault. I heard *one* day of her illness, the *next* of her death. Thank God her last moments were most tranquil. I am told she was in little pain, and not aware of her situation. I now feel the truth of Mr. Gray's observation, 'That we can only have *one* mother.' Peace be with her! I have to thank you for your expressions of regard; and as in six weeks I shall be in Lancashire on business, I may extend to Liverpool and Chester,—at least I shall endeavour.

If it will be any satisfaction, I have to inform you that in November next the Editor of the *Scourge* will be tried for two different libels on the late Mrs. B. and myself (the decease of Mrs. B. makes no difference in the proceedings); and as he is guilty, by his very foolish and unfounded assertion of a breach of privilege, he will be prosecuted with the utmost rigour.

I inform you of this, as you seem interested in the affair, which is now in the hands of the Attorney-general.

T

I shall remain at Newstead the greater part of this month, where I shall be happy to hear from you, after my two years' absence in the East. I am, dear Pigot, yours very truly.

BYRON

TO JOHN MURRAY

Ravenna, 9bre 19, 1820

What you said of the late Charles Skinner Matthews has set me to my recollections; but I have not been able to turn up any thing which would do for the purposed Memoir of his brother,—even if he had previously done enough during his life to sanction the introduction of anecdotes so merely personal. He was, however, a very extraordinary man, and would have been a great one. No one ever succeeded in a more surpassing degree than he did as far as he went. He was indolent, too; but whenever he stripped, he overthrew all antagonists. His conquests will be found registered at Cambridge, particularly his *Downing* one, which was hotly and highly contested, and yet easily *won*. Hobhouse was his most intimate friend, and can tell you more of him than any man. William Bankes also a great deal. I myself recollect more of his oddities than of his academical qualities, for we lived most together at a very idle period of *my* life. When I went up to Trinity, in 1805, at the age of seventeen and a half, I was miserable and untoward to a degree. I was wretched at leaving Harrow, to which I had become attached during the two last years of my stay there; wretched at going to Cambridge instead of Oxford (there were no rooms vacant at Christchurch); wretched from some private domestic circumstances of different kinds, and consequently about as unsocial as a wolf taken from the troop. So that, although I knew Matthews, and met him often *then* at Bankes's, (who was my collegiate pastor, and master, and patron,) and at Rhode's, Milnes's, Price's, Dick's, Macnamara's, Farrell's, Gally Knight's, and others of that *set* of contemporaries, yet I was neither intimate with him nor with any one else, except my old schoolfellow Edward Long (with whom I used to pass the day in riding and swimming), and William Bankes, who was good-naturedly tolerant of my ferocities.

It was not till 1807, after I had been upwards of a year away from Cambridge, to which I had returned again to *reside* for my degree, that I became one of Matthews's familiars, by means of Hobhouse, who, after hating me for two years, because I wore a *white hat*, and a *grey* coat, and rode a *grey* horse (as he says himself), took me into his good graces because I had written some poetry. I had always lived a good deal, and got drunk occasionally, in their company—but now we became really friends in a morning. Matthews, however, was not at this period resident in College. I met *him* chiefly in London, and at uncertain periods at Cambridge. Hobhouse, in the mean time, did great things: he founded the Cambridge 'Whig Club' (which he seems to have forgotten), and the 'Amicable Society,' which was dissolved in consequence of the members constantly quarrelling, and made himself very popular with 'us youth,' and no less formidable to all tutors, professors, and heads of Colleges. William Bankes was gone; while he stayed, he ruled the roast—or rather the *roasting*—and was father of all mischiefs.

Matthews and I, meeting in London, and elsewhere, became great cronies. He was not good tempered—nor am I—but with a little tact his temper was manageable, and I thought him so superior a man, that I was willing to sacrifice something to his humours, which were often, at the same time, amusing and provoking. What became of his *papers* (and he certainly had many), at the time of his death, was never known. I mention this by the way, fearing to skip it over, and *as* he *wrote* remarkably well, both in Latin and English. We went down to Newstead together, where I had got a famous cellar, and *Monks'* dresses from a masquerade warehouse. We were a company of some seven or eight, with an occasional neighbour or so for visiters, and used to sit up late in our friars' dresses, drinking burgundy, claret, champagne, and what not, out of the *skull-cup*, and all sorts of glasses, and buffooning all round the house, in our conventual garments. Matthews always denominated me 'the Abbot,' and never called me by any other name in his good humours, to the day of his death. The harmony of these our symposia was somewhat interrupted, a few days after our assembling, by Matthews's threatening to throw Hobhouse out of a *window*, in consequence of I know not what commerce of jokes ending in this epigram. Hobhouse came to me and said, that 'his respect and regard for me as host would not permit him to call out any of my guests, and that he should go to town next morning.' He did. It was in vain that I represented to him that the window was not high, and that the turf under it was particularly soft. Away he went.

Matthews and myself had travelled down from London together, talking all the way incessantly upon one single topic. When we got to Loughborough, I know not what chasm had made us diverge for a moment to some other subject, at which he was indignant. 'Come,' said he, 'don't let us break through —let us go on as we began, to our journey's end;' and so he continued, and was as entertaining as ever to the very end. He had previously occupied, during my year's absence from Cambridge, my rooms in Trinity, with the furniture; and Jones, the tutor, in his odd way, had said, on putting him in, 'Mr. Matthews, I recommend to your attention not to damage any of the moveables, for Lord Byron, Sir, is a young man of *tumultuous passions*.' Matthews was delighted with this; and whenever anybody came to visit him, begged them to handle the very door with caution; and used to repeat Jones's admonition in his tone and manner. There was a large mirror in the room, on which he remarked, 'that he thought his friends were grown uncommonly assiduous in coming to *see him*, but he soon discovered that they only came to *see themselves*.' Jones's phrase of '*tumultuous passions*,' and the whole scene, had put him into such good humour, that I verily believe that I owed to it a portion of his good graces.

When at Newstead, somebody by accident rubbed against one of his white silk stockings, one day before dinner; of course the gentleman apologised. 'Sir,' answered Matthews, 'it may be all very well for you, who have a great many silk stockings, to dirty other people's; but to me, who have only this *one pair*, which I have put on in honour of the Abbot here, no apology can compensate for such carelessness; besides, the expense of washing.' He had the same sort of droll sardonic way about every thing. A wild Irishman, named Farrell, one evening beginning to say something at a large supper at Cambridge, Matthews roared out 'Silence!' and then, pointing to Farrell, cried out, in the words of the oracle, '*Orson is endowed with reason.*' You may easily suppose that Orson lost what reason he had acquired, on hearing this compliment. When Hobhouse published his volume of poems, the *Miscellany* (which Matthews *would* call the '*Miss-sell-any*'), all that could be drawn from him was, that the preface was 'extremely like *Walsh.*' Hobhouse thought this at first a compliment; but we never could make out what it was, for all we know of *Walsh* is his Ode to King William, and Pope's epithet of '*knowing Walsh.*' When the Newstead party broke up for London, Hobhouse and Matthews, who were the greatest friends possible, agreed, for a whim, to *walk together* to town. They quarrelled by the way, and actually walked the latter half of the journey, occasionally passing and repassing, without speaking. When Matthews had got to Highgate, he had spent all his money but three-pence halfpenny, and determined to spend that also in a pint of beer, which I believe he was drinking before a public-house, as Hobhouse passed him (still without speaking) for the last time on their route. They were reconciled in London again.

One of Matthews's passions was 'the Fancy;' and he sparred uncommonly well. But he always got beaten in rows, or combats with the bare fist. In swimming, too, he swam well; but with *effort* and *labour*, and *too high* out of the water; so that Scrope Davies and myself, of whom he was therein somewhat emulous, always told him that he would be drowned if ever he came to a difficult pass in the water. He was so; but surely Scrope and myself would have been most heartily glad that

> the Dean had lived,
> And our prediction proved a lie.

His head was uncommonly handsome, very like what Pope's was in his youth.

His voice, and laugh, and features, are strongly resembled by his brother Henry's, if Henry be *he* of *King's College*. His passion for boxing was so great, that he actually wanted me to match him with Dogherty (whom I had backed and made the match for against Tom Belcher), and I saw them spar together at my own lodgings with the gloves on. As he was bent upon it, I would have backed Dogherty to please him, but the match went off. It was of course to have been a private fight, in a private room.

On one occasion, being too late to go home and dress, he was equipped by a friend (Mr. Baillie, I believe,) in a magnificently fashionable and somewhat exaggerated shirt and neckcloth. He proceeded to the Opera, and took his station in Fops' Alley. During the interval between the opera and the ballet, an acquaintance took his station by him and saluted him: 'Come round,' said Matthews, 'come round.'—'Why should I come round?' said the other; 'you have only to turn your head—I am close by you.'—'That is exactly what I cannot do,' said Matthews; 'don't you see the state I am in?' pointing to his buckram shirt collar and inflexible cravat,—and there he stood with his head always in the same perpendicular position during the whole spectacle.

One evening, after dining together, as we were going to the Opera, I happened to have a spare Opera ticket (as subscriber to a box), and presented it to Matthews. 'Now, sir,' said he to Hobhouse afterwards, 'this I call *courteous* in the Abbot—another man would never have thought that I might do better with half a guinea than throw it to a door-keeper;—but here is a man not only asks me to dinner, but gives me a ticket for the theatre.' These were only his oddities, for no man was more liberal, or more honourable in all his doings and dealings, than Matthews. He gave Hobhouse and me, before we set out for Constantinople, a most splendid entertainment, to which we did ample justice. One of his fancies was dining at all sorts of out-of-the-way places. Somebody popped upon him in I know not what coffee-house in the Strand—and what do you think was the attraction? Why, that he paid a shilling (I think) to *dine with his hat on*. This he called his '*hat* house,' and used to boast of the comfort of being covered at meal-times.

When Sir Henry Smith was expelled from Cambridge for a row with a tradesman named 'Hiron,' Matthews solaced himself with shouting under Hiron's windows every evening,

> *Ah me! what perils do environ*
> *The man who meddles with* hot Hiron.

He was also of that band of profane scoffers who, under the auspices of ——, used to rouse Lort Mansel (late Bishop of Bristol) from his slumbers in the lodge of Trinity; and when he appeared at the window foaming with wrath, and crying out, 'I know you, gentlemen, I know you!' were wont to reply, 'We beseech thee to hear us, good *Lort!*'—'Good *Lort* deliver us!' (Lort was his Christian name.) As he was very free in his speculations upon all kinds of subjects, although by no means either dissolute or intemperate in his conduct, and as I was no less independent, our conversation and correspondence used to alarm our friend Hobhouse to a considerable degree.

You must be almost tired of my packets, which will have cost a mint of postage.

Salute Gifford and all my friends.

Yours, B.

TO SCROPE DAVIES

Newstead Abbey, August 7, 1811

My dearest Davies,

Some curse hangs over me and mine. My mother lies a corpse in this house; one of my best friends is drowned in a ditch. What can I say, or think, or do? I received a letter from him the day before yesterday. My dear Scrope, if you can spare a moment, do come down to me—I want a friend. Matthews's last letter was written on *Friday*.—on Saturday he was not. In ability, who was like Matthews? How did we all shrink before him? You do me but justice in saying, I would have risked my paltry existence to have preserved his. This very evening did I mean to write, inviting him, as I invite you, my very dear friend, to visit me. God forgive —— for his apathy! What will our poor Hobhouse feel? His letters breathe but of Matthews. Come to me, Scrope, I am almost desolate—left almost alone in the world—I had but you, and H., and M., and let me enjoy the survivors whilst I can. Poor M., in his letter of Friday, speaks of his intended contest for Cambridge, and a speedy journey to London. Write or come, but come if you can, or one or both.

Yours ever.

TO —— BOLTON, ESQ.

Newstead Abbey, August 12, 1811

Sir,

I enclose a rough draught of my intended will, which I beg to have drawn up as soon as possible, in the firmest manner. The alterations are principally made in consequence of the death of Mrs. Byron. I have only to request that it may be got ready in a short time, and have the honour to be,

Your most obedient, humble servant,

BYRON

Newstead Abbey, August 12, 1811

DIRECTIONS FOR THE CONTENTS OF A WILL TO BE DRAWN UP IMMEDIATELY.

The estate of Newstead to be entailed (subject to certain deductions) on George Anson Byron, heir-at-law, or whoever may be the heir-at-law on the death of Lord B. The Rochdale property to be sold in part or the whole, according to the debts and legacies of the present Lord B.

To Nicolo Giraud of Athens, subject of France, but born in Greece, the sum of seven thousand pounds sterling, to be paid from the sale of such parts of Rochdale, Newstead, or elsewhere, as may enable the said Nicolo Giraud (resident at Athens and Malta in the year 1810) to receive the above sum on his attaining the age of twenty-one years.

To William Fletcher, Joseph Murray, and Demetrius Zograffo (native of Greece), servants, the sum of fifty pounds pr. ann. each, for their natural lives. To Wm. Fletcher, the Mill at Newstead, on condition that he payeth rent, but not subject to the caprice of the landlord. To Rt. Rushton the sum of fifty pounds per ann. for life, and a further sum of one thousand pounds on attaining the age of twenty-five years.

To Jn. Hanson, Esq. the sum of two thousand pounds sterling.

The claims of S. B. Davies, Esq. to be satisfied on proving the amount of the same.

The body of Lord B. to be buried in the vault of the garden of Newstead, without any ceremony or burial-service whatever, or any inscription, save his name and age. His dog not to be removed from the said vault.

My library and furniture of every description to my friends Jn. Cam Hobhouse, Esq., and S. B. Davies, Esq., my executors. In case of their decease, the Rev. J. Becher, of Southwell, Notts., and R. C. Dallas, Esq., of Mortlake, Surrey, to be executors.

The produce of the sale of Wymondham in Norfolk, and the late Mrs. B.'s Scotch property, to be appropriated in aid of the payment of debts and legacies. . . .

TO —— BOLTON, ESQ.

Newstead Abbey, August 16, 1811

Sir,

I have answered the queries on the margin. I wish Mr. Davies's claims to be most fully allowed, and, further, that he be one of my executors. I wish the will to be made in a manner to prevent all discussion, if possible, after my decease; and this I leave to you as a professional gentleman.

With regard to the few and simple directions for the disposal of my *carcass*, I must have them implicitly fulfilled, as they will, at least, prevent trouble and expense,—and (what would be of little consequence to me, but may quiet the conscience of the survivors) the garden is *consecrated* ground. These directions are copied verbatim from my former will; the alterations in other parts have arisen from the death of Mrs. B. I have the honour to be

Your most obedient, humble servant,

BYRON

TO FRANCIS HODGSON

Newstead Abbey, August 22, 1811

You may have heard of the sudden death of my mother, and poor Matthews, which, with that of Wingfield (of which I was not fully aware till just before I left town, and indeed hardly believed it,) has made a sad chasm in my connections. Indeed the blows followed each other so rapidly that I am yet stupid from the shock; and though I do eat, and drink, and talk, and even laugh, at times, yet I can hardly persuade myself that I am awake, did not every morning convince me mournfully to the contrary.—I shall now wave the subject,— the dead are at rest, and none but the dead can be so.

You will feel for poor Hobhouse,—Matthews was the 'god of his idolatry;' and if intellect could exalt a man above his fellows, no one could refuse him pre-eminence. I knew him most intimately, and valued him proportionably; but I am recurring—so let us talk of life and the living.

If you should feel a disposition to come here, you will find 'beef and a sea-coal fire,' and not ungenerous wine. Whether Otway's two other requisites for an Englishman or not, I cannot tell, but probably one of them.—Let me know when I may expect you, that I may tell you when I go and when return. I have not yet been to Lancs. Davies has been here, and has invited me to Cambridge for a week in October, so that, per-adventure, we may encounter glass to glass. His gaiety (death cannot mar it) has done me service; but, after all, ours was a hollow laughter.

You will write to me? I am solitary, and I never felt solitude irksome before. Your anxiety about the critique on ——'s book is amusing; as it was anonymous, certes it was of little consequence: I wish it had produced a little more confusion, being a lover of literary malice. Are you doing nothing?

writing nothing? printing nothing? why not your Satire on Methodism? the subject (supposing the public to be blind to merit) would do wonders. Besides, it would be as well for a destined deacon to prove his orthodoxy.—It really would give me pleasure to see you properly appreciated. I say *really*, as, being an author, my humanity might be suspected. Believe me, dear H., yours always.

TO ROBERT DALLAS

Newstead Abbey, Aug. 27, 1811

I was so sincere in my note on the late Charles Matthews, and do feel myself so totally unable to do justice to his talents, that the passage must stand for the very reason you bring against it. To him all the men I ever knew were pigmies. He was an intellectual giant. It is true I loved Wingfield better; he was the earliest and the dearest, and one of the few one could never repent of having loved: but in ability—ah! you did not know Matthews!

Childe Harold may wait and welcome—books are never the worse for delay in the publication. So you have got our heir, George Anson Byron, and his sister, with you.

You may say what you please, but you are one of the *murderers* of Blackett, and yet you won't allow Harry White's genius. Setting aside his bigotry, he surely ranks next Chatterton. It is astonishing how little he was known; and at Cambridge no one thought or heard of such a man till his death rendered all notice useless. For my own part, I should have been most proud of such an acquaintance: his very prejudices were respectable. There is a sucking epic poet at Granta, a Mr. Townsend, *protégé* of the late Cumberland. Did you ever hear of him and his *Armageddon?* I think his plan (the man I don't know) borders on the sublime: though, perhaps, the anticipation of the 'Last Day' (according to you Nazarenes) is a little too daring: at least, it looks like telling the Lord what he is to do, and might remind an ill-natured person of the line,

And fools rush in where angels fear to tread.

But I don't mean to cavil, only other folks will, and he may bring all the lambs of Jacob Behmen about his ears. However, I hope he will bring it to a conclusion, though Milton is in his way.

Write to me—I dote on gossip—and make a bow to Ju—, and shake George by the hand for me; but, take care, for he has a sad sea paw.

P.S.—I would ask George here, but I don't know how to amuse him—all my horses were sold when I left England, and I have not had time to replace them. Nevertheless, if he will come down and shoot in September, he will be very welcome: but he must bring a gun, for I gave away all mine to Ali Pacha, and other Turks. Dogs, a keeper, and plenty of game, with a very large manor, I have—a lake, a boat, houseroom, and *neat wines*.

TO FRANCIS HODGSON

Newstead Abbey, Sept. 25, 1811

My dear Hodgson,

I fear that before the latest of October or the first of November, I shall hardly be able to make Cambridge. My everlasting agent puts off his coming like the accomplishment of a prophecy. However, finding me growing serious he hath promised to be here on Thursday, and about Monday we shall remove to Rochdale. I have only to give discharges to the tenantry here (it seems the poor creatures must be raised, though I wish it was not necessary), and arrange the receipt of sums, and the liquidation of some debts, and I shall be ready to enter upon new subjects of vexation. I intend to visit you in Granta, and hope to prevail on you to accompany me here or there or anywhere.

I am plucking up my spirits, and have begun to gather my little sensual comforts together. Lucy is extracted from Warwickshire; some very bad faces have been warned off the premises, and more promising substituted in their stead; the partridges are plentiful, hares fairish, pheasants not quite so good, and the Girls on the Manor . . . . Just as I had formed a tolerable establishment my travels commenced, and on my return I find all to do over again; my former flock were all scattered; some married, not before it was needful. As I am a great disciplinarian, I have just issued an edict for the abolition of caps; no hair to be cut on any pretext; stays permitted, but not too low before; full uniform always in the evening; Lucinda to be commander—*vice* the present, about to be wedded (*mem.* she is 35 with a flat face and a squeaking voice), of all the makers and unmakers of beds in the household.

My tortoises (all Athenians), my hedgehog, my mastiff and the other live Greek, are all purely. The tortoises lay eggs, and I have hired a hen to hatch them. I am writing notes for *my* quarto (Murray would have it a *quarto*), and Hobhouse is writing text for *his* quarto; if you call on Murray or Cawthorn you will hear news of either. I have attacked De Pauw, Thornton, Lord Elgin, Spain, Portugal, the *Edinburgh Review*, travellers, Painters, Antiquarians, and others, so you see what a dish of Sour Crout Controversy I shall prepare for myself. It would not answer for me to give way, now; as I was forced into bitterness at the beginning, I will go through to the last. *Væ Victis!* If I fall, I shall fall gloriously, fighting against a host.

Felicissima Notte a Voss. Signoria,

B.

TO THOMAS MOORE

8 St. James's Street, October 29, 1811

Sir,

Soon after my return to England, my friend, Mr. Hodgson, apprised me that a letter for me was in his possession; but a domestic event hurrying me from London immediately after, the letter (which may most probably be your own) is still *unopened in his keeping*. If, on examination of the address, the similarity of the handwriting should lead to such a conclusion, it shall be opened in your presence, for the satisfaction of all parties. Mr. H. is at present out of town;—on Friday I shall see him, and request him to forward it to my address.

With regard to the latter part of both your letters, until the principal point was discussed between us, I felt myself at a loss in what manner to reply. Was I to anticipate friendship from one, who conceived me to have charged him with falsehood? Were not *advances*, under such circumstances, to be misconstrued,—not, perhaps, by the person to whom they were addressed, but by others? In *my* case such a step was impracticable. If you, who conceived yourself to be the offended person, are satisfied that you had no cause for offence, it will not be difficult to convince me of it. My situation, as I have before stated, leaves me no choice. I should have felt proud of your acquaintance, had it commenced under other circumstances; but it must rest with you to determine how far it may proceed after so *auspicious* a beginning. I have the honour to be, etc.

TO WILLIAM HARNESS

St. James's Street, Dec. 8, 1811

Behold a most formidable sheet, without gilt or black edging, and consequently very vulgar and indecorous, particularly to one of your precision; but this being Sunday, I can procure no better, and will atone for its length by not filling it. Bland I have not seen since my last letter; but on Tuesday he dines with me, and will meet Moore, the epitome of all that is exquisite in poetical or personal accomplishments. How Bland has settled with Miller, I know not. I have very little interest with either, and they must arrange their concerns according to their own gusto. I have done my endeavours, *at your request*, to bring them together, and hope they may agree to their mutual advantage.

Coleridge has been lecturing against Campbell. Rogers was present, and from him I derive the information. We are going to make a party to hear this Manichean of poesy. Pole is to marry Miss Long, and will be a very miserable dog for all that. The present ministers are to continue, and his Majesty *does* continue in the same state; so there's folly and madness for you, both in a breath.

I never heard but of one man truly fortunate, and he was Beaumarchais, the author of *Figaro*, who buried two wives and gained three lawsuits before he was thirty.

And now, child, what art thou doing? *Reading, I trust.* I want to see you take a degree. Remember, this is the most important period of your life; and don't disappoint your papa and your aunt, and all your kin—besides myself. Don't you know that all male children are begotten for the express purpose of being graduates? and that even I am an A.M., though how I became so the Public Orator only can resolve. Besides, you are to be a priest; and to confute Sir William Drummond's late book about the Bible (printed, but not published,) and all other infidels whatever. Now leave Master H.'s gig, and Master S.'s Sapphics, and become as immortal as Cambridge can make you.

You see, *Mio Carissimo*, what a pestilent correspondent I am likely to become; but then you shall be as quiet at Newstead as you please, and I won't disturb your studies as I do now. When do you fix the day, that I may take you up according to contract? Hodgson talks of making a third in our journey; but we can't stow him, inside at least. Positively you shall go with me as was agreed, and don't let me have any of your *politesse* to H. on the occasion. I shall manage to arrange for both with a little contrivance. I wish H. was not quite so fat, and we should pack better. You will want to know what I am doing—chewing tobacco.

You see nothing of my allies, Scrope Davies and Matthews —they don't suit you; and how does it happen that I—who am a pipkin of the same pottery—continue in your good graces? Good night,—I will go on in the morning.

Dec. 9th.—In a morning, I am always sullen, and to-day is as sombre as myself. Rain and mist are worse than a sirocco, particularly in a beef-eating and beer-drinking country. My bookseller, Cawthorne, has just left me, and tells me, with a most important face, that he is in treaty for a novel of Madame D'Arblay's, for which 1000 guineas are asked! He wants me to read the MS. (if he obtains it), which I shall do with pleasure; but I should be very cautious in venturing an opinion on her whose *Cecilia* Dr. Johnson superintended. If he lends it to me, I shall put it into the hands of Rogers and Moore, who are truly men of taste. I have filled the sheet, and beg your pardon; I will not do it again. I shall, perhaps, write again; but if not, believe, silent or scribbling, that I am, my dearest William, ever, etc.

TO WILLIAM HARNESS

8 St. James's Street, Dec. 15, 1811

I wrote you an answer to your last, which, on reflection, pleases me as little as it probably has pleased yourself. I will not wait for your rejoinder; but proceed to tell you, that I had just then been greeted with an epistle of ——'s, full of his petty grievances, and this at the moment when (from circumstances it is not necessary to enter upon) I was bearing up against recollections to which *his* imaginary sufferings are as a scratch to a cancer. These things combined, put me out of humour with him and all mankind. The latter part of my life has been a perpetual struggle against affections which embittered the earliest portion; and though I flatter myself I have in a great measure conquered them, yet there are moments (and this was one) when I am as foolish as formerly. I never said so much before, nor had I said this now, if I did not suspect myself of having been rather savage in my letter, and wish to inform you this much of the cause. You know I am not one of your dolorous gentlemen: so now let us laugh again.

Yesterday I went with Moore to Sydenham to visit Campbell. He was not visible, so we jogged homeward merrily enough. To-morrow I dine with Rogers, and am to hear Coleridge, who is a kind of rage at present. Last night I saw Kemble in Coriolanus;—he *was glorious*, and exerted himself wonderfully. By good luck I got an excellent place in the best part of the house, which was more than overflowing. Clare and Delawarr, who were there on the same speculation, were less fortunate. I saw them by accident,—we were not together. I wished for you, to gratify your love of Shakspeare and of fine acting to its fullest extent. Last week I saw an exhibition of a different kind in a Mr. Coates, at the Haymarket, who performed Lothario in a *damned* and damnable manner.

I told you the fate of B[land] and H[odgson] in my last. So much for these sentimentalists, who console themselves in their stews for the loss—the never to be recovered loss—the despair of the refined attachment of a couple of drabs! You censure *my* life, Harness,—when I compare myself with these men, my elders and my betters, I really begin to conceive myself a monument of prudence—a walking statue—without feeling or failing; and yet the world in general hath given me a proud pre-eminence over them in profligacy. Yet I like the men, and, God knows, ought not to condemn their aberrations. But I own I feel provoked when they dignify all this by the name of *love*—romantic attachments for things marketable for a dollar!

Dec. 16th.—I have just received your letter;—I feel your kindness very deeply. The foregoing part of my letter, written yesterday, will, I hope, account for the tone of the former, though it cannot excuse it. I do *like* to hear from you—more than *like*. Next to seeing you, I have no greater satisfaction. But you have other duties, and greater pleasures, and I should regret to take a moment from either. H—— was to call to-day, but I have not seen him. The circumstances you mention at the close of your letter is another proof in favour of my opinion of mankind. Such you will always find them—selfish and distrustful. I except none. The cause of this is the state of society. In the world, every one is to stir for himself—it is useless, perhaps selfish, to expect any thing from his neighbour. But I do not think we are born of this disposition; for you find *friendship* as a schoolboy, and *love* enough before twenty.

I went to see ——; he keeps me in town, where I don't wish to be at present. He is a good man, but totally without conduct. And now, my dearest William, I must wish you good morrow, and remain ever, most sincerely and affectionately yours, etc.

TO FRANCIS HODGSON

8 St. James's Street, February 16, 1812

Dear Hodgson,

I send you a proof. Last week I was very ill and confined to bed with stone in the kidney, but I am now quite recovered. The women are gone to their relatives, after many attempts to explain what was already too clear. If the stone had got into my heart instead of my kidneys, it would have been all the better. However, I have quite recovered *that* also, and only wonder at my folly in excepting my own strumpets from the general corruption,—albeit a two months' weakness is better than ten years. I have one request to make, which is, never mention a woman again in any letter to me, or even allude to the existence of the sex. I won't even read a word of the feminine gender;—it must all be *propria quæ maribus.*

In the spring of 1813 I shall leave England for ever. Every thing in my affairs tends to this, and my inclinations and health do not discourage it. Neither my habits nor constitution are improved by your customs or your climate. I shall find employment in making myself a good Oriental scholar. I shall retain a mansion in one of the fairest islands, and retrace, at intervals, the most interesting portions of the East. In the mean time, I am adjusting my concerns, which will (when arranged) leave me with wealth sufficient even for home, but enough for a principality in Turkey. At present they are involved, but I hope, by taking some necessary but unpleasant steps, to clear every thing. Hobhouse is expected daily in London: we shall be very glad to see him; and, perhaps, you will come up and 'drink deep ere he depart,' if not, 'Mahomet must go to the mountain;'—but Cambridge will bring sad recollections to him, and worse to me, though for very different reasons. I believe the only human being, that ever loved me in truth and entirely, was of, or belonging to, Cambridge, and, in that, no change can now take place. There is one consolation in death—where he sets his seal, the im-

pression can neither be melted nor broken, but endureth
for ever.

Yours always,

B.

TO FRANCIS HODGSON

8 St. James's Street, March 5, 1812

My dear Hodgson,

We are not answerable for reports of speeches in the papers;
they are always given incorrectly, and on this occasion more
so than usual, from the debate in the Commons on the same
night. The *Morning Post* should have said *eighteen years*.
However, you will find the speech, as spoken, in the Parliamentary Register, when it comes out. Lords Holland and
Grenville, particularly the latter, paid me some high compliments in the course of their speeches, as you may have seen in
the papers, and Lords Eldon and Harrowby answered me. I
have had many marvellous eulogies repeated to me since, in
person and by proxy, from divers persons *ministerial*—yea,
ministerial!—as well as oppositionists; of them I shall only
mention Sir F. Burdett. *He* says it is the best speech by a *lord*
since the '*Lord* knows when,' probably from a fellow-feeling
in the sentiments. Lord H. tells me I shall beat them all if I
persevere; and Lord G. remarked that the construction of
some of my periods are very like *Burke's*!! And so much for
vanity. I spoke very violent sentences with a sort of modest
impudence, abused every thing and every body, and put the
Lord Chancellor very much out of humour; and if I may
believe what I hear, have not lost any character by the experiment. As to my delivery, loud and fluent enough, perhaps a
little theatrical. I could not recognise myself or any one else
in the newspapers.

. . . My poesy comes out on Saturday. Hobhouse is here; I
shall tell him to write. My stone is gone for the present, but I
fear is part of my habit. We *all* talk of a visit to Cambridge.

Yours ever,

B.

TO THOMAS MOORE

March 25, 1812

Know all men by these presents, that you, Thomas Moore, stand indicted—no—invited, by special and particular solicitation, to Lady Caroline Lamb's to-morrow evening, at half-past nine o'clock, where you will meet with a civil reception and decent entertainment. Pray, come—I was so examined after you this morning, that I entreat you to answer in person,

Believe me, etc.

TO THOMAS MOORE

May 8, 1812

I am too proud of being your friend, to care with whom I am linked in your estimation, and, God knows, I want friends more at this time than at any other. I am 'taking care of myself' to no great purpose. If you knew my situation in every point of view, you would excuse apparent and unintentional neglect. I shall leave town, I think; but do not you leave it without seeing me. I wish you, from my soul, every happiness you can wish yourself; and I think you have taken the road to secure it. Peace be with you! I fear she has abandoned me.

Ever, etc.

TO THOMAS MOORE

May 20, 1812

On Monday, after sitting up all night, I saw Bellingham launched into eternity, and at three the same day I saw —— launched into the country.

I believe, in the beginning of June, I shall be down for a few days in Notts. If so, I shall beat you up *en passant* with Hobhouse, who is endeavouring, like you and every body else, to keep me out of scrapes.

I meant to have written you a long letter, but I find I cannot.

If any thing remarkable occurs, you will hear it from me—if good; if *bad*, there are plenty to tell it. In the mean time, do you be happy.

> Ever yours, etc.

P.S.—My best wishes and respects to Mrs. Moore;—she is beautiful. I may say so even to you, for I was never more struck with a countenance.

TO LADY CAROLINE LAMB

> [*Undated.*]

I never supposed you artful: we are all selfish,—nature did that for us. But even when you attempt deceit occasionally, you cannot maintain it, which is all the better; want of success will curb the tendency. Every word you utter, every line you write, proves you to be either *sincere* or a *fool*. Now as I know you are not the one, I must believe you the other.

I never knew a woman with greater or more pleasing talents, *general* as in a woman they should be, something of everything, and too much of nothing. But these are unfortunately coupled with a total want of common conduct. For instance, the *note* to your *page*—do you suppose I delivered it? or did you mean that I should? I did not of course.

Then your heart, my poor Caro (what a little volcano!), that pours *lava* through your veins; and yet I cannot wish it a bit colder, to make a *marble slab* of, as you sometimes see (to understand my foolish metaphor) brought in vases, tables, etc., from Vesuvius, when hardened after an eruption. To drop my detestable tropes and figures, you know I have always thought you the cleverest, most agreeable, absurd, amiable, perplexing, dangerous, fascinating little being that lives now, or ought to have lived 2000 years ago. I won't talk to you of beauty; I am no judge. But our beauties cease to be so when near you, and therefore you have either some, or something better. And now, Caro, this nonsense is the first and last compliment (if it be such) I ever paid you. You have often reproached me as wanting in that respect; but others will make up the deficiency.

Come to Lord Grey's; at least do not let me keep you away. All that you so often *say*, I *feel*. Can more be said or felt? This same prudence is tiresome enough; but one *must* maintain it, or what *can* one do to be saved? Keep to it.

TO SIR WALTER SCOTT

St. James's Street, July 6, 1812

Sir,

I have just been honoured with your letter.—I feel sorry that you should have thought it worth while to notice the 'evil works of my nonage,' as the thing is suppressed *voluntarily*, and your explanation is too kind not to give me pain. The Satire was written when I was very young and very angry, and fully bent on displaying my wrath and my wit, and now I am haunted by the ghosts of my wholesale assertions. I cannot sufficiently thank you for your praise; and now, waving myself, let me talk to you of the Prince Regent. He ordered me to be presented to him at a ball; and after some sayings peculiarly pleasing from royal lips, as to my own attempts, he talked to me of you and your immortalities: he preferred you to every bard past and present, and asked which of your works pleased me most. It was a difficult question. I answered, I thought the *Lay*. He said his own opinion was nearly similar. In speaking of the others, I told him that I thought you more particularly the poet of *Princes*, as *they* never appeared more fascinating than in *Marmion* and the *Lady of the Lake*. He was pleased to coincide, and to dwell on the description of your Jameses as no less royal than poetical. He spoke alternately of Homer and yourself, and seemed well acquainted with both; so that (with the exception of the Turks and your humble servant) you were in very good company. I defy Murray to have exaggerated his Royal Highness's opinion of your powers, nor can I pretend to enumerate all he said on the subject; but it may give you pleasure to hear that it was conveyed in language which would only suffer by my attempting to transcribe it, and with a tone and taste which gave me a very high idea of his abilities and accomplishments, which I had hitherto considered as confined to *manners*, certainly superior to those of any living *gentleman*.

This interview was accidental. I never went to the levee; for having seen the courts of Mussulman and Catholic sovereigns, my curiosity was sufficiently allayed; and my politics being as perverse as my rhymes, I had, in fact, 'no business there.' To be thus praised by your Sovereign must be gratifying to you; and if that gratification is not alloyed by the communication being made through me, the bearer of it will consider himself very fortunately and sincerely,

> Your obliged and obedient servant,
>
> BYRON

P.S.—Excuse this scrawl, scratched in a great hurry, and just after a journey.

TO LADY MELBOURNE

Cheltenham, September 13, 1812

My dear Lady M.,

The end of Lady B[essborough]'s letter shall be the beginning of mine. 'For Heaven's sake do not lose your hold on him.' Pray don't, *I* repeat, and assure you it is a very firm one, 'but the yoke is easy, and the burthen is light,' to use one of my scriptural phrases.

So far from being ashamed of being governed like Lord Delacour or any *other Lord* or *master*, I am always but too happy to find one to regulate or misregulate me, and I am as docile as a dromedary, and can bear almost as much. Will you undertake me? If you are sincere (which I still a little hesitate in believing), give me but time, let *hers* retain her in Ireland— the 'gayer' the better. I want her just to be sufficiently gay that I may have enough to bear me out on my own part. Grant me but till December, and if I do not disenchant the Dulcinea and Don Quichotte, both, then I must attack the windmills, and leave the land in quest of adventures. In the meantime I must, and do write the greatest absurdities to keep her 'gay,' and the more so because the last epistle informed me that 'eight guineas, a mail, and a packet could soon bring her to London,' a threat which immediately called forth a letter worthy of the Grand Cyrus or the Duke of York, or any other hero of Madame Scudery or Mrs. Clarke.

Poor Lady Bessborough! with her hopes and her fears. In fact it is no jest for her, or indeed any of us. I must let you into one little secret—*her* folly half did this. At the commencement she piqued that 'vanity' (which it would be the vainest thing in the world to deny) by telling me she was certain I was not beloved, 'that I was only led on for the sake of etc. etc.' This raised a devil between us, which now will only be laid, I really do believe, in the *Red* Sea; I made no answer, but determined, not to *pursue*, for pursuit it was not, but to sit still, and in a week after I was convinced—not that [Caroline] loved me, for I do not believe in the existence of what is called Love—but that any other man in my situation would have believed that he was loved.

Now, my dear Lady M., you are all out as to my real sentiments. I was, am, and shall be, I fear, attached to another, one to whom I have never said much, but have never lost sight of, and the whole of this interlude has been the result of circumstances which it may be too late to regret. Do you suppose that at my *time* of *life*, were I so very *far* gone, that I should not be in Ireland, or at least have followed into Wales, as it was hinted was *expected*. Now they have crossed the Channel, I feel anything but regret. I told you in my two last, that I did not 'like any other, etc. etc.' I deceived you and myself in saying so; there was, and is one whom I wished to marry, had not this affair intervened, or had not some occurrences rather discouraged me. When our drama was 'rising' ('I'll be d—d if it falls off,' I may say with Sir Fretful), in the 5th Act, it was no time to hesitate. I had made up my mind to bear the consequences of my own folly; honour, pity, and a kind of affection all forbade me to shrink, but now if I can *honorably* be off, if *you* are not deceiving me, and if she does not take some accursed step to precipitate her own inevitable fall (if not with me, with some less lucky successor)—if these impossibilities can be got over, all will be well. If not—she will travel.

As I have said so much, I may as well say all. The woman I

mean is Miss Milbanke; I know nothing of her fortune, and I am told that her father is ruined, but my own will, when my Rochdale arrangements are closed, be sufficient for both. My debts are not £25,000, and the deuce is in it, if with R[ochdale] and the surplus of N[ewstead], I could not contrive to be as independent as half the peerage.

I know little of her, and have not the most distant reason to suppose that I am at all a favourite in that quarter. But I never saw a woman whom I *esteemed* so much. But that chance is gone, and there's an end.

Now, my dear Lady M., I am completely in your power. I have not deceived you as to —— [C. L.]. I hope you will not deem it vanity, when I soberly say that it would have been want of gallantry, though the acme of virtue, if I had played the Scipio on this occasion. If through your means, or any means, I can be free, or at least change my fetters, my regard and admiration would not be increased, but my gratitude would. In the meantime, it is by no means unfelt for what you have already done.

To Lady B[essborough] I could not say all this, for she would with the best intentions make the most absurd use of it. What a miserable picture does her letter present of this daughter! She seems afraid to know her, and, blind herself, writes in such a manner as to open the eyes of all others.

I am still here in Holland's house, quiet and alone, without any wish to add to my acquaintances. Your departure was, I assure you, much more regretted than that of any of your lineals or collaterals, so do not you go to Ireland, or I shall follow you o'er 'flood and fen,' a complete Ignis fatuus—that is *I*, the epithet will not apply to you, so we will divide the expression; you would be the *light*, and I the *fool*.

I send you back the letter, and this fearful ream of my own. Lady Caroline is suspicious about our counter-plots, and I am obliged to be as treacherous as Talleyrand, but remember *that treachery* is *truth* to you; I write as rarely as I can, but when I do, I must lie like George Rose. Your name I never mention when I can help it; and all my amatory tropes and figures are exhausted.

I have a glimmering of hope. I *had* lost it—it is renewed—all depends on it; her worst enemy could not wish her such a fate as *now* to be thrown back upon me.

Yours ever most truly,

B.

P.S.—Dear Lady M.,—Don't think me careless. My correspondence since I was sixteen has not been of a nature to allow of any trust except to a lock and key, and I have of late been doubly guarded. The few letters of yours, and all others in case of the worst, shall be sent back or burnt. Surely after returning the one with *Mr. L.'s message*, you will hardly suspect me of wishing to take any advantage; *that* was the only important one in behalf of my own interests. Think me bad if you please, but not *meanly* so. Lady B.'s under another cover accompanies this.

TO LADY MELBOURNE

Cheltenham, September 18, 1812

My dear Lady Melbourne,

I only wish you thought your influence worth a '*boast*,' I should ask, when it is the highest compliment paid to myself. To you it would be none, for (besides the little value of the thing) you have seen enough to convince you how easily I am governed by anyone's *presence*, but *you* would be obeyed even in absence. All persons in this situation are so, from having too much *heart*, or too little head, one or both. Set mine down according to your calculations. You and yours seem to me much the same as the Ottoman family to the faithful; they frequently change their rulers, but never the reigning race. I am perfectly convinced if I fell in love with a woman of Thibet, she would turn out an *emigrée cousine* of some of you.

You ask, 'Am I sure of myself?' and I answer no, but *you* are, which I take to be a much better thing. Miss M[ilbanke] I admire because she is a clever woman, an amiable woman, and of high blood, for I have still a few Norman and Scotch inherited prejudices on the last score, were I to marry. As to *love*, that is done in a week (provided the lady has a reasonable share); besides, marriage goes on better with esteem and confidence than romance, and she is quite pretty enough to be loved by her husband, without being so glaringly beautiful as to attract too many rivals. She always reminds me of 'Emma' in the modern Griselda, and whomever I *may* marry, that is the woman I would wish to *have married.* It is odd enough that my acquaintance with Caroline commenced with a confidence on my part about your niece; C. herself (as I have often told her) was *then* not at all to my taste, nor I (and I may believe her) to hers, and we shall end probably as we began. However, if after all 'it is decreed on high,' that, like James the fatalist, I *must* be hers, she shall be *mine* as long as it pleases her, and the circumstances under which she becomes so, will at least make me devote my life to the vain attempt of reconciling her to herself. Wretched as it would render me, she should never know it; the sentence once past, I could never restore that which she had lost, but all the reparation I could make should be made, and the cup drained to the very dregs by myself, so that its bitterness passed from her.

In the meantime, till it *is* irrevocable, I must and may fairly endeavour to extricate both from a situation which, from our total want of all but selfish considerations, has brought us to the brink of the gulf. Before I sink I will at least have a *swim* for it, though I wish with all my heart it was the Hellespont instead, or that I could cross *this* as easily as I did ye other. One reproach I cannot escape. Whatever happens hereafter, *she* will charge it on me, and so shall I, and I fear that

> *The first step or error none e'er could recall,*
> *And the woman once fallen for ever must fall;*
> *Pursue to the last the career she begun,*
> *And be* false *unto* many, *as* faithless *to* one.

Forgive one stanza of my own sad rhymes; you know I never did inflict any upon you before, nor will again.

What think you of Lady Bessborough's last? She is losing those brilliant hopes expressed in the former epistle. I have written three letters to Ireland and cannot compass more, the last to Lady B. herself, in which I never mentioned Lady C.'s name nor yours (if I recollect aright), nor alluded to either. It is an odd thing to say, but I am sure Lady B. will be a little provoked, if *I* am the first to change, for, like the Governor of Tilbury Fort, although 'the Countess is resolved,' the mother *intenerisce un poco*, and doubtless will expect her daughter to be adored (like an Irish lease) for a term of 99 years. I say it again, that happy as she must and will be to have it broken off *anyhow*, she will hate me if *I* don't break my heart; now is it not so? Laugh—but answer me truly.

I am sorry that Caroline sends you extracts from my epistles. I deserve it for the passage I showed once to you, but remember that was in the *outset*, and when everything said or sung was exculpatory and innocent and what not. Moreover, recollect what absurdities a man must write to his idol, and that 'garbled extracts' prove nothing without the context; for my own part I declare that I recollect no such proposal of an *epistolary truce*, and the gambols at divers houses of entertainment with ye express, etc., tend ye rather to confirm my statement. But I cannot be sure, or answerable for all I have said or unsaid, since 'Jove' himself (some with Mrs. Malaprop would read *Job*) has forgotten to 'laugh at our perjuries.' I am certain that I tremble for the trunkfuls of my contradictions, since, like a minister or a woman, she may one day exhibit them in some magazine or some quartos of villainous memories written in her 7000th love-fit.

Now, dear Lady M., my *paper* spares you.

Believe me, with great regard, Yours ever,

B.

P.S.—In your last you say you are 'surrounded by fools;' Why then 'motley's the only wear:'

> *Oh that I were a fool, a motley fool;*
> *I am ambitious of a motley coat.*

Well, will you answer, 'Thou shalt have one.'

> *Chi va piano va sano,*
> *E chi va sano va lontano.*

My progress has been 'lontano,' but alas! ye 'sano' and 'piano' are past praying for.

TO MR. WILLIAM BANKES

Cheltenham, September 28, 1812

My dear Bankes,

When you point out to one how people can be intimate at the distance of some seventy leagues, I will plead guilty to your charge, and accept your farewell, but not *wittingly*, till you give me some better reason than my silence, which merely proceeded from a notion founded on your own declaration of *old*, that you hated writing and receiving letters. Besides, how was I to find out a man of many residences? If I had addressed you *now*, it had been to your borough, where I must have conjectured you were amongst your constituents. So now, in despite of Mr. N. and Lady W., you shall be as 'much better' as the Hexham post-office will allow me to make you. I do assure you I am much indebted to you for thinking of me at all, and can't spare you even from amongst the superabundance of friends with whom you suppose me surrounded.

You heard that Newstead is sold—the sum 140,000*l.*; sixty to remain in mortgage on the estate for three years, paying interest, of course. Rochdale is also likely to do well—so my worldly matters are mending. I have been here some time drinking the waters, simply because there are waters to drink, and they are very medicinal, and sufficiently disgusting. In a few days I set out for Lord Jersey's, but return here, where I am quite alone, go out very little, and enjoy in its fullest extent the *dolce far niente*. What you are about I cannot guess, even from your date;—not dauncing to the sound of the gitourney in the Halls of the Lowthers? one of whom is here, ill, poor thing, with a phthisic. I heard that you passed through here (at the sordid inn where I first alighted) the very day before I arrived in these parts. We had a very pleasant set here; at first the Jerseys, Melbournes, Cowpers, and Hollands, but all gone; and the only persons I know are the Rawdons and Oxfords, with some later acquaintances of less brilliant descent.

But I do not trouble them much; and as for your rooms and

your assemblies 'they are not dreamed of in our philosophy!!'
—Did you read of a sad accident in the Wye t' other day?
A dozen drowned; and Mr. Rossoe, a corpulent gentleman,
preserved by a boat-hook or an eel-spear, begged, when he
heard his wife was saved—no—*lost*—to be thrown in again!!—
as if he could not have thrown himself in, had he wished it;
but this passes for a trait of sensibility. What strange beings
men are, in and out of the Wye!

I have to ask you a thousand pardons for not fulfilling
some orders before I left town; but if you knew all the cursed
entanglements I *had* to wade through, it would be unnecessary
to beg your forgiveness.—When will Parliament (the new one)
meet?—in sixty days, on account of Ireland, I presume: the
Irish election will demand a longer period for completion
than the constitutional allotment. Yours, of course, is safe,
and all your side of the question. Salamanca is the ministerial
watchword, and all will go well with you. I hope you will
speak more frequently, I am sure at least you *ought*, and it
will be expected. I see Portman means to stand again. Good
night.

Ever yours most affectionately,

Mπαίρων.

TO LADY MELBOURNE

Eywood, Presteign, November 6, 1812

My dear Lady M.,

Not being aware of any amusement which can possibly last
four-and-twenty hours, by 'Shrewsbury clock,' sans intermission, I suppose one may look at a Roman encampment
now and then, and yet be exceedingly occupied nevertheless
with more serious entertainments.

Your 'Coach horse' is admirable, but *not* apropos. I am
glad you recommend 'cupping;' I wanted to be so, but Lady
O[xford] says I *shan't* (God knows why), and you know I am
too tractable to oppose a negative to anything.

I believe I mentioned in my last that I have taken Kinsham
Court in this vicinity, with the description of which I shall not

trouble you. I shall be here at Christmas to look after my arrangements.

Seriously (and I am *very* serious), I have so completely rendered a renewal with C. next to impossible, that you will at least give me credit for sincerity; and to mend the matter, all this is infinitely more to my taste than the A[nnabella] scheme, to which my principal inducement was the tie to yourself, which I confess would have delighted me.

I have had a tremulous letter from Mrs. [George] L[amb], who is in a panic about C. This I have answered, and announced, as a simple piece of information, that I have taken a seat in Herefordshire, an intimation which, with 'Lady Blarney's' marginal notes, will have a miraculous effect on the arrival of Pandora (and her boxes of evil for all her acquaintance) at Tixal.

So, a new accusation of imposition! At *M[iddleton]*, and before—my memory really fails me—I never laughed at P. (by the bye, this is an initial which might puzzle posterity when our correspondence bursts forth in the 20th century), nor can I possibly pronounce where all was 'proper' who was the 'properest,' but I am sure no one can regret the general *propriety* half so much as I do.

Though *we* are very quiet, and wish to remain so as much as C. and *others* may permit, yet *we* are also determined to abide by our Articles, and not to relinquish a single *right* (read '*wrong*' instead, if you like) which devolves to the conquerors on such occasions. As to the Lady Blarney, though I expected some absurd dissatisfaction on her part, I own it provokes me. 'Unfair!' Who could act fairly with people who are sending couriers, and threatening to follow them? As to C., she will find her in *fits* for the winter, without me to help her, depend upon it; and unless Providence sends another illness and journey, it is all over with my successor. I guess at Webster (who is now in Parliament, and will be in town more) as the first essay; but I doubt the Bart. himself as somewhat of the coldest. Besides, he must sacrifice his senatorial duties, and do nothing else but attend to his perplexities, which will be manifold.

I presume that I may now have access to the lower regions of Melbourne House, from which my *ascent* had long excluded me. I doubt if C. and I will be on speaking terms; and it is on the whole much better we should not, but I trust the taciturnity is not to be general. Your threatened visit of *C.* to this place would have no effect in this *quarter*, all being secure. I shall go to Middleton shortly after the 12th inst.; address your answer *there*, or to *Cheltenham*. I hope to find you at M[iddleton].

You see, nothing makes me unmindful of *you*, and I feel but too much obliged by your reciprocal remembrance.

Ever, my dear Lady M., Yrs. most affectionately,

B.

TO THOMAS MOORE

June 22, 1813

Yesterday I dined in company with Stael, the 'Epicene,' whose politics are sadly changed. She is for the Lord of Israel and the Lord of Liverpool—a vile antithesis of a Methodist and a Tory—talks of nothing but devotion and the ministry, and, I presume, expects that God and the government will help her to a pension.

Murray, the αναξ of publishers, the Anak of stationers, has a design upon you in the paper line. He wants you to become the staple and stipendiary editor of a periodical work. What say you? Will you be bound, like 'Kit Smart, to write for ninety-nine years in the *Universal Visitor?*' Seriously, he talks of hundreds a year, and—though I hate prating of the beggarly elements—his proposal may be to your honour and profit, and, I am very sure, will be to our pleasure.

I don't know what to say about 'friendship.' I never was in friendship but once, in my nineteenth year, and then it gave me as much trouble as love. I am afraid, as Whitbread's sire said to the king, when he wanted to knight him, that I am 'too old;' but nevertheless, no one wishes you more friends, fame, and felicity, than

Yours, etc.

TO LADY MELBOURNE

July 6, 1813

Dear Lady M[elbourne],

Since I wrote ye enclosed I have heard a strange story of C.'s scratching herself with glass, and I know not what besides; of all this I was ignorant till this evening. What I did, or said to provoke her I know not. I told her it was better to *waltz*; 'because she danced well, and it would be imputed to *me*, if she did not'—but I see nothing in this to produce cutting and maiming; besides, before supper I saw her, and though she said, and did even then a foolish thing, I could not suppose her so frantic as to be in earnest. She took hold of my hand as I passed, and pressed it against some sharp instrument, and said, 'I mean to use this.' I answered, 'Against me, I presume?' and passed on with Lady R[ancliffe], trembling lest Lord Y. or Lady R. should overhear her; though not believing it possible that this was more than one of her, not uncommon, *bravadoes*, for *real feeling* does not disclose its intentions, and always shuns display. I thought little more of this, and leaving the table in search of her would have appeared more particular than proper—though, of course, had I guessed her to be serious, or had I been conscious of offending I should have done everything to pacify or prevent her. I know not what to say, or do. I am quite unaware of what I did to displease; and useless regret is all I can feel on the subject. Can she be in her senses? Yet I would rather think myself to *blame—than that she were so silly* without cause.

I really remained at Lady H[eathcote's] till 5, totally ignorant of all that passed. Nor do I now know where this cursed scarification took place, nor when—I mean the room—and the hour.

TO THOMAS MOORE

4 Benedictine Street, St. James's, July 8, 1813

I presume by your silence that I have blundered into something noxious in my reply to your letter, for the which I beg

u

leave to send beforehand a sweeping apology, which you may apply to any, or all, parts of that unfortunate epistle. If I err in my conjecture, I expect the like from you in putting our correspondence so long in quarantine. God he knows what I have said; but he also knows (if he is not as indifferent to mortals as the *nonchalant* deities of Lucretius), that you are the last person I want to offend. So, if I have,—why the devil don't you say it at once, and expectorate your spleen?

Rogers is out of town with Madame de Stael, who hath published an Essay against Suicide, which, I presume, will make somebody shoot himself;—as a sermon by Blinkensop, in *proof* of Christianity, sent a hitherto most orthodox acquaintance of mine out of a chapel of ease a perfect atheist. Have you found or founded a residence yet? and have you begun or finished a poem? If you won't tell me what *I* have done, pray say what you have done, or left undone, yourself. I am still in equipment for voyaging, and anxious to hear from, or of, you *before* I go, which anxiety you should remove more readily, as you think I sha'n't cogitate about you afterwards. I shall give the lie to that calumny by fifty foreign letters, particularly from any place where the plague is rife,—without a drop of vinegar or a whiff of sulphur to save you from infection.

The Oxfords have sailed almost a fortnight, and my sister is in town, which is a great comfort,—for, never having been much together, we are naturally more attached to each other. I presume the illuminations have conflagrated to Derby (or wherever you are) by this time. We are just recovering from tumult and train oil, and transparent fripperies, and all the noise and nonsense of victory. Drury Lane had a large *M. W.*, which some thought was Marshal Wellington; others, that it might be translated into Manager Whitbread; while the ladies of the vicinity of the saloon conceived the last letter to be complimentary to themselves. I leave this to the commentators to illustrate. If you don't answer this, I sha'n't say what *you* deserve, but I think *I* deserve a reply. Do you conceive there is no Post-Bag but the Twopenny? Sunburn me, if you are not too bad.

TO THOMAS MOORE

July 13, 1813

Your letter set me at ease; for I really thought (as I hear of your susceptibility) that I had said—I know not what—but something I should have been very sorry for, had it, or I, offended you;—though I don't see how a man with a beautiful wife—*his own* children,—quiet—fame—competency and friends, (I will vouch for a thousand, which is more than I will for a unit in my own behalf,) can be offended with any thing.

Do you know, Moore, I am amazingly inclined—remember I say but *inclined*—to be seriously enamoured with Lady A. F. —but this —— has ruined all my prospects. However, you know her; is she *clever*, or sensible, or good-tempered? either *would* do—I scratch out the *will*. I don't ask as to her beauty— that I see; but my circumstances are mending, and were not my other prospects blackening, I would take a wife, and that should be the woman, had I a chance. I do not yet know her much, but better than I did.

I want to get away, but find difficulty in compassing a passage in a ship of war. They had better let me go; if I cannot, patriotism is the word—'nay, an they'll mouth, I'll rant as well as they.' Now, what are you doing?—writing, we all hope, for our own sakes. Remember you must edit my posthumous works, with a Life of the Author, for which I will send you Confessions, dated 'Lazaretto,' Smyrna, Malta, or Palermo— one can die any where.

There is to be a thing on Tuesday ycleped a national fête. The Regent and —— are to be there, and every body else, who has shillings enough for what was once a guinea. Vauxhall is the scene—there are six tickets issued for the modest women, and it is supposed there will be three to spare. The passports for the lax are beyond my arithmetic.

P.S.—The Stael last night attacked me most furiously—said that I had 'no right to make love—that I had used —— barbarously—that I had no feeling, and was totally *in*sensible to *la belle passion*, and *had* been all my life.' I am very glad to hear it, but did not know it before. Let me hear from you anon.

TO THOMAS MOORE

July 25, 1813

I am not well versed enough in the ways of single woman to make much matrimonial progress.

I have been dining like the dragon of Wantley for this last week. My head aches with the vintage of various cellars, and my brains are muddled as their dregs. I met your friends the Daltons:—she sang one of your best songs so well, that, but for the appearance of affectation, I could have cried; he reminds me of Hunt, but handsomer, and more musical in soul, perhaps. I wish to God he may conquer his horrible anomalous complaint. The upper part of her face is beautiful, and she seems much attached to her husband. He is right, nevertheless, in leaving this nauseous town. The first winter would infallibly destroy her complexion,—and the second, very probably, every thing else.

I must tell you a story. Morris (of indifferent memory) was dining out the other day, and complaining of the Prince's coldness to his old wassailers. D'Israeli (a learned Jew) bored him with questions—why this? and why that? 'Why did the Prince act thus?'—'Why, sir, on account of Lord ——, who ought to be ashamed of himself.'—'And why ought Lord —— to be ashamed of himself?'—'Because the Prince, sir—— ——'—'And why, sir, did the Prince cut *you*?'—'Because, G—d d—mme, sir, I stuck to my principles.'—'And *why* did you stick to your principles?'

Is not this last question the best that was ever put, when you consider to whom? It nearly killed Morris. Perhaps you may think it stupid, but, as Goldsmith said about the peas, it was a very good joke when I heard it—as I did from an ear-witness—and is only spoilt in my narration.

The season has closed with a dandy ball;—but I have dinners with the Harrowbys, Rogers, and Frere and Mackintosh, where I shall drink your health in a silent bumper, and regret your absence till 'too much canaries' wash away my memory, or render it superfluous by a vision of you at the opposite side of the table. Canning has disbanded his party by a speech from his . . . —the true throne of a Tory. Conceive his turning them off in a formal harangue, and bidding them think for themselves. 'I have led my ragamuffins where they are well peppered. There are but three of the 150 left alive', and they are for the *Townsend* (*query*, might not Falstaff mean the Bow Street officer? I dare say Malone's posthumous edition will have it so) for life.

Since I wrote last, I have been into the country. I journeyed by night—no incident, or accident, but an alarm on the part of my valet on the outside, who, in crossing Epping Forest, actually, I believe, flung down his purse before a mile-stone, with a glow-worm in the second figure of number XIX—mistaking it for a footpad and dark lantern. I can only attribute his fears to a pair of new pistols wherewith I had armed him; and he thought it necessary to display his vigilance by calling out to me whenever we passed any thing—no matter whether moving or stationary. Conceive ten miles, with a tremor every furlong. I have scribbled you a fearfully long letter. This sheet must be blank, and is merely a wrapper, to preclude the tabellarians of the post from peeping. You once complained of my *not* writing;—I will 'heap coals of fire upon your head' by *not* complaining of your *not* reading. Ever, my dear Moore, your'n (isn't that the Staffordshire termination?)

BYRON

TO THOMAS MOORE

Bennet Street, August 22, 1813

As our late—I might say, deceased—correspondence had too much of the town-life leaven in it, we will now, *paulo majora*, prattle a little of literature in all its branches; and first of the first—criticism. The Prince is at Brighton, and Jackson, the boxer, gone to Margate, having, I believe, decoyed Yarmouth to see a milling in that polite neighbourhood. Made. de Stael Holstein has lost one of her young

barons, who has been carbonadoed by a vile Teutonic adjutant,
—kilt and killed in a coffee-house at Scrawsenhawsen.
Corinne is, of course, what all mothers must be,—but will, I
venture to prophesy, do what few mothers could—write an
Essay upon it. She cannot exist without a grievance—and
somebody to see, or read, how much grief becomes her. I have
not seen her since the event; but merely judge (not very chari-
tably) from prior observation.

In a 'mail-coach copy' of the *Edinburgh*, I perceive *The
Giaour* is second article. The numbers are still in the Leith
smack—*pray which way is the wind?* The said article is so very
mild and sentimental, that it must be written by Jeffrey *in
love*;—you know he is gone to America to marry some fair one,
of whom he has been, for several *quarters*, *éperdument
amoureux*. Seriously—as Winifred Jenkins says of Lismahago
—Mr. Jeffrey (or his deputy) 'has done the handsome thing by
me,' and I say *nothing*. But this I will say, if you and I had
knocked one another on the head in this quarrel, how he
would have laughed, and what a mighty bad figure we should
have cut in our posthumous works. By the by, I was call'd *in*
the other day to mediate between two gentlemen bent upon
carnage, and,—after a long struggle between the natural
desire of destroying one's fellow-creatures, and the dislike of
seeing men play the fool for nothing,—I got one to make an
apology, and the other to take it, and left them to live happy
ever after. One was a peer, the other a friend untitled, and both
fond of high play;—and one, I can swear for, though very
mild, 'not fearful,' and so dead a shot, that, though the other
is the thinnest of men, he would have split him like a cane.
They both conducted themselves very well, and I put them out
of *pain* as soon as I could.

There is an American *Life* of G. F. Cooke, *Scurra* deceased,
lately published. Such a book!—I believe, since *Drunken
Barnaby's Journal*, nothing like it has drenched the press.
All green-room and tap-room—drams and the drama—
brandy, whisky-punch, and, *latterly*, toddy, overflow every
page. Two things are rather marvellous,—first, that a man
should live so long drunk, and, next, that he should have

found a sober biographer. There are some very laughable
things in it, nevertheless;—but the pints he swallowed, and
the parts he performed, are too regularly registered.

All this time you wonder I am not gone; so do I; but the
accounts of the plague are very perplexing—not so much for
the thing itself as the quarantine established in all ports, and
from all places, even from England. It is true, the forty or
sixty days would, in all probability, be as foolishly spent on
shore as in the ship; but one likes to have one's choice, nevertheless. Town is awfully empty; but not the worse for that. I
am really puzzled with my perfect ignorance of what I mean to
do;—not stay, if I can help it, but where to go? Sligo is for the
North;—a pleasant place, Petersburgh, in September, with
one's ears and nose in a muff, or else tumbling into one's neckcloth or pocket-handkerchief! If the winter treated Buonaparte with so little ceremony, what would it inflict upon your
solitary traveller?—Give me a *sun*, I care not how hot, and
sherbet, I care not how cool, and *my* Heaven is as easily made
as your Persian's. The *Giaour* is now a thousand and odd
lines. 'Lord Fanny spins a thousand such a day', eh, Moore?—
thou wilt needs be a wag, but I forgive it.

Yours ever,

BYRON

TO THOMAS MOORE

August 28, 1813

Ay, my dear Moore, 'there *was* a time'—I have heard of
your tricks, when 'you was campaigning at the King of
Bohemy.' I am much mistaken if, some fine London spring,
about the year 1815, that time does not come again. After all,
we must end in marriage; and I can conceive nothing more
delightful than such a state in the country, reading the county
newspaper, etc., and kissing one's wife's maid. Seriously, I
would incorporate with any woman of decent demeanour to-
morrow—that is, I would a month ago, but, at present, . . .

Why don't you 'parody that Ode?'—Do you think I should
be *tetchy*? or have you done it, and won't tell me?—You are

quite right about Giamschid, and I have reduced it to a dissyllable within this half hour. I am glad to hear you talk of Richardson, because it tells me what you won't—that you are going to beat Lucien. At least tell me how far you have proceeded. Do you think me less interested about your works, or less sincere than our friend Ruggiero? I am not—and never was. In that thing of mine, the *English Bards*, at the time when I was angry with all the world, I never 'disparaged your parts,' although I did not know you personally;—and have always regretted that you don't give us an *entire* work, and not sprinkle yourself in detached pieces—beautiful, I allow, and quite *alone* in our language, but still giving us a right to expect a *Shah Nameh* (is that the name?) as well as gazelles. Stick to the East;—the oracle, Stael, told me it was the only poetical policy. The North, South, and West, have all been exhausted; but from the East, we have nothing but Southey's unsaleables, —and these he has contrived to spoil, by adopting only their most outrageous fictions. His personages don't interest us, and yours will. You will have no competitor; and, if you had, you ought to be glad of it. The little I have done in that way is merely a 'voice in the wilderness' for you; and if it has had any success, that also will prove that the public are orientalising, and pave the path for you.

I have been thinking of a story, grafted on the amours of a Peri and a mortal—something like, only more *philanthropical* than, Cazotte's *Diable Amoureux*. It would require a good deal of poesy, and tenderness is not my forte. For that, and other reasons, I have given up the idea, and merely suggest it to you, because, in intervals of your greater work, I think it a subject you might make much of. If you want any more books, there is ' Castellan's *Mœurs des Ottomans* ', the best compendium of the kind I ever met with, in six small tomes. I am really taking a liberty by talking in this style to my 'elders and my betters;'—pardon it, and don't *Rochefoucault* my motives.

TO THOMAS MOORE

August—September, I mean—1, 1813

I send you, begging your acceptance, Castellan, and three vols. on Turkish literature, not yet looked into. The *last* I will thank you to read, extract what you want, and return in a week, as they are lent to me by that brightest of Northern constellations, Mackintosh,—amongst many other kind things into which India has warmed him; for I am sure your *home* Scotsman is of a less genial description.

Your Peri, my dear M., is sacred and inviolable; I have no idea of touching the hem of her petticoat. Your affectation of a dislike to encounter me is so flattering, that I begin to think myself a very fine fellow. But you are laughing at me—'Stap my vitals, Tam! thou art a very impudent person;' and, if you are not laughing at me, you deserve to be laughed at. Seriously, what on earth can you, or have you, to dread from any poetical flesh breathing? It really puts me out of humour to hear you talk thus.

The Giaour I have added to a good deal; but still in foolish fragments. It contains about 1200 lines, or rather more— now printing. You will allow me to send you a copy. You delight me much by telling me that I am in your good graces, and more particularly as to temper; for, unluckily, I have the reputation of a very bad one. But they say the devil is amusing when pleased, and I must have been more venomous than the old serpent, to have hissed or stung in your company. It may be, and would appear to a third person, an incredible thing, but I know *you* will believe me when I say, that I am as anxious for your success as one human being can be for another's,— as much as if I had never scribbled a line. Surely the field of fame is wide enough for all; and if it were not, I would not willingly rob my neighbour of a rood of it. Now you have a pretty property of some thousand acres there, and when you have passed your present Inclosure Bill, your income will be doubled, (there's a metaphor, worthy of a Templar, namely, pert and low,) while my wild common is too remote to incommode you, and quite incapable of such fertility. I send you (which return per post, as the printer would say) a curious letter from a friend of mine, which will let you into the origin of *The Giaour*. Write soon. Ever, dear Moore, yours most entirely, etc.

P.S.—This letter was written to me on account of a *different story* circulated by some gentlewomen of our acquaintance, a little too close to the text. The part erased contained merely some Turkish names, and circumstantial evidence of the girl's detection, not very important or decorous.

TO LADY MELBOURNE

September 5, 1813

Dear Lady Melbourne,

I return you the plan of A[nnabella]'s spouse elect, of which I shall say nothing because I do not understand it; though I dare say it is exactly what it ought to be. Neither do I know why I am writing this note, as I mean to call on you, unless it be to try your 'new patent pens' which delight me infinitely with their colours. I have pitched upon a yellow one to begin with.

Very likely you will be out, and I must return all the annexed epistles. I would rather have seen your answer. She seems to have been spoiled—not as children usually are—but systematically Clarissa Harlowed into an awkward kind of correctness, with a dependence upon her own infallibility which will or may lead her into some egregious blunder. I don't mean the usual error of young gentlewomen, but she will find exactly what she wants, and then discover that it is much more dignified than entertaining.

TO LADY MELBOURNE

Aston Hall, Rotherham, September 21, 1813

My dear Lady Me.,

My stay at Cambridge was very short, but feeling feverish and restless in town I flew off, and here I am on a visit to my friend Webster, now married, and (according to yᵉ Duke of Buckingham's curse) 'settled in yᵉ country.' His bride, Lady Frances, is a pretty, pleasing woman, but in delicate health, and, I fear, going—if not gone—into a decline. Stanhope and his wife—pretty and pleasant too, but not at all consumptive— left us to-day, leaving only yᵉ family, another single gentleman, and your slave. The sister, Lady Catherine, is here too, and looks very pale from a *cross* in her love for Lord Bury (Lord Alb[emarl]e's son); in short, we are a society of happy wives and unfortunate maidens. The place is very well, and quiet, and the children only scream in a low voice, so that I am not much disturbed, and shall stay a few days in tolerable repose.

W[ebster] don't want sense, nor good nature, but both are occasionally obscured by his suspicions, and absurdities of all descriptions; he is passionately fond of having his wife admired, and at the same time jealous to jaundice of every-thing and everybody. I have hit upon the medium of praising her to him perpetually behind her back, and never looking at her before his face; as for her, I believe she is disposed to be very faithful, and I don't think anyone now here is inclined to put her to the test. W[ebster] himself is, with all his jealousy and admiration, a little tired; he has been lately at Newstead, and wants to go again. I suspected this sudden *penchant*, and soon discovered that a foolish nymph of the Abbey, about whom fortunately I care not, was the attraction. Now if I wanted to make mischief I could extract much good perplexity from a proper management of such events; but I am grown so good, or so indolent, that I shall not avail myself of so pleasant an opportunity of tormenting mine host, though he deserves it for poaching. I believe he has hitherto been unsuccessful, or rather it is too astonishing to be believed.

He proposed to me, with great gravity, to carry him over there, and I replied with equal candour, that *he* might set out when he pleased, but that I should remain here to take care of his household in the interim—a proposition which I thought very much to the purpose, but which did not seem at all to his satisfaction. By way of opiate he preached me a sermon on his wife's good qualities, concluding by an assertion that in all moral and mortal qualities, she was very like 'Christ!!!' I think the Virgin Mary would have been a more appropriate typification; but it was the first comparison of the kind I ever heard, and made me laugh till he was angry, and then I got out of humour too, which pacified him, and shortened the panegyric.

Lord Petersham is coming here in a day or two, who will certainly flirt furiously with Lady F[rances], and I shall have some comic Iagoism with our little Othello. I should have no chance with his Desdemona myself, but a more lively and better dressed and formed personage might, in an innocent way, for I really believe the girl is a very good, well-disposed wife, and will do very well if she lives, and he himself don't tease her into some dislike of her lawful owner.

I passed through Hatfield the night of your *ball*. Suppose we had jostled at a turnpike!! At Bugden I blundered on a Bishop; the Bishop put me in mind of ye Government—the Government of the Governed—and the governed of their *indifference* towards their governors, which you must have remarked as to all *parties*. These reflections expectorated as follows—you know I *never* send you my scribblings—and when you read these, you will wish I never may:

> '*Tis said* Indifference *marks the present time,*
> *Then hear the reason—though* '*tis told in rhyme—*
> *A king who* can't, *a Prince of Wales who* don't,
> *Patriots who* sha'n't, *and Ministers who* won't,
> *What matters who are* in *or* out *of place,*
> *The* Mad, *the* Bad, *the* Useless, *or the* Base?

You may read the 2nd couplet *so*, if you like,

> *A King who* cannot, *and a Prince who don't,*
> *Patriots who would not, ministers who won't.*

I am asked to stay for the Doncaster races, but I am not in plight, and am a miserable beau at the best of times; so I shall even return to town, or elsewhere; and in the meantime ever am

Yours, dear Lady M^e.,

B.

P.S.—If you write, address to *B[enne]t Street*; were I once gone, I should not wish my letters to travel *here* after me, for fear of *accidents*.

TO THOMAS MOORE

September 27, 1813

Thomas Moore,

(Thou wilt never be called '*true* Thomas,' like he of Ercildoune,) why don't you write to me?—as you won't, I must. I was near you at Aston the other day, and hope I soon shall be again. If so, you must and shall meet me, and go to Matlock and elsewhere, and take what, in *flash* dialect, is poetically termed 'a lark,' with Rogers and me for accomplices. Yesterday, at Holland House, I was introduced to Southey—the best-looking bard I have seen for some time. To have that poet's head and shoulders, I would almost have written his Sapphics. He is certainly a prepossessing person to look on, and a man of talent, and all that, and—*there* is his eulogy.

— read me *part* of a letter from you. By the foot of Pharaoh, I believe there was abuse, for he stopped short, so he did, after a fine saying about our correspondence, and *looked*—I wish I could revenge myself by attacking you, or by telling you that I have *had* to defend you—an agreeable way which one's friends have of recommending themselves by saying—'Ay, ay, *I* gave it Mr. Such-a-one for what he said about your being a plagiary, and a rake, and so on.' But do you know that you are one of the very few whom I never have the satisfaction of hearing abused, but the reverse;—and do you suppose I will forgive *that*?

I have been in the country, and ran away from the Doncaster races. It is odd,—I was a visitor in the same house which came to my sire as a residence with Lady Carmarthen (with whom he adulterated before his majority—by the by, remember *she* was not my mamma,)—and they thrust me into an old room, with a nauseous picture over the chimney, which I should suppose my papa regarded with due respect, and which, inheriting the family taste, I looked upon with great satisfaction. I stayed a week with the family, and behaved very well—though the lady of the house is young, and religious, and pretty, and the master is my particular friend. I felt no wish for any thing but a poodle dog, which they kindly gave me. Now, for a man of my courses not even to have *coveted*, is a sign of great amendment. Pray pardon all this nonsense, and don't 'snub me when I'm in spirits.'

Ever yours,

Bn.

Here's an impromptu for you by a 'person of quality,' written last week, on being reproached for low spirits:

> *When from the heart where Sorrow sits,*
> *Her dusky shadow mounts too high,*
> *And o'er the changing aspect flits,*
> *And clouds the brow, or fills the eye:*
> *Heed not that gloom, which soon shall sink;*
> *My Thoughts their dungeon know too well—*
> *Back to my breast the wanderers shrink,*
> *And bleed within their silent cell.*

TO LADY MELBOURNE

October 8, 1813

My dear Lady M.,

I have volumes, but neither time nor space. I have already trusted too deeply to hesitate now; besides, for certain reasons, you will not be sorry to hear that I am anything but what I was. Well then, to begin, and first, a word of mine host.—He has lately been talking *at*, rather than *to*, me before the party (with the exception of the women) in a tone, which as I never use it myself, I am not particularly disposed to tolerate in others. What *he* may do with impunity, it seems, but not suffer, till at last I told him that the whole of his argument involved the interesting contradiction that 'he might love where he liked, but that no one else might like what he ever thought proper to love,' a doctrine which, as the learned Partridge observed, contains a 'non sequitur' from which I, for one, begged leave as a general proposition to dissent. This nearly produced a scene with me, as well as another guest, who seemed to admire my sophistry the most of the two; and as it was after dinner, and debating time, might have ended in more than *wineshed*, but that the devil, for some wise purpose of his own, thought proper to restore good humour, which has not as yet been further infringed.

In these last few days I have had a good deal of conversation with an amiable person, whom (as we deal in *letters* and initials only) we will denominate *Ph.* Well, these things are dull in detail. Take it once, I have made love, and if I am to believe mere *words* (for there we have hitherto stopped), it is returned.

I must tell you the place of declaration, however, a billiard room. I did not, as C. says: 'kneel in the middle of the room,' but, like Corporal Trim to the Nun, 'I made a speech,' which as you might not listen to it with the same patience, I shall not transcribe. We were before on very amicable terms, and I remembered being asked an odd question, 'how a woman who liked a man could inform him of it when he did not perceive it.' I also observed that we went on with our game (of billiards) without *counting the hazards*; and supposed that, as mine certainly were not, the thoughts of the other party also were not exactly occupied by what was our ostensible pursuit. Not quite, though pretty well satisfied with my progress, I took a very imprudent step with pen and paper, in tender and tolerably turned *prose* periods (no poetry even when in earnest). Here were risks, certainly: first, how to convey, then how would it be received? It was received, however, and deposited not very far from the heart which I wished it to reach when, who should enter the room but the person who ought at that moment to have been in the Red Sea, if Satan had any civility. But *she* kept her countenance, and the paper; and I my composure as well as I could. It was a risk, and *all* had been lost by failure; but then recollect how much more I had to gain by the reception, if not declined, and how much one always hazards to obtain anything worth having. My billet prospered, it did more, it even (I am this moment interrupted by the *Marito*, and write this before him, he has brought me a political pamphlet in MS. to decypher and applaud, I shall content myself with the last; oh, he is gone again), my billet produced an *answer*, a very unequivocal one too, but a little too much about virtue, and indulgence of attachment in some sort of etherial process, in which the soul is principally concerned, which I don't very well understand, being a bad metaphysician; but one generally *ends* and *begins* with platonism, and, as my proselyte is only twenty, there is time enough to materialize. I hope nevertheless this spiritual system won't last long, and at any rate must make the experiment. I remember my last case was the reverse, as Major O'Flaherty recommends, 'we fought first and explained afterwards.'

This is the present state of things: much mutual profession, a good deal of melancholy, which, I am sorry to say, was remarked by 'the Moor,' and as much love as could well be made, considering the time, place and circumstances.

I need not say that the folly and petulance of [Webster] has tended to all this. If a man is not contented with a pretty woman, and not only runs after any little country girl he meets with, but absolutely boasts of it; he must not be surprised if others admire that which he knows not how to value. Besides, he literally provoked, and goaded me into it, by something not unlike bullying, *indirect* to be sure, but tolerably obvious: 'he *would* do this, and he would do that,' 'if any man,' etc. etc., and *he* thought that every 'woman' was *his* lawful prize, nevertheless. Oons! who is this strange monopolist? It is odd enough, but on other subjects he is like other people, on this he seems infatuated. If he had been rational, and not prated of his pursuits, I should have gone on very well, as I did at Middleton. Even now, I shan't quarrel with him if I can help it; but one or two of his speeches have blackened the blood about my heart, and curdled the milk of kindness. If put to the proof, I shall behave like other people, I presume.

I have heard from A., but her letter to me is *melancholy*, about her old friend Miss My's departure, etc. etc. I wonder who will have her at last; her letter to you is *gay* you say; that to me must have been written at the same time; the little demure nonjuror!

I wrote to C. the other day, for I was afraid she might repeat last year's epistle, and make it *circular* among my friends.

Good evening, I am now going to *billiards*.

Ever yrs.,

B.

P.S. 6 o'clock. This business is growing serious, and I think *Platonism* in some peril. There has been very nearly a scene, almost an *hysteric*, and really without cause, for I was conducting myself with (to me) very irksome decorum. Her expressions astonish me, so young and cold as she appeared. But these professions must end as usual, and *would* I think *now*, had 'l'occasion' been *not* wanting. Had any one come in during the *tears*, and consequent consolation, all had been spoiled; we must be more cautious, or less *larmoyante*.

P.S. second, 10 o'clock. I write to you, just escaped from claret and vocification on G—d knows what paper. My landlord is a rare gentleman. He has just proposed to me a bet that *he*, for a certain sum, 'wins any given *woman*, against any given *homme* including *all friends* present,' which I declined with becoming deference to him, and the rest of the company. Is not this, at the moment, a perfect comedy?

I forgot to mention that on his entrance yesterday during the letter scene, it reminded me so much of an awkward passage in 'The Way to Keep Him' between Lovemore, Sir Bashful, and my Lady, that, embarrassing as it was, I could hardly help laughing. I hear his voice in the passage; he wants me to go to a ball at Sheffield, and is talking to me as I write. Good night. I am in the act of praising his pamphlet.

I don't half like your story of *Corinne*, some day I will tell you why, if I can, but at present, good night.

TO LADY MELBOURNE

Newstead Abbey, October 10, 1813

My dear Lady M.,

I write to you from the melancholy mansion of my fathers, where I am dull as the longest deceased of my progenitors. I hate reflection on irrevocable things, and won't now turn sentimentalist.

[Webster] alone accompanied me here (I return to-morrow to [Aston]). He is now sitting opposite; and between us are red and white Cham[pagn]e, Burgundy, two sorts of Claret, and lighter vintages, the relics of my youthful cellar, which is yet in formidable number and famous order. But I leave the wine to him, and prefer conversing soberly with you.

Ah! if you knew what a quiet Mussulman life (except in wine) I led here for a few years. But no matter.

Yesterday I sent you a long letter, and must recur to the same subject which is uppermost in my thoughts. I am as much astonished, but I hope not so much mistaken, as Lord Ogleby at the dénouement or rather commencement of the last week. It has changed my views, my wishes, my hopes, my everything, and will furnish you with additional proof of my weakness. Mine guest (late host) has just been congratulating himself on possessing a partner without *passion*. I don't know, and cannot yet speak with certainty, but I never yet saw more decisive preliminary symptoms.

As I am apt to take people at their word, on receiving my answer, that whatever the weakness of her heart might be, I should never derive further proof of it than the confession, instead of pressing the point, I told her that I was willing to be hers on her own terms, and should never attempt to infringe upon the conditions. I said this without pique, and believing her perfectly in earnest for the time; but in the midst of our mutual professions, or, to use her own expression, 'more than mutual,' she bursts into an agony of crying, and at such a time, and in such a place, as rendered such a scene particularly perilous to both—her sister in the next room, and [her husband] not far off. Of course I said and did almost everything proper on the occasion, and fortunately we restored sunshine in time to prevent anyone from perceiving the cloud that had darkened our horizon.

She says she is convinced that my own declaration was produced solely because I perceived her previous *penchant*, which by-the-bye, as I think I said to you before, I neither per-

ceived nor expected. I really did not suspect her of a predilection for anyone, and even now in public, with the exception of
those little indirect, yet mutually understood—I don't know
how and it is unnecessary to name, or describe them—her
conduct is as coldly correct as her still, fair, Mrs. L[amb]-like
aspect.

She, however, managed to give me a note and to receive
another, and a ring before [Webster's] very face, and yet she is
a thorough devotee, and takes prayers, morning and evening,
besides being measured for a new Bible once a quarter.

The only alarming thing is that [Webster] complains of her
aversion from being beneficial to population and posterity. If
this is an invariable maxim, I shall lose my labour. Be this as
it may, she owns to more than I ever heard from any woman
within the time, and I shan't take [Webster's] word any more
for her feelings than I did for that celestial comparison, which
I once mentioned. I think her eye, her change of colour, and
the trembling of her hand, and above all her devotion, tell a
different tale.

Good night. We return to-morrow, and now I drink your
health; you are my only correspondent, and I believe friend.

> Ever yours,
> B.

TO LADY MELBOURNE

Newstead Abbey, October 17, 1813

My dear Lady M.,

The whole party are here—and now to my narrative. But
first I must tell you that I am rather unwell, owing to a folly of
last night. About midnight, after deep and drowsy potations,
I took it into my head to empty my *skull cup*, which holds
rather better than a bottle of claret, at *one draught*, and nearly
died the death of Alexander—which I shall be content to do
when I have achieved his conquests. I had just sense enough
left to feel that I was not fit to join the ladies, and went to bed,
where, my valet tells me, that I was first convulsed, and afterwards so motionless, that he thought, 'Good night to Marmion.'

I don't know how I came to do so very silly a thing; but I believe my guests were boasting, and 'company, villainous company, hath been the spoil of me.' I detest drinking in general, and beg your pardon for this excess. I *can't* do so any more.

To my theme. You were right. I have been a little too sanguine as to the *conclusion*—but hear. One day, left entirely to ourselves, was nearly fatal—another such *victory*, and with Pyrrhus we were lost—it came to this. 'I am entirely at your *mercy*. I own it. I give myself up to you. I am not *cold*—whatever I seem to others; but I know that I cannot bear the reflection hereafter. Do not imagine that these are mere words. I tell you the truth—now act as you will.' Was I wrong? I spared her. There was a something so very peculiar in her manner—a kind of mild decision—no scene—not even a struggle; but still I know not what, that convinced me that she was serious. It was not the mere '*No*,' which one has heard forty times before, and always with the same accent; but the *tone*, and the aspect —yet I sacrificed much—the hour *two* in the morning—away —the Devil whispering that it was mere *verbiage*, etc. And yet I know not whether I can regret it—she seems so very thankful for my forbearance—a proof, at least, that she was not playing merely the usual decorous reluctance, which is sometimes so tiresome on these occasions.

You ask if I am prepared to go 'all lengths.' If you mean by 'all lengths' anything including duel, or divorce? I answer, *Yes*. I love her. If I did not, and much too, I should have been more selfish on the occasion before mentioned. I have offered to go away with her, and her answer, whether sincere or not, is 'that on *my account* she declines it.' In the meantime we are all as wretched as possible; he scolding on *account* of *unaccountable* melancholy; the sister very suspicious, but rather amused—the friend very suspicious too (why I know not), not at all amused—il Marito something like Lord Chesterfield in De Grammont, putting on a martial physiognomy, prating with his worthy ally; swearing at servants, sermonizing both sisters; and buying sheep; but never quitting her side now; so that we are in despair. *I* am very feverish, restless, and silent, as indeed seems to be the tacit agreement of everyone else. In short I can foresee nothing—it may end in nothing; but here are half a dozen persons very much occupied, and two, if not three, in great perplexity; and, as far as I can judge, so we must continue.

She *don't* and *won't* live with him, and they have been so far separate for a long time; therefore I have nothing to answer for on that point. Poor thing—she is either the most *artful* or *artless* of her age (20) I ever encountered. She *owns* to so much, and perpetually says, 'Rather than you should be angry,' or 'Rather than you should like anyone else, I will do whatever you please'; 'I won't speak to this, that, or the other if you dislike it,' and throws, or seems to throw, herself so entirely upon my discretion in every respect, that it disarms me quite; but I am really wretched with the perpetual conflict with myself. Her health is so very delicate; she is so thin and pale, and seems to have lost her appetite so entirely, that I doubt her living much longer. This is also her own opinion. But these fancies are common to all who are not very happy; if she were once my wife, or likely to be so, a warm climate should be the first resort, nevertheless, for her recovery.

The most perplexing—and yet I can't prevail upon myself to give it up—is the caressing system. In her it appears perfectly childish, and I do think innocent; but it really puzzles all the Scipio about me to confine myself to the laudable portion of these endearments.

What a cursed situation I have thrust myself into! Potiphar (it used to be O[xford]'s name) putting some stupid question to me the other day, I told him that I rather admired the *sister*, and what does he? but tell her this; and his *wife* too, who a little too hastily asked him 'if he was mad?' which put him to demonstration that a man ought not to be asked if he was mad, for relating that a friend thought his wife's sister a pretty woman. Upon this topic he held forth with great fervour for a customary period. I wish he had a quinsey.

Tell L[or]d H[ollan]d that Clarke is the name, and Craven Street (No. forgotten) the residence—may be heard of at Trin. Coll.—excellent man—able physician—shot a friend in a duel (about his sister) and I believe killed him professionally after-wards. Lord H. may have him for self or friends. I don't know where I am going—my mind is a chaos. I always am setting all upon single stakes, and this is one. Your story of the French-man Matta, in 'Grammont,' and the Marquis. Heigh ho! Good night. Address to Aston.

Ever yrs.,

B.

P.S. My stay is quite uncertain—a moment may overturn everything; but you shall hear—happen what may—nothing or something.

TO THOMAS MOORE

November 30, 1813

Since I last wrote to you, much has occurred, good, bad, and indifferent,—not to make me forget you, but to prevent me from reminding you of one who, nevertheless, has often thought of you, and to whom *your* thoughts, in many a measure, have frequently been a consolation. We were once very near neighbours this autumn; and a good and bad neigh-bourhood it has proved to me. Suffice it to say, that your French quotation was confoundedly to the purpose,—though very *unexpectedly* pertinent, as you may imagine by what I *said* before, and my silence since. However, 'Richard's himself again,' and except all night and some part of the morning, I don't think very much about the matter.

All convulsions end with me in rhyme; and to solace my midnights, I have scribbled another Turkish story—not a Fragment—which you will receive soon after this. It does not trench upon your kingdom in the least, and if it did, you would soon reduce me to my proper boundaries. You will think, and justly, that I run some risk of losing the little I have gained in fame, by this further experiment on public patience; but I have really ceased to care on that head. I have written this, and published it, for the sake of the *employment*,—to wring my thoughts from reality, and take refuge in 'imaginings,' how-

ever 'horrible;' and, as to success! those who succeed will console me for a failure—excepting yourself and one or two more,
whom luckily I love too well to wish one leaf of their laurels a
tint yellower. This is the work of a week, and will be the
reading of an hour to you, or even less,—and so, let it go . . . .

P.S.—Ward and I *talk* of going to Holland. I want to see
how a Dutch canal looks after the Bosphorus. Pray respond.

TO THOMAS MOORE

December 8, 1813

Your letter, like all the best, and even kindest things in this
world, is both painful and pleasing. But, first, to what sits
nearest. Do you know I was actually about to dedicate to you,
—not in a formal inscription, as to one's *elders,*—but through
a short prefatory letter, in which I boasted myself your intimate, and held forth the prospect of *your* poem; when, lo! the
recollection of your strict injunctions of secrecy as to the said
poem, more than *once* repeated by word and letter, flashed
upon me, and marred my intents. I could have no motive for
repressing my own desire of alluding to you (and not a day
passes that I do not think and talk of you), but an idea that
you might, yourself, dislike it. You cannot doubt my sincere
admiration, waving personal friendship for the present,
which, by the by, is not less sincere and deep rooted. I have
you by rote and by heart; of which *ecce signum!* When I was
at Aston, on my first visit, I have a habit, in passing my time a
good deal alone, of—I won't call it singing, for that I never
attempt except to myself—but of uttering, to what I think
tunes, your 'Oh breathe not,' 'When the last glimpse,' and
'When he who adores thee,' with others of the same minstrel;
—they are my matins and vespers. I assuredly did not intend
them to be overheard, but, one morning, in comes, not *La
Donna,* but *Il Marito,* with a very grave face, saying, 'Byron, I
must request you won't sing any more, at least of *those* songs.'
I stared, and said, 'Certainly, but why?'—'To tell you the
truth,' quoth he, 'they make my wife *cry,* and so melancholy,
that I wish her to hear no more of them.'

Now, my dear M., the effect must have been from your words, and certainly not my music. I merely mention this foolish story to show you how much I am indebted to you for even my pastimes. A man may praise and praise, but no one recollects but that which pleases—at least, in composition. Though I think no one equal to you in that department, or in satire,—and surely no one was ever so popular in both,—I certainly am of opinion that you have not yet done all *you* can do, though more than enough for any one else. I want, and the world expects, a longer work from you; and I see in you what I never saw in poet before, a strange diffidence of your own powers, which I cannot account for, and which must be un-accountable, when a *Cossac* like me can appal a *cuirassier*. Your story I did not, could not, know,—I thought only of a Peri. I wish you had confided in me, not for your sake, but mine, and to prevent the world from losing a much better poem than my own, but which, I yet hope, this *clashing* will not even now deprive them of. Mine is the work of a week, written, *why* I have partly told you, and partly I cannot tell you by letter—some day I will.

Go on—I shall really be very unhappy if I at all interfere with you. The success of mine is yet problematical; though the public will probably purchase a certain quantity, on the pre-sumption of their own propensity for *The Giaour* and such 'horrid mysteries.' The only advantage I have is being on the spot; and that merely amounts to saving me the trouble of turning over books which I had better read again. If *your chamber* was furnished in the same way, you have no need to *go there* to describe—I mean only as to *accuracy*—because I drew it from recollection.

This last thing of mine *may* have the same fate, and I assure you I have great doubts about it. But, even if not, its little day will be over before you are ready and willing. Come out—'screw your courage to the sticking-place.' Except the *Post Bag* (and surely you cannot complain of a want of success there), you have not been *regularly* out for some years. No man stands higher,—whatever you may think on a rainy day, in your provincial retreat. 'Aucun homme, dans aucune

angue, n'a été, peut-être, plus complètement le poëte du cœur
et le poëte des femmes. Les critiques lui reprochent de n'avoir
représenté le monde ni tel qu'il est, ni tel qu'il doit être; *mais
les femmes répondent qu'il l'a représenté tel qu'elles le désirent.'*
—I should have thought Sismondi had written this for you
instead of Metastasio.

Write to me, and tell me of *yourself.* Do you remember
what Rousseau said to some one—'Have we quarrelled? you
have talked to me often, and never once mentioned yourself.'

P.S.—The last sentence is an indirect apology for my
egotism,—but I believe in letters it is allowed. I wish it was
mutual. I have met with an odd reflection in Grimm; it shall
not—at least the bad part—be applied to you or me, though
one of us has certainly an indifferent name—but this it is:—
'Many people have the reputation of being wicked, with whom
we should be too happy to pass our lives.' I need not add it is a
woman's saying—a Mademoiselle de Sommery's.

JOURNAL, BEGUN NOVEMBER 14, 1813

If this had been begun ten years ago, and faithfully kept!!!—
heigho! there are too many things I wish never to have remembered, as it is. Well,—I have had my share of what are called
the pleasures of this life, and have seen more of the European
and Asiatic world than I have made a good use of. They say
'Virtue is its own reward,'—it certainly should be paid well for
its trouble. At five-and-twenty, when the better part of life is
over, one should be *something*;—and what am I? nothing but
five-and-twenty—and the odd months. What have I seen? the
same man all over the world,—ay, and woman too. Give *me*
a Mussulman who never asks questions, and a she of the same
race who saves one the trouble of putting them. But for this
same plague—yellow fever—and Newstead delay, I should
have been by this time a second time close to the Euxine. If I
can overcome the last, I don't so much mind your pestilence;
and, at any rate, the spring shall see me there,—provided I
neither marry myself, nor unmarry any one else in the interval.

I wish one was—I don't know what I wish. It is odd I never set myself seriously to wishing without attaining it—and repenting. I begin to believe with the good old Magi, that one should only pray for the nation, and not for the individual;—but, on my principle, this would not be very patriotic.

No more reflections.—Let me see—last night I finished 'Zuleika,' my second Turkish Tale. I believe the composition of it kept me alive—for it was written to drive my thoughts from the recollection of—

> *Dear sacred name, rest ever unreveal'd.*

At least, even here, my hand would tremble to write it. This afternoon I have burnt the scenes of my commenced comedy. I have some idea of expectorating a romance, or rather a tale in prose;—but what romance could equal the events—

> *quæque ipse . . . vidi,*
> *Et quorum pars magna fui.*

To-day Henry Byron called on me with my little cousin Eliza. She will grow up a beauty and a plague; but, in the mean time, it is the prettiest child! dark eyes and eyelashes, black and long as the wing of a raven. I think she is prettier even than my niece, Georgina,—yet I don't like to think so neither; and though older, she is not so clever.

Dallas called before I was up, so we did not meet. Lewis, too,—who seems out of humour with every thing. What can be the matter? he is not married—has he lost his own mistress, or any other person's wife? Hodgson, too, came. He is going to be married, and he is the kind of man who will be the happier. He has talent, cheerfulness, every thing that can make him a pleasing companion; and his intended is handsome and young, and all that. But I never see any one much improved by matrimony. All my coupled contemporaries are bald and discontented. W[ordsworth] and S[outhey] have both lost their hair and good humour; and the last of the two had a good deal to lose. But it don't much signify what falls *off* a man's temples in that state.

Mem. I must get a toy to-morrow for Eliza, and send the device for the seals of myself and —— Mem. too, to call on the Stael and Lady Holland to-morrow, and on ——, who has advised me (without seeing it, by the by) not to publish Zuleika;' I believe he is right, but experience might have taught him that not to print is *physically* impossible. No one has seen it but Hodgson and Mr. Gifford. I never in my life read a composition, save to Hodgson, as he pays me in kind. It is a horrible thing to do too frequently;—better print, and they who like may read, and if they don't like, you have the satisfaction of knowing that they have, at least, *purchased* the right of saying so.

I have declined presenting the Debtors' Petition, being sick of parliamentary mummeries. I have spoken thrice; but I doubt my ever becoming an orator. My first was liked; the second and third—I don't know whether they succeeded or not. I have never yet set to it *con amore*;—one must have some excuse to one's self for laziness, or inability, or both, and this is mine. 'Company, villanous company, hath been the spoil of me;'—and then, I 'have drunk medicines,' not to make me love others, but certainly enough to hate myself.

Two nights ago I saw the tigers sup at Exeter 'Change. Except Veli Pacha's lion in the Morea,—who followed the Arab keeper like a dog,—the fondness of the hyæna for her keeper amused me most. Such a conversazione!—There was a 'hippopotamus,' like Lord Liverpool in the face; and the 'Ursine Sloth' had the very voice and manner of my valet— but the tiger talked too much. The elephant took and gave me my money again—took off my hat—opened a door—*trunked* a whip—and behaved so well, that I wish he was my butler. The handsomest animal on earth is one of the panthers; but the poor antelopes were dead. I should hate to see one *here*:— the sight of the *camel* made me pine again for Asia Minor. *Oh quando te aspiciam?*

November 16

Went last night with Lewis to see the first of *Antony and Cleopatra*. It was admirably got up, and well acted—a salad of Shakspeare and Dryden. Cleopatra strikes me as the epitome of her sex—fond, lively, sad, tender, teasing, humble, haughty, beautiful, the devil!—coquettish to the last, as well with the 'asp' as with Antony. After doing all she can to persuade him that—but why do they abuse him for cutting off that poltroon Cicero's head? Did not Tully tell Brutus it was a pity to have spared Antony? and did he not speak the Philippics? and are not '*words things?*' and such '*words*' very pestilent '*things*' too? If he had had a hundred heads, they deserved (from Antony) a rostrum (his was stuck up there) apiece—though, after all, he might as well have pardoned him, for the credit of the thing. But to resume—Cleopatra, after securing him, says, 'yet go—it is your interest,' etc.—how like the sex! and the questions about Octavia—it is woman all over.

To-day received Lord Jersey's invitation to Middleton—to travel sixty miles to meet Madame De Stael! I once travelled three thousand to get among silent people; and this same lady writes octavos, and *talks* folios. I have read her books—like most of them, and delight in the last; so I won't hear it, as well as read.

Read Burns to-day. What would he have been, if a patrician? We should have had more polish—less force—just as much verse, but no immortality—a divorce and a duel or two, the which had he survived, as his potations must have been less spirituous, he might have lived as long as Sheridan, and outlived as much as poor Brinsley. What a wreck is that man! and all from bad pilotage; for no one had ever better gales, though now and then a little too squally. Poor dear Sherry! I shall never forget the day he and Rogers and Moore and I passed together; when *he* talked, and *we* listened, without one yawn, from six till one in the morning.

Got my seals —— Have again forgot a plaything for *ma petite cousine* Eliza; but I must send for it to-morrow. I hope Harry will bring her to me. I sent Lord Holland the proofs of the last *Giaour*, and *The Bride of Abydos*. He won't like the latter, and I don't think that I shall long. It was written in four nights to distract my dreams from —— Were it not thus, it had never been composed; and had I not done something at that time, I must have gone mad, by eating my own heart,—bitter diet;—Hodgson likes it better than *The Giaour*, but nobody else will,—and he never liked the Fragment. I am sure, had it not been for Murray, *that* would never have been published, though the circumstances which are the ground-work make it —— heigh-ho!

To-night I saw both the sisters of ——; my God! the youngest so like! I thought I should have sprung across the house, and am so glad no one was with me in Lady H.'s box. I hate those likenesses—the mock-bird, but not the nightingale—so like as to remind, so different as to be painful. One quarrels equally with the points of resemblance and of distinction.

Nov. 17

No letter from ——; but I must not complain. The respectable Job says, 'Why should a *living man* complain?' I really don't know, except it be that a *dead man* can't; and he, the said patriarch, *did* complain, nevertheless, till his friends were tired and his wife recommended that pious prologue, 'Curse—and die;' the only time, I suppose, when but little relief is to be found in swearing. I have had a most kind letter from Lord Holland on *The Bride of Abydos*, which he likes, and so does Lady H. This is very good-natured in both, from whom I don't deserve any quarter. Yet I *did* think, at the time, that my cause of enmity proceeded from Holland House, and am glad I was wrong, and wish I had not been in such a hurry with that confounded satire, of which I would suppress even the memory;—but people, now they can't get it, make a fuss, I verily believe, out of contradiction.

George Ellis and Murray have been talking something about Scott and me, George *pro Scoto*,—and very right too. If they want to depose him, I only wish they would not set me up as a competitor. Even if I had my choice, I would rather be the Earl of Warwick than all the *kings* he ever made! Jeffrey and Gifford I take to be the monarch-makers in poetry and prose. The *British Critic*, in their Rokeby Review, have presupposed a comparison which I am sure my friends never thought of, and W. Scott's subjects are injudicious in descending to. I like the man—and admire his works to what Mr. Braham calls *Entusymusy*. All such stuff can only vex him, and do me no good. Many hate his politics—(I hate all politics); and, here, a man's politics are like the Greek *soul*—an εἴδωλον, besides God knows what *other soul*; but their estimate of the two generally go together.

Harry has not brought *ma petite cousine*. I want us to go to the play together;—she has been but once. Another short note from Jersey, inviting Rogers and me on the 23d. I must see my agent to-night. I wonder when that Newstead business will be finished. It cost me more than words to part with it—and to *have* parted with it! What matters it what I do? or what becomes of me?—but let me remember Job's saying, and console myself with being 'a living man.'

I wish I could settle to reading again,—my life is monotonous, and yet desultory. I take up books, and fling them down again. I began a comedy, and burnt it because the scene ran into *reality*;—a novel, for the same reason. In rhyme, I can keep more away from facts; but the thought always runs through, through . . . yes, yes, through. I have had a letter from Lady Melbourne—the best friend I ever had in my life, and the cleverest of women.

Not a word from ——. Have they set out from ——? or has my last precious epistle fallen into the lion's jaws? If so—and this silence looks suspicious—I must clap on my 'musty morion' and 'hold out my iron.' I am out of practice—but I won't begin again at Manton's now. Besides, I would not return his shot. I was once a famous wafer-splitter; but then the bullies of society made it necessary. Ever since I began to feel that I had a bad cause to support, I have left off the exercise.

What strange tidings from that Anakim of anarchy—Buonaparte! Ever since I defended my bust of him at Harrow against the rascally time-servers, when the war broke out in 1803, he has been *a Héros de Roman* of mine—on the Continent; I don't want him here. But I don't like those same flights—leaving of armies, etc. etc. I am sure when I fought for his bust at school, I did not think he would run away from himself. But I should not wonder if he banged them yet. To be beat by men would be something; but by three stupid, legitimate-old-dynasty boobies of regular-bred sovereigns— O-hone-a-rie!—O-hone-a-rie! It must be, as Cobbett says, his marriage with the thick-lipped and thick-headed *Autrichienne* brood. He had better have kept to her who was kept by Barras. I never knew any good come of your young wife, and legal espousals, to any but your 'sober-blooded boy' who 'eats fish' and drinketh 'no sack.' Had he not the whole opera? all Paris? all France? But a mistress is just as perplexing—that is, *one*—two or more are manageable by division.

I have begun, or had begun, a song, and flung it into the fire. It was in remembrance of Mary Duff, my first of flames, before most people begin to burn. I wonder what the devil is the matter with me! I can do nothing, and—fortunately there is nothing to do. It has lately been in my power to make two persons (and their connections) comfortable, *pro tempore*, and one happy, *ex tempore*,—I rejoice in the last particularly, as it is an excellent man. I wish there had been more inconvenience and less gratification to my self-love in it, for then there had been more merit. We are all selfish—and I believe, ye gods of Epicurus! I believe in Rochefoucault about *men*, and in Lucretius (not Busby's translation) about yourselves. Your bard has made you very *nonchalant* and blest; but as he has excused *us* from damnation, I don't envy you your blessedness *much*—a little, to be sure. I remember, last year, —— said to me, at ——, 'Have we not passed our last month like the gods of Lucretius?' And so we had. She is an adept in the text of the original (which I like too); and when that booby Bus. sent his translating prospectus, she subscribed. But, the devil prompting him to add a specimen, she transmitted him a subsequent answer, saying, that 'after perusing it, her conscience would not permit her to allow her name to remain on the list of sub-scribblers.' Last night, at Lord H.'s—Mackintosh, the Ossul-stones, Puységur, etc. there—I was trying to recollect a quotation (as *I* think) of Stael's, from some Teutonic sophist about architecture. 'Architecture,' says this Macoronico Tedescho, 'reminds me of frozen music.' It is somewhere—but where?—

the demon of perplexity must know and won't tell. I asked M., and he said it was not in her: but Puységur said it must be *hers*, it was so *like*. H. laughed, as he does at all *De l'Allemagne*,— in which, however, I think he goes a little too far. B., I hear, contemns it too. But there are fine passages;—and, after all, what is a work—any—or every work—but a desert with fountains, and, perhaps, a grove or two, every day's journey? To be sure, in Madame, what we often mistake, and 'pant for,' as the 'cooling stream,' turns out to be the '*mirage*' (criticè *verbiage*); but we do, at last, get to something like the temple of Jove Ammon, and then the waste we have passed is only remembered to gladden the contrast.

Called on C——, to explain — She is very beautiful, to my taste, at least; for on coming home from abroad, I recollect being unable to look at any woman but her—they were so fair, and unmeaning, and *blonde*. The darkness and regularity of her features reminded me of my 'Jannat al Aden.' But this impression wore off; and now I can look at a fair woman, without longing for a Houri. She was very good-tempered, and every thing was explained.

To-day, great news—'the Dutch have taken Holland,'— which, I suppose, will be succeeded by the actual explosion of the Thames. Five provinces have declared for young Stadt, and there will be inundation, conflagration, constupration, consternation, and every sort of nation and nations, fighting away, up to their knees, in the damnable quags of this will-o'- the-wisp abode of Boors. It is said Bernadotte is amongst them, too; and, as Orange will be there soon, they will have (Crown) Prince Stork and King Log in their Loggery at the same time. Two to one on the new dynasty!

Mr. Murray has offered me one thousand guineas for *The Giaour* and *The Bride of Abydos*. I won't—it is too much, though I am strongly tempted, merely for the *say* of it. No bad price for a fortnight's (a week each) what?—the gods know— it was intended to be called poetry.

I have dined regularly to-day, for the first time since Sunday last—this being Sabbath, too. All the rest, tea and dry biscuits —six *per diem*. I wish to God I had not dined now!—It kills me with heaviness, stupor, and horrible dreams;—and yet it was but a pint of bucellas, and fish. Meat I never touch,—nor much vegetable diet. I wish I were in the country, to take exercise,—instead of being obliged to *cool* by abstinence, in lieu of it. I should not so much mind a little accession of flesh, —my bones can well bear it. But the worst is, the devil always came with it,—till I starved him out,—and I will *not* be the slave of *any* appetite. If I do err, it shall be my heart, at least, that heralds the way. Oh, my head—how it aches?—the horrors of digestion! I wonder how Buònaparte's dinner agrees with him?

Mem. I must write to-morrow to 'Master Shallow, who owes me a thousand pounds,' and seems, in his letter, afraid I should ask him for it;—as if I would!—I don't want it (just now, at least,) to begin with; and though I have often wanted that sum, I never asked for the repayment of 10*l.* in my life— from a friend. His bond is not due this year, and I told him when it was, I should not enforce it. How often must he make me say the same thing?

I am wrong—I did once ask —— to repay me. But it was under circumstances that excused me *to him*, and would to any one. I took no interest, nor required security. He paid me soon,—at least, his *padre*. My head! I believe it was given me to ache with. Good even.

Nov. 22, 1813

'Orange Boven!' So the bees have expelled the bear that broke open their hive. Well,—if we are to have new De Witts and De Ruyters, God speed the little republic! I should like to see the Hague and the village of Brock, where they have such primitive habits. Yet, I don't know,—their canals would cut a poor figure by the memory of the Bosphorus; and the Zuyder Zee look awkwardly after 'Ak-Denizi.' No matter,—the bluff burghers, puffing freedom out of their short tobacco-pipes, might be worth seeing; though I prefer a cigar or a hooka, with the rose-leaf mixed with the milder herb of the Levant. I don't know what liberty means,—never having seen it,—but wealth is power all over the world; and as a shilling performs

x

the duty of a pound (besides sun and sky and beauty for nothing) in the East,—*that* is the country. How I envy Herodes Atticus!—more than Pomponius. And yet a little *tumult*, now and then, is an agreeable quickener of sensation; such as a revolution, a battle, or an *aventure* of any lively description. I think I rather would have been Bonneval, Ripperda, Alberoni, Hayreddin, or Horuc Barbarossa, or even Wortley Montague, than Mahomet himself.

Rogers will be in town soon?—the 23d is fixed for our Middleton visit. Shall I go? umph!—In this island, where one can't ride out without overtaking the sea, it don't much matter where one goes.

I remember the effect of the *first Edinburgh Review* on me. I heard of it six weeks before,—read it the day of its denunciation,—dined and drank three bottles of claret, (with S. B. Davies, I think,) neither ate nor slept the less, but, nevertheless, was not easy till I had vented my wrath and my rhyme, in the same pages, against every thing and every body. Like George, in the *Vicar of Wakefield*, 'the fate of my paradoxes' would allow me to perceive no merit in another. I remembered only the maxim of my boxing-master, which, in my youth, was found useful in all general riots,—'Whoever is not for you is against you—*mill* away right and left,' and so I did;—like Ishmael, my hand was against all men, and all men's anent me. I did wonder, to be sure, at my own success—

And marvels so much wit is all his own,

as Hobhouse sarcastically says of somebody (not unlikely myself, as we are old friends);—but were it to come over again, I would *not*. I have since redde the cause of my couplets, and it is not adequate to the effect. C——told me that it was believed I alluded to poor Lord Carlisle's nervous disorder in one of the lines. I thank Heaven I did not know it—and would not, could not, if I had. I must naturally be the last person to be pointed on defects or maladies.

Rogers is silent,—and, it is said, severe. When he does talk, he talks well; and, on all subjects of taste, his delicacy of expression is pure as his poetry. If you enter his house—his drawing-room—his library—you of yourself say, this is not the dwelling of a common mind. There is not a gem, a coin, a book thrown aside on his chimney-piece, his sofa, his table, that does not bespeak an almost fastidious elegance in the possessor. But this very delicacy must be the misery of his existence. Oh the jarrings his disposition must have encountered through life!

Southey, I have not seen much of. His appearance is *Epic*; and he is the only existing entire man of letters. All the others have some pursuit annexed to their authorship. His manners are mild, but not those of a man of the world, and his talents of the first order. His prose is perfect. Of his poetry there are various opinions: there is, perhaps, too much of it for the present generation;—posterity will probably select. He has *passages* equal to any thing. At present, he has *a party*, but no *public*—except for his prose writings. The life of Nelson is beautiful.

Sotheby is a *Littérateur*, the Oracle of the Coteries, of the ——s, Lydia White (Sydney Smith's 'Tory Virgin'), Mrs. Wilmot (she, at least, is a swan, and might frequent a purer stream,) Lady Beaumont, and all the Blues, with Lady Charlemont at their head—but I say nothing of *her*—'look in her face and you forget them all,' and every thing else. Oh that face!—by *te, Diva potens Cypri*, I would, to be beloved by that woman, build and burn another Troy.

Moore has a peculiarity of talent, or rather talents,—poetry, music, voice, all his own; and an expression in each, which never was, nor will be, possessed by another. But he is capable of still higher flights in poetry. By the by, what humour, what—every thing, in the *Post-Bag!* There is nothing Moore may not do, if he will but seriously set about it. In society, he is gentlemanly, gentle, and, altogether, more pleasing than any individual with whom I am acquainted. For his honour, principle, and independence, his conduct to —— speaks 'trumpet-tongued.' He has but one fault—and that one I daily regret—he is not *here*.

Nov. 23

Ward—I like Ward. By Mahomet! I begin to think I like every body;—a disposition not to be encouraged;—a sort of

social gluttony that swallows every thing set before it. But I
like Ward. He is *piquant*; and, in my opinion, will stand *very*
high in the House, and every where else, if he applies *regularly*.
By the by, I dine with him to-morrow, which may have some
influence on my opinion. It is as well not to trust one's gratitude *after* dinner. I have heard many a host libelled by his
guests, with his burgundy yet reeking on their rascally lips.

I have taken Lord Salisbury's box at Covent Garden for the
season; and now I must go and prepare to join Lady Holland
and party, in theirs, at Drury Lane, *questa sera*.

Holland doesn't think the man *is Junius*; but that the yet unpublished journal throws great light on the obscurities of that
part of George the Second's reign.—What is this to George
the Third's? I don't know what to think. Why should Junius
be yet dead? If suddenly apoplexed, would he rest in his grave
without sending his εἰδωλον to shout in the ears of posterity,
'Junius was X. Y. Z., Esq., buried in the parish of ——. Repair
his monument, ye churchwardens! Print a new edition of his
Letters, ye booksellers!' Impossible,—the man must be alive,
and will never die without the disclosure. I like him;—he was
a good hater.

Came home unwell and went to bed,—not so sleepy as
might be desirable.

Tuesday morning

I awoke from a dream!—well! and have not others dreamed?
—Such a dream!—but she did not overtake me. I wish the
dead would rest, however. Ugh! how my blood chilled,—and I
could not wake—and—and—heigho!

Shadows to-night
Have struck more terror to the soul of Richard,
Than could the substance of ten thousand ——s,
Arm'd all in proof, and led by shallow ——.

I do not like this dream,—I hate its 'foregone conclusion.'
And am I to be shaken by shadows? Ay, when they remind us
of—no matter—but, if I dream thus again, I will try whether

all sleep has the like visions. Since I rose, I've been in consider-able bodily pain also; but it is gone, and now, like Lord Ogleby, I am wound up for the day.

A note from Mountnorris—I dine with Ward;—Canning is to be there, Frere and Sharpe, perhaps Gifford. I am to be one of 'the five' (or rather six), as Lady —— said a little sneeringly yesterday. They are all good to meet, particularly Canning, and ——Ward, when he likes. I wish I may be well enough to listen to these intellectuals.

No letters to-day;—so much the better,—there are no answers. I must not dream again;—it spoils even reality. I will go out of doors, and see what the fog will do for me. Jackson has been here: the boxing world much as usual;—but the club increases. I shall dine at Crib's to-morrow. I like energy—even animal energy—of all kinds; and I have need of both mental and corporeal. I have not dined out, nor, indeed *at all*, lately: have heard no music—have seen nobody. Now for a *plunge*—high life and low life. *Amant* alterna *Camœnæ!*

I have burnt my *Roman*—as I did the first scenes and sketch of my comedy—and, for aught I see, the pleasure of burning is quite as great as that of printing. These two last would not have done. I ran into *realities* more than ever; and some would have been recognised and others guessed at.

Redde the *Ruminator*—a collection of Essays, by a strange, but able, old man (Sir Egerton Brydges), and a half-wild young one, author of a poem on the Highlands, called *Childe Alarique.* The word 'sensibility' (always my aversion) occurs a thousand times in these Essays; and, it seems, is to be an excuse for all kinds of discontent. This young man can know nothing of life; and, if he cherishes the disposition which runs through his papers, will become useless, and, per-haps, not even a poet, after all, which he seems determined to be. God help him! no one should be a rhymer who could be any thing better. And this is what annoys one, to see Scott and Moore, and Campbell and Rogers, who might have all been agents and leaders, now mere spectators. For, though they may have other ostensible avocations, these last are reduced to a secondary consideration. ——, too, frittering away his

time among dowagers and unmarried girls. If it advanced any
serious affair, it were some excuse; but, with the unmarried,
that is a hazardous speculation, and tiresome enough, too;
and, with the veterans, it is not much worth trying, unless, perhaps, one in a thousand.

If I had any views in this country, they would probably be
parliamentary. But I have no ambition; at least, if any, it
would be *aut Cæsar aut nihil.* My hopes are limited to the
arrangement of my affairs, and settling either in Italy or the
East (rather the last), and drinking deep of the languages and
literature of both. Past events have unnerved me; and all I can
now do is to make life an amusement, and look on while others
play. After all, even the highest game of crowns and sceptres,
what is it? *Vide* Napoleon's last twelvemonth. It has completely upset my system of fatalism. I thought, if crushed, he
would have fallen, when *fractus illabitur orbis,* and not have
been pared away to gradual insignificance; that all this was
not a mere *jeu* of the gods, but a prelude to greater changes
and mightier events. But men never advance beyond a certain
point; and here we are, retrograding, to the dull, stupid old
system,—balance of Europe—poising straws upon kings'
noses, instead of wringing them off! Give me a republic, or a
despotism of one, rather than the mixed government of one,
two, three. A republic!—look in the history of the Earth—
Rome, Greece, Venice, France, Holland, America, our short
(*eheu!*) Commonwealth, and compare it with what they did
under masters. The Asiatics are not qualified to be republicans,
but they have the liberty of demolishing despots, which is the
next thing to it. To be the first man—not the Dictator—not the
Sylla, but the Washington or the Aristides—the leader in
talent and truth—is next to the Divinity! Franklin, Penn, and,
next to these, either Brutus or Cassius—even Mirabeau—or
St. Just. I shall never be any thing, or rather always be nothing.
The most I can hope is, that some will say, 'He might, perhaps,
if he would.'

12, midnight

Here are two confounded proofs from the printer. I have
looked at the one, but for the soul of me, I can't look over that

Giaour again,—at least, just now, and at this hour—and yet there is no moon.

Ward talks of going to Holland, and we have partly discussed an *ensemble* expedition. It must be in ten days, if at all, if we wish to be in at the Revolution. And why not? —— is distant, and will be at ——, still more distant, till spring. No one else, except Augusta, cares for me; no ties—no trammels —*andiamo dunque—se torniamo, bene—se non, ch' importa?* Old William of Orange talked of dying in 'the last ditch' of his dingy country. It is lucky I can swim, or I suppose I should not well weather the first. But let us see. I have heard hyænas and jackalls in the ruins of Asia; and bull-frogs in the marshes; besides wolves and angry Mussulmans. Now, I should like to listen to the shout of a free Dutchman.

Alla! Viva! For ever! Hourra! Huzza!—which is the most rational or musical of these cries? 'Orange Boven,' according to the *Morning Post*.

Wednesday, 24

No dreams last night of the dead, nor the living; so—I am 'firm as the marble, founded as the rock,' till the next earthquake.

Ward's dinner went off well. There was not a disagreeable person there—unless *I* offended any body, which I am sure I could not by contradiction, for I said little, and opposed nothing. Sharpe (a man of elegant mind, and who has lived much with the best—Fox, Horne Tooke, Windham, Fitzpatrick, and all the agitators of other times and tongues,) told us the particulars of his last interview with Windham, a few days before the fatal operation which sent 'that gallant spirit to aspire the skies.' Windham,—the first in one department of oratory and talent, whose only fault was his refinement beyond the intellect of half his hearers,—Windham, half his life an active participator in the events of the earth, and one of those who governed nations,—*he* regretted,—and dwelt much on that regret, that 'he had not entirely devoted himself to literature and science!!!' His mind certainly would have carried him to eminence there, as elsewhere;—but I cannot comprehend what debility of that mind could suggest such a wish. I, who have heard him, cannot regret any thing but that I shall never hear him again. What! would he have been a plodder? a metaphysician?—perhaps a rhymer? a scribbler? Such an exchange must have been suggested by illness. But he is gone and Time 'shall not look upon his like again.'

I am tremendously in arrear with my letters,—except to ——, and to her my thoughts overpower me:—my words never compass them. To Lady Melbourne I write with most pleasure—and her answers, so sensible, so *tactique*—I never met with half her talent. If she had been a few years younger, what a fool she would have made of me, had she thought it worth her while,—and I should have lost a valuable and most agreeable *friend*. Mem. a mistress never is nor can be a friend. While you agree, you are lovers; and, when it is over, any thing but friends.

I have not answered W. Scott's last letter,—but I will. I regret to hear from others, that he has lately been unfortunate in pecuniary involvements. He is undoubtedly the Monarch of Parnassus, and the most *English* of bards. I should place Rogers next in the living list (I value him more as the last of the *best* school)—Moore and Campbell both *third*—Southey and Wordsworth and Coleridge—the rest, ὁι πολλοι—thus:—

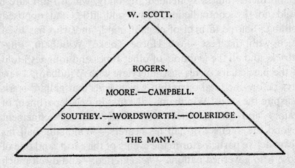

There is a triangular *Gradus ad Parnassum!*—the names are too numerous for the base of the triangle. Poor Thurlow has gone wild about the poetry of Queen Bess's reign—*c'est dom-*

mage. I have ranked the names upon my triangle more upon what I believe popular opinion, than any decided opinion of my own. For, to me, some of Moore's last *Erin* sparks—'As a beam o'er the face of the waters'—'When he who adores thee'—'Oh blame not'—and 'Oh breathe not his name'—are worth all the Epics that ever were composed.

Rogers thinks the *Quarterly* will attack me next. Let them. I have been 'peppered so highly' in my time, *both* ways, that it must be cayenne or aloes to make me taste. I can sincerely say, that I am not very much alive *now* to criticism. But—in tracing this—I rather believe that it proceeds from my not attaching that importance to authorship which many do, and which, when young, I did also. 'One gets tired of every thing, my angel,' says Valmont. The 'angels' are the only things of which I am not a little sick—but I do think the preference of *writers* to *agents*—the mighty stir made about scribbling and scribes, by themselves and others—a sign of effeminacy, degeneracy, and weakness. Who would write, who had any thing better to do? 'Action—action—action'—said Demosthenes: 'Action*s*—action*s*,' I say, and not writing,—least of all, rhyme. Look at the querulous and monotonous lives of the 'genus;'—except Cervantes, Tasso, Dante, Ariosto, Kleist (who were brave and active citizens), Æschylus, Sophocles, and some other of the antiques also—what a worthless, idle brood it is!

12, Mezza Notte

Just returned from dinner with Jackson (the Emperor of Pugilism) and another of the select, at Crib's, the champion's. I drank more than I like, and have brought away some three bottles of very fair claret—for I have no headach. We had Tom Crib up after dinner;—very facetious, though somewhat prolix. He don't like his situation—wants to fight again—pray Pollux (or Castor, if he was the *miller*) he may! Tom has been a sailor—a coal-heaver—and some other genteel profession, before he took to the cestus. Tom has been in action at sea, and is now only three-and-thirty. A great man! has a wife and a mistress, and conversations well—bating some sad omissions and misapplications of the aspirate. Tom is an old friend of mine; I have seen some of his best battles in my nonage. He is now a publican, and, I fear, a sinner;—for Mrs. Crib is on alimony, and Tom's daughter lives with the champion. *This* Tom told me,—Tom, having an opinion of my morals, passed her off as a legal spouse. Talking of her, he said, 'she was the truest of women'—from which I immediately inferred she could *not* be his wife, and so it turned out.

These panegyrics don't belong to matrimony;—for, if 'true,' a man don't think it necessary to say so; and if not, the less he says the better. Crib is the only man except ——, I ever heard harangue upon his wife's virtue; and I listened to both with great credence and patience, and stuffed my handkerchief into my mouth, when I found yawning irresistible— By the by, I am yawning now—so, good night to thee.— Νωαίρων.

Thursday, November 26

Awoke a little feverish, but no headach—no dreams neither, thanks to stupor! Two letters; one from ——, the other from Lady Melbourne—both excellent in their respective styles. ——'s contained also a very pretty lyric on 'concealed griefs;' if not her own, yet very like her. Why did she not say that the stanzas were, or were not, of her composition? I do not know whether to wish them *hers* or not. I have no great esteem for poetical persons, particularly women; they have so much of the 'ideal' in *practics*, as well as *ethics*.

I have been thinking lately a good deal of Mary Duff. How very odd that I should have been so utterly, devotedly fond of that girl, at an age when I could neither feel passion, nor know the meaning of the word. And the effect! My mother used always to rally me about this childish amour; and, at last, many years after, when I was sixteen, she told me one day, 'Oh, Byron, I have had a letter from Edinburgh, from Miss Abercromby, and your old sweetheart Mary Duff is married to a Mr. Coe.' And what was my answer? I really cannot explain or account for my feelings at that moment; but they nearly threw me into convulsions, and alarmed my mother so much, that after I grew better, she generally avoided the subject—to *me*—and contented herself with telling it to all her acquaintance. Now, what could this be? I had never seen her since her mother's *faux pas* at Aberdeen had been the cause of her removal to her grandmother's at Banff; we were both the merest children. I had and have been attached fifty times since that period; yet I recollect all we said to each other, all our caresses, her features, my restlessness, sleeplessness, my tormenting my mother's maid to write for me to her, which she at last did, to quiet me. Poor Nancy thought I was wild, and, as I could not write for myself, became my secretary. I remember, too, our walks, and the happiness of sitting by Mary, in the children's apartment, at their house not far from the Plain-stanes at Aberdeen, while her lesser sister Helen played with the doll, and we sat gravely making love, in our way.

How the deuce did all this occur so early? where could it originate? I certainly had no sexual ideas for years afterwards; and yet my misery, my love for that girl were so violent, that I sometimes doubt if I have ever been really attached since. Be that as it may, hearing of her marriage several years after was like a thunder-stroke—it nearly choked me—to the horror of my mother and the astonishment and almost incredulity of every body. And it is a phenomenon in my existence (for I was not eight years old) which has puzzled, and will puzzle me to the latest hour of it; and lately, I know not why, the *recollection* (*not* the attachment) has recurred as forcibly as ever. I wonder if she can have the least remembrance of it or me? or remember pitying her sister Helen for not having an admirer too? How very pretty is the perfect image of her in my memory —her brown, dark hair, and hazel eyes; her very dress! I should be quite grieved to see *her now*; the reality, however beautiful, would destroy, or at least confuse, the features of the lovely Peri which then existed in her, and still lives in my imagination, at the distance of more than sixteen years. I am now twenty-five and odd months. . . .

I think my mother told the circumstances (on my hearing of her marriage) to the Parkynses, and certainly to the Pigot family, and probably mentioned it in her answer to Miss A., who was well acquainted with my childish *penchant*, and had sent the news on purpose for *me*,—and thanks to her!

Next to the beginning, the conclusion has often occupied my reflections, in the way of investigation. That the facts are thus, others know as well as I, and my memory yet tells me so, in more than a whisper. But, the more I reflect, the more I am bewildered to assign any cause for this precocity of affection.

Lord Holland invited me to dinner to-day; but three days' dining would destroy me. So, without eating at all since yesterday, I went to my box at Covent Garden.

Saw —— looking very pretty, though quite a different style of beauty from the other two. She has the finest eyes in the world, out of which she pretends *not* to see, and the longest eyelashes I ever saw, since Leila's and Phannio's Moslem curtains of the light. She has much beauty,—just enough,—but is, I think, *méchante*.

I have been pondering on the miseries of separation, that—oh how seldom we see those we love! yet we live ages in moments, *when met*. The only thing that consoles me during absence is the reflection that no mental or personal estrangement, from ennui or disagreement, can take place; and when people meet hereafter, even though many changes may have taken place in the mean time, still, unless they are *tired* of each other, they are ready to reunite, and do not blame each other for the circumstances that severed them.

> *Saturday 27, (I believe—or rather am in doubt, which is the ne plus ultra of mortal faith.)*

I have missed a day; and, as the Irishman said, or Joe Miller says for him, 'have gained a loss,' or *by* the loss. Every thing is settled for Holland, and nothing but a cough, or a caprice of my fellow-traveller's, can stop us. Carriage ordered, funds prepared, and, probably, a gale of wind into the bargain. *N'importe*—I believe, with Clym o' the Clow, or Robin Hood, 'By our Mary, (dear name!) thou art both Mother and May, I think it never was a man's lot to die before his day.' Heigh for Helvoetsluys, and so forth!

To-night I went with young Henry Fox to see *Nourjahad*, a drama, which the *Morning Post* hath laid to my charge, but of which I cannot even guess the author. I wonder what they will next inflict upon me. They cannot well sink below a melo-drama; but that is better than a satire, (at least, a personal one,) with which I stand truly arraigned, and in atonement of which I am resolved to bear silently all criticisms, abuses, and even praises, for bad pantomimes never composed by me, without even a contradictory aspect. I suppose the root of this report is my loan to the manager of my Turkish drawings for his dresses, to which he was more welcome than to my name. I suppose the real author will soon own it, as it has succeeded; if not, Job be my model, and Lethe my beverage!

—— has received the portrait safe; and, in answer, the only remark she makes upon it is, 'indeed it is like'—and again, 'indeed it is like.' With her the likeness 'covered a multitude of sins;' for I happen to know that this portrait was not a flatterer, but dark and stern,—even black as the mood in which my mind was scorching last July, when I sat for it. All the others of me, like most portraits whatsoever, are, of course, more agreeable than nature.

Redde the *Edinburgh Review* of Rogers. He is ranked highly; but where he should be. There is a summary view of us all—*Moore* and *me* among the rest; and both (the *first* justly) praised—though, by implication (justly again) placed beneath our memorable friend. Mackintosh is the writer, and also of the critique on the Stael. His grand essay on Burke, I hear, is for the next number. But I know nothing of the *Edinburgh*, or of any other *Review*, but from rumour; and I have long ceased —indeed, I could not, in justice, complain of any, even though I were to rate poetry. in general, and my rhymes in particular, more highly than I really do. To withdraw *myself* from *myself* (oh that cursed selfishness!) has ever been my sole, my entire, my sincere motive in scribbling at all; and publishing is also the continuance of the same object, by the action it affords to the mind, which else recoils upon itself. If I valued fame, I should flatter received opinions, which have gathered strength by time, and will yet wear longer than any living works to the contrary. But, for the soul of me, I cannot and will not give the lie to my own thoughts and doubts, come what may. If I am a fool, it is, at least, a doubting one; and I envy no one the certainty of his self-approved wisdom.

All are inclined to believe what they covet, from a lottery-ticket up to a passport to Paradise,—in which, from the description, I see nothing very tempting. My restlessness tells me I have something 'within that passeth show.' It is for Him, who made it, to prolong that spark of celestial fire which illuminates, yet burns, this frail tenement; but I see no such horror in a 'dreamless sleep,' and I have no conception of any existence which duration would not render tiresome. How else 'fell the angels,' even according to your creed? They were immortal, heavenly, and happy, as their *apostate Abdiel* is now by his treachery. Time must decide; and eternity won't be the less agreeable or more horrible because one did not expect it. In the mean time, I am grateful for some good, and tolerably patient under certain evils—*grace à Dieu et mon bon tempérament.*

Tuesday, 30th

Two days missed in my log-book;—*hiatus* haud *deflendus.* They were as little worth recollection as the rest; and, luckily, laziness or society prevented me from *notching* them.

Sunday, I dined with the Lord Holland in St. James's Square. Large party—among them Sir S. Romilly and Lady Ry.—General Sir Somebody Bentham, a man of science and talent, I am told—Horner—*the* Horner, an Edinburgh Reviewer, an excellent speaker in the 'Honourable House,' very pleasing, too, and gentlemanly in company, as far as I have seen—Sharpe—Philips of Lancashire—Lord John Russell, and others, 'good men and true.' Holland's society is very good; you always see some one or other in it worth knowing. Stuffed myself with sturgeon, and exceeded in champagne and wine in general, but not to confusion of head. When I *do* dine, I gorge like an Arab or a Boa snake, on fish and vegetables, but no meat. I am always better, however, on my tea and biscuit than any other regimen, and even *that* sparingly.

Why does Lady H. always have that damned screen between the whole room and the fire? I, who bear cold no better than an antelope, and never yet found a sun quite *done* to my taste, was absolutely petrified, and could not even shiver. All the rest, too, looked as if they were just unpacked, like salmon from an ice-basket, and set down to table for that day only. When she retired, I watched their looks as I dismissed the screen, and every cheek thawed, and every nose reddened with the anticipated glow.

Saturday, I went with Harry Fox to *Nourjahad;* and, I believe, convinced him, by incessant yawning, that it was not mine. I wish the precious author would own it, and release me from his fame. The dresses are pretty, but not in costume;— Mrs. Horn's, all but the turban, and the want of a small dagger (if she is a sultana), *perfect*. I never saw a Turkish woman with a turban in my life—nor did any one else. The sultanas have a small poniard at the waist. The dialogue is drowsy—the action heavy—the scenery fine—the actors tolerable. I can't say much for their seraglio—Teresa, Phannio, or ——, were worth them all.

Sunday, a very handsome note from Mackintosh, who is a rare instance of the union of very transcendent talent and great good nature. To-day (Tuesday) a very pretty billet from M. la Baronne de Stael Holstein. She is pleased to be much pleased with my mention of her and her last work in my notes. I spoke as I thought. Her works are my delight, and so is she herself, for—half an hour. I don't like her politics—at least, her *having changed* them; had she been *qualis ab incepto*, it were nothing. But she is a woman by herself, and has done more than all the rest of them together, intellectually;—she ought to have been a man. She *flatters* me very prettily in her note;—but I *know* it. The reason that adulation is not displeasing is, that, though untrue, it shows one to be of consequence enough, in one way or other, to induce people to lie, to make us their friend:— that is their concern.

—— is, I hear, thriving on the repute of a *pun* which was mine (at Mackintosh's dinner some time back), on Ward, who was asking, 'how much it would take to *re-whig* him?' I answered that, probably, 'he must first, before he was *re-whigged*, be re-*warded*.' This foolish quibble, before the Stael and Mackintosh, and a number of conversationers, has been mouthed about, and at last settled on the head of ——, where long may it remain!

George is returned from afloat to get a new ship. He looks thin, but better than I expected. I like George much more than most people like their heirs. He is a fine fellow, and every inch a sailor. I would do any thing, *but apostatise*, to get him on in his profession.

Lewis called. It is a good and good-humoured man, but pestilently prolix and paradoxical and *personal*. If he would but talk half, and reduce his visits to an hour, he would add to his popularity. As an author he is very good, and his vanity is *ouverte*, like Erskine's, and yet not offending.

Yesterday, a very pretty letter from Annabella, which I answered. What an odd situation and friendship is ours!— without one spark of love on either side, and produced by circumstances which in general lead to coldness on one side, and aversion on the other. She is a very superior woman, and very little spoiled, which is strange in an heiress—a girl of twenty—a peeress that is to be, in her own right—an only child, and a *savante*, who has always had her own way. She is a poetess—a mathematician—a metaphysician, and yet, withal, very kind, generous, and gentle, with very little pretension. Any other head would be turned with half her acquisitions, and a tenth of her advantages.

Wednesday, December 1, 1813

To-day responded to La Baronne de Stael Holstein, and sent to Leigh Hunt (an acquisition to my acquaintance— through Moore—of last summer) a copy of the two Turkish tales. Hunt is an extraordinary character, and not exactly of the present age. He reminds me more of the Pym and Hampden times—much talent, great independence of spirit, and an austere, yet not repulsive, aspect. If he goes on *qualis ab incepto*, I know few men who will deserve more praise or obtain it. I must go and see him again;—the rapid succession

of adventure, since last summer, added to some serious un-
easiness and business, have interrupted our acquaintance; but
he is a man worth knowing; and though, for his own sake, I
wish him out of prison, I like to study character in such
situations. He has been unshaken, and will continue so. I don't
think him deeply versed in life;—he is the bigot of virtue (not
religion), and enamoured of the beauty of that 'empty name,'
as the last breath of Brutus pronounced, and every day proves
it. He is, perhaps, a little opinionated, as all men who are the
centre of *circles*, wide or narrow—the Sir Oracles, in whose
name two or three are gathered together—must be, and as
even Johnson was; but, withal, a valuable man, and less vain
than success and even the consciousness of preferring 'the
right to the expedient' might excuse.

To-morrow there is a party of *purple* at the 'blue' Miss
Berry's. Shall I go? um!—I don't much affect your blue-
bottles;—but one ought to be civil. There will be, 'I guess
now' (as the Americans say), the Staels and Mackintoshes—good—the ——s and ——s—not so good—the ——s,
etc., etc.—good for nothing. Perhaps that blue-winged Kash-
mirian butterfly of book-learning, Lady Charlemont, will be
there. I hope so; it is a pleasure to look upon that most
beautiful of faces.

Wrote to H.:—he has been telling that I——. I am sure, at
least, *I* did not mention it, and I wish he had not. He is a good
fellow, and I obliged myself ten times more by being of use
than I did him,—and there's an end on't.

Baldwin is boring me to present their King's Bench petition.
I presented Cartwright's last year; and Stanhope and I stood
against the whole House, and mouthed it valiantly—and had
some fun and a little abuse for our opposition. But 'I am not i'
th' vein' for this business. Now, had —— been here, she would
have *made* me do it. *There* is a woman, who, amid all her
fascination, always urged a man to usefulness or glory. Had
she remained, she had been my tutelar genius.

Baldwin is very importunate—but, poor fellow, 'I can't get
out, I can't get out—said the starling.' Ah, I am as bad as that
dog Sterne, who preferred whining over 'a dead ass to relieving

a living mother'—villain—hypocrite—slave—sycophant! but *I* am no better. Here I cannot stimulate myself to a speech for the sake of these unfortunates, and three words and half a smile of —— had she been here to urge it (and urge it she infallibly would—at least she always pressed me on senatorial duties, and particularly in the cause of weakness) would have made me an advocate, if not an orator. Curse on Rochefoucault for being always right! In him a lie were virtue,—or, at least, a comfort to his readers.

George Byron has not called to-day; I hope he will be an admiral, and, perhaps, Lord Byron into the bargain. If he would but marry, I would engage never to marry myself, or cut him out of the heirship. He would be happier, and I should like nephews better than sons.

I shall soon be six-and-twenty (January 22d, 1814). Is there any thing in the future that can possibly console us for not being always *twenty-five?*

Oh Gioventu!
Oh Primavera! gioventu dell' anno.
Oh Gioventu! primavera della vita.

Sunday, December 5

Dallas's nephew (son to the American Attorney-general) is arrived in this country, and tells Dallas that my rhymes are very popular in the United States. These are the first tidings that have ever sounded like *Fame* to my ears—to be redde on the banks of the Ohio! The greatest pleasure I ever derived, of this kind, was from an extract, in Cooke the actor's life, from his journal, stating that in the reading-room at Albany, near Washington, he perused *English Bards, and Scotch Reviewers.* To be popular in a rising and far country has a kind of *posthumous feel,* very different from the ephemeral *éclat* and fêteing, buzzing and party-ing compliments of the well-dressed multitude. I can safely say that, during my *reign* in the spring of 1812, I regretted nothing but its duration of six weeks instead of a fortnight, and was heartily glad to resign.

Last night I supped with Lewis; and, as usual, though I

neither exceeded in solids nor fluids, have been half dead ever since. My stomach is entirely destroyed by long abstinence, and the rest will probably follow. Let it—I only wish the *pain* over. The 'leap in the dark' is the least to be dreaded.

The Duke of —— called. I have told them forty times that, except to half-a-dozen old and specified acquaintances, I am invisible. His Grace is a good, noble, ducal person; but I am content to think so at a distance, and so—I was not at home.

Galt called.—Mem.—to ask some one to speak to Raymond in favour of his play. We are old fellow-travellers, and, with all his eccentricities, he has much strong sense, experience of the world, and is, as far as I have seen, a good-natured philosophical fellow. I showed him Sligo's letter on the reports of the Turkish girl's *aventure* at Athens soon after it happened. He and Lord Holland, Lewis, and Moore, and Rogers, and Lady Melbourne have seen it. Murray has a copy. I thought it had been *unknown*, and wish it were; but Sligo arrived only some days after, and the *rumours* are the subject of his letter. That I shall preserve,—*it is as well.* Lewis and Galt were both *horrified*; and L. wondered I did not introduce the situation into *The Giaour*. He *may* wonder;—he might wonder more at that production's being written at all. But to describe the *feelings* of *that situation* were impossible—it is *icy* even to recollect them.

The *Bride of Abydos* was published on Thursday the second of December; but how it is liked or disliked, I know not. Whether it succeeds or not is no fault of the public, against whom I can have no complaint. But I am much more indebted to the tale than I can ever be to the most partial reader; as it wrung my thoughts from reality to imagination—from selfish regrets to vivid recollections—and recalled me to a country replete with the *brightest* and *darkest*, but always most *lively* colours of my memory. Sharpe called, but was not let in—which I regret.

Saw [Rogers] yesterday. I have not kept my appointment at Middleton, which has not pleased him, perhaps; and my projected voyage with [Ward] will, perhaps, please him less. But I wish to keep well with both. They are instruments that don't do in concert; but, surely, their separate tones are very musical, and I won't give up either.

It is well if I don't jar between these great discords. At present I stand tolerably well with all, but I cannot adopt their *dislikes*;—so many *sets*. Holland's is the first;—every thing *distingué* is welcome there, and certainly the *ton* of his society is the best. Then there is Madame de Stael's—there I never go, though I might, had I courted it. It is composed of the ——s and the —— family, with a strange sprinkling,—orators, dandies, and all kinds of *Blue*, from the regular Grub Street uniform, down to the azure jacket of the *Littérateur*. To see —— and —— sitting together, at dinner, always reminds me of the grave, where all distinctions of friend and foe are levelled; and they—the Reviewer and Reviewée—the Rhinoceros and Elephant—the Mammoth and Megalonyx—all will lie quietly together. They now *sit* together, as silent, but not so quiet, as if they were already immured.

I did not go to the Berrys' the other night. The elder is a woman of much talent, and both are handsome, and must have been beautiful. To-night asked to Lord H.'s—shall I go? um!—perhaps.

Morning, two o'clock

Went to Lord H.'s—party numerous—*mi*lady in perfect good humour, and consequently *perfect*. No one more agreeable, or perhaps so much so, when she will. Asked for Wednesday to dine and meet the Stael—asked particularly, I believe, out of mischief to see the first interview after the *note*, with which Corinne professes herself to be so much taken. I don't much like it; she always talks of *my*self or *her*self, and I am not (except in soliloquy, as now,) much enamoured of either subject—especially one's works. What the devil shall I say about *De l'Allemagne?* I like it prodigiously; but unless I can twist my admiration into some fantastical expression, she won't believe me; and I know, by experience, I shall be overwhelmed with fine things about rhyme, etc., etc. The lover, Mr. —— [Rocca], was there to-night, and C—— said 'it was the only proof *he* had seen of her good taste.' Monsieur

L' Amant is remarkably handsome; but *I* don't think more so than her book.

C—— [Campbell] looks well,—seems pleased, and dressed to *sprucery*. A blue coat becomes him,—so does his new wig. He really looked as if Apollo had sent him a birthday suit, or a wedding-garment, and was witty and lively. He abused Corinne's book, which I regret; because, firstly, he understands German, and is consequently a fair judge; and, secondly, he is *first-rate*, and, consequently, the best of judges. I reverence and admire him; but I won't give up my opinion— why should I? I read *her* again and again, and there can be no affectation in this. I cannot be mistaken (except in taste) in a book I read and lay down, and take up again; and no book can be totally bad which finds *one*, even *one* reader, who can say as much sincerely.

Campbell talks of lecturing next spring; his last lectures were eminently successful. Moore thought of it, but gave it up,—I don't know why. —— had been prating *dignity* to him, and such stuff; as if a man disgraced himself by instructing and pleasing at the same time.

Introduced to Marquis Buckingham—saw Lord Gower—he is going to Holland; Sir J. and Lady Mackintosh and Horner, G. Lamb, with I know not how many (Richard Wellesley, one —a clever man), grouped about the room. Little Henry Fox, a very fine boy, and very promising in mind and manner,—he went away to bed, before I had time to talk to him. I am sure I had rather hear him than all the *savans*.

Monday, Dec. 6

Murray tells me that Croker asked him why the thing was called the *Bride* of Abydos? It is a cursed awkward question, being unanswerable. *She* is not a *bride*, only about to be one; but for, etc., etc., etc.

I don't wonder at his finding out the *Bull*; but the detection —— is too late to do any good. I was a great fool to make it, and am ashamed of not being an Irishman.

Campbell last night seemed a little nettled at something or other—I know not what. We were standing in the ante-

saloon, when Lord H. brought out of the other room a vessel
of some composition similar to that which is used in Catholic
churches, and, seeing us, he exclaimed, 'Here is some *incense*
for you.' Campbell answered—'Carry it to Lord Byron, *he is
used to it.*'

Now, this comes of 'bearing no brother near the throne.'
I, who have no throne, nor wish to have one *now*, whatever I
may have done, am at perfect peace with all the poetical
fraternity: or, at least, if I dislike any, it is not *poetically*, but
personally. Surely the field of thought is infinite; what does it
signify who is before or behind in a race where there is no
goal? The temple of fame is like that of the Persians, the universe; our altar, the tops of mountains. I should be equally
content with Mount Caucasus, or Mount Anything; and those
who like it, may have Mount Blanc or Chimborazo, without
my envy of their elevation.

I think I may *now* speak thus; for I have just published a
poem, and am quite ignorant whether it is *likely* to be *liked* or
not. I have hitherto heard little in its commendation, and no
one can *downright* abuse it to one's face, except in print. It
can't be good, or I should not have stumbled over the threshold, and blundered in my very title. But I began it with my
heart full of ——, and my head of oriental*ities* (I can't call
them *isms*), and wrote on rapidly.

This journal is a relief. When I am tired—as I generally am
—out comes this, and down goes every thing. But I can't read
it over; and God knows what contradictions it may contain.
If I am sincere with myself (but I fear one lies more to one's
self than to any one else), every page should confute, refute,
and utterly abjure its predecessor.

Another scribble from Martin Baldwin the petitioner; I
have neither head nor nerves to present it. That confounded
supper at Lewis's has spoiled my digestion and my philanthropy. I have no more charity than a cruet of vinegar. Would
I were an ostrich, and dieted on fire-irons,—or any thing that
my gizzard could get the better of.

To-day saw Ward. His uncle is dying, and W. don't much
affect our Dutch determinations. I dine with him on Thursday,

provided *l'oncle* is not dined upon, or peremptorily bespoke by the posthumous epicures before that day. I wish he may recover—not for *our* dinner's sake, but to disappoint the undertaker, and the rascally reptiles that may well wait, since they *will* dine at last.

Gell called—he of Troy—after I was out. Mem.—to return his visit. But my Mems. are the very land-marks of forgetfulness;—something like a light-house, with a ship wrecked under the nose of its lantern. I never look at a Mem. without seeing that I have remembered to forget. Mem.—I have forgotten to pay Pitt's taxes, and suppose I shall be surcharged. 'An I do not turn rebel when thou art king'—oons! I believe my very biscuit is leavened with that impostor's imposts.

Lady Melbourne returns from Jersey's to-morrow;—I must call. A Mr. Thomson has sent a song, which I must applaud. I hate annoying them with censure or silence;—and yet I hate *lettering*.

Saw Lord Glenbervie and his Prospectus, at Murray's, of a new Treatise on Timber. Now here is a man more useful than all the historians and rhymers ever planted. For, by preserving our woods and forests, he furnishes materials for all the history of Britain worth reading, and all the odes worth nothing.

Redde a good deal, but desultorily. My head is crammed with the most useless lumber. It is odd that when I do read, I can only bear the chicken broth of—*any thing* but Novels. It is many a year since I looked into one, (though they are sometimes ordered, by way of experiment, but never taken,) till I looked yesterday at the worst parts of the *Monk*. These descriptions ought to have been written by Tiberius at Caprea —they are forced—the *philtered* ideas of a jaded voluptuary. It is to me inconceivable how they could have been composed by a man of only twenty—his age when he wrote them. They have no nature—all the sour cream of cantharides. I should have suspected Buffon of writing them on the death-bed of his detestable dotage. I had never redde this edition, and merely looked at them from curiosity and recollection of the noise they made, and the name they have left to Lewis. But they could do no harm, except . . . .

Called this evening on my agent—my business as usual. Our strange adventures are the only inheritances of our family that have not diminished.

I shall now smoke two cigars, and get me to bed. The cigars don't keep well here. They get as old as a *donna di quaranti anni* in the sun of Africa. The Havannah are the best;—but neither are so pleasant as a hooka or chiboque. The Turkish tobacco is mild, and their horses entire—two things as they should be. I am so far obliged to this Journal, that it preserves me from verse,—at least from keeping it. I have just thrown a poem into the fire (which it has relighted to my great comfort), and have smoked out of my head the plan of another. I wish I could as easily get rid of thinking, or,'at least, the confusion of thought.

Tuesday, December 7

Went to bed, and slept dreamlessly, but not refreshingly. Awoke, and up an hour before being called; but dawdled three hours in dressing. When one subtracts from life infancy (which is vegetation),—sleep, eating, and swilling—buttoning and unbuttoning—how much remains of downright existence? The summer of a dormouse.

Redde the papers and *tea*-ed and soda-watered, and found out that the fire was badly lighted. Lord Glenbervie wants me to go to Brighton—um!

This morning, a very pretty billet from the Stael about meeting her at Ld. H.'s to-morrow. She has written, I dare say, twenty such this morning to different people, all equally flattering to each. So much the better for her and those who believe all she wishes them, or they wish to believe. She has been pleased to be pleased with my slight eulogy in the note annexed to *The Bride*. This is to be accounted for in several ways,—firstly, all women like all, or any, praise; secondly, this was unexpected, because I have never courted her; and, thirdly, as Scrub says, those who have been all their lives regularly praised, by regular critics, like a little variety, and are glad when any one goes out of his way to say a civil thing; and, fourthly, she is a very good-natured creature, which is the best reason, after all, and, perhaps, the only one.

A knock—knocks single and double. Bland called. He says Dutch society (he has been in Holland) is second-hand French; but the women are like women every where else. This is a bore: I should like to see them a little *un*like; but that can't be expected.

Went out—came home—this, that, and the other—and 'all is vanity, saith the preacher,' and so say I, as part of his congregation. Talking of vanity, whose praise do I prefer? Why, Mrs. Inchbald's, and that of the Americans. The first, because her *Simple Story* and *Nature and Art* are, to me, *true* to their *titles*; and, consequently, her short note to Rogers about *The Giaour* delighted me more than any thing, except the *Edinburgh Review*. I like the Americans, because *I* happened to be in *Asia*, while the *English Bards, and Scotch Reviewers* were redde in *America*. If I could have had a speech against the *Slave Trade in Africa*, and an epitaph on a dog in *Europe* (i.e. in the *Morning Post*), my *vertex sublimis* would certainly have displaced stars enough to overthrow the Newtonian system.

Friday, December 10, 1813

I am *ennuyé* beyond my usual tense of that yawning verb, which I am always conjugating; and I don't find that society much mends the matter. I am too lazy to shoot myself—and it would annoy Augusta, and perhaps ——; but it would be a good thing for George, on the other side, and no bad one for me; but I won't be tempted.

I have had the kindest letter from Moore. I *do* think that man is the best-hearted, the only *hearted* being I ever encountered; and, then, his talents are equal to his feelings.

Dined on Wednesday at Lord H.'s—the Staffords, Staels, Cowpers, Ossulstones, Melbournes, Mackintoshes, etc., etc.—and was introduced to the Marquis and Marchioness of Stafford,—an unexpected event. My quarrel with Lord Carlisle (their or his brother-in-law) having rendered it improper, I suppose, brought it about. But, if it was to happen at all, I wonder it did not occur before. She is handsome, and must have been beautiful—and her manners are *princessly*.

The Stael was at the other end of the table, and less loquacious than heretofore. We are now very good friends; though she asked Lady Melbourne whether I had really any *bonhommie*. She might as well have asked that question before she told C. L. '*c'est un démon*.' True enough, but rather premature, for *she* could not have found it out, and so—she wants me to dine there next Sunday.

Murray prospers, as far as circulation. For my part, I adhere (in liking) to my Fragment. It is no wonder that I wrote one—my mind is a fragment.

Saw Lord Gower, Tierney, etc. in the square. Took leave of Lord Gower, who is going to Holland and Germany. He tells me that he carries with him a parcel of *Harolds* and *Giaours*, etc., for the readers of Berlin, who, it seems, read English, and have taken a caprice for mine. Um!—have I been *German* all this time, when I thought myself *Oriental*?

Lent Tierney my box for to-morrow; and received a new comedy sent by Lady C. A.—but *not hers*. I must read it, and endeavour not to displease the author. I hate annoying them with cavil; but a comedy I take to be the most difficult of compositions, more so than tragedy.

Galt says there is a coincidence between the first part of *The Bride* and some story of his—whether published or not, I know not, never having seen it. He is almost the last person on whom any one would commit literary larceny, and I am not conscious of any *witting* thefts on any of the genus. As to originality, all pretensions are ludicrous,—'there is nothing new under the sun.'

Went last night to the play. Invited out to a party, but did not go;—right. Refused to go to Lady ——'s on Monday;—right again. If I must fritter away my life, I would rather do it alone. I was much tempted;—C—— looked so Turkish with her red turban, and her regular, dark, and clear features. Not that *she* and *I* ever were, or could be, any thing; but I love any aspect that reminds me of the 'children of the sun.'

To dine to-day with Rogers and Sharpe, for which I have some appetite, not having tasted food for the preceding forty-eight hours. I wish I could leave off eating altogether.

Sunday, December 12

By Galt's answer, I find it is some story in *real life*, and not any work with which my late composition coincides. It is still more singular, for mine is drawn from *existence* also.

I have sent an excuse to Madame de Stael. I do not feel sociable enough for dinner to-day;—and I will not go to Sheridan's on Wednesday. Not that I do not admire and prefer his unequalled conversation; but—that '*but*' must only be intelligible to thoughts I cannot write. Sheridan was in good talk at Rogers's the other night, but I only stayed till *nine*. All the world are to be at the Stael's to-night, and I am not sorry to escape any part of it. I only go out to get me a fresh appetite for being alone. Went out—did not go to the Stael's but to Ld. Holland's. Party numerous—conversation general. Stayed late—made a blunder—got over it—came home and went to bed, not having eaten. Rather empty, but *fresco*, which is the great point with me.

Monday, December 13, 1813

Called at three places—read, and got ready to leave town to-morrow. Murray has had a letter from his brother biblio-pole of Edinburgh, who says, 'he is lucky in having such a *poet*'—something as if one was a pack-horse, or 'ass, or any thing that is his:' or, like Mrs. Packwood, who replied to some inquiry after the Odes on Razors,—'Laws, sir, we keeps a poet.' The same illustrious Edinburgh bookseller once sent an order for books, poesy, and cookery, with this agreeable postscript—'The *Harold* and *Cookery* are much wanted.' Such is fame, and, after all, quite as good as any other 'life in others' breath.' 'Tis much the same to divide purchasers with Hannah Glasse or Hannah More.

Some editor of some magazine has *announced* to Murray his intention of abusing the thing '*without reading it.*' So much the better; if he redde it first, he would abuse it more.

Allen (Lord Holland's Allen—the best informed and one of the ablest men I know—a perfect Magliabecchi—a devourer, a *Helluo* of books, and an observer of men,) has lent me a quantity of Burns's unpublished and never-to-be published

Letters. They are full of oaths and obscene songs. What an antithetical mind!—tenderness, roughness—delicacy, coarseness—sentiment, sensuality—soaring and grovelling, dirt and deity—all mixed up in that one compound of inspired clay!

It seems strange; a true voluptuary will never abandon his mind to the grossness of reality. It is by exalting the earthly, the material, the *physique* of our pleasures, by veiling these ideas, by forgetting them altogether, or, at least, never naming them hardly to one's self, that we alone can prevent them from disgusting.

December 14, 15, 16

Much done, but nothing to record. It is quite enough to set down my thoughts,—my actions will rarely bear retrospection.

December 17, 18

Lord Holland told me a curious piece of sentimentality in Sheridan. The other night we were all delivering our respective and various opinions on him and other *hommes marquans*, and mine was this:—'Whatever Sheridan has done or chosen to do has been, *par excellence*, always the *best* of its kind. He has written the *best* comedy (*School for Scandal*), the *best* drama (in my mind, far before that St. Giles's lampoon, the *Beggar's Opera*), the best farce (the *Critic*—it is only too good for a farce), and the best Address (Monologue on Garrick), and, to crown all, delivered the very best Oration (the famous Begum Speech) ever conceived or heard in this country.' Somebody told S. this the next day, and on hearing it he burst into tears!

Poor Brinsley! if they were tears of pleasure, I would rather have said these few, but most sincere, words than have written the Iliad or made his own celebrated Philippic. Nay, his own comedy never gratified me more than to hear that he had derived a moment's gratification from any praise of mine, humble as it must appear to 'my elders and my betters.'

Went to my box at Covent Garden to-night; and my delicacy felt a little shocked at seeing S——'s mistress (who, to my certain knowledge, was actually educated, from her birth, for her profession) sitting with her mother, 'a three-piled b——d, b——d-Major to the army,' in a private box opposite. I felt rather indignant; but, casting my eyes round the house, in the next box to me, and the next, and the next, were the most distinguished old and young Babylonians of quality;— so I burst out a laughing. It was really odd; Lady —— *divorced* —Lady —— and her daughter, Lady ——, both *divorceable*—Mrs. ——, in the next the *like*, and still nearer ——! What an assemblage to *me*, who know all their histories. It was as if the house had been divided between your public and your *understood* courtesans;—but the intriguantes much outnumbered the regular mercenaries. On the other side were only Pauline and *her* mother, and, next box to her, three of inferior note. Now, where lay the difference between *her* and *mamma*, and Lady —— and daughter? except that the two last may enter Carleton and any *other house*, and the two first are limited to the opera and b—— house. How I do delight in observing life as it really is!—and myself, after all, the worst of any. But no matter—I must avoid egotism, which, just now, would be no vanity.

I have lately written a wild, rambling, unfinished rhapsody, called *The Devil's Drive*, the notion of which I took from Porson's *Devil's Walk*.

Redde some Italian, and wrote two Sonnets on —— I never wrote but one sonnet before, and that was not in earnest, and many years ago, as an exercise—and I will never write another. They are the most puling, petrifying, stupidly platonic compositions. I detest the Petrarch so much, that I would not be the man even to have obtained his Laura, which the metaphysical, whining dotard never could.

January 16, 1814

To-morrow I leave town for a few days. I saw Lewis to-day, who is just returned from Oatlands, where he has been squabbling with Mad. de Stael about himself, Clarissa Harlowe, Mackintosh, and me. My homage has never been paid in that quarter, or we would have agreed still worse. I don't talk—I can't flatter, and won't listen, except to a pretty or a foolish woman. She bored Lewis with praises of himself till he sickened—found out that Clarissa was perfection, and Mackintosh the first man in England. There I agree, at least *one* of the first—but Lewis did not. As to Clarissa, I leave to those who can read it to judge and dispute. I could not do the one, and am, consequently, not qualified for the other. She told Lewis wisely, he being my friend, that I was affected, in the first place; and that, in the next place, I committed the heinous offence of sitting at dinner with my *eyes* shut, or half shut. I wonder if I really have this trick. I must cure myself of it, if true. One insensibly acquires awkward habits, which should be broken in time. If this is one, I wish I had been told of it before. It would not so much signify if one was always to be checkmated by a plain woman, but one may as well see some of one's neighbours, as well as the plate upon the table.

I should like, of all things, to have heard the Amabæan eclogue between her and Lewis—both obstinate, clever, odd, garrulous, and shrill. In fact, one could have heard nothing else. But they fell out, alas!—and now they will never quarrel again. Could not one reconcile them for the 'nonce?' Poor Corinne—she will find that some of her fine sayings won't suit our fine ladies and gentlemen.

I am getting rather into admiration of [Lady C. Annesley], the youngest sister of [Lady F. Webster]. A wife would be my salvation. I am sure the wives of my acquaintances have hitherto done me little good. Catherine is beautiful, but very young, and, I think, a fool. But I have not seen enough to judge; besides, I hate an *esprit* in petticoats. That she won't love me is very probable, nor shall I love her. But, on my system, and the modern system in general, that don't signify. The business (if it came to business) would probably be arranged between papa and me. She would have her own way; I am good-humoured to women, and docile; and, if I did not fall in love with her, which I should try to prevent, we should be a very comfortable couple. As to conduct, *that* she must look to. But *if* I love, I shall be jealous;— and for that reason I will not be in love. Though, after all, I doubt my temper, and fear I should not be so patient as becomes the *bienséance* of a married man in my station. Divorce ruins the poor *femme*, and damages are a paltry compensation. I do fear my temper would lead me into some of our oriental tricks of vengeance, or, at any rate, into a summary appeal to the court of twelve paces. So 'I'll none on't,' but e'en remain single and solitary;—though I should like to have somebody now and then to yawn with one.

Ward, and, after him, ——, has stolen one of my buffooneries about Mde. de Stael's Metaphysics and the Fog, and passed it, by speech and letter, as their own. As Gibbet says, 'they are the most of a gentleman of any on the road.' W. is in sad enmity with the Whigs about this Review of Fox (if he *did* review him);—all the epigrammatists and essayists are at him. I hate *odds*, and wish he may beat them. As for me, by the blessing of indifference, I have simplified my politics into an utter detestation of all existing governments; and, as it is the shortest and most agreeable and summary feeling imaginable, the first moment of an universal republic would convert me into an advocate for single and uncontradicted despotism. The fact is, riches are power, and poverty is slavery all over the earth, and one sort of establishment is no better nor worse for a *people* than another. I shall adhere to my party, because it would not be honourable to act otherwise; but, as to *opinions*, I don't think politics *worth* an *opinion*. *Conduct* is another thing:—if you begin with a party, go on with them. I have no consistency, except in politics; and *that* probably arises from my indifference on the subject altogether.

Feb. 18

Better than a month since I last journalised:—most of it out of London and at Notts., but a busy one and a pleasant, at least three weeks of it. On my return, I find all the newspapers in hysterics, and town in an uproar, on the avowal and republication of two stanzas on Princess Charlotte's weeping at Regency's speech to Lauderdale in 1812. They are daily at it still;—some of the abuse good, all of it hearty. They talk of a motion in our House upon it—be it so.

Got up—redde the *Morning Post* containing the battle of Buonaparte, the destruction of the Custom-house, and a paragraph on me as long as my pedigree, and vituperative, as usual.

Hobhouse is returned to England. He is my best friend, the most lively, and a man of the most sterling talents extant.

The Corsair has been conceived, written, published, etc. since I last took up this journal. They tell me it has great success;—it was written *con amore*, and much from *existence*. Murray is satisfied with its progress; and if the public are equally so with the perusal, there's an end of the matter.

Nine o'clock

Been to Hanson's on business. Saw Rogers, and had a note from Lady Melbourne, who says, it is said I am 'much out of spirits.' I wonder if I really am or not? I have certainly enough of 'that perilous stuff which weighs upon the heart,' and it is better they should believe it to be the result of these attacks than of the real cause; but—ay, ay, always *but*, to the end of the chapter.

Hobhouse has told me ten thousand anecdotes of Napoleon, all good and true. My friend H. is the most entertaining of companions, and a fine fellow to boot.

Redde a little—wrote notes and letters, and am alone, which Locke says is bad company. 'Be not solitary, be not idle.'—Um!—the idleness is troublesome; but I can't see so much to regret in the solitude. The more I see of men, the less I like them. If I could but say so of women too, all would be well. Why can't I? I am now six-and-twenty; my passions have had enough to cool them; my affections more than enough to wither them,—and yet—and yet—always *yet* and *but*—'Excellent well, you are a fishmonger—get thee to a nunnery.'—'They fool me to the top of my bent.'

Midnight

Began a letter, which I threw into the fire. Redde—but to little purpose. Did not visit Hobhouse, as I promised and ought. No matter, the loss is mine. Smoked cigars.

Napoleon!—this week will decide his fate. All seems against him; but I believe and hope he will win—at least, beat back the invaders. What right have we to prescribe sovereigns to France? Oh for a Republic! 'Brutus, thou sleepest.' Hobhouse abounds in continental anecdotes of this extraordinary man; all in favour of his intellect and courage, but against his *bon-hommie*. No wonder;—how should he, who knows mankind well, do other than despise and abhor them?

The greater the equality, the more impartially evil is distributed, and becomes lighter by the division among so many—therefore, a Republic!

More notes from Madame de Stael unanswered—and so they shall remain. I admire her abilities, but really her society is overwhelming—an avalanche that buries one in glittering nonsense—all snow and sophistry.

Shall I go to Mackintosh's on Tuesday? um!—I did not go to Marquis Lansdowne's, nor to Miss Berry's, though both are pleasant. So is Sir James's,—but I don't know—I believe one is not the better for parties; at least, unless some *regnante* is there.

I wonder how the deuce any body could make such a world; for what purpose dandies, for instance, were ordained —and kings—and fellows of colleges—and women of 'a certain age'—and many men of any age—and myself, most of all!

> *Divesne prisco natus ab Inacho*
> *Nil interest, an pauper, et infimâ*
> *De gente, sub dio moreris,*
> *Victima nil miserantis Orci.*
> *Omnes eodem cogimur, etc.*

Is there any thing beyond?—*who* knows? *He* that can't tell. Who tells that there *is*? He who don't know. And when shall he know? perhaps, when he don't expect, and generally when he don't wish it. In this last respect, however, all are not alike: it depends a good deal upon education,—something upon nerves and habits—but most upon digestion.

Saturday, Feb. 19

Just returned from seeing Kean in Richard. By Jove, he is a soul! Life—nature—truth without exaggeration or diminu-

Y

tion. Kemble's Hamlet is perfect;—but Hamlet is not Nature. Richard is a man; and Kean is Richard. Now to my own concerns.

Went to Waite's. Teeth are all right and white; but he says that I grind them in my sleep and chip the edges. That same sleep is no friend of mine, though I court him sometimes for half the twenty-four.

February 20

Got up and tore out two leaves of this Journal—I don't know why. Hodgson just called and gone. He has much *bonhommie* with his other good qualities, and more talent than he has yet had credit for beyond his circle.

An invitation to dine at Holland House to meet Kean. He is worth meeting; and I hope, by getting into good society, he will be prevented from falling like Cooke. He is greater now on the stage, and off he should never be less. There is a stupid and underrating criticism upon him in one of the newspapers. I thought that, last night, though great, he rather under-acted more than the first time. This may be the effect of these cavils; but I hope he has more sense than to mind them. He cannot expect to maintain his present eminence, or to advance still higher, without the envy of his green-room fellows, and the nibbling of their admirers. But, if he don't beat them all, why then—merit hath no purchase in 'these coster-monger days.'

I wish that I had a talent for the drama; I would write a tragedy *now*. But no,—it is gone. Hodgson talks of one,—he will do it well;—and I think Moore should try. He has wonderful powers, and much variety; besides, he has lived and felt. To write so as to bring home to the heart, the heart must have been tried,—but, perhaps, ceased to be so. While you are under the influence of passions, you only feel, but cannot describe them,—any more than, when in action, you could turn round and tell the story to your next neighbour! When all is over,—all, all, and irrevocable,—trust to memory—she is then but too faithful.

Went out, and answered some letters, yawned now and then, and redde the *Robbers*. Fine,—but *Fiesco* is better;

and Alfieri and Monti's *Aristodemo best*. They are more
equal than the Tedeschi dramatists.

Answered—or rather acknowledged—the receipt of young
Reynolds's poem, *Safie*. The lad is clever, but much of his
thoughts are borrowed,—*whence*, the Reviewers may find out.
I hate discouraging a young one; and I think,—though wild
and more oriental than he would be, had he seen the scenes
where he has placed his tale,—that he has much talent, and,
certainly, fire enough.

Received a very singular epistle; and the mode of its conveyance, through Lord H.'s hands, as curious as the letter itself.
But it was gratifying and pretty.

Sunday, February 27

Here I am, alone, instead of dining at Lord H.'s, where I
was asked,—but not inclined to go any where. Hobhouse says
I am growing a *loup garou*,—a solitary hobgoblin. True;—'I
am myself alone.' The last week has been passed in reading—
seeing plays—now and then visitors—sometimes yawning and
sometimes sighing, but no writing,—save of letters. If I could
always read, I should never feel the want of society. Do I
regret it?—um!—'Man delights not me,' and only one woman
—at a time.

There is something to me very softening in the presence of a
woman,—some strange influence, even if one is not in love
with them—which I cannot at all account for, having no very
high opinion of the sex. But yet,—I always feel in better
humour with myself and every thing else, if there is a woman
within ken. Even Mrs. Mule, my fire-lighter,—the most
ancient and withered of her kind,—and (except to myself) not
the best-tempered—always makes me laugh,—no difficult task
when I am 'i' the vein.'

Heigho! I would I were in mine island!—I am not well; and
yet I look in good health. At times, I fear, 'I am not in my perfect mind;'—and yet my heart and head have stood many a
crash, and what should ail them now? They prey upon themselves, and I am sick—sick—'Prithee, undo this button—why
should a cat, a rat, a dog have life—and *thou* no life at all?'

Six-and-twenty years, as they call them, why, I might and should have been a Pasha by this time. 'I 'gin to be a-weary of the sun.'

Buonaparte is not yet beaten; but has rebutted Blucher, and repiqued Schwartzenburg. This it is to have a head. If he again wins, *Væ victis!*

Sunday, March 6

On Tuesday last dined with Rogers,—Madame de Staël, Mackintosh, Sheridan, Erskine, and Payne Knight, Lady Donegal, and Miss R. there. Sheridan told a very good story of himself and Madame de Recamier's handkerchief; Erskine a few stories of himself only. *She* is going to write a big book about England, she says;—I believe her. Asked by her how I liked Miss Edgeworth's thing, called *Patronage*, and answered (very sincerely) that I thought it very bad for *her*, and worse than any of the others. Afterwards thought it possible Lady Donegal, being Irish, might be a patroness of Miss Edgeworth, and was rather sorry for my opinion, as I hate putting people into fusses, either with themselves or their favourites; it looks as if one did it on purpose. The party went off very well, and the fish was very much to my gusto. But we got up too soon after the women; and Mrs. Corinne always lingers so long after dinner that we wish her in—the drawing-room.

To-day Campbell called, and while sitting here in came Merivale. During our colloquy, C. (ignorant that Merivale was the writer) abused the 'mawkishness of the *Quarterly Review* of Grimm's *Correspondence*. I (knowing the secret) changed the conversation as soon as I could; and C. went away, quite convinced of having made the most favourable impression on his new acquaintance. Merivale is luckily a very good-natured fellow, or God he knows what might have been engendered from such a malaprop. I did not look at him while this was going on, but I felt like a coal—for I like Merivale, as well as the article in question.

Asked to Lady Keith's to-morrow evening—I think I will go; but it is the first party invitation I have accepted this 'season,' as the learned Fletcher called it, when that youngest brat of Lady ——'s cut my eye and cheek open with a mis-directed pebble—'Never mind, my Lord, the scar will be gone before the *season*;' as if one's eye was of no importance in the mean time.

Lord Erskine called, and gave me his famous pamphlet, with a marginal note and corrections in his handwriting. Sent it to be bound superbly, and shall treasure it.

Sent my fine print of Napoleon to be framed. It *is* framed; and the Emperor becomes his robes as if he had been hatched in them.

March 7

Rose at seven—ready by half-past eight—went to Mr. Hanson's, Bloomsbury Square—went to church with his eldest daughter, Mary Anne (a good girl), and gave her away to the Earl of Portsmouth. Saw her fairly a countess—congratulated the family and groom (bride)—drank a bumper of wine (whole-some sherris) to their felicity, and all that—and came home. Asked to stay to dinner, but could not. At three sat to Phillips for faces. Called on Lady Melbourne—I like her so well, that I always stay too long. (Mem. to mend of that.)

Passed the evening with Hobhouse, who has begun a poem, which promises highly;—wish he would go on with it. Heard some curious extracts from a life of Morosini, the blundering Venetian, who blew up the Acropolis at Athens with a bomb, and be damned to him! Waxed sleepy—just come home— must go to bed, and am engaged to meet Sheridan to-morrow at Rogers's.

Queer ceremony that same of marriage—saw many abroad, Greek and Catholic—one, at *home*, many years ago. There be some strange phrases in the prologue (the exhortation), which made me turn away, not to laugh in the face of the surplice-man. Made one blunder, when I joined the hands of the happy —rammed their left hands, by mistake, into one another. Cor-rected it—bustled back to the altar-rail, and said 'Amen.' Portsmouth responded as if he had got the whole by heart;

and, if any thing, was rather before the priest. It is now midnight and . . . .

On Tuesday dined with Rogers,—Mackintosh, Sheridan, Sharpe,—much talk, and good,—all, except my own little prattlement. Much of old times—Horne Tooke—the Trials—evidence of Sheridan, and anecdotes of those times, when *I*, alas! was an infant. If I had been a man, I would have made an English Lord Edward Fitzgerald.

Set down Sheridan at Brookes's,—where, by the by, he could not have well set down himself, as he and I were the only drinkers. Sherry means to stand for Westminster, as Cochrane (the stock-jobbing hoaxer) must vacate. Brougham is a candidate. I fear for poor dear Sherry. Both have talents of the highest order, but the youngster has *yet* a character. We shall see, if he lives to Sherry's age, how he will pass over the redhot ploughshares of public life. I don't know why, but I hate to see the *old* ones lose; particularly Sheridan, notwithstanding all his *méchanceté*.

Received many, and the kindest, thanks from Lady Portsmouth, *père* and *mère*, for my match-making. I don't regret it, as she looks the countess well, and is a very good girl. It is odd how well she carries her new honours. She looks a different woman, and high-bred, too. I had no idea that I could make so good a peeress.

Went to the play with Hobhouse. Mrs. Jordan superlative in Hoyden, and Jones well enough in Foppington. *What plays!* what wit!—*hélas!* Congreve and Vanbrugh are your only comedy. Our society is too insipid now for the like copy. Would *not* go to Lady Keith's. Hobhouse thought it odd. I wonder *he* should like parties. If one is in love, and wants to break a commandment and covet any thing that is there, they do very well. But to go out amongst the mere herd, without a motive, pleasure, or pursuit—'sdeath! 'I'll none of it.' He told me an odd report,—that *I* am the actual Conrad, the veritable Corsair, and that part of my travels are supposed to have passed in privacy. Um!—people sometimes hit near the truth;

but never the whole truth. H. don't know what I was about the year after he left the Levant; nor does any one—nor—nor— nor—however, it is a lie—but, 'I doubt the equivocation of the fiend that lies like truth!'

I shall have letters of importance to-morrow. Which ——, ——, or ——? heigho! . . . —— is in my heart, —— in my head, —— in my eye, and the *single* one, Heaven knows where. All write, and will be answered. 'Since I have crept in favour with myself, I must maintain it;' but *I* never 'mistook my person,' though I think others have.

—— called to-day in great despair about his mistress, who has taken a freak of——. He began a letter to her, but was obliged to stop short—I finished it for him, and he copied and sent it. If *he* holds out, and keeps to my instructions of affected indifference, she will lower her colours. If she don't, he will, at least, get rid of her, and she don't seem much worth keeping. But the poor lad is in love—if that is the case, she will win. When they once discover their power, *finita è la musica.*

Sleepy, and must go to bed.

Tuesday, March 15

Dined yesterday with Rogers, Mackintosh, and Sharpe. Sheridan could not come. Sharpe told several very amusing anecdotes of Henderson, the actor. Stayed till late, and came home, having drunk so much *tea*, that I did not get to sleep till six this morning. R. says I am to be in *this Quarterly*—cut up, I presume, as they 'hate us youth.' *N'importe.* As Sharpe was passing by the doors of some debating society (the West-minster Forum), in his way to dinner, he saw rubricked on the walls *Scott's* name and *mine*—'Which the best poet?' being the question of the evening; and I suppose all the Templars and *would-bes* took our rhymes in vain in the course of the contro-versy. Which had the greater show of hands, I neither know nor care; but I feel the coupling of the names as a compliment, —though I think Scott deserves better company.

Wedderburn Webster called—Lord Erskine, Lord Holland, etc., etc. Wrote to —— the *Corsair* report. She says she don't wonder, since 'Conrad is so *like*.' It is odd that one, who knows me so thoroughly, should tell me this to my face. However, if she don't know, nobody can.

Mackintosh is, it seems, the writer of the defensive letter in the *Morning Chronicle*. If so, it is very kind, and more than I did for myself.

Told Murray to secure for me Bandello's Italian Novels at the sale to-morrow. To me they will be *nuts*. Redde a satire on myself, called 'Anti-Byron,' and told Murray to publish it if he liked. The object of the author is to prove me an atheist and a systematic conspirator against law and government. Some of the verse is good; the prose I don't quite understand. He asserts that my 'deleterious works' have had 'an effect upon civil society, which requires,' etc., etc., etc., and his own poetry. It is a lengthy poem, and a long preface, with an harmonious title-page. Like the fly in the fable, I seem to have got upon a wheel which makes much dust; but, unlike the said fly, I do not take it all for my own raising.

A letter from *Bella*, which I answered. I shall be in love with her again, if I don't take care.

I shall begin a more regular system of reading soon.

Thursday, March 17

I have been sparring with Jackson for exercise this morning; and mean to continue and renew my acquaintance with the muffles. My chest, and arms, and wind are in very good plight, and I am not in flesh. I used to be a hard hitter, and my arms are very long for my height (5 feet 8½ inches). At any rate, exercise is good, and this the severest of all; fencing and the broad-sword never fatigued me half so much.

Redde the *Quarrels of Authors* (another sort of *sparring*)— a new work, by that most entertaining and researching writer, Israeli. They seem to be an irritable set, and I wish myself well out of it. 'I'll not march through Coventry with them, that's flat.' What the devil had I to do with scribbling? It is too late to inquire, and all regret is useless. But, an it were to do again,—I should write again, I suppose. Such is human nature, at least my share of it;—though I shall think better of myself, if I have sense to stop now. If I have a wife, and that wife has a son—by any body—I will bring up mine heir in the most anti-poetical way—make him a lawyer, or a pirate, or—any thing. But, if he writes too, I shall be sure he is none of mine, and cut him off with a Bank token. Must write a letter—three o'clock.

Sunday, March 20

I intended to go to Lady Hardwicke's, but won't. I always begin the day with a bias towards going to parties; but, as the evening advances, my stimulus fails, and I hardly ever go out—and, when I do, always regret it. This might have been a pleasant one;—at least, the hostess is a very superior woman. Lady Lansdowne's to-morrow—Lady Heathcote's Wednesday. Um!—I must spur myself into going to some of them, or it will look like rudeness, and it is better to do as other people do—confound them!

Redde Machiavel, parts of Chardin, and Sismondi, and Bandello—by starts. Redde the *Edinburgh*, 44, just come out. In the beginning of the article on Edgeworth's *Patronage*, I have gotten a high compliment, I perceive. Whether this is creditable to me, I know not; but it does honour to the editor, because he once abused me. Many a man will retract praise; none but a high-spirited mind will revoke its censure, or *can* praise the man it has once attacked. I have often, since my return to England, heard Jeffrey most highly commended by those who know him for things independent of his talents. I admire him for *this*—not because he has *praised me* (I have been so praised elsewhere and abused, alternately, that mere habit has rendered me as indifferent to both as a man at twenty-six can be to any thing), but because he is, perhaps, the *only man* who, under the relations in which he and I stand, or stood, with regard to each other, would have had the liberality to act thus; none but a great soul dared hazard it. The height on which he stands has not made him giddy;—a little scribbler would have gone on cavilling to the end of the chapter. As to the justice of his panegyric, that is matter of taste. There are plenty to question it, and glad, too of the opportunity.

Lord Erskine called to-day. He means to carry down his reflections on the war—or rather wars—to the present day.

I trust that he will. Must send to Mr. Murray to get the binding of my copy of his pamphlet finished, as Lord E. has promised me to correct it, and add some marginal notes to it. Any thing in his handwriting will be a treasure, which will gather compound interest from years. Erskine has high expectations of Mackintosh's promised History. Undoubtedly it must be a classic, when finished.

Sparred with Jackson again yesterday morning, and shall to-morrow. I feel all the better for it, in spirits, though my arms and shoulders are very stiff from it. Mem. to attend the pugilistic dinner:—Marquess Huntley is in the chair.

Lord Erskine thinks that ministers must be in peril of going out. So much the better for him. To me it is the same who are in or out;—we want something more than a change of ministers, and some day we will have it.

I remember, in riding from Chrisso to Castri (Delphos), along the sides of Parnassus, I saw six eagles in the air. It is uncommon to see so many together; and it was the number—not the species, which is common enough—that excited my attention.

The last bird I ever fired at was an *eaglet*, on the shore of the Gulf of Lepanto, near Vostitza. It was only wounded, and I tried to save it, the eye was so bright; but it pined, and died in a few days; and I never did since, and never will, attempt the death of another bird. I wonder what put these two things into my head just now? I have been reading Sismondi, and there is nothing there that could induce the recollection.

I am mightily taken with Braccio di Montone, Giovanni Galeazzo, and Eccelino. But the last is *not* Bracciaferro (of the same name), Count of Ravenna, whose history I want to trace. There is a fine engraving in Lavater, from a picture by Fuseli, of *that* Ezzelin, over the body of Meduna, punished by him for a *hitch* in her constancy during his absence in the Crusades. He was right—but I want to know the story.

Tuesday, March 22

Last night, *party* at Lansdowne House. To-night, *party* at Lady Charlotte Greville's—deplorable waste of time, and something of temper. Nothing imparted—nothing acquired—

talking without ideas:—if any thing like *thought* in my mind, it was not on the subjects on which we were gabbling. Heigho!—and in this way half London pass what is called life. To-morrow there is Lady Heathcote's—shall I go? yes—to punish myself for not having a pursuit.

Let me see—what did I see? The only person who much struck me was Lady Stafford's eldest daughter, Lady Charlotte Leveson. They say she is *not* pretty. I don't know—every thing is pretty that pleases; but there is an air of *soul* about her—and her colour changes—and there is that shy-ness of the antelope (which I delight in) in her manner so much, that I observed her more than I did any other woman in the rooms, and only looked at anything else when I thought she might perceive and feel embarrassed by my scrutiny. After all, there may be something of association in this. She is a friend of Augusta's, and whatever she loves I can't help liking.

Her mother, the Marchioness, talked to me a little; and I was twenty times on the point of asking her to introduce me to *sa fille*, but I stopped short. This comes of that affray with the Carlisles.

Earl Grey told me laughingly of a paragraph in the last *Moniteur*, which has stated, among other symptoms of rebel-lion, some particulars of the *sensation* occasioned in all our government gazettes by the 'tear' lines,—*only* amplifying, in its re-statement, an epigram (by the by, no epigram except in the *Greek* acceptation of the word) into a *roman*. I wonder the *Couriers*, etc., etc., have not translated that part of the *Moni-teur*, with additional comments.

The Princess of Wales has requested Fuseli to paint from *The Corsair*,—leaving to him the choice of any passage for the subject: so Mr. Locke tells me. Tired, jaded, selfish, and supine—must go to bed.

Roman, at least, *Romance*, means a song sometimes, as in the Spanish. I suppose this is the *Moniteur's* meaning, unless he has confused it with *The Corsair*.

Albany, March 28

This night got into my new apartments, rented of Lord Althorpe, on a lease of seven years. Spacious, and room for my books and sabres. *In* the *house*, too, another advantage. The last few days, or whole week, have been very abstemious, regular in exercise, and yet very *un*well.

Yesterday, dined *tête-à-tête* at the Cocoa with Scrope Davies—sat from six till midnight—drank between us one bottle of champagne and six of claret, neither of which wines ever affect me. Offered to take Scrope home in my carriage; but he was tipsy and pious, and I was obliged to leave him on his knees praying to I know not what purpose or pagod. No headach, nor sickness, that night nor to-day. Got up, if any thing, earlier than usual—sparred with Jackson *ad sudorem*, and have been much better in health than for many days. I have heard nothing more from Scrope. Yesterday paid him four thousand eight hundred pounds, a debt of some standing, and which I wished to have paid before. My mind is much relieved by the removal of that *debit*.

Augusta wants me to make it up with Carlisle. I have refused *every* body else, but I can't deny her any thing;—so I must e'en do it, though I had as lief 'drink up Eisel—eat a crocodile.' Let me see—Ward, the Hollands, the Lambs, Rogers, etc., etc., —every body, more or less, have been trying for the last two years to accommodate this *couplet* quarrel, to no purpose. I shall laugh if Augusta succeeds.

Redde a little of many things—shall get in all my books to-morrow. Luckily this room will hold them—with 'ample room and verge, etc., the characters of hell to trace.' I must set about some employment soon; my heart begins to eat *itself* again.

April 8

Out of town six days. On my return, find my poor little pagod, Napoleon, pushed off his pedestal;—the thieves are in Paris. It is his own fault. Like Milo, he would rend the oak; but it closed again, wedged his hands, and now the beasts— lion, bear, down to the dirtiest jackal—may all tear him. That Muscovite winter *wedged* his arms;—ever since, he has fought with his feet and teeth. The last may still leave their marks; and 'I guess now' (as the Yankees say) that he will yet play them a pass. He is in their rear—between them and their homes. Query—will they ever reach them?

Saturday, April 9, 1814

I mark this day!

Napoleon Buonaparte has abdicated the throne of the world. 'Excellent well.' Methinks Sylla did better; for he revenged and resigned in the height of his sway, red with the slaughter of his foes—the finest instance of glorious contempt of the rascals upon record. Dioclesian did well too—Amurath not amiss, had he become aught except a dervise—Charles the Fifth but so so—but Napoleon, worst of all. What! wait till they were in his capital, and then talk of his readiness to give up what is already gone!! 'What whining monk art thou— what holy cheat?' 'Sdeath!—Dionysius at Corinth was yet a king to this. The 'Isle of Elba' to retire to!—Well—if it had been Caprea, I should have marvelled less. 'I see men's minds are but a parcel of their fortunes.' I am utterly bewildered and confounded.

I don't know—but I think *I*, even *I* (an insect compared with this creature), have set my life on casts not a millionth part of this man's. But, after all, a crown may be not worth dying for. Yet, to outlive *Lodi* for this!!! Oh that Juvenal or Johnson could rise from the dead! *Expende—quot libras in duce summo invenies?* I knew they were light in the balance of mortality; but I thought their living dust weighed more *carats*. Alas! this imperial diamond hath a flaw in it, and is now hardly fit to stick in a glazier's pencil:—the pen of the historian won't rate it worth a ducat.

Psha! 'something too much of this.' But I won't give him up even now; though all his admirers have, 'like the thanes, fallen from him.'

April 10

I do not know that I am happiest when alone; but this I am sure of, that I never am long in the society even of *her* I love, (God knows too well, and the devil probably too,) without a yearning for the company of my lamp and my utterly confused and tumbled-over library. Even in the day, I send away my carriage oftener than I use or abuse it. *Per esempio,*—I have not stirred out of these rooms for these four days past: but I have sparred for exercise (windows open) with Jackson an hour daily, to attenuate and keep up the ethereal part of me. The more violent the fatigue, the better my spirits for the rest of the day; and then, my evenings have that calm nothingness of languor, which I most delight in. To-day I have boxed an hour—written an ode to Napoleon Buonaparte—copied it— eaten six biscuits—drunk four bottles of soda water—redde away the rest of my time—besides giving poor —— a world of advice about this mistress of his, who is plaguing him into a phthisic and intolerable tediousness. I am a pretty fellow truly to lecture about 'the sect.' No matter, my counsels are all thrown away.

April 19, 1814

There is ice at both poles, north and south—all extremes are the same—misery belongs to the highest and the lowest only, —to the emperor and the beggar, when unsixpenced and un-throned. There is, to be sure, a damned insipid medium—an equinoctial line—no one knows where, except upon maps and measurement.

> *And all our* yesterdays *have lighted fools*
> *The way to dusty death.*

I will keep no further journal of that same hesternal torch-light; and, to prevent me from returning, like a dog, to the vomit of memory, I tear out the remaining leaves of this volume, and write, in *Ipecacuanha,*—'that the Bourbons are restored!!!'—'Hang up philosophy.' To be sure, I have long despised myself and man, but I never spat in the face of my species before—'O fool! I shall go mad.'

TO THOMAS MOORE

January 6, 1814

I have got a devil of a long story in the press, entitled *The Corsair,* in the regular heroic measure. It is a pirate's isle, peopled with my own creatures, and you may easily suppose they do a world of mischief through the three cantos. Now for your dedication—if you will accept it. This is positively my last experiment on public *literary* opinion, till I turn my thirtieth year,—if so be I flourish until that downhill period. I have a confidence for you—a perplexing one to me, and, just at present, in a state of abeyance in itself. . . .

However, we shall see. In the mean time, you may amuse yourself with my suspense, and put all the justices of peace in requisition, in case I come into your county with 'hackbut bent.'

Seriously, whether I am to hear from her or him, it is a *pause*, which I shall fill up with as few thoughts of my own as I can borrow from other people. Any thing is better than stagnation ; and now, in the interregnum of my autumn and a strange summer adventure, which I don't like to think of, (I don't mean ——'s, however, which is laughable only), the antithetical state of my lucubrations makes me alive, and Macbeth can 'sleep no more :'—he was lucky in getting rid of the drowsy sensation of waking again.

Pray write to me. I must send you a copy of the letter of dedication. When do you come out? I am sure we don't *clash* this time, for I am all at sea, and in action,—and a wife, and a mistress, etc.

Thomas, thou art a happy fellow ; but if you wish us to be so, you must come up to town, as you did last year ; and we shall have a world to say, and to see, and to hear. Let me hear from you.

P.S.—Of course you will keep my secret, and don't even talk in your sleep of it. Happen what may, your dedication is ensured, being already written ; and I shall copy it out fair tonight, in case business or amusement—*Amant alterna Camœnæ*.

TO THOMAS MOORE

February 10, 1814

I arrived in town late yesterday evening, having been absent three weeks, which I passed in Notts. quietly and pleasantly. You can have no conception of the uproar the eight lines on the little Royalty's weeping in 1812 (now republished) have occasioned. The Regent, who had always thought them *yours*, chose—God knows why—on discovering them to be mine, to be *affected* 'in sorrow rather than anger.' The *Morning Post*, *Sun, Herald, Courier*, have all been in hysterics ever since. M[urray] is in a fright, and wanted to shuffle; and the abuse against me in all directions is vehement, unceasing, loud—some of it good, and all of it hearty. I feel a little compunctious as to the Regent's *regret*;—'would he had been only angry! but I fear him not.'

Some of these same assailments you have probably seen. My person (which is excellent for the 'nonce') has been denounced in verses, the more like the subject, inasmuch as they halt exceedingly. Then, in another, I am an *atheist*, a *rebel*, and, at last, the *devil* (*boiteux*, I presume). My demonism seems to be a female's conjecture; if so, perhaps, I could convince her that I am but a mere mortal,—if a queen of the Amazons may be believed, who says αριστον χωλος οιθει. I quote from memory, so my Greek is probably deficient; but the passage is *meant* to mean——.

Seriously, I am in, what the learned call, a dilemma, and the vulgar, a scrape; and my friends desire me not to be in a passion; and, like Sir Fretful, I assure them that I am 'quite calm,'—but I am nevertheless in a fury.

Since I wrote thus far, a friend has come in, and we have been talking and buffooning till I have quite lost the thread of my thoughts; and as I won't send them unstrung to you, good morning, and

Believe me ever, etc.

P.S.—Murray, during my absence, *omitted* the Tears in several of the copies. I have made him replace them, and am very wroth with his qualms;—'as the wine is poured out, let it be drunk to the dregs.'

TO THOMAS MOORE

March 3, 1814

My dear Friend,

I have a great mind to tell you that I *am* 'uncomfortable,' if only to make you come to town; where no one ever more delighted in seeing you, nor is there any one to whom I would sooner turn for consolation in my most vapourish moments. The truth is, I have 'no lack of argument' to ponder upon of the most gloomy description, but this arises from *other* causes. Some day or other, when we are *veterans*, I may tell you a tale of present and past times; and it is not from want of confidence that I do not now,—but—but—always a *but* to the end of the chapter.

There is nothing, however, upon the *spot* either to love or hate;—but I certainly have subjects for both at no very great distance, and am besides embarrassed between *three* whom I know, and one (whose name, at least) I do not know. All this would be very well if I had no heart; but, unluckily, I have found that there is such a thing still about me, though in no very good repair, and, also, that it has a habit of attaching it-self to *one* whether I will or no. *Divide et impera*, I begin to think, will only do for politics.

If I discover the 'toad,' as you call him, I shall 'tread,'—and put spikes in my shoes to do it more effectually. The effect of all these fine things I do not inquire much nor perceive. I believe —— felt them more than either of us. People are civil enough, and I have had no dearth of invitations,—none of which, however, I have accepted. I went out very little last year, and mean to go about still less. I have no passion for circles, and have long regretted that I ever gave way to what is called a town life;—which, of all the lives I ever saw (and they are nearly as many as Plutarch's), seems to me to leave the least for the past and future.

How proceeds the poem? Do not neglect it, and I have no fears. I need not say to you that your fame is dear to me,—I really might say *dearer* than my own; for I have lately begun to think my things have been strangely over-rated; and, at any rate, whether or not, I have done with them for ever. I may say to you what I would not say to every body, that the last two were written, *The Bride* in four, and *The Corsair* in ten days,— which I take to be a most humiliating confession, as it proves my own want of judgment in publishing, and the public's in reading things, which cannot have stamina for permanent attention. 'So much for Buckingham.'

I have no dread of your being too hasty, and I have still less of your failing. But I think a *year* a very fair allotment of time to a composition which is not to be Epic; and even Horace's 'Nonum prematur' must have been intended for the Millennium, or some longer-lived generation than ours. I wonder how much we should have had of *him*, had he observed his own doctrines to the letter. Peace be with you! Remember that I am always and most truly yours, etc.

P.S.—I never heard the 'report' you mention, nor, I dare say, many others. But, in course, you, as well as others, have 'damned good-natured friends,' who do their duty in the usual way. One thing will make you laugh. . . .

TO THOMAS MOORE

Albany, April 20, 1814

I *am* very glad to hear that you are to be transient from Mayfield so very soon, and was taken in by the first part of your letter. Indeed, for aught I know, you may be treating me, as Slipslop says, with 'ironing' even now. I shall say nothing of the *shock*, which had nothing of *humeur* in it; as I am apt to take even a critic, and still more a friend, at his word, and never to doubt that I have been writing cursed nonsense, if they say so. There was a mental reservation in my pact with the public, in behalf of *anonymes*; and, even had there not, the provocation was such as to make it physically impossible to pass over this damnable epoch of triumphant tameness. 'Tis a cursed business; and, after all, I shall think higher of rhyme and reason, and very humbly of your heroic people, till—Elba becomes a volcano, and sends him out again. I can't think it all over yet.

My departure for the Continent depends, in some measure, on the *in*continent. I have two country invitations at home, and don't know what to say or do. In the mean time, I have bought a macaw and a parrot, and have got up my books; and I box and fence daily, and go out very little.

At this present writing, Louis the Gouty is wheeling in triumph into Piccadilly, in all the pomp and rabblement of royalty. I had an offer of seats to see them pass; but, as I have seen a Sultan going to mosque, and been at *his* reception of an ambassador, the Most Christian King 'hath no attractions for me:'—though in some coming year of the Hegira, I should not dislike to see the place where he *had* reigned, shortly after the second revolution, and a happy sovereignty of two months, the last six weeks being civil war.

Pray write, and deem me ever, etc.

TO LADY MELBOURNE

April 25, 1814

My dear Ly. Me.

Thanks as to C—— though the task will be difficult; if she is to determine as to kindness or unkindness, the best way will be to avoid each other *without appearing* to do so, or if we jostle, at any rate not to bite.

Oh! but it is 'worth while,' I can't tell you why, and it is *not* an '*Ape,*' and if it is, that must be my fault; however, I will positively reform. You must however allow that it is utterly impossible I can ever be half so well liked elsewhere, and I have been all my life trying to make someone love me, and never got the sort that I preferred before. But positively she and I will grow good and all that, and so we are *now* and shall be these three weeks and more too.

Yesterday I dined at the Princess's, where I deported myself like a white stick; till, as the Devil would have it, a man with a flute played a solemn and somewhat tedious piece of music. Well, I got through that, but down sate Lady Anne H. to give evidence at the pianoforte with a Miss Somebody (the 'privy purse,' in a pair of spectacles—dark green) these, and the flute man, and the 'damnable faces' (as Hamlet says) of the whole party, threw me into a convulsion of uncourtly laughter, which Gell and Lady Crewe encouraged; at least the *last* joined in it so heartily that the whooping-cough would have been an Æolian harp in comparison to us both. At last I half strangled it, and myself, with my kerchief; and here I am grave and sedate again.

You will be sorry to hear that I have got a physician just in time for an old complaint, 'troublesome, but not dangerous,' like Lord Stair and Ld. Stair's, of which I am promised an eventual removal. It is very odd; he is a staid grave man, and puts so many questions to me about *my mind*, and the state of it, that I begin to think he half suspects my senses. He asked me how I felt 'when anything weighed upon my mind?' and I answered him by a question, why he should suppose that anything did? I was laughing and sitting quietly in my chair the whole time of his visits, and yet he thinks me horribly restless and irritable, and talks about my having lived *excessively* 'out of all compass' some time or other; which has no more to do with the malady he has to deal with than I have with the Wisdom of Solomon.

To-morrow I go to the Berrys; on Wednesday to the Jerseys; on Thursday I dine at Ld. Grey's, and there is Ly. Hard[wick]e in the evening; and on Friday I am asked to a Lady Charleville's, whom I don't know, and where I shan't go. We shall meet, I hope, at one or two of these places.

I don't often bore you with rhyme—but as a wrapper to this note I send you some upon a brunette, which I have shown to no one else. If you think them not much beneath the common places you may give them to any of your 'album' acquaintances.

Ever yrs most truly, B.

TO LADY MELBOURNE

April 30, 1814

My dear Lady Me.

You—or rather *I*—have done *my A* much injustice. The expression which you recollect as objectionable meant only 'loving' in the *senseless* sense of that wide word, and it must be some selfish stupidity of mine in telling my own story, but really and truly—as I hope mercy and happiness for her—by that God who made me for my own misery, and not much for the good of others, *she* was not to blame, one thousandth part in comparison. She was not aware of her own peril till it was too late, and I can only account for her subsequent '*abandon*' by an observation which I think is not unjust, that women are much more *attached* than men if they are treated with anything like fairness or tenderness.

As for *your* A, I don't know what to make of her. I enclose her last but one, and *my* A's last but one, from which you may form your own conclusions on both. I think you will allow mine to be a very extraordinary person in point of *talent*, but I won't say more, only do not allow your good nature to lean to my side of this question; on all others I shall be glad to avail myself of your partiality.

Now for *common* life. There is a party at Lady J[erse]y's on Monday and on Wednesday. I am asked to both, and excused myself out of Tuesday's dinner because I want to see Kean in Richard again.

Pray *why* did you say I am getting into a *scrape* with R.'s moiety? We must talk to somebody. I always give you the preference when you are disposed to listen, and when you seem fidgeted, as you do now and then (and no wonder, for latterly I do but repeat), I turn to anyone, and she was the first that I stumbled upon. As for anything more, I have not even advanced to the tip of her little finger, and never shall unless she gives it.

You won't believe me, and won't care if you do, but I really believe that I have more true regard and affection for yourself than for any other existence. As for my A, my feelings towards her are a mixture of good and diabolical. I hardly know one passion which has not some share in them, but I won't run into the subject.

Your niece has committed herself perhaps, but it can be of no consequence; if I pursued and succeeded in that quarter, of course I must give up all other pursuits, and the fact is that my wife, if she had common sense, would have more power over me than any other whatsoever, for my heart always alights on the nearest *perch*—if it is withdrawn it goes God knows where —but one must like something.

Ever yrs., B.

TO THOMAS MOORE

May 4, 1814

Last night we supp'd at R——fe's board, etc.

. . . I wish people would not shirk their *dinners*—ought it not to have been a dinner?—and that damned anchovy sandwich!

That plaguy voice of yours made me sentimental, and almost fall in love with a girl who was recommending herself, during your song, by *hating* music. But the song is past, and my passion can wait, till the *pucelle* is more harmonious.

Do you go to Lady Jersey's to-night? It is a large party, and you won't be bored into 'softening rocks,' and all that. *Othello* is to-morrow and Saturday too. Which day shall we go? When shall I see you? If you call, let it be after three, and as near four as you please.

Ever, etc.

TO THOMAS MOORE

Sunday matin

Was not Iago perfection? particularly the last look. I was *close* to him (in the orchestra), and never saw an English countenance half so expressive.

I am acquainted with no *im*material sensuality so delightful as good acting; and, as it is fitting there should be good plays, now and then, besides Shakspeare's, I wish you or Campbell would write one:—the rest of 'us youth' have not heart enough.

You were cut up in the *Champion*—is it not so? this day so am I—even to *shocking* the editor. The critic writes well; and as, at present, poesy is not my passion predominant, and my snake of Aaron has swallowed up all the other serpents, I don't feel fractious. I send you the paper, which I mean to take in for the future. We go to M.'s together. Perhaps I shall see you before, but don't let me *bore* you, now nor ever.

Ever, as now, truly and affectionately, etc.

TO THOMAS MOORE

May 31, 1814

As I shall probably not see you here to-day, I write to request that, if not inconvenient to yourself, you will stay in town till *Sunday*; if not to gratify me, yet to please a great many others, who will be very sorry to lose you. As for myself, I can only repeat that I wish you would either remain a long time with us, or not come at all; for these *snatches* of society make the subsequent separations bitterer than ever.

I believe you think that I have not been quite fair with that Alpha and Omega of beauty, etc. with whom you would willingly have united me. But if you consider what her sister said on the subject, you will less wonder that my pride should have taken the alarm; particularly as nothing but the every-day flirtation of every-day people ever occurred between your heroine and myself. Had Lady —— appeared to wish it—or even *not* to oppose it—I would have gone on, and very possibly married (that is, *if* the other had been equally accordant) with the same indifference which has frozen over the 'Black Sea' of almost all my passions. It is that very indifference which makes me so uncertain and apparently capricious. It is not eagerness of new pursuits, but that nothing impresses me sufficiently to *fix*; neither do I feel disgusted, but simply indifferent to almost all excitements. The proof of this is, that obstacles, the slightest even, *stop* me. This can hardly be *timidity*, for I have done some impudent things too, in my time; and in almost all cases, opposition is a stimulus. In mine, it is not; if a straw were in my way, I could not stoop to pick it up.

I have sent this long tirade, because I would not have you suppose that I have been *trifling* designedly with you or others. If you think so, in the name of St. Hubert (the patron of antlers and hunters) let me be married out of hand—I don't care to whom, so it amuses any body else, and don't interfere with me much in the day time.

Ever, etc.

TO THOMAS MOORE

June 14, 1814

I *could* be very sentimental now, but I won't. The truth is, that I have been all my life trying to harden my heart, and have not yet quite succeeded—though there are great hopes—and you do not know how it sunk with your departure. What adds to my regret is having seen so little of you during your stay in this crowded desert, where one ought to be able to bear thirst like a camel,—the springs are so few, and most of them so muddy.

The newspapers will tell you all that is to be told of emperors, etc. They have dined, and supped, and shown their flat faces in all thoroughfares, and several saloons. Their uniforms are very becoming, but rather short in the skirts; and their conversation is a catechism, for which and the answers I refer you to those who have heard it.

I think of leaving town for Newstead soon. If so, I shall not be remote from your recess, and (unless Mrs. M. detains you at home over the caudle-cup and a new cradle) we will meet. You shall come to me, or I to you, as you like it;—but *meet* we will. An invitation from Aston has reached me, but I do not think I shall go. I have also heard of—— . . . I should like to see her again, for I have not met her for years; and though 'the light that ne'er can shine again' is set, I do not know that 'one dear smile like those of old' might not make me for a moment forget the 'dulness' of 'life's stream.'

I am going to R——'s to-night—to one of those suppers which '*ought* to be dinners.' I have hardly seen her, and never *him*, since you set out. I told you, you were the last link of that chain. As for ——, we have not syllabled one another's names since. The post will not permit me to continue my scrawl. More anon.

Ever, dear Moore, etc.

P.S.—Keep the Journal; I care not what becomes of it; and if it has amused you, I am glad that I kept it. *Lara* is finished, and I am copying him for my third vol., now collecting;—but *no separate* publication.

TO THOMAS MOORE

Hastings, August 3, 1814

By the time this reaches your dwelling, I shall (God wot) be in town again probably. I have been here renewing my acquaintance with my old friend Ocean; and I find his bosom as pleasant a pillow for an hour in the morning as his daughters of Paphos could be in the twilight. I have been swimming and eating turbot, and smuggling neat brandies and silk handkerchiefs,—and listening to my friend Hodgson's raptures about a pretty wife-elect of his,—and walking on cliffs, and tumbling down hills, and making the most of the *dolce far-niente* for the last fortnight. I met a son of Lord Erskine's, who says he has been married a year, and is the 'happiest of men;' and I have met the aforesaid H., who is also the 'happiest of men;' so, it is worth while being here, if only to witness the superlative felicity of these foxes, who have cut off their tails, and would persuade the rest to part with their brushes to keep them in countenance.

It rejoiceth me that you like *Lara*. Jeffrey is out with his 45th Number, which I suppose you have got. He is only too kind to me, in my share of it, and I begin to fancy myself a golden pheasant, upon the strength of the plumage wherewith he hath bedecked me. But then, *surgit amari*, etc.—the gentlemen of the *Champion*, and Perry, have got hold (I know not how) of the condolatory address to Lady Jersey on the picture-abduction by our Regent, and have published them—with my name, too, smack—without even asking leave, or inquiring whether or no! Damn their impudence, and damn every thing. It has put me out of patience, and so, I shall say no more about it.

You shall have *Lara* and *Jacque* (both with some additions) when out; but I am still demurring and delaying, and in a fuss, and so is Rogers in his way.

Newstead is to be mine again. Claughton forfeits twenty-five thousand pounds; but that don't prevent me from being very prettily ruined. I mean to bury myself there—and let my beard grow—and hate you all.

Oh! I have had the most amusing letter from Hogg, the Ettick minstrel and shepherd. He wants me to recommend him to Murray; and, speaking of his present bookseller, whose 'bills' are never 'lifted,' he adds, *totidem verbis*, 'God damn him and them both.' I laughed, and so would you too, at the way in which this execration is introduced. The said Hogg is a strange being, but of great, though uncouth, powers. I think very highly of him, as a poet; but he, and half of these Scotch and Lake troubadours, are spoilt by living in little circles and petty societies. London and the world is the only place to take the conceit out of a man— in the milling phrase. Scott, he says, is gone to the Orkneys in a gale of wind;— during which wind, he affirms, the said Scott, 'he is sure, is not at his ease,—to say the best of it.' Lord, Lord, if these home-keeping minstrels had crossed your Atlantic or my Mediterranean, and tasted a little open boating in a white squall—or a gale in 'the Gut'—or the 'Bay of Biscay,' with no gale at all— how it would enliven and introduce them to a few of the sensations!—to say nothing of an illicit amour or two upon shore, in the way of essay upon the Passions, beginning with simple adultery, and compounding it as they went along.

I have forwarded your letter to Murray,—by the way, you had addressed it to *Miller*. Pray write to me, and say what art thou doing? 'Not finished!'—Oons! how is this?—these 'flaws and starts' must be 'authorised by your grandam,' and are unbecoming of any other author. I was sorry to hear of your discrepancy with the ——s, or rather your abjuration of agreement. I don't want to be impertinent, or buffoon on a serious subject, and am therefore at a loss what to say.

I hope nothing will induce you to abate from the proper price of your poem, as long as there is a prospect of getting it. For my own part, I have *seriously* and *not whiningly* (for that is not my way—at least, it used not to be) neither hopes, nor prospects, and scarcely even wishes. I am, in some respects, happy, but not in a manner that can or ought to last,—but enough of that. The worst of it is, I feel quite enervated and indifferent. I really do not know, if Jupiter were to offer me my choice of the contents of his benevolent cask, what I would pick out of it. If I was born, as the nurses say, with a 'silver spoon in my mouth,' it has stuck in my throat, and spoiled my palate, so that nothing put into it is swallowed with much relish,—unless it be cayenne. However, I have grievances enough to occupy me that way too ;—but for fear of adding to yours by this pestilent long diatribe, I postpone the reading of them, *sine die*.

Ever, dear M., yours, etc.

P.S.—Don't forget my godson. You could not have fixed on a fitter porter for his sins than me, being used to carry double without inconvenience. . . .

TO THOMAS MOORE

August 12, 1814

I was *not* alone, nor will be while I can help it. Newstead is not yet decided. Claughton is to make a grand effort by Saturday week to complete,—if not, he must give up twenty-five thousand pounds and the estate, with expenses, etc., etc. If I resume the Abbacy, you shall have due notice, and a cell set apart for your reception, with a pious welcome. Rogers I have not seen, but Larry and Jacky came out a few days ago. Of their effect I know nothing. . . .

There is something very amusing in *your* being an *Edinburgh Reviewer*. You know, I suppose, that Thurlow is none of the placidest, and may possibly enact some tragedy on being told that he is only a fool. If, now, Jeffrey were to be slain on account of an article of yours, there would be a fine conclusion. For my part, as Mrs. Winifred Jenkins says, 'he has done the handsome thing by me,' particularly in his last number ; so, he is the best of men and the ablest of critics, and I won't have him killed—though I dare say many wish he were, for being so good-humoured.

Before I left Hastings I got in a passion with an ink-bottle, which I flung out of the window one night with a vengeance ;— and what then? Why, next morning I was horrified by seeing that it had struck, and split upon, the petticoat of Euterpe's graven image in the garden, and grimed her as if it were on purpose. Only think of my distress,—and the epigrams that might be engendered on the Muse and her misadventure.

I had an adventure almost as ridiculous, at some private theatricals near Cambridge—though of a different description —since I saw you last. I quarrelled with a man in the dark for asking me who I was (insolently enough to be sure), and followed him into the green-room (a *stable*) in a rage, amongst a set of people I never saw before. He turned out to be a low comedian, engaged to act with the amateurs, and to be a civil-spoken man enough, when he found out that nothing very pleasant was to be got by rudeness. But you would have been amused with the row, and the dialogue, and the dress—or rather the undress—of the party, where I had introduced myself in a devil of a hurry, and the astonishment that ensued. I had gone out of the theatre, for coolness, into the garden;— there I had tumbled over some dogs, and, coming away from them in very ill humour, encountered the man in a worse, which produced all this confusion.

Well—and why don't you 'launch?'—Now is your time. The people are tolerably tired with me, and not very much enamoured of Wordsworth, who has just spawned a quarto of metaphysical blank verse, which is nevertheless only a part of a poem.

Murray talks of divorcing Larry and Jacky—a bad sign for the authors, who, I suppose, will be divorced too, and throw the blame upon one another. Seriously, I don't care a cigar about it, and I don't see why Sam should.

Let me hear from and of you and my godson. If a daughter, the name will do quite as well. Ever, etc.

TO THOMAS MOORE

Newstead Abbey, September 15, 1814

This is the fourth letter I have begun to you within the month. Whether I shall finish or not, or burn it like the rest, I know not. When we meet, I will explain *why* I have not written— *why* I have not asked you here, as I wished—with a great many other *whys* and wherefores, which will keep cold. In short, you must excuse all my seeming omissions and commissions, and grant me more *re*mission than St. Athanasius will to yourself, if you lop off a single shred of mystery from his pious puzzle. It is my creed (and it may be St. Athanasius's too) that your article on Thurlow will get somebody killed, and *that*, on the *Saints* get him damned afterwards, which will be quite enow for one number. Oons, Tom! you must not meddle just now with the incomprehensible; for if Johanna Southcote turns out to be . . . .

Now for a little egotism. My affairs stand thus. To-morrow I shall know whether a circumstance of importance enough to change many of my plans will occur or not. If it does not, I am off for Italy next month, and London, in the mean time, next week. I have got back Newstead and twenty-five thousand pounds (out of twenty-eight paid already),—as a 'sacrifice,' the late purchaser calls it, and he may choose his own name. I have paid some of my debts, and contracted others; but I have a few thousand pounds, which I can't spend after my own heart in this climate, and so, I shall go back to the south. Hobhouse, I think and hope, will go with me; but, whether he will or not, I shall. I want to see Venice, and the Alps, and Parmesan cheeses, and look at the coast of Greece, or rather Epirus, from Italy, as I once did—or fancied I did— that of Italy, when off Corfu. All this, however, depends upon an event, which may, or may not, happen. Whether it will, I shall know probably to-morrow; and, if it does, I can't well go abroad at present.

Pray pardon this parenthetical scrawl. You shall hear from me again soon;—I don't call this an answer.

Ever most affectionately, etc.

TO THOMAS MOORE

Newstead Abbey, Sept. 20, 1814

Here's to her who long
    Hath waked the poet's sigh!
The girl who gave to song
    What gold could never buy.

My dear Moore,

I am going to be married—that is, I am accepted, and one usually hopes the rest will follow. My mother of the Gracchi (that *are* to be), *you* think too strait-laced for me, although the paragon of only children, and invested with 'golden opinions of all sorts of men,' and full of 'most blest conditions' as Desdemona herself. Miss Milbanke is the lady, and I have her father's invitation to proceed there in my elect capacity,—which, however, I cannot do till I have settled some business in London, and got a blue coat.

She is said to be an heiress, but of that I really know nothing certainly, and shall not enquire. But I do know, that she has talents and excellent qualities; and you will not deny her judgment, after having refused six suitors and taken me.

Now, if you have any thing to say against this, pray do; my mind's made up, positively fixed, determined, and therefore I will listen to reason, because now it can do no harm. Things may occur to break it off, but I will hope not. In the mean time, I tell you (a *secret*, by the by,—at least till I know she wishes it to be public) that I have proposed and am accepted. You need not be in a hurry to wish me joy, for one mayn't be married for months. I am going to town to-morrow; but expect to be here, on my way there, within a fortnight.

If this had not happened, I should have gone to Italy. In my way down, perhaps, you will meet me at Nottingham, and come over with me here. I need not say that nothing will give me greater pleasure. I must, of course, reform thoroughly; and, seriously, if I can contribute to her happiness, I shall secure my own. She is so good a person, that—that—in short, I wish I was a better. Ever, etc.

TO THOMAS MOORE

October 14, 1814

An there were any thing in marriage that would make a difference between my friends and me, particularly in your case, I would 'none on't.' My agent sets off for Durham next

week, and I shall follow him, taking Newstead and you in my
way. I certainly did not address Miss Milbanke with these
views, but it is likely she may prove a considerable *parti*. All
her father can give, or leave her, he will; and from her childless uncle, Lord Wentworth, whose barony, it is supposed,
will devolve on Ly. Milbanke (*his* sister), she has expectations.
But these will depend upon his own disposition, which seems
very partial towards her. She is an only child, and Sir R.'s
estates, though dipped by electioneering, are considerable.
Part of them are settled on her; but whether *that* will be
dowered now, I do not know,—though, from what has been
intimated to me, it probably will. The lawyers are to settle this
among them, and I am getting my property into matrimonial
array, and myself ready for the journey to Seaham, which I
must make in a week or ten days.

I certainly did not dream that she was attached to me,
which it seems she has been for some time. I also thought her
of a very cold disposition, in which I was also mistaken—it is a
long story, and I won't trouble you with it. As to her virtues,
etc., etc., you will hear enough of them (for she is a kind of
pattern in the north), without my running into a display on the
subject. It is well that *one* of us is of such fame, since there is
sad deficit in the *morale* of that article upon my part,—all
owing to my 'bitch of a star,' as Captain Tranchemont says of
his planet.

Don't think you have not said enough of me in your article
on T[hurlow]; what more could or need be said?

Your long-delayed and expected work—I suppose you will
take fright at *The Lord of the Isles* and Scott now. You must
do as you like,—I have said my say. You ought to fear comparison with none, and any one would stare, who heard you
were so tremulous,—though, after all, I believe it is the surest
sign of talent. Good morning. I hope we shall meet soon, but I
will write again, and perhaps you will meet me at Nottingham.
Pray say so.

P.S.—If this union is productive, you shall name the first
fruits.

TO THOMAS MOORE

Halnaby, Darlington, January 10, 1815

I was married this day week. The parson has pronounced it
—Perry has announced it—and the *Morning Post*, also, under
the head of 'Lord Byron's Marriage'—as if it were a fabrica-
tion, or the puff-direct of a new stay-maker.

Now for thine affairs. I have redde thee upon the Fathers,
and it is excellent well. Positively, you must not leave off
reviewing. You shine in it—you kill in it: and this article has
been taken for Sydney Smith's (as I heard in town), which
proves not only your proficiency in parsonology, but that you
have all the airs of a veteran critic at your first onset. So,
prithee, go on and prosper.

Scott's *Lord of the Isles* is out—'the mail-coach copy' I
have, by special licence, of Murray. . . .

Now is *your* time;—you will come upon them newly and
freshly. It is impossible to read what you have lately done
(verse or prose) without seeing that you have trained on tenfold. —— has floundered ; —— has foundered. *I* have tried the
rascals (*i.e.* the public) with my Harrys and Larrys, Pilgrims
and Pirates. Nobody but S——y [Southey] has done any thing
worth a slice of bookseller's pudding, and *he* has not luck
enough to be found out in doing a good thing. Now, Tom, is
thy time—'Oh, joyful day!—I would not take a knighthood
for thy fortune.' Let me hear from you soon, and believe me
ever, etc.

P.S.—Lady Byron is vastly well. How are Mrs. Moore and
Joe Atkinson's 'Graces'? We must present our women to one
another.

TO THOMAS MOORE

Seaham, Stockton-on-Tees, February 2, 1815

I have heard from London that you have left Chatsworth
and all the women full of 'entusymusy' about you, personally
and poetically; and, in particular, that 'When first I met thee'
has been quite overwhelming in its effect. I told you it was one

of the best things you ever wrote, though that dog Power wanted you to omit part of it. They are all regretting your absence at Chatsworth, according to my informant—'all the ladies quite,' etc., etc., etc. Stap my vitals!

Well, now you have got home again—which I dare say is as agreeable as a 'draught of cool small beer to the scorched palate of a waking sot'—now you have got home again, I say, probably I shall hear from you. Since I wrote last, I have been transferred to my father-in-law's, with my lady and my lady's maid, etc., etc., etc., and the treacle-moon is over, and I am awake, and find myself married. My spouse and I agree to— and in—admiration. Swift says 'no *wise* man ever married;' but, for a fool, I think it the most ambrosial of all possible future states. I still think one ought to marry upon *lease*; but am very sure I should renew mine at the expiration, though next term were for ninety and nine years.

I wish you would respond, for I am here *oblitusque meorum obliviscendus et illis*. Pray tell me what is going on in the way of intriguery, and how the w——s and rogues of the upper Beggar's Opera go on—or rather go off—in or after marriage; or who are going to break any particular command- ment. Upon this dreary coast, we have nothing but county meetings and shipwrecks: and I have this day dined upon fish, which probably dined upon the crews of several colliers lost in the late gales. But I saw the sea once more in all the glories of surf and foam,—almost equal to the Bay of Biscay, and the interesting white squalls and short seas of Archipelago memory.

My papa, Sir Ralpho, hath recently made a speech at a Durham tax-meeting; and not only at Durham, but here, several times since after dinner. He is now, I believe, speaking it to himself (I left him in the middle) over various decanters, which can neither interrupt him nor fall asleep,—as might possibly have been the case with some of his audience. Ever thine,
                                                                    B.

I must go to tea—damn tea. I wish it was Kinnaird's brandy, and with you to lecture me about it.

z

TO THOMAS MOORE

February 10, 1815

My dear Tom,

Jeffrey has been so very kind about me and my damnable works, that I would not be indirect or equivocal with him, even for a friend. So, it may be as well to tell him that it is not mine; but that if I did not firmly and truly believe it to be much better than I could offer, I would never have troubled him or you about it. You can judge between you how far it is admissible, and reject it, if not of the right sort. For my own part, I have no interest in the article one way or the other, further than to oblige ——; and should the composition be a good one, it can hurt neither party,—nor, indeed, any one, saving and excepting Mr. ——.

Curse catch me if I know what H[obhouse] means or meaned about the demonstrative pronoun, but I admire your fear of being inoculated with the same. Have you never found out that you have a particular style of your own, which is as distinct from all other people, as Hafiz of Shiraz from Hafiz of the *Morning Post?*

So you allowed B—— and such like to hum and haw you, or, rather, Lady Jersey out of her compliment, and *me* out of mine. Sun-burn me, but this was pitiful-hearted. However, I will tell her all about it when I see her.

Bell desires me to say all kinds of civilities, and assure you of her recognition and high consideration. I will tell you of our movements south, which may be in about three weeks from this present writing. By the way, don't engage yourself in any travelling expedition, as I have a plan of travel into Italy, which we will discuss. And then, think of the poesy where-withal we should overflow, from Venice to Vesuvius, to say nothing of Greece, through all which—God willing—we might perambulate in one twelve months. If I take my wife, you can take yours; and if I leave mine, you may do the same. 'Mind you stand by me in either case, Brother Bruin.'

And believe me, inveterately yours,

                                                            B.

TO THOMAS MOORE

March 2, 1815

My dear Thom,

Jeffrey has sent me the most friendly of all possible letters, and has accepted H[obhouse]'s article. He says he has long liked not only, etc., etc., but my character. This must be *your* doing, you dog—ar'nt you ashamed of yourself, knowing me so well? This is what one gets for having you for a father confessor.

I feel merry enough to send you a sad song. You once asked me for some words which you would set. Now you may set or not, as you like,—but there they are in a legible hand; and not in mine, but of my own scribbling; so you may say of them what you please. Why don't you write to me? I shall make you 'a speech' if you don't respond quickly.

I am in such a state of sameness and stagnation, and so totally occupied in consuming the fruits—and sauntering—and playing dull games at cards—and yawning—and trying to read old Annual Registers and the daily papers—and gathering shells on the shore—and watching the growth of stunted gooseberry bushes in the garden—that I have neither time nor sense to say more than yours ever,   B.

P.S.—I open my letter again to put a question to you. What would Lady Cork, or any other fashionable Pidcock, give to collect you and Jeffrey and me to *one* party? I have been answering his letter, which suggested this dainty query. I can't help laughing at the thoughts of your face and mine; and our anxiety to keep the Aristarch in good humour during the *early* part of a compotation, till we got drunk enough to make him 'a speech.' I think the critic would have much the best of us— of one, at least—for I don't think diffidence (I mean social) is a disease of yours.

TO THOMAS MOORE

April 23, 1815

Lord Wentworth died last week. The bulk of his property (from seven to eight thousand per ann.) is entailed on Lady

Milbanke and Lady Byron. The first is gone to take possession in Leicestershire, and attend the funeral, etc. this day. . . .

I have mentioned the facts of the settlement of Lord W.'s property, because the newspapers, with their usual accuracy, have been making all kinds of blunders in their statement. His will is just as expected—the principal part settled on Lady Milbanke (now Noel) and Bell, and a separate estate left for sale to pay debts (which are not great) and legacies to his natural son and daughter.

Mrs. Wilmot's tragedy was last night damned. They may bring it on again, and probably will; but damned it was,—not a word of the last act audible. I went (*malgré* that I ought to have stayed at home in sackcloth for unc., but I could not resist the *first* night of any thing) to a private and quiet nook of my private box, and witnessed the whole process. The first three acts, with transient gushes of applause, oozed patiently but heavily on. I must say it was badly acted, particularly by Kean, who was groaned upon in the third act,—something about 'horror—such a horror' was the cause. Well! the fourth act became as muddy and turbid as need be; but the fifth— what Garrick used to call (like a fool) the *concoction* of a play —the fifth act stuck fast at the king's prayer. You know he says, 'he never went to bed without saying them, and did not like to omit them now.' But he was no sooner upon his knees, than the audience got upon their legs—the damnable pit—and roared, and groaned, and hissed, and whistled. Well, that was choked a little; but the ruffian-scene—the penitent peasantry —and killing the bishop and princes—oh, it was all over! The curtain fell upon unheard actors, and the announcement attempted by Kean for Monday was equally ineffectual. Mrs. Bartley was so frightened, that, though the people were tolerably quiet, the epilogue was quite inaudible to half the house. In short,—you know all. I clapped till my hands were skinless, and so did Sir James Mackintosh, who was with me in the box. All the world were in the house, from the Jerseys, Greys, etc., etc., downwards. But it would not do. It is, after all, not an *acting* play; good language, but no power. . . . Women (saving Joanna Baillie) cannot write tragedy: they have not seen enough nor felt enough of life for it. I think Semiramis or Catherine II. might have written (could they have been un-queened) a rare play. . . .

It is, however, a good warning not to risk or write tragedies. I never had much bent that way; but if I had, this would have cured me.

Ever, *carissime* Thom.,
Thine, B.

TO THOMAS MOORE

13 Piccadilly Terrace, June 12, 1815

I have nothing to offer in behalf of my late silence, except the most inveterate and ineffable laziness; but I am too supine to invent a lie, or I *certainly* should, being ashamed of the truth. Kinnaird, I hope, has appeased your magnanimous indignation at his blunders. I wished and wish you were in the Committee, with all my heart. It seems so hopeless a business, that the company of a friend would be quite consoling,—but more of this when we meet. In the mean time, you are en-treated to prevail upon Mrs. Esterre to engage herself. I believe she has been written to, but your influence, in person or proxy, would probably go further than our proposals. What they are, I know not; all *my* new function consists in listening to the despair of Cavendish Bradshaw, the hopes of Kinnaird, the wishes of Lord Essex, the complaints of Whitbread, and the calculations of Peter Moore, all of which, and whom, seem totally at variance. C. Bradshaw wants to light the theatre with *gas*, which may, perhaps (if the vulgar be be-lieved), poison half the audience, and all the *dramatis personæ*. Essex has endeavoured to persuade Kean not to get drunk; the consequence of which is, that he has never been sober since. Kinnaird, with equal success, would have convinced Raymond that he, the said Raymond, had too much salary. Whitbread wants us to assess the pit another sixpence,—a damned insidious proposition,—which will end in an O. P. combustion. To crown all, Robins, the auctioneer has the impudence to be displeased, because he has no dividend. The villain is a proprietor of shares, and a long-lunged orator in the meetings. I hear he has prophesied our incapacity,—'a fore-gone conclusion,' whereof I hope to give him signal proofs before we are done.

Will you give us an opera? No, I'll be sworn; but I wish you would. . . .

To go on with the poetical world, Walter Scott has gone back to Scotland. Murray, the bookseller, has been cruelly cudgelled of misbegotten knaves, 'in Kendal Green,' at Newington Butts, in his way home from a purlieu dinner,—and robbed—would you believe it?—of three or four bonds of forty pound a piece, and a seal-ring of his grandfather's, worth a million! This is his version,—but others opine that D'Israeli, with whom he dined, knocked him down with his last publication, *The Quarrels of Authors*, in a dispute about copyright. Be that as it may, the newspapers have teemed with his *injuria formæ*, and he has been embrocated, and invisible to all but the apothecary ever since.

Lady B. is better than three months advanced in her progress towards maternity, and, we hope, likely to go well through with it. We have been very little out this season, as I wish to keep her quiet in her present situation. Her father and mother have changed their names to Noel, in compliance with Lord Wentworth's will, and in complaisance to the property bequeathed by him.

I hear that you have been gloriously received by the Irish,—and so you ought. But don't let them kill you with claret and kindness at the national dinner in your honour, which, I hear and hope, is in contemplation. If you will tell me the day, I'll get drunk myself on this side of the water, and waft you an applauding hiccup over the Channel.

Of politics, we have nothing but the yell for war; and C——h [Castlereagh] is preparing his head for the pike, on which we shall see it carried before he has done. The loan has made every body sulky. I hear often from Paris, but in direct contradiction to the home statements of our hirelings. Of domestic doings, there has been nothing since Lady D——. Not a divorce stirring,—but a good many in embryo, in the shape of marriages.

I enclose you an epistle received this morning from I know not whom; but I think it will amuse you. The writer must be a rare fellow.

P.S.—A gentleman named D'Alton (not your Dalton) has sent me a National Poem called *Dermid*. The same cause which prevented my writing to you operated against my wish to write to him an epistle of thanks. If you see him, will you make all kinds of fine speeches for me, and tell him that I am the laziest and most ungrateful of mortals?

A word more;—don't let Sir John Stevenson (as an evidence on trials for copy-right, etc.) talk about the price of your next poem, or they will come upon you for the *property tax* for it. I am serious, and have just heard a long story of the rascally tax-men making Scott pay for his. So, take care. Three hundred is a devil of a deduction out of three thousand.

TO THOMAS MOORE

Terrace, Piccadilly, October 31, 1815

I have not been able to ascertain precisely the time of duration of the stock market; but I believe it is a good time for selling out, and I hope so. First, because I shall see you; and, next, because I shall receive certain monies on behalf of Lady B., the which will materially conduce to my comfort,—I wanting (as the duns say) 'to make up a sum.'

Yesterday, I dined out with a large-ish party, where were Sheridan and Colman, Harry Harris of Covent Garden, and his brother, Sir Gilbert Heathcote, Douglas Kinnaird, and others, of note and notoriety. Like other parties of the kind, it was first silent, then talky, then argumentative, then disputatious, then unintelligible, then altogethery, then inarticulate, and then drunk. When we had reached the last step of this glorious ladder, it was difficult to get down again without stumbling; and, to crown all, Kinnaird and I had to conduct Sheridan down a damned corkscrew staircase, which had certainly been constructed before the discovery of fermented liquors, and to which no legs, however crooked, could possibly accommodate themselves. We deposited him safe at home, where his man, evidently used to the business, waited to receive him in the hall.

Both he and Colman were, as usual, very good; but I carried away much wine, and the wine had previously carried away my memory; so that all was hiccup and happiness for the last hour or so, and I am not impregnated with any of the conversation. Perhaps you heard of a late answer of Sheridan to the watchman who found him bereft of that 'divine particle of air,' called reason, ... He, the watchman, who found Sherry in the street, fuddled and bewildered, and almost insensible, 'Who are *you*, sir?'—no answer. 'What's your name?'—a hiccup. 'What's your name?'—Answer, in a slow, deliberate, and impassive tone—'Wilberforce!!!' Is not that Sherry all over?—and, to my mind, excellent. Poor fellow, *his* very dregs are better than the 'first sprightly runnings' of others.

My paper is full, and I have a grievous head-ach.

P.S.—Lady B. is in full progress. Next month will bring to light (with the aid of 'Juno Lucina, *fer opem*,' or rather *opes*, for the last are most wanted,) the tenth wonder of the world—Gil Blas being the eighth, and he (my son's father) the ninth.

TO THOMAS MOORE

January 5, 1816

I hope Mrs. M. is quite re-established. The little girl was born on the 10th of December last; her name is Augusta *Ada* (the second a very antique family name,—I believe not used since the reign of King John). She was, and is, very flourishing and fat, and reckoned very large for her days—squalls and sucks incessantly. Are you answered? Her mother is doing very well, and up again.

I have now been married a year on the second of this month—heigh-ho! I have seen nobody lately much worth noting, except Sebastiani and another general of the Gauls, once or twice at dinners out of doors. Sebastiani is a fine, foreign, villanous-looking, intelligent, and very agreeable man; his compatriot is more of the *petit-maître* and younger, but I should think not at all of the same intellectual calibre with the Corsican—which Sebastiani, you know, is, and a cousin of Napoleon's.

Are you never to be expected in town again? To be sure, there is no one here of the fifteen hundred fillers of hot rooms, called the fashionable world. My approaching papa-ship detained us for advice, etc., etc., though I would as soon be here as any where else on this side of the Straits of Gibraltar.

I would gladly—or, rather, sorrowfully—comply with your request of a dirge for the poor girl you mention. But how can I write on one I have never seen or known? Besides, you will do it much better yourself. I could not write upon any thing, without some personal experience and foundation: far less on a theme so peculiar. Now, you have both in this case; and, if you had neither, you have more imagination, and would never fail.

This is but a dull scrawl, and I am but a dull fellow. Just at present, I am absorbed in 500 contradictory contemplations, though with but one object in view—which will probably end in nothing, as most things we wish do. But never mind,—as somebody says, 'for the blue sky bends over all.' I only could be glad, if it bent over me where it is a little bluer; like the 'skyish top of blue Olympus,' which, by the way, looked very white when I last saw it.   Ever, etc.

TO THOMAS MOORE

February 29, 1816

I have not answered your letter for a time; and, at present, the reply to part of it might extend to such a length, that I shall delay it till it can be made in person, and then I will shorten it as much as I can.

In the mean time, I am at war 'with all the world and his wife;' or rather, 'all the world and *my* wife' are at war with me, and have not yet crushed me,—whatever they *may* do. I don't know that in the course of a hair-breadth existence I was ever, at home or abroad, in a situation so completely uprooting of present pleasure, or rational hope for the future, as this same. I say this, because I think so, and feel it. But I shall not sink under it the more for that mode of considering the question—I have made up my mind.

By the way, however, you must not believe all you hear on the subject; and don't attempt to defend me. If you succeeded in that, it would be a mortal, or an immortal, offence—who can bear refutation? I have but a very short answer for those whom it concerns; and all the activity of myself and some vigorous friends have not yet fixed on any tangible ground or personage, on which or with whom I can discuss matters, in a summary way, with a fair pretext;—though I nearly had *nailed one* yesterday, but he evaded by—what was judged by others—a satisfactory explanation. I speak of *circulators*— against whom I have no enmity, though I must act according to the common code of usage, when I hit upon those of the serious order.

Now for other matters—poesy, for instance. Leigh Hunt's poem is a devilish good one—quaint, here and there, but with the substratum of originality, and with poetry about it, that will stand the test. I do not say this because he has inscribed it to me, which I am sorry for, as I should otherwise have begged you to review it in the *Edinburgh*. It is really deserving of much praise, and a favourable critique in the *E. R.* would but do it justice, and set it up before the public eye, where it ought to be.

How are you? and where? I have not the most distant idea what I am going to do myself—or with myself—or where—or what. I had a few weeks ago, some things to say that would have made you laugh; but they tell me now that I must not laugh, and so I have been very serious—and am.

I have not been very well—with a *liver* complaint—but am much better within the last fortnight, though still under Iatrical advice. I have latterly seen a little of——.

I must go and dress to dine. My little girl is in the country, and, they tell me, is a very fine child, and now nearly three months old. Lady Noel (my mother-in-law, or, rather, *at* law) is at present overlooking it. Her daughter (Miss Milbanke

that was) is, I believe, in London with her father. A Mrs. C.
(now a kind of housekeeper and spy of Lady N.'s), who, in her
better days, was a washerwoman, is supposed to be—by the
learned—very much the occult cause of our late domestic
discrepancies.

In all this business, I am the sorriest for Sir Ralph. He and I
are equally punished, though *magis pares quam similes* in our
affliction. Yet it is hard for both to suffer for the fault of one,
and so it is—I shall be separated from my wife; he will retain
his.   Ever, etc.

TO THOMAS MOORE

March 8, 1816

I rejoice in your promotion as Chairman and Charitable
Steward, etc. etc. These be dignities which await only the
virtuous. But then, recollect you are *six* and *thirty*, (I speak this
enviously—not of your age, but the 'honour—love—obedience
—troops of friends,' which accompany it,) and I have eight
years good to run before I arrive at such hoary perfection; by
which time,—if I *am* at all,—it will probably be in a state of
grace or progressing merits.

I must set you right in one point, however. The fault was
not—no, nor even the misfortune—in my 'choice' (unless in
choosing at all)—for I do not believe—and I must say it, in the
very dregs of all this bitter business—that there ever was a
better, or even a brighter, a kinder, or a more amiable and
agreeable being than Lady B. I never had, nor can have, any
reproach to make her, while with me. Where there is blame, it
belongs to myself, and, if I cannot redeem, I must bear it.

Her nearest relatives are a . . . . —my circumstances have been
and are in a state of great confusion—my health has been a
good deal disordered, and my mind ill at ease for a considerable period. Such are the causes (I do not name them as
excuses) which have frequently driven me into excess, and dis-
qualified my temper for comfort. Something also may be
attributed to the strange and desultory habits which, becoming

my own master at an early age, and scrambling about, over and through the world, may have induced. I still, however, think that, if I had a fair chance, by being placed in even a tolerable situation, I might have gone on fairly. But that seems hopeless,—and there is nothing more to be said. At present— except my health, which is better (it is odd, but agitation or contest of any kind gives a rebound to my spirits and sets me up for the time)—I have to battle with all kinds of unpleasant-nesses, including private and pecuniary difficulties, etc., etc.

I believe I may have said this before to you, but I risk repeating it. It is nothing to bear the *privations* of adversity, or, more properly, ill fortune; but my pride recoils from its *indignities*. However, I have no quarrel with that same pride, which will, I think, buckler me through every thing. If my heart could have been broken, it would have been so years ago, and by events more afflicting than these.

I agree with you (to turn from this topic to our shop), that I have written too much. The last things were, however, pub-lished very reluctantly by me, and for reasons I will explain when we meet. I know not why I have dwelt so much on the same scenes, except that I find them fading, or *confusing* (if such a word may be) in my memory, in the midst of present turbulence and pressure, and I felt anxious to stamp before the die was worn out. I now break it. With those countries, and events connected with them, all my really poetical feelings begin and end. Were I to try, I could make nothing of any other subject, and that I have apparently exhausted. 'Wo to him,' says Voltaire, 'who says all he could say on any subject.' There are some on which, perhaps, I could have said still more: but I leave them all, and too soon.

Do you remember the lines I sent you early last year, which you still have? I don't wish (like Mr. Fitzgerald, in the *Morning Post*) to claim the character of 'Vates' in all its translations, but were they not a little prophetic? I mean those beginning, 'There's not a joy the world can,' etc., etc., on which I rather pique myself as being the truest, though the most melancholy, I ever wrote.

What a scrawl have I sent you! You say nothing of yourself,

except that you are a Lancasterian churchwarden, and an encourager of mendicants. When are you out? and how is your family? My child is very well and flourishing, I hear; but I must see also. I feel no disposition to resign it to the contagion of its grandmother's society, though I am unwilling to take it from the mother. It is weaned, however, and something about it must be decided. Ever, etc.

A JOURNAL

Clarens, Septr. 18, 1816

Yesterday September 17th, 1816—I set out (with H[obhouse]) on an excursion of some days to the Mountains. I shall keep a short journal of each day's progress for my Sister Augusta.

Septr. 17th

Rose at five; left Diodati about seven, in one of the country carriages (a Charaban), our servants on horseback: weather very fine; the Lake calm and clear; Mont Blanc and the Aiguille of Argentières both very distinct; the borders of the Lake beautiful. Reached Lausanne before Sunset; stopped and slept at Ouchy.

H. went to dine with a Mr. Okeden. I remained at our Caravansera (though invited to the house of H.'s friend—too lazy or tired, or something else, to go), and wrote a letter to Augusta. Went to bed at nine—sheets damp: swore and stripped them off and flung them—Heaven knows where: wrapt myself up in the blankets, and slept like a child of a month's existence till 5 o'Clock of

Septr. 18th

Called by Berger (my Courier who acts as Valet for a day or two, the learned Fletcher being left in charge of Chattels at Diodati): got up. H. walked on before. A mile from Lausanne the road overflowed by the lake; got on horseback and rode till within a mile of Vevay. The Colt young, but went very well; overtook H., and resumed the carriage, which is an open one. Stopped at Vevay two hours (the *second* time I had visited it); walked to the church; view from the Churchyard superb; within it General Ludlow's (the Regicide's) monument—black marble—long inscription—Latin, but simple, particularly the latter part, in which his wife (Margaret de Thomas) records her long, her tried, and unshaken affection; he was an Exile *two and thirty years*—one of King's (Charles's) Judges—a fine fellow. I remember reading his memoirs in January 1815 (at Halnaby)—the first part of them very amusing, the latter less so; I little thought, at the time of their perusal by me, of seeing his tomb. Near him Broughton (who read King Charles's sentence to Charles Stuart) is buried, with a queer and rather canting, but still a Republican, epitaph. Ludlow's house shown; it retains still its inscription—*Omne solum forti patria*. Walked down to the Lake side; servants, Carriage, saddle-horses—all set off and left us *plantés là*, by some mistake; and we walked on after them towards Clarens: H—— ran on before, and overtook them at last. Arrived the second time (1st time was by water) at Clarens, beautiful Clarens! Went to Chillon through Scenery worthy of I know not whom; went over the Castle of Chillon again. On our return met an English party in a carriage; a lady in it fast asleep!—fast asleep in the most anti-narcotic spot in the world —excellent! I remember, at Chamouni, in the very eyes of Mont Blanc, hearing another woman, English also, exclaim to her party 'did you ever see any thing more *rural?*'—as if it was Highgate, or Hampstead, or Brompton, or Hayes,— '*Rural!*' quotha!—Rocks, pines, torrents, Glaciers, Clouds and Summits of eternal snow far above them—and '*Rural!*' I did not know the thus exclaiming fair one, but she was a very good kind of a woman.

After a slight and short dinner, we visited the Château de Clarens; an English woman has rented it recently (it was not let when I saw it first); the roses are gone with their Summer; the family out, but the servants desired us to walk over the interior of the mansion. Saw on the table of the saloon Blair's

sermons and somebody else's (I forget who's) sermons, and a
set of noisy children. Saw all worth seeing, and then descended
to the 'Bosquet de Julie,' etc., etc.; our guide full of *Rousseau*,
whom he is eternally confounding with *St. Preux*, and mixing
the man and the book. On the steps of a cottage in the village,
I saw a young paysan*ne*, beautiful as Julie herself. Went again
as far as Chillon to revisit the little torrent from the hill behind
it. Sunset reflected in the lake. Have to get up at 5 to-morrow
to cross the mountains on horseback—carriage to be sent
round; lodged at my old Cottage—hospitable and comfortable; tired with a longish ride on the Colt, and the subsequent
jolting of the Charaban, and my scramble in the hot sun. Shall
go to bed, thinking of you, dearest Augusta.

Mem. The Corporal who showed the wonders of Chillon
was as drunk as Blucher, and (to my mind) as great a man. He
was *deaf* also, and thinking every one else so, roared out the
legends of the castle so fearfully that H. got out of humour.
However, we saw things from the Gallows to the Dungeons
(the *Potence* and the *Cachots*), and returned to Clarens with
more freedom than belonged to the 15th Century.

September 19

At Clarens—the only book (except the Bible), a translation
of '*Cecilia*' (Miss Burney's *Cecilia*); and the owner of the
Cottage had also called her dog (a fat Pug ten years old, and
hideous as *Tip*) after Cecilia's (or rather Delville's) dog, Fidde.

Rose at five: order the carriage round. Crossed the mountains to Montbovon on horseback, and on Mules, and, by
dint of scrambling on foot also; the whole route beautiful as a
Dream, and now to me almost as indistinct. I am so tired; for
though healthy, I have not the strength I possessed but a few
years ago. At Mont Davant we breakfasted; afterwards, on a
steep ascent dismounted, tumbled down, and cut a finger open;
the baggage also got loose and fell down a ravine, till stopped
by a large tree; swore; recovered baggage; horse tired and
dropping; mounted Mule. At the approach of the summit of
Dent Jamant dismounted again with H. and all the party.
Arrived at a lake in the very nipple of the bosom of the Moun-

tain; left our quadrupeds with a Shepherd, and ascended further; came to some snow in patches, upon which my forehead's perspiration fell like rain, making the same dints as in a sieve; the chill of the wind and the snow turned me giddy, but I scrambled on and upwards. H. went to the highest *pinnacle*; I did not, but paused within a few yards (at an opening of the Cliff). In coming down, the Guide tumbled three times; I fell a laughing, and tumbled too—the descent luckily soft, though steep and slippery: H. also fell, but nobody hurt. The whole of the Mountain superb. A Shepherd on a very steep and high cliff playing upon his *pipe*; very different from *Arcadia*, (where I saw the pastors with a long Musquet instead of a Crook, and pistols in their Girdles). Our Swiss Shepherd's pipe was sweet, and his tune agreeable. Saw a cow strayed; am told that they often break their necks on and over the crags. Descended to Montbovon; pretty scraggy village, with a wild river and a wooden bridge. H. went to fish—caught one. Our carriage not come; our horses, mules, etc. knocked up; ourselves fatigued; but so much the better—I shall sleep.

The view from the highest points of to-day's journey comprized on one side the greatest part of Lake Leman; on the other, the valleys and mountains of the Canton of Fribourg, and an immense plain, with the Lakes of Neuchâtel and Morat, and all which the borders of these and of the Lake of Geneva inherit; we had both sides of the Jura before us in one point of view, with Alps in plenty. In passing a ravine, the Guide recommended strenuously a quickening of pace, as the Stones fall with great rapidity and occasional damage; the advice is excellent, but, like most good advice, impracticable, the road being so rough in this precise point, that neither mules, nor mankind, nor horses, can make any violent progress. Passed without fractures or menace thereof.

The music of the Cows' bells (for their wealth, like the Patriarchs', is cattle) in the pastures, (which reach to a height far above any mountains in Britain), and the Shepherds' shouting to us from crag to crag, and playing on their reeds where the steeps appeared almost inaccessible, with the surrounding scenery, realized all that I have ever heard or imagined of a pastoral existence:—much more so than Greece or Asia Minor, for there we are a little too much of the sabre and musquet order; and if there is a Crook in one hand, you are sure to see a gun in the other:—but this was pure and un-mixed—solitary, savage, and patriarchal: the effect I cannot describe. As we went, they played the 'Ranz des Vaches' and other airs, by way of farewell. I have lately repeopled my mind with Nature.

September 20

Up at 6. Off at 8. The whole of this day's journey at an average of between from 2700 to 3000 feet above the level of the Sea. This valley, the longest, narrowest, and considered the finest of the Alps, little traversed by travellers. Saw the bridge of La Roche. The bed of the river very low and deep, between immense rocks, and rapid as anger:—a man and mule said to have tumbled over without damage (the mule was lucky at any rate: unless I knew the *man*, I should be loth to pronounce *him* fortunate). The people looked free, and happy, and *rich* (which last implies neither of the former); the cows superb; a Bull nearly leapt into the Charaban—'agreeable companion in a post-chaise;' Goats and Sheep very thriving. A mountain with enormous Glaciers to the right—the Kletsgerberg; further on, the Hockthorn—nice names—so soft!—Hockthorn, I believe, very lofty and craggy, patched with snow only; no Glaciers on it, but some good epaulettes of clouds.

Passed the boundaries, out of Vaud and into Bern Canton; French exchanged for a bad German; the district famous for Cheese, liberty, property, and no taxes. H. went to fish—caught none. Strolled to river; saw boy and kid; kid followed him like a dog; kid could not get over a fence, and bleated piteously; tried myself to help kid, but nearly overset both self and kid into the river. Arrived here about six in the evening. Nine o'clock—going to bed. H. in next room knocked his head against the door, and exclaimed of course against doors; not tired to-day, but hope to sleep nevertheless. Women gabbling below: read a French translation of Schiller. Good Night, Dearest Augusta.

September 21

Off early. The valley of Simmenthal, as before. Entrance to
the plain of Thoun very narrow; high rocks, wooded to the
top; river; new mountains, with fine Glaciers. Lake of Thoun;
extensive plain with a girdle of Alps. Walked down to the
Château de Schadau; view along the lake; crossed the river
in a boat rowed by women. . . . Thoun a very pretty town.
The whole day's journey Alpine and proud.

September 22

Left Thoun in a boat, which carried us the length of the lake
in three hours. The lake small; but the banks fine: rocks down
to the water's edge. Landed at Neuhause; passed Interlachen;
entered upon a range of scenes beyond all description or
previous conception. Passed a rock; inscription—2 brothers
—one murdered the other; just the place for it. After a variety
of windings came to an enormous rock. Girl with fruit—very
pretty; blue eyes, good teeth, very fair: long but good features
—reminded me rather of Fy. Bought some of her pears, and
patted her upon the cheek; the expression of her face very
mild, but good, and not at all coquettish. Arrived at the foot of
the Mountain (the Yung frau, *i.e.* the Maiden); Glaciers;
torrents; one of these torrents *nine hundred feet* in height of
visible descent. Lodged at the Curate's. Set out to see the
Valley; heard an Avalanche fall, like thunder; saw Glacier—
enormous. Storm came on, thunder, lightning, hail; all in
perfection, and beautiful. I was on horseback; Guide wanted
to carry my cane; I was going to give it him, when I recollected
that it was a Swordstick, and I thought the lightning might be
attracted towards him; kept it myself; a good deal encumbered with it, and my cloak, as it was too heavy for a whip, and
the horse was stupid, and stood still with every other peal.
Got in, not very wet; the Cloak being staunch. H. wet through;
H. took refuge in cottage; sent man, umbrella, and cloak (from
the Curate's when I arrived) after him. Swiss Curate's house
very good indeed,—much better than most English Vicarages.
It is immediately opposite the torrent I spoke of. The torrent
is in shape curving over the rock, like the *tail* of a white horse

streaming in the wind, such as it might be conceived would be that of the '*pale* horse' on which *Death* is mounted in the Apocalypse. It is neither mist nor water, but a something between both; it's immense height (nine hundred feet) gives it a wave, a curve, a spreading here, a condensation there, wonderful and indescribable. I think, upon the whole, that this day has been better than any of this present excursion.

September 23

Before ascending the mountain, went to the torrent (7 in the morning) again; the Sun upon it forming a *rainbow* of the lower part of all colours, but principally purple and gold; the bow moving as you move; I never saw any thing like this; it is only in the Sunshine. Ascended the Wengen Mountain; at noon reached a valley on the summit; left the horses, took off my coat, and went to the summit, 7000 feet (English feet) above the level of the *sea*, and about 5000 above the valley we left in the morning. On one side, our view comprized the *Yung frau*, with all her glaciers; then the *Dent d'Argent* shining like truth; then the *little Giant* (the Kleiner Eigher); and the great Giant (the Grosser Eigher), and last, not least, the Wetterhorn. The height of Jungfrau is 13,000 feet above the sea, 11,000 above the valley; she is the highest of this range. Heard the Avalanches falling every five minutes nearly—as if God was pelting the Devil down from Heaven with snow balls. From where we stood, on the *Wengen* Alp, we had all these in view on one side; on the other, the clouds rose from the opposite valley, curling up perpendicular precipices like the foam of the Ocean of Hell, during a Spring tide—it was white, and sulphury, and immeasurably deep in appearance. The side we ascended was (of course) not of so precipitous a nature; but on arriving at the summit, we looked down the other side upon a boiling sea of cloud, dashing against the crags on which we stood (these crags on one side quite perpendicular). Staid a quarter of an hour; began to descend; quite clear from cloud on that side of the mountain. In passing the masses of snow, I made a snowball and pelted H. with it.

Got down to our horses again; eat something; remounted;

heard the Avalanches still; came to a morass; H. dismounted;
H. got over well; I tried to pass my horse over; the horse sunk
up [to] the chin, and of course he and I were in the mud
together; bemired all over, but not hurt; laughed, and rode on.
Arrived at the Grindenwald; dined, mounted again, and rode
to the higher Glacier—twilight, but distinct—very fine Glacier,
like *a frozen hurricane*. Starlight, beautiful, but a devil of a
path! Never mind, got safe in; a little lightning; but the whole
of the day as fine in point of weather as the day on which
Paradise was made. Passed *whole woods of withered pines, all
withered;* trunks stripped and barkless, branches lifeless; done
by a single winter,—their appearance reminded me of me and
my family.

September 24

Set off at seven; up at five. Passed the black Glacier, the
Mountain Wetterhorn on the right; crossed the Scheideck
mountain; came to the *Rose* glacier, said to be the largest and
finest in Switzerland. *I* think the Bossons Glacier at Chamouni
as fine; H. does not. Came to the Reichenback waterfall, two
hundred feet high; halted to rest the horses. Arrived in the
valley of Oberhasli; rain came on; drenched a little; only 4
hours' rain, however, in 8 days. Came to Lake of Brientz, then
to town of Brientz; changed. H. hurt his head against door.
In the evening, four Swiss Peasant Girls of Oberhasli came and
sang the airs of their country; two of the voices beautiful—the
tunes also: they sing too that *Tyrolese air* and song which you
love, Augusta, because I love it—and I love, because you love
it; they are still singing. Dearest, you do not know how I
should have liked this, were you with me. The airs are so wild
and original, and at the same time of great sweetness. The
singing is over: but below stairs I hear the notes of a Fiddle
which bode no good to my night's rest. The *Lord* help us—
shall go down and see the dancing.

September 25

The whole town of Brientz were apparently gathered together in the rooms below; pretty music and excellent Waltz

ing; none but peasants; the dancing much better than in England; the English can't Waltz, never could, nor ever will. One man with his pipe in his mouth, but danced as well as the others; some other dances in pairs and in fours, and very good. I went to bed, but the revelry continued below late and early. Brientz but a village. Rose early. Embarked on the Lake of Brientz, rowed by the women in a long boat; (one very young and very pretty—seated myself by her, and began to row also): presently we put to shore, and another woman jumped in. It seems it is the custom here for the boats to be *manned* by *women*: for of five men and three women in our bark, all the women took an oar, and but one man.

Got to Interlachen in three hours; pretty lake, not so large as that of Thoun. Dined at Interlachen. Girl gave me some flowers, and made me a speech in German, of which I know nothing: I do not know whether the speech was pretty, but as the woman was, I hope so. Saw another—very pretty too, and tall, which I prefer: I hate short women, for more reasons than one. Re-embarked on the lake of Thoun; fell asleep part of the way: sent our horses round; found people on the shore, blowing up a rock with gunpowder: they blew it up near our boat, only telling us a minute before:—mere stupidity, but they might have broke our noddles. Got to Thoun in the Evening; the weather has been tolerable the whole day; but as the wild part of our tour is finished, it don't matter to us; in all the desirable part, we have been most lucky in warmth and clearness of Atmosphere, for which 'Praise we the Lord!!'

September 26

Being out of the mountains, my journal must be as flat as my journey. From Thoun to Bern, good road, hedges, villages, industry, property, and all sorts of tokens of insipid civilisation. From Bern to Fribourg; different Canton—Catholics; passed a field of Battle; Swiss beat the French in one of the late wars against the French Republic. Bought a dog—a very ugly dog, but '*très méchant*'; this was his great recommendation in the owner's eyes and mine, for I mean him to watch the carriage. He hath no tail, and is called '*Mutz*', which signifies

'*Short-tail*': he is apparently of the Shepherd dog genus! The greater part of this tour has been on horseback, on foot, and on mule.

The Filly (which is one of the two young horses I bought of the Baron de Vincy), carried me very well: she is young and as quiet as any thing of her sex can be—very good tempered, and perpetually neighing when she wants any thing, which is every five minutes. I have called her *Biche*, because her manners are not unlike a little dog's; but she is a very tame pretty childish quadruped.

September 28

Saw the tree planted in honour of the battle of Morat; 340 years old; a good deal decayed. Left Fribourg, but first saw the Cathedral; high tower. Overtook the baggage of the Nuns of La Trappe, who are removing to Normandy from their late abode in the Canton of Fribourg; afterwards a coach, with a quantity of Nuns in it—Nuns old. Proceeded along the banks of the Lake of Neufchâtel; very pleasing and soft, but not so mountainous—at least, the Jura, not appearing so, after the Bernese Alps. Reached Yverdun in the dusk; a long line of large trees on the border of the lake—fine and sombre; the Auberge nearly full—a German—with princess and suite; got rooms. . . .

We hope to reach Diodati the day after tomorrow, and I wish for a letter from you, my own dearest Sis. May your sleep be soft, and your dreams of me. I am going to bed—good night.

September 29

Passed through a fine and flourishing country, but not mountainous. In the evening reached Aubonne (the entrance and bridge something like that of Durham), which commands by far the fairest view of the Lake of Geneva; twilight; the Moon on the Lake; a grove on the height, and of very noble trees. Here Tavernier (the eastern traveller) bought (or built) the Château, because the site resembled and equalled that of *Erivan* (a frontier city of Persia); here he finished his voyages, and I this little excursion,—for I am within a few hours of Diodati, and have little more to see, and no more to say.

In the weather for this tour (of 13 days), I have been very fortunate—fortunate in a companion (Mr. He.)—fortunate in our prospects, and exempt from even the little petty accidents and delays which often render journeys in a less wild country disappointing. I was disposed to be pleased. I am a lover of Nature and an admirer of Beauty. I can bear fatigue and welcome privation, and have seen some of the noblest views in the world. But in all this—the recollections of bitterness, and more especially of recent and more home desolation, which must accompany me through life, have preyed upon me here; and neither the music of the Shepherd, the crashing of the Avalanche, nor the torrent, the mountain, the Glacier, the Forest, nor the Cloud, have for one moment lightened the weight upon my heart, nor enabled me to lose my own wretched identity in the majesty, and the power, and the Glory, around, above, and beneath me.

I am past reproaches; and there is a time for all things. I am past the wish of vengeance, and I know of none like for what I have suffered; but the hour will come, when what I feel must be felt, and the—but enough.

To you, dearest Augusta, I send, and *for* you I have kept this record of what I have seen and felt. Love me as you are beloved by me.

TO THOMAS MOORE

Verona, November 6, 1816

My dear Moore,

Your letter, written before my departure from England, and addressed to me in London, only reached me recently. Since that period, I have been over a portion of that part of Europe which I had not already seen. About a month since, I crossed the Alps from Switzerland to Milan, which I left a few days ago, and am thus far on my way to Venice, where I shall probably winter. Yesterday I was on the shores of the Benacus,

with his *fluctibus et fremitu.* Catullus's Sirmium has still its
name and site, and is remembered for his sake: but the very
heavy autumnal rains and mists prevented our quitting our
route, (that is, Hobhouse and myself, who are at present
voyaging together,) as it was better not to see it at all than to a
great disadvantage.

I found on the Benacus the same tradition of a city, still
visible in calm weather below the waters, which you have preserved of Lough Neagh, 'When the clear, cold eve's declining.'
I do not know that it is authorised by records; but they tell
you such a story, and say that the city was swallowed up by an
earthquake. We moved to-day over the frontier to Verona, by
a road suspected of thieves,—'the wise *convey* it call,'—but
without molestation. I shall remain here a day or two to gape
at the usual marvels,—amphitheatre, paintings, and all that
time-tax of travel,—though Catullus, Claudian, and Shakspeare have done more for Verona than it ever did for itself.
They still pretend to show, I believe, the 'tomb of all the
Capulets'—we shall see.

Among many things at Milan, one pleased me particularly,
viz. the correspondence (in the prettiest love-letters in the
world) of Lucretia Borgia with Cardinal Bembo, (who, *you
say,* made a very good cardinal,) and a lock of her hair, and
some Spanish verses of hers,—the lock very fair and beautiful.
I took one single hair of it as a relic, and wished sorely to get a
copy of one or two of the letters; but it is prohibited: *that* I
don't mind; but it was impracticable; and so I only got some
of them by heart. They are kept in the Ambrosian Library,
which I often visited to look them over—to the scandal of the
librarian, who wanted to enlighten me with sundry valuable
MSS., classical, philosophical, and pious. But I stick to the
Pope's daughter, and wish myself a cardinal.

I have seen the finest parts of Switzerland, the Rhine, the
Rhone, and the Swiss and Italian lakes; for the beauties of
which, I refer you to the Guide-book. The north of Italy is
tolerably free from the English; but the south swarms with
them, I am told. Madame de Stael I saw frequently at Copet,
which she renders remarkably pleasant. She has been parti-

cularly kind to me. I was for some months her neighbour, in a country-house called Diodati, which I had on the Lake of Geneva. My plans are very uncertain; but it is probable that you will see me in England in the spring. I have some business there. If you write to me, will you address to the care of Mons. Hentsch, *Banquier*, Geneva, who receives and forwards my letters. Remember me to Rogers, who wrote to me lately, with a short account of your poem, which, I trust, is near the light. He speaks of it most highly.

My health is very endurable, except that I am subject to casual giddiness and faintness, which is so like a fine lady, that I am rather ashamed of the disorder. When I sailed, I had a physician with me, whom, after some months of patience, I found it expedient to part with, before I left Geneva some time. On arriving at Milan, I found this gentleman in very good society, where he prospered for some weeks: but, at length, at the theatre, he quarrelled with an Austrian officer, and was sent out by the government in twenty-four hours. I was not present at his squabble; but, on hearing that he was put under arrest, I went and got him out of his confinement, but could not prevent his being sent off, which, indeed, he partly deserved, being quite in the wrong, and having begun a row for row's sake. I had preceded the Austrian government some weeks myself, in giving him his congé from Geneva. He is not a bad fellow, but very young and hot-headed, and more likely to incur diseases than to cure them. Hobhouse and myself found it useless to intercede for him. This happened some time before we left Milan. He is gone to Florence.

At Milan I saw, and was visited by, Monti, the most celebrated of the living Italian poets. He seems near sixty; in face he is like the late Cooke the actor. His frequent changes in politics have made him very unpopular as a man. I saw many more of their literati; but none whose names are well known in England, except Acerbi. I lived much with the Italians, particularly with the Marquis of Breme's family, who are very able and intelligent men, especially the Abbate. There was a famous improvvisatore who held forth while I was there. His fluency astonished me; but, although I understand Italian, and speak it (with more readiness than accuracy), I could only carry off a few very common-place mythological images, and one line about Artemisia, and another about Algiers, with sixty words of an entire tragedy about Eteocles and Polynices. Some of the Italians liked him—others called his performance '*seccatura*' (a devilish good word, by the way) and all Milan was in controversy about him.

The state of morals in these parts is in some sort lax. A mother and son were pointed out at the theatre, as being pronounced by the Milanese world to be of the Theban dynasty—but this was all. The narrator (one of the first men in Milan) seemed to be not sufficiently scandalised by the taste or the tie. All society in Milan is carried on at the opera: they have private boxes, where they play at cards, or talk, or any thing else; but (except at the Cassino) there are no open houses, or balls, etc., etc. . . .

The peasant girls have all very fine dark eyes, and many of them are beautiful. There are also two dead bodies in fine preservation—one Saint Carlo Boromeo, at Milan; the other not a saint, but a chief, named Visconti, at Monza—both of which appeared very agreeable. In one of the Boromean isles (the Isola bella), there is a large laurel—the largest known—on which Buonaparte, staying there just before the battle of Marengo, carved with his knife the word 'Battaglia'. I saw the letters, now half worn out and partly erased.

Excuse this tedious letter. To be tiresome is the privilege of old age and absence; I avail myself of the latter, and the former I have anticipated. If I do not speak to you of my own affairs, it is not from want of confidence, but to spare you and myself. My day is over—what then?—I have had it. To be sure, I have shortened it; and if I had done as much by this letter, it would have been as well. But you will forgive that, if not the other faults of

Yours ever and most affectionately, B.

P.S.—*November 7, 1816*

I have been over Verona. The amphitheatre is wonderful—beats even Greece. Of the truth of Juliet's story they seem tenacious to a degree, insisting on the fact—giving a date (1303), and showing a tomb. It is a plain, open, and partly decayed sarcophagus, with withered leaves in it, in a wild and desolate conventual garden, once a cemetery, now ruined to the very graves. The situation struck me as very appropriate to the legend, being blighted as their love. I have brought away a few pieces of the granite, to give to my daughter and my nieces. Of the other marvels of this city, paintings, antiquities, etc., excepting the tombs of the Scaliger princes, I have no pretensions to judge. The Gothic monuments of the Scaligers pleased me, but 'a poor virtuoso am I,' and ever yours.

TO THOMAS MOORE

Venice, November 17, 1816

I wrote to you from Verona the other day in my progress hither, which letter I hope you will receive. Some three years ago, or it may be more, I recollect your telling me that you had received a letter from our friend Sam, dated 'On board his gondola.' *My* gondola is, at this present, waiting for me on the canal; but I prefer writing to you in the house, it being autumn—and rather an English autumn than otherwise. It is my intention to remain at Venice during the winter, probably, as it has always been (next to the East) the greenest island of my imagination. It has not disappointed me; though its evident decay would, perhaps, have that effect upon others. But I have been familiar with ruins too long to dislike desolation. Besides, I have fallen in love, which, next to falling into the canal, (which would be of no use, as I can swim,) is the best or the worst thing I could do. I have got some extremely good apartments in the house of a 'Merchant of Venice,' who is a good deal occupied with business, and has a wife in her twenty-second year. Marianna (that is her name) is in her appearance altogether like an antelope. She has the large, black, oriental eyes, with that peculiar expression in them which is seen rarely among *Europeans*—even the Italians—and which many of the Turkish women give themselves by tinging the eyelid,—an art not known out of that country, I believe. This expression she has *naturally*,—and something more than this. In short, I cannot describe the effect of this kind of eye,— at least upon me. Her features are regular, and rather aquiline —mouth small—skin clear and soft, with a kind of hectic colour—forehead remarkably good: her hair is of the dark gloss, curl, and colour of Lady J[ersey]'s: her figure is light and pretty, and she is a famous songstress—scientifically so; her natural voice (in conversation, I mean) is very sweet; and the naïveté of the Venetian dialect is always pleasing in the mouth of a woman.

November 23

You will perceive that my description, which was proceeding with the minuteness of a passport, has been interrupted for several days. . . .

December 5

Since my former dates, I do not know that I have much to add on the subject, and, luckily, nothing to take away; for I am more pleased than ever with my Venetian, and begin to feel very serious on that point—so much so, that I shall be silent. . . .

TO THOMAS MOORE

Venice, December 24, 1816

I have taken a fit of writing to you, which portends postage —once from Verona—once from Venice, and again from Venice—*thrice* that is. For this you may thank yourself; for I heard that you complained of my silence—so, here goes for garrulity.

I trust that you received my other twain of letters. My 'way of life' (or 'May of life,' which is it, according to the commentators?)—my 'way of life' is fallen into great regularity. In the mornings I go over in my gondola to babble Armenian with the friars of the convent of St. Lazarus, and to help one of them in correcting the English of an English and Armenian grammar which he is publishing. In the evenings I do one of many nothings—either at the theatres, or some of the conversaziones, which are like our routs, or rather worse, for the women sit in a semicircle by the lady of the mansion, and the men stand about the room. To be sure, there is one improvement upon ours—instead of lemonade with their ices, they hand about stiff *rum-punch*—*punch*, by my palate; and this they think *English*. I would not disabuse them of so agreeable an error,—'no, not for Venice.' . . .

My flame (my *Donna* whom I spoke of in my former epistle, my Marianna) is still my Marianna, and I her—what she pleases. She is by far the prettiest woman I have seen here, and the most loveable I have met with any where—as well as one of the most singular. I believe I told you the rise and progress of our *liaison* in my former letter. Lest that should not have reached you, I will merely repeat, that she is a Venetian, two-and-twenty years old, married to a merchant well to do in the world, and that she has great black oriental eyes, and all the qualities which her eyes promise. Whether being in love with her has steeled me or not, I do not know; but I have not seen many other women who seem pretty. The nobility, in particular, are a sad-looking race—the gentry rather better. And now, what art *thou* doing?

> *What are you doing now,*
> *Oh Thomas Moore?*
> *What are you doing now,*
> *Oh Thomas Moore?*
> *Sighing or suing now,*
> *Rhyming or wooing now,*
> *Billing or cooing now,*
> *Which, Thomas Moore?*

Are you not near the Luddites? By the Lord! if there's a row, but I'll be among ye! How go on the weavers—the breakers of frames—the Lutherans of politics—the reformers?

As the Liberty lads o'er the sea
Bought their freedom, and cheaply, with blood,
So we, boys, we
Will die fighting, or live free,
And down with all kings but King Ludd!

When the web that we weave is complete,
And the shuttle exchanged for the sword,
We will fling the winding-sheet
O'er the despot at our feet,
And dye it deep in the gore he has pour'd.

Though black as his heart its hue,
Since his veins are corrupted to mud,
Yet this is the dew
Which the tree shall renew
Of Liberty, planted by Ludd!

There's an amiable *chanson* for you—all impromptu. I have
written it principally to shock your neighbour ——, who is all
clergy and loyalty—mirth and innocence—milk and water.

But the Carnival's coming,
Oh Thomas Moore,
The Carnival's coming,
Oh Thomas Moore;
Masking and humming,
Fifing and drumming,
Guitarring and strumming,
Oh Thomas Moore....

TO THOMAS MOORE

Venice, January 28, 1817

... Venice is in the *estro* of her carnival, and I have been up
these last two nights at the ridotto and the opera, and all that
kind of thing. Now for an adventure. A few days ago a
gondolier brought me a billet without a subscription, intimating a wish on the part of the writer to meet me either in
gondola or at the island of San Lazaro, or at a third rendez-

vous, indicated in the note. 'I know the country's disposition well'—in Venice 'they do let Heaven see those tricks they dare not show,' etc., etc.; so, for all response, I said that neither of the three places suited me; but that I would either be at home at ten at night *alone*, or be at the ridotto at midnight, where the writer might meet me masked. At ten o'clock I was at home and alone (Marianna was gone with her husband to a conversazione), when the door of my apartment opened, and in walked a well-looking and (for an Italian) *bionda* girl of about nineteen, who informed me that she was married to the brother of my *amorosa*, and wished to have some conversation with me. I made a decent reply, and we had some talk in Italian and Romaic (her mother being a Greek of Corfu), when lo! in a very few minutes in marches, to my very great astonishment, Marianna Segati, *in propriâ personâ*, and after making a most polite courtesy to her sister-in-law and to me, without a single word seizes her said sister-in-law by the hair, and bestows upon her some sixteen slaps, which would have made your ear ache only to hear their echo. I need not describe the screaming which ensued. The luckless visitor took flight. I seized Marianna, who, after several vain efforts to get away in pursuit of the enemy, fairly went into fits in my arms; and, in spite of reasoning, eau de Cologne, vinegar, half a pint of water, and God knows what other waters beside, continued so till past midnight.

After damning my servants for letting people in without apprizing me, I found that Marianna in the morning had seen her sister-in-law's gondolier on the stairs, and, suspecting that his apparition boded her no good, had either returned of her own accord, or been followed by her maids or some other spy of her people to the conversazione, from whence she returned to perpetrate this piece of pugilism. I had seen fits before, and also some small scenery of the same genus in and out of our island: but this was not all. After about an hour, in comes— who? why, Signor Segati, her lord and husband, and finds me with his wife fainting upon the sofa, and all the apparatus of confusion, dishevelled hair, hats, handkerchiefs, salts, smelling bottles—and the lady as pale as ashes, without sense or motion. His first question was, 'What is all this?' The lady could not reply—so I did. I told him the explanation was the easiest thing in the world; but in the meantime it would be as well to recover his wife—at least, her senses. This came about in due time of suspiration and respiration.

You need not be alarmed—jealousy is not the order of the day in Venice, and daggers are out of fashion; while duels, on love matters, are unknown—at least, with the husbands. But, for all this, it was an awkward affair; and though he must have known that I made love to Marianna, yet I believe he was not, till that evening, aware of the extent to which it had gone. It is very well known that almost all the married women have a lover; but it is usual to keep up the forms, as in other nations. I did not, therefore, know what the devil to say. I could not out with the truth, out of regard to her, and I did not choose to lie for my sake;—besides, the thing told itself. I thought the best way would be to let her explain it as she chose (a woman being never at a loss—the devil always sticks by them)—only determining to protect and carry her off, in case of any ferocity on the part of the Signor. I saw that he was quite calm. She went to bed, and next day—how they settled it, I know not, but settle it they did. Well—then I had to explain to Marianna about this never-to-be-sufficiently-confounded sister-in-law; which I did by swearing innocence, eternal constancy, etc., etc. . . . But the sister-in-law, very much discomposed with being treated in such wise, has (not having her own shame before her eyes) told the affair to half Venice, and the servants (who were summoned by the fight and the fainting) to the other half. But, here, nobody minds such trifles, except to be amused by them. I don't know whether you will be so, but I have scrawled a long letter out of these follies.

Believe me ever, etc.

TO JOHN MURRAY

Venice, May 30, 1817

I returned from Rome two days ago, and have received your letter; but no sign nor tidings of the parcel sent through Sir [C.]

Stuart, which you mention. After an interval of months, a packet of *Tales*, etc. found me at Rome; but this is all, and may be all that ever will find me. The post seems to be the only sane conveyance; and *that only for letters*. From Florence I sent you a poem on Tasso, and from Rome the new third act of *Manfred*, and by Dr. Polidori two pictures for my sister. I left Rome, and made a rapid journey home. You will continue to direct here as usual. Mr. Hobhouse is gone to Naples: I should have run down there too for a week, but for the quantity of English whom I heard of there. I prefer hating them at a distance; unless an earthquake, or a good real eruption of Vesuvius, were insured to reconcile me to their vicinity. . . .

The day before I left Rome I saw three robbers guillotined. The ceremony—including the *masqued* priests; the half-naked executioners; the bandaged criminals; the black Christ and his banner; the scaffold; the soldiery; the slow procession, and the quick rattle and heavy fall of the axe; the splash of the blood, and the ghastliness of the exposed heads—is altogether more impressive than the vulgar and ungentlemanly dirty 'new drop,' and dog-like agony of infliction upon the sufferers of the English sentence. Two of these men behaved calmly enough, but the first of the three died with great terror and reluctance, which was very horrible. He would not lie down; then his neck was too large for the aperture, and the priest was obliged to drown his exclamations by still louder exhortations. The head was off before the eye could trace the blow; but from an attempt to draw back the head, notwithstanding it was held forward by the hair, the first head was cut off close to the ears: the other two were taken off more cleanly. It is better than the oriental way, and (I should think) than the axe of our ancestors. The pain seems little; and yet the effect to the spectator, and the preparation to the criminal, are very striking and chilling. The first turned me quite hot and thirsty, and made me shake so that I could hardly hold the opera-glass (I was close, but determined to see, as one should see every thing, once, with attention); the second and third (which shows how dreadfully soon things grow indifferent), I am ashamed to say, had no effect on me as a horror, though I would have saved them if I could. . . . Yours, etc.

2 A

TO THOMAS MOORE

La Mira, Venice, July 10, 1817

Murray, the Mokanna of booksellers, has contrived to send me extracts from *Lalla Rookh* by the post. They are taken from some magazine, and contain a short outline and quotations from the two first Poems. I am very much delighted with what is before me, and very thirsty for the rest. You have caught the colours as if you had been in the rainbow, and the tone of the East is perfectly preserved. I am glad you have changed the title from 'Persian Tale.' . . .

I suspect you have written a devilish fine composition, and I rejoice in it from my heart; because 'the Douglas and the Percy both together are confident against a world in arms.' I hope you won't be affronted at my looking on us as 'birds of a feather;' though, on whatever subject you had written, I should have been very happy in your success.

There is a simile of an orange-tree's 'flowers and fruits,' which I should have liked better if I did not believe it to be a reflection on . . . .

Do you remember Thurlow's poem to Sam—'*When* Rogers;' and that damned supper at Rancliffe's that ought to have been a *dinner*? 'Ah, Master Shallow, we have heard the chimes at midnight.' But,

> *My boat is on the shore,*
> *And my bark is on the sea;*
> *But, before I go, Tom Moore,*
> *Here's a double health to thee!*

> *Here's a sigh to those who love me,*
> *And a smile to those who hate;*
> *And whatever sky's above me,*
> *Here's a heart for every fate.*

> *Though the ocean roar around me,*
> *Yet it still shall bear me on;*
> *Though a desert should surround me,*
> *It hath springs that may be won.*

Were't the last drop in the well,
  As I gasp'd upon the brink,
Ere my fainting spirit fell,
  'Tis to thee that I would drink.

With that water, as this wine,
  The libation I would pour
Should be—peace with thine and mine,
  And a health to thee, Tom Moore.

This should have been written fifteen moons ago—the first stanza was. I am just come out from an hour's swim in the Adriatic; and I write to you with a black-eyed Venetian girl before me, reading Boccaccio.

Last week I had a row on the road (I came up to Venice from my casino, a few miles on the Paduan road, this blessed day, to bathe) with a fellow in a carriage, who was impudent to my horse. I gave him a swingeing box on the ear, which sent him to the police, who dismissed his complaint. Witnesses had seen the transaction. He first shouted, in an unseemly way, to frighten my palfry. I wheeled round, rode up to the window, and asked him what he meant. He grinned, and said some foolery, which produced him an immediate slap in the face, to his utter discomfiture. Much blasphemy ensued, and some menace, which I stopped by dismounting and opening the carriage door, and intimating an intention of mending the road with his immediate remains, if he did not hold his tongue. He held it.

Monk Lewis is here—'how pleasant!' He is a very good fellow, and very much yours. So is Sam—so is every body—and amongst the number,

                                    Yours ever,   B.

P.S.—What think you of *Manfred?* . . .

TO JOHN MURRAY

Venice, Feb. 20, 1818

I have to thank Mr. Croker for the arrival, and you for the Continents [contents] of the parcel which came last week, much quicker than any before, owing to Mr. C's kind attention, and the official exterior of the bags; and all safe, except much friction amongst the magnesia, of which only two bottles came entire; but it is all very well, and I am exceedingly obliged to you.

The books I have read, or rather am reading. Pray, who may be the Sexagenarian, whose gossip is very amusing? Many of his sketches I recognise, particularly Gifford, Mackintosh, Drummond, Dutens, H. Walpole, Mrs. Inchbald, Opie, etc., with the Scotts, Loughborough, and most of the divines and lawyers, besides a few shorter hints of authors, and a few lines about a certain '*Noble Author*,' characterised as Malignant and Sceptical, according to the good old story, 'as it was in the beginning, is now, but *not* always shall be:' do you know such a person, Master Murray? eh?—And pray, of the Booksellers, which be *you*? the dry, the dirty, the honest, the opulent, the finical, the splendid, or the Coxcomb Bookseller? 'Stap my vitals,' but the author grows scurrilous in his grand Climacteric!

I remember to have seen Porson at Cambridge, in the Hall of our College, and in private parties, but not frequently: and I never can recollect him except as drunk or brutal, and generally both: I mean in an evening, for in the hall he dined at the Dean's table, and I at the Vice-master's, so that I was not near him; and he then and there appeared sober in his demeanour, nor did I ever hear of excess or outrage on his part in public,— Commons, college, or Chapel; but I have seen him in a private party of undergraduates, many of them freshmen and strangers—take up a poker to one of them, and heard him use language as blackguard as his action. I have seen Sheridan drunk, too, with all the world; but his intoxication was that of Bacchus, and Porson's that of Silenus. Of all the disgusting brutes, sulky, abusive, and intolerable, Porson was the most bestial, as far as the few times that I saw him went, which were only at William Bankes's (the Nubian Discoverer's) rooms. I saw him once go away in a rage, because nobody knew the name of the 'Cobbler of Messina,' insulting their ignorance with the most vulgar terms of reprobation. He was tolerated in this state amongst the young men for his talents—as the Turks think a Madman inspired, and bear with him. He used to recite, or rather vomit, pages of all languages, and could hiccup Greek like a Helot; and certainly Sparta never shocked her children with a grosser exhibition than this man's intoxication.

I perceive, in the book you sent me, a long account of him; of Gilbert Wakefield's account of him, which is very savage, I cannot judge, as I never saw him sober, except in *Hall* or Combination-room; and then I was never near enough to hear, and hardly to see him. Of his drunken deportment I can be sure, because I saw it.

With the Reviews I have been much entertained. It requires to be as far from England as I am to relish a periodical paper properly: it is like Soda-water in an Italian Summer. But what cruel work you make with Lady Morgan!—You should recollect that she is a woman; though, to be sure, they are now and then very provoking: still, as authoresses, they can do no great harm; and I think it a pity so much good invective should have been laid out upon her, when there is such a fine field of us Jacobin gentlemen for you to work upon. . . .

I heard from Moore lately, and was very sorry to be made aware of his domestic loss. Thus it is—*medio de fonte leporum* —in the acmé of his fame and of his happiness comes a drawback as usual. . . .

Mr. Hoppner, whom I saw this morning, has been made the father of a very fine boy.—Mother and child doing very well indeed. By this time Hobhouse should be with you, and also certain packets, letters, etc., of mine, sent since his departure.— I am not at all well in health within this last eight days. My remembrances to Gifford and all friends.

Yours,

B.

P.S.—In the course of a month or two, Hanson will have probably to send off a clerk with conveyances to sign (Newstead being sold in November last for ninety-four thousand and five hundred pounds), in which case I supplicate supplies of articles as usual, for which desire Mr. Kinnaird to settle from funds in their bank, and deduct from my account with him.

P.S.—To-morrow night I am going to see *Otello*, an opera from our *Othello*, and one of Rossini's best, it is said. It will be curious to see in Venice the Venetian story itself represented, besides to discover what they will make of Shakspeare in Music.

TO JOHN MURRAY

Ravenna, August 1, 1819

... Since you desire the story of Margarita Cogni, you shall be told it, though it may be lengthy.

Her face is of the fine Venetian cast of the old Time, and her figure, though perhaps too tall, not less fine—taken altogether in the national dress.

In the summer of 1817, Hobhouse and myself were sauntering on horseback along the Brenta one evening, when, amongst a group of peasants, we remarked two girls as the prettiest we had seen for some time. About this period, there had been great distress in the country, and I had a little relieved some of the people. Generosity makes a great figure at very little cost in Venetian livres, and mine had probably been exaggerated—as an Englishman's. Whether they remarked us looking at them or no, I know not; but one of them called out to me in Venetian, 'Why do not you, who relieve others, think of us also?' I turned round and answered her—*Cara, tu sei troppo bella e giovane per aver' bisogna del' soccorso mio.* She answered, 'If you saw my hut and my food, you would not say so.' All this passed half jestingly, and I saw no more of her for some days.

A few evenings after, we met with these two girls again, and they addressed us more seriously, assuring us of the truth of their statement. They were cousins; Margarita married, the other single. As I doubted still of the circumstances, I took the business in a different light, and made an appointment with them for the next evening. ... In short, in a few evenings we arranged our affairs, and for two years, in the course of which I had more women than I can count or recount, she was the only one who preserved over me an ascendency which was often disputed, and never impaired. . . .

The reasons of this were, firstly, her person—very dark, tall, the Venetian face, very fine black eyes. . . . She was two-and-twenty years old, . . . She was, besides, a thorough Venetian in her dialect, in her thoughts, in her countenance, in every thing, with all their *naïveté* and Pantaloon humour. Besides, she could neither read nor write, and could not plague me with letters,—except twice that she paid sixpence to a public scribe, under the piazza, to make a letter for her, upon some occasion, when I was ill and could not see her. In other respects, she was somewhat fierce and *prepotente*, that is, overbearing, and used to walk in whenever it suited her, with no very great regard to time, place, nor persons; and if she found any women in her way, she knocked them down.

When I first knew her, I was in *relazione* (*liaison*) with la Signora Segati, who was silly enough one evening at Dolo, accompanied by some of her female friends, to threaten her; for the Gossips of the Villeggiatura had already found out, by the neighing of my horse one evening, that I used to 'ride late in the night' to meet the Fornarina. Margarita threw back her veil (*fazziolo*), and replied in very explicit Venetian, '*You* are *not* his *wife*: *I* am *not* his *wife*: you are his *Donna*, and *I* am his *Donna*: your husband is a cuckold, and mine is another. For the rest, what *right* have you to reproach me? if he prefers what is mine to what is yours, is it my fault? if you wish to secure him, tie him to your petticoat-string; but do not think to speak to me without a reply, because you happen to be richer than I am.' Having delivered this pretty piece of eloquence (which I translate as it was related to me by a bye-stander), she went on her way, leaving a numerous audience with Madame Segati, to ponder at her leisure on the dialogue between them.

When I came to Venice for the Winter, she followed; . . . and as she found herself out to be a favourite, she came to me pretty often. But she had inordinate Self-love, and was not tolerant of other women. . . . At the *Cavalchina*, the masqued ball on the last night of the Carnival, where all the World goes, she snatched off the mask of Madame Contarini, a lady noble by birth, and decent in conduct, for no other reason, but because she happened to be leaning on my arm. You may suppose what a cursed noise this made; but this is only one of her pranks.

At last she quarrelled with her husband, and one evening ran away to my house. I told her this would not do: she said she would lie in the street, but not go back to him; that he beat her (the gentle tigress), spent her money, and scandalously neglected his Oven. As it was Midnight I let her stay, and next day there was no moving her at all. Her husband came, roaring and crying, and entreating her to come back:—*not* she! He then applied to the Police, and they applied to me: I told them and her husband to *take* her; I did not want her; she had come, and I could not fling her out of the window; but they might conduct her through that or the door if they chose it. She went before the Commissary, but was obliged to return with that *becco ettico* ('consumptive cuckold'), as she called the poor man, who had a Ptisick. In a few days she ran away again. After a precious piece of work, she fixed herself in my house, really and truly without my consent, but, owing to my indolence, and not being able to keep my countenance; for if I began in a rage, she always finished by making me laugh with some Venetian pantaloonery or another; and the Gipsy knew this well enough, as well as her other powers of persuasion, and exerted them with the usual tact and success of all She-things; high and low, they are all alike for that.

Madame Benzone also took her under her protection, and then her head turned. She was always in extremes, either crying or laughing; and so fierce when angered, that she was the terror of men, women, and children—for she had the strength of an Amazon, with the temper of Medea. She was a fine animal, but quite untameable. *I* was the only person that could at all keep her in any order, and when she saw me really angry (which they tell me is a savage sight), she subsided. But she had a thousand fooleries: in her *fazziolo*, the dress of the lower orders, she looked beautiful; but, alas! she longed for a hat and feathers, and all I could say or do (and I said much) could not prevent this travestie. I put the first into the fire; but I got tired of burning them, before she did of buying them, so that she made herself a figure—for they did not at all become her.

Then she would have her gowns with a *tail*—like a lady, forsooth; nothing would serve her but '*l'abita colla coua*,' or *cua*, (that is the Venetian for '*la Coda*,' the tail or train,) and as her cursed pronunciation of the word made me laugh, there was an end of all controversy, and she dragged this diabolical tail after her every where.

In the mean time, she beat the women and stopped my letters. I found her one day pondering over one: she used to try to find out by their shape whether they were feminine or no; and she used to lament her ignorance, and actually studied her Alphabet, on purpose (as she declared) to open all letters addressed to me and read their contents.

I must not omit to do justice to her housekeeping qualities: after she came into my house as *donna di governo*, the expences were reduced to less than half, and every body did their duty better—the apartments were kept in order, and every thing and every body else, except herself.

That she had a sufficient regard for me in her wild way, I had many reasons to believe. I will mention one. In the autumn, one day, going to the Lido with my Gondoliers, we were overtaken by a heavy Squall, and the Gondola put in peril—hats blown away, boat filling, oar lost, tumbling sea, thunder, rain in torrents, night coming, and wind encreasing. On our return, after a tight struggle, I found her on the open steps of the Mocenigo palace, on the Grand Canal, with her great black eyes flashing through her tears, and the long dark hair, which was streaming drenched with rain over her brows and breast. She was perfectly exposed to the storm; and the wind blowing her hair and dress about her thin tall figure, and the lightning flashing round her, and the waves rolling at her feet, made her look like Medea alighted from her chariot, or the Sibyl of the tempest that was rolling around her, the only living thing within hail at that moment except ourselves. On seeing me safe, she did not wait to greet me, as might be expected, but calling out to me—*Ah! can' della Madonna, xe esto il tempo per andar' al' Lido?* (Ah! Dog of the Virgin, is this a time to go to Lido?) ran into the house, and solaced herself with scolding the boatmen for not foreseeing the '*temporale.*' I was told by the servants that she had only been prevented from coming in a boat to look after me, by the refusal of all the Gondoliers of the Canal to put out into the harbour in such a moment; and that then she sat down on the steps in all the thickest of the Squall, and would neither be removed nor comforted. Her joy at seeing me again was moderately mixed with ferocity, and gave me the idea of a tigress over her recovered Cubs.

But her reign drew near a close. She became quite ungovernable some months after; and a concurrence of complaints, some true, and many false—'a favourite has no friend'—determined me to part with her. I told her quietly that she must return home, (she had acquired a sufficient provision for herself and mother, etc., in my service,) and She refused to quit the house. I was firm, and she went, threatening knives and revenge. I told her that I had seen knives drawn before her time, and that if she chose to begin, there was a knife, and fork also, at her service on the table, and that intimidation would not do. The next day, while I was at dinner, she walked in, (having broke open a glass door that led from the hall below to the staircase, by way of prologue,) and, advancing strait up to the table, snatched the knife from my hand, cutting me slightly in the thumb in the operation. Whether she meant to use this against herself or me, I know not—probably against neither—but Fletcher seized her by the arms, and disarmed her. I then called my boatmen, and desired them to get the Gondola ready, and conduct her to her own house again, seeing carefully that she did herself no mischief by the way. She seemed quite quiet, and walked down stairs. I resumed my dinner.

We heard a great noise: I went out, and met them on the staircase, carrying her up stairs. She had thrown herself into the Canal. That she intended to destroy herself, I do not believe; but when we consider the fear women and men who can't swim have of deep or even of shallow water, (and the Venetians in particular, though they live on the waves,) and that it was also night, and dark, and very cold, it shows that she had a devilish spirit of some sort within her. They had got her out without much difficulty or damage, excepting the salt water she had swallowed, and the wetting she had undergone.

I foresaw her intention to refix herself, and sent for a Surgeon, enquiring how many hours it would require to restore her from her agitation; and he named the time. I then said, 'I give you that time, and more if you require it; but at the expiration of the prescribed period, if *She* does not leave the house, *I* will.'

All my people were consternated—they had always been frightened at her, and were now paralyzed: they wanted me to apply to the police, to guard myself, etc., etc., like a pack of sniveling servile boobies as they were. I did nothing of the kind, thinking that I might as well end that way as another; besides, I had been used to savage women, and knew their ways.

I had her sent home quietly after her recovery, and never saw her since, except twice at the opera, at a distance amongst the audience. She made many attempts to return, but no more violent ones. And this is the story of Margarita Cogni, as far as it belongs to me.

I forgot to mention that she was very devout, and would cross herself if she heard the prayer time strike—sometimes when that ceremony did not appear to be much in unison with what she was then about.

She was quick in reply; as, for instance—One day when she had made me very angry with beating somebody or other, I called her a *Cow* (*Cow*, in Italian, is a sad affront and tantamount to the feminine of dog in English). I called her '*Vacca*.' She turned round, curtesied, and answered, '*Vacca tua*, *'Celenza*' (*i.e. Eccelenza*). '*Your* Cow, please your Excellency.' In short, she was, as I said before, a very fine Animal, of considerable beauty and energy, with many good and several amusing qualities, but wild as a witch and fierce as a demon. She used to boast publicly of her ascendancy over me, contrasting it with that of other women, and assigning for it sundry reasons. True it was, that they all tried to get her away, and no one succeeded till her own absurdity helped them. . . .

TO THOMAS MOORE

Venice, September 19, 1818

An English newspaper here would be a prodigy, and an opposition one a monster; and except some extracts *from* extracts in the vile, garbled Paris gazettes, nothing of the kind reaches the Veneto-Lombard public, who are, perhaps, the most oppressed in Europe. My correspondences with England are mostly on business, and chiefly with my attorney, who has no very exalted notion, or extensive conception, of an author's attributes; for he once took up an *Edinburgh Review*, and, looking at it a minute, said to me, 'So, I see you have got into the magazine,'—which is the only sentence I ever heard him utter upon literary matters, or the men thereof.

My first news of your Irish Apotheosis has, consequently, been from yourself. But, as it will not be forgotten in a hurry, either by your friends or your enemies, I hope to have it more in detail from some of the former, and, in the mean time, I wish you joy with all my heart. Such a moment must have been a good deal better than Westminster Abbey,—besides being an assurance of *that* one day (many years hence, I trust), into the bargain.

I am sorry to perceive, however, by the close of your letter, that even *you* have not escaped the *surgit amari*, etc., and that your damned deputy has been gathering such 'dew from the still *vext* Bermoothes'—or rather *vexatious*. Pray, give me some items of the affair, as you say it is a serious one; and, if it grows more so, you should make a trip over here for a few months, to see how things turn out. I suppose you are a violent admirer of England by your staying so long in it. For my own part, I have passed, between the age of one-and-twenty and thirty, half the intervenient years out of it without regretting any thing, except that I ever returned to it at all, and the gloomy prospect before me of business and parentage obliging me, one day, to return to it again,—at least, for the transaction of affairs, the signing of papers, and inspecting of children.

I have here my natural daughter, by name Allegra,—a pretty little girl enough, and reckoned like papa. Her mamma is English,—but it is a long story, and—there's an end. She is about twenty months old. . . .

I have finished the first canto (a long one, of about 180 octaves) of a poem in the style and manner of *Beppo*, encouraged by the good success of the same. It is called *Don Juan*, and is meant to be a little quietly facetious upon every thing. But I doubt whether it is not—at least, as far as it has yet gone—too free for these very modest days. However, I shall try the experiment, anonymously; and if it don't take, it will be discontinued. It is dedicated to Southey in good, simple, savage verse, upon the Laureat's politics, and the way he got them. But the bore of copying it out is intolerable; and if I had an amanuensis he would be of no use, as my writing is so difficult to decipher.

> *My poem's Epic, and is meant to be*
> *Divided in twelve books, each book containing,*
> *With love and war, a heavy gale at sea—*
> *A list of ships, and captains, and kings reigning—*
> *New characters, etc., etc.*

The above are two stanzas, which I send you as a brick of my Babel, and by which you can judge of the texture of the structure.

In writing the *Life* of Sheridan, never mind the angry lies of the humbug Whigs. Recollect that he was an Irishman and a clever fellow, and that *we* have had some very pleasant days with him. Don't forget that he was at school at Harrow, where, in my time, we used to show his name—R. B. Sheridan, 1765,—as an honour to the walls. Remember . . . . Depend upon it that there were worse folks going, of that gang, than ever Sheridan was.

What did Parr mean by 'haughtiness and coldness?' I listened to him with admiring ignorance, and respectful silence. What more could a talker for fame have?—they don't like to be answered. It was at Payne Knight's I met him, where he gave me more Greek than I could carry away. But I certainly meant to (and *did*) treat him with the most respectful deference.

I wish you a good night, with a Venetian benediction, '*Benedetto te, e la terra che ti fara!*'—'May you be blessed, and the *earth* which you will *make*!'—is it not pretty? You would think it still prettier if you had heard it, as I did two hours ago, from the lips of a Venetian girl, with large black eyes, a face like Faustina's, and the figure of a Juno—tall and energetic as a Pythoness, with eyes flashing, and her dark hair streaming in the moonlight—one of those women who may be made any thing. I am sure if I put a poniard into the hand of this one, she would plunge it where I told her,—and into *me*, if I offended her. I like this kind of animal, and am sure that I should have preferred Medea to any woman that ever breathed. You may, perhaps, wonder that I don't in that case . . . . I could have forgiven the dagger or the bowl,—any thing, but the deliberate desolation piled upon me, when I stood alone upon my hearth, with my household gods shivered around me. . . . Do you suppose I have forgotten it? It has comparatively swallowed up in me every other feeling, and I am only a spectator upon earth, till a tenfold opportunity offers. It may come yet. There are others more to be blamed than—, and it is on these that my eyes are fixed unceasingly.

TO JOHN MURRAY

May 15, 1819

. . . The story of Shelley's agitation is true. I can't tell what seized him, for he don't want courage. He was once with me in a gale of Wind, in a small boat, right under the rocks between Meillerie and St. Gingo. We were five in the boat—a servant, two boatmen, and ourselves. The sail was mismanaged, and the boat was filling fast. He can't swim. I stripped off my coat—made him strip off his, and take hold of an oar, telling him that I thought (being myself an expert swimmer) I could save him, if he would not struggle when I took hold of him—unless we got smashed against the rocks, which were high and sharp, with an awkward surf on them at that minute. We were then about a hundred yards from shore, and the boat in peril. He answered me with the greatest coolness, that 'he had no notion of being saved, and that I would have enough to do to save myself, and begged not to trouble me.' Luckily, the boat righted, and, baling, we got round a point into St. Gingo, where the inhabitants came down and embraced the boatmen on their escape, the Wind having been high enough to tear up some huge trees from the Alps above us, as we saw next day.

And yet the same Shelley, who was as cool as it was possible to be in such circumstances, (of which I am no judge myself, as the chance of swimming naturally gives self-possession when near shore,) certainly had the fit of phantasy which Polidori describes, though *not exactly* as he describes it.

The story of the agreement to write the Ghost-books is true; but the ladies are *not* sisters. . . . Mary Godwin (now Mrs. Shelley) wrote *Frankenstein*, which you have reviewed, thinking it Shelley's. Methinks it is a wonderful book for a girl of nineteen,—*not* nineteen, indeed, at that time. I enclose you the beginning of mine, by which you will see how far it resembles Mr. Colburn's publication. If you choose to publish it in the *Edinburgh Magazine*, you may, *stating why*, and with such explanatory proem as you please. I never went on with it, as you will perceive by the date. I began it in an old account-book of Miss Milbanke's, which I kept because it contains the word 'Household,' written by her twice on the inside blank page of the covers, being the only two scraps I have in the world in her writing, except her name to the Deed of Separation. Her letters I sent back except those of the quarrelling correspondence, and those, being documents, are placed in the hands of a third person, with copies of several of my own; so that I have no kind of memorial whatever of her, but these *two* words,—and her actions. I have torn the leaves containing the part of the Tale out of the book, and enclose them with this sheet. . . .

TO JOHN MURRAY

Ravenna, June 29, 1819

The letters have been forwarded from Venice, but I trust that you will not have waited for further alterations—I will make none. . . .

I have no time to return you the proofs—publish without them. I am glad you think the poesy good; and as to 'thinking of the effect,' think *you* of the sale, and leave me to pluck the Porcupines who may point their quills at you.

I have been here (at Ravenna) these four weeks, having left Venice a month ago;—I came to see my *Amica*, the Countess Guiccioli, who has been, and still continues, very unwell. . . . She is only twenty years old, but not of a strong constitution. . . . She has a perpetual cough and an intermittent fever, but bears up most *gallantly* in every sense of the word. Her husband (this is his third wife) is the richest noble of Ravenna, and almost of Romagna; he is also *not* the youngest, being upwards of threescore, but in good preservation. All this will appear strange to you, who do not understand the Meridian morality, nor our way of life in such respects, and I cannot at present expound the difference;—but you would find it much the same in these parts. At Faenza there is Lord Kinnaird with an opera girl; and at the inn in the same town is a Neapolitan Prince, who serves the wife of the Gonfaloniere of that city. I am on duty here—so you see 'Così fan tut*ti* e tut*te*.'

I have my horses here—*saddle* as well as carriage—and ride or drive every day in the forest, the *Pineta*, the scene of Boccaccio's novel, and Dryden's fable of Honoria, etc., etc.; and I see my *Dama* every day at the proper (and improper) hours; but I feel seriously uneasy about her health, which seems very precarious. In losing her, I should lose a being who has run great risks on my account, and whom I have every reason to love— but I must not think this possible. I do not know what I *should* do if she died, but I ought to blow my brains out—and I hope that I should. Her husband is a very polite personage, but I wish he would not carry me out in his Coach and Six, like Whittington and his Cat

You ask me if I mean to continue *D. J.*, etc. How should I know? what encouragement do you give me, all of you, with your nonsensical prudery? publish the two Cantos, and then you will see. I desired Mr. Kinnaird to speak to you on a little matter of business; either he has not spoken, or you have not answered. You are a pretty pair, but I will be even with you both. I perceive that Mr. Hobhouse has been challenged by Major Cartwright—Is the Major 'so cunning of fence?'—why did not they fight?—they ought.

Yours, etc.

TO JOHN MURRAY

Bologna, August 12, 1819

I do not know how far I may be able to reply to your letter, for I am not very well to-day. Last night I went to the representation of Alfieri's *Mirra*, the two last acts of which threw me into convulsions. I do not mean by that word a lady's hysterics, but the agony of reluctant tears, and the choaking shudder, which I do not often undergo for fiction. This is but the second time for any thing under reality; the first was on seeing Kean's Sir Giles Overreach. The worst was, that the '*dama*,' in whose box I was, went off in the same way, I really believe more from fright than any other sympathy—at least with the players: but she has been ill, and I have been ill, and we are all languid and pathetic this morning, with great expenditure of Sal Volatile. But, to return to your letter of the 23d of July.

You are right, Gifford is right, Crabbe is right, Hobhouse is right—you are all right, and I am all wrong; but do, pray, let me have that pleasure. Cut me up root and branch; quarter me in the *Quarterly*; send round my *disjecti membra poetæ*, like those of the Levite's Concubine; make me, if you will, a spectacle to men and angels; but don't ask me to alter, for I can't:—I am obstinate and lazy—and there's the truth.

But, nevertheless, I will answer your friend C[ohen], who objects to the quick succession of fun and gravity, as if in that case the gravity did not (in intention, at least) heighten the fun. His metaphor is, that 'we are never scorched and drenched at the same time.' Blessings on his experience! Ask him these questions about 'scorching and drenching.' Did he never play at Cricket, or walk a mile in hot weather? Did he never spill a dish of tea over himself in handing the cup to his charmer, to the great shame of his nankeen breeches? Did he never swim in the sea at Noonday with the Sun in his eyes and on his head, which all the foam of Ocean could not cool? Did he never draw his foot out of a tub of too hot water, damning his eyes and his valet's? . . . Did he never tumble into a river or lake, fishing, and sit in his wet cloathes in the boat, or on the bank, afterwards 'scorched and drenched,' like a true sportsman? 'Oh for breath to utter!'—but make him my compliments; he is a clever fellow for all that—a very clever fellow.

You ask me for the plan of Donny Johnny: I *have* no plan—I *had* no plan; but I had or have materials; though if, like Tony Lumpkin, I am 'to be snubbed so when I am in spirits,' the poem will be naught, and the poet turn serious again. If it don't take, I will leave it off where it is, with all due respect to the Public; but if continued, it must be in my own way. You might as well make Hamlet (or Diggory) 'act mad' in a strait waistcoat as trammel my buffoonery, if I am to be a buffoon; their gestures and my thoughts would only be pitiably absurd and ludicrously constrained. Why, Man, the Soul of such writing is its licence; at least the *liberty* of that *licence*, if one likes—*not* that one should abuse it: it is like Trial by Jury and Peerage and the Habeas Corpus—a very fine thing, but chiefly in the *reversion*; because no one wishes to be tried for the mere pleasure of proving his possession of the privilege.

But a truce with these reflections. You are too earnest and eager about a work never intended to be serious. Do you suppose that I could have any intention but to giggle and make giggle?—a playful satire, with as little poetry as could be helped, was what I meant: and as to the indecency, do, pray, read in Boswell what *Johnson*, the sullen moralist, says of *Prior* and Paulo Purgante. . . .

TO JOHN MURRAY

Bologna, August 24, 1819

I wrote to you by last post, enclosing a buffooning letter for publication, addressed to the buffoon Roberts, who has thought proper to tie a cannister to his own tail. It was written off hand, and in the midst of circumstances not very favourable to facetiousness, so that there may, perhaps, be more bitterness than enough for that sort of small acid punch. You will tell me.

Keep the *anonymous*, in every case: it helps what fun there may be; but if the matter grows serious about *Don Juan*, and you feel *yourself* in a scrape, or *me* either, *own that I am the author. I* will never *shrink*; and if *you* do, I can always answer you in the question of Guatimozin to his minister—each being on his own coals.

I wish that I had been in better spirits, but I am out of sorts, out of nerves; and now and then (I begin to fear) out of my senses. All this Italy has done for me, and not England: I defy all you, and your climate to boot, to make me mad. But if ever I do really become a Bedlamite, and wear a strait waistcoat, let me be brought back among you; your people will then be proper compagny.

I assure you what I here say and feel has nothing to do with England, either in a literary or personal point of view. All my present pleasures or plagues are as Italian as the Opera. And after all, they are but trifles, for all this arises from my *dama's* being in the country for three days (at Capofiume); but as I could never live but for one human being at a time, (and, I assure you, *that one* has never been *myself,* as you may know by the consequences, for the *Selfish* are *successful* in life,) I feel alone and unhappy.

I have sent for my daughter from Venice, and I ride daily, and walk in a Garden, under a purple canopy of grapes, and sit by a fountain, and talk with the Gardener of his toils, which seem greater than Adam's, and with his wife, and with his Son's wife, who is the youngest of the party, and, I think, talks

best of the three. Then I revisit the Campo Santo, and my old
friend, the Sexton, has two—but *one* the prettiest daughter
imaginable; and I amuse myself with contrasting her beautiful
and innocent face of fifteen with the skulls with which he has
peopled several cells, and particularly with that of one skull
dated 1766, which was once covered (the tradition goes,) by
the most lovely features of Bologna—noble and rich. When I
look at these, and at this girl—when I think of what *they were*,
and what *she* must be—why, then, my dear Murray, I won't
shock you by saying what I think. It is little matter what becomes of us 'bearded men,' but I don't like the notion of a
beautiful woman's lasting less than a beautiful tree—than her
own picture—her own shadow, which won't change so to the
Sun as her face to the mirror. I must leave off, for my head
aches consumedly: I have never been quite well since the night
of the representation of Alfieri's *Mirra*, a fortnight ago.

Yours ever.

TO COUNTESS GUICCIOLI

Bologna, August 25, 1819

My dear Teresa,

I have read this book in your garden;—my love, you were
absent, or else I could not have read it. It is a favourite book of
yours, and the writer was a friend of mine. You will not understand these English words, and *others* will not understand
them—which is the reason I have not scrawled them in
Italian. But you will recognise the hand-writing of him who
passionately loved you, and you will divine that, over a book
which was yours, he could only think of love. In that word,
beautiful in all languages, but most so in yours—*Amor mio*—is
comprised my existence here and hereafter. I feel I exist here,
and I fear that I shall exist hereafter,—to *what* purpose you
will decide; my destiny rests with you, and you are a woman,
seventeen years of age, and two out of a convent. I wish that
you had stayed there, with all my heart,—or, at least, that I
had never met you in your married state.

But all this is too late. I love you, and you love me,—at least, you *say so*, and *act* as if you *did* so, which last is a great consolation in all events. But *I* more than love you, and cannot cease to love you.

Think of me, sometimes, when the Alps and the ocean divide us,—but they never will, unless you *wish* it.

BYRON

TO R. B. HOPPNER

October 29, 1819

The Ferrara story is of a piece with all the rest of the Venetian manufacture,—you may judge. I only changed horses there since I wrote to you after my visit in June last. '*Convent*,' and '*carry off*,' quotha! and '*girl*'—I should like to know *who* has been carried off, except poor dear *me*. I have been more ravished myself than any body since the Trojan war; but as to the arrest and it's causes—one is as true as the other, and I can account for the invention of neither. I suppose it is some confusion of the tale of the F[ornarina]—and of M^e. Guiccioli—and half a dozen more—but it is useless to unravel the web, when one has only to brush it away. I shall settle with Muster Edgecombe who looks very blue at your *in-decision*, and swears that he is the best arithmetician in Europe; and so I think also, for he makes out two and two to be five.

You may see me next week. I have a horse or two more (five in all) and I shall repossess myself of Lido, and I will rise earlier, and we will go and shake our livers over the beach as heretofore—if you like, and we will make the Adriatic roar again with our hatred of that now empty Oyster shell, without it's pearl—the city of Venice.

Murray sent me a letter yesterday; the impostors have published *two* new *third* Cantos of *Don Juan*; the devil take the impudence of some blackguard bookseller or other there*for*.

Perhaps I did not make myself understood. He told me the sale had been great—1200 out of 1500 quarto I believe (which is nothing after selling 13,000 of *The Corsair* in one day) but that the 'best judges,' etc., had said it was very fine, and clever, and particularly good English, and poetry, and all those consolatory things which are not, however, worth a single copy to a bookseller;—and as to the author—of course I am in a damned passion at the bad taste of the times, and swear there is nothing like posterity, who of course must know more of the matter than their Grandfathers. There has been an eleventh commandment to the women not to read it—and what is still more extraordinary they seem not to have broken it. But that can be of little import to them, poor things, for the reading or non-reading a book will never. . . .

Count G. comes to Venice next week and I am requested to consign his wife to him, which shall be done—with all her linen. What you say of the long evenings at the Mira, or Venice, reminds me of what *Curran* said to Moore—'So—I hear—you have married a pretty woman—and a very good creature too—an excellent creature pray—um! *how do you pass your evenings?*' it is a devil of a question that, and perhaps as easy to answer with a wife as with a mistress. . . .

If you go to Milan, pray leave at least a *Vice-Consul*—the only Vice that will ever be wanting in Venice. D'Orville is a good fellow. But you should go to England in the Spring with me, and plant Mrs. Hoppner at Berne with her relations for a few months. I wish you had been here (at Venice I mean not the Mira) when Moore was here; we were very merry and tipsy—he *hated* Venice by the way, and swore it was a sad place.

So Madame Albrizzi's death is in danger, poor woman . . . Moore told me that at Geneva they had made a devil of a story of the Fornaretta:—'young lady seduced—subsequent abandonment—leap into the grand canal—her being in the hospital of *fous* in consequence.' I should like to know who was nearest being made '*fou*' and be damned to them. Don't you think me in the interesting character of a very ill used gentleman? I hope your little boy is well. Allegrina is flourishing like a pome-granate blossom. Yours ever.

TO JOHN MURRAY

Venice, 10th 10bre, 1819

Since I last wrote, I have changed my mind, and shall not come to England. The more I contemplate, the more I dislike the place and the prospect. You may, therefore, address to me as usual *here*, though I mean to go to another city. I have finished the third canto of *D[on] J[uan]*, but the things I have read and heard discourage all further publication—at least for the present. You may try the copy question, but you'll lose it: the cry is up, and cant is up. I should have no objection to return the price of the copyright, and have written to Mr. Kin^d. by this post on the subject. Talk with him.

I have not the patience, nor do I feel interest enough in the question, to contend with the fellows in their own slang; but I perceive Mr. Blackwood Magazine and one or two others of your missives have been hyperbolical in their praise, and diabolical in their abuse. I like and admire Wilson, and *he* should not have indulged himself in such outrageous license: it is overdone and defeats itself. What would he say to the grossness without passion, and the misanthropy without feeling, of *Gulliver's Travels?* When he talks of Lady Byron's business, he talks of what he knows nothing about; and you may tell him that no one can more desire a public investigation of that affair than I do.

I sent home by Moore (*for* Moore only, who has my Journal too) my memoir written up to 1816, and I gave him leave to show it to whom he pleased, but *not to publish*, on any account. You may read it, and you may let Wilson read it, if he likes—not for his *public* opinion, but his private; for I like the man, and care very little about his magazine. And I could wish Lady B. herself to read it, that she may have it in her power to mark any thing mistaken or misstated; as it will probably appear after my extinction, and it would be but fair she should see it,—that is to say, herself willing.

Perhaps I may take a journey to you in the Spring; but I *have* been ill, and *am* indolent and indecisive, because few things interest me. These fellows first abused me for being gloomy, and now they are wroth that I am, or attempted to be, facetious. I have got such a cold and headache that I can hardly see what I scrawl: the winters here are as sharp as needles. Some time ago, I wrote to you rather fully about my Italian affairs; at present I can say no more, except that you shall know further by and bye.

Your Blackwood accuses me of treating women harshly: it may be so, but I have been their martyr. My whole life has been sacrificed *to* them and *by* them. I mean to leave Venice in a few days, but you will address your letters *here* as usual. When I fix elsewhere, you shall know.

Yours.

TO R. B. HOPPNER

Ravenna, January 31, 1820

You would hardly have been troubled with the removal of my furniture but there is none to be had nearer than Bologna, and I have been fain to have that of the rooms which I fitted up for my daughter there in the summer removed here. The expense will be at least as great of the land carriage, so that you see it was necessity, and not choice. Here they get every thing from Bologna, except some lighter articles from Forli or Faenza.

If Scott is returned, pray remember me to him, and plead laziness the whole and sole cause of my not replying:—dreadful is the exertion of letter-writing. The Carnival here is less boisterous, but we have balls and a theatre. I carried Bankes to both, and he carried away, I believe, a much more favourable impression of the society here than of that of Venice,—recollect that I speak of the *native* society only.

I am drilling very hard to learn how to double a shawl, and should succeed to admiration if I did not always double it the wrong side out; and then I sometimes confuse and bring away two, so as to put all the *Serventi* out, besides keeping their *Servite* in the cold till every body can get back their property. But it is a dreadfully moral place, for you must not look at anybody's wife except your neighbour's,—if you go to the next door but one, you are scolded, and presumed to be perfidious. And then a *relazione* or an *amicizia* seems to be a regular affair of from five to fifteen years, at which period, if there occur a widowhood, it finishes by a *sposalizio*; and in the mean time it has so many rules of its own, that it is not much better. A man actually becomes a piece of female property,—they won't let their *Serventi* marry until there is a vacancy for themselves. I know two instances of this in one family here. . . .

TO THOMAS MOORE

Ravenna, May 24, 1820

I wrote to you a few days ago. There is also a letter of January last for you at Murray's, which will explain to you why I am here. Murray ought to have forwarded it long ago. I enclose you an epistle from a countrywoman of yours at Paris, which has moved my entrails. You will have the goodness, perhaps, to enquire into the truth of her story, and I will help her as far as I can,—though not in the useless way she proposes. Her letter is evidently unstudied, and so natural, that the orthography is also in a state of nature.

Here is a poor creature, ill and solitary, who thinks, as a last resource, of translating you or me into French! Was there ever such a notion? It seems to me the consummation of despair. Pray enquire, and let me know, and, if you could draw a bill on me *here* for a few hundred francs, at your banker's, I will duly honour it,—that is, if she is not an impostor. If not, let me know, that I may get something remitted by my banker Longhi, of Bologna, for I have no correspondence myself at Paris: but tell her she must not translate;—if she does, it will be the height of ingratitude.

I had a letter (not of the same kind, but in French and flattery) from a Madame Sophie Gail, of Paris, whom I take to be the spouse of a Gallo-Greek of that name. Who is she? and what is she? and how came she to take an interest in my *poeshie* or its author? If you know her, tell her, with my compliments, that, as I only *read* French, I have not answered her letter; but would have done so in Italian, if I had not thought it would look like an affectation. I have just been scolding my monkey for tearing the seal of her letter, and spoiling a mock book, in which I put rose leaves. I had a civet-cat the other day, too; but it ran away, after scratching my monkey's cheek, and I am in search of it still. It was the fiercest beast I ever saw, and like —— in the face and manner.

I have a world of things to say; but, as they are not come to a *dénouement*, I don't care to begin their history till it is wound up. After you went, I had a fever, but got well again without bark. Sir Humphry Davy was here the other day, and liked Ravenna very much. He will tell you any thing you may wish to know about the place and your humble servitor.

Your apprehensions (arising from Scott's) were unfounded. There are *no damages* in this country, but there will probably be a separation between them, as her family, which is a principal one, by its connections, are very much against *him*, for the whole of his conduct;—and he is old and obstinate, and she is young and a woman, determined to sacrifice every thing to her affections. I have given her the best advice, viz. to stay with him,—pointing out the state of a separated woman, (for the priests won't let lovers live openly together, unless the husband sanctions it,) and making the most exquisite moral reflections, —but to no purpose. She says, 'I will stay with him, if he will let you remain with me. It is hard that I should be the only woman in Romagna who is not to have her *Amico*; but, if not, I will not live with him; and as for the consequences, love, etc. etc. etc.'—you know how females reason on such occasions.

He says he has let it go on till he can do so no longer. But he wants her to stay, and dismiss me; for he doesn't like to pay back her dowry and to make an alimony. Her relations are rather for the separation, as they detest him,—indeed, so does every body. The populace and the women are, as usual, all for those who are in the wrong, viz. the lady and her lover. I should have retreated, but honour, and an erysipelas which has attacked her, prevent me,—to say nothing of love, for I love her most entirely, though not enough to persuade her to sacrifice every thing to a frenzy. 'I see how it will end; she will be the sixteenth Mrs. Shuffleton.'

My paper is finished, and so must this letter.

Yours ever, B.

P.S.—I regret that you have not completed the Italian Fudges. Pray, how come you to be still in Paris? Murray has four or five things of mine in hand—the new *Don Juan*, which his back-shop synod don't admire;—a translation of the first canto of Pulci's *Morgante Maggiore*, excellent;—a short ditto from Dante, not so much approved; the *Prophecy of Dante*, very grand and worthy, etc. etc. etc.:—a furious prose answer to Blackwood's 'Observations on *Don Juan*,' with a savage Defence of Pope—likely to make a row. The opinions above I quote from Murray and his Utican senate;—you will form your own, when you see the things.

You will have no great chance of seeing me, for I begin to think I must finish in Italy. But, if you come my way, you shall have a tureen of macaroni. Pray tell me about yourself, and your intents.

My trustees are going to lend Earl Blessington sixty thousand pounds (at six per cent.) on a Dublin mortgage. Only think of my becoming an Irish absentee!

TO JOHN MURRAY

Ravenna, 8bre 12°, 1820

By land and Sea Carriage a considerable quantity of books have arrived; and I am obliged and grateful. But 'medio de fonte leporum surgit amari aliquid,' etc. etc.; which, being interpreted, means,

> *I'm thankful for your books, dear Murray;*
> *But why not send Scott's Monast*urry?

the only book in four *living* volumes I would give a baiocco to see—abating the rest by the same author, and an occasional *Edinburgh* and *Quarterly*, as brief Chroniclers of the times.

Instead of this, here are Johnny Keats's *p——a-bed* poetry, and three novels by God knows whom, except that there is Peg Holford's name to one of them—a Spinster whom I thought we had sent back to her spinning. Crayon is very good; Hogg's Tales rough, but RACY, and welcome. . . .

Books of *travels* are expensive, and I don't want them, having travelled already; besides, they lie. Thank the author of 'The Profligate, a Comedy,' for his (or her) present. Pray send me *no more* poetry but what is rare and decidedly good. There is such a trash of Keats and the like upon my tables, that I am ashamed to look at them. I say nothing against your parsons, your Smedleys and your Crolys: it is all very fine; but pray dispense me from the pleasure, as also from Mrs. Hemans. Instead of poetry if you will favour me with a few Soda powders, I shall be delighted: but all prose (bating travels and *novels* NOT by Scott) is welcome, especially Scott's *Tales of my Landlord*, and so on. . . .

I am in a very fierce humour at not having Scott's *Monastery*. You are *too liberal* in *quantity*, and somewhat careless of the quality, of your missives. All the *Quarterlies* (four in number) I had had before from you, and *two* of the *Edinburghs*; but no matter; we shall have new ones by and bye. No more Keats, I entreat:—flay him alive; if some of you don't, I must skin him myself: there is no bearing the drivelling idiotism of the Mankin.

I don't feel inclined to care further about *Don Juan*. What do you think a very pretty Italian lady said to me the other day? She had read it in the French, and paid me some compliments, with due DRAWBACKS, upon it. I answered that what she said was true, but that I suspected it would live longer than *Childe Harold*. '*Ah but* (said She) *I would rather have the fame of Childe Harold for* THREE YEARS *than an* IMMORTALITY *of Don Juan!*' The truth is that *it is* TOO TRUE, and the women hate every thing which strips off the tinsel of *Sentiment*; and they are right, as it would rob them of their weapons. I never knew a woman who did not hate *De Grammont's memoirs* for the same reason: even Lady Oxford used to abuse them. . . .

TO THOMAS MOORE

Ravenna, Dec. 9, 1820

I open my letter to tell you a fact, which will show the state of this country better than I can. The commandant of the troops is *now* lying *dead* in my house. He was shot at a little past eight o'clock, about two hundred paces from my door. I was putting on my great-coat to visit Madame la Contessa G. when I heard the shot. On coming into the hall, I found all my servants on the balcony, exclaiming that a man was murdered. I immediately ran down, calling on Tita (the bravest of them) to follow me. The rest wanted to hinder us from going, as it is the custom for every body here, it seems, to run away from 'the stricken deer.'

However, down we ran, and found him lying on his back, almost, if not quite, dead, with five wounds; one in the heart, two in the stomach, one in the finger, and the other in the arm. Some soldiers cocked their guns, and wanted to hinder me from passing. However, we passed, and I found Diego, the adjutant, crying over him like a child—a surgeon, who said nothing of his profession—a priest, sobbing a frightened prayer—and the commandant, all this time, on his back, on the hard, cold pavement, without light or assistance, or any thing around him but confusion and dismay.

As nobody could, or would, do any thing but howl and pray, and as no one would stir a finger to move him, for fear of consequences, I lost my patience—made my servant and a couple of the mob take up the body—sent off two soldiers to the guard—despatched Diego to the Cardinal with the news, and had the commandant carried upstairs into my own quarter. But it was too late, he was gone—not at all disfigured—bled inwardly—not above an ounce or two came out.

I had him partly stripped—made the surgeon examine him, and examined him myself. He had been shot by cut balls or slugs. I felt one of the slugs, which had gone through him, all but the skin. Everybody conjectures why he was killed, but no one knows how. The gun was found close by him—an old gun, half filed down.

He only said, 'O Dio!' and 'Gesu!' two or three times, and appeared to have suffered very little. Poor fellow! he was a brave officer, but had made himself much disliked by the people. I knew him personally, and had met with him often at conversazioni and elsewhere. My house is full of soldiers, dragoons, doctors, priests, and all kinds of persons,—though I have now cleared it, and clapt sentinels at the doors. To-morrow the body is to be moved. The town is in the greatest confusion, as you may suppose.

You are to know that, if I had not had the body moved, they would have left him there till morning in the street, for fear of consequences. I would not choose to let even a dog die in such a manner, without succour:—and, as for consequences, I care for none in a duty.

Yours, etc.

P.S.—The lieutenant on duty by the body is smoking his pipe with great composure.—A queer people this.

EXTRACTS FROM A DIARY

Ravenna, January 4, 1821

'A sudden thought strikes me.' Let me begin a Journal once more. The last I kept was in Switzerland, in record of a tour made in the Bernese Alps, which I made to send to my sister in 1816, and I suppose that she has it still, for she wrote to me that she was pleased with it. Another, and longer, I kept in 1813–1814, which I gave to Thomas Moore in the same year.

This morning I gat me up late, as usual—weather bad—bad as England—worse. The snow of last week melting to the sirocco of to-day, so that there were two damned things at once. Could not even get to ride on horseback in the forest. Stayed at home all the morning—looked at the fire—wondered when the post would come. Post came at the Ave Maria, instead of half-past one o'clock, as it ought. Galignani's *Messengers*, six in number—a letter from Faenza, but none from England. Very sulky in consequence (for there ought to have been letters), and ate in consequence a copious dinner; for when

I am vexed, it makes me swallow quicker—but drank very little.

I was out of spirits—read the papers—thought what *fame* was, on reading, in a case of murder, that 'Mr. Wych, grocer, at Tunbridge, sold some bacon, flour, cheese, and, it is believed, some plums, to some gipsy woman accused. He had on his counter (I quote faithfully) a *book*, the Life of *Pamela*, which he was *tearing* for *waste* paper, etc. etc. In the cheese was found, etc. and a *leaf* of *Pamela wrapt round the bacon.*' What would Richardson, the vainest and luckiest of *living* authors (*i.e.* while alive)—he who, with Aaron Hill, used to prophesy and chuckle over the presumed fall of Fielding (the *prose* Homer of human nature) and of Pope (the most beautiful of poets)—what would he have said, could he have traced his pages from their place on the French prince's toilets (see Boswell's Johnson) to the grocer's counter and the gipsy-murderess's bacon!!!

What would he have said? What can any body say, save what Solomon said long before us? After all, it is but passing from one counter to another, from the bookseller's to the other tradesman's—grocer or pastry-cook. For my part, I have met with most poetry upon trunks; so that I am apt to consider the trunk-maker as the sexton of authorship.

Wrote five letters in about half an hour, short and savage, to all my rascally correspondents. Carriage came. Heard the news of three murders at Faenza and Forli—a carabinier, a smuggler, and an attorney—all last night. The two first in a quarrel, the latter by premeditation.

Three weeks ago—almost a month—the 7th it was—I picked up the commandant, mortally wounded, out of the street; he died in my house; assassins unknown, but presumed political. His brethren wrote from Rome last night to thank me for having assisted him in his last moments. Poor fellow! it was a pity; he was a good soldier, but imprudent. It was eight in the evening when they killed him. We heard the shot; my servants and I ran out, and found him expiring, with five wounds, two whereof mortal—by slugs they seemed. I examined him, but did not go to the dissection next morning.

Carriage at 8 or so—went to visit La Contessa G.—found her playing on the piano-forte—talked till ten, when the Count, her father, and the no less Count, her brother, came in from the theatre. Play, they said, Alfieri's *Fileppo*—well received.

Two days ago the King of Naples passed through Bologna on his way to congress. My servant Luigi brought the news. I had sent him to Bologna for a lamp. How will it end? Time will show.

Came home at eleven, or rather before. If the road and weather are comfortable, mean to ride to-morrow. High time —almost a week at this work—snow, sirocco, one day—frost and snow the other—sad climate for Italy. But the two seasons, last and present, are extraordinary. Read a Life of Leonardo da Vinci by Rossi—ruminated—wrote this much, and will go to bed.

January 5, 1821

Rose late—dull and drooping—the weather dripping and dense. Snow on the ground, and sirocco above in the sky, like yesterday. Roads up to the horse's belly, so that riding (at least for pleasure) is not very feasible. Added a postscript to my letter to Murray. Read the conclusion, for the fiftieth time (I have read all W. Scott's novels at least fifty times), of the third series of *Tales of my Landlord*,—grand work—Scotch Fielding, as well as great English poet—wonderful man! I long to get drunk with him.

Dined *versus* six o' the clock. Forgot that there was a plum-pudding, (I have added, lately, *eating* to my 'family of vices,') and had dined before I knew it. Drank half a bottle of some sort of spirits—probably spirits of wine; for what they call brandy, rum, etc. etc. here is nothing but spirits of wine, coloured accordingly. Did *not* eat two apples, which were placed by way of dessert. Fed the two cats, the hawk, and the tame (but *not* tamed) crow. Read Mitford's *History of Greece* —Xenophon's *Retreat of the Ten Thousand*. Up to this present moment writing, 6 minutes before eight o' the clock— French hours, not Italian.

Hear the carriage—order pistols and great coat, as usual—

necessary articles. Weather cold—carriage open, and inhabitants somewhat savage—rather treacherous and highly inflamed by politics. Fine fellows, though—good materials for a nation. Out of chaos God made a world, and out of high passions comes a people.

Clock strikes—going out to make love. Somewhat perilous, but not disagreeable. Memorandum—a new screen put up today. It is rather antique, but will do with a little repair.

Thaw continues—hopeful that riding may be practicable tomorrow. Sent the papers to All¹.—grand events coming.

11 o' the clock and nine minutes. Visited La Contessa G[uiccioli] *nata* G[hisleri] G[amba]. Found her beginning my letter of answer to the thanks of Alessio del Pinto of Rome for assisting his brother the late Commandant in his last moments, as I had begged her to pen my reply for the purer Italian, I being an ultramontane, little skilled in the set phrase of Tuscany. Cut short the letter—finish it another day. Talked of Italy, patriotism, Alfieri, Madame Albany, and other branches of learning. Also Sallust's *Conspiracy of Catiline*, and the *War of Jugurtha*. At 9 came in her brother, Il Conte Pietro—at 10, her father, Conte Ruggiero.

Talked of various modes of warfare—of the Hungarian and Highland modes of broad-sword exercise, in both whereof I was once a moderate 'master of fence.' Settled that the R. will break out on the 7th or 8th of March, in which appointment I should trust, had it not been settled that it was to have broken out in October, 1820. But those Bolognese shirked the Romagnuoles.

'It is all one to Ranger.' One must not be particular, but take rebellion when it lies in the way. Come home—read the *Ten Thousand* again, and will go to bed.

Mem.—Ordered Fletcher (at four o'clock this afternoon) to copy out seven or eight apophthegms of Bacon, in which I have detected such blunders as a schoolboy might detect rather than commit. Such are the sages! What must they be, when such as I can stumble on their mistakes or misstatements? I will go to bed, for I find that I grow cynical.

January 6, 1821

Mist—thaw—slop—rain. No stirring out on horseback. Read Spence's *Anecdotes*. Pope a fine fellow—always thought him so. Corrected blunders in *nine* apophthegms of Bacon—all historical—and read Mitford's *Greece*. Wrote an epigram. Turned to a passage in Guinguené—ditto in Lord Holland's *Lope de Vega*. Wrote a note on *Don Juan*.

At eight went out to visit. Heard a little music—like music. Talked with Count Pietro G. of the Italian comedian Vestris, who is now at Rome—have seen him often act in Venice—a good actor—very. Somewhat of a mannerist; but excellent in broad comedy, as well as in the sentimental pathetic. He has made me frequently laugh and cry, neither of which is now a very easy matter—at least, for a player to produce in me.

Thought of the state of women under the ancient Greeks— convenient enough. Present state a remnant of the barbarism of the chivalric and feudal ages—artificial and unnatural. They ought to mind home—and be well fed and clothed—but not mixed in society. Well educated, too, in religion—but to read neither poetry nor politics—nothing but books of piety and cookery. Music—drawing—dancing—also a little garden- ing and ploughing now and then. I have seen them mending the roads in Epirus with good success. Why not, as well as hay- making and milking?

Came home, and read Mitford again, and played with my mastiff—gave him his supper. Made another reading to the epigram, but the turn the same. To-night at the theatre, there being a prince on his throne in the last scene of the comedy,— the audience laughed, and asked him for a *Constitution*. This shows the state of the public mind here, as well as the assassin- ations. It won't do. There must be an universal republic,—and there ought to be.

The crow is lame of a leg—wonder how it happened—some fool trod upon his toe, I suppose. The falcon pretty brisk—the cats large and noisy—the monkeys I have not looked to since the cold weather, as they suffer by being brought up. Horses must be gay—get a ride as soon as weather serves. Deuced muggy still—an Italian winter is a sad thing, but all the other seasons are charming.

What is the reason that I have been, all my lifetime, more or less *ennuyé*? and that, if any thing, I am rather less so now than I was at twenty, as far as my recollection serves? I do not know how to answer this, but presume that it is constitutional,—as well as the waking in low spirits, which I have invariably done for many years. Temperance and exercise, which I have practised at times, and for a long time together vigorously and violently, made little or no difference. Violent passions did;—when under their immediate influence—it is odd, but—I was in agitated, but *not* in depressed, spirits.

A dose of salts has the effect of a temporary inebriation, like light champagne, upon me. But wine and spirits make me sullen and savage to ferocity—silent, however, and retiring, and not quarrelsome, if not spoken to. Swimming also raises my spirits,—but in general they are low, and get daily lower. That is *hopeless*; for I do not think I am so much *ennuyé* as I was at nineteen. The proof is, that then I must game, or drink, or be in motion of some kind, or I was miserable. At present, I can mope in quietness; and like being alone better than any company—except the lady's whom I serve. But I feel a something, which makes me think that, if I ever reach near to old age, like Swift, 'I shall die at top' first. Only I do not dread idiotism or madness so much as he did. On the contrary, I think some quieter stages of both must be preferable to much of what men think the possession of their senses.

January 7, 1821. Sunday

Still rain—mist—snow—drizzle—and all the incalculable combinations of a climate where heat and cold struggle for mastery. Read Spence, and turned over Roscoe, to find a passage I have not found. Read the fourth vol. of W. Scott's second series of *Tales of my Landlord*. Dined. Read the *Lugano Gazette*. Read—I forget what. At eight went to conversazione. Found there the Countess Geltrude, Betti V. and her husband, and others. Pretty black-eyed woman that—*only* nineteen—same age as Teresa, who is prettier, though.

The Count Pietro G[amba] took me aside to say that the Patriots have had notice from Forli (twenty miles off) that to-night the government and its party mean to strike a stroke —that the Cardinal here has had orders to make several arrests immediately, and that, in consequence, the Liberals are arming, and have posted patroles in the streets, to sound the alarm and give notice to fight for it.

He asked me 'what should be done?' I answered, 'Fight for it, rather than be taken in detail;' and offered, if any of them are in immediate apprehension of arrest, to receive them in my house (which is defensible), and to defend them, with my servants and themselves (we have arms and ammunition), as long as we can, —or try to get them away under cloud of night. On going home, I offered him the pistols which I had about me—but he refused, but said he would come off to me in case of accidents.

It wants half an hour of midnight, and rains;—as Gibbet says, 'a fine night for their enterprise—dark as hell, and blows like the devil.' If the row don't happen *now*, it must soon. I thought that their system of shooting people would soon produce a re-action—and now it seems coming. I will do what I can in the way of combat, though a little out of exercise. The cause is a good one.

Turned over and over half a score of books for the passage in question, and can't find it. Expect to hear the drum and the musquetry momently (for they swear to resist, and are right,) —but I hear nothing, as yet, save the plash of the rain and the gusts of the wind at intervals. Don't like to go to bed, because I hate to be waked, and would rather sit up for the row, if there is to be one.

Mended the fire—have got the arms—and a book or two, which I shall turn over. I know little of their numbers, but think the Carbonari strong enough to beat the troops, even here. With twenty men this house might be defended for twenty-four hours against any force to be brought against it *now* in this place, for the same time; and, in such a time, the country would have notice, and would rise,—if ever they *will* rise, of which there is some doubt. In the mean time, I may as well read as do any thing else, being alone.

January 8, 1821. Monday

Rose, and found Count P. G. in my apartments. Sent away the servant. Told me that, according to the best information, the Government had not issued orders for the arrests apprehended; that the attack in Forli had not taken place (as expected) by the *Sanfedisti*—the opponents of the *Carbonari* or Liberals—and that, as yet, they are still in apprehension only. Asked me for some arms of a better sort, which I gave him. Settled that, in case of a row, the Liberals were to assemble *here* (with me), and that he had given the word to Vincenzo G. and others of the *Chiefs* for that purpose. He himself and father are going to the chase in the forest; but V. G. is to come to me, and an express to be sent off to him, P. G., if any thing occurs. Concerted operations. They are to seize—but no matter.

I advised them to attack in detail, and in different parties, in different *places* (though at the *same* time), so as to divide the attention of the troops, who, though few, yet being disciplined, would beat any body of people (not trained) in a regular fight —unless dispersed in small parties, and distracted with different assaults. Offered to let them assemble here if they choose. It is a strongish post—narrow street, commanded from within—and tenable walls.

Dined. Tried on a new coat. Letter to Murray, with corrections of Bacon's *Apophthegms* and an epigram—the *latter not* for publication. At eight went to Teresa, Countess G. At nine and a half came in Il Conte P. and Count P. G. Talked of a certain proclamation lately issued. Count R. G. had been with —— (the ——), to sound him about the arrests. He, ——, is a *trimmer*, and deals, at present, his cards with both hands. If he don't mind, they'll be full. —— pretends (*I* doubt him— *they* don't,—we shall see) that there is no such order, and seems staggered by the immense exertions of the Neapolitans, and the fierce spirit of the Liberals here. The truth is, that —— cares for little but his place (which is a good one), and wishes to play pretty with both parties. He has changed his mind thirty times these last three moons, to my knowledge, for he corresponds with me. But he is not a bloody fellow—only an avaricious one.

It seems that, just at this moment (as Lydia Languish says), 'there will be no elopement after all'. I wish that I had known as much last night—or, rather, this morning—I should have gone to bed two hours earlier. And yet I ought not to complain; for, though it is a sirocco, and heavy rain, I have not *yawned* for these two days.

Came home—read *History of Greece*—before dinner had read Walter Scott's *Rob Roy*. Wrote address to the letter in answer to Alessio del Pinto, who has thanked me for helping his brother (the late Commandant, murdered here last month) in his last moments. Have told him I only did a duty of humanity—as is true. The brother lives at Rome.

Mended the fire with some *sgobole* (a Romagnuole word), and gave the falcon some water. Drank some Seltzer-water. Mem.—received to-day a print, or etching, of the story of Ugolino, by an Italian painter—different, of course, from Sir Joshua Reynolds's, and I think (as far as recollection goes) *no worse*, for Reynolds's is not good in history. Tore a button in my new coat.

I wonder what figure these Italians will make in a regular row. I sometimes think that, like the Irishman's gun (somebody had sold him a crooked one), they will only do for 'shooting round a corner;' at least, this sort of shooting has been the late tenor of their exploits. And yet there are materials in this people, and a noble energy, if well directed. But who is to direct them? No matter. Out of such times heroes spring. Difficulties are the hotbeds of high spirits, and Freedom the mother of the few virtues incident to human nature.

Tuesday, January 9, 1821

Rose—the day fine. Ordered the horses; but Lega (my *secretary*, an Italianism for steward or chief servant) coming to tell me that the painter had finished the work in fresco for the room he has been employed on lately, I went to see it before I set out. The painter has not copied badly the prints from Titian, etc. considering all things.

Dined. Read Johnson's *Vanity of Human Wishes*,—all the examples and mode of giving them sublime, as well as the latter part, with the exception of an occasional couplet. I do not so much admire the opening. I remember an observation of Sharpe's, (the *Conversationist*, as he was called in London, and a very clever man,) that the first line of this poem was superfluous, and that Pope (the best of poets, *I* think,) would have begun at once, only changing the punctuation—

Survey mankind from China to Peru.

The former line, 'Let observation,' etc., is certainly heavy and useless. But 'tis a grand poem—and *so true!*—true as the 10th of Juvenal himself. The lapse of ages *changes* all things—time —language—the earth—the bounds of the sea—the stars of the sky, and every thing 'about, around, and underneath' man, *except man himself*, who has always been, and always will be, an unlucky rascal. The infinite variety of lives conduct but to death, and the infinity of wishes lead but to disappoint-ment. All the discoveries which have yet been made have multiplied little but existence. An extirpated disease is suc-ceeded by some new pestilence; and a discovered world has brought little to the old one, except the p—— first and freedom afterwards—the *latter* a fine thing, particularly as they gave it to Europe in exchange for slavery. But it is doubtful whether 'the Sovereigns' would not think the *first* the best present of the two to their subjects.

At eight went out—heard some news. They say the King of Naples has declared by couriers from Florence, to the *Powers* (as they call now those wretches with crowns), that his Consti-tution was compulsive, etc., etc., and that the Austrian bar-barians are placed again on *war* pay, and will march. Let them—'they come like sacrifices in their trim,' the hounds of hell! Let it still be a hope to see their bones piled like those of the human dogs at Morat, in Switzerland, which I have seen.

Heard some music. At nine the usual visitors—news, *war*, or rumours of war. Consulted with P. G. etc., etc. They mean to *insurrect* here, and are to honour me with a call thereupon.

I shall not fall back; though I don't think them in force or heart sufficient to make much of it. But, *onward!*—it is now the time to act, and what signifies *self*, if a single spark of that which would be worthy of the past can be bequeathed unquenchedly to the future? It is not one man, nor a million, but the *spirit* of liberty which must be spread. The waves which dash upon the shore are, one by one, broken, but yet the *ocean* conquers, nevertheless. It overwhelms the Armada, it wears the rock, and, if the *Neptunians* are to be believed, it has not only destroyed, but made a world. In like manner, whatever the sacrifice of individuals, the great cause will gather strength, sweep down what is rugged, and fertilise (for *sea-weed* is *manure*) what is cultivable. And so, the mere selfish calculation ought never to be made on such occasions; and, at present, it shall not be computed by me. I was never a good arithmetician of chances, and shall not commence now.

January 10, 1821

Day fine—rained only in the morning. Looked over accounts. Read Campbell's *Poets*—marked errors of Tom (the author) for correction. Dined—went out—music—Tyrolese air, with variations. Sustained the cause of the original simple air against the variations of the Italian school.

Politics somewhat tempestuous, and cloudier daily. To-morrow being foreign post-day, probably something more will be known.

Came home—read. Corrected Tom Campbell's slips of the pen. A good work, though—style affected—but his defence of Pope is glorious. To be sure, it is his *own cause* too,—but no matter, it is very good, and does him great credit.

Midnight

I have been turning over different *Lives* of the Poets. I rarely read their works, unless an occasional flight over the classical ones, Pope, Dryden, Johnson, Gray, and those who approach them nearest (I leave the *rant* of the rest to the *cant* of the day), and—I had made several reflections, but I feel sleepy, and may as well go to bed.

January 11, 1821

Read the letters. Corrected the tragedy and the *Hints from Horace*. Dined, and got into better spirits. Went out—returned—finished letters, five in number. Read *Poets*, and an anecdote in Spence.

All¹. writes to me that the Pope, and Duke of Tuscany, and King of Sardinia, have also been called to Congress; but the Pope will only deal there by proxy. So the interests of millions are in the hands of about twenty coxcombs, at a place called Leibach!

I should almost regret that my own affairs went well, when those of nations are in peril. If the interests of mankind could be essentially bettered (particularly of these oppressed Italians), I should not so much mind my own 'sma peculiar.' God grant us all better times, or more philosophy!

In reading, I have just chanced upon an expression of Tom Campbell's;—speaking of Collins, he says that 'no reader cares any more about the *characteristic manners* of his Eclogues than about the authenticity of the tale of Troy.' 'Tis false—we *do* care about 'the authenticity of the tale of Troy.' I have stood upon that plain *daily*, for more than a month in 1810; and if any thing diminished my pleasure, it was that the blackguard Bryant had impugned its veracity. It is true I read *Homer Travestied* (the first twelve books), because Hobhouse and others bored me with their learned localities, and I love quizzing. But I still venerated the grand original as the truth of *history* (in the material *facts*) and of *place*. Otherwise, it would have given me no delight. Who will persuade me, when I reclined upon a mighty tomb, that it did not contain a hero?—its very magnitude proved this. Men do not labour over the ignoble and petty dead—and why should not the *dead* be *Homer*'s dead? The secret of Tom Campbell's defence of *inaccuracy* in costume and description is, that his *Gertrude*, etc. has no more locality in common with Pennsylvania than with Penmanmaur. It is notoriously full of grossly false scenery, as all Americans declare, though they praise parts of the poem. It is thus that self-love for ever creeps out, like a snake, to sting any thing which happens, even accidentally, to stumble upon it.

January 12, 1821

The weather still so humid and impracticable, that London, in its most oppressive fogs, were a summer-bower to this mist and sirocco, which has now lasted (but with one day's interval), chequered with snow or heavy rain only, since the 30th of December, 1820. It is so far lucky that I have a literary turn;—but it is very tiresome not to be able to stir out, in comfort, on any horse but Pegasus, for so many days. The roads are even worse than the weather, by the long splashing, and the heavy soil, and the growth of the waters.

Read the Poets—English, that is to say—out of Campbell's edition. There is a good deal of taffeta in some of Tom's prefatory phrases, but his work is good as a whole. I like him best, though, in his own poetry.

Murray writes that they want to act the Tragedy of *Marino Faliero*—more fools they, it was written for the closet. I have protested against this piece of usurpation, (which, it seems, is legal for managers over any printed work, against the author's will) and I hope they will not attempt it. Why don't they bring out some of the numberless aspirants for theatrical celebrity, now encumbering their shelves, instead of lugging me out of the library? I have written a fierce protest against any such attempt; but I still would hope that it will not be necessary, and that they will see, at once, that it is not intended for the stage. It is too regular—the time, twenty-four hours—the change of place not frequent—nothing *melo*-dramatic—no surprises, no starts, nor trap-doors, nor opportunities 'for tossing their heads and kicking their heels'—and no *love*—the grand ingredient of a modern play.

I have found out the seal cut on Murray's letter. It is meant for Walter Scott—or *Sir* Walter—he is the first poet knighted since Sir Richard Blackmore. But it does not do him justice. Scott's—particularly when he recites—is a very intelligent countenance, and this seal says nothing.

Scott is certainly the most wonderful writer of the day. His novels are a new literature in themselves, and his poetry as good as any—if not better (only on an erroneous system)—and only ceased to be so popular, because the vulgar learned were tired of hearing 'Aristides called the Just,' and Scott the Best, and ostracised him.

I like him, too, for his manliness of character, for the extreme pleasantness of his conversation, and his good-nature towards myself, personally. May he prosper!—for he deserves it. I know no reading to which I fall with such alacrity as a work of W. Scott's. I shall give the seal, with his bust on it, to Madame la Comtesse G. this evening, who will be curious to have the effigies of a man so celebrated.

How strange are my thoughts!...

Midnight

Read the Italian translation by Guido Sorelli of the German Grillparzer—a devil of a name, to be sure, for posterity; but they *must* learn to pronounce it. With all the allowance for a *translation*, and above all, an *Italian* translation (they are the very worst of translators, except from the Classics—Annibale Caro, for instance—and *there*, the bastardy of their language helps them, as, by way of *looking legitimate*, they ape their father's tongue);—but with every allowance for such a disadvantage, the tragedy of *Sappho* is superb and sublime! There is no denying it. The man has done a great thing in writing that play. And *who is he?* I know him not; but *ages will*. 'Tis a high intellect.

I must premise, however, that I have read *nothing* of Adolph Müllner's (the author of *Guilt*, and much less of Goethe, and Schiller, and Wieland, than I could wish. I only know them through the medium of English, French, and Italian translations. Of the *real* language I know absolutely nothing,—except oaths learned from postillions and officers in a squabble! I can *swear* in German potently, when I like—'Sacrament—Verfluchter—Hundsfott'—and so forth; but I have little else of their energetic conversation.

I like, however, their women, (I was once *so desperately* in love with a German woman, Constance,) and all that I have read, translated, of their writings, and all that I have seen on the Rhine of their country and people—all, except the Austrians, whom I abhor, loathe, and—I cannot find words for my hate of them, and should be sorry to find deeds correspondent to my hate; for I abhor cruelty more than I abhor the Austrians—except on an impulse, and then I am savage— but not deliberately so.

Grillparzer is grand—antique—*not so simple* as the ancients, but very simple for a modern—too Madame de Stael*ish*, now and then—but altogether a great and goodly writer.

January 13, 1821, Saturday

Sketched the outline and Drams. Pers. of an intended tragedy of Sardanapalus, which I have for some time meditated. Took the names from Diodorus Siculus, (I know the history of Sardanapalus, and have known it since I was twelve years old,) and read over a passage in the ninth vol. octavo, of Mitford's *Greece*, where he rather vindicates the memory of this last of the Assyrians.

Dined—news come—the *Powers* mean to war with the peoples. The intelligence seems positive—let it be so—they will be beaten in the end. The king-times are fast finishing. There will be blood shed like water, and tears like mist; but the peoples will conquer in the end. I shall not live to see it, but I foresee it.

I carried Teresa the Italian translation of Grillparzer's *Sappho*, which she promises to read. She quarrelled with me, because I said that love was *not the loftiest* theme for true tragedy; and, having the advantage of her native language, and natural female eloquence, she overcame my fewer arguments. I believe she was right. I must put more love into *Sardanapalus* than I intended. I speak, of course, *if* the times will allow me leisure. That *if* will hardly be a peace-maker.

January 14, 1821

Turned over Seneca's tragedies. Wrote the opening lines of the intended tragedy of *Sardanapalus*. Rode out some miles into the forest. Misty and rainy. Returned—dined—wrote some more of my tragedy.

Read Diodorus Siculus—turned over Seneca, and some other books. Wrote some more of the tragedy. Took a glass of grog. After having ridden hard in rainy weather, and scribbled, and scribbled again, the spirits (at least mine) need a little exhilaration, and I don't like laudanum now as I used to do. So I have mixed a glass of strong waters and single waters, which I shall now proceed to empty. Therefore and thereunto I conclude this day's diary.

The effect of all wines and spirits upon me is, however, strange. It *settles*, but it makes me gloomy—gloomy at the very moment of their effect, and not gay hardly ever. But it composes for a time, though sullenly.

January 15, 1821

Weather fine. Received visit. Rode out into the forest—fired pistols. Returned home—dined—dipped into a volume of Mitford's *Greece*—wrote part of a scene of *Sardanapalus*. Went out—heard some music—heard some politics. More ministers from the other Italian powers gone to Congress. War seems certain—in that case, it will be a savage one. Talked over various important matters with one of the initiated. At ten and half returned home.

I have just thought of something odd. In the year 1814, Moore ('the poet,' *par excellence*, and he deserves it) and I were going together, in the same carriage, to dine with Earl Grey, the *Capo Politico* of the remaining Whigs. Murray, the magnificent (the illustrious publisher of that name), had just sent me a Java gazette—I know not why, or wherefore. Pulling it out, by way of curiosity, we found it to contain a dispute (the said Java gazette) on Moore's merits and mine. I think, if I had been there, that I could have saved them the trouble of disputing on the subject. But, there is *fame* for you at six and twenty! Alexander had conquered India at the same age; but I doubt if he was disputed about, or his conquests compared with those of Indian Bacchus, at Java.

It was a great fame to be named with Moore; greater to be compared with him; greatest—*pleasure*, at least—to be *with* him; and, surely, an odd coincidence, that we should be dining together while they were quarrelling about us beyond the equinoctial line.

Well, the same evening, I met Lawrence the painter, and heard one of Lord Grey's daughters (a fine, tall, spirit-looking girl, with much of the *patrician thorough-bred look* of her father, which I dote upon) play on the harp, so modestly and ingenuously, that she *looked music*. Well, I would rather have had my talk with Lawrence (who talked delightfully) and heard the girl, than have had all the fame of Moore and me put together.

The only pleasure of fame is that it paves the way to pleasure; and the more intellectual our pleasure, the better for the pleasure and for us too. It was, however, agreeable to have heard our fame before dinner, and a girl's harp after.

January 16, 1821

Read—rode—fired pistols—returned—dined—wrote—visited—heard music—talked nonsense—and went home.

Wrote part of a Tragedy—advanced in Act 1st with 'all deliberate speed.' Bought a blanket. The weather is still muggy as a London May—mist, mizzle, the air replete with Scotticisms, which, though fine in the descriptions of Ossian, are somewhat tiresome in real, prosaic perspective. Politics still mysterious.

January 17, 1821

Rode i' the forest—fired pistols—dined. Arrived a packet of books from England and Lombardy—English, Italian, French, and Latin. Read till eight—went out.

January 18, 1821

To-day, the post arriving late, did not ride. Read letters—only two gazettes instead of twelve now due. Made Lega write to that negligent Galignani, and added a postscript. Dined.

At eight proposed to go out. Lega came in with a letter about a bill *unpaid* at Venice, which I thought paid months ago. I flew into a paroxysm of rage, which almost made me faint. I have not been well ever since. I deserve it for being such a fool—but it *was* provoking—a set of scoundrels! It is, however, but five and twenty pounds.

January 19, 1821

Rode. Winter's wind somewhat more unkind than ingratitude itself, though Shakspeare says otherwise. At least, I am so much more accustomed to meet with ingratitude than the north wind, that I thought the latter the sharper of the two. I had met with both in the course of the twenty-four hours, so could judge.

Thought of a plan of education for my daughter Allegra, who ought to begin soon with her studies. Wrote a letter—afterwards a postscript. Rather in low spirits—certainly hippish—liver touched—will take a dose of salts.

I have been reading the Life, by himself and daughter, of Mr. R. L. Edgeworth, the father of *the* Miss Edgeworth. It is altogether a great name. In 1813, I recollect to have met them in the fashionable world of London (of which I then formed an item, a fraction, the segment of a circle, the unit of a million, the nothing of something) in the assemblies of the hour, and at a breakfast of Sir Humphry and Lady Davy's, to which I was invited for the nonce. I had been the lion of 1812 : Miss Edgeworth and Madame de Stael, with 'the Cossack,' towards the end of 1813, were the exhibitions of the succeeding year.

I thought Edgeworth a fine old fellow, of a clarety, elderly, red complexion, but active, brisk, and endless. He was seventy, but did not look fifty—no, nor forty-eight even. I had seen poor Fitzpatrick not very long before—a man of pleasure, wit, eloquence, all things. He tottered—but still talked like a gentleman, though feebly. Edgeworth bounced about, and talked loud and long; but he seemed neither weakly nor decrepit, and hardly old.

He began by telling 'that he had given Dr. Parr a dressing, who had taken him for an Irish bogtrotter,' etc., etc. Now I, who know Dr. Parr, and who know (*not* by experience—for I never should have presumed so far as to contend with him—but by hearing him *with* others, and *of* others) that it is not so easy a matter to 'dress him,' thought Mr. Edgeworth an assertor of what was not true. He could not have stood before Parr an instant. For the rest, he seemed intelligent, vehement, vivacious, and full of life. He bids fair for a hundred years.

He was not much admired in London, and I remember a 'ryghte merrie' and conceited jest which was rife among the gallants of the day,—viz. a paper had been presented for the *recall of Mrs. Siddons to the stage*, (she having lately taken leave, to the loss of ages,—for nothing ever was, or can be, like her,) to which all men had been called to subscribe. Whereupon Thomas Moore, of profane and poetical memory, did propose that a similar paper should be *sub*scribed and *circum*scribed 'for the recall of Mr. Edgeworth to Ireland.'

The fact was—every body cared more about *her*. She was a nice little unassuming 'Jeanie Deans-looking body,' as we Scotch say—and, if not handsome, certainly not ill-looking. Her conversation was as quiet as herself. One would never have guessed she could write *her name*; whereas her father talked, *not* as if he could write nothing else, but as if nothing else was worth writing.

As for Mrs. Edgeworth, I forget—except that I think she was the youngest of the party. Altogether, they were an excellent cage of the kind; and succeeded for two months, till the landing of Madame de Stael.

To turn from them to their works, I admire them; but they excite no feeling, and they leave no love—except for some Irish steward or postillion. However, the impression of intellect and prudence is profound—and may be useful.

January 21, 1821

Rode—fired pistols. Read from Grimm's *Correspondence*. Dined—went out—heard music—returned—wrote a letter to the Lord Chamberlain to request him to prevent the theatres from representing the Doge, which the Italian papers say that they are going to act. This is pretty work—what! without asking my consent, and even in opposition to it!

January 21, 1821

Fine, clear, frosty day—that is to say, an Italian frost, for their winters hardly get beyond snow; for which reason nobody knows how to skate (or skait)—a Dutch and English accomplishment. Rode out, as usual, and fired pistols. Good shooting—broke four common, and rather small, bottles, in four shots, at fourteen paces, with a common pair of pistols and indifferent powder. Almost as good *wafering* or shooting—considering the difference of powder and pistol,—as when, in 1809, 1810, 1811, 1812, 1813, 1814, it was my luck to split walking-sticks, wafers, half-crowns, shillings, and even the *eye* of a walking-stick, at twelve paces, with a single bullet—and all by *eye* and calculation; for my hand is not steady, and apt to change with the very weather. To the prowess which I here note, Joe Manton and others can bear testimony; for the former taught, and the latter has seen me do, these feats.

Dined—visited—came home—read. Remarked on an anecdote in Grimm's *Correspondence*, which says that 'Regnard et la plûpart des poëtes comiques étaient gens bilieux et mélancoliques; et que M. de Voltaire, qui est très gai, n'a jamais fait que des tragédies—et que la comédie gaie est le seul genre où il n'ait point réussi. C'est que celui qui rit et celui qui fait rire sont deux hommes fort différens.'—Vol. VI.

At this moment I feel as bilious as the best comic writer of them all, (even as Regnard himself, the next to Molière, who has written some of the best comedies in any language, and who is supposed to have committed suicide,) and am not in spirits to continue my proposed tragedy of *Sardanapalus*, which I have, for some days,' ceased to compose.

To-morrow is my birth-day—that is to say, at twelve o' the clock, midnight, *i. e.* in twelve minutes, I shall have completed thirty and three years of age!!!—and I go to my bed with a heaviness of heart at having lived so long, and to so little purpose.

It is three minutes past twelve.—' 'Tis the middle of the night by the castle clock,' and I am now thirty-three!

> *Eheu, fugaces, Posthume, Posthume,*
> *Labuntur anni;—*

but I don't regret them so much for what I have done, as for what I *might* have done.

> *Through life's road, so dim and dirty,*
> *I have dragged to three-and-thirty.*
> *What have these years left to me?*
> *Nothing—except thirty-three.*

January 22, 1821

1821.
Here lies
interred in the Eternity
of the Past,
from whence there is no
Resurrection
for the Days—Whatever there may be
for the Dust—
the Thirty-Third Year
of an ill-spent Life,
Which, after
a lingering disease of many months,
sunk into a lethargy,
and expired,
January 22d, 1821, A. D.
Leaving a successor
Inconsolable
for the very loss which
occasioned its
Existence.

January 23, 1821

Fine day. Read—rode—fired pistols, and returned. Dined—read. Went out at eight—made the usual visit. Heard of nothing but war,—'the cry is still, They come.' The Carbonari seem to have no plan—nothing fixed among themselves, how, when, or what to do. In that case, they will make nothing of this project, so often postponed, and never put in action.

Came home, and gave some necessary orders, in case of circumstances requiring a change of place. I shall act according to what may seem proper, when I hear decidedly what the Barbarians mean to do. At present, they are building a bridge of boats over the Po, which looks very warlike. A few days will probably show. I think of retiring towards Ancona, nearer the northern frontier; that is to say, if Teresa and her father are obliged to retire, which is most likely, as all the family are Liberals. If not, I shall stay. But my movements will depend upon the lady's wishes—for myself, it is much the same.

I am somewhat puzzled what to do with my little daughter, and my effects, which are of some quantity and value,—and neither of them do in the seat of war, where I think of going. But there is an elderly lady who will take charge of *her*, and T. says that the Marchese C. will undertake to hold the chattels in safe keeping. Half the city are getting their affairs in marching trim. A pretty Carnival! The blackguards might as well have waited till Lent.

January 24, 1821

Returned—met some masques in the Corso—*Vive la bagatelle!*—the Germans are on the Po, the Barbarians at the gate, and their masters in council at Leybach (or whatever the eructation of the sound may syllable into a human pronunciation), and lo! they dance and sing and make merry, 'for to-morrow they may die.' Who can say that the Arlequins are not right? Like the Lady Baussiere, and my old friend Burton—I 'rode on.'

Dined—(damn this pen!)—beef tough—there is no beef in Italy worth a curse; unless a man could eat an old ox with the hide on, singed in the sun.

The principal persons in the events which may occur in a few days are gone out on a *shooting party*. If it were like a '*highland* hunting,' a pretext of the chase for a grand re-union of counsellors and chiefs, it would be all very well. But it is nothing more or less than a real snivelling, popping, small-shot, water-hen waste of powder, ammunition, and shot, for their own special amusement: a rare set of fellows for 'a man to risk his neck with,' as 'Marishall Wells' says in the *Black Dwarf.*

If they gather,—'whilk is to be doubted,'—they will not muster a thousand men. The reason of this is, that the populace are not interested,—only the higher and middle orders. I wish that the peasantry *were*; they are a fine savage race of two-legged leopards. But the Bolognese won't—the Romagnuoles can't without them. Or, if they try—what then? They will try, and man can do no more—and, if he *would* but try his utmost, much might be done. The Dutch, for instance, against the Spaniards—*then* the tyrants of Europe, since, the slaves, and, lately, the freedmen.

The year 1820 was not a fortunate one for the individual me, whatever it may be for the nations. I lost a lawsuit, after two decisions in my favour. The project of lending money on an Irish mortgage was finally rejected by my wife's trustee after a year's hope and trouble. The Rochdale lawsuit had endured fifteen years, and always prospered till I married; since which, every thing has gone wrong—with me at least.

In the same year, 1820, the Countess T. G. *nata* G^i. G^i., in despite of all I said and did to prevent it, *would* separate from her husband, Il Cavalier Commendatore G^i. etc., etc., etc., and all on the account of 'P. P. clerk of this parish.' The other little petty vexations of the year—overturns in carriages—the murder of people before one's door, and dying in one's beds—the cramp in swimming—colics—indigestions and bilious attacks, etc., etc., etc.—

> *Many small articles make up a sum,*
> *And hey ho for Caleb Quotem, oh!*

January 25, 1821

Received a letter from Lord S[idney] O[sborne], state secretary of the Seven Islands—a fine fellow—clever—dished in England five years ago, and came abroad to retrench and to renew. He wrote from Ancona, in his way back to Corfu, on some matters of our own. He is son of the late Duke of L[eeds] by a second marriage. He wants me to go to Corfu. Why not?—perhaps I may, next spring.

Answered Murray's letter—read—lounged. Scrawled this additional page of life's log-book. One day more is over of it and of me:—but 'which is best, life or death, the gods only know,' as Socrates said to his judges, on the breaking up of the tribunal. Two thousand years since that sage's declaration of ignorance have not enlightened us more upon this important point; for, according to the Christian dispensation, no one can know whether he is *sure* of salvation—even the most righteous —since a single slip of faith may throw him on his back, like a skaiter, while gliding smoothly to his paradise. Now, there-fore, whatever the certainty of faith in the facts may be, the certainty of the individual as to his happiness or misery is no greater than it was under Jupiter.

It has been said that the immortality of the soul is a *grand peut-être*—but still it is a *grand* one. Every body clings to it— the stupidest, and dullest, and wickedest of human bipeds is still persuaded that he is immortal.

January 26, 1821

Fine day—a few mares' tails portending change, but the sky clear, upon the whole. Rode—fired pistols—good shooting. Coming back, met an old man. Charity—purchased a shilling's worth of salvation. If that was to be bought, I have given more to my fellow-creatures in this life—sometimes for *vice*, but, if not more *often*, at least more *considerably*, for virtue—than I now possess. I never in my life gave a mistress so much as I have sometimes given a poor man in honest distress; but no matter. The scoundrels who have all along persecuted me (with the help of —— who has crowned their efforts) will triumph;—and, when justice is done to me, it will be when this hand that writes is as cold as the hearts which have stung me.

Returning, on the bridge near the mill, met an old woman. I asked her age—she said '*Tre croci.*' I asked my groom (though myself a decent Italian) what the devil *her* three crosses meant. He said, ninety years, and that she had five years more to boot!! I repeated the same three times—not to mistake—ninety-five years!!!—and she was yet rather active—*heard* my question, for she answered it—*saw* me, for she advanced towards me; and did not appear at all decrepit, though certainly touched with years. Told her to come to-morrow, and will examine her myself. I love phenomena. If she *is* ninety-five years old, she must recollect the Cardinal Alberoni, who was legate here.

On dismounting, found Lieutenant E. just arrived from Faenza. Invited him to dine with me to-morrow. Did *not* invite him for to-day, because there was a small *turbot*, (Friday, fast regularly and religiously,) which I wanted to eat all myself. Ate it.

Went out—found T. as usual—music. The gentlemen, who make revolutions and are gone on a shooting, are not yet returned. They don't return till Sunday—that is to say, they have been out for five days, buffooning, while the interests of a whole country are at stake, and even they themselves compromised.

It is a difficult part to play amongst such a set of assassins and blockheads—but, when the scum is skimmed off, or has boiled over, good may come of it. If this country could but be freed, what would be too great for the accomplishment of that desire? for the extinction of that Sigh of Ages? Let us hope. They have hoped these thousand years. The very revolvement of the chances may bring it—it is upon the dice.

If the Neapolitans have but a single Massaniello amongst them, they will beat the bloody butchers of the crown and sabre. Holland, in worse circumstances, beat the Spains and Philips; America beat the English; Greece beat Xerxes; and France beat Europe, till she took a tyrant; South America beats her old vultures out of their nest; and, if these men are but firm in themselves, there is nothing to shake them from without.

January 28, 1821

Lugano Gazette did not come. Letters from Venice. It appears that the Austrian brutes have seized my three or four pounds of English powder. The scoundrels!—I hope to pay them in *ball* for that powder. Rode out till twilight.

Pondered the subjects of four tragedies to be written (life and circumstances permitting), to wit, Sardanapalus, already begun; Cain, a metaphysical subject, something in the style of Manfred, but in five *acts*, perhaps, with the chorus; Francesca of Rimini, in five acts; and I am not sure that I would not try Tiberius. I think that I could extract a something, of *my* tragic, at least, out of the gloomy sequestration and old age of the tyrant—and even out of his sojourn at Caprea—by softening the *details*, and exhibiting the despair which must have led to those very vicious pleasures. For none but a powerful and gloomy mind overthrown would have had recourse to such solitary horrors,—being also, at the same time, *old*, and the master of the world.

Memoranda.

What is Poetry?—The feeling of a Former world and Future.

Thought Second.

Why, at the very height of desire and human pleasure,— worldly, social, amorous, ambitious, or even avaricious,— does there mingle a certain sense of doubt and sorrow—a fear of what is to come—a doubt of what *is*—a retrospect to the past, leading to a prognostication of the future? (The best of Prophets of the future is the Past.) Why is this, or these?—I know not, except that on a pinnacle we are most susceptible of giddiness, and that we never fear falling except from a preci- pice—the higher, the more awful, and the more sublime; and, therefore, I am not sure that Fear is not a pleasurable sensation; at least, *Hope* is; and *what Hope* is there without a deep leaven of Fear? and what sensation is so delightful as Hope? and, if it were not for Hope, where would the Future be?—in hell. It is useless to say *where* the Present is, for most of us know; and as for the Past, *what* predominates in memory?— *Hope baffled.* Ergo, in all human affairs, it is Hope—Hope— Hope. I allow sixteen minutes, though I never counted them, to any given or supposed possession. From whatever place we commence, we know where it all must end. And yet, what good is there in knowing it? It does not make men better or wiser. During the greatest horrors of the greatest plagues, (Athens and Florence, for example—see Thucydides and Machiavelli,) men were more cruel and profligate than ever. It is all a mystery. I feel most things, but I know nothing, except

— — — — — — — — — — — —
— — — — — — — — — — — —
— — — — — — — — — — —

*Thought for a Speech of Lucifer, in the
Tragedy of Cain:—*

Were Death *an* evil, *would* I *let thee* live?
*Fool! live as I live—as thy father lives,
And thy son's sons shall live for evermore.*

Past Midnight. One o' the clock

I have been reading Frederick Schlegel (brother to the other of the name) till now, and I can make out nothing. He evidently shows a great power of words, but there is nothing to be taken hold of. He is like Hazlitt, in English, who *talks pimples* —a red and white corruption rising up (in little imitation of mountains upon maps), but containing nothing, and discharging nothing, except their own humours.

I dislike him the worse, (that is, Schlegel,) because he always seems upon the verge of meaning; and, lo, he goes down like sunset, or melts like a rainbow, leaving a rather rich confusion,—to which, however, the above comparisons do too much honour.

Continuing to read Mr. Frederick Schlegel. He is not such a fool as I took him for, that is to say, when he speaks of the North. But still he speaks of things *all over the world* with a kind of authority that a philosopher would disdain, and a man of common sense, feeling, and knowledge of his own ignorance, would be ashamed of. The man is evidently wanting to make an impression, like his brother,—or like George in the Vicar of Wakefield, who found out that all the good things had been said already on the right side, and therefore 'dressed up some paradoxes' upon the wrong side—ingenious, but false, as he himself says—to which 'the learned world said nothing, nothing at all, sir.' The 'learned world,' however, *has* said something to the brothers Schlegel.

It is high time to think of something else. What they say of the antiquities of the North is best.

January 29, 1821

Yesterday, the woman of ninety-five years of age was with me. She said her eldest son (if now alive) would have been seventy. She is thin—short, but active—hears, and sees, and talks incessantly. Several teeth left—all in the lower jaw, and single front teeth. She is very deeply wrinkled, and has a sort of scattered grey beard over her chin, at least as long as my mustachios. Her head, in fact, resembles the drawing in crayons of Pope the poet's mother, which is in some editions of his works.

I forgot to ask her if she remembered Alberoni (legate here), but will ask her next time. Gave her a louis—ordered her a new suit of clothes, and put her upon a weekly pension. Till now, she had worked at gathering wood and pine-nuts in the forest,—pretty work at ninety-five years old! She had a dozen children, of whom some are alive. Her name is Maria Montanari.

Met a company of the sect (a kind of Liberal Club) called the *Americani* in the forest, all armed, and singing, with all their might, in Romagnuole—'*Sem* tutti soldat' per la liberta' ('we are all soldiers for liberty'). They cheered me as I passed— I returned their salute, and rode on. This may show the spirit of Italy at present.

My to-day's journal consists of what I omitted yesterday. To-day was much as usual. Have rather a better opinion of the writings of the Schlegels than I had four-and-twenty hours ago; and will amend it still further, if possible.

They say that the Piedmontese have at length arisen—*ça ira!*

Read Schlegel. Of Dante he says, 'that at no time has the greatest and most national of all Italian poets ever been much the favourite of his countrymen.' 'Tis false! There have been more editors and commentators (and imitators, ultimately) of Dante than of all their poets put together. *Not* a favourite! Why, they talk Dante—write Dante—and think and dream Dante at this moment (1821) to an excess, which would be ridiculous, but that he deserves it.

In the same style this German talks of gondolas on the Arno —a precious fellow to dare to speak of Italy!

He says also that Dante's chief defect is a want, in a word, of gentle feelings. Of gentle feelings!—and Francesca of Rimini —and the father's feelings in Ugolino—and Beatrice—and 'La Pia!' Why, there is gentleness in Dante beyond all gentleness, when he is tender. It is true that, treating of the Christian Hades, or Hell, there is not much scope or site for gentleness— but who *but* Dante could have introduced any 'gentleness' at all into *Hell*? Is there any in Milton's? No—and Dante's Heaven is all love, and glory and majesty.

One o'clock

I have found out, however, where the German is right—it is about the *Vicar of Wakefield*. 'Of all romances in miniature (and, perhaps, this is the best shape in which romance can appear) the *Vicar of Wakefield* is, I think, the most exquisite.' He *thinks!*—he might be sure. But it is very well for a Schlegel. I feel sleepy, and may as well get me to bed. To-morrow there will be fine weather.

Trust on, and think to-morrow will repay.

January 30, 1821

The Count P. G. this evening (by commission from the Ci.) transmitted to me the new *words* for the next six months. —— and ——. The new sacred word is —— . . . the reply ——

. . . the rejoinder ———. The former word (now changed) was
——— . . . there is also ——— . . . ———. Things seem fast coming
to a crisis—*ça ira!*

We talked over various matters of moment and movement.
These I omit;—if they come to any thing, they will speak for
themselves. After these, we spoke of Kosciusko. Count R. G.
told me that he has seen the Polish officers in the Italian war
burst into tears on hearing his name.

Something must be up in Piedmont—all the letters and
papers are stopped. Nobody knows anything, and the
Germans are concentrating near Mantua. Of the decision of
Leybach nothing is known. This state of things cannot last
long. The ferment in men's minds at present cannot be conceived without seeing it.

January 31, 1821

For several days I have not written any thing except a few
answers to letters. In momentary expectation of an explosion
of some kind, it is not easy to settle down to the desk for the
higher kinds of composition. I *could* do it, to be sure, for, last
summer, I wrote my drama in the very bustle of Madame la
Contessa G.'s divorce, and all its process of accompaniments.
At the same time, I also had the news of the loss of an important lawsuit in England. But these were only private and
personal business; the present is of a different nature.

I suppose it is this, but have some suspicion that it may be
laziness, which prevents me from writing; especially as Rochefoucault says that 'laziness often masters them all'—speaking of
the *passions*. If this were true, it could hardly be said that 'idleness is the root of all evil,' since this is supposed to spring
from the passions only: ergo, that which masters all the
passions (laziness, to wit) would in so much be a good. Who
knows?

Midnight

I have been reading Grimm's *Correspondence*. He repeats
frequently, in speaking of a poet, or a man of genius in any
department, even in music, (Grétry, for instance,) that he must

have *une ame qui se tourmente, un esprit violent.* How far this may be true, I know not; but if it were, I should be a poet '*per excellenza*;' for I have always had *une ame*, which not only tormented itself but every body else in contact with it; and an *esprit violent*, which has almost left me without any *esprit* at all. As to defining what a poet *should* be, it is not worth while, for what are *they* worth? what have they done?

Grimm, however, is an excellent critic and literary historian. His *Correspondence* forms the annals of the literary part of that age of France, with much of her politics, and still more of her 'way of life.' He is as valuable, and far more entertaining than Muratori or Tiraboschi—I had almost said, than Ginguené—but there we should pause. However, 't is a great man in its line.

Monsieur St. Lambert has,

> *Et lorsqu'à ses regards la lumière est ravie,*
> *Il n'a plus, en mourant, à perdre que la vie.*

This is, word for word, Thomson's

> *And dying, all we can resign is breath,*

without the smallest acknowledgment from the Lorrainer of a poet. M. St. Lambert is dead as a man, and (for any thing I know to the contrary) damned, as a poet, by this time. However, his *Seasons* have good things, and, it may be, some of his own.

February 2, 1821

I have been considering what can be the reason why I always wake, at a certain hour in the morning, and always in very bad spirits—I may say, in actual despair and despondency, in all respects—even of that which pleased me over night. In about an hour or two, this goes off, and I compose either to sleep again, or, at least, to quiet. In England, five years ago, I had the same kind of hypochondria, but accompanied with so violent a thirst that I have drank as many as fifteen bottles of soda-water in one night, after going to bed, and been still thirsty—calculating, however, some lost from the bursting out and effervescence and overflowing of the soda-water, in drawing the corks, or striking off the necks of the bottles from mere thirsty impatience. At present, I have *not* the thirst; but the depression of spirits is no less violent.

I read in Edgeworth's *Memoirs* of something similar (except that his thirst expended itself on *small beer*) in the case of Sir F. B. Delaval;—but then he was, at least, twenty years older. What is it?—liver? In England, Le Man (the apothecary) cured me of the thirst in three days, and it had lasted as many years. I suppose that it is all hypochondria.

What I feel most growing upon me are laziness, and a disrelish more powerful than indifference. If I rouse, it is into fury. I presume that I shall end (if not earlier by accident, or some such termination) like Swift—'dying at top.' I confess I do not contemplate this with so much horror as he apparently did for some years before it happened. But Swift had hardly *begun life* at the very period (thirty-three) when I feel quite an *old sort* of feel.

Oh! there is an organ playing in the street—a waltz, too! I must leave off to listen. They are playing a waltz which I have heard ten thousand times at the balls in London, between 1812 and 1815. Music is a strange thing.

February 5, 1821

At last, 'the kiln's in a low.' The Germans are ordered to march, and Italy is, for the ten thousandth time, to become a field of battle. Last night the news came.

This afternoon—Count P. G. came to me to consult upon divers matters. We rode out together. They have sent off to the C. for orders. To-morrow the decision ought to arrive, and then something will be done. Returned—dined—read—went out—talked over matters. Made a purchase of some arms for the new enrolled Americani, who are all on tiptoe to march. Gave order for some *harness* and pormanteaus necessary for the horses.

Read some of Bowles's dispute about Pope, with all the replies and rejoinders. Perceive that my name has been lugged into the controversy, but have not time to state what I know of the subject. On some 'piping day of peace' it is probable that I may resume it.

February 9, 1821

Before dinner wrote a little; also, before I rode out, Count P. G. called upon me, to let me know the result of the meeting of the Ci. at F. and at B. —— returned late last night. Every thing was combined under the idea that the Barbarians would pass the Po on the 15th inst. Instead of this, from some previous information or otherwise, they have hastened their march and actually passed two days ago; so that all that can be done at present in Romagna is, to stand on the alert and wait for the advance of the Neapolitans. Every thing was ready, and the Neapolitans had sent on their own instructions and intentions, all calculated for the *tenth* and *eleventh*, on which days a general rising was to take place, under the supposition that the Barbarians could not advance before the 15th.

As it is, they have but fifty or sixty thousand troops, a number with which they might as well attempt to conquer the world as secure Italy in its present state. The artillery marches *last*, and alone, and there is an idea of an attempt to cut part of them off. All this will much depend upon the first steps of the Neapolitans. *Here*, the public spirit is excellent, provided it be kept up. This will be seen by the event.

It is probable that Italy will be delivered from the Barbarians if the Neapolitans will but stand firm, and are united among themselves. *Here* they appear so.

February 10, 1821

Day passed as usual—nothing new. Barbarians still in march—not well equipped, and, of course, not well received on their route. There is some talk of a commotion at Paris.

Rode out between four and six—finished my letter to Murray on Bowles's pamphlets—added postscript. Passed the evening as usual—out till eleven—and subsequently at home.

February 11, 1821

Wrote—had a copy taken of an extract from Petrarch's Letters, with reference to the conspiracy of the Doge, Marino Faliero, containing the poet's opinion of the matter. Heard a heavy firing of cannon towards Comacchio—the Barbarians rejoicing for their principal pig's birthday, which is to-morrow—or Saint day—I forget which. Received a ticket for the first ball to-morrow. Shall not go to the first, but intend going to the second, as also to the Veglioni.

February 13, 1821

To-day read a little in Louis B.'s *Hollande*, but have writ-ten nothing since the completion of the letter on the Pope controversy. Politics are quite misty for the present. The Bar-barians still upon their march. It is not easy to divine what the Italians will now do.

Was elected yesterday *Socio* of the Carnival Ball Society. This is the fifth carnival that I have passed. In the four former, I racketed a good deal. In the present, I have been as sober as Lady Grace herself.

February 14, 1821

Much as usual. Wrote, before riding out, part of a scene of *Sardanapalus*. The first act nearly finished. The rest of the day and evening as before—partly without, in conversazione—partly at home.

Heard the particulars of the late fray at Russi, a town not far from this. It is exactly the fact of Roměo and Giulietta—*not* Roměo, as the Barbarian writes it. Two families of *Conta-dini* (peasants) are at feud. At a ball, the younger part of the families forget their quarrel, and dance together. An old man of one of them enters, and reproves the young men for dancing with the females of the opposite family. The male relatives of the latter resent this. Both parties rush home and arm them-selves. They meet directly, by moonlight, in the public way, and fight it out. Three are killed on the spot, and six wounded, most of them dangerously,—pretty well for two families, methinks—and all *fact*, of the last week. Another assassination has taken place at Cesenna,—in all about *forty* in Romagna within the last three months. These people retain much of the middle ages.

February 15, 1821

Last night finished the first act of *Sardanapalus*. To-night, or to-morrow, I ought to answer letters.

February 16, 1821

Last night Il Conte P. G. sent a man with a bag full of bayonets, some muskets, and some hundreds of cartridges to my house, without apprizing me, though I had seen him not half an hour before. About ten days ago, when there was to be a rising here, the Liberals and my brethren C^i. asked me to purchase some arms for a certain few of our ragamuffins. I did so immediately, and ordered ammunition, etc., and they were armed accordingly. Well—the rising is prevented by the Barbarians marching a week sooner than appointed; and an *order* is issued, and in force, by the Government, 'that all persons having arms concealed, etc., etc., shall be liable to, etc., etc.'—and what do my friends, the patriots, do two days afterwards? Why, they throw back upon my hands, and into my house, these very arms (without a word of warning previously) with which I had furnished them at their own request, and at my own peril and expense.

It was lucky that Lega was at home to receive them. If any of the servants had (except Tita and F. and Lega) they would have betrayed it immediately. In the mean time, if they are denounced or discovered, I shall be in a scrape.

At nine went out—at eleven returned. Beat the crow for stealing the falcon's victuals. Read *Tales of my Landlord*—wrote a letter—and mixed a moderate beaker of water with other ingredients.

February 18, 1821

The news are that the Neapolitans have broken a bridge, and slain four pontifical carabiniers, whilk carabiniers wished to oppose. Besides the disrespect to neutrality, it is a pity that the first blood shed in this German quarrel should be Italian. However, the war seems begun in good earnest: for, if the Neapolitans kill the Pope's carabiniers, they will not be more delicate towards the Barbarians. If it be even so, in a short time 'there will be news o' thae craws,' as Mrs. Alison Wilson says of Jenny Blane's 'unco cockernony' in the *Tales of my Landlord.*

In turning over Grimm's *Correspondence* to-day, I found a thought of Tom Moore's in a song of Maupertuis to a female Laplander

> *Et tous les lieux*
> *Où sont ses yeux,*
> *Font la zone brûlante.*

This is Moore's,
> *And those eyes make my climate, wherever I roam.*

But I am sure that Moore never saw it; for this was published in Grimm's *Correspondence*, in 1813, and I knew Moore's by heart in 1812. There is also another, but an antithetical coincidence—

> *Le soleil luit,*
> *Des jours sans nuit*
> *Bientôt il nous destine;*
> *Mais ces longs jours*
> *Seront trop courts,*
> *Passés près de Christine.*

This is the *thought reversed*, of the last stanza of the ballad on Charlotte Lynes, given in Miss Seward's *Memoirs of Darwin*, which is pretty—I quote from memory of these last fifteen years.

> *For my first night I'd go*
> *To those regions of snow,*
> *Where the sun for six months never shines;*
> *And think, even then,*
> *He too soon came again,*
> *To disturb me with fair Charlotte Lynes.*

2 C

To-day I have had no communication with my Carbonari cronies; but, in the mean time, my lower apartments are full of their bayonets, fusils, cartridges, and what not. I suppose that they consider me as a depôt, to be sacrificed, in case of accidents. It is no great matter, supposing that Italy could be liberated, who or what is sacrificed. It is a grand object—the very *poetry* of politics. Only think—a free Italy!!! Why, there has been nothing like it since the days of Augustus. I reckon the times of Cæsar (Julius) free; because the commotions left every body a side to take, and the parties were pretty equal at the set out. But, afterwards, it was all prætorian and legionary business—and since!—we shall see, or, at least, some will see, what card will turn up. It is best to hope, even of the hopeless. The Dutch did more than these fellows have to do, in the Seventy Years' War.

February 19, 1821

Came home *solus*—very high wind—lightning—moonshine —solitary stragglers muffled in cloaks—women in masks— white houses—clouds hurrying over the sky, like spilt milk blown out of the pail—altogether very poetical. It is still blowing hard—the tiles flying, and the house rocking—rain splashing—lightning flashing—quite a fine Swiss Alpine evening, and the sea roaring in the distance.

Visited—conversazione. All the women frightened by the squall: they *won't* go to the masquerade because it lightens— the pious reason!

Still blowing away. A. has sent me some news to-day. The war approaches nearer and nearer. Oh those scoundrel sovereigns! Let us but see them beaten—let the Neapolitans but have the pluck of the Dutch of old, or the Spaniards of now, or of the German Protestants, the Scotch Presbyterians, the Swiss under Tell, or the Greeks under Themistocles—*all* small and solitary nations (except the Spaniards and German Lutherans), and there is yet a resurrection for Italy, and a hope for the world.

February 20, 1821

The news of the day are, that the Neapolitans are full of energy. The public spirit *here* is certainly well kept up. The *Americani* (a patriotic society here, an under branch of the *Carbonari*) give a dinner in *the Forest* in a few days, and have invited me, as one of the C[l]. It is to be in *the Forest* of Boccacio's and Dryden's 'Huntsman's Ghost;' and, even if I had not the same political feelings, (to say nothing of my old convivial turn, which every now and then revives,) I would go as a poet, or, at least, as a lover of poetry. I shall expect to see the spectre of 'Ostasio degli Onesti' (Dryden has turned him into Guido Cavalcanti—an essentially different person, as may be found in Dante) come 'thundering for his prey in the midst of the festival'. At any rate, whether he does or no, I will get as tipsy and patriotic as possible.

Within these few days I have read, but not written.

February 21, 1821

As usual, rode—visited, etc. Business begins to thicken. The Pope has printed a declaration against the patriots, who, he says, meditate a rising. The consequence of all this will be, that, in a fortnight, the whole country will be up. The proclamation is not yet published, but printed, ready for distribution. —— sent me a copy privately—a sign that he does not know what to think. When he wants to be well with the patriots, he sends to me some civil message or other.

For my own part, it seems to me, that nothing but the most decided success of the Barbarians can prevent a general and immediate rise of the whole nation.

February 23, 1821

Almost ditto with yesterday—rode, etc.—visited—wrote nothing—read Roman History.

Had a curious letter from a fellow, who informs me that the Barbarians are ill-disposed towards me. He is probably a spy, or an impostor. But be it so, even as he says. They cannot bestow their hostility on one who loathes and execrates them more than I do, or who will oppose their views with more zeal, when the opportunity offers.

February 24, 1821

Rode, etc. as usual. The secret intelligence arrived this morning from the frontier to the C^l. is as bad as possible. The *plan* has missed—the Chiefs are betrayed, military, as well as civil—and the Neapolitans not only have *not* moved, but have declared to the P. government, and to the Barbarians, that they know nothing of the matter!!!

Thus the world goes; and thus the Italians are always lost for lack of union among themselves. What is to be done *here*, between the two fires, and cut off from the N^n. frontier, is not decided. My opinion was,—better to rise than be taken in detail; but how it will be settled now, I cannot tell. Messengers are despatched to the delegates of the other cities to learn their resolutions.

I always had an idea that it would be *bungled*; but was willing to hope, and am so still. Whatever I can do by money, means, or person, I will venture freely for their freedom; and have so repeated to them (some of the Chiefs here) half an hour ago. I have two thousand five hundred scudi, better than five hundred pounds, in the house, which I offered to begin with.

February 25, 1821

Came home—my head aches—plenty of news, but too tiresome to set down. I have neither read nor written, nor thought, but led a purely animal life all day. I mean to try to write a page or two before I go to bed. But, as Squire Sullen says, 'My head aches consumedly: Scrub, bring me a dram!' Drank some Imola wine, and some punch!

Log-book continued

February 27, 1821

I have been a day without continuing the log, because I could not find a blank book. At length I recollected this.

Rode, etc.—wrote down an additional stanza for the 5th canto of *D[on] J[uan]* which I had composed in bed this morning. Visited *l'Amica*. We are invited, on the night of the

Veglione (next Dominica) with the Marchesa Clelia Cavalli and the Countess Spinelli Rusponi. I promised to go. Last night there was a row at the ball, of which I am a *socio*. The Vice-legate had the imprudent insolence to introduce *three* of his servants in masque—*without tickets*, too! and in spite of remonstrances. The consequence was, that the young men of the ball took it up, and were near throwing the Vice-legate out of the window. His servants, seeing the scene, withdrew, and he after them. His reverence Monsignore ought to know, that these are not times for the predominance of priests over decorum. Two minutes more, two steps further, and the whole city would have been in arms, and the government driven out of it.

Such is the spirit of the day, and these fellows appear not to perceive it. As far as the simple fact went, the young men were right, servants being prohibited always at these festivals.

Yesterday wrote two notes on the 'Bowles and Pope' controversy, and sent them off to Murray by the post. The old woman whom I relieved in the forest (she is ninety-four years of age) brought me two bunches of violets. *Nam vita gaudet mortua floribus.* I was much pleased with the present. An English woman would have presented a pair of worsted stockings, at least, in the month of February. Both excellent things; but the former are more elegant. The present, at this season, reminds one of Gray's stanza, omitted from his elegy:—

> *Here scatter'd oft, the* earliest *of the year,*
> *By hands unseen, are showers of violets found;*
> *The red-breast loves to build and warble here,*
> *And little footsteps lightly print the ground.*

As fine a stanza as any in his elegy. I wonder that he could have the heart to omit it.

Last night I suffered horribly—from an indigestion, I believe. I *never* sup—that is, never at home. But, last night, I was prevailed upon by the Countess Gamba's persuasion, and the strenuous example of her brother, to swallow, at supper, a quantity of boiled cockles, and to dilute them, *not* reluctantly, with some Imola wine. When I came home, apprehensive of the consequences, I swallowed three or four glasses of spirits, which men (the venders) call brandy, rum, or hollands, but which gods would entitle spirits of wine, coloured or sugared. All was pretty well till I got to bed, when I became somewhat swollen, and considerably vertiginous. I got out, and mixing some soda-powders, drank them off. This brought on temporary relief. I returned to bed; but grew sick and sorry once and again. Took more soda-water. At last I fell into a dreary sleep. Woke, and was ill all day, till I had galloped a few miles. Query—was it the cockles, or what I took to correct them, that caused the commotion? I think both. I remarked in my illness the complete inertion, inaction, and destruction of my chief mental faculties. I tried to rouse them, and yet could not —and this is the *Soul!!!* I should believe that it was married to the body, if they did not sympathise so much with each other. If the one rose, when the other fell, it would be a sign that they longed for the natural state of divorce. But as it is, they seem to draw together like post-horses.

Let us hope the best—it is the grand possession.

TO R. B. HOPPNER

Ravenna, April 3, 1821

Thanks for the translation. I have sent you some books, which I do not know whether you have read or no—you need not return them, in any case. I enclose you also a letter from Pisa. I have neither spared trouble nor expense in the care of the child; and as she was now four years old complete, and quite above the control of the servants—and as a *man* living without any woman at the head of his house cannot much attend to a nursery—I had no resource but to place her for a time (at a high pension too) in the convent of Bagna-Cavalli (twelve miles off), where the air is good, and where she will, at least, have her learning advanced, and her morals and religion inculcated. I had also another reason;—things were and are in such a state here, that I had no reason to look upon my own personal safety as particularly insurable; and I thought the infant best out of harm's way, for the present.

It is also fit that I should add that I by no means intended, nor intend, to give a *natural* child an *English* education, because with the disadvantages of her birth, her after settlement would be doubly difficult. Abroad, with a fair foreign education and a portion of five or six thousand pounds, she might and may marry very respectably. In England such a dowry would be a pittance, while elsewhere it is a fortune. It is, besides, my wish that she should be a Roman Catholic, which I look upon as the best religion, as it is assuredly the oldest of the various branches of Christianity. I have now explained my notions as to the *place* where she now is—it is the best I could find for the present; but I have no prejudices in its favour.

I do not speak of politics, because it seems a hopeless subject, as long as those scoundrels are to be permitted to bully states out of their independence. Believe me,

Yours ever and truly.

P.S.—There is a report here of a change in France; but with what truth is not yet known.

P.S.—My respects to Mrs. H. I *have* the 'best opinion' of her countrywomen; and at my time of life, (three and thirty, 22d January, 1821,) that is to say, after the life I have led, a *good* opinion is the only rational one which a man should entertain of the whole sex—up to *thirty*, the worst possible opinion a man can have of them in *general*, the better for himself. Afterwards, it is a matter of no importance to *them*, nor to him either, *what opinion* he entertains—his day is over, or, at least, should be.

You see how sober I am become.

Ravenna, May 1, 1821

Amongst various journals, memoranda, diaries, etc., which I have kept in the course of my living, I began one about three months ago, and carried it on till I had filled one paper-book (thinnish), and two sheets or so of another. I then left off, partly because I thought we should have some business here, and I had furbished up my arms, and got my apparatus ready for taking a turn with the Patriots, having my drawers full of their proclamations, oaths, and resolutions, and my lower rooms of their hidden weapons of most calibres; and partly because I had filled my paper book. But the Neapolitans have betrayed themselves and all the World, and those who would have given their blood for Italy can now only give her their tears.

Some day or other, if dust holds together, I have been enough in the Secret (at least in this part of the country) to cast perhaps some little light upon the atrocious treachery which has replunged Italy into Barbarism. At present I have neither the time nor the temper. However, the *real* Italians are *not* to blame—merely the scoundrels at the *Heel of the Boot*, which the *Hun* now wears, and will trample them to ashes with for their Servility.

I have risked myself with the others *here*, and how far I may or may not be compromised is a problem at this moment: some of them like 'Craigengelt' would 'tell all and more than all to save themselves;' but, come what may, the cause was a glorious one, though it reads at present as if the Greeks had run away from Xerxes.

Happy the few who have only to reproach themselves with believing that these rascals were less *rascaille* than they proved. *Here* in Romagna the efforts were necessarily limited to preparations and good intentions, until the Germans were fairly engaged in *equal* warfare, as we are upon their very frontiers without a single fort, or hill, nearer than San Marino. Whether 'Hell will be paved with' those 'good intentions,' I know not; but there will probably be good store of Neapolitans to walk upon the pavement, whatever may be it's composition. Slabs of lava from their mountain, with the bodies of their own damned Souls for cement, would be the fittest causeway for Satan's *Corso*.

But what shall I write? another Journal? I think not. Anything that comes uppermost—and call it 'my Dictionary.'

MY DICTIONARY

Augustus.—I have often been puzzled with his character. Was he a great Man? Assuredly. But not one of *my* great men. I have always looked upon Sylla as the greatest Character in History, for laying down his power at the moment when it was

too great to keep or to resign,

and thus despising them all. As to the retention of his power by Augustus, the thing was already settled. If he had given it up, the Commonwealth was gone, the republic was long past all resuscitation. Had Brutus and Cassius gained the battle of Philippi, it would not have restored the republic—its days ended with the Gracchi, the rest was a mere struggle of parties. You might as well cure a Consumption, restore a broken egg, as revive a state so long a prey to every uppermost Soldier as Rome had long been.

As for a despotism, if Augustus could have been sure that all his Successors would have been like himself (I mean *not* as *Octavius,* but Augustus), or Napoleon would have insured the world that *none* of his Successors would have been like himself, the antient or modern World might have gone on like the Empire of China—in a state of lethargic prosperity.

Suppose, for instance, that, instead of Tiberius and Caligula, Augustus had been immediately succeeded by Nerva, Trajan, the Antonines, or even by Titus and his father, what a difference in our estimate of himself? So far from gaining by the *contrast,* I think that one half of our dislike arises from his having been heired by Tiberius, and one half of Julius Caesar's fame from his having had his empire consolidated by Augustus.

Suppose that there had been *no Octavius,* and Tiberius had 'jumped the life' between, and at once succeeded Julius? And yet it is difficult to say whether hereditary right, or popular choice, produce the worse Sovereigns. The Roman Consuls make a goodly show, but then they only reigned for a year, and were under a sort of personal obligation to distinguish themselves. It is still more difficult to say which form of

Government is the *worst*—all are so bad. As for democracy, it is the worst of the whole; for what is (*in fact*) democracy? an Aristocracy of Blackguards.

ABERDEEN—OLD AND NEW, OR THE AULDTOUN AND NEWTOUN

For several years of my earliest childhood I was in that City, but have never revisited it since I was ten years old. I was sent at five years old, or earlier, to a School kept by a Mr. *Bowers*, who was called '*Bodsy* Bowers' by reason of his dapperness. It was a School for both sexes. I learned little there, except to repeat by rote the first lesson of Monosyllables—'God made man, let us love him'—by hearing it often repeated, without acquiring a letter. Whenever proof was made of my progress at home, I repeated these words with the most rapid fluency; but on turning over a new leaf, I continued to repeat them, so that the narrow boundaries of my first year's accomplishments were detected, my ears boxed (which they did not deserve, seeing that it was by *ear* only that I had acquired my letters), and my intellects consigned to a new preceptor. He was a very decent, clever, little Clergyman, named Ross, afterwards Minister of one of the Kirks (*East* I think). Under *him* I made an astonishing progress, and I recollect to this day his mild manners and good-natured pains-taking.

The moment I could read, my grand passion was *history*; and why, I know not, but I was particularly taken with the battle near the Lake Regillus in the Roman History, put into my hands the first.

Four years ago, when standing on the heights of Tusculum, and looking down upon the little round Lake, that was once Regillus, and which dots the immense expanse below, I remembered my young enthusiasm and my old instructor.

Afterwards I had a very serious, saturnine, but kind young man, named Paterson, for a Tutor: he was the son of my Shoemaker, but a good Scholar, as is common with the Scotch. He was a rigid Presbyterian also. With him I began Latin in Ruddiman's Grammar, and continued till I went to the 'Grammar School' (*Scotice* 'Schule'—*Aberdonice* 'Squeel'), where I threaded all the Classes to the *fourth*, when I was recalled to England (where I had been hatched) by the demise of my Uncle.

I acquired this handwriting, which I can hardly read myself, under the fair copies of Mr. Duncan of the same city. I don't think that he would plume himself upon my progress. However, I wrote much better then than I have ever done since. Haste and agitation of one kind or another have quite spoilt as pretty a scrawl as ever scratched over a frank.

The Grammar School might consist of a hundred and fifty of all ages under age. It was divided into five classes, taught by four masters, the Chief teaching the fifth and fourth himself, as in England the fifth, sixth forms, and Monitors are heard by the Head Masters.

DETACHED THOUGHTS

Octr. 15, 1821

I have been thinking over the other day on the various comparisons, good or evil, which I have seen published of myself in different journals English and foreign. This was suggested to me by accidentally turning over a foreign one lately; for I have made it a rule latterly never to *search* for anything of the kind, but not to avoid the perusal if presented by Chance.

To begin then—I have seen myself compared personally or poetically, in English, French, *German* (*as* interpreted to me), Italian, and Portuguese, within these nine years, to Rousseau—Göethe—Young—Aretino—Timon of Athens—'An Alabaster Vase lighted up within'—Satan—Shakespeare—Buonaparte — Tiberius — Aeschylus — Sophocles — Euripides —Harlequin—The Clown—Sternhold and Hopkins—to the Phantasmagoria—to Henry the 8th.—to Chenies—to Mirabeau —to young R. Dallas (the Schoolboy)—to Michael Angelo— to Raphael—to a *petit maître*—to Diogenes—to Childe Harold—to Lara—to the Count in Beppo—to Milton—to Pope—to Dryden—to Burns—to Savage—to Chatterton—to 'oft have I heard of thee my Lord Biron' in Shakespeare—

to Churchill the poet—to Kean the Actor—to Alfieri, etc. etc. etc. The likeness to Alfieri was asserted very seriously by an Italian, who had known him in his younger days: it of course related merely to our apparent personal dispositions. He did not assert it to *me* (for we were not then good friends), but in society.

The Object of so many contradictory comparisons must probably be like something different from them all; but what *that* is, is more than *I* know, or any body else.

My Mother, before I was twenty, would have it that I was like Rousseau, and Madame de Staël used to say so too in 1813, and the *Edinh. Review* has something of the sort in its critique on the 4th. Canto of *Che. Had.* I can't see any point of resemblance: he wrote prose, I verse: he was of the people, I of the Aristocracy: he was a philosopher, I am none: he published his first work at forty, I mine at eighteen: his first essay brought him universal applause, mine the contrary: he married his housekeeper, I could not keep house with my wife: he thought all the world in a plot against *him*, my little world seems to think *me* in a plot against it, if I may judge by their abuse in print and coterie: he liked Botany, I like flowers, and herbs, and trees, but know nothing of their pedigrees: he wrote Music, I limit my knowledge of it to what I catch by *Ear* —I never could learn any thing by *study*, not even a language, it was all by rote and ear and memory: he had a bad memory, I *had* at least an excellent one (ask Hodgson the poet, a good judge, for he has an astonishing one): he wrote with hesitation and care, I with rapidity and rarely with pains: *he* could never ride nor swim 'nor was cunning of fence,' *I* am an excellent swimmer, a decent though not at all a dashing rider (having staved in a rib at eighteen in the course of scampering), and was sufficient of fence—particularly of the Highland broadsword; not a bad boxer when I could keep my temper, which was difficult, but which I strove to do ever since I knocked down Mr. Purling and put his knee-pan out (with the gloves on) in Angelo's and Jackson's rooms in 1806 during the sparring; and I was besides a very fair cricketer—one of the Harrow Eleven when we play[ed] against Eton in 1805. Besides,

Rousseau's way of life, his country, his manners, his whole character, were so very different, that I am at a loss to conceive how such a comparison could have arisen, as it has done three several times, and all in rather a remarkable manner. I forgot to say, that *he* was also short-sighted, and that hitherto my eyes have been the contrary to such a degree, that, in the largest theatre of Bologna, I distinguished and read some busts and inscriptions painted near the stage, from a box so distant, and so *darkly* lighted, that none of the company (composed of young and very bright-eyed people—some of them in the same box) could make out a letter, and thought it was a trick, though I had never been in that theatre before.

Altogether, I think myself justified in thinking the comparison not well founded. I don't say this out of pique, for Rousseau was a great man, and the thing if true were flattering enough; but I have no idea of being pleased with a chimera.

1

When I met old Courtenay, the Orator, at Rogers the poet's in 1811–1812, I was much taken with the portly remains of his fine figure, and the still acute quickness of his conversation. It was *he* who silenced Flood in the English House by a crushing reply to a hasty debût of the rival of Grattan in Ireland. I asked Courtenay (for I like to trace motives), if he had not some personal provocation; for the acrimony of his answer seemed to me as I had read it) to involve it. Courtenay said 'he had— that when in Ireland (being an Irishman) at the *bar* of the Irish house of Commons that Flood had made a personal and unfair attack upon *himself*, who, not being a member of that house, could not defend himself; and that some years afterwards, the opportunity of retort offering in the English Parliament, he could not resist it.' He certainly repaid F. with interest, for Flood never made any figure, and only a speech or two afterwards in the E. H. of Commons. I must except, however, his speech on Reform in 1790, which 'Fox called the best he ever heard upon that Subject.'

2

When Fox was asked what he thought the best speech he had ever heard, he replied 'Sheridan's on the Impeachment of Hastings in the house of Commons' (*not* that in Westminster Hall). When asked what he thought of his *own* speech on the breaking out of the War? he replied 'that was a damned good speech too.'—From Ld. Holland.

3

When Sheridan made his famous speech already alluded to, Fox advised him to speak it over again in Westminster Hall on the trial, as nothing better *could* be made of the subject; but Sheridan made his new speech as different as possible, and, according to the best Judges, very inferior to the former, notwithstanding the laboured panegyric of Burke upon his *Colleague*.—Ld. H.

4

Burke spoilt his own speaking afterwards by an imitation of Sheridan's in Westminster Hall: this Speech he called always 'the grand desideratum, which was neither poetry nor eloquence, but something *better* than both.'

5

I have never heard any one who fulfilled my Ideal of an Orator. Grattan would have been near it but for his Harlequin delivery. Pitt I never heard. Fox but once, and then he struck me as a debater, which to me seems as different from an Orator as an Improvisatore or a versifier from a poet. Grey is great, but it is not oratory. Canning is sometimes very like one, Windham I did not admire, though all the world did: it seemed such sophistry. Whitbread was the Demosthenes of bad taste and vulgar vehemence, but strong and English. Holland is impressive from sense and sincerity. Lord Lansdowne good, but still a debater only. Grenville I like vastly, if he would prune his speeches down to an hour's delivery. Burdett is sweet and silvery as Belial himself, and *I* think the greatest favourite in Pandemonium; at least I always heard the

Country Gentlemen and the ministerial devilry praise his *speeches* upstairs, and run down from Bellamy's when he was upon his legs. I heard Bob. Milnes make his *second* speech : it made no impression. I like Ward—studied, but keen, and sometimes eloquent. Peel, my School and form-fellow (we sate within two of each other) strange to say I have never heard, though I often wished to do so ; but, from what I remember of him at Harrow, he *is*, or *should* be, among the best of them. Now, I do *not* admire Mr. Wilberforce's speaking ; it is nothing but a flow of *words*—'words, words alone.'

I doubt greatly if the English *have* any eloquence, properly so called, and am inclined to think that the Irish *had* a great deal, and that the French *will* have, and have had in Mirabeau. Lord Chatham and Burke are the nearest approaches to Orators in England. I don't know what Erskine may have been at the *bar*, but in the house I wish him at the Bar once more. Lauderdale is shrill, and Scotch, and acute. Of Brougham I shall say nothing, as I have a personal feeling of dislike to the man.

But amongst all these—good, bad, and indifferent—I never heard the speech which was not too long for the auditors, and not very intelligible except here and there. The whole thing is a grand deception, and as tedious and tiresome as may be to those who must be often present. I heard Sheridan only once, and that briefly ; but I liked his voice, his manner, and his wit : he is the only one of them I ever wished to hear at greater length. In society I have met him frequently : he was superb! He had a sort of liking for me, and never attacked me—at least to my face, and he did every body else—high names, and wits, and orators, some of them poets also. I have seen [him] cut up Whitbread, quiz Me. de Stael, annihilate Colman, and do little less by some others (whose names as friends I set not down), of good fame and abilities. Poor fellow! he got drunk very thoroughly and very soon. It occasionally fell to my lot to convoy him home—no sinecure, for he was so tipsy that I was obliged to put on his cock'd hat for him : to be sure it tumbled off again, and I was not myself so sober as to be able to pick it up again.

6

There was something odd about Sheridan. One day at a dinner he was slightly praising that pert pretender and impostor, Lyttelton (The Parliament puppy, still alive, I believe). I took the liberty of differing from him: he turned round upon me, and said, 'Is that your real opinion?' I confirmed it. Then said he, 'Fortified by this concurrence, I beg leave to say that it in fact is also *my* opinion, and that he is a person whom I do absolutely and utterly despise, abhor, and detest.' He then launched out into a description of his despicable qualities, at some length, and with his usual wit, and evidently in earnest (for he hated Lyttelton). His former compliment had been drawn out by some preceding one, just as it's reverse was by my hinting that it was unmerited.

7

One day I saw him take up his own 'Monody on Garrick.' He lighted upon the dedication to the Dowager Lady Spencer: on seeing it he flew into a rage, and exclaimed 'that it must be a forgery—that he had never dedicated anything of his to such a d——d canting b——h,' etc. etc. etc.; and so went on for half an hour abusing his own dedication, or at least the object of it. If all writers were equally sincere, it would be ludicrous.

8

He told me that, on the night of the grand success of his S[chool] for S[candal], he was knocked down and put into the watch house for making a row in the Street, and being found intoxicated by the watchmen.

9

Latterly, when found drunk one night in the kennel, and asked his *Name* by the Watchmen, he answered '*Wilberforce*.'

The last time I met him was, I think, at Sir Gilbert Elliot's, where he was as quick as ever. No, it was not the last time: the last time was at Douglas Kd.'s I have met him in all places and parties—at Whitehall with the Melbournes, at the Marquis of Tavistock's, at Robins the Auctioneer's, at Sir Humphrey

Davy's, at Sam Rogers's, in short, in most kinds of company, and always found him very convivial and delightful.

10

Sheridan's liking for me (whether he was not mystifying me I do not know; but Lady Ce. L. and others told me he said the same both before and after he knew me) was founded upon *English Bards and S. Reviewers*. He told me that he did not care about poetry (or about mine—at least, any but *that* poem of mine), but he was sure, from *that* and other symptoms, I should make an Orator, if I would but take to speaking, and grow a parliament man. He never ceased harping upon this to me, to the last; and I remember my old tutor Dr. Drury had the same notion when I was a *boy*: but it never was my turn of inclination to try. I spoke once or twice as all young peers do, as a kind of introduction into public life; but dissipation, shyness, haughty and reserved opinions, together with the short time I lived in England—after my majority (only about five years in all)—prevented me from resuming the experiment. As far as it went, it was not discouraging—particularly my *first* speech (I spoke three or four times in all); but just after it my poem of *Ce. Hd.* was published, and nobody ever thought about my *prose* afterwards: nor indeed did I; it became to me a secondary and neglected object, though I sometimes wonder to myself *if* I should have succeeded?

11

The Impression of Parliament upon me was that it's members are not formidable as *Speakers*, but very much so as an *audience*; because in so numerous a body there may be little Eloquence (after all there were but *two* thorough Orators in all Antiquity, and I suspect still *fewer* in modern times), but must be a leaven of thought and good sense sufficient to make them *know* what is right, though they can't express it nobly.

12

Horne Tooke and Roscoe both are said to have declared, that they left Parliament with a higher opinion of its aggregate integrity and abilities than that with which they had entered it.

The general amount of both in most parliaments is probably about the same, as also the number of *Speakers* and their *talent*. I except *Orators*, of course, because *they* are things of Ages and not of Septennial or triennial reunions.

Neither house ever struck me with more awe or respect than the same number of Turks in a Divan, or of Methodists in a barn would have done. Whatever diffidence or nervousness I felt (and I felt both in a great degree) arose from the number rather than the quality of the assemblage, and the thought rather of the *public without* than the persons within—knowing (as all know) that Cicero himself, and probably the Messiah, could never have alter'd the vote of a single Lord of the Bed-chamber or Bishop.

I thought *our* house dull, but the other animating enough upon great days.

12 [so repeated by Byron]

Sheridan dying was requested to undergo 'an Operation:' he replied that he had already submitted to *two*, which were enough for one man's life time. Being asked what they were, he answered, 'having his hair cut, and sitting for his picture.'

13

Whenever an American requests to see me (which is *not* un-frequently), I comply: 1stly, because I respect a people who acquired their freedom by firmness without excess; and 2ndly, because these trans-atlantic visits, 'few and far between,' make me feel as if talking with Posterity from the other side of the Styx. In a century or two, the new English and Spanish Atlantides will be masters of the old Countries in all probability, as Greece and Europe overcame their Mother Asia in the older, or earlier ages as they are called.

14

Sheridan was one day offered a bet by M. G. Lewis. 'I will bet you, Mr. Sheridan, a very large sum: I will bet you what you *owe me* as Manager, for my "Castle Spectre."' 'I never make *large bets*,' said Sheridan: 'but I will lay you a *very small* one; I will bet you *what it is* WORTH!'

15

Lewis, though a kind man, hated Sheridan; and we had some words upon that score when in Switzerland in 1816. Lewis afterwards sent me the following epigram upon Sheridan from Saint Maurice:—

> *For worst abuse of finest parts*
> *Was Misophil begotten;*
> *There might indeed be* blacker *hearts,*
> *But none could be more* rotten.

16

Lewis at Oatlands was observed one morning to have his eyes red, and his air sentimental: being asked why? replied, 'that when people said any thing *kind* to him, it affected him deeply; and just now the Duchess has said something *so* kind to me that . . .' here 'tears began to flow' again. 'Never mind, Lewis,' said Col. Armstrong to him, 'never mind, don't cry. *She could not mean it.*'

17

Lewis was a good man, a clever man, but a bore, a damned bore, one may say. My only revenge or consolation used to be, setting him by the ears with some vivacious person who hated Bores, especially Me. de Stael, or Hobhouse, for example. But I liked Lewis: he was a Jewel of a Man had he been better set. I don't mean *personally*, but less *tiresome*; for he was tedious, as well as contradictory, to every thing and every body.

Being short-sighted, when we used to ride out together near the Brenta in the twilight in Summer, he made me go *before* to pilot him. I am absent at times, especially towards evening; and the consequence of this pilotage was some narrow escapes to the Monk on horseback. Once I led him *into* a ditch, over which I had passed as usual forgetting to warn my convoy. Once I led him nearly into the river, instead of *on* the *moveable* bridge which *in*commodes passengers; and twice did we both run against the diligence, which, being heavy and slow, did communicate less damage than it received in its leaders, who were *terrassé*'d by the charge. Thrice did I lose him in the gray of the Gloaming, and was obliged to bring to to his distant signals of distance and distress. All the time he went on talking without intermission, for he was a man of many words.

Poor fellow, he died, a martyr to his new riches, of a second visit to Jamaica—

> *I'll give the lands of Deloraine*
> *Dark Musgrave were alive again!*

that is

I would give many a Sugar Cane
Monk Lewis were alive again!

18

Lewis said to me, 'Why do you talk *Venetian*' (such as I could talk, not very fine to be sure) 'to the Venetians? and not the usual Italian?' I answered, partly from habit, and partly to be understood, if possible. 'It may be so,' said Lewis, 'but it sounds to me like talking with a *brogue* to an *Irishman*.'

19

Baillie (commonly called Long Baillie, a very clever man, but odd), complained in riding to our friend Scrope B. Davies, 'that he had a *stitch* in his side.' 'I don't wonder at it' (said Scrope) 'for you ride *like* a *tailor*.' Whoever had seen B. on horseback, with his very tall figure on a small nag, would not deny the justice of the repartée.

20

In 1808, Scrope and myself being at Supper at Steevens's (I think Hobhouse was there too) after the Opera, young Goulburne (of the Blues and of the Blueviad) came in full of the praises of his horse, Grimaldi, who had just won a race at Newmarket. 'Did he win easy?' said Scrope. 'Sir,' replied Goulburne, 'he did not even condescend to *puff* at coming in.' 'No' (said Scrope) 'and so *you puff for* him.'

21

Captain Wallace, a notorious character of that day, and *then* intimate with most of the more dissipated young men of the day, asked me one night at the Gaming table, where I thought *his Soul* would be found after death? I answered him, 'In *Silver Hell*' (a cant name for a second rate Gambling house).

22

When the Honble. J. W. Ward quitted the Whigs, he facetiously demanded, at Sir James Macintosh's table, in the presence of Made. de Staël, Malthus, and a large and goodly company of all parties and countries, 'what it would take to *re-whig him*, as he thought of turning again.' 'Before you can be *re-whigged*' (said I), 'I am afraid you must be *re-Warded*.' This pun has been attributed to others: they are welcome to it; but it was mine notwithstanding, as a numerous company and Ward himself doth know. I believe Luttrel versified it afterwards to put into the *M. Chronicle*—at least the late Lady Melbourne told me so. Ward took it good-humouredly at the time.

23

When Sheridan was on his death-bed, Rogers aided him with purse and person: this was particularly kind in Rogers, who always spoke ill of Sheridan (to me at least); but indeed he does that of every-body to any body. Rogers is the reverse of the line

> *The* best good man *with the* worst natured *Muse*,

being

> *The* worst *good man with the* best *natured Muse*.

His Muse being all Sentiment and Sago and Sugar, while he himself is a venomous talker. I say '*worst good* man' because he is (perhaps) a *good* man—at least he does good now and then, as well he may, to purchase himself a shilling's worth of Salvation for his Slanders. They are so *little* too—small talk, and old Womanny; and he is malignant too, and envious, and —he be damned!

24

Curran! Curran's the Man who struck me most. Such Imagination! There never was any thing like it, that ever I saw or heard of. His *published* life, his published speeches, give you *no* idea of the Man—none at all. He was a *Machine* of Imagination, as some one said that Piron was an 'Epigrammatic Machine.'

I did not see a great deal of Curran—only in 1813; but I met him at home (for he used to call on me), and in society, at Mac'Intosh's, Holland House, etc. etc. etc., and he was wonderful, even to me, who had seen many remarkable men of the time.

25

A young American, named Coolidge, called on me not many months ago: he was intelligent, very handsome, and not more than twenty years old according to appearances. A little romantic, but that sits well upon youth, and mighty fond of poesy as may be suspected from his approaching me in my cavern. He brought me a message from an old Servant of my family (Joe Murray), and told me that *he* (Mr. Coolidge) had obtained a copy of my bust from Thorwal[d]sen at Rome, to send to America. I confess I was more flattered by this young enthusiasm of a solitary trans-atlantic traveller, than if they had decreed me a Statue in the Paris Pantheon (I have seen Emperors and demagogues cast down from their pedestals even in my own time, and Grattan's name razed from the Street called after him in Dublin) I say that I was more flattered by it, because it was *single, un-political*, and was without motive or ostentation—the pure and warm feeling of a boy for the poet he admired. It must have been expensive though. *I* would not pay the price of a Thorwaldsen bust for any human head and shoulders, except Napoleon's, or my children's, or some '*absurd Womankind*'s' as Monkbarns calls them, or my Sister's. If asked, *why* then I sate for my own—answer, that it was at the request particular of J. C. Hobhouse, Esqre., and for no one else. A *picture* is a different matter—every body sits for their picture; but a bust looks like putting up pretensions to permanency, and smacks something of a hankering for *public* fame rather than private remembrance.

26

One of the cleverest men I ever knew in Conversation was Scrope Beardmore Davies. Hobhouse is also very good in that line, though it is of less consequence to a man who has other ways of showing his talents than in company. Scrope was always ready, and often witty: Hobhouse as witty, but not always so ready, being more diffident.

27

A drunken man ran against Hobhouse in the Street. A companion of the Drunkard, not much less so, cried out to Hobhouse, '*An't* you ashamed to run against a drunken man? couldn't you see that he was *drunk*?' 'Damn him' (answered Hobhouse) 'isn't *he* ashamed to run against *me*? couldn't he see that *I* was *sober*?'

28

When Brummell was obliged (by that affair of poor Meyler, who thence acquired the name of 'Dick the Dandy-killer'—it was about money and debt and all that) to retire to France, he knew no French; and having obtained a Grammar for the purposes of Study, our friend Scrope Davies was asked what progress Brummell had made in French, to which he responded, 'that B. had been stopped like Buonaparte in Russia by the *Elements*.' I have put this pun into 'Beppo,' which is 'a fair exchange and no robbery;' for Scrope made his fortune at several dinners (as he owned himself), by repeating occasionally as his own some of the buffooneries with which I had encountered him in the Morning.

29

I liked the Dandies; they were always very civil to *me*, though in general they disliked literary people, and persecuted and mystified Me. de Staël, Lewis, Horace Twiss, and the like, damnably. They persuaded Me. de Staël that Alvanley had a hundred thousand a year, etc. etc., till she praised him to his *face* for his *beauty*! and made a set at him for Albertine (*Libertine*, as Brummell baptized her, though the poor Girl was and is as correct as maid or wife can be, and very amiable withal), and a hundred fooleries besides.

The truth is, that, though I gave up the business early, I had a tinge of Dandyism in my minority, and probably retained enough of it, to conciliate the great ones; at four and twenty, I had gamed, and drank, and taken my degrees in most dissipations; and having no pedantry, and not being overbearing, we ran quietly together. I knew them all more or less, and they made me a Member of Watier's (a superb Club at that time), being, I take it, the only literary man (except *two others*, both men of the world, M. and S.) in it.

Our Masquerade was a grand one; so was the Dandy Ball, too, at the Argyle, but *that* (the latter) was given by the four Chiefs, B., M., A., and P., if I err not.

30

I was a Member of the Alfred too, being elected while in Greece. It was pleasant—a little too sober and literary, and bored with Sotheby and Sir Francis D'Ivernois! but one met Peel, and Ward, and Valentia, and many other pleasant or known people; and was upon the whole a decent resource on a rainy day, in a dearth of parties, or parliament, or an empty season.

31

I belonged, or belong, to the following Clubs or Societies:— to the Alfred, to the Cocoa tree, to Watier's, to the Union, to Racket's (at Brighton), to the Pugilistic, to the Owls or 'Fly by Night,' to the *Cambridge* Whig Club, to the Harrow Club, Cambridge, and to one or two private Clubs, to the Hampden political Club, and to the Italian Carbonari, etc. etc. etc., 'though last *not least*.' I got into all these, and never stood for any other—at least to my own knowledge. I declined being proposed to several others; though pressed to stand Candidate.

32

If the papers lie not (which they generally do), Demetrius Zograffo of Athens is at the head of the Athenian part of the present Greek Insurrection. He was my Servant in 1809, 1810, 1811, 1812, at different intervals in those years (for I left him in Greece when I went to Constantinople), and accompanied me to England in 1811. He returned to Greece, Spring 1812. He was a clever, but not *apparently* an enterprizing, man; but Circumstances make men. His two sons (*then* infants) were named Miltiades and Alcibiades. May the Omen be happy!

33

I have a notion that Gamblers are as happy as most people, being always *excited*. Women, wine, fame, the table, even Ambition, *sate* now and then; but every turn of the card, and cast of the dice, keeps the Gamester alive: besides one can Game ten times longer than one can do any thing else.

I was very fond of it when young, that is to say, of 'Hazard;' for I hate all *Card* Games, even Faro. When Macco (or whatever they spell it) was introduced, I gave up the whole thing; for I loved and missed the *rattle* and *dash* of the box and dice, and the glorious uncertainty, not only of good luck or bad luck, but of *any luck at all*, as one had sometimes to throw *often* to decide at all.

I have thrown as many as fourteen mains running, and carried off all the cash upon the table occasionally; but I had no coolness or judgement or calculation. It was the *delight* of the thing that pleased me. Upon the whole, I left off in time without being much a winner or loser. Since one and twenty years of age, I played but little, and then never above a hundred or two, or three.

34

As far as Fame goes (that is to say *living* Fame) I have had my share—perhaps, indeed, *certainly* more than my *deserts*. Some odd instances have occurred to my own experience of the wild and strange places, to which a name may penetrate, and where it may impress. Two years ago (almost three, being in August or July 1819), I received at Ravenna a letter in *English* verse from *Drontheim* in Norway, written by a Norwegian, and full of the usual compliments, etc. etc. It is still somewhere amongst my papers. In the same month, I received an invitation into *Holstein* from a Mr. Jacobsen (I think), of Hamburgh; also (by the same medium), a translation of Medora's song in the 'Corsair' by a Westphalian Baroness (not 'Thunderton-tronck'), with some original verses of hers (very pretty and Klopstock-ish), and a prose translation annexed to them, on the subject of my wife. As they concerned *her* more than me, I sent them to her together with Mr. J.'s letter. It was odd enough to receive an invitation to pass the *summer* in *Holstein*, while in *Italy*, from people I never knew. The letter was addressed to Venice. Mr. J. talked to me of the 'wild roses growing in the Holstein summer:' why then did the Cimbri and Teutones emigrate?

What a strange thing is life and man? Were I to present myself at the door of the house, where my daughter now is, the door would be shut in my face, unless (as is not impossible) I knocked down the porter; and if I had gone in that year (and perhaps now) to Drontheim (the furthest town in Norway), or into Holstein, I should have been received with open arms into the mansions of Strangers and foreigners, attached to me by no tie but that of mind and rumour.

As far as *Fame* goes, I have had my share: it has indeed been leavened by other human contingencies, and this in a greater degree than has occurred to most literary men of a *decent* rank in life; but on the whole I take it that such equipoise is the condition of humanity.

I doubt sometimes whether, after all, a quiet and unagitated life would have suited me: yet I sometimes long for it. My earliest dreams (as most boys' dreams are) were martial; but a little later they were all for *love* and retirement, till the hopeless attachment to M. C. began, and continued (though sedulously concealed) *very* early in my teens; and so upwards for a time. *This* threw me out again 'alone on a wide, wide sea.'

In the year 1804, I recollect meeting my Sister at General Harcourt's in Portland Place. I was then *one* thing, and *as* she had always till then found me. When we met again in 1805 (she told me since), that my temper and disposition were so completely altered, that I was hardly to be recognized. I was not then sensible of the change, but I can believe it, and account for it.

35

A private play being got up at Cambridge, a Mr. *Tulk*, greatly to the inconvenience of Actors and audience, declined his part on a sudden, so that it was necessary to make an apology to the Company. In doing this, Hobhouse (indignant like all the rest at this inopportune caprice of the Seceder) stated to the audience 'that in consequence of *a* Mr. Tulk having unexpectedly thrown up his part, they must request their indulgence, etc. etc. Next day, the furious Tulk demanded of Hobhouse, 'did you, Sir, or did you not use *that* expression?' 'Sir,' (said Hobhouse) 'I *did* or *did not* use that expression.' 'Perhaps' (said Scrope Davies, who was present), 'you object to the *indefinite article*, and prefer being entitled *the* Mr. *Tulk*?' *The* Tulk eyed Scrope indignantly; but aware, probably, that the said Scrope, besides being a profane Jester, had the misfortune to be a very good shot, and had already fought two or three duels, he retired without further objections to either article, except a conditional menace—*if* he should ascertain that an intention, etc. etc. etc.

36

I have been called in as Mediator or Second at least twenty times in violent quarrels, and have always contrived to settle the business without compromising the honour of the parties, or leading them to mortal consequences; and this too some-times in very difficult and delicate circumstances, and having to deal with very hot and haughty Spirits—Irishmen, Game-sters, Guardsmen, Captains and Cornets of horse, and the like. This was of course in my youth, when I lived in hot-headed company. I have had to carry challenges from Gentlemen to Noblemen, from Captains to Captains, from lawyers to

Counsellors, and once from a Clergyman to an officer in the Lifeguards. It may seem strange, but I found the latter by far the most difficult

> ... *to compose*
> *The bloody duel without blows.*

The business being about a woman. I must add too that I never saw a *woman* behave so ill, like a cold-blooded heartless whore as she was; but very handsome for all that. A certain Susan C. was she called. I never saw her but once, and that was to induce her but to say two words (which in no degree compromised herself), and which would have had the effect of saving a priest or a Lieutenant of Cavalry. She would *not* say them, and neither N. or myself (the Son of Sir E. N., and a friend of one of the parties) could prevail upon her to say them, though both of us used to deal in some sort with Woman-kind. At last I managed to quiet the combatants without her talisman, and, I believe, to her great disappointment. She was the d——st b——h that I ever saw, and I have seen a great many. Though my Clergyman was sure to lose either his life or his living, he was as warlike as the Bishop of Beauvais, and would hardly be pacified: but then he was in love, and that is a martial passion.

37

[Scrawled out by Byron.]

38

Somebody asked Schlegel (the Dousterswivel of Madame de Stael) 'whether he did not think *Canova* a great Sculptor?' 'Ah!' replied the modest Prussian, 'did you ever see *my bust* by *Tiecke*?'

39

At Venice, in the year 1817, an order came from Vienna for the Archbishop to go in State to Saint Mark's in his Carriage and four horses, which is much the same as commanding the Lord Mayor of London to proceed through Temple Bar in his Barge.

40

When I met Hudson Lowe, the Jailor, at Lord Holland's, before he sailed for Saint Helena, the discourse turned on the battle of Waterloo. I asked him whether the dispositions of Napoleon were those of a great General: he answered disparagingly, 'that they were very *simple*.' I had always thought that a degree of Simplicity was an ingredient of Greatness.

41

I was much struck with the simplicity of Grattan's manners in private life: they were odd, but they were natural. Curran used to take him off bowing to the very ground, and 'thanking God that he had no peculiarities of gesture or appearance,' in a way irresistibly ludicrous. And Rogers used to call him 'a Sentimental Harlequin;' but Rogers back-bites every body; and Curran, who used to quiz his great friend Godwin to his very face, would hardly respect a fair mark of mimicry in another. To be sure, Curran *was* admirable! To hear his description of the examination of an Irish witness, was next to hearing his own speeches: the latter I never heard, but I have the former.

42

I have heard that, when Grattan made his first speech in the English Commons, it was for some minutes doubtful whether to laugh at or cheer him. The debût of his predecessor, Flood, had been a complete failure, under nearly similar circumstances. But when the ministerial part of our Senators had watched Pitt (their thermometer) for their cue, and saw him nod repeatedly his stately nod of approbation, they took the hint from their huntsman, and broke out into the most rapturous cheers. Grattan's speech indeed deserved them: it was a *chef d'œuvre*. I did not hear *that* speech of his (being then at Harrow), but heard most of his others on the same question; also that on the war of 1815. I differed from his opinion on the latter question, but coincided in the general admiration of his eloquence.

43

At the Opposition Meeting of the peers in 1812 at Lord Grenville's, when Ld. Grey and he read to us the correspondence upon Moira's negociation, I sate next to the present Duke of Grafton. When it was over, I turned to him, and said, 'What is to be done next?' 'Wake the Duke of Norfolk' (who was snoring near us) replied he, 'I don't think the Negociators have left anything else for us to do this turn.'

44

In the debate, or rather discussion, afterwards in the House of Lords upon that very question, I sate immediately behind Lord Moira, who was extremely annoyed at G.'s speech upon the subject, and while G. was speaking, turned round to me repeatedly, and asked me whether I agreed with him? It was an awkward question to me who had not heard both sides. Moira kept repeating to me, 'it was *not so*, it was so and so, etc.' I did not know very well what to think, but I sympathized with the acuteness of his feelings upon the subject.

45

Lord Eldon affects an Imitation of two very different Chancellors, Thurlow and Loughborough, and can indulge in an oath now and then. On one of the debates on the Catholic question, when we were either equal or within one (I forget which), I had been sent for in great haste to a Ball, which I quitted, I confess, somewhat reluctantly, to emancipate five Millions of people. I came in late, and did not go immediately into the body of the house, but stood just behind the Woolsack. Eldon turned round, and, catching my eye, immediately said to a peer (who had come to him for a few minutes on the Woolsack, as is the custom of his friends), 'Damn them! they'll have it now, by G—d! The vote that is just come in will give it them.'

46

When I came of age, some delays on account of some birth and marriage certificates from Cornwall occasioned me not to take my seat for several weeks. When these were over, and I had taken the Oaths, the Chancellor apologized to me for the delay, observing 'that these forms were a part of his *duty*.' I begged of him to make no apology, and added (as he certainly had shown no violent hurry) 'Your Lordship was exactly like "Tom Thumb" (which was then being acted), You did your *duty*, and you did *no more*.'

47

In a certain Capital abroad, the Minister's Secretary (the Minister being then absent) was piqued that I did not call upon him. When I was going away, Mr. W., an acquaintance of mine, applied to him for my passport, which was sent, but at the same time accompanied by a formal note from the Secretary stating 'that at *Mr. W.'s request* he had granted, etc.,' and in such a manner as appeared to *hint* that it was only to oblige *Mr. W.* that he had given me that which in fact he had no right to refuse to Any-body. I wrote to him the following answer:—'Lord B. presents his Compliments to L., and is extremely obliged to *Mr. W.* for the passport.'

48

There was a Madman of the name of Battersby, that frequented Steevens's and the Prince of Wales's Coffee-houses, about the time when I was leading a loose life about town, before I was of age. One night he came up to some hapless Stranger, whose coat was not to his liking, and said, 'Pray, Sir, did the tailor cut your coat in that fashion, or the rats gnaw it?'

49

The following is (I believe) better known. A beau (*dandies* were not then christened) came into the P. of W.'s, and exclaimed, 'Waiter, bring me a glass of Madeira Negus with a Jelly, and rub my plate with a Chalotte.' This in a very soft tone of voice. A Lieutenant of the Navy, who sate in the next box, immediately roared out the following rough parody: 'Waiter, bring me a glass of d——d stiff Grog, and rub . . . with a brick-bat.'

50

Sotheby is a good man, rhymes well (if not wisely), but is a
bore. He seizes you by the button. One night of a route at
Mrs. Hope's, he had fastened upon me (something about Agamemnon, or Orestes, or some of his plays), notwithstanding
my symptoms of manifest distress (for I was in love, and had
just nicked a minute, when neither mothers, nor husbands, nor
rivals, nor gossips, were near my then idol, who was beautiful
as the Statues of the Gallery where we stood at the time)—
Sotheby I say had seized upon me by the button and the
heart-strings, and spared neither. W. Spencer, who likes
fun, and don't dislike mischief, saw my case, and coming up
to us both, took me by the hand, and pathetically bade me
farewell: 'for,' said he, 'I see it is all over with you.' Sotheby
then went away. 'Sic me servavit Apollo.'

51

It is singular how soon we lose the impression of what
ceases to be *constantly* before us. A year impairs, a lustre
obliterates. There is little distinct left without an *effort* of
memory: *then* indeed the lights are rekindled for a moment;
but who can be sure that Imagination is not the torch-bearer?
Let any man try at the end of *ten* years to bring before him the
features, or the mind, or the sayings, or the habits, of his best
friend, or his *greatest* man (I mean his favourite—his Buonaparte, his this, that or 'tother), and he will be surprized at the
extreme confusion of his ideas. I speak confidently on this
point, having always past for one who had a good, aye, an
excellent memory. I except indeed our recollections of
Womankind: there is no forgetting *them* (and be d——d to
them) any more than any other remarkable Era, such as 'the
revolution,' or 'the plague,' or 'the Invasion,' or 'the Comet,'
or 'the War' of such and such an Epoch—being the favourite
dates of Mankind, who have so many *blessings* in their lot,
that they never make their Calendars from them, being too
common. For instance, you see 'the great drought,' 'the
Thames frozen over,' 'the Seven years war broke out,' the E.

or F. or S. 'Revolution commenced,' 'The Lisbon Earthquake,' 'the Lima Earthquake,' 'The Earthquake of Calabria,' the 'Plague of London,' 'Ditto of Constantinople,' 'the Sweating Sickness,' 'The Yellow fever of Philadelphia,' etc. etc. etc.; but you don't see 'the abundant harvest,' 'the fine Summer,' 'the long peace,' 'the wealthy speculation,' the 'wreckless voyage,' recorded so emphatically? By the way, there has been a *thirty years war*, and a *Seventy years war*: was there ever a *Seventy or a thirty years Peace*? Or was there ever even a *day's Universal* peace, except perhaps in China, where they have found out the miserable happiness of a stationary and unwar-like mediocrity? And is all this, because Nature is niggard or savage? or Mankind ungrateful? Let philosophers decide. I am none.

52

In the year 1814, as Moore and I were going to dine with Lord Grey in P. Square, I pulled out a 'Java Gazette' (which Murray had sent to me), in which there was a controversy on our respective merits as poets. It was amusing enough that we should be proceeding peaceably to the same table, while they were squabbling about us in the Indian Seas (to be sure, the paper was dated six months before), and filling columns with Batavian Criticism. But this is fame, I presume.

53

In general, I do not draw well with literary men: not that I dislike them, but I never know what to say to them after I have praised their last publication. There are several exceptions, to be sure; but then they have either been men of the world, such as Scott, and Moore, etc., or visionaries out of it, such as Shelley, etc.: but your literary every day man and I never went well in company—especially your foreigner, whom I never could abide. Except Giordani, and—and—and—(I really can't name any other) I do not remember a man amongst them, whom I ever wished to see twice, except perhaps Mezzo-phanti, who is a Monster of Languages, the Briareus of parts of Speech, a walking Polyglott and more, who ought to have

2 D

existed at the time of the tower of Babel as universal Inter-preter. He is indeed a Marvel—unassuming also: I tried him in all the tongues of which I knew a single oath (or adjuration to the Gods against Postboys, Lawyers, Tartars, boatmen, Sailors, pilots, Gondoliers, Muleteers, Camel-drivers, Vetturini, Post-masters, post-horses, post-houses, post-every-thing), and Egad! he astounded me even to my English.

54

Three Swedes came to Bologna, knowing no tongue but Swedish. The inhabitants in despair presented them to Mezzo-phanti. Mezzophanti (though a great Linguist) knew no more Swedish than the Inhabitants. But in two days, by dint of dictionary, he talked with them fluently and freely, so that they were astonished, and every body else, at his acquisition of another tongue in forty eight hours. I had this anecdote first from Me. Albrizzi, and afterwards confirmed by *himself*—and he is not a boaster.

55

I sometimes wish that I had studied languages with more attention: those which I know, even the classical (Greek and Latin, in the usual proportion of a sixth form boy), and a smattering of modern Greek, the Armenian and Arabic Alpha-bets, a few Turkish and Albanian phrases, oaths, or requests, Italian tolerably, Spanish less than tolerably, French to read with ease but speak with difficulty—or rather not at all—all have been acquired by ear or eye, and never by anything like Study. Like 'Edie Ochiltree,' 'I never dowed to bide a hard turn o' wark in my life.'

To be sure, I set in zealously for the Armenian and Arabic, but I fell in love with some absurd womankind both times, before I had overcome the Characters; and at Malta and Venice left the profitable Orientalists for—for—(no matter what), notwithstanding that my master, the Padre Pasquale Aucher (for whom, by the way, I compiled the major part of two Armenian and English Grammars), assured me 'that the terrestrial Paradise had been certainly in *Armenia*.' I went seeking it—God knows where—did I find it? Umph! Now and then, for a minute or two. '

56

Of Actors, Cooke was the most natural, Kemble the most supernatural, Kean a medium between the two, but Mrs. Siddons worth them all put together, of those whom I remember to have seen in England.

57

I have seen Sheridan weep two or three times: it may be that he was maudlin; but this only renders it more impressive, for who would see—

> *From Marlborough's eyes the tears of dotage flow,*
> *And Swift expire a driveller and a show?*

Once I saw him cry at Robins's, the Auctioneer's, after a splendid dinner full of great names and high Spirits. I had the honour of sitting next to Sheridan. The occasion of his tears was some observation or other upon the subject of the sturdiness of the Whigs in resisting Office, and keeping to their principles. Sheridan turned round—'Sir, it is easy for my Lord G., or Earl G., or Marquis B., or Ld. H., with thousands upon thousands a year—some of it either *presently* derived or *inherited* in Sinecures or acquisitions from the public money— to boast of their patriotism, and keep aloof from temptation; but they do not know from what temptations those have kept aloof, who had equal pride—at least equal talents, and not unequal passions, and nevertheless knew not in the course of their lives what it was to have a shilling of their own.' And in saying this he wept.

58

I have more than once heard Sheridan say, that he never 'had a shilling of his own:' to be sure, he contrived to extract a good many of other people's.

In 1815, I had occasion to visit my Lawyer in Chancery Lane: he was with Sheridan. After mutual greetings, etc., Sheridan retired first. Before recurring to my own business, I could not help enquiring *that* of S. 'Oh' (replied the Attorneo), 'the usual thing—to stave off an action from his Wine-Merchant, my Client.' 'Well' (said I) 'and what do you mean to do?' 'Nothing at all for the present,' said he: 'would you have us proceed against old Sherry? What would be the use of it?' And here he began laughing, and going over Sheridan's good gifts of Conversation. Now, from personal experience, I can vouch that my Attorneo is by no means the tenderest of men, or particularly accessible to any kind of impression out of the Statute or record. And yet Sheridan, in half an hour, had found the way to soften and seduce him in such a manner, that I almost think he would have thrown his Client (an honest man with all the laws and some justice on his side) out of the window, had he come in at the moment. Such was Sheridan! He could soften an Attorney! There has been nothing like it since the days of Orpheus.

59

When the Bailiffs (for I have seen most kinds of life) came upon me in 1815, to seize my chattels (being a peer of parliament my person was beyond him), being curious (as is my habit), I first asked him 'what Extents elsewhere he had for Government?' upon which he showed me one upon *one house only* for *seventy thousand pounds!* Next I asked him, if he had nothing for Sheridan? 'Oh, Sheridan,' said he: 'aye, I have this' (pulling out a pocket-book, etc.). 'But, my L., I have been in Mr. Sheridan's house a twelve-month at a time: a civil gentleman—knows how to deal with *us*, etc. etc. etc.' Our own business was then discussed, which was none of the easiest for me at that time. But the Man was civil, and, (what I valued more), communicative. I had met many of his brethren years before in affairs of my friends (commoners, that is), but this was the first (or second) on my own account. A civil Man, feed accordingly: probably he anticipated as much.

60

No man would live his life over again, is an old and true saying, which all can resolve for themselves. At the same time, there are probably *moments* in most men's lives, which they would live over the rest of life to *regain*? Else, why do we live at all? Because Hope recurs to Memory, both false; but—but—but—but—and this *but* drags on till—What? I do not know, and who does? 'He that died o' Wednesday.' By the way, there is a poor devil to be shot tomorrow here (Ravenna) for murder. He hath eaten half a Turkey for his dinner, besides fruit and pudding; and he refuses to confess? Shall I go to see him exhale? No. And why? Because it is to take place at *Nine*. Now, could I *save* him, or a fly even from the same catastrophe, I would out-match years; but as I cannot, I will not get up earlier to see another man shot, than I would to run the same risk in person. Besides, I have seen more men than one die that death (and other deaths) before to-day.

It is not cruelty which actuates mankind, but excitement, on such occasions; at least, I suppose so. It is detestable to *take* life in that way, unless it be to preserve two lives.

61

Old Edgeworth, the fourth or fifth Mrs. Edgeworth, and *the* Miss Edgeworth were in London, 1813. Miss Edgeworth liked, Mrs. Edgeworth not disliked, old Edgeworth a bore—the worst of bores—a boisterous Bore. I met them in society once at a breakfast of Sir H. D.'s. Old Edgeworth came in late, boasting that he had given 'Dr. Parr a dressing the night before' (no such easy matter by the way). I thought *her* pleasant. They all abused Anna Seward's memory.

62

When, on the road, they heard of *her* brother's, and *his* Son's, death. What was to be done? Their *London* Apparel was all ordered and made! So they sunk his death for the six weeks of their Sojourn, and went into mourning on their way back to Ireland. *Fact!*

63

While the Colony were in London, there was a book, with a Subscription for the 'recall of Mrs. Siddons to the Stage,' going about for signatures. Moore moved for a similar subscription for the 'recall of *Mr. Edgeworth to Ireland*!'

64

Sir Humphrey Davy told me, that the Scene of the French Valet and Irish postboy in 'Ennui' was taken from *his* verbal description to the Edgeworths in Edgeworthtown of a similar fact on the road occurring to himself. So much the better—being *life*.

65

When I was fifteen years of age, it happened that in a Cavern in Derbyshire I had to cross in a boat (in which two people only could lie down) a stream which flows under a rock, with the rock so close upon the water, as to admit the boat only to be pushed on by a ferry-man (a sort of Charon), who wades at the stern stooping all the time. The Companion of my transit was M. A. C., with whom I had been long in love, and never told it, though *she* had discovered it without. I recollect my sensations, but cannot describe them—and it is as well.

We were a party—a Mr. W., two Miss W.'s, Mr. and Mrs. Cl——ke, Miss M., and *my* M. A. C. Alas! why do I say *My*? Our Union would have healed feuds, in which blood had been shed by our fathers; it would have joined lands, broad and rich; it would have joined at least *one* heart, and two persons not ill-matched in years (she is two years my elder); and—and—and—what has been the result? *She* has married a man older than herself, been wretched, and separated. I have married, and am separated: and yet *We* are *not* united.

66

One of my notions, different from those of my co-temporaries, is, that the present is not a high age of English Poetry: there are *more* poets (soi-disant) than ever there were, and proportionally *less* poetry.

This *thesis* I have maintained for some years, but, strange to say, it meeteth not with favour from my brethren of the Shell. Even Moore shakes his head, and firmly believes that it is the grand Era of British Poesy.

67

When I belonged to the D. L. Committee, and was one of the S. C. of Management, the number of plays upon the shelves were about *five* hundred. Conceiving that amongst these there must be *some* of merit, in person and by proxy I caused an investigation. I do not think that, of those which I saw, there was one which could be conscientiously tolerated. There never were such things as most of them.

Mathurin was very kindly recommended to me by Walter Scott, to whom I had recourse; firstly, in the hope that he would do something for us himself; and secondly, in my despair, that he would point out to us any young (or old) writer of promise. Mathurin sent his Bertram, and a letter *without* his address, so that at first I could give him no answer. When I at last hit upon his residence, I sent him a favourable answer, and something more substantial. His play succeeded. but I was at that time absent from England.

I tried Coleridge, too; but he had nothing feasible in hand at the time. Mr. Sotheby obligingly offered *all* his tragedies, and I pledged myself; and, notwithstanding many squabbles with my Committe[e]d Brethren, did get 'Ivan' accepted, read, and the parts distributed. But lo! in the very heart of the matter, upon some *tepid*-ness on the part of Kean, or warmth on that of the Authour, Sotheby withdrew his play.

Sir J. B. Burgess did also present four tragedies and a farce, and I moved Green-room and S. Committee; but they would not.

Then the Scenes I had to go through! The authours, and the authoresses, the Milliners, the wild Irishmen, the people from Brighton, from Blackwall, from Chatham, from Cheltenham, from Dublin, from Dundee, who came in upon me! To all of whom it was proper to give a civil answer, and a hearing, and a reading. Mrs. Glover's father, an Irish dancing-Master of Sixty years, called upon me to request to play 'Archer,' drest in silk stockings on a frosty morning, to show his legs (which were certainly good and Irish for his age, and had been still better). Miss Emma Somebody, with a play entitled the 'Bandit of Bohemia,' or some such title or production. Mr.

O'Higgins, then resident at Richmond, with an Irish tragedy, in which the unities could not fail to be observed, for the protagonist was chained by the leg to a pillar during the chief part of the performance. He was a wild man, of a salvage (*sic*) appearance; and the difficulty of *not* laughing at him was only to be got over by reflecting upon the probable consequences of such cachinnation.

As I am really a civil and polite person, and *do* hate giving pain, when it can be avoided, I sent them up to Douglas Kinnaird, who is a man of business, and sufficiently ready with a negative, and left them to settle with him. And, as at the beginning of next year, I went abroad, I have since been little aware of the progress of the theatres.

68

Players are said to be an impracticable people. They are so. But I managed to steer clear of any disputes with them, and, excepting one debate with the Elder Byrne about Miss Smith's Pas de (Something—I forget the technicals), I do not remember any litigation of my own. I used to protect Miss Smith, because she was like Lady Jane Harley in the face; and likenesses go a great way with me. Indeed, in general, I left such things to my more bustling colleagues, who used to reprove me seriously for not being able to take such things in hand without buffooning with the Histrions, and throwing things into confusion by treating light matters with levity.

69

Then the Committee!—then the Sub-Committee! We were but few, and never agreed! There was Peter Moore who contradicted Kinnaird, and Kinnaird who contradicted everybody: then our two managers, Rae and Dibdin, and our Secretary, Ward! And yet we were all very zealous and in earnest to do good, and so forth. Hobhouse furnished us with prologues to our revived Old English plays, but was not pleased with me for complimenting him as 'the *Upton*' of our theatre (Mr. Upton is or was the poet who writes the songs for Astley's), and almost gave up prologuizing in consequence.

70

In the Pantomime of 1815–16, there was a Representation of the Masquerade of 1814, given by 'us Youth' of Watier's Club to Wellington and Co. Douglas Kinnaird, and one or two others with myself, put on Masques, and went *on* the Stage amongst the 'οἱ πολλοί,' to see the effect of a theatre from the Stage. It is very grand. Douglas danced among the figuranti, too; and they were puzzled to find out who we were, as being more than their number. It was odd enough that D. K. and I should have been both at the *real* Masquerade, and afterwards in the Mimic one of the same on the stage of D. L. Theatre.

71

When I was a youth, I was reckoned a good actor. Besides 'Harrow Speeches' (in which I shone) I enacted 'Penruddock' in the 'Wheel of Fortune,' and 'Tristram Fickle' in Allingham's farce of 'the Weathercock,' for three nights (the duration of our compact), in some private theatricals at Southwell in 1806, with great applause. The occasional prologue for our volunteer play was also of my composition. The other performers were young ladies and gentlemen of the neighbourhood; and the whole went off with great effect upon our good-natured audience.

72

When I first went up to College, it was a new and a heavy hearted scene for me. Firstly, I so much disliked leaving Harrow, that, though it was time (I being seventeen), it broke my very rest for the last quarter with counting the days that remained. I always *hated* Harrow till the last year and half, but then I liked it. Secondly, I wished to go to Oxford and not to Cambridge. Thirdly, I was so completely alone in this new world, that it half broke my Spirits. My companions were not unsocial, but the contrary—lively, hospitable, of rank, and fortune, and gay far beyond my gaiety. I mingled with, and dined and supped, etc., with them; but, I know not how, it was one of the deadliest and heaviest feelings of my life to feel that

I was no longer a boy. From that moment I began to grow old in my own esteem; and in my esteem age is not estimable. I took my gradations in the vices with great promptitude, but they were not to my taste; for my early passions, though violent in the extreme, were concentrated, and hated division or spreading abroad. I could have left or lost the world with or for that which I loved; but, though my temperament was naturally burning, I could not share in the common place libertinism of the place and time without disgust. And yet this very disgust, and my heart thrown back upon itself, threw me into excesses perhaps more fatal than those from which I shrunk, as fixing upon one (at a time) the passions, which, spread amongst many, would have hurt only myself.

73

People have wondered at the Melancholy which runs through my writings. Others have wondered at my personal gaiety; but I recollect once, after an hour, in which I had been sincerely and particularly gay, and rather brilliant, in company, my wife replying to me when I said (upon her remarking my high spirits) 'and yet, Bell, I have been called and mis-called Melancholy—you must have seen how falsely, frequently.' 'No, B.,' (she answered) 'it is not so: at *heart* you are the most melancholy of mankind, and often when apparently gayest.'

74

If I could explain at length the *real* causes which have contributed to increase this perhaps *natural* temperament of mine, this Melancholy which hath made me a bye-word, nobody would wonder; but this is impossible without doing much mischief. I do not know what other men's lives have been, but I cannot conceive anything more strange than some of the earlier parts of mine. I have written my memoirs, but omitted *all* the really *consequential* and *important* parts, from deference to the dead, to the living, and to those who must be both.

75

I sometimes think that I should have written the *whole* as a *lesson*, but it might have proved a *lesson* to be *learnt* rather than *avoided*; for passion is a whirlpool, which is not to be viewed nearly without attraction from its Vortex.

76

I must not go on with these reflections, or I shall be letting out some secret or other to paralyze posterity.

77

One night, Scrope Davies at a gaming house (before I was of age), being tipsy as he usually was at the Midnight hour, and having lost monies, was in vain intreated by his friends, one degree less intoxicated than himself, to come or go home. In despair, he was left to himself, and to the demons of the dice-box. Next day, being visited, about two of the Clock, by some friends just risen with a severe headache and empty pockets (who had left him losing at four or five in the morning), he was found in a sound sleep, without a night-cap, and not particularly encumbered with bed-cloathes: a Chamber-pot stood by his bed-side, *brim-full* of —— *Bank Notes!* all won, God knows how, and crammed, Scrope knew not where; but *there* they were, all good legitimate notes, and to the amount of some thousand pounds.

78

At Brighthelmstone (I love orthography at length), in the year 1808, Hobhouse, Scrope Davies, Major Cooper, and myself, having dined together with Lord Delvin, Count (I forget the french Emigrant nomenclature) and others, did about the middle of the night (we *four*) proceed to a house of Gambling, being then *amongst us* possest of about *twenty guineas* of ready cash, with which we had to maintain as many of your whorson horses and servants, besides house-hold and whore-hold expenditure. We had, I say, twenty guineas or so, and we lost them, returning home in bad humour. Cooper went home.

Scrope and Hobhouse and I (it being high Summer), did firstly strip and plunge into the Sea, whence, after half an hour's swimming of those of us (Scrope and I) who could swim, we emerged in our dressing-gowns to discuss a bottle or two of Champaigne and Hock (according to choice) at our quarters. In course of this discussion, words arose; Scrope seized H. by the throat; H. seized a knife in self-defence, and stabbed Scrope in the shoulder to avoid being throttled. Scrope fell bathed in blood and wine—for the *bottle* fell with him, being infinitely intoxicated with Gaming, Sea-bathing at two in the morning, and Supplementary Champaigne. The skirmish had past before I had time or thought to interfere. Of course I lectured against gambling—

Pugnare Thracum est,

and then examined Scrope's wound, which proved to be a gash long and broad, but not deep nor dangerous. Scrope was furious: first he wanted to fight, then to go away in a post-chaise, and then to *shoot* himself, which latter intention I offered to forward, provided that he did not use *my pistols*, which, in case of suicide, would become a deo-dand to the King. At length, with many oaths and some difficulty, he was gotten to bed. In the morning, Cool reflection and a Surgeon came, and, by dint of loss of blood, and sticking plaister, the quarrel (which Scrope had begun), was healed as well as the wound, and we were all friends as for years before and after.

79

My first dash into poetry was as early as 1800. It was the ebullition of a passion for my first Cousin Margaret Parker (daughter and grand-daughter of the two Admirals Parker), one of the most beautiful of evanescent beings. I have long forgotten the verses, but it would be difficult for me to forget her. Her dark eyes! her long eye-lashes! her completely Greek cast of face and figure! I was then about twelve—She rather older, perhaps a year. She died about a year or two afterwards, in consequence of a fall which injured her spine and induced consumption. Her Sister, Augusta (by some thought still more beautiful), died of the same malady; and it was indeed in attending her that Margaret met with the accident, which occasioned her own death. My Sister told me that, when she went to see her shortly before her death, upon accidentally mentioning my name, Margaret coloured through the paleness of mortality to the eyes, to the great astonishment of my Sister, who (residing with her Grandmother, Lady Holderness) saw at that time but little of me for family reasons, knew nothing of our attachment, nor could conceive why my name should affect her at such a time. I knew nothing of her illness (being at Harrow and in the country), till she was gone.

Some years after, I made an attempt at an Elegy. A very dull one. I do not recollect scarcely any thing equal to the *transparent* beauty of my cousin, or to the sweetness of her temper, during the short period of our intimacy. She looked as if she had been made out of a rainbow—all beauty and peace.

My passion had its usual effects upon me: I could not sleep, could not eat; I could not rest; and although I had reason to know that she loved me, it was the torture of my life to think of the time which must elapse before we could meet again— being usually about *twelve hours* of separation! But I was a fool then, and am not much wiser now.

80

My passions were developed very early—so early, that few would believe me, if I were to state the period, and the facts which accompanied it. Perhaps this was one of the reasons which caused the anticipated melancholy of my thoughts— having anticipated life.

My earlier poems are the thoughts of one at least ten years older than the age at which they were written: I don't mean for their solidity, but their Experience. The two first Cantos of Ce. Hd. were completed at twenty two, and they are written as if by a man older than I shall probably ever be.

[81 omitted by Byron.]

82

Upon Parnassus, going to the fountain of Delphi (Castri), in 1809, I saw a flight of twelve Eagles (Hobhouse says they are Vultures—at least in conversation), and I seized the Omen. On the day before, I composed the lines to Parnassus (in Childe Harold), and, on beholding the birds, had a hope that Apollo had accepted my homage. I have at least had the name and fame of a Poet during the poetical period of life (from twenty to thirty): whether it will last is another matter; but I *have been* a votary of the Deity and the place, and am grateful for what he has done in my behalf, leaving the future in his hands as I left the past.

83

Like Sylla, I have always believed that all things depend upon Fortune, and nothing upon ourselves. I am not aware of any one thought or action worthy of being called good to myself or others, which is not to be attributed to the Good Goddess, Fortune!

84

Two or three years ago, I thought of going to one of the Americas, English or Spanish. But the accounts sent from England, in consequence of my enquiries, discouraged me. After all, I believe most countries, properly balanced, are equal to *a Stranger* (by no means to the *native*, though). I remembered General Ludlow's domal inscription:—

Omne solum forti patria—

And sate down free in a country of Slavery for many centuries. But there is *no* freedom, even for *Masters*, in the midst of slaves: it makes my blood boil to see the thing. I sometimes wish that I was the Owner of Africa, to do at once, what Wilberforce will do in time, viz.—sweep Slavery from her desarts, and look on upon the first dance of their Freedom.

As to *political* slavery—so general—it is man's own fault; if they *will* be slaves, let them! Yet it is but 'a word and a blow.' See how England formerly, France, Spain, Portugal,

America, Switzerland, freed themselves! There is no one
instance of a *long* contest, in which *men* did not triumph over
Systems. If Tyranny misses her *first* spring, she is cowardly as
the tiger, and retires to be hunted.

85

An Italian (the younger Count Ruota), writing from
Ravenna to his friend at Rome in 1820, says of me, by way of
compliment, 'that in society no one would take me for an
Englishman, though he believes that I *am* English at bottom—
my manners were so different.' This he meant as a grand
eulogy, and I accept it as such. The letter was shown to me this
year by the Correspondent, Count P. G., or by his Sister.

86

I have been a reviewer. In 'the Monthly Review' I wrote
some articles, which were inserted. This was in the latter part
of 1811. In 1807, in a Magazine called 'Monthly Literary Re-
creations,' I reviewed Wordsworth's trash of that time.
Excepting these, I cannot accuse myself of anonymous
Criticism (that I recollect), though I have been *offered* more
than one review in our principal Journals.

87

Till I was eighteen years old (odd as it may seem), I had
never read a review. But, while at Harrow, my general information was so great on modern topics, as to induce a suspicion
that I could only collect so much information from *reviews*,
because I was never *seen* reading, but always idle and in mischief, or at play. The truth is that I read eating, read in bed,
read when no one else reads; and had read all sorts of reading
since I was five years old, and yet never *met* with a review,
which is the only reason that I know of why I should not have
read them. But it is true; for I remember when Hunter and
Curzon, in 1804, told me this opinion at Harrow, I made them
laugh by my ludicrous astonishment in asking them, '*what is* a
review?' To be sure, they were then less common. In three

years more, I was better acquainted with that same, but the first I ever read was in 1806–7.

88

At School, I was (as I have said) remarked for the extent and readiness of my *general* information; but in all other respects idle; capable of great sudden exertions (such as thirty or forty Greek Hexameters—of course with such prosody as it pleased God), but of few continuous drudgeries. My qualities were much more oratorical and martial, than poetical; and Dr. D., my grand patron (our head-master), had a great notion that I should turn out an Orator, from my fluency, my turbulence, my voice, my copiousness of declamation, and my action. I remember that my first declamation astonished him into some unwonted (for he was economical of such), and sudden compliments, before the declaimers at our first rehearsal. My first Harrow verses (that is, English as exercises), a translation of a chorus from the Prometheus of Aeschylus, were received by him but cooly: no one had the least notion that I should subside into poesy.

89

Peel, the Orator and Statesman ('that was, or is, or is to be'), was my form fellow, and we were both at the top of our remove (a public School Phrase). We were on good terms, but his brother was my intimate friend. There were always great hopes of Peel amongst us all—Masters and Scholars, and he has not disappointed them. As a Scholar, he was greatly my superior: as a declaimer, and Actor, I was reckoned at least his equal. As a school boy *out* of school, I was always *in* scrapes, and *he never*; and *in School* he *always* knew his lesson, and I rarely; but when I knew it, I knew it nearly as well. In general information, history, etc. etc., I think I was *his* Superior, as also of most boys of my standing.

89 [twice].

The prodigy of our School days was George Sinclair (son of Sir John): he made exercises for half the School (*literally*), verses at will, and themes without it. When in the Shell, he made exercises for his Uncle, Dudley Macdonald (a dunce who could only play upon the flute), in the sixth. He was a friend of mine, and in the same remove, and used at times to beg me to let him do my exercise—a request always most readily accorded, upon a pinch, or when I wanted to do something else, which was usually once an hour. On the other hand, he was pacific, and I savage; so I fought for him, or thrashed others for him, or thrashed himself to make him thrash others, whom it was necessary, as a point of honour and stature, that he should so chastise. Or, we talked politics, for he was a great politician, and were very good friends. I have some of his letters, written to me from School, still.

90

Clayton was another School Monster of learning, and talent, and hope; but what has become of him I do not know: he was certainly a Genius.

91

My School friendships were with *me passions* (for I was always violent), but I do not know that there is one which has endured (to be sure, some have been cut short by death) till now. That with Lord Clare began one of the earliest and lasted longest, being only interrupted by distance, that I know of. I never hear the word 'Clare' without a beating of the heart even *now*, and I write it with the feelings of 1803–4–5 ad infinitum.

92

In 1812, at Middelton (Lord Jersey's), amongst a goodly company of Lords, Ladies, and wits, etc., there was poor old Vice Leach, the lawyer, attempting to play off the fine gentleman. His first exhibition—an attempt on horseback, I think, to escort the women—God knows where, in the month of November, ended in a fit of the Lumbago—as Lord Ogleby says, 'a grievous enemy to Gallantry and address'—and if he could but have heard Lady Jersey quizzing him (as I did) next day for the *cause* of his malady, I don't think that he would have turned a 'Squire of dames' in a hurry again. He seemed to me the greatest fool (in that line) I ever saw. This was the last I saw of old Vice Leach, except in town, where he was creeping into assemblies, and trying to look young and gentlemanly.

93

Erskine too! Erskine was there—good, but intolerable. He jested, he talked, he did every thing admirably, but then he *would* be applauded for the same thing twice over: he would read his own verses, his own paragraphs, and tell his own story, again and again—and then 'the trial by Jury!!!' I almost wished it abolished, for I sate next him at dinner. As I had read his published speeches, there was no occasion to repeat them to me.

Chester (the fox hunter), surnamed '*Cheeks Chester*,' and I sweated the Claret, being the only two who did so. Cheeks, who loves his bottle, and had no notion of meeting with a 'bon vivant' in a scribbler, in making my eulogy to somebody one evening, summed it up in—'By G—d, he *drinks like a Man!*'

94

Nobody drank, however, but Cheeks and I. To be sure, there was little occasion, for we swept off what was on the table (a most splendid board, as may be supposed, at Jersey's) very sufficiently. However, we carried our liquor discreetly, like 'the Baron of Bradwardine.'

95

If I had to live over again, I do not know what I would change in my life, unless it were *for not to have lived at all.* All history and experience, and the rest, teaches us that the good and evil are pretty equally balanced in this existence, and that what is most to be desired is an easy passage out of it.

What can it give us but *years*? and those have little of good but their ending.

96

Of the Immortality of the Soul, it appears to me that there can be little doubt, if we attend for a moment to the action of Mind. It is in perpetual activity. I used to doubt of it, but reflection has taught me better. It acts also so very independent of body: in dreams for instance incoherently and madly, I grant you; but still it is *Mind*, and much more *Mind* than when we are awake. Now, that *this* should not act *separately*, as well as jointly, who can pronounce? The Stoics, Epictetus and Marcus Aurelius, call the present state 'a Soul which drags a Carcase:' a heavy chain, to be sure; but all chains, being material, may be shaken off.

How far our future life will be individual, or, rather, how far it will at all resemble our *present* existence, is another question; but that the *Mind* is *eternal*, seems as probable as that the body is not so. Of course, I have ventured upon the question without recurring to Revelation, which, however, is at least as rational a solution of it as any other.

A *material* resurrection seems strange, and even absurd, except for purposes of punishment; and all punishment, which is to *revenge* rather than *correct*, must be *morally wrong*. And *when* the *World is at an end*, what moral or warning purpose *can* eternal tortures answer? Human passions have probably disfigured the divine doctrines here, but the whole thing is inscrutable. It is useless to tell me *not* to *reason*, but to *believe*. You might as well tell a man not to wake but *sleep*. And then to *bully* with torments! and all that! I cannot help thinking that the *menace* of Hell makes as many devils, as the severe penal codes of inhuman humanity make villains.

Man is born *passionate* of body, but with an innate though secret tendency to the love of Good in his Mainspring of Mind. But God help us all! It is at present a sad jar of atoms.

97

Matter is eternal, always changing, but reproduced, and, as far as we can comprehend Eternity, Eternal; and why not *Mind*? Why should not the Mind act with and upon the

Universe? as portions of it act upon and with the congregated dust called Mankind? See, how one man acts upon himself and others, or upon multitudes? The same Agency, in a higher and purer degree, may act upon the Stars, etc., ad infinitum.

98

I have often been inclined to Materialism in philosophy but could never bear its introduction into *Christianity*, which appears to me essentially founded upon the *Soul*. For this reason, Priestley's Christian Materialism always struck me as deadly. Believe the resurrection of the body, if you will, but *not without* a *Soul*. The devil's in it, if, after having had a Soul (as surely the *Mind*, or whatever you call it, *is*) in this world, we must part with it in the next, even for an Immortal Materiality. I own my partiality for *Spirit*.

99

I am always most religious upon a sun-shiny day; as if there was some association between an internal approach to greater light and purity, and the kindler of this dark lanthorn of our external existence.

100

The Night is also a religious concern; and even more so, when I viewed the Moon and Stars through Herschell's telescope, and saw that they were worlds.

101

If, according to some speculations, you could prove the World many thousand years older than the Mosaic Chronology, or if you could knock up Adam and Eve and the Apple and Serpent, still what is to be put up in their stead? or how is the difficulty removed? Things must have had a beginning, and what matters it *when* or *how*?

I sometimes think that *Man* may be the relic of some higher material being, wrecked in a former world, and degenerated in the hardships and struggle through Chaos into Conformity— or something like it; as we see Laplanders, Esquimaux, etc., inferior in the present state, as the Elements become more inexorable. But even then this higher pre-Adamite supposititious Creation must have had an Origin and a *Creator*; for a *Creator* is a more natural imagination than a fortuitous concourse of atoms. All things remount to a fountain, though they may flow to an Ocean.

102

What a strange thing is the propagation of life! A bubble of Seed . . . might (for aught we know) have formed a Caesar or a Buonaparte: there is nothing remarkable recorded of their Sires, that I know of.

103

Lord Kames has said (if I misquote not), 'that a power to call up agreeable ideas at will would be something greater for mortals than all the boons of a fairy tale.'

I have found increasing upon me (without sufficient cause at times) the depression of Spirits (with few intervals), which I have some reason to believe constitutional or inherited.

104

Plutarch says, in his life of Lysander, that Aristotle observes, 'that in general great Geniuses are of a melancholy turn, and instances Socrates, Plato, and Hercules (or Heracleitus), as examples, and Lysander, though not *while* young, yet as inclined to it when approaching towards age.' Whether I am a Genius or not, I have been called such by my friends as well as enemies, and in more countries and languages than one, and also within a no very long period of existence. Of my Genius, I can say nothing, but of my melancholy, that it is 'increasing and ought to be diminished'—but how?

105

I take it that most men are so at bottom, but that it is only remarked in the remarkable. The Duchesse de Broglie, in reply to a remark of mine on the errors of clever people, said, 'that they were not *worse* than others, only being more in view, more noted, especially in all that could reduce them to the rest, or raise the rest to them.' In 1816, this was.

106

In fact (I suppose that), if the follies of fools were all set down like those of the wise, the wise (who seem at present only a better sort of fools), would appear almost intelligent.

107

I have met George Colman occasionally, and thought him extremely pleasant and convivial. Sheridan's humour, or rather wit, was always saturnine, and sometimes savage: he never laughed (at least that *I* saw, and I watched him), but Colman did. I have got very drunk with them both; but, if I had to *choose*, and could not have both at a time, I should say, 'let me begin the evening with Sheridan, and finish it with Colman.' Sheridan for dinner—Colman for Supper. Sheridan for Claret or port; but Colman for every thing, from the Madeira and Champaigne at dinner—the Claret with a *layer* of *port* between the Glasses—up to the Punch of the Night, and down to the Grog or Gin and water of day-break. All these I have threaded with both the same. Sheridan was a Grenadier Company of Life-Guards, but Colman a whole regiment—of *light Infantry*, to be sure, but still a *regiment*.

108

Alcibiades is said to have been 'successful in all his battles;' but *what* battles? Name them! If you mention Caesar, or Annibal, or Napoleon, you at once rush upon Pharsalia, Munda, Alesia, Cannae, Thrasimene, Trebia, Lodi, Marengo, Jena, Austerlitz, Friedland, Wagram, Moskwa; but it is less easy to pitch upon the victories of Alcibiades, though they may be named too—though not so readily as the Leuctra and Mantinea of Epaminondas, the Marathon of Miltiades, the Salamis of Themistocles, and the Thermopylae of Leonidas.

Yet upon the whole it may be doubted, whether there be a name of Antiquity, which comes down with such a general charm as that of *Alcibiades*. *Why?* I cannot answer: who can?

109

The vanity of Victories is considerable. Of all who fell at Waterloo or Trafalgar, ask any man in company to *name you ten off hand*: they will stick at Nelson; the other will survive himself. *Nelson was* a hero: the other is a mere Corporal, dividing with Prussians and Spaniards the luck, which he never deserved. He even—but I hate the fool, and will be silent.

110

The Miscreant Wellington is the Cub of Fortune, but she will never lick him into shape: if he lives, he will be beaten— that's certain. Victory was never before wasted upon such an unprofitable soil, as this dunghill of Tyranny, whence nothing springs but Viper's eggs.

111

I remember seeing Blucher in the London Assemblies, and never saw anything of his age less venerable. With the voice and manners of a recruiting Sergeant, he pretended to the honours of a hero; just as if a stone could be worshipped, because a Man had stumbled over it.

112

There is nothing left for Mankind but a Republic, and I think that there are hopes of such. The two Americas (South and North) have it; Spain and Portugal approach it; all thirst for it. Oh Washington!

113

Pisa, Novr. 5th 1821

'There is a strange coincidence sometimes in the little things of this world, Sancho,' says Sterne in a letter (if I mistake not); and so I have often found it.

Page 128 [833], article 91, of this collection of scattered things, I had alluded to my friend Lord Clare in terms such as my feelings suggested. About a week or two afterwards, I met him on the road between Imola and Bologna, after not having met for seven or eight years. He was abroad in 1814, and came home just as I set out in 1816.

This meeting annihilated for a moment all the years between the present time and the days of *Harrow*. It was a new and inexplicable feeling, like rising from the grave, to me. Clare, too, was much agitated—*more* in appearance than even myself; for I could feel his heart beat to his fingers' ends, unless, indeed, it was the pulse of my own which made me think so. He told me that I should find a note from him, left at Bologna. I did. We were obliged to part for our different journeys—he for Rome, I for Pisa; but with the promise to meet again in Spring. We were but five minutes together, and in the public road; but I hardly recollect an hour of my existence which could be weighed against them. He had heard that I was coming on, and had left his letter for me at B., because the people with whom he was travelling could not wait longer.

Of all I have ever known, he has always been the least altered in every thing from the excellent qualities and kind affections which attached me to him so strongly at School. I should hardly have thought it possible for Society (or the World as it is called), to leave a being with so little of the leaven of bad passions. I do not speak from personal experience only, but from all I have ever heard of him from others during absence and distance.

114

I met with Rogers at Bologna: staid a day there, crossed the Appennines with him. He remained at Florence; I went on to Pisa—8bre. 29, 30th etc., 1821.

115

I re-visited the Florence Gallery, etc. My former impressions were confirmed; but there were too many visitors there, to allow me to *feel* any thing properly. When we were (about thirty or forty) all stuffed into the Cabinet of Gems, and knick-knackeries, in a corner of one of the Galleries, I told R. that it 'felt like being in the Watch-house.' I left him to make his obeisances to some of his acquaintances, and strolled on alone—the only few minutes I could snatch of any feeling for the works around me. I do not mean to apply this to a *tête à tête* scrutiny with Rogers, who has an excellent taste and deep feeling for the Arts (indeed much more of both than I can possess; for of the *former* I have not much); but to the crowd of jostling starers and travelling talkers around me.

I heard one bold Briton declare to the woman on his arm, looking at the Venus of Titian, 'Well, now, this is really very fine indeed,'—an observation, which, like that of the landlord in Joseph Andrews 'on the certainty of death,' was (as the landlord's wife observed), 'extremely true.'

In the Pitti palace, I did not omit Goldsmith's prescription for a Connoisseur, viz: 'that the pictures would have been better, if the painter had taken more pains, and to praise the works of Pietro Perugino.'

116

I have lately been reading Fielding over again. They talk of Radicalism, Jacobinism, etc., in England (I am told), but they should turn over the pages of 'Jonathan Wild the Great.' The inequality of conditions, and the littleness of the great, were never set forth in stronger terms; and his contempt for Conquerors and the like is such, that, had he lived *now*, he would have been denounced in 'the Courier' as the grand Mouthpiece and Factionary of the revolutionists. And yet I never recollect to have heard this turn of Fielding's mind noticed, though it is obvious in every page.

117

The following dialogue passed between me and a very pretty peasant Girl (Rosa Benini, married to Domenico Ovioli, or Oviuoli, the Vetturino) at Ravenna.

Rosa.   '*What* is the Pope?'

I.   'Don't *you* know?'

Rosa.   'No, I don't know. What or who is he? Is he a *Saint*?'

I.   'He is an old man.'

Rosa.   'What nonsense to make such a fuss about an old man. Have you ever seen him?'

I.   'Yes, at Rome.'

Rosa.   'You English don't obey the Pope?'

I.   'No, we don't; but you do.'

Rosa.   'I don't know what I believe, but the priests talk
about him. I am sure I did not know what he was.'

This dialogue I have translated nearly verbatim, and I don't
think that I have either added to or taken away from it. The
speaker was under eighteen, and an old acquaintance of mine.
It struck me as odd that I should have to instruct her *who* the
Pope was: I think they might have found it out without me by
this time. The fact is indisputable, and occurred but a few
weeks ago, before I left Ravenna.

Pisa, Novr. 6th 1821

118

1

Oh! talk not to me of a name great in story
The days of our Youth are the days of our Glory
And the myrtle and ivy of sweet two and twenty
Are worth all your laurels though ever so plenty.

2

What are garlands and crowns to the brow that is
  wrinkled?
'Tis but as a dead flower with May-dew besprinkled:
Then away with all such from the head that is hoary,
What care I for the wreaths that can only *give Glory?*

3

Oh! Fame! if I e'er took delight in thy praises,
'Twas less for the sake of thy high-sounding phrases,
Than to see the bright eyes of the dear One discover
She thought that I was not unworthy to love her.

4

There chiefly *I sought thee, there* only *I found thee;*
Her Glance was the best of the rays that surround thee,
When it sparkled o'er aught that was bright in my story,
I knew it was love, and I felt it was Glory.

I composed these stanzas (except the fourth added now) a
few days ago, on the road from Florence to Pisa.

Pisa, Novr. 6th 1821

119

My daughter Ada, on her recent birthday the other day (the 10th of December 1821), completed her sixth year. Since she was a Month old, or rather better, I have not seen her. But I hear that she is a fine child, with a violent temper.

I have been thinking of an odd circumstance. My daughter, my wife, my half sister, my mother, my sister's mother [1], my natural daughter [2,3,4], and myself, are or were all *only* [5] children. My sister's Mother [6] (Lady Conyers) had only my half *sister* by that second marriage (herself too an only child), and my father had only me (an only child) by his second marriage with my Mother (an only child too). Such a complication of *only* children, all tending to *one family*, is singular enough, and looks like fatality almost. But the fiercest Animals have the rarest numbers in their litters, as Lions, tigers, and even Elephants which are mild in comparison.

120

May 18th 1822

I have not taken up this sort of Journal for many months: shall I continue it? 'Chi cosa?'

I have written little this year, but a good deal last (1821). *Five* plays in all (two yet unpublished), some Cantos, etc. I have begun one or two things since, but under some discouragement, or rather indignation at the brutality of the attacks, which I hear (for I have seen but few of them) have been multiplied in every direction against me and my recent writings. But the English dishonour themselves more than me by such conduct. It is strange, but the Germans say that I am more popular in Germany by far than in England, and I have heard the Americans say as much of America. The French, too, have printed a considerable number of translations—in prose! with good success; but *their* predilection (if it exists) depends, I suspect, upon their belief that I have no great passion for England or the English. It would be singular if I had; however, I wish them no harm.

TO JOHN MURRAY

Ravenna, August 23, 1821

Enclosed are the two acts corrected. With regard to the charges about the Shipwreck,—I think that I told both you and Mr. Hobhouse, years ago, that [there] was not a *single circumstance* of it *not* taken from *fact*; not, indeed, from any *single* shipwreck, but all from *actual* facts of different wrecks. Almost all *Don Juan* is *real* life, either my own, or from people I knew. By the way, much of the description of the *furniture*, in Canto third, is taken from *Tully's Tripoli* (pray *note this*), and the rest from my own observation. Remember I never meant to conceal this at all, and have only not stated it, because *Don Juan* had no preface nor name to it. If you think it worth while to make this statement, do so, in your own way. *I* laugh at such charges, convinced that no writer ever borrowed less, or made his materials more his own. Much is coincidence: for instance, Lady Morgan (in a really *excellent* book, I assure you, on Italy) calls Venice an *ocean Rome*; I have the very same expression in *Foscari*, and yet *you* know that the play was written months ago, and sent to England. The 'Italy' I received only on the 16th instant.

Your friend, like the public, is not aware, that my dramatic simplicity is *studiously* Greek, and must continue so: *no* reform ever succeeded at first. I admire the old English dramatists; but this is quite another field, and has nothing to do with theirs. I want to make a *regular* English drama, no matter whether for the Stage or not, which is not my object,—but a *mental theatre*.

Yours ever.

Is the bust arrived?

P.S.—*Can't* accept your courteous offer.

> *For Orford and for Waldegrave*
> *You give much more than me you gave;*
> *Which is not fairly to behave,*
> *My Murray!*

Because if a live dog, 'tis said,
Be worth a Lion fairly sped,
A live lord *must be worth* two *dead,*
　　　　　My Murray!

And if, as the opinion goes,
Verse hath a better sale than prose—
Certes, I should have more than those,
　　　　　My Murray!

But now this sheet is nearly cramm'd,
So, if you *will, I* sha'n't *be shamm'd,*
And if you *won't,—you* may be damn'd,
　　　　　My Murray!

These matters must be arranged with Mr. Douglas K[innaird]. He is my trustee, and a man of honour. To him you can state all your mercantile reasons, which you might not like to state to me personally, such as 'heavy season'—'flat public'—'don't go off'—'Lordship writes too much'—'won't take advice'—'declining popularity'—'deductions for the trade'—'make very little'—'generally lose by him'—'pirated edition'—'foreign edition'—'severe criticisms,' etc. with other hints and howls for an oration, which I leave Douglas, who is an orator, to answer.

You can also state them more freely to a third person, as between you and me they could only produce some smart postscripts, which would not adorn our mutual archives.

I am sorry for the Queen, and that's more than you are.

　　　　　Yours ever, etc.

　　　　　　　　　BYRON

TO THOMAS MOORE

　　　　　Ravenna, September 19, 1821

I am in all the sweat, dust, and blasphemy of an universal packing of all my things, furniture, etc. for Pisa, whither I go for the winter. The cause has been the exile of all my fellow

Carbonics, and, amongst them, of the whole family of Madame G.; who, you know, was divorced from her husband last week, 'on account of P.P. clerk of this parish,' and who is obliged to join her father and relatives, now in exile there, to avoid being shut up in a monastery, because the Pope's decree of separation required her to reside in *casa paterna*, or else, for decorum's sake, in a convent. As I could not say with Hamlet, 'Get thee to a nunnery,' I am preparing to follow them.

It is awful work, this love, and prevents all a man's projects of good or glory. I wanted to go to Greece lately (as every thing seems up here) with her brother, who is a very fine, brave fellow (I have seen him put to the proof), and wild about liberty. But the tears of a woman who has left her husband for a man, and the weakness of one's own heart, are paramount to these projects, and I can hardly indulge them.

We were divided in choice between Switzerland and Tuscany, and I gave my vote for Pisa, as nearer the Mediterranean, which I love for the sake of the shores which it washes, and for my young recollections of 1809. Switzerland is a curst selfish, swinish country of brutes, placed in the most romantic region of the world. I never could bear the inhabitants, and still less their English visitors; for which reason, after writing for some information about houses, upon hearing that there was a colony of English all over the cantons of Geneva, etc., I immediately gave up the thought, and persuaded the Gambas to do the same. . . .

TO JOHN MURRAY

Ravenna, September 20, 1821

You need not send 'The Blues,' which is a mere buffoonery, never meant for publication.

The papers to which I allude, in case of Survivorship, are collections of letters, etc., since I was sixteen years old, contained in the trunks in the care of Mr. Hobhouse. This collection is at least doubled by those I have now here; all received since my last Ostracism. To these I should wish the Editor to have access, *not* for the purpose of *abusing confidences*, or of *hurting* the feelings of correspondents living, or the memories of the dead; but there are things which would do neither, that I have left unnoticed or unexplained, and which (like all such things) Time only can permit to be noticed or explained, though some are to my credit. The task will, of course, require delicacy; but that will not be wanting, if Moore and Hobhouse survive me, and, I may add, yourself; and that you may all three do so, is, I assure you, my very sincere wish. I am not sure that long life is desirable for one of my temper and constitutional depression of Spirits, which of course I suppress in society; but which breaks out when alone, and in my writings, in spite of myself. It has been deepened, perhaps, by some long-past events (I do not allude to my marriage, etc.—on the contrary, *that* raised them by the persecution giving a fillip to my Spirits); but I call it constitutional, as I have reason to think it. You know, or you do *not* know, that my maternal Grandfather (a very clever man, and amiable, I am told) was strongly suspected of Suicide (he was found drowned in the Avon at Bath), and that another very near relative of the same branch took poison, and was merely saved by antidotes. For the first of these events there was no apparent cause, as he was rich, respected, and of considerable intellectual resources, hardly forty years of age, and not at all addicted to any unhinging vice. It was, however, but a strong suspicion, owing to the manner of his death and to his melancholy temper. The *second had* a cause, but it does not become me to touch upon it; it happened when I was far too young to be aware of it, and I never heard of it till after the death of that relative, many years afterwards. I think, then, that I may call this dejection *constitutional*. I had always been told that in *temper* I more resembled my maternal Grandfather than any of my *father's* family—that is, in the gloomier part of his temper, for he was what you call a good natured man, and I am not.

The Journal here I sent by Mawman to Moore the other day; but as it is a mere diary, only *parts* of it would ever do for publication. The other Journal, of the tour in 1816, I should think Augusta might let you have a copy of. . . .

I am much mortified that Gifford don't take to my new dramas: to be sure, they are as opposite to the English drama as one thing can be to another; but I have a notion that, if understood, they will in time find favour (though *not* on the stage) with the reader. The Simplicity of plot is intentional, and the avoidance of *rant* also, as also the compression of the speeches in the more severe situations. What I seek to show in *The Foscaris* is the *suppressed* passion, rather than the rant of the present day. For that matter—

> *Nay, if thou'lt mouth,*
> *I'll rant as well as thou—*

would not be difficult, as I think I have shown in my younger productions—*not dramatic* ones, to be sure. But, as I said before, I am mortified that Gifford don't like them; but I see no remedy, our notions on the subject being so different. How is he? well, I hope: let me know. I regret his demur the more that he has been always my grand patron, and I know no praise which would compensate me in my own mind for his censure. I do not mind *reviews*, as I can work them at their own weapons.

Yours, etc.

. . . Address to me at *Pisa*, whither I am going. The reason is, that all my Italian friends here have been exiled, and are met there for the present; and I go to join them, as agreed upon, for the Winter.

TO THOMAS MOORE

October 6, 1821

By this post I have sent my nightmare to balance the incubus of Southey's impudent anticipation of the Apotheosis of George the Third. I should like you to take a look over it, as I think there are two or three things in it which might please 'our puir hill folk.'

By the last two or three posts I have written to you at length. My *ague* bows to me every two or three days, but we

are not as yet upon intimate speaking terms. I have an intermittent generally every two years, when the climate is favourable (as it is here), but it does me no harm. What I find worse,
and cannot get rid of, is the growing depression of my spirits,
without sufficient cause. I ride—I am not intemperate in
eating or drinking—and my general health is as usual, except
a slight ague, which rather does good than not. It must be constitutional; for I know nothing more than usual to depress me
to that degree.

How do *you* manage? I think you told me, at Venice, that
your spirits did not keep up without a little claret. I *can* drink,
and bear a good deal of wine (as you may recollect in England); but it don't exhilarate—it makes me savage and suspicious, and even quarrelsome. Laudanum has a similar effect;
but I can take much of *it* without any effect at all. The thing
that gives me the highest spirits (it seems absurd, but true) is
a dose of *salts*—I mean in the afternoon, after their effect.
But one can't take *them* like champagne.

Excuse this old woman's letter; but my *lemancholy* don't
depend upon health, for it is just the same, well or ill, or here
or there.

Yours, etc.

TO LADY BYRON

(TO THE CARE OF THE HON. MRS. LEIGH, LONDON.)

Pisa, November 17, 1821

I have to acknowledge the receipt of 'Ada's hair,' which is
very soft and pretty, and nearly as dark already as mine was at
twelve years old, if I may judge from what I recollect of some
in Augusta's possession, taken at that age. But it don't curl,—
perhaps from its being let grow.

I also thank you for the inscription of the date and name,
and I will tell you why;—I believe that they are the only two
or three words of your hand-writing in my possession. For
your letters I returned; and except the two words, or rather
the one word, 'Household,' written twice in an old account
book, I have no other. I burnt your last note, for two reasons:

2 E

—firstly, it was written in a style not very agreeable; and, secondly, I wished to take your word without documents, which are the worldly resources of suspicious people.

I suppose that this note will reach you somewhere about Ada's birthday—the 10th of December, I believe. She will then be six, so that in about twelve more I shall have some chance of meeting her;—perhaps sooner, if I am obliged to go to England by business or otherwise. Recollect, however, one thing, either in distance or nearness;—every day which keeps us asunder should, after so long a period, rather soften our mutual feelings, which must always have one rallying-point as long as our child exists, which I presume we both hope will be long after either of her parents.

The time which has elapsed since the separation has been considerably more than the whole brief period of our union, and the not much longer one of our prior acquaintance. We both made a bitter mistake; but now it is over, and irrevocably so. For, at thirty-three on my part, and a few years less on yours, though it is no very extended period of life, still it is one when the habits and thought are generally so formed as to admit of no modification; and as we could not agree when younger, we should with difficulty do so now.

I say all this, because I own to you, that, notwithstanding every thing, I considered our re-union as not impossible for more than a year after the separation;—but then I gave up the hope entirely and for ever. But this very impossibility of re-union seems to me at least a reason why, on all the few points of discussion which can arise between us, we should preserve the courtesies of life, and as much of its kindness as people who are never to meet may preserve perhaps more easily than nearer connections. For my own part, I am violent, but not malignant; for only fresh provocations can awaken my resentments. To you, who are colder and more concentrated, I would just hint, that you may sometimes mistake the depth of a cold anger for dignity, and a worse feeling for duty. I assure you that I bear you *now* (whatever I may have done) no resentment whatever. Remember, that *if you have injured me* in aught, this forgiveness is something; and that, if I have *injured you*, it is something more still, if it be true, as the moralists say, that the most offending are the least forgiving.

Whether the offence has been solely on my side, or reciprocal, or on yours chiefly, I have ceased to reflect upon any but two things,—viz. that you are the mother of my child, and that we shall never meet again. I think if you also consider the two corresponding points with reference to myself, it will be better for all three.

> Yours ever,
> NOEL BYRON

TO JOHN MURRAY

Pisa, December 10, 1821

This day and this hour, (one, on the clock,) my daughter is six years old. I wonder when I shall see her again, or if ever I shall see her at all.

I have remarked a curious coincidence, which almost looks like a fatality.

My *mother*, my *wife*, my *daughter*, my *half-sister*, my *sister's mother*, my *natural daughter* (as far at least as *I* am concerned), and *myself*, are all *only children*.

My father, by his first marriage with Lady Conyers (an only child), had only my sister; and by his second marriage with another only child, an only child again. Lady Byron, as you know, was one also, and so is my daughter, etc.

Is not this rather odd—such a complication of only children? By the way, send me my daughter Ada's miniature. I have only the print, which gives little or no idea of her complexion. . . .

> Yours, etc.
> N.B.

TO SIR WALTER SCOTT

Pisa, May 4, 1822

My dear Sir Walter,

Your account of your family is very pleasing: would that I 'could answer this comfort with the like!' but I have just lost my natural daughter, Allegra, by a fever. The only consolation,

save time, is the reflection that she is either at rest or happy;
for her few years (only five) prevented her from having
incurred any sin, except what we inherit from Adam.

Whom the gods love die young.

I need not say that your letters are particularly welcome,
when they do not tax your time and patience; and now that
our correspondence is resumed, I trust it will continue.

I have lately had some anxiety, rather than trouble, about
an awkward affair here, which you may perhaps have heard
of; but our minister has behaved very handsomely, and the
Tuscan Government as well as it is possible for such a government to behave, which is not saying much for the latter.
Some other English and Scots, and myself, had a brawl with
a dragoon, who insulted one of the party, and whom we mistook for an officer, as he was medalled and well mounted, etc.;
but he turned out to be a serjeant-major. He called out the
guard at the gates to arrest us (we being unarmed); upon
which I and another (an Italian) rode through the said guard;
but they succeeded in detaining others of the party. I rode to
my house, and sent my secretary to give an account of the
attempted and illegal arrest to the authorities, and then, without dismounting, rode back towards the gates, which are near
my present mansion. Half-way I met my man vapouring away
and threatening to draw upon me (who had a cane in my
hand, and no other arms). I, still believing him an officer,
demanded his name and address, and gave him my hand and
glove thereupon. A servant of mine thrust in between us
(totally without orders), but let him go on my command. He
then rode off at full speed; but about forty paces further was
stabbed, and very dangerously (so as to be in peril), by some
Callum Beg or other of my people (for I have some rough-
handed folks about me), I need hardly say without my direction or approval. The said dragoon had been sabring our unarmed countrymen, however, at the *gate, after they were in
arrest,* and held by the guards, and wounded one, Captain
Hay, very severely. However, he got his paiks—having acted
like an assassin, and being treated like one. *Who* wounded

him, though it was done before thousands of people, they have never been able to ascertain, or prove, nor even the *weapon*; some said a *pistol*, an *air-gun*, a stiletto, a sword, a lance, a pitchfork, and what not. They have arrested and examined servants and people of all descriptions, but can make out nothing. Mr. Dawkins, our minister, assures me that no suspicion is entertained of the man who wounded him having been instigated by me, or any of the party. I enclose you copies of the depositions of those with us, and Dr. Crauford, a canny Scot (*not* an acquaintance), who saw the latter part of the affair. They are in Italian.

These are the only literary matters in which I have been engaged since the publication and row about *Cain*;—but Mr. Murray has several things of mine in his obstetrical hands. Another *Mystery*—a *Vision*—a Drama—and the like. But *you won't* tell me what *you* are doing—however, I shall find you out, write what you will. You say that I should like your son-in-law—it would be very difficult for me to dislike any one connected with you; but I have no doubt that his own qualities are all that you describe.

I am sorry you don't like Lord Orford's new work. My aristocracy, which is very fierce, makes him a favourite of mine. Recollect that those 'little factions' comprised Lord Chatham and Fox, the father; and that *we* live in gigantic and exaggerated times, which make all under Gog and Magog appear pigmean. After having seen Napoleon begin like Tamerlane and end like Bajazet in our own time, we have not the same interest in what would otherwise have appeared important history. But I must conclude.

Believe me ever and most truly yours,

NOEL BYRON

TO THOMAS MOORE

Montenero, Villa Dupuy, near Leghorn,
June 8, 1822

I have written to you twice through the medium of Murray, and on one subject, *trite* enough,—the loss of poor little

Allegra by a fever; on which topic I shall say no more—there is nothing but time.

A few days ago, my earliest and dearest friend, Lord Clare, came over from Geneva on purpose to see me before he returned to England. As I have always loved him (since I was thirteen, at Harrow) better than any (*male*) thing in the world, I need hardly say what a melancholy pleasure it was to see him for a *day* only; for he was obliged to resume his journey immediately. . . . Do you recollect, in the year of revelry 1814, the pleasantest parties and balls all over London? and not the least so at——'s. Do you recollect your singing duets with Lady ——, and my flirtation with Lady ——, and all the other fooleries of the time? while —— was sighing, and Lady —— ogling him with her clear hazel eyes. *But* eight years have passed, and, since that time, —— has . . . . . . ; —— has run away with ——; and *mysen* (as my Nottinghamshire friends call themselves) might as well have thrown myself out of the window while you were singing, as intermarried where I did. You and —— have come off the best of us. I speak merely of my marriage, and its consequences, distresses, and calumnies; for I have been much more happy, on the whole, *since*, than I ever could have been with ——.

I have read the recent article of Jeffrey in a faithful transcription of the impartial Galignani. I suppose the long and short of it is, that he wishes to provoke me to reply. But I won't, for I owe him a good turn still for his kindness by-gone. Indeed, I presume that the present opportunity of attacking me again was irresistible; and I can't blame him, knowing what human nature is. I shall make but one remark:—what does he mean by elaborate? The whole volume was written with the greatest rapidity, in the midst of evolutions, and revolutions, and persecutions, and proscriptions of all who interested me in Italy. They said the same of *Lara*, which, *you* know, was written amidst balls and fooleries, and after coming home from masquerades and routs, in the summer of the sovereigns. Of all I have ever written, they are perhaps the most carelessly composed; and their faults, whatever they may be, are those of negligence, and not of labour. I do not think this a merit, but it is a fact.

Yours ever and truly,

N. B.

P.S.—You see the great advantage of my new signature;— it may either stand for 'Nota Bene' or 'Noel Byron,' and, as such, will save much repetition, in writing either books or letters. Since I came here, I have been invited on board of the American squadron, and treated with all possible honour and ceremony. They have asked me to sit for my picture; and, as I was going away, an American lady took a rose from me (which had been given to me by a very pretty Italian lady that very morning), because, she said, 'She was determined to send or take something which I had about me to America.' *There* is a kind of Lalla Rookh incident for you! However, all these American honours arise, perhaps, not so much from their enthusiasm for my 'Poeshie,' as their belief in my dislike to the English,—in which I have the satisfaction to coincide with them. I would rather, however, have a nod from an American, than a snuff-box from an emperor.

TO THOMAS MOORE

Pisa, August 27, 1822

It is boring to trouble you with 'such small gear;' but it must be owned that I should be glad if you would enquire whether my Irish subscription ever reached the committee in Paris from Leghorn. My reasons, like Vellum's, 'are three-fold:'—First, I doubt the accuracy of all almoners, or remitters of benevolent cash; second, I do suspect that the said Committee, having in part served its time to time-serving, may have kept back the acknowledgement of an obnoxious politician's name in their lists; and third, I feel pretty sure that I shall one day be twitted by the government scribes for having been a professor of love for Ireland, and not coming forward with the others in her distresses.

It is not, as you may opine, that I am ambitious of having my name in the papers, as I can have that any day in the week gratis. All I want is to know if the Reverend Thomas Hall did or did not remit my subscription (200 scudi of Tuscany, or about a thousand francs, more or less,) to the Committee at Paris.

The other day at Viareggio, I thought proper to swim off to my schooner (the Bolivar) in the offing, and thence to shore again—about three miles, or better, in all. As it was at mid-day, under a broiling sun, the consequence has been a feverish attack, and my whole skin's coming off, after going through the process of one large continuous blister, raised by the sun and sea together. I have suffered much pain; not being able to lie on my back, or even side; for my shoulders and arms were equally St. Bartholomewed. But it is over,—and I have got a new skin, and am as glossy as a snake in its new suit.

We have been burning the bodies of Shelley and Williams on the sea-shore, to render them fit for removal and regular interment. You can have no idea what an extraordinary effect such a funeral pile has, on a desolate shore, with mountains in the back-ground and the sea before, and the singular appearance the salt and frankincense gave to the flame. All of Shelley was consumed, except his *heart*, which would not take the flame, and is now preserved in spirits of wine.

Your old acquaintance Londonderry has quietly died at North Cray! and the virtuous De Witt was torn in pieces by the populace! What a lucky —— the Irishman has been in his life and end. In him your Irish Franklin *est mort*!

Leigh Hunt is sweating articles for his new Journal; and both he and I think it somewhat shabby in *you* not to contribute. Will you become one of the *properrioters*? 'Do, and we go snacks.' I recommend you to think twice before you respond in the negative.

I have nearly (*quite three*) four new cantos of *Don Juan* ready. I obtained permission from the female Censor Morum of *my* morals to continue it, provided it were immaculate; so I have been as decent as need be. There is a deal of war—a siege, and all that, in the style, graphical and technical, of the ship-wreck in Canto Second, which 'took,' as they say in the Row.

Yours, etc.

P.S.—That —— Galignani has about ten lies in one paragraph. It was not a Bible that was found in Shelley's pocket, but John Keats's poems. However, it would not have been strange, for he was a great admirer of Scripture as a composition. *I* did not send my bust to the academy of New York; but I sat for my picture to young West, an American artist, at the request of some members of that Academy to *him* that he would take my portrait,—for the Academy, I believe.

I had, and still have, thoughts of South America, but am fluctuating between it and Greece. I should have gone, long ago, to one of them, but for my liaison with the Countess G[1].; for love, in these days, is little compatible with glory. *She* would be delighted to go too; but I do not choose to expose her to a long voyage, and a residence in an unsettled country, where I shall probably take a part of some sort.

TO LADY —— [HARDY]

Albaro, November 10, 1822

The Chevalier persisted in declaring himself an ill-used gentleman, and describing you as a kind of cold Calypso, who lead astray people of an amatory disposition without giving them any sort of compensation, contenting yourself, it seems, with only making *one* fool instead of two, which is the more approved method of proceeding on such occasions. For my part, I think you are quite right; and be assured from me that a woman (as society is constituted in England) who gives any advantage to a man may expect a lover, but will sooner or later find a tyrant; and this is not the man's fault either, perhaps, but is the necessary and natural result of the circumstances of society, which, in fact, tyrannise over the man equally with the woman; that is to say, if either of them have any feeling or honour.

You can write to me at your leisure and inclination. I have always laid it down as a maxim, and found it justified by experience, that a man and a woman make far better friendships than can exist between two of the same sex; but *these* with this condition, that they never have made, or are to make, love with each other. Lovers may, and, indeed, generally *are* enemies, but they never can be friends; because there must always be a spice of jealousy and a something of self in all their speculations.

Indeed, I rather look upon love altogether as a sort of hostile transaction, very necessary to make or to break matches, and keep the world going, but by no means a sinecure to the parties concerned.

Now, as my love perils are, I believe, pretty well over, and yours, by all accounts, are never to begin, we shall be the best friends imaginable, as far as both are concerned; and with this advantage, that we may both fall to loving right and left through all our acquaintance, without either sullenness or sorrow from that amiable passion, which are its inseparable attendants.

Believe me, etc.
N. B.

TO THOMAS MOORE

Genoa, February 20, 1823

My dear Tom,

I must again refer you to those two letters addressed to you at Passy before I read your speech in Galignani, etc., and which you do not seem to have received.

Of Hunt I see little—once a month or so, and then on his own business, generally. You may easily suppose that I know too little of Hampstead and his satellites to have much communion or community with him. My whole present relation to him arose from Shelley's unexpected wreck. You would not have had me leave him in the street with his family, would you? and as to the other plan you mention, you forget how it would *humiliate* him—that his writings should be supposed to be dead weight! Think a moment—he is perhaps the vainest man on earth, at least his own friends say so pretty loudly; and if he were in other circumstances, I might be tempted to take him down a peg; but not now,—it would be cruel. It is a cursed business; but neither the motive nor the means rest upon my conscience, and it happens that he and his brother *have* been so far benefited by the publication in a pecuniary point of view. His brother is a steady, bold fellow, such as *Prynne*, for example, and full of moral, and, I hear, physical courage.

And *you* are *really* recanting, or softening to the clergy! It will do little good for you—it is *you*, not the poem, they are at. They will say they frightened you—forbid it, Ireland! Believe me

Yours ever,

N. B.

TO THE EARL OF BLESSINGTON

April 5, 1823

My dear Lord,

How is your gout? or rather, how are you? I return the Count D'Orsay's Journal, which is a very extraordinary production, and of a most melancholy truth in all that regards high life in England. I know, or knew personally, most of the personages and societies which he describes; and after reading his remarks, have the sensation fresh upon me as if I had seen them yesterday. I would however plead in behalf of some few exceptions, which I will mention by and by. The most singular thing is, *how* he should have penetrated *not* the *fact*, but the *mystery* of the English *ennui*, at two-and-twenty. I was about the same age when I made the same discovery, in almost precisely the same circles,—(for there is scarcely a person mentioned whom I did not see nightly or daily, and was acquainted more or less intimately with most of them,)—but I never could have described it so well. *Il faut être Français*, to effect this.

But he ought also to have been in the country during the hunting season, with 'a select party of distinguished guests,' as the papers term it. He ought to have seen the gentlemen after dinner (on the hunting days), and the soirée ensuing thereupon, —and the women looking as if they had hunted, or rather been hunted; and I could have wished that he had been at a dinner in town, which I recollect at Lord Cowper's—small, but select, and composed of the most amusing people. The dessert was hardly on the table, when, out of twelve, I counted *five asleep*; of that five, there were *Tierney*, Lord Lansdowne, and Lord Darnley—I forget the other two, but they were either wits or orators—perhaps poets.

My residence in the East and in Italy has made me some-what indulgent of the siesta;—but then they set regularly about it in warm countries, and perform it in solitude (or at most in a tête-à-tête with a proper companion), and retire quietly to their rooms to get out of the sun's way for an hour or two.

Altogether, your friend's Journal is a very formidable pro-duction. Alas! our dearly beloved countrymen have only dis-covered that they are tired, and not that they are tiresome; and I suspect that the communication of the latter unpleasant verity will not be better received than truths usually are. I have read the whole with great attention and instruction. I am too good a patriot to say *pleasure*—at least I won't say so, what-ever I may think. I showed it (I hope no breach of confidence) to a young Italian lady of rank, *très instruite* also; and who passes, or passed, for being one of the three most celebrated belles in the district of Italy, where her family and connections resided in less troublesome times as to politics, (which is not Genoa, by the way,) and she was delighted with it, and says that she has derived a better notion of English society from it than from all Madame de Stael's metaphysical disputations on the same subject, in her work on the Revolution. I beg that you will thank the young philosopher, and make my compli-ments to Lady B. and her sister.

Believe me your very obliged and faithful

N. B.

P.S.—There is a rumour in letters of some disturbance or complot in the French Pyrenean army—generals suspected or dismissed, and ministers of war travelling to see what's the matter. 'Marry (as David says), this hath an angry favour.'

Tell Count D' Orsay that some of the names are not quite intelligible, especially of the clubs; he speaks of *Watts*—perhaps he is right, but in my time *Watier's* was the Dandy Club, of which (though no dandy) I was a member, at the time too of its greatest glory, when Brummel and Mildmay, Alvanley and Pierrepoint, gave the Dandy Balls; and we (the club, that is,) got up the famous masquerade at Burlington House and Garden, for Wellington. He does not speak of the *Alfred*, which was the most *recherché* and most tiresome of any, as I know, by being a member of that too.

TO THE COUNTESS OF BLESSINGTON

Albaro, May 6, 1823

My dear Lady ——,

I send you the letter which I had forgotten, and the book, which I ought to have remembered. It contains (the book, I mean,) some melancholy truths; though I believe that it is too triste a work ever to have been popular. The first time I ever read it (not the edition I send you,—for I got it since,) was at the desire of Madame de Stael, who was supposed by the good-natured world to be the heroine;—which she was not, however, and was furious at the supposition. This occurred in Switzerland, in the summer of 1816, and the last season in which I ever saw that celebrated person.

I have a request to make to my friend Alfred (since he has not disdained the title), viz. that he would condescend to add a *cap* to the gentleman in the jacket,—it would complete his costume,—and smooth his brow, which is somewhat too inveterate a likeness of the original, God help me!

I did well to avoid the water-party,—*why*, is a mystery, which is not less to be wondered at than all my other mysteries. Tell Milor that I am deep in his MS., and will do him justice by a diligent perusal.

The letter which I enclose I was prevented from sending by my despair of its doing any good. I was perfectly sincere when I wrote it, and am so still. But it is difficult for me to withstand the thousand provocations on that subject, which both friends and foes have for seven years been throwing in the way of a man whose feelings were once quick, and whose temper was never patient. But 'returning were as tedious as go o'er.' I feel this as much as ever Macbeth did; and it is a dreary sensation, which at least avenges the real or imaginary wrongs of one of the two unfortunate persons whom it concerns.

But I am going to be gloomy;—so 'to bed, to bed.' Good night,—or rather morning. One of the reasons why I wish to avoid society is, that I can never sleep after it, and the pleasanter it has been the less I rest.

Ever most truly, etc. etc.

TO GOETHE

Leghorn, July 24, 1823

Illustrious Sir,

I cannot thank you as you ought to be thanked for the lines which my young friend, Mr. Sterling, sent me of yours; and it would but ill become me to pretend to exchange verses with him who, for fifty years, has been the undisputed sovereign of European literature. You must therefore accept my most sincere acknowledgments in prose—and in hasty prose too; for I am at present on my voyage to Greece once more, and surrounded by hurry and bustle, which hardly allow a moment even to gratitude and admiration to express themselves.

I sailed from Genoa some days ago, was driven back by a gale of wind, and have since sailed again and arrived here, 'Leghorn,' this morning, to receive on board some Greek passengers for their struggling country.

Here also I found your lines and Mr. Sterling's letter; and I could not have had a more favourable omen, a more agreeable surprise, than a word of Goethe, written by his own hand.

I am returning to Greece, to see if I can be of any little use there: if ever I come back, I will pay a visit to Weimar, to offer the sincere homage of one of the many millions of your admirers. I have the honour to be, ever and most respectfully, y[our],

Obliged adm[irer] and se[rvant],

NOEL BYRON

TO THE HON. DOUGLAS KINNAIRD

Cephalonia, December 23, 1823

I shall be as saving of my purse and person as you recommend; but you know that it is as well to be in readiness with one or both in the event of either being required.

I presume that some agreement has been concluded with Mr. Murray about *Werner*. Although the copyright should only be worth two or three hundred pounds, I will tell you what can be done with them. For three hundred pounds I can maintain in Greece, at more than the *fullest pay* of the Provisional Government, rations included, one hundred armed men for *three months*. You may judge of this when I tell you, that the four thousand pounds advanced by me to the Greeks is likely to set a fleet and an army in motion for some months.

A Greek vessel has arrived from the squadron to convey me to Missolonghi, where Mavrocordato now is, and has assumed the command, so that I expect to embark immediately. Still address, however, to Cephalonia, through Messrs. Webb and Barry of Genoa, as usual; and get together all the means and credit of mine you can, to face the war establishment, for it is 'in for a penny, in for a pound,' and I must do all that I can for the ancients.

I have been labouring to reconcile these parties, and there is *now* some hope of succeeding. Their public affairs go on well. The Turks have retreated from Acarnania without a battle, after a few fruitless attempts on Anatoliko. Corinth is taken, and the Greeks have gained a battle in the Archipelago. The squadron here, too, has taken a Turkish corvette with some money and a cargo. In short, if they can obtain a Loan, I am of opinion that matters will assume and preserve a steady and favourable aspect for their independence.

In the mean time I stand paymaster, and what not; and lucky it is that, from the nature of the warfare and of the country, the resources even of an individual can be of a partial and temporary service.

Colonel Stanhope is at Missolonghi. Probably we shall attempt Patras next. The Suliotes, who are friends of mine, seem anxious to have me with them, and so is Mavrocordato. If I can but succeed in reconciling the two parties (and I have left no stone unturned), it will be something; and if not, we must go over to the Morea with the Western Greeks—who are the bravest, and at present the strongest, having beaten back the Turks—and try the effect of a little *physical* advice, should they persist in rejecting *moral* persuasion.

Once more recommending to you the reinforcement of my strong box and credit from all lawful sources and resources of mine to their practicable extent—for, after all, it is better playing at nations than gaming at Almack's or Newmarket—and requesting you to write to me as often as you can,

I remain ever yours,

N. BYRON

TO THOMAS MOORE

Cephalonia, December 27, 1823

I received a letter from you some time ago. I have been too much employed latterly to write as I could wish, and even now must write in haste.

I embark for Missolonghi to join Mavrocordato in four-and-twenty hours. The state of parties (but it were a long story) has kept me here till *now*; but now that Mavrocordato (their Washington, or their Kosciusko) is employed again, I can act with a *safe conscience*. I carry money to pay the squadron, etc., and I have influence with the Suliotes, *supposed* sufficient to keep them in harmony with some of the dissentients;—for there are plenty of differences, but trifling.

It is imagined that we shall attempt either Patras or the castles on the Straits; and it seems, by most accounts, that the Greeks, at any rate the Suliotes, who are in affinity with me of 'bread and salt,'—expect that I should march with them, and —be it even so! If any thing in the way of fever, fatigue, famine, or otherwise, should cut short the middle age of a brother warbler,—like Garcilasso de la Vega, Kleist, Korner,

Joukoffsky (a Russian nightingale—see Bowring's *Anthology*), or Thersander, or,—or somebody else—but never mind—I pray you to remember me in your 'smiles and wine.'

I have hopes that the cause will triumph; but whether it does or no, still 'honour must be minded as strictly as milk diet.' I trust to observe both.

Ever, etc.

TO CHARLES HANCOCK

Missolonghi, January 13, 1824

Dear Sir,

Many thanks for yours of the fifth; ditto to Muir for his. You will have heard that Gamba and my vessel got out of the hands of the Turks safe and intact; nobody knows well how or why, for there is a mystery in the story somewhat melo-dramatic. Captain Valsamachi has, I take it, spun a long yarn by this time in Argostoli. I attribute their release entirely to Saint Dionysius, of Zante, and the Madonna of the Rock, near Cephalonia.

The adventures of my separate bark were also not finished at Dragomestri: we were conveyed out by some Greek gun-boats, and found the *Leonidas*, brig-of-war at sea to look after us. But blowing weather coming on, we were driven on the rocks *twice* in the passage of the Scrofes, and the dollars had another narrow escape. Two thirds of the crew got ashore over the bowsprit: the rocks were rugged enough, but water very deep close in-shore, so that she was, after much swearing and some exertion, got off again, and away we went with a third of our crew, leaving the rest on a desolate island, where they might have been now, had not one of the gun-boats taken them off, for we were in no condition to take them off again.

Tell Muir that Dr. Bruno did not show much fight on the occasion; for besides stripping to his flannel waistcoat, and running about like a rat in an emergency, when I was talking to a Greek boy (the brother of the Greek girls in Argostoli), and telling him the fact that there was no danger for the passengers, whatever there might be for the vessel, and assur-ing him I could save both him and myself without difficulty (though he can't swim), as the water, though deep, was not very rough,—the wind *not* blowing *right* on shore (it was a blunder of the Greeks who missed stays),—the Doctor exclaimed, 'Save *him*, indeed! by G—d! save *me* rather—I'll be first if I can'—a piece of egotism which he pronounced with such emphatic simplicity as to set all who had leisure to hear him laughing, and in a minute after the vessel drove off again after striking twice. She sprang a small leak, but nothing further happened, except that the captain was very nervous afterwards.

To be brief, we had bad weather almost always, though not contrary; slept on deck in the wet generally for seven or eight nights, but never was in better health (I speak personally)—so much so that I actually bathed for a quarter of an hour on the evening of the 4th instant in the sea (to kill the fleas, and other, etc.), and was all the better for it.

We were received at Missolonghi with all kinds of kindness and honours; and the sight of the fleet saluting, etc., and the crowds and different costumes was really picturesque. We think of undertaking an expedition soon, and I expect to be ordered with the Suliotes to join the army.

All well at present. We found Gamba already arrived, and everything in good condition. Remembrance to all friends.

Yours ever,

N. B.

P.S.—You will, I hope, use every exertion to realise the *assets*. For besides what I have already advanced, I have undertaken to maintain the Suliotes for a year, (and will accompany them either as a Chief, or—whichever is most agreeable to the Government,) besides sundries. I do not understand Browne's '*letter of credit*.' I neither gave nor ordered a letter of credit that I know of; and though of course, if you have done it, I will be responsible, I was not aware of any thing, except that I would have backed his bills, which you said was unnecessary. As to *orders*—I ordered nothing but some *red cloth* and *oil cloths*, both of which I am ready to receive; but if Gamba has exceeded my commission, *the other things must be sent back*, *for I cannot permit any thing of the kind, nor will.* The servants' journey will of course be paid for, though *that* is exorbitant. As for Browne's letter, I do not know any thing more than I have said, and I really cannot defray the charges of half Greece and the Frank adventurers besides. Mr. Barff must send us some dollars soon, for the expenses fall on me for the present.

TO THOMAS MOORE

Missolonghi, Western Greece, March 4, 1824

My dear Moore,

Your reproach is unfounded—I have received two letters from you, and answered both previous to leaving Cephalonia. I have not been 'quiet' in an Ionian island, but much occupied with business, as the Greek deputies (if arrived) can tell you. Neither have I continued *Don Juan*, nor any other poem. You go, as usual, I presume, by some newspaper report or other.

When the proper moment to be of some use arrived, I came here; and am told that my arrival (with some other circumstances) *has* been of, at least, temporary advantage to the cause. I had a narrow escape from the Turks, and another from shipwreck, on my passage. On the 15th (or 16th) of February I had an attack of apoplexy, or epilepsy,—the physicians have not exactly decided which, but the alternative is agreeable. My constitution, therefore, remains between the two opinions, like Mahomet's sarcophagus between the magnets. All that I can say is, that they nearly bled me to death, by placing the leeches too near the temporal artery, so that the blood could with difficulty be stopped, even with caustic. I am supposed to be getting better, slowly, however. But my homilies will, I presume, for the future, be like the Archbishop of Grenada's—in this case, 'I order you a hundred ducats from my treasurer, and wish you a little more taste.'

For public matters I refer you to Colonel Stanhope's and Capt. Parry's reports,—and to all other reports whatsoever. There is plenty to do—war without, and tumult within—they 'kill a man a week,' like Bob Acres in the country. Parry's artificers have gone away in alarm, on account of a dispute in which some of the natives and foreigners were engaged, and a Swede was killed, and a Suliote wounded. In the middle of their fright there was a strong shock of an earthquake; so, between that and the sword, they boomed off in a hurry, in despite of all dissuasions to the contrary. A Turkish brig run ashore, etc., etc., etc.

You, I presume, are either publishing or meditating that same. Let me hear from and of you, and believe me, in all events,

Ever and affectionately yours,
N. B.

P.S.—Tell Mr. Murray that I wrote to him the other day, and hope that he has received, or will receive, the letter.

NOTES

ENGLISH BARDS, AND SCOTCH REVIEWERS

A first edition of this spirited satire appeared, without the author's name, in March 1809. The present text is based on that of the suppressed fifth edition of 1812

Page 3, line 1: 'hoarse Fitzgerald'. Nicknamed by Cobbett the 'Small-Beer Poet'. A contemporary poetaster inclined to spout his verses at convivial literary gatherings.

p. 4, l. 55: 'This Lamb must own'. The Hon. George Lamb, son of Lady Melbourne, whose family was afterwards closely connected with the poet's life.

p. 5, l. 61: 'Not seek great Jeffrey's'. Francis (afterwards Lord) Jeffrey, editor of the *Edinburgh* and *Quarterly Reviews*.

p. 6, l. 128: 'Little's Lyrics.' 'Little' was the pseudonym adopted by Tom Moore; at a happier period one of Byron's closest friends.

p. 7, l. 142: 'grovelling Stott'. A versifier who embellished the columns of the *Morning Post*, under the name of 'Hafiz'.

p. 7, l. 153: 'Thus Lays of Minstrels'. Interesting to compare this attack on Scott with the veneration expressed by Byron at a later date.

p. 9, l. 211: *Thalaba* and Southey's other major efforts, though seldom read, are still sufficiently well known. *The Old Woman of Berkeley*, however (which describes how an aged female is carried off by the Devil), demands a note.

p. 10, l. 265: 'Oh! wonder-working Lewis!' 'Monk' Lewis, author of celebrated tales of horror; intimate of the Holland House circle; afterwards, like many of his early victims, Byron's friend.

p. 11, l. 297: 'Hibernian Strangford'. Lord Strangford, author of *Translations from Camoëns*.

p. 11, l. 310: 'Hayley's last work'. William Hayley, author of *The Triumphs of Temper*. A prosperous dilettante. Friend of Miss Anna Seward. Patron of William Blake.

p. 12, l. 321: 'Sepulchral Grahame'. A pious nonentity who had to his discredit two volumes, entitled 'Sabbath Walks' and 'Biblical Lectures'.

p. 12, l. 331: 'harmonious Bowles'. The Rev. William Lisle Bowles. Author of numerous and undistinguished works, including 'Sonnet to Oxford' and 'Stanzas on Hearing the Bells of Ostend'.

p. 13, l. 372: 'Consult Lord Fanny, and confide in Curll'. 'Lord Fanny', otherwise 'Sporus', in real life the brilliant, effeminate Lord Hervey, and Curll, the bookseller, were two chief victims of Pope's satire.

p. 13, l. 378: 'What Mallet did for hire'. Mallet was hired by Bolingbroke to attack Pope after his death.

p. 13, l. 380: 'To rave with Dennis, and with Ralph to rhyme'. Two inconsiderable personages, badly belaboured in the *Dunciad*.

p. 14, l. 396: 'Amos Cottle strikes the lyre in vain'. In these and in subsequent lines, Amos Cottle—a harmless, if entirely untalented, versifier—receives his sole immortality. No doubt it was his name that fascinated Byron.

p. 15, l. 425: Byron refers here to 'poor Montgomery', a poet whose work had been roughly handled by the *Edinburgh Review*.

p. 16, l. 466: 'When Little's leadless pistol'. Jeffrey's duel with Tom Moore had had a ridiculous conclusion, when it was discovered that one of the two duelling pistols was unloaded.

p. 17, l. 509: 'Athenian Aberdeen'. Lord Aberdeen, an occasional reviewer and much travelled peer.

p. 17, l. 510: 'Herbert shall wield Thor's hammer'. The Hon. W. Herbert translated Icelandic poetry.

p. 17, l. 512: 'Smug Sydney'. Sydney Smith; favourite of Lady Holland, and one of the greatest ornaments of the Holland House circle.

p. 17, l. 513: 'classic Hallam'. Henry Hallam, a frequenter of Holland House and *Edinburgh Review* critic.

p. 17, l. 515: 'paltry Pillans'. An Eton tutor.

p. 17, l. 519: 'Thy Holland's banquets'. Byron soon regretted this attack on Lord Holland—an entirely estimable character, both from the intellectual and from the political point of view.

p. 17, l. 524: 'blundering Brougham'. Henry (afterwards Lord) Brougham, the Machiavellian Whig politician.

p. 18, l. 551: 'Declare his landlord can at least translate!' Lord Holland had translated Lope de Vega.

p. 18, l. 557: 'My lady skims the cream of each critique'. Lady Holland's early life had been unconventional. Her first child by Lord Holland was illegitimate.

p. 18, l. 562: 'Puns, and a Prince within a barrel pent'. In the melodrama of *Tekeli*, the hero was 'clapt into a barrel on the stage'.

p. 18, l. 563: 'Dibdin's nonsense'. It seems doubtful to which of the Dibdins Byron refers—whether to Charles Dibdin the older (1745–1814) or to Thomas John Dibdin (1771–1841). Both were authors of plays and songs.

p. 18, l. 564: 'Though now, thank Heaven! the Rosciomania's o'er'. Master Betty—known as the Infant Roscius—first appeared on the stage at the age of twelve. His success in adult parts paved the way for a long series of juvenile actors.

p. 19, l. 591: 'Skeffington'. Sir Lumley Skeffington; dandy, eccentric, and amateur playwright of the period.

p. 19, l. 601: 'Greenwood's gay designs'. Greenwood was scene-painter at Drury Lane.

p. 20, ll. 613 and 615: 'Naldi's face': 'Catalini's pantaloons'. Naldi and Catalini, two itinerant Italian mimes. Signora Catalini was one of the first actresses to appear on the stage in trousers, thus creating a tremendous popular hubbub.

p. 20, l. 639: 'Argyle'. The Argyle Rooms were notorious for heavy gambling.

p. 21, l. 661: 'Now in loose waltz'. Byron had a very strong prejudice against dancing, since his own lameness prevented his taking part in it.

p. 22, l. 686: 'like Falkland fall'. Byron's friend Lord Falkland had been killed in a duel. Byron befriended his widow and orphans—with disastrous results: for Lady Falkland decided that she was in love with him.

p. 23, l. 726: 'The paralytic puling of Carlisle'. Against Lord Carlisle, his guardian, Byron nursed an undying resentment. Carlisle had cold-shouldered him when he made his first appearance in London.

p. 24, l. 756: 'The lovely Rosa's prose'. Rosa, 'daughter of the noted Jew King', had published two collections of verse and various highly romantic novels.

p. 24, l. 774: 'And Capel Lofft declares 'tis quite sublime'. Capel Lofft, described by Byron as 'the Maecenas of shoemakers and preface-writer-general to distressed versemen'.

p. 24, l. 777: 'Bloomfield'. Robert Bloomfield; bred up a shoemaker; author of *The Farmer's Boy* (published in 1800) of which 25,000 copies were sold.

p. 24, l. 782: 'brother Nathan'. Nathaniel Bloomfield, author of a poem 'on the enclosures of Honington Green'.

p. 25, l. 818: 'Sotheby, Macneil'. Sotheby, author of translations and an epic poem : Macneil, a popular Scottish versifier.

p. 26, l. 831: 'Unhappy White!' Henry Kirke White had died of over-study at Cambridge in the year 1806. Like several other third- and fourth-rate poets, he was much admired by Byron.

p. 27, l. 859: 'Shee and Genius'. Shee was President of the Royal Academy and author of poems.

p. 27, l. 877: 'Wright! 'twas thy happy lot'. W. R. Wright, author of a poem on Greece and the Ionian Islands.

p. 27, l. 893: 'flimsy Darwin'. Erasmus Darwin; author of *The Botanic Garden*, published in 1781.

p. 30, l. 973: 'There Clarke'. Hewson Clarke, the journalist here attacked, never forgave the insult, and afterwards revenged himself with a ferocious libel on Byron's person and family.

p. 30, l. 983 : Francis Hodgson was a poor poet and prosy personality; but he had the merit of being Byron's devoted supporter.

p. 31, l. 1034: 'rapid Gell'. Gell's *Topography of Troy and Ithaca* was a work that Byron much admired.

CHILDE HAROLD

Composed during the second year of Byron's Near-Eastern tour, Cantos I and II of *Childe Harold* were published, at the instigation of the poet's friend, Dallas, in the opening week of March, 1812. Their success —contrary to their author's expectation, for he had been greatly discouraged by certain unfavourable criticisms he had received in Greece— was instantaneous. Then followed the years of his highest celebrity, during which he dashed off the series of Eastern Tales and one or two admirable short poems. In disgrace and exile, he once more took up the theme. Canto III appeared on November 18th, 1816; Canto IV on April 28th, 1818. There was an interval of eight years between the composition of the first and last cantos, and meanwhile an immense change had taken place both in Byron's mood and in the style through which it was expressed.

To Ianthe: This dedicatory poem, written during the Autumn of 1812, was added to the seventh edition, published in February 1814. It is addressed to the thirteen-year-old Lady Charlotte Harley, daughter of Lady Oxford.

p. 37, *Canto I.* V. 3: 'though he loved but one'. Byron here refers to Mary Chaworth, his early love, in later years a focus of sentimental reverie. She had made an unhappy marriage with the dissipated Jack Musters.

p. 38, VII. 2: 'It was a vast and venerable pile'. Byron was deeply attached to Newstead, and dwelt with some complaisance both on the venerable monastic associations of the Abbey and on the revels that he himself had organized there.

p. 39, X. 3: 'A sister whom he loved'. Byron kept up an affectionate, though not very regular, correspondence with his half-sister, Augusta Leigh; but, till his return to England from the Near East, they were rarely able to meet.

p. 66, XCI. 1: 'And thou, my friend!' John Wingfield had died in Portugal of a fever on May 14th, 1811. His memory belonged to what Byron afterwards described as the happiest and most untroubled period of his life—his days at Harrow.

p. 70, *Canto II*. XI. 1: 'But who, of all the plunderers of yon Fane'. Byron was no great lover of antiquity; but he felt the keenest resentment at Lord Elgin's spoliation of the Parthenon marbles.

p. 76, XXX. 5: 'Sweet Florence!' Mrs. Spencer Smith was the heroine of a somewhat inconclusive love affair in which Byron became involved during his stay in Malta.

p. 97, *Canto III*. I. 2: 'Ada! sole daughter of my house and heart'. Ada Byron had been born in December, 1815.

p. 105, XXIX. 4: 'And partly that I did his Sire some wrong'. The father of 'young gallant Howard' was Lord Carlisle, Byron's guardian, so savagely attacked in *English Bards, and Scotch Reviewers*.

p. 133, *Canto IV*. IV. 7: 'And Pierre'. Byron was a great reader of plays and had a very proper admiration for Otway's *Venice Preserved*.

SHORTER POEMS

p. 159, *Remember Thee! Remember Thee!*: This violent little poem—originally published by Medwin in his indiscreet but illuminating volume of Byronic reminiscences—was directed at the poet's first fashionable mistress, Lady Caroline Lamb, who had burst into his lodgings and, on the flyleaf of a copy of *Vathek* which she found on his table, had scribbled the admonition: 'Remember Me!'

p. 159, *Remember him, whom Passion's power*: Composed in 1813, these lines appear to have been precipitated by Byron's relationship with Lady Frances Wedderburn Webster.

p. 161, from *The Bride of Abydos*: There is very little in Byron's Eastern Tales that appears to deserve re-reading; but the conclusion of *The Bride of Abydos* (published in 1814) marks an unusually high level. For details of this poem's composition, see the first Journal.

p. 163, *She walks in Beauty*: Wedderburn Webster, the husband of the exquisite and disconsolate Lady Frances, describes how he persuaded Byron to attend a party given by the famous blue-stocking Lady Sitwell, where the poet encountered the wife of a second cousin, the beautiful Mrs. Wilmot, who wore a black dress sewn with luminous spangles. On returning home, Byron desired his valet to give him a '*tumbler* of *Brandy*' which he drank to Mrs. Wilmot's health. He was 'in a sad state all night'; but, next morning, he dashed off this delightful lyric.

p. 164, *If that high world*: Written at the end of 1815: published among *Hebrew Melodies*.

p. 164, *Oh! snatch'd away in Beauty's bloom*: Published among *Hebrew Melodies*.

p. 165, *Sun of the sleepless*: Published among *Hebrew Melodies*.

pp. 165–6, *Stanzas for Music*: Written in 1815. Byron was intensely susceptible to music; though his musical tastes were not of a very high order.

p. 167, *A Sketch*: Just before leaving England, Byron bade a characteristic *Farewell* to the unforgiving Annabella and fired off a parting broadside at his mother-in-law's detested confidante, 'the respectable Mrs. Clermont'.

p. 170, *The Dream*: This autobiographical poem (composed in July 1816) contains a sort of poetic résumé of Byron's emotional life—his unhappy youthful love-affair with Mary Chaworth and his own singularly unfortunate marriage.

p. 176, *Churchill's Grave*: The 'fact literally rendered' in this poem was Byron's visit to the grave of Churchill the day before he set sail from England. Its references to his own existence—to the glory that he had enjoyed and to the disgrace that had overtaken him—need no amplification.

p. 177, *Epistle to Augusta*: Though, like so many of Byron's productions, extremely unequal, the *Epistle to Augusta* has a grave and tragic beauty. Byron's mention of his 'heritage of storms' and 'our grandsire's fate' is explained by the legend that surrounded Admiral the Hon. John Byron, known in the navy as 'Foulweather Jack', since a hurricane sprang up whenever he sailed.

p. 181, *So we'll go no more a-roving*: Byron never came nearer to pure poetry than in this little poem, written during the aftermath of the Venetian Carnival in 1817.

p. 182, *Stanzas to the Po*: Written in the Spring of 1819, these lines are addressed to Teresa Guiccioli and reflect the calm flow of a quasi-domestic love affair.

p. 184, *On This Day I Complete My Thirty-Sixth Year*: Byron's last poem, written at Missolonghi on January 22nd, 1824. Those who are familiar with the background of his life in Greece may find matter for speculation in the eighth verse.

THE VISION OF JUDGMENT

An attack both on the 'renegade' Southey, whose 'epic' appearance Byron had admired at Holland House, and on the entire Tory faction, *The Vision of Judgment* was published in the first number of the ill-fated *Liberal*, October 15th, 1822.

DON JUAN

At one pole of Byron's achievement stands *Childe Harold*, at the other *Don Juan*. To gain a true impression of his genius and of his relationship to the social period in which he lived, both must be taken into account. Whereas *Childe Harold* represents the romantic Byron—the 'wandering prioner of his own dark mind'—who made so deep an impression on London society between 1812 and 1816, *Don Juan* conveys the cheerful, disabused and ironic being who endeared himself to Hobhouse, Rogers and Moore. Like *Childe Harold*, the poem—at any rate, in the opening Cantos—is very largely autobiographical. Donna Inez, Juan's prudish and mathematical mother, is a portrait of Annabella Milbanke, the formidable 'Princess of Parallelograms'. Sir Samuel Romilly, who had earned Byron's hatred during the separation proceedings, comes in for a ferocious and unjust sneer. Later episodes recall the feverish excitement of the poet's London life—his acquaintanceship with Sydney Smith (whose volubility Byron admired but resented) and his mingled love and loathing of the English scene.

Cantos I and II were published in 1819; Cantos III, IV and V in 1821; VI to XIV in 1823; XV and XVI in 1824; the fragment of XVII in 1903.

LETTERS AND JOURNALS

p. 529 : Elizabeth Bridget Pigot and her brother, John Pigot, were neighbours at Burgage Green, Southwell. Byron and Mrs. Byron inhabited a modest Georgian house on the Green, Burgage Manor, while Newstead was let to Lord Grey de Ruthyn.

p. 530 : The Pigots, brother and sister, sympathised with Byron in his frequent and impassioned quarrels with Mrs. Byron, here referred to as 'my amiable Alecto'.

p. 531 : By the year 1806, Byron was already poet, man of pleasure and dandy. This letter gives some indication of his worldly progress.

p. 534: For an account of his passionate friendship with Lord Clare, see the journal of *Detached Thoughts* compiled at Ravenna in 1821. His friendships at Harrow (Byron records) 'were with *me passions* . . . That with Lord Clare began one of the earliest and lasted longest . . . I never hear the word 'Clare' without a beating of the heart even *now. . . .*'

p. 535, l. 21 : By 'the hero of *my Cornelian*', Byron intends his protégé, the good-looking Cambridge chorister, John Edleston, who had been his 'almost constant associate since October 1805' and had presented his patron with a cornelian heart.

p. 537, l. 25 : Lady Elizabeth Butler and Miss Ponsonby are better known as the 'ladies of Llangollen'. Their devotion and eccentricities were already celebrated.

p. 539, l. 33 : Lord Carlisle was Byron's guardian; but the one-time dandy and gambler was now a strait-laced court-official; and he avoided the Byrons as far as he could.

p. 541 : John Jackson, 'the Emperor of Pugilism', was a celebrated ex-bruiser. He taught Byron boxing and, according to Hobhouse, was also employed in other and more discreditable capacities.

p. 543, l. 5 : Lord Falkland was killed in a duel. See Note on *English Bards, and Scotch Reviewers.* 1, 686. John Hanson, who advised the sale of Newstead, acted as Byron's man of business throughout his lifetime.

p. 543 : William Harness had met Byron at Harrow and ranked at least third or fourth in the catalogue of his schoolboy 'passions'. The satire mentioned is, of course, *English Bards, and Scotch Reviewers*.

p. 545, l. 31 : Robert Rushton, who sailed with Byron as his servant in 1809, had been brought up on the Newstead estate. His portrait is included in the engraved picture, *Lord Byron at the Age of Nineteen*, published in early editions of Moore's *Life*.

p. 546, l. 4 : John Cam Hobhouse, afterwards Lord Broughton, remained Byron's most faithful, though perhaps one of his least understanding, friends. His annotations on a copy of Moore's *Life* and his memories of the poet published in *Recollections of a Long Life* are extremely illuminating.

p. 548, l. 19 : The 'lock of hair about three feet in length' is still preserved in the archives of Byron's original publisher.

p. 554, l. 29 : The 'married woman at Malta' was Mrs. Spencer Smith—the 'fair Florence' celebrated in *Childe Harold*: the 'three Greek girls', Teresa Macri—the Maid of Athens—and her two red-headed sisters.

p. 561 : It is said that Mrs. Byron—always hot-tempered and, latterly, alcoholic—expired in a fit of passion on opening one of her son's bills.

p. 567 : Scrope Davies represented, among Byron's friends, the type of hard-headed man of the world whom he most admired. References to Davies' prowess will be found in subsequent letters and journals.

p. 567, l. 27: 'one of my best friends' was Charles Skinner Matthews. See preceding letter.

p. 568: Among the most remarkable features of Byron's altogether remarkable will was the legacy of seven thousand pounds to Nicolo Giraud, the handsome Levantine youth who had acted as Italian master during his Near-Eastern tour.

p. 571, l. 14: John Wingfield, a close Harrow friend, had died of fever in Portugal during the May of this year.

For details of the career of Henry Kirke White, see note on *English Bards, and Scotch Reviewers*, 1. 831.

p. 573: Byron's gibes at Moore in *English Bards, and Scotch Reviewers* had evoked a challenge. Owing to Byron's departure for Greece, this challenge had gone astray; and Moore, in the meantime, had acquired the responsibility of a wife and child.

p. 575, l. 11: Sir William Drummond had recently had the effrontery to suggest that the Old Testament was a collection of astronomical myths. There are frequent references to his 'profane' book in Byron's correspondence.

p. 576 l. 33: For Lord Clare, see note to p. 534. Lord Delawarr was another Harrow friend. His neglect of Byron, after they had left school, caused the poet much unhappiness.

p. 578: In this letter, Byron refers to a somewhat mysterious quarrel that had broken out among his Newstead favourites.

p. 579: Byron's brilliant maiden speech against the reactionary Frame Breaking Bill was delivered on February 27th 1812.

p. 579, l. 32: 'My poesy'—due to appear—'on Saturday'—was the first instalment of *Childe Harold*.

p. 580, l. 5: Here Lady Caroline Lamb—daughter of Lady Bessborough, daughter-in-law of Lady Melbourne—makes her first tempestuous appearance in Byron's life.

p. 580, l. 24: John Bellingham, a lunatic with a grievance, had assassinated the Prime Minister, Spencer Perceval, in the lobby of the House of Commons.

p. 582: Compare the virulent attacks on Sir Walter Scott scattered throughout *English Bards, and Scotch Reviewers*.

p. 587, l. 4: ' "Emma" in the modern Griselda. Maria Edgeworth's novel had appeared in 1804.

p. 589, l. 18: Newstead was not, in fact, sold till many years later.

When this letter was written, Byron was rusticating at Cheltenham after a strenuous London season. His love-affair with Lady Oxford had already begun.

p. 591, l. 27: 'As to the Lady Blarney'. 'Lady Blarney' was Byron's nickname for Lady Caroline Lamb's mother, Lady Bessborough.

p. 592, l. 15: Byron respected and liked, though he often made fun of, Madame de Staël. On her side, she complained that he was quite incapable of real love, and often sat at dinner parties with his eyes shut!

p. 593, l. 28: At Lady Heathcote's ball, the irrepressible Lady Caroline had staged a mock suicide, thus throwing the party into a pandemonium.

p. 595, l. 12: 'Lady A.F.' stands for Lady Adelaide Forbes, daughter of Lord Granard, who interested Byron because she reminded him of the Apollo Belvedere.

p. 596, l. 35: John Hookham Frere was a member of the Holland House circle: Sir James Mackintosh, a supporter and friend of Madame de Staël.

p. 597, l. 36: Madame de Staël's son had been killed in a duel.

p. 602, l. 14: While Byron was carrying on a sentimental correspondence with Miss Milbanke, she drew up and sent to her aunt a list of the qualities that she would require in her future husband. Lady Melbourne forwarded the document to Byron.

p. 602, l. 30: In this, and in the four following letters, Byron describes his tragi-comic love-affair with Lady Frances, the wife of an old but somewhat ridiculous acquaintance, Wedderburn Webster.

p. 617, *Journal* 1813: Byron's journals need very little annotation. They are self-explanatory and, according to the modern taste, with their easy flow and amusing mixture of irony, cynicism and sentiment, some of the best things he ever wrote. Here we find a fluent day-to-day chronicle of thoughts, fancies and adventures. We notice an increasing restlessness and the gradual drift towards marriage which culminated in his disastrous alliance with Annabella Milbanke at the beginning of January 1815. Meanwhile, he had completed *The Bride of Abydos*—otherwise called *Zuleika*—a memorial of an episode in his past life that (as he told Tom Moore) he hardly liked to think of. One of the greatest charms of this—his earliest—journal is that it shows us Byron in so many different aspects at the same time. He is tragic, serious, deeply introspective—yet frivolity is perpetually breaking through!

p. 671, l. 37: Attached to *The Corsair* were some lines entitled *Stanzas to a Lady Weeping* which referred to a recent and painful scene at Carlton House, when Princess Charlotte had burst into tears at one of her father's dinner parties.

p. 674, l. 35: During April, 1814, Louis XVIII, returning in triumph from his English exile, was escorted with royal honours towards Paris.

p. 675, l. 16: The words 'it is *not* an "Ape" ' are thought to refer to Augusta Leigh's latest child, Medora. It has been conjectured that Byron had in mind the mediaeval legend that the children of incest were born monsters.

p. 676, l. 29: '*My* A' seems to have been Byron's pseudonym for Augusta Leigh, so called to distinguish her from '*your* A', Annabella Milbanke.

p. 678, l. 5: Invited to supper by Lady Radcliffe, Byron who, at that moment, had given up his strictly Spartan régime, found himself regaled with a 'damned anchovy sandwich'. This, Moore tells us, long remained a subject of jocular resentment.

p. 678, l. 18: The actor, whose performance Byron so much admired, was the incomparable Charles Kean.

p. 680, l. 11: The allied Sovereigns, the Emperor of Russia and the King of Prussia, were in London from June 6th to June 27th.

p. 681, l. 19: *Lara* was published in combination with Rogers' *Jacqueline* during August 1814. 'The condolatory address to Lady Jersey' here mentioned was certain verses, written during the same month, commiserating with Lady Jersey on her quarrel with the Prince Regent over his matrimonial affairs.

p. 683, l. 14: Byron was '*not* alone' at Newstead, since he had been accompanied thither by Mrs. Leigh. It is interesting to note the slightly defiant and defensive tone of the opening paragraph.

p. 685, l. 11: The 'circumstance of importance', which *might* change all his plans, actually materialised a few days later. His proposal of marriage was accepted by Annabella Milbanke. 'It never rains but it pours!' observed Byron, as he handed her letter across the table to Mrs. Leigh.

p. 689, . 36: The Hon. Douglas Kinnaird—the excellence of whose brandy Byron compares with the insipidity of his father-in-law's after-dinner speeches—was the kind of *homme du monde* for whom Byron appears always to have felt a somewhat envious admiration.

p. 691, l. 23: Lady Cork was a notorious blue-stocking, celebrated for her literary parties.

p. 693, l. 16: During the unhappy months that he spent in London after his marriage, Byron found some consolation in the Drury Lane Committee, which had been charged with the management of that famous theatre.

p. 698, l. 35: Lady Byron left London on January 15th. At the beginning of February, Byron received a letter in which Sir Ralph Milbanke announced that her parents could not feel justified in permitting her return. The 'Mrs. C.' of the penultimate paragraph was Mrs. Clairmont, Lady Byron's former governess, now Lady Noel's friend and adviser. See *A Sketch* among Shorter Poems. Lady Milbanke had changed her name to Noel after inheriting the Wentworth estates.

p. 701, *Extracts from a Journal*: This Journal was kept for the benefit of Mrs. Leigh, to whom Byron had bidden farewell on Easter Sunday, April 14th, 1816.

p. 713, l. 13: The private physician, who had become involved in a quarrel with an officer at Milan, was Dr. I. W. Polidori, an over-romantic and somewhat ridiculous young man.

p. 715, l. 30: For a further description of the wife of the merchant of Venice—Marianna Segati—see the next letter.

p. 733, l. 5: Allegra—Byron's natural daughter by Claire Clairmont —had been born at Bath on January 12th, 1817.

p. 735, l. 18: Byron here alludes to an incident that had occurred when, after 'having perused a German work called Phantasmagoria' and exchanged ghost stories with Shelley, Mary and Claire Clairmont, he 'recited the beginning of Christabel, then unpublished'. The effect upon Shelley was so disturbing 'that he suddenly started up and ran out of the room. The physician and Lord Byron followed, and discovered him leaning against a mantel-piece, with cold drops of perspiration trickling down his face. . . . Enquiring into the cause of his alarm, they found that his wild imagination having pictured him the bosom of one of the ladies with eyes. . . . he was obliged to leave the room in order to destroy the impression'.

p. 736, l. 11: Byron's quasi-domestic *liaison* with the Countess Guiccioli had begun in Venice during the previous April.

p. 739, l. 4: William Roberts was the editor of the *British Review*. The first and second cantos of *Don Juan* were published, anonymously, on July 15th.

p. 742, l. 27: Madame Albrizzi kept a famous literary salon. She had been nicknamed 'the de Stael of Italy'.

p. 743: The Memoir, referred to in the third paragraph, was the autobiographical document burnt by his friends after Byron's death. Its loss—and the folly and prudery of his executors—cannot be sufficiently regretted.

p. 749, l. 4: Partly because he was himself by disposition and tradition a Liberal, partly because he had now cast in his lot with the Guiccioli family, Byron had become involved in Italian revolutionary politics. Tita, the bravest of his servants, was the Venetian gondolier whom he had brought with him to Ravenna.

p. 790: Richard Belgrave Hoppner, English Consul General in Venice, had acted as intermediary between Byron, on the one hand, and the Shelleys and Claire Clairmont on the other, in their difficult discussions as to what was to become of Claire's natural child.

p. 797, *Detached Thoughts* (1): 'Old Courtenay'—John Courtenay, though private secretary to a Lord-Lieutenant of Ireland, was not himself an Irishman.

p. 798 (5): 'Whitbread'—Sir Samuel Whitbread, member of a rich brewing family and prominent Whig.

p. 800 (6): 'Lyttelton'—The Lyttelton here mentioned was the third Lord Lyttelton, *not* 'the Wicked Lord Lyttleton', author of *Poems by a Young Nobleman lately deceased*.

p. 806 (24): 'Curran!'—John Curran, the Irish patriot, had transferred his activities to Westminster after the disappearance of the Irish Parliament. He was a fine orator, a brilliant talker and an irrepressible mimic.

p. 807 (29): 'Alvanley'—For a superb impression of Lord Alvanley see Dighton's celebrated caricature, *Going to Whites*.

p. 809 (33): 'I have a notion that Gamblers are as happy as most people, being always *excited*.'—Compare this sentence with *Don Juan*:

> The best of life is but intoxication

and Lady Byron's remark to Mrs. Leigh, that Byron's undoing was his 'habitual passion for excitement'.

p. 822 (65): '*My* M.A.C.'—M.A.C. or M.C. (as she is called in an earlier jotting) was Mary Chaworth. Byron continued to cherish her memory, but displayed a curious reluctance to meet Mary Chaworth (or, as she latterly became, Mrs. Chaworth Musters) in real life.

p. 823 (67): 'The D.L. Committee'—This was the Drury Lane Committee, on which Byron served—much to his own amusement and Lady Byron's distress—during his last year in London.

p. 844, l. 3: The third, fourth and fifth cantos of *Don Juan* were published in August 1821.

p. 846, l. 2: The Guiccioli family having been expelled from Ravenna, Byron was following in their train.

p. 848, l. 28: Byron's counterblast to Southey's apotheosis of George III was, of course, *The Vision of Judgment*.

p. 857: The Lady Hardy, to whom Byron wrote, was the wife of the naval officer who attended Nelson's last moments and evoked that famous and controversial plea: 'Kiss me, Hardy!' Her 'Chevalier', strangely enough, was 'bold Webster', who still wrote pamphlets but was now estranged from his wife, Lady Frances, with whom Byron had enjoyed a fugitive passage in the year 1813.

p. 865: Charles Hancock was a partner in the firm of Barff and Hancock, bankers of Zante and Argostoli.

INDEX OF FIRST LINES
to the Shorter Poems

Date Due